WOMEN'S LIFE AND WORK
IN THE SOUTHERN COLONIES

Women's Life and Work

IN THE

Southern Colonies

JULIA CHERRY SPRUILL

New Introduction by Anne Firor Scott

W · W · NORTON & COMPANY
New York · London

Frontispiece: Julia Cherry Spruill, 1921

Library of Congress Cataloging in Publication Data

Spruill, Julia Cherry.
    Women's life and work in the Southern colonies.

    (The Norton library)
    Reprint of the 1938 ed., with a new introd.
    Bibliography: p.
    1. Woman—History and condition of women.
2. Women in the Southern States.   3. Southern
States—Social life and customs—Colonial period.
I. Title.
HQ1416.S65   1972   301.41´2´0975   72-6149

ISBN 0-393-31758-7

W.W. Norton & Company, Inc.
500 Fifth Avenue, New York, N.Y. 10110
www.wwnorton.com
W.W. Norton & Company, Ltd.
Castle House, 75/76 Wells Street London WIT 3QT

2 3 4 5 6 7 8 9 0

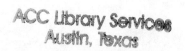

CONTENTS

Illustrations between pages 207 and 208

Introduction to the Norton Paperback Edition

IN THE 1920s, when this story begins, the southern colonies had attracted much less attention from historians than had those of New England, and southern colonial women had attracted none at all. I like to picture the lovely young woman who traveled each day to the Massachusetts Historical Society or the Widener Library, and in those unequivocally New England settings sought to answer a question no historian had asked before: what was life like for the *women* who lived in the colonial South?

Born in 1899 into a highly respected middle class family in eastern North Carolina, Julia Cherry had been raised by a talented mother who supported suffrage and birth control—both radical causes in the South in the early twentieth century. Julia herself joined the suffrage campaign while she was in high school and when she was sixteen benefited from the efforts of activists who, not long before she was born, had worked to create a state-supported college for women in North Carolina. At the North Carolina Normal and Industrial College she became a campus leader and graduated with honors in 1920.[1]

By then she was engaged to Corydon Spruill, himself an academic star—a Rhodes scholar, an honor then confined to single men. When he returned from England in 1922 the two were married and set up house in Chapel Hill where he was on the faculty of the University of North Carolina. In what was then a very small town, Julia—a bright, engaging, faculty wife—soon made friends among the historians, all men. Enrolled as the only woman in a graduate seminar for master's degree candidates, she was its star member and wrote a prize-winning thesis on Orestes Brownson.

After this early foray into the intellectual history of New England and a stint at high school teaching, Howard Odum, the director of the Institute for Research in the Social Sciences, suggested that she undertake a book on changing attitudes toward southern women

[1]While Julia Cherry was a student the college acquired full accreditation and was renamed the North Carolina College for Women.

in the nineteenth century. When she discovered that nothing whatever had yet been published about southern women of any period,
she concluded that she had to begin with an examination of women's
experience in the earliest European settlements—and thus embarked
on what would become *Women's Life and Work in the Southern
Colonies.*[2] She remembered her initial year of research as "sort of scat-
terbrained . . ." in that she had gone to the Library of Congress and
from place to place in search of data.

When Corydon was invited to spend two years at Harvard, Julia
found a sympathetic mentor in Arthur M. Schlesinger, Sr., who had
recently written a compelling essay about the need for historical study
of women. With his encouragement she began exploring the vast re-
sources of Boston and Cambridge.

There was very little in the secondary literature to guide her, so
she simply set out to read every colonial document that might throw
light on her subject. She cast a wide net, and though the Spruills returned to North Carolina with a steamer trunk of her notes, she
spent the ensuing decade visiting one depository after another in
search of documents that might tell her something more about colonial women.

In a totally untouched field she had to make up her own methods, and in doing so she began to create the kind of social history
which would come to be a central focus of mainstream historians half
a century later. As she searched she examined nearly every source that
any social historian of recent times has thought to use: parish records,
court minutes, land records, contemporary accounts, inventories, wills,
guardian bonds, letter books, colonial newspapers (especially their advertisements), formal colonial records (including those of the assemblies), and the records of the British Board of Trade. Her
bibliography of primary sources ran to twenty-four pages and suggests
extraordinary diligence in tracking evidence. Though modern colo-
nialists have done impressive work, few have matched her in command of primary sources. Her findings appeared first in a series of
articles in historical journals, and then in 1938 in the book itself.

Most of the reviewers, including several leading male historians,

---

[2] The only exception to this generalization was a pre-Civil War study of southern
women writers. Though Spruill did not know it, at the University of Wisconsin a young
woman named Virginia Gearheart had recently embarked on a dissertation about antebel-
lum southern women. See Anne F. Scott, *Unheard Voices: The First Historians of Southern
Women* (University Press of Virginia, 1993).

recognized the innovative nature of her study; Philip Davidson, writing in the *Journal of Southern History,* closed by saying it was a book by a woman, about women, and for everybody. Schlesinger himself wrote that it was "an important contribution to American social history to which students will constantly turn." He was right, but more than three decades would pass before his forecast came true.

Although academic jobs were not plentiful in the 1930s, a talented young man who had published so impressive a book would soon have been snapped up by some university; he would have gone on to write more books and to become a respected figure in the small community of historians of the South. But Julia Spruill was a young woman, and a married woman at that. Though she was well known to the historians in a university that considered itself, and may indeed have been, the outstanding intellectual center of the region, none of them gave evidence of having read her work and no one offered her a proper job. She spent some time teaching in high school, and the Institute for Research in the Social Sciences supported her research for a time, but when the Great Depression came the women were the first to be cut off.

Meantime Corydon Spruill, whose star had risen rapidly, became a dean. In the 1940s a dean's wife had clearly defined responsibilities. Julia conscientiously studied student folders before successive waves of freshman came to dinner. She entertained faculty members and visiting dignitaries in the approved manner of southern hospitality. When, at the end of the war, the university was overwhelmed with returning veterans, she was allowed to teach a course usually assigned to graduate students. In such time as she had for herself she joined the local book club and steered some of its reading toward history. She was a member of the North Carolina Historical Society and the American Association of University Women. So her life went on.

Her book, though widely available in libraries, had no effect whatever on the way southern history was being written. Despite all the favorable reviews, it appeared to have dropped into a void. Neither her subject—women—nor her innovative methodology seem to have affected the thinking of scholars in the field or the training of graduate students. C. Vann Woodward in his reflective memoir, *Thinking Back,* has testified to the stultifying nature of graduate education in history, especially in southern history, when he began in the 1930s. "I began to wonder," he wrote, "if I had ever encountered prose so pedestrian, pages so dull, chapters so devoid of ideas, whole volumes so wrongheaded . . ." None of his mentors suggested that Spruill had shown one way out of the abstractions and rigidities which so offended him.

Julia Spruill lived on as a faculty wife, a hard-working member of the Christian Science church, good citizen, and reader of history. She was resigned to the fact that her work had been ignored and contented herself by sharing all she knew with me when I turned up with the idea of writing the book she had initially thought to write on nineteenth-century southern women.

We became fast friends, and I read and reread her book in search of ideas, as a model for my own work. In 1971 or so I happened to sit by an editor from W. W. Norton on an airplane. He spoke of having just made arrangements with the University of North Carolina Press to reprint books from its backlist. Seizing the moment, I offered a spirited recommendation for *Women's Life and Work*. He was convinced, and so when Julia was seventy-three, in the context of the new feminism and the burgeoning interest in the history of women, a happy accident brought her book into a paperback edition. It began to appear on reading lists. Colonial Williamsburg adopted it as a training document. She was overwhelmed with pleasure and could hardly believe what was happening so belatedly. When she was eighty the University of North Carolina at long last conferred a distinguished alumna award upon her. And when, in 1984, the Southern Association of Women Historians created a Julia Cherry Spruill Prize for the best book published each year in southern women's history, she responded with a moving letter, quoting Pericles: "For it is only the love of honor that never grows old, not gain as some would have it that rejoices the heart of age . . ." Three years later she was dead. Corydon Spruill lived a little longer and in his will provided for a Julia Cherry Spruill Chair in the department of history of the university which had so long ignored her.

But what of the book itself?

Once it was widely available, it quickly made its way among historians of women and of the South. It became an inspiration and a model for students beginning to think seriously about the social history of women, and especially for those concerned with colonial history.

Now the book is nearly sixty years old, and more than twenty-five years of vigorous activity in the field of women's history have passed since that first Norton edition. Very few monographs published in the 1930s are opened any more, much less reprinted. Yet here is yet another edition of this one. Why?

The book's longevity is a tribute to the extraordinary care and patience with which Spruill examined the colonial record. Her careful scholarship is well illustrated in the paragraphs about the so-called "brideships" (see pp. 8–10) that were a part of southern folklore. Instead of simply repeating the story, Spruill tracked down an obscure article which examined the fate of the 140 women who came on those ships—and discovered that a few years later only thirty-five had survived. The brides from those ships had very little part in peopling the new colony.

One can open the book at almost any point and find data to stimulate thinking. In her description of the instability of colonial family life due to the high death rate among both men and women, she anticipated the modern work of Lois Green Carr and Lorena S. Walsh.[3] Her reading in court records foreshadowed, and in some cases inspired, work in legal history on the part of scholars such as Marylynn Salmon, Donna Spindel, Joan Gunderson, Gwen Gampel, and Linda Speth.[4]

Spruill recognized the limitations of traditional sources—i.e., that literate people who made records represented only a small part of colonial society—and was diligent in her effort to find evidence for the experience of women in other classes. Court records turned out to be useful for this purpose, as did travelers' accounts. She paid as much attention as her data permitted to "women of the back settlements" and to indentured servants. For descriptions of the clothing of servants she

[3] See Carr and Walsh, "The Planter's Wife: The Experience of White Women in Seventeenth Century Maryland," *William and Mary Quarterly,* 3rd. ser., no. 34 (1977): 547–71.

[4] These are only samples, since the subject has aroused wide interest. Marylynn Salmon, *Women and the Law of Property in Early America* (Chapel Hill: University of North Carolina Press, 1986); Donna J. Spindel, "Women's Civil Actions in the North Carolina Higher Courts 1670–1730," *North Carolina Historical Review* LXXI, no. 2 (April 1994); Joan R. Gunderson and Gwen Victor Gampel, "Married Women's Legal Status in New York and Virginia," *William and Mary Quarterly,* 3rd ser., no. 39 (January 1982): 113–34; Linda Speth, "More Than Her 'Thirds': Wives and Widows in Colonial Virginia," *Women and History* 4 (New York: Institute for Research in History, 1982). Terri Lynn Snyder's 1992 Ph.D. dissertation at the University of Iowa and Kathleen Brown's 1990 University of Wisconsin dissertation are among the most recent fine works dealing with southern colonial women.

turned to advertisements for those who ran away. In recent years students of slavery have followed her lead and have drawn a good bit of interesting evidence from advertisements for runaway slaves.

Court records also led her to understand the numerous ways colonial women had worked to earn money in a wide variety of trades and crafts. She found women practicing medicine, appearing in court, and taking an active part in public affairs. She discovered many women planters patenting land. She provided abundant evidence of the work of "deputy husbands," as they have been labeled by a modern scholar.

She was probably the first to formulate the now widely accepted view that as men acquired more education and shaped their work into professions, women lost opportunities in law and medicine—fields which they had practiced in the earlier, less organized society. She also anticipated John Murrin's thesis that as the colonies grew more prosperous they grew more like England.

Though she was in many ways a very proper southern lady, she dealt straightforwardly with the evidence of sexual behavior which turned up in the court records, and though she knew that southerners liked to believe that deviance was confined to the lower classes, she noted that prominent men contributed their share to cases of fornication, bastardy, adultery, and the "widespread admixture of the races." She observed that well-to-do people were better able to stay out of court and to cover up their misdeeds than their poorer contemporaries. She also recognized that the concern of town fathers for bastards was based more on the possible drain on town budgets than on the behavior of women.

Her treatment of marriage was judicious: she contrasted felicity and discord, and from contemporary sources showed that not all marriages were carefully contracted. Her sources convinced her—contrary to the view of modern demographers—that women married very young.

Spruill may be faulted for piling up examples to the point of tediousness, but aware as she was that nobody had documented the lives of these women before, she was determined to prove her points beyond argument.

The world of historical writing has changed dramatically in the past two or three decades, and historians of southern women now have the benefit of massive microfilm collections, of methodological innovation, of theoretical discussion which would amaze Spruill could she return. She was writing long before concerns with theory, with "social construction," had come on the scene. Asked for her theoretical framework she might have looked puzzled and responded that her goal was—in words she did use—to "get it right," to find out what happened and record it. "History" for her was not quite as slippery as it now seems.

In two or three areas present-day students and scholars find Spruill wanting. In the 1930s it had not occurred to any white scholar to examine slavery from the point of view of the slaves themselves. Spruill was a child of her day, and her references to slave women reflect this. So does her view of Native Americans, whom she does not hesitate to call savages. For this reason, undergraduates with late-twentieth-century sensibilities are sometimes put off by their first encounter with this book; it is necessary to introduce them also to the more recent work of Suzanne Lebsock, Peter Wood, and Allan Kulikoff on African Americans and to that of Theda Perdue on Indians.[5]

With these caveats, what we have in this volume still stands as the best single overview of its subject. The most recent general survey of southern women's history has, in its colonial chapter, more references to Spruill than to any other secondary work.[6] The perceptive reader will still find leads to research projects not yet undertaken.

For all these reasons we can welcome this new edition, which will be read well into the twenty-first century. Truly the good that we do lives after us . . .

ANNE FIROR SCOTT
Chapel Hill, N.C.
November 1997

[5] Peter Wood, *Black Majority* (New York: Knopf, 1973); Suzanne Lebsock, *Share of Honor: Virginia Women 1600–1945* (Richmond: Virginia Women's Cultural History Project, 1984); Allan Kulikoff, *Tobacco and Slaves: The Development of Southern Cultures in the Chesapeake, 1680–1800* (Chapel Hill: University of North Carolina Press, 1986).

[6] Margaret Ripley Wolfe, *Daughters of Canaan: A Saga of Southern Women* (Lexington: The University Press of Kentucky, 1995). See footnotes to Chapter 1.

PREFACE

THIS WORK was begun ten years ago as a project in the Institute for Research in Social Science at the University of North Carolina. My original plan was to make a study of the changing attitudes toward women in the South. But as work proceeded, I realized that such a very limited amount of research had been attempted in the whole field of social history of the South that groundwork would have to be done for every phase of the study. So I decided to limit the subject to the life and status of women in the English colonies of the South. My purpose was to find out as much as possible about the everyday life of women, their function in the settlement of colonies, their homes and domestic occupations, their social life and recreations, the aims and methods of their education, their participation in affairs outside the home, and the manner in which they were regarded by the law and by society in general.

I have obtained the data chiefly from contemporary records. The generosity of the Institute has made it possible for me to visit the depositories of records and to work wherever needed materials have been accessible. The Library of the University of North Carolina, the Library of Duke University, the Library of Harvard University, the Library of Congress, and the state libraries and historical societies of Maryland, Virginia, North Carolina, South Carolina, and Georgia have furnished most of the materials.

Many persons have had a part in this work. Dr. W. W. Pierson, professor of history at the University of North Carolina, secured for me a place as research assistant in the Institute. Dr. Howard W. Odum and the other directors of the Institute furnished the financial means which made the research possible, and many librarians and their assistants have contributed their services. Dr. R. D. W. Connor, formerly Kenan professor of history in the University of North Carolina, now archivist of the United States, directed the project in its early stages, and Dr. Arthur M. Schlesinger, professor of history in Harvard University, and Mr. Worthington C. Ford, historian and formerly editor of the Massachusetts Historical Society, also gave valuable advice. Dr. Katharine Jocher, assistant director of the Institute, coöperated in many ways, and Mrs. Treva Williams Bevacqua of her secretarial staff has given most efficient help. Dr. C. C. Crittenden, secretary of the North Carolina Historical Commission; Dr. A. C. McIntosh, professor emeritus of law at the University of North Carolina; Mrs. Mary R. Beard, author; Mrs. Eleanore Elliott Carroll and Mrs. Mildred Cherry Hill of Chapel Hill; and my husband, Corydon Perry Spruill, Jr., professor of economics in the University of North Carolina, all have read the manuscript and have given many suggestions for its improvement. To each of them and to many others who have helped I should like to express my gratitude.

J. C. S.

Chapel Hill
North Carolina

WOMEN'S LIFE AND WORK
IN THE SOUTHERN COLONIES

CHAPTER I

WOMEN WANTED

"WHEN THE PLANTATION grows to strength, then it is time to plant with women as well as with men; that the plantation may spread into generations, and not be ever pieced from without."[1] Thus wrote Lord Bacon, member of His Majesty's Council for Virginia, and so described the general idea of the function of women in the settlement of colonies. They were to supply an increase of population. Also they were needed, according to other promoters of plantations, to make the masculine settlers more comfortable that "their minds might be faster tyed to Virginia." The founders of the colonies early realized that mothers and housewives were indispensable to the success of their undertaking and urged women to emigrate. They made special appeals to young and marriageable females, offering them not only generous land grants but also advantageous matrimonial matches.

Women, however, did not wait to come until inducements had been offered and the plantations had become settled and secure, but they were found in each of the colonies almost from its beginning. The first group of settlers sent by Sir Walter Raleigh was of men only, but seventeen women suffered the unknown fate of the famous "Lost Colony," which came to Roanoke Island in 1587.[2] No mention was made of women among the first persons to arrive at Jamestown with Captain Newport in 1607 or in the "First Supply" in January, 1608, but in the "Second Supply," arriving in the fall of 1608, were the wife of Thomas Forrest and Anne Burras, her maid. Captain John Smith wrote of them in his *Generall Historie* as "the first gentlewoman and woman-servant that arrived in our colony." Not long after, when Anne was married to John Laydon, one of the

[1] Alexander Brown, ed., *The Genesis of the United States*, II, 799-801. (Publication facts of primary sources are given in the Bibliography.)

[2] Samuel A'Court Ashe, *History of North Carolina* (2 vols. Raleigh. Vol. I, 1908; Vol. II, 1925), I, 11-12.

4 WOMEN IN THE SOUTHERN COLONIES

first emigrants, Smith noted that it was the first marriage they had in Virginia.[3]

In the next few years women continued to come to Virginia, though in much smaller numbers than men. In a broadside of 1609, women as well as men were solicited for "the better strengthening of the colony," and the *Blessing*, which arrived at Jamestown in August of that year, brought twenty women and children.[4] In the "Great Supply" sailing in the nine ships under the command of Gates, Somers, Newport, and others from England in 1609, there were about one hundred women with the four hundred to five hundred men. Some were the wives and daughters of gentlemen. John Rolfe and his first wife were with Somers and Gates, and among those that arrived with Lord Delaware in June, 1610, was Jane, daughter of William Pierce, who later became the third wife of John Rolfe.[5] With Sir Thomas Gates in 1611 were his wife and two daughters, but his wife died on the way and his daughters were sent back to England.[6] The *John and Francis*, which sailed from England in November, 1614, brought thirty-four men and eleven women.[7]

These first women and those who soon followed them suffered inexpressible hardships and privation. Smith, in a letter dated December, 1608, described the colonists as "the one halfe sicke, the other little better," and added, "our dyet is of a little meale and water, and not sufficient of that."[8] Only by means of help from the Indians and by obtaining oysters and fish from the near-by waters did the little band survive until July, when Captain Argall arrived at Jamestown in a ship supplied with wine and biscuit. The next winter, following Smith's departure for England in October, came famine, pestilence, and an Indian massacre. To agues and fevers, which had carried away many before, were added yellow fever and the plague; and the Indians, instead of supplying the settlers with corn, pillaged their homes and murdered them. Of the whole population of about five hundred, there remained "not past sixty men,

[3] *Works* (ed., Edward Arber), pp. 446, 447.
[4] Brown, *op. cit.*, I, 248-49, 329.
[5] Alexander Brown, *The First Republic in America* (Boston, Cambridge, and New York, 1898), p. 132. Hereafter cited as *The First Republic*.
[6] Edward D. Neill, *History of the Virginia Company of London (1606-24) with Letters to and from the First Colony never before Printed* (Albany, 1869), p. 70.
[7] Brown, *The First Republic*, p. 224. [8] *Works*, p. 444.

women and children, most miserable and poore creatures, and those were preserved for the most part by roots, herbes, acornes, walnuts, berries and now and then a little fish."[9]

Incredible stories were told of this horrible winter. "Famine compelled us wholly to devoure those Hogges, Dogges & horses that weare then in the Collony, together with Rates, mice, snakes . . . ," wrote one of the "ancient Planters," and "[we] weare driven through unsufferable hunger unnaturallie to eat those thinges which nature most abhorred, the flesh . . . of man, as well of our owne nation as of an Indian, digged by some out of his grave after he had laien buried three daies & wholly devoured; . . . others, envyinge the better state of bodie of any whom hunger had not yet so much wasted as there owne, lay weight and threatened to kill and eat them; one amonge the rest slue his wife as she slept in his bosome, cutt her in pieces, powdered her & fedd upon her till he had clean devoured all her partes saveinge her heade, & was for soe barbarouse a fact and cruelty justly executed."[10] This "tragicall histoire" of the man's eating his wife, however, was denied as a "scandalous report" in a pamphlet published under the direction of the Council of Virginia, which gave this version of the gruesome incident: "There was one of the companie who mortally hated his wife, and therefore secretly killed her, then cut her in pieces and hid her in diuers parts of his house: when the woman was missing, the man suspected, his house searched, and parts of her mangled body were discouered, to excuse himself he said that his wife died, that he had hid her to satisfie his hunger, and that he fed daily upon her. . . . Hee . . . confessed the murder and was burned for his horrible villany."[11]

Whether the desperate colonists actually resorted to cannibalism or not, when Sir Thomas Gates and Sir George Somers arrived with one hundred and fifty persons in June, 1610, conditions were so discouraging that it was decided to abandon Jamestown. Their ship with the wretched remnants of the colonists on board was sailing for England when, before they had passed out of James River, they met

[9] *Ibid.*, p. 498.

[10] "A Briefe Declaration of the Plantation of Virginia duringe the First Twelve Years . . . By the Ancient Planters nowe remaining Alive in Virginia. 1624." *Colonial Records of Virginia*, p. 71.

[11] "A True Declaration of the estate of the Colonie in Virginia . . . 1610," Peter Force, ed., *Tracts and Other Papers* . . . III (No. 1), 16: Hereafter cited as *Force Tracts.*

Lord Delaware, who had been sent as governor with three ships supplied with provisions. Encouraged by the aid of fresh recruits and supplies, they returned to Jamestown and began life anew.

During these first years, the colonists had been organized as a communal body, with each person working for the group as a whole and receiving rations from the "common kettell." But when Sir Thomas Dale arrived as governor in 1611, he encouraged the establishment of separate households and gardens. He assured to every man with a family a house of four rooms or more and sufficient provisions for twelve months, allowed him twelve acres of fenced-in ground, furnished him with tools, and gave him a cow, several goats, and a start of poultry and swine.[12] A majority of the female settlers were probably mistresses of households, but regulations drawn up at the time[13] show that women, probably the poor and unmarried, were performing services for the company's tenants in return for their allowance out of the common store. One regulation provided that any laundress appointed to wash for the company's laborers and soldiers as her particular duty who should take payment for her work, withhold linen committed to her to wash, or return old and torn linen for good, was to be whipped and imprisoned. Another provided severe punishment for "what man or woman soever" who should rob any garden which he or she had been "set to weed." Other regulations throw light upon the domestic economy of the time. All persons, men and women, were forbidden to "wash any uncleane Linen, . . . throw out water or suds of fowle cloathes" in the streets or within the palisades, or to "rench, and make cleane, any kettle, pot, or pan, or such like vessell, within twenty foote of the old well, or new Pumpe." Extreme punishment was prescribed for any baker or cook who should ask or take payment for his work or detain any part of the flour, meal, or flesh committed to him to prepare. Bakers and cooks were apparently men.

In the next few years after Dale's coming, peace was secured with the Indians through the instrumentality of Pocahontas, daughter and "dearest Jewell" of the Indian chief, Powhatan. Pocahontas had befriended the first settlers at Jamestown, bringing them provisions and serving as mediator between them and her people. But

[12] Ralph Hamor, *A True Discourse of the Present State of Virginia*, p. 19. Hereafter cited as *True Discourse*.

[13] "Articles, Lawes, and Orders, Diuine, Politique, and Martiall for the Colony of Virginea . . . 1611," *Force Tracts*, III, No. 2.

after Smith's departure she was not seen again in the town until in 1612, when she was brought there captive. Captain Argall, an unscrupulous Englishman, had found her with a friendly Indian named Japazaws, and, remembering her former usefulness in dealing with her father, had plotted to take her to Jamestown as a hostage. With the aid of Japazaws and his wife, whom he bribed with the promise of a copper kettle, he had got Pocahontas aboard his ship, and when he arrived in Jamestown had notified her father that he would release her upon the Indians' return of some English prisoners and arms that they were holding.[14]

While Argall was parleying with Powhatan, Governor Dale and John Rolfe, then a widower, were attempting to convert their pagan captive to Christianity, and in the course of his instructions Rolfe conceived the idea of marrying her. She was baptized and christened Rebecca, and with the consent of Powhatan, who sent her uncle and two brothers to attend her, she was married in the church at Jamestown.[15] Whether Rolfe felt a genuine attachment for the young Indian girl,[16] or sought to advance his interests at Jamestown by a union with an Indian princess, of which scheming he was accused, or married her, as claimed by his friend and defender, Ralph Hamor, "Meerely for the good and honour of the Plantation," the union was apparently approved by all and brought peace with the savages. Letters sent home by Reverend Alexander Whitaker and Sir Thomas Dale told of the peace following the marriage, and Hamor wrote: ". . . euer since we haue had friendly commerce and trade, not only with Powhatan, himselfe, but also his subjects round about vs."[17]

Though the marriage of Pocahontas and Rolfe was generally regarded as an auspicious occasion, no other union between Indians and whites is recorded in the early years of the colony. Sir Thomas Dale, whose wife was living in England, besought Powhatan to give him his youngest daughter, sister of Pocahontas, for "his neerest companion, wife, and bedfellow" as a bond of "perpetual friendship," and sent Hamor with presents of beads, copper, wooden combs, fishhooks, and knives, to make his proposal. But the chief refused to

---

[14] Smith, *Works*, pp. 511-12.   [15] Hamor, *True Discourse*, pp. 10-11.
[16] His letter of apology for marrying "one whose education hath been rude, her manners barbarous, her generation accursed," hardly suggests the romantic lover. The letter is given in full in *The Narratives of Early Virginia* (ed., Lyon Gardiner Tyler), pp. 239-44.   [17] *True Discourse*, pp. 10-11.

listen, declaring it unbrotherly of Dale to request another daughter as a pledge of friendship.[18]

Whether other men at Jamestown had scruples against being "unequally yoked with unbelievers" or objected to Indian women for other reasons, they did not take them for wives. As the proportion of white women to men was small, there were naturally a large number of bachelors and widowers. These unmarried men were not interested in building permanent homes in Virginia or in cultivating lands to be enjoyed by future generations, but planned to make their fortunes and then return to England. Recognizing this unsettled character of their tenants, promoters of the London Company realized that it was very important to induce their bachelor farmers to marry and settle down in Virginia. Richard Martin, the company's attorney, in a speech before the House of Lords in May, 1614, declared that Virginia's greatest need was for honest laborers with wives and children and moved that a committee be appointed to consider means of securing them.[19]

At a meeting of the company, November 3, 1619, Sir Edwin Sandys, the treasurer, made several recommendations for improving their plantations. One was the sending of a hundred women to Virginia as wives to "make the men more setled & lesse moveable who by defect thereof (as is credibly reported) stay there but to gett something and then return for England." Such instability, he was sure, would "breed a dissolucon, and so an overthrow of the Plantation."[20] The transportation of the maids, he declared, should be paid for by the planters who took them for wives. The company approved these suggestions and the following spring sent ninety maids to Virginia. The next year Sandys urged sending a hundred more maids, but the lack of funds in the treasury prevented it. Later, explaining that from "the want of wives have sprung up the greatest of hindrances of the encrease of the plantation,"[21] the company attempted to raise money by subscription for sending maids and succeeded in getting enough to pay the charges of twelve.

The letter of instructions accompanying these young women stated that special care had been taken in choosing them, for "not one had been received but upon good recommendation," and urged

---

[18] *Ibid.*, p. 41; Smith, *Works*, pp. 517-20.

[19] Neill, *op. cit.*, p. 70.

[20] *Records of the Virginia Company of London* (ed., Susan M. Kingsbury), I, 256.   [21] *Ibid.*, p. 566.

the Virginia authorities to place them in the homes of married house-holders and allow them food until they could be "provided with husbands." For defraying the charges of their transportation, each planter who married one of the maids was to pay one hundred and twenty pounds of the best leaf tobacco. They were not to be married to servants, but only to freemen with the means of maintaining them. "We pray you, therefore," said the letter, "to be fathers to them in this business, not enforcing them to marry against their will." Also the letter declared that the company would consign the first servants they could send over to the planters who married these maids, as it was their intent "to preserve families and proper married men before single persons."[22]

The same letter stated that fifty more maids would be sent shortly by the Earl of Southampton and other worthy gentlemen, who realized "that the plantation can never flourish till families be planted and the respect of wives and children fix the people on the soil." Accordingly, in September, 1621, "an extraordinary choice lot of thirty-eight maids for wives" were dispatched with a letter asking that they be received "with the same Christian piety and charity as they were sent from hence" and that they be married to "honest and sufficient men."[23] For the charges disbursed in setting them forth, the adventurers asked one hundred and fifty pounds of tobacco for each maid.

In its efforts to anchor its discontented bachelors to the soil of Virginia, the company sent in all one hundred and forty maids, ninety in 1620 and fifty in 1621 and 1622.[24] Afterward it did not concern itself with supplying wives to its colonists. But the importance of women continued to be appreciated. The Virginia House of Burgesses, in a petition of July 31, 1619, asked that lots of land be allowed them for their wives as well as for themselves, declaring, "because that in a newe plantation it is not knowen whether man or woman be the most necessary."[25] The petition was granted and husbands were allowed shares for their wives equal to those given for their own ventures.

[22] H. R. McIlwaine, "The Maids Who Came to Virginia in 1620 and 1621 for Husbands," *The Reviewer*, I (April 1, 1921), 109-10.

[23] *Ibid.*, p. 111; Edward D. Neill, *English Colonization of America during the Seventeenth Century* (London, 1871), p. 155.

[24] McIlwaine, "The Maids Who Came to Virginia . . . ," *The Reviewer*, I, 113.

[25] *Journals of the House of Burgesses* (ed., H. R. McIlwaine), I, 7; *Records of the Virginia Company*, I, 566.

According to a letter sent from Virginia in 1622, all the maids sent over by the company had already been married.[26] But they did not "live happily ever after." The same year came a terrible Indian massacre, in which about four hundred of the twelve hundred and forty inhabitants were murdered. From a study of a muster of the inhabitants in Virginia in 1625, it has been estimated that only thirty-five of the one hundred and forty maids were then alive.[27] After 1624, when the company turned the colony over to the crown, it became more secure and prosperous, and women were courted and won in marriage and lived more as they did in the Mother Country.

Virginia had passed through its early critical years when in 1633 Lord Baltimore, soon after the departure of the *Ark* and the *Dove* from England, wrote a friend that he had finally succeeded in sending a "hopeful colony" into Maryland, in which were two of his brothers, twenty other gentlemen of "very good fashion," and three hundred laboring men.[28] The letter made no mention of women, but that women were among these first Marylanders appears in an account of the voyage of Father Andrew White, one of the passengers. Writing of the arrival of the little ships at an island in Chesapeake Bay, he declared: "Here by the overturning of a shallop we had allmost lost our mades which we brought along. The linnen they went to wash was much of it lost, which is noe small matter in these partes."[29]

Another narrator described the settlers' arrival at the place they named St. Mary's, which was then an Indian village. They presented the natives with English cloth, axes, hoes, and knives, and in return received permission to dwell in a part of their town. They moved at once into the half allowed them, using the natives' wigwams as well as their corn fields. Seating themselves thus upon lands already cleared, they were able to start at once to plant corn, make gardens, and build a guardhouse, storehouse, and dwellings. They procured hogs, poultry, cattle, and fruit trees from Virginia, and the Indians helped them in fishing and in hunting deer and turkeys. By virtue of their peaceful relations with the natives and

[26] Mary Newton Stanard, *Colonial Virginia* . . . (Philadelphia, 1917), p. 168.
[27] McIlwaine, "The Maids Who Came to Virginia . . . ," *The Reviewer*, I, 105-13.
[28] J. Thomas Scharf, *History of Maryland from its Earliest Period to the Present Day* (3 vols. Baltimore, 1879), I, 68.
[29] "Briefe Relation of the Voyage unto Maryland," *Narratives of Early Maryland* (ed., Clayton Colman Hall), p. 40.

the advantages of having a settled neighboring province, they escaped the horrors of war and famine, and within six months advanced as far in founding their colony as Virginia had done in six years.[30]

Lord Baltimore encouraged the coming of women to Maryland. His first "conditions of plantation" offered to each adventurer a hundred acres for himself, a hundred for his wife, fifty for each child, a hundred for each manservant, and sixty for a woman servant. Women heads of families were treated just as men. Later the grants were reduced to fifty acres for each man or woman and twenty-five for a child, and the conditions required that men be between sixteen and fifty years old and women between fourteen and forty.[31] Among those arriving during the first years of settlement were wives of adventurers, a larger number of maidservants, and several women adventurers, who came at their own expense, brought in servants, claimed large tracts, and set up plantations. The names of Mistresses Mary Tranton (also spelled Throughton), Frances White, Winifred Seaborne, Elizabeth Beach, and Mary and Margaret Brent appear frequently in the records as recipients of generous land grants and also in numerous lawsuits.[32]

A bill passed by the assembly in 1634 suggests some opposition to the holding of lands by unmarried women. A letter to Lord Baltimore in 1638 complained against the measure: "That it may be prevented that noe woman here vow chastety in the world, unlesse she marry within seven years after land shall fall to hir, she must either dispose away of hir land, or else she shall forfeite it to the nexte of kinne, and if she have but one Mannor, whereas she canne not alienate it, it is gonne unlesse she git a husband."[33] Spinsters were unpopular in an infant colony. But this early limitation of their rights did not become the law, for the Proprietor vetoed all the measures of the first assembly.[34]

The Lords Proprietors of Carolina, like Lord Baltimore and the London Company, encouraged the emigration of families to their colony by offering lands for the transportation of wives, servants, and children. The first permanent settlements in the northern part of

[30] "A Relation of Maryland, 1635," *Narratives of Early Maryland*, pp. 70-112.
[31] *Archives of Maryland*, III, 47-49, 99.
[32] "Land Notes," *Maryland Historical Magazine*, V, 166-74, 261-71, 365-74 (hereafter cited as *Maryland Magazine*); *Archives of Maryland*, I, Index.
[33] "Calvert Papers," Maryland Historical Society, *Fund Publication*, No. 28, p. 165.　　　[34] Scharf, *op. cit.*, I, 121.

Carolina were not made by persons directly from Europe, as in Virginia and Maryland, but by an overflow of population from Virginia. Adventurous or dissatisfied persons in search of cheaper and better lands gradually moved down those rivers of southeastern Virginia which flow into the Carolina sounds. Their favorable reports of the new country brought other settlers, until by 1663, when the Proprietors received their charter, there was a steady stream of immigrants into the Albemarle region.[35] The first expeditions, interested chiefly in exploring the country, probably consisted only of men, but later migrations were doubtless of whole families bringing their household goods and bent on setting up permanent homes. Unfortunately no record was kept of these movements which might throw light upon the first North Carolina women.

More information is available concerning those who helped in the founding of South Carolina. Among the passengers of the *Carolina,* the *Port Royal,* and the *Albemarle,* which in August, 1669, the Lords Proprietors sent under the command of Joseph West to found a colony at Port Royal in the lower part of their province, were wives and women servants. After experiencing many adventures on their passage,[36] they made the first settlement in April, 1670, at Albemarle Point on the west bank of the Ashley River. As this location proved unfavorable, ten years later the government and most of the settlers moved to the neck between the Cooper and Ashley rivers, the site of the present city of Charleston.

Letters of these first arrivals tell something of the life in the early years of the colony. Though their provisions sometimes ran low and they feared the Spaniards, who had a settlement below them, their difficulties were small when compared with those of the first Virginians, for they were able to obtain food and other supplies from neighboring colonies.[37] Thomas Newe, writing his father soon after

[35] Ashe, *op. cit.,* I, 59-60.

[36] The fleet reached Barbadoes in October, where it was struck by a gale, and the *Albemarle,* having been wrecked, was replaced by a shallop called *The Three Brothers.* Later the *Port Royal* was cast away near one of the Bahama Islands, but her passengers reached the shore and got transportation to Bermuda, where the other two vessels had already arrived. Here a sloop was obtained to replace the stranded *Port Royal.* Then *The Three Brothers* was separated from the other vessels and did not reach Carolina until a month after the others had arrived.—*Narratives of Early Carolina, 1650-1708* (ed., Alexander S. Salley), pp. 111-12.

[37] Joseph West, writing Lord Ashley from Albermarle Point, June 27, 1670, explained that it had been necessary to send the Barbadoes shallop to Bermuda for sup-

arriving at Charles Town in 1682, declared that the town, which two years before had had only three or four houses, had then about a hundred. Charles Town housewives were probably having many troubles, for all provisions in town were very dear. The common drink was molasses and water; malt was not yet being made. Country housekeepers fared better, he thought, for each family had a stock of hogs and cattle, and those who understood how to do it made as good butter and cheese as in England. They raised all sorts of English fruit and garden herbs, besides many others he had never seen in England, and were furnished with venison, fish, and fowl by the Indians for trifles.[38] Thomas Ashe, advertising Carolina in the same year, declared that numerous fruit trees and vines grew wild, and in the gardens were cultivated all European plants and herbs necessary for the kitchen, such as potatoes, lettuce, coleworts, parsnips, turnips, carrots, and radishes. Even flower gardens were being started, with roses, carnations, tulips, and lilies.[39]

The hardships suffered by some of the first women are suggested by the painful experiences related in a letter of Judith Manigault, one of the French Huguenots. As Judith Giton, a young woman of about twenty, with relatives and friends, she had escaped from her native land, abandoning home and household goods. Arriving penniless in South Carolina sometime in 1685, she soon married another refugee, Noe Royer, a weaver. With her husband she grubbed the land, felled trees, and operated the whipsaw. For six months together, she declared in a letter to her brother, she went without bread while working the ground like a slave, and for a period of three or four years did not always have food when she wanted

---

plies, lest the *Carolina* sent to Virginia for that purpose miscarry, for, he declared, "we have but 7 weeks provision left and that onely pease at a pint a day a man . . . and we cannot employ our servants as wee would because we have not victualls for them." The following September Governor Sayle wrote of the arrival of the *Carolina*, which brought enough Indian corn, peas, and meal for eight months and some cows and hogs from Virginia. The people, he declared, were much in need of clothing and "overprest with watching" [guard duty], but only four of the colonists had died from the "distempers usual in other parts."—*Narratives of Early Carolina*, pp. 121, 123.

[38] "Letters of Thomas Newe, 1682," *Narratives of Early Carolina*, pp. 181-82, 184.

[39] "Carolina, or a Description of the Present State of That Country," *Narratives of Early Carolina*, p. 145.

it.[40]   After the death of her first husband, she married Pierre Manigault, who with his brother Gabriel had come to Carolina after the
revocation of the Edict of Nantes.   Pierre, having brought a limited
amount of money, obtained a house, where Judith kept boarders and
lodgers while he operated a distillery and cooperage.   Their earnings from these enterprises formed the basis of the large fortune
later enjoyed by their distinguished son, Gabriel Manigault.   But
this son was only seven years old when in 1711 Judith died without
knowing that her hard labor and privation had helped lay the foundation of a great family.

Affra Coming, one of the first English settlers, wrote her sister
March 6, 1698/99, regarding their difficulties: "I am sorry that I
should be the messenger of so sad tidings as to desire you not to
come to me till you can hear better times than here is now, for the
whole country is full of trouble and sickness, 'tis the Small pox which
has been mortal to all sorts of the inhabitants & especially the Indians
who tis said to have swept away a whole neighboring nation, all to
5 or 6 which ran away and left their dead unburied, lying upon the
ground for the vultures to devouer; besides the want of shipping
this fall winter & spring is the cause of another trouble, & has been
followed by an earthquake & burning of the town or one third of it
which they say was of equal value with what remains, besides the
great loss of cattle which I know by what has been found dead of
mine . . . all these things put together makes the place look with a
terrible aspect & none knows what will be the end of it."[41]

Declarations and instructions of the Lords Proprietors and pamphlets advertising Carolina show that appeals to emigrate were made
to women as well as to men.   Adventurers were given land grants
for the transportation of their wives, children, and servants as for
their own ventures.   Women heads of families were offered lands on

[40] This letter is given in full in Charles Washington Baird's *History of the
Huguenot Immigration to America* (2 vols.   New York, 1885), II, 396-97.   See
also Edward McCrady, *The History of South Carolina under the Proprietary Government, 1679-1719* (New York and London, 1897), pp. 320-21; Arthur Henry
Hirsch, *The Huguenots of Colonial South Carolina* (Durham, N. C., 1928), pp. 174,
229-31; and David Ramsay, *The History of South-Carolina from its First Settlement in 1670 to the Year 1808* (2 vols.   Charleston, 1809), pp. 5-8.

[41] McCrady, *op. cit.*, p. 308.   Affra Harleston, a servant, arrived on the *Carolina*
with the first immigrants, and within the next two years married John Coming.   At
his death she came into possession of a considerable estate.—*South Carolina Historical
and Genealogical Magazine* (hereafter cited as *South Carolina Magazine*), III, 153.

the same terms as men, and women servants were given lands at the expiration of their terms, though in most cases their grants were smaller than those allowed menservants.[42]

Publicists offered women prospects inducements besides generous land grants. One, after expatiating on the wonders of the climate and natural products of Carolina, declared: "the Women are very fruitful and the Children have fresh sanguine Complexions."[43] Another offered this encouragement: "If any Maid or single Woman have a desire to go over, they will think themselves in the Golden Age, when Men paid a Dowry for their Wives; for if they be but civil, and under 50 years of Age, some honest Man or other, will purchase them for their Wives."[44]

The colonies of Virginia and Maryland were over a hundred years old and the Carolinas had passed through the first stages of colonization when in January, 1733, James Oglethorpe with thirty-five families ascended the Savannah River to Yamacraw Bluff and made a settlement at Savannah. The next year arrived about forty families of Salzburgers, who, having been driven first from the Tyrol and then from Germany, had taken advantage of Oglethorpe's offer of toleration in Georgia. After seeing his first colonists settled, Oglethorpe returned in 1735 to England, and in the fall of that year brought back a body of German and English and settled on St. Simon's Island a town which they called Frederica. In January, 1736, one hundred and thirty Scotch Highlanders with fifty women and children founded a settlement called New Inverness.[45]

Not much is known of the women in any of these groups. But of those who came with Oglethorpe in 1735 glimpses are to be had in a record kept by one of the passengers.[46] On board the ship they were given thread, worsted, and knitting needles and were employed in making stockings and caps and in mending clothes for their families. During the passage four children were born. Upon their

[42] "A Declaration and Proposal to all that will Plant in Carolina," *Colonial Records of North Carolina*, I, 43-46.

[43] Samuel Wilson, "An Account of the Province of Carolina, 1682," *Narratives of Early Carolina*, p. 169.

[44] Robert Horne (?), "A Briefe Description of the Province of Carolina, 1666," *Narratives of Early Carolina*, p. 78.

[45] Charles C. Jones, *History of Georgia* (2 vols. Boston and New York, 1883), I, 119-20, 201.

[46] Francis Moore, "A Voyage to Georgia Begun in the Year 1735, by Francis Moore," *Georgia Historical Society, Collections*, I, 88, 111-12, 114.

arrival at Savannah, when Oglethorpe found it impossible to get ships to carry them to Frederica, he called the freeholders together and explained the hardships to be undergone in getting to the island. He pointed out that it would mean traveling one hundred and thirty miles in open boats and lying at nights in the woods exposed to cold and frost, and perhaps hard rains. After explaining these difficulties, which he said were almost insuperable to women and children, of whom there were a large number in the company, he told the men to talk it over with their wives and decide whether they chose to remain in Savannah or attempt the proposed settlement on the island. The women were apparently unafraid of hardships, for the answer brought back was that they wished to go on and settle the town of Frederica. When they arrived on the island, they found that Oglethorpe had built a bower thatched with palmetto leaves for each family. "These palmetto bowers," the chronicler declared, "were very convenient shelters, being tight in the hardest rains; they were about twenty foot long, and fourteen foot wide, and in regular rows, looked very pretty, the palmetto leaves lying smooth and handsome and of a good color. The whole appeared something like a camp; for the bowers looked like tents, only being larger, and covered with palmetto leaves instead of canvas."

As the promoters of Georgia appealed to the poorer classes for settlers, among the advantages they offered men to emigrate was the gainful employment of their wives and children. Pamphlets advertising Georgia compared the scanty earnings of a family in England with the generous rewards awaiting them in Georgia. They pointed out that women and children would find pleasant and remunerative work in the production of silk, one of the trustees' most cherished enterprises. This glowing picture was painted for the poor English workman who would take his family to the new colony: "Let him see the People all in Employment of various Kinds, Women and Children feeding and nursing Silkworms, winding off the Silk, or gathering the Olives; the Men ploughing and planting their Lands, tending the Cattle, or felling the Forest . . . let him see these in content and Affluence . . . and think if they are not happier than those supported by Charity and Idleness [in England]."[47]

But while the trustees offered employment for wives and prom-

[47] Benjamin Martyn, "Reasons for Establishing the Colony of Georgia," Georgia Historical Society, *Collections*, I, 231.

ised maintenance for one year for the family of each man who would
go to Georgia, they did so to enable poor men encumbered with de-
pendents to emigrate rather than to obtain women colonists. At first
they made no bid for female settlers. They granted lands to men
only, restricted their descent to male heirs, and provided that on the
failure of male issue they were to revert to the trust.[48] Thus women
colonists were prevented even from inheriting land. The trustees
explained that this policy was due to the military character of the
colony. Because of the hostile Spaniards on her southern frontier,
Georgia required a large body of soldiers for defense. Therefore
it was necessary to establish such tenures of land as would keep the
number of soldiers equal to the number of lots. If women were
allowed to inherit lots, the military strength of each township would
soon be diminished, for every female heir would take one soldier
from the garrison. Other inconveniences which would result from
allowing lands to descend to women were that "women being equally
incapable to act as soldiers or serve on juries, these duties and many
others such as watchings and wardings etc., would return so much
oftener to each man in proportion as the number of men in the township was lessened, and by that means become very burdensome to the
remaining male lot-holders."[49]

But after the first establishment of the colony, the importance of
women settlers came to be recognized. There was much grumbling
against the system of land tenure, which finally the trustees modified,
first allowing fathers to appoint daughters as their successors when
they had no male children, and later permitting them to bequeath
daughters lands whether or not there were sons.[50] Also, the bachelor
soldiers and farmers had not long been subjected to masculine housewifery before they began to demand wives.

In 1738 a minister of the Salzburgers urged that some unmarried
Christian Salzburger women be brought over, or "other honest members of the female sex" who "would not regret to marry" in Georgia
and "establish an orderly household." Hitherto, he declared, the
bachelors had "endured much disorder in their dwellings rather than

[48] *Colonial Records of Georgia*, III, 418.
[49] "An Account Showing the Progress of the Colony of Georgia . . . 1742,"
American Colonial Tracts (ed., G. P. Humphrey), I (No. 5), 5-6; Moore, *op. cit.*,
Georgia Historical Society, *Collections*, I, 97.
[50] *Colonial Records of Georgia*, I, 164, 345-46; II, 7, 393-94; III, 378-79;
V, 170.

marry such persons in whom they did not discover the token of a
genuine fear of God and an exceptionally honest life."[51]   In the same
year another appeal came from the Salzburgers, asking that at least
half a dozen unmarried women be sent to them.[52]   So great was their
need for wives that they requested Oglethorpe to leave with them
some German servant women, declaring that the young men who
married them would pay their passage.[53]   Householders took Dutch
servants into their homes, giving them temporal and spiritual instruction in preparation for marriage with their young men.[54]

The Salzburgers were not alone in realizing the need for wives,
for, after seeing the discomforts of his unmarried soldiers, Oglethorpe
began to urge the trustees to send marriageable women to Georgia.
In January, 1739-40, he asked them to give passage to the wives of
some recruits, suggesting that it would be "a cheap way of increasing
the Colony by 30 families," and declaring, "from single men there
are great Inconveniences."[55]   The trustees evidently approved his
recommendations, for a report of their meeting, February 2, 1741-42,
stated: "We agreed that it would help to people the Colony, that
Women should go over, who would soon get husbands among the
soldiers, and be an inducement to those soldiers to settle in the Colony when the time of their service should expire: and therefore
Order'd that 30 head of women and children should go, the freight
of whom would come to £180, and that 6 pence a day should be
allow'd them for their maintenance till they were ship'd."[56]

A pamphlet describing conditions in Georgia in 1741 declared
that the married soldiers were "the most industrious, and willing to
plant."[57]   The same year Oglethorpe suggested that the greatest service which could be done for the colony was to send over "married
recruits with industrious wives."[58]   Again, emphasizing the same
urgent need, he wrote: "The first Measure for us as Trustees to take
is after supporting Religion to encourage Marriage and the rearing of
Children . . . there is now in this place [Frederica] only above 700
men more than there are Women, most of these would marry if they

[51] *Ibid.*, XXII (Part I), 348.   [52] *Ibid.*, p. 250.

[53] "Letters from Oglethorpe," Georgia Historical Society, *Collections*, III, 100.

[54] *Colonial Records of Georgia*, XXII (Part II), 464.

[55] Georgia Historical Society, *Collections*, III, 104-5.

[56] *Colonial Records of Georgia*, V, 591.

[57] John Percival, "Impartial Inquiry into the State and Utility of the Province
of Georgia," Georgia Historical Society, *Collections*, I, 181.

[58] "Letters from Oglethorpe," Georgia Historical Society, *Collections*, III, 113.

could get Wives. The sending over single Women Without Familys that could protect them might be attended with Indecencys, but the giving of passage to the Wives, Sisters, and Daughters of Recruits and a small Maintenance till they go on board would be a remedy to this and much the cheapest way of peopling the Country. . . . We have found also that the married Soldiers live easiest, many of them having turned out very industrious Planters."[59]

Oglethorpe, Sandys, and the proprietors of Maryland and Carolina were of one mind regarding the importance of women in founding colonies. Masculine settlers might explore new territories, clear the lands, and defend them against the Spaniards and the Indians, but alone they could establish only temporary camps in the wilderness. Women were necessary for the founding of permanent homes.

[59] *Ibid.*, p. 144.

CHAPTER II

FROM HUT TO MANSION

WHEN MISTRESS FORREST and Anne Burras arrived at Jamestown, they found there hardly more than an armed camp. Enclosing a little more than an acre of land and defended by palisades made of large poles, stood a triangular fort with three gates in the center of each side. In the market-place were a storehouse, "Corps du Gard," and a church, described by Smith as "a homely thing like a barne, set upon Cratchets covered with rafts, sedge, and earth."[1] Of even worse construction were the dwellings within the fort, flimsy huts arranged in lines facing the palisades of its two shorter sides.

For fifteen or more years after the first settlement at Jamestown, the dwellings continued to be rude shanties of such green timber and poor workmanship that they were constantly falling into decay. Struggling for existence amid famine, sickness, and hostile savages, the miserable colonists had no time, or heart either, perhaps, to build lasting and substantial residences. Also, many who were bachelors were more interested in digging for gold or amassing a fortune to take back to England than in importing unnecessary household goods.[2]

But gradually dwellings became more substantial and comfortable. Rude huts gave way to improved frame houses, which in turn were replaced by brick residences of impressive dimensions. Governor Sir John Harvey, in a letter to the Privy Council in 1638, told of twelve new houses at Jamestown. One of brick erected by the secretary was "the fairest that was ever known in this countrye"; others were framed but were constructed "consonant to his Ma'ties Instruction that we should not suffer men to build slight cottages as heretofore."[3]

[1] Smith, *Works*, p. 957.

[2] Captain Nathaniel Butler wrote in 1622 that the Virginia houses were generally the worst he ever saw, "the meanest Cottages in England being every ways equall (if not superior) with the most of the best." The Virginians resented this criticism, replying that their dwellings had been built for use and not for ornament. But later their assembly, looking back upon this early period, declared that the houses were "so meane and poore . . . that they could not stand above one or two yeares."— *Records of the Virginia Company of London*, II, 383.

[3] *Virginia Magazine of History and Biography*, III, 29-30. Hereafter cited as *Virginia Magazine*.

Outside Jamestown a majority of the planters used brick for foundations and chimneys only, as the abundance of wood made framing
less expensive. Typical of many Virginia dwellings at the time, doubtless, was the parsonage which the vestry of Northampton County
resolved to build in 1635. It was to be forty feet long, eighteen feet
wide, and "nyne foot to the wall plates," with a chimney at each end.
A partition running through the middle was to divide it into two
apartments, a "Kitchinge" and a "Chamber," and at each end of the
house there was to be a room, one a study and the other a buttery.[4]
In the last half of the century, while houses varied from one-story,
two-room cottages to two-and-a-half-story brick structures, the most
frequent style, whether of frame or brick, was the story-and-a-half
type, sometimes with a wing at the rear, and often with a "shedd-
room" kitchen. According to Beverley, the Virginians built many
rooms on a floor because the frequent high winds would "incommode
a towring Fabrick."[5]

Some of the most prosperous planters had residences of four to
seven rooms and a few had larger homes, but generally seventeenth-
century houses were small. Governor Berkeley's brick residence at
Green Spring had six apartments, and that of Colonel Nathaniel
Bacon contained seven, besides a kitchen, dairy, and storeroom.[6] The
inventory of Mrs. Elizabeth Digges described the divisions in her
residence as the yellow room, the red room, the hall parlor, the large
room opposite the yellow room, and the chamber back of this. All
of these were apparently on one floor. Above was a garret with a
room attached, and below was a cellar.[7] Homes generally were
much less pretentious. Robert Beverley, planter of large estate, lived
in a house containing only three chambers besides a dairy, kitchen, and
overseer's room; and the dwelling of Edmund Cobbs had only a
hall and kitchen on the lower floor and one room above.[8]

From contemporary observations it appears that the seventeenth-
century houses, though simple and plain, were sometimes surprisingly
attractive inside. John Hammond in 1655 described the Virginia
dwellings as "Pleasant in their building, which although for most

[4] Esther Singleton, *The Furniture of Our Forefathers* (New York, 1913), p. 6.
[5] *The History and Present State of Virginia*, p. 251.
[6] Philip Alexander Bruce, *Economic History of Virginia in the Seventeenth Century* (2 vols. New York, 1896), II, 155-56.
[7] *Ibid.*, p. 155.   [8] *Ibid.*, pp. 155, 156.

part they are but one story besides the loft, and built of wood, yet contrived so delightfull, that your ordinary houses in England are not so handsome, for usually the rooms are daubed and whitelimed, glazed and flowered, and if not glazed windows, shutters which are made very pritty and convenient."[9]

A visitor in 1686 declared there were very good houses in the colony. Those in the country were of wood sheathed with chestnut plank and sealed inside with the same. "As they get on in the world," he added, "they refinish the interior with plaster, for which they use oyster shell lime, making it as white as snow; so that although these houses seem poor enough on the outside because one sees only the weathered sheathing, within they are most agreeable. Most of the houses are amply pierced with glazed windows." Commenting further upon the general style of architecture, he declared: "Whatever their estates, for what reason I do not know, they build their houses consisting only of two ground floor rooms, with some closets and one or two prophet's chambers above. According to his means, each planter provides as many of such houses as he needs. They build also a separate kitchen, a house for the Christian slaves, another for Negro slaves, and several tobacco barns, so that in arriving at a plantation of a person of importance you think you are entering a considerable village."[10]

This custom of providing houses for special purposes and removing household occupations from the residence prevailed wherever wealth was sufficient to make it possible and continued through the eighteenth and into the nineteenth century. Beverley declared the "Drudgeries of Cookery, Washing, Dairies, &c.," were performed in outside offices in order to keep the dwelling house "more cool and sweet."[11] Hugh Jones explained that the kitchen was removed from the main house because of "the Smell of hot Victuals, offensive in hot Weather."[12] The number of these outbuildings, rather than the size or grandeur of the dwelling house, doubtless accounted for its being referred to as the "Great House."

A description of the home of a representative prosperous planter with its outbuildings and other surroundings appears in this letter

[9] "Leah and Rachel," *Narratives of Early Maryland*, pp. 297-98.
[10] Durand of Dauphiné, *A Frenchman in Virginia, being the Memoirs of a Huguenot Refugee in 1686* (trans., Fairfax Harrison), pp. 111-13.
[11] *Op. cit.*, p. 251.
[12] *Present State of Virginia*, p. 36.

from William Fitzhugh to a friend in 1686: ". . . the Plantation where I now live contains a thousand acres . . . upon it there is three quarters well furnished with all necessary houses; grounds and fencing, together with a choice crew of negro's at each plantation . . . with stocks of cattle & hogs at each quarter, upon the same land, is my Dwelling house furnished with all accomodations for a comfortable & gentile living, as a very good dwelling house with rooms in it, four of the best of them are hung & nine of them plentifully furnished with all things necessary and convenient, & all houses for use furnished with brick chimneys, four good Cellars, a Dairy, Dovecot, Stable, Barn, Henhouse, Kitchen, & all other conveniencys & all in a manner new, a large Orchard, of about 2500 Apl trees most grafted, well fenced with a Locust fence a Garden, a hundred square foot square, well pailed in, a Yeard wherein is most of the said necessary houses pallizado'd in with locust Puncheons . . . together with a good Stock of Cattle, hogs, horses, mares, sheep, &c. and necessary servants belonging to it, . . . About a mile & half distance a good Water Grist miln, whose tole I find sufficient to find my own family with wheat & Indian corn. . . ."[13]

The divisions in the seventeenth-century dwelling were not designed and furnished for particular purposes such as dining, sleeping, and entertaining, but differed very little from each other in their appointments. As the size of the family, even among the wealthiest, was ordinarily greatly out of proportion to that of the house, it was necessary to make of every room a possible sleeping apartment and dressing room. The hall, where the family usually had their meals and sat, contained several tables, a cupboard, various kinds of chairs, chests of drawers, a looking glass, a cabinet, a trunk or two, a couch-bed, and even a "standing-bed" with appurtenances. The parlor was furnished very much like the chamber, often with a large four-poster and one or two trundle beds in addition to tables, chairs, chests, and trunks. Clothing and household linen were stored, apparently according to no general rule, in hall, parlor, or chamber.

The most prominent article of furniture in the colonies as in the Mother Country was the bed, which was found in every room except possibly the kitchen. The feeling of impropriety in entertaining mixed company in a bedroom was not present in America or Europe in the seventeenth century. It will be remembered that at the time

[13] *Virginia Magazine*, I, 395-96.

kings and queens received their courtiers in their sleeping apartments. So, the "bedd standing in ye parlour" was the most expensive and luxurious object on display in many homes. It was often an imposing four-poster covered with a soft feather bed and surrounded by curtains of bright-colored fabrics upheld by a rod, and by valances of the same material suspended from the sides to the floor.[14] Other furnishings of the bed were pillows and bolsters, pillowberes and sheets of oznaburg, canvas, Holland, or linen, blankets or "duffields," and coverlets and quilts of gay colors. A brass warming pan in which coals could be placed was used to take the chill from the sheets in winter.

Besides the bed and its furnishings were chests, trunks, tables, and chairs. There were costly Russian leather and Turkey-worked chairs, plainer chairs with bottoms of rush, calfskin, cane, or white oak strips, and plain joint stools, many kinds of tables, chests with and without drawers, and various kinds of boxes and trunks. Furniture was of oak, pine, cypress, bay, cedar, maple, and walnut. Mahogany did not appear until the next century, and then only in the homes of the wealthy. The chest of drawers with a looking glass and the bureau, though far less common than the trunk or ordinary chest, were found in the better homes, and cupboards were fairly common among the most prosperous, along with such refinements as brass and iron andirons, shovel, tongs, and bellows at each fireplace, curtains at the windows, and "cloths" and cushions for chairs and tables. The carpets often mentioned in inventories were coverings for tables or other furniture. Floor coverings were not in general use until the next century.

Some of the most affluent housewives, by the latter part of the century, were well equipped with linens and tableware. In 1677 Mistress Elizabeth Beasley, describing her losses in Bacon's Rebellion the year before, mentioned "twenty-two pairs of fine dowlas sheets, six pairs of Holland sheets, forty-six pillow cases, twenty-four fine napkins, two tablecloths and thirty-six towels, most of them fine dowlas."[15] The size of the families, the hospitable manners, and the

[14] Hugh Jones declared that the Virginians pulled the down of their living geese and both wild and tame ducks "wherewith they make the softest and sweetest Beds."—*Present State of Virginia*, p. 42. The "flock bed" often mentioned in the wills and inventories was of wool or wool ravelings. The wives of the poorer planters sometimes made beds of cat-tails, a plant growing in the marshes of the colony.—Bruce, *op. cit.*, II, 163.   [15] *Virginia Magazine*, V, 372.

rarity of forks made it important to have on hand a large quantity of table linen. For everyday purposes this was of cotton, oznaburg, dowlas, or Holland, but that saved for special occasions was of damask. Mistress Elizabeth Digges possessed nine tablecloths and thirty napkins of this expensive material, besides three diaper and forty-eight flaxen tablecloths and thirty-six diaper and sixty flaxen napkins.[16]

Plates used in serving food were sometimes of earthenware, though because of its durability and inexpensiveness, pewter was the material of which the larger number were made. Wooden trenchers or hollowed-out pieces of board, were much used. Dishes of various kinds were made of pewter, a material so much used that in most houses the raw metal was kept on hand for molding new and re-pairing old utensils. Forks were rare, but knives and spoons of tin, pewter, or alchemy were in general use. Tumblers, mugs, flagons, tankards, beakers, and cups were used for drinking. Other articles on dining tables were saltcellars, porringers, sugar-pots, butter-dishes, castors, cruets, bowls, and jugs. Wealthier families had silver drinking vessels, spoons, and saltcellars, and the most prosperous possessed silver services engraved with their coats of arms.

The Virginia kitchen, though usually less picturesque than that of New England, was a very important adjunct to the house. At one end was a vast chimney of brick or stone built with an inner projecting ledge, on which rested a bar called a lug-pole or back-bar. Suspended from this bar, which was six or eight feet from the floor, were iron hooks or chains with hooks of various lengths called pothooks or trammels. On these hooks, huge pots and kettles hung at varying distances over the fire. Some of the best-equipped homes had copper boilers embedded in brick and mortar and heated from underneath. The oven was a brick structure in a hole in the ground. Enormous iron pots, weighing forty pounds or more, and copper, tin, and brass kettles holding as much as fifteen gallons were used for boiling large quantities of food at a time. Trivets, or three-legged stands of varying heights, on which food could be placed at exactly the right distance from the coals, iron spits for roasting meats above the fire, gridirons for broiling, iron and brass skillets for baking, long toasting forks for turning the meats, and ladles for basting them were also part of the kitchen equipment. In addition were long-handled waffle irons, chafing dishes, pudding pans, saucepans, wooden bowls, tin and

[16] Bruce, *op. cit.*, p. 182.

earthenware pans, graters, sifters, cullenders, funnels, iron or brass mortars and pestles, rolling-pins, scales and weights, pincers, and various kinds of knives. In the dairy were churns, pails, tubs, cheese press, trays, strainers, butter-sticks, noggins, piggins, and earthen butter-pots.

The variety and quantity of household furniture described above were found only in homes of persons of easy circumstances. Those of narrower means had much less, and even affluent families sometimes possessed only the essential articles. The Reverend John Fontaine, who in 1715 visited in the home of Robert Beverley, declared that, though rich, Beverley had nothing in or about his house but what was necessary, that he had good beds but no curtains, and instead of cane chairs, used stools made of wood.[17] Inventories show that many persons owned hardly more equipment than what was absolutely required for sleeping and the preparation of food.

Homes in early Maryland were very much like those in Virginia. Lord Baltimore's instructions to his colonists in 1633 directed that they build their houses in "as decent and uniforme a manner as their abilities and the place will afford, and neere adjoyning on to an other"; that streets be marked out, upon which the houses should face; and that divisions of land adjoining the house plots be allotted for gardens.[18] Father White, writing to Lord Baltimore in 1638, recommended that he send a brickmaker to the colony and oblige each planter to take from him as many bricks as would be necessary to build an abode according to his own degree, explaining that brick houses would be cheaper, more healthful "against heate and coale," and "fitter for defense against the infidels."[19] But this suggestion was not carried out by the planters. The order of development in Maryland, as in Virginia, was from huts of hewn logs to framed story-and-a-half houses. Thomas Cornwallis, one of the first emigrants and most prominent inhabitants, wrote the proprietor in 1638: "I am building of A house toe put my head in, of sawn Timber frame A story and half hygh, with a sellar and Chimnies of brick toe Encourage others toe follow my Example, for hithertoe wee Live in Cottages."[20] Charles Calvert in 1672 declared his intention of building

[17] Ann Maury, *Memoirs of a Huguenot Family*, p. 265. Quoted in *Virginia Magazine*, III, 171.

[18] *Narratives of Early Maryland*, pp. 21-22; "Calvert Papers," Maryland Historical Society, *Fund Publication*, No. 28, p. 138.

[19] *Ibid.*, p. 207.   [20] *Ibid.*, p. 174.

a brick house for his son. His example may have been followed by a few of the most prosperous, but generally the houses at the time appear to have been but plain wooden structures. Lord Baltimore declared in 1678 that in St. Mary's, excepting his own home and the public buildings, there were not more than thirty houses, and "those . . . as in all other parts of the Provynce very meane and Little and Generally after the manner of the meanest farme houses in England."[21]

The inventory of the estate of Governor Leonard Calvert, who died in 1647, gives some idea of the home of a prominent gentleman during the infancy of the colony. His residence was a large framed house with one hundred acres of land. His furniture consisted of the following: an old bed and bolster with an old green rug for coverlet; a very old feather bed; an old flock bed, bolster, and old red rug; an old trunk with lock and key; a small trunk; a white box without lock or key; a great old square chest; a "joined" table, two chairs, and a form; an old frame of a chair; and a "rugge." For tableware he had a blue jug, five old pewter dishes, one "bason," five plates, twelve pewter spoons, a silver sack cup, and "3 small bitts of Syluer plate." The only kitchen utensils mentioned were an iron pot and an old brass kettle.[22]

Nicholas Wyatt's inventory describes a home probably represent-ative of those of well-to-do Marylanders toward the close of the century. The dwelling consisted of a hall, parlor, hall-chamber, porch-chamber, parlor-chamber, kitchen, kitchen-chamber, kitchen loft, cellar, milk house, and buttery. The hall, as in Virginia houses, was a combination dining room, living room, and bedroom, and con-tained furniture appropriate to all three—an oblong table, a side cupboard, six "joint stools," sixteen "Turkey-work chairs" and seven leather chairs, a couch-bed with its appurtenances, a round table, a chest of drawers, a looking glass, a trunk, and a cabinet. Brass and-irons, tongs, shovel, and a pair of bellows stood at the fireplace; a "window-cloth" hung at the window; and seven framed pictures decorated the walls. In the parlor stood a four-post bedstead, with curtains and valance, feather bed, bolster and pillows, and a gaily colored rug for coverlet, a couch with its furnishings, a chest of draw-ers with a looking glass, a sealskin trunk, a cupboard, and eleven chairs. This room also had window curtains, framed pictures, and fire-

[21] *Archives of Maryland*, V, 266.   [22] *Ibid.*, IV, 320-21.

place furniture. The parlor-chamber, hall-chamber, kitchen-chamber, and porch-chamber each contained beds, chests, trunks, looking glasses, chairs, and stools. There were no floor coverings, but window curtains, pictures, cushions, and table covers gave evidence of comfortable living. In this house there were six large beds, three couch-beds, and one trundle bed. The household linen, which was kept in a chest and a box in the parlor-chamber, consisted of seventeen "pillow-coats," seven pairs of sheets, two diaper tablecloths, five other tablecloths, twelve diaper napkins and four dozen and four other napkins, seven towels, three small tablecloths, and one old tablecloth.[23]

North Carolina was settled too late in the century to have advanced far beyond the rude cabin stage before 1700. Though there were a few substantial planters among them, the first inhabitants of the Albemarle region generally were men of little capital. They lacked sufficient wealth to build large houses, and, because of the dangerous coast line, found it difficult to import furniture. Yet John Lawson, writing about 1700, declared there were few housekeepers "but what lived very nobly."[24] According to this early historian, good bricks were made throughout the settlement, and carpenters, joiners, masons, and plasterers were present.[25] Many different kinds of trees provided building materials for substantial residences and attractive woods for furniture. Framing of houses was of chestnut; window frames were of the durable live oak; post and sills were of red cedar, and shingles of white cedar. Wainscoting, tables, and chests were made of cedar; tables and chests of drawers of black walnut, and trenchers and other turnery ware of maple and holly.[26]

The household furnishings of Captain Valentine Bird, whose estate was described in an inventory of 1680,[27] were probably representative of those of the better sort of seventeenth-century Carolinians. Captain Bird possessed a plantation with the usual outhouses and stock of cows, sheep, and hogs, eleven Negro slaves, an Indian slave woman, and a white indentured woman servant. In his house were two bedsteads, one couch, a cradle, and a "Hammacker"; two feather beds, twelve pillows, and four bolsters; a large trunk, two iron-bound chests, and two small chests, one of which had drawers;

[23] Singleton, op. cit., pp. 58-61.
[24] History of Carolina . . . , p. 111.   [25] Ibid., p. 273.
[26] Ibid., pp. 156, 157, 161, 165, 166, 167.
[27] J. Bryan Grimes, North Carolina Wills and Inventories . . . , pp. 472-74.

two tables with frames, ten chairs, a looking glass, a dressing box, a warming pan, and two hairbrushes. Tableware consisted of two tankards, two dozen plates, nineteen porringers, fifty-one dishes, and four basins, all of pewter. Kitchen utensils included a brass kettle weighing thirty-two pounds, one iron pot of fifty pounds, another of thirty-six, and two of thirty-three pounds, three skillets, a frying pan, three spits, a mortar and pestle, a pair of andirons, three pairs of pothooks, one pair of racks, a flesh fork, and a "Parcel of Tining ware." There were ten pairs of Holland sheets and three of brown oznaburg, seventeen towels, five cupboard cloths, four diaper table-cloths and two dozen and nine diaper napkins, and six coarse table-cloths and two dozen and four coarse napkins.

Of the Ashley River settlement, a new arrival wrote in 1682 that it had about a hundred houses, all of which were built wholly of wood, that though excellent brick was made in the colony, there was very little of it.[28] Doubtless these wooden houses resembled the first rude huts of the neighboring colonies. Lawson wrote of staying in the home of a Frenchman thirty-six miles from Charles Town in "a very curious contrived house built of brick and stone,"[29] but there were probably very few buildings of these materials in the colony at the time.

A letter from South Carolina in 1710 gives this illuminating description of the steps usually taken in the establishment of a planta-tion home: "The first thing to be done is, after having cutt down a few Trees, to split Palisades, or Clapboards, and therewith make small Houses or Huts, to shelter the Slaves. After that, whilst some Servants are clearing the Land, others are to be employed in squaring or sawing Wall-plats, Posts, Rafters, Boards and Shingles, for a small House for the Family, which usually serves for a Kitchen after-wards, when they are in better Circumstances to build a larger. Dur-ing the Time of this Preparation, the Master Overseer, or white Servants, go every Evening to the next Neighbour's house, where they are lodg'd and entertain'd kindly, without Charges. And if the Person have any Wife or Children, they are commonly left in some Friend's House, till a suitable dwelling Place and Conveniences are provided, fit for them to live decently. . . . In the second Fall, or Winter, after a Plantation is settled they make Gardens, plant Or-

---

[28] "Letters of Thomas Newe, 1682," *Narratives of Early Carolina*, p. 181.

[29] *Op. cit.*, p. 30. For descriptions of some early Carolina houses see McCrady, *op. cit.*, pp. 705-8.

chards, build Barns, and other convenient Houses. The third or fourth Winter, Persons of any Substance provide Brick, Lime, or other Materials, in order to build a good House."[30]

As suggested in this letter, the modest dwellings built by emigrants upon their arrival in the colonies were later converted into outhouses or became merely wings of more palatial residences, as the owners made their way in the world. During the seventeenth century, while planters generally were busy laying the foundations of their fortunes, their homes were small and unpretentious. But with the accumulation of wealth during the eighteenth century, a social and political aristocracy developed, desirous of more comforts and luxuries and ambitious to display their success in their homes. Members of this privileged class built handsome mansions and imported sumptuous furnishings from England. Generally, in the settled regions, the dwellings became larger, better-proportioned, and more expensively furnished.

Wealthy South Carolina families, by the middle of the century, had fine houses both in Charles Town and in the country. Lord Adam Gordon, who visited the colony in 1764, wrote that almost every planter of note had a town residence, to which he and his family repaired on public occasions and during the three "sickly months" in the fall. Many of these town houses, he observed, were "large and handsome, having all the conveniences one sees at home [England] . . . the most considerable are of Brick, the other Cypress and yellow Pine."[31] The first floor of a Charles Town dwelling, before 1760, was usually two feet above the grade. The street frontage was narrow, but the lots were deep enough not only for the house and its appendages of kitchen and washroom, but for servants' quarters, stables, and kitchen and flower gardens. The drawing room was on the second floor, overlooking the street. The more important rooms were paneled, but the woodwork was simple. After 1760,

[30] Thomas Nairne, *Letter from South Carolina:* . . . (1710).

[31] "Journal," *Travels in the American Colonies* (ed., N. D. Mereness), pp. 397, 398. Hereafter cited as *Journal*. For descriptions of Charles Town houses, see Albert Simons and Samuel Lapham (eds.), "Charleston, South Carolina," *The Octagon Library of American Architecture* (New York, 1927), Vol. I; A. R. Huger Smith and D. E. Huger Smith, *Dwelling Houses of Charleston* (Philadelphia and London, 1917); Joseph Everett Chandler, *Some Charleston Mansions*, Vol. XIV, No. 4, of The White Pine Monograph Series on Early American Architecture (New York, 1928); and E. A. Crane and E. E. Soderholtz, *Colonial Architecture in South Carolina and Georgia* (1898).

houses were larger and more elaborately decorated. In their general design, as well as in their well-proportioned, paneled rooms and hand-carved woodwork, they showed clearly the influence of English Georgian architecture.

The country seats of well-to-do Charlestonians, situated on the banks of the Ashley and Cooper rivers and their tributaries, were noted for the beauty of their grounds, which were often tended by imported English gardeners. Eliza Pinckney left a charming picture of "Crowfield," the country place of the Middletons on Goose Creek. "The house stands a mile from, but in sight of the road, and makes a very handsome appearance," she wrote, adding, "as you draw near it new beauties discover themselves; first the fruit vine mantleing the wall, loaded with delicious clusters. Next a spacious Basin in the midst of a large Green presents itself." The mansion house was "neatly finish'd, the rooms well contrived and Elegantly furnish'd." Leading from the back door was a spacious walk a thousand feet long, on each side of which was a "grass plat ornamented in a Serpentine manner with Flowers." Round this plot on the right was a thicket of young, tall live oaks, and opposite on the left was a large square bowling green, sunk a little below the level of the garden. Surrounding this was a walk, bordered by a double row of fine, large, flowering laurels and catalpas, which afforded both shade and beauty. At the bottom of this "charming spott" was a large fish pond with a mount rising out of the middle, upon which stood a Roman temple.[32]

Similar to "Crowfield" were many country places in Virginia and Maryland. Situated on the bank of a stream, a country place of this kind had a waterfront looking out over the river, which was frequently used as a highway, and a landward front, where the drive leading from the road terminated. The "Great House," often a large, square, two-storied brick building with impressive doorways and imposing steps at each entrance, had on each side a cluster of outbuildings, which were generally better proportioned and more symmetrically arranged than the service houses of the preceding century. Surrounding the houses were broad lawns with terraced gardens, hedged with boxwood and lilacs and bordered with elms, cedars, catalpas, crape myrtles, and poplars. The mansion usually had a hall running through the center connecting the two fronts, and often it had four rooms on each floor, though some houses contained

[32] Harriott Horry Ravenel, *Eliza Pinckney*, pp. 53-55.

as many as fourteen or seventeen rooms in all. These rooms were sometimes as large as twenty-five feet square, with a pitch of from twelve to seventeen feet, and were finished with elegant and delicate taste. The smoothly paneled walls, cornices, and other woodwork of fine detail, and the graceful stairways with carved step ends and newel posts, delicately turned balusters, and rich mahogany handrails were probably what the visitor John Bernard had in mind when he declared that the planters' dwellings were "internally palaces."[33]

Philip Fithian left a description of "Nomini Hall," the country seat of Councillor Robert Carter, where he was tutor a few years before the Revolution. The mansion house, seventy-six feet long and forty-four wide, was constructed of brick and covered with a mortar so white that it looked like marble. On the first floor were the dining room, where the family usually sat, the children's dining room, Mr. Carter's study, and a ballroom thirty feet long. Above stairs were four chambers, one for Mr. and Mrs. Carter, another for the five Carter girls, and two reserved for guests. This main house stood in the center of a square, at each of the four corners of which and at a hundred yards distance stood an outbuilding of considerable size. In one of these, a five-room, story-and-a-half brick house, school was kept and Mr. Carter's clerk, the tutor, the two Carter sons, and a nephew lodged. Corresponding to the schoolhouse, at the other corners were stables, coach house, and washhouse. Other buildings grouped near by were kitchen, bakehouse, dairy, and storehouse. Fronting the mansion were tastefully designed and carefully tended grounds, a "curious Terrace" covered with green turf, a bowling green, and rectangular walks paved with bricks. On one side was a pleasant avenue of two rows of tall poplars leading to the county road.[34]

"Nomini Hall" is a good example of many plantation homes in the eighteenth century, though other places like "Westover," the seat of the Byrd family, "Mount Airy," the home of the Tayloes, and "Rosewell," built by the Pages, were larger and more magnificent.[35] These are said to have had room for scores of guests. Gen-

---

[33] *Retrospections of America, 1797-1811*, p. 149.

[34] *Journal and Letters, 1767-1774*, pp. 127-32. Hereafter cited as *Journal*.

[35] For descriptions of these and other Virginia mansions, see Thomas Allen Glenn, *Some Colonial Mansions and Those who Lived in them with Genealogies of the Various Families Mentioned. . . .* (2 vols. Philadelphia, 1898); Fiske Kimball, *Domestic Architecture of the American Colonies and of the Early Republic* (New

erally, however, colonial residences were not of such enormous proportions as tradition has made them. Neither did all the best houses conform in structure and shape to the type of which "Nomini" and "Westover" are examples. Of a different plan was "Tuckahoe," home of the Randolphs on the James River. According to Thomas Anburey, a British officer who was a guest there in 1779, this house seemed to have been built solely to answer the purposes of hospitality. Constructed in the form of an H, it had the appearance of two houses joined by a large saloon. Each wing had two stories and four rooms on a floor. The family resided in one wing and the other was reserved for guests. The saloon, having doors on four sides and a very high pitch, was a cool retreat in summer and was so large that it was used sometimes as a ballroom.[36] Other houses resembled the plan of "Tuckahoe," and the story-and-a-half type also continued, though usually it was larger and more handsomely finished than its predecessors of the seventeenth century.

In the towns, as on the plantations, were large two-story brick residences of the Georgian style and rambling wooden houses with many wings and appendages. The grounds of these homes were usually less spacious than those in the country, but they were large enough for separate kitchens, servants' quarters, and gardens. Inside the dwellings were the same well-proportioned, smoothly paneled rooms, fine woodwork, and majestic stairways found in the best plantation mansions.

Abbé Robin, a French visitor approaching Maryland from the North in 1781, was struck by the contrast between the luxury in Annapolis and the smallness and meagerness of the abodes farther north. He wrote: "As we advance towards the south, we observe a sensible difference in the manners and customs of the people. We no longer find, as in Connecticut, houses situated along the road at small distances, just large enough to contain a single family, and the household furniture nothing more than is barely necessary; here are spacious habitations, consisting of different buildings, at some distance from each other, surrounded with plantations that extend be-

York, 1927); Robert Alexander Lancaster, *Historic Virginia Homes and Churches* (Philadelphia, 1915); Edith Dabney (Tunis) Sale, *Interiors of Virginia Houses of Colonial Times* (Richmond, 1927); and Thomas Tileston Waterman and John A. Barrows, *Domestic Colonial Architecture of Tidewater Virginia* (New York and London, 1932).

[36] *Travels through the Interior Parts of America*, II, 358-59.

yond the reach of the eye. . . . Their furniture here, is constructed out of the most costly kinds of wood, and that most valuable marble, enriched by the elegant devices of the artists hand."[37] William Eddis wrote of many "pleasant villas" in the vicinity of Annapolis. One was the dwelling of Colonel Sharp, which was "on a large scale, with apartments well fitted up, and perfectly convenient." Beautifully situated on the Severn, was the governor's mansion, which, when its alterations were completed, would be a "regular, convenient, and elegant building."[38]

One of the handsomest Maryland residences was that of Matthias Hammond built at Annapolis just before the Revolution. This house, which was of the best of the Georgian mansions throughout the colonies, stands today as an example of the splendid setting in which the wives and daughters of prosperous colonial gentlemen passed their lives. It is a two-story, almost square house with a two-story wing on each side connected by single-story passages. The first floor is divided into a large hall, a separate stair hall, a very large room, which has been called the "State Dining Room," and three smaller rooms. Divisions on the second floor are like those on the first. The large space over the dining room was used before the Revolution for a ballroom; the other apartments were probably bedrooms. One wing, in which there is a huge fireplace, was the kitchen, and the other was used for offices. The most distinguishing features of the house are its beautifully carved doorways and cornices and the rich though delicate ornamentation of its interior woodwork.[39]

Though the inhabitants of North Carolina did not possess such stately residences as their wealthier neighbors, they were not without comfortable homes. Governor Burrington wrote in 1735 that it had many "good Brick and wooden Mansion Houses with Suitable Outhouses" and orchards and gardens "handsomely laid out."[40] John Brickell declared that the homes of the most substantial planters were of brick and lime and had "large and decent Rooms."[41] Janet

[37] New Travels Through North-America, pp. 50-51.

[38] Letters from America, . . . 1769 to 1777, pp. 17, 20.

[39] Effingham C. Desmond, "A Pre-Revolutionary Annapolis House," The Monograph Series Recording the Architecture of the American Colonies and the Early Republic, XV, Nos. 4 and 5. For descriptions of other Maryland colonial houses see Glenn, op. cit., and John Martin Hammond, Colonial Mansions of Maryland and Delaware (Philadelphia, 1914).

[40] Colonial Records of North Carolina, IV, 305.

[41] Natural History of North Carolina, p. 37.

Schaw, who visited near Wilmington just before the Revolution, wrote that the town houses, though not spacious, were "very commodious and well furnished," and described the seat of Cornelius Harnett as "a very handsome house . . . properly situated to enjoy every advantage."[42] The English traveler Smyth, visiting Halifax shortly before the Revolution, saw there many handsome residences, most of which, he wrote, were constructed of timber and painted white.[43] William Attmore found in New Bern many large and commodious dwellings, which usually were built of wood and had balconies or piazzas in front and sometimes also at the back. The former governor's mansion was a large and elegant brick edifice finished in a splendid manner.[44]

"Buncombe Hall," built by Colonel Edward Buncombe in 1766, was representative of the residences of many of the more prosperous North Carolinians. The original was a frame two-story building with four rooms, wide halls, and three cellars, but a long wing containing two rooms on the first floor and one above was later added, making it L-shaped. The lower rooms had high ceilings, but those above had low, sloping walls pierced by numerous little dormer windows. The kitchen was in the cellar. On the front of the house facing the road was a double piazza, and at the rear broad piazzas extended the length of both wings. At the front were a plot of flowers, ornamental shrubs, and border plants, at one side of which a walk led to Colonel Buncombe's office. At the rear was a sloping hillside planted with orchards, to the west of which in a grove of virgin oaks were the slave quarters. Near by stood a smithy and a wood shop, where many utensils and farm implements used on the plantation were manufactured.[45] There were many hospitable residences on the Cape Fear,[46] but generally these were not so imposing as the mansions in the neighboring colonies.

[42] *Journal of a Lady of Quality* (ed., Evangeline Walker Andrews with Charles McLean Andrews), pp. 155, 178. This residence on the Cape Fear a short distance north of Wilmington was a brick structure with gambrel roof surrounded by a grove of splendid oaks and cedars. Including the cellar, it contained twelve rooms, most of which were finished in ornamented woodwork of red cedar.—R. D. W. Connor, *Cornelius Harnett* (Raleigh, 1909), pp. 201-2.
[43] *Tour in the United States of America*, I, 84.
[44] "Journal of a Tour," *James Sprunt Historical Publications*, XVII (No. 2), 45.
[45] Thomas Blount, "Buncombe Hall," *North Carolina Booklet*, II (No. 8), 14-31.
[46] See Col. A. M. Waddell, "Historic Homes in the Cape Fear Country," *North Carolina Booklet*, II (No. 9), 16-22.

Most of the furnishings of the eighteenth-century mansions were imported from the Mother Country and were of the kind found in the homes of the English aristocracy. Smoothly polished mahogany and walnut tables, chests of drawers, escritoires, and desks, works of the best English cabinet-makers; graceful chairs and sofas upholstered in velvets and rich brocades; hand-carved beds with hand-turned legs and sumptuous curtains and hangings; rosewood spinets, harpsichords, and writing tables; costly framed mirrors and pier glasses; graceful candle stands and japanned tea tables; Turkey rugs and richly woven Axminster and Wilton carpets were in keeping with the excellence of the interior architecture. Table furnishings were luxurious. Pewter, which was so popular in the former period, was gradually replaced by silver, china, and glass in the more expensive homes. The wealthy took particular pride in their silverware, often investing large sums in silver decanters, goblets, teapots, bowls, platters, pitchers, and candlesticks, as well as spoons, knives, and forks.[47] Chinaware and linens were also often costly. Anne Le Brasseur of South Carolina in 1742 owned among many pieces of valuable china two large dishes worth four pounds each.[48] Mary Mullins of the same colony in 1730 owned a damask tablecloth valued at seven pounds and two other tablecloths and twenty-four napkins valued at thirty-six pounds. The real costliness of this table linen is emphasized by the fact that in the inventory with it were a dozen leather-bottom chairs valued at only fifteen pounds.[49] Madam d'Harriette, another wealthy South Carolinian, had at the time of her decease in 1760 china and glassware worth one hundred and twenty-nine pounds, and bed and table

[47] Janet Schaw wrote of dining at a newly established plantation on the Cape Fear, where, though the house was no better than a Negro hut, she ate out of china and was served in plate.—*Journal*, p. 185. The silver at "Westover," which was valued at £662, included the following pieces: an epergne, a pitcher and stand, a bread basket, ten candlesticks, a snuffer stand, a large cup, two large punch bowls, two coffee pots, six cans, a sugar dish, a sugar basket, two sauce-boats, eight salt-cellars and spoons, two sets of castors, a cruet, a large waiter, two middle-sized waiters, four small castors, a cream-boat, four chafing dishes, a tea kettle, a "reine," two pudding dishes, a fish slice, a "sucking bottle," a large sauce-pan, a punch strainer, a punch ladle, a soup ladle, a small sauce-pan, four ragout spoons, two large sauce spoons, three marrow spoons, seven dozen knives and six dozen and eleven forks, eleven old-fashioned tablespoons, four dozen best large tablespoons, two dozen dessert spoons, three pairs of tea tongs, two tea strainers, one mustard spoon, one dozen new teaspoons, eleven second best teaspoons, six camp teaspoons, seven old teaspoons, five children's spoons, a large camp spoon, two small camp spoons, a camp cup, and a broad candlestick.—*Virginia Magazine*, IX, 81-82.

[48] Singleton, *op. cit.*, p. 131.   [49] *Ibid.*, p. 133.

linen valued at three hundred and one pounds, besides some very valuable plate.[50]

The following list from the inventory of Joseph Wragg of South Carolina gives some idea of the amount and kind of tableware found in the best-equipped homes of the middle of the century:

561	ounces three pennyweights of silver plate	£1,139-1-6
3	doz. knives and forks	71-0-0
25	enamelled china bowls	27-15-0
6	flowered china bowls	0-15-0
5	blue-and-white soup dishes	8-0-0
5	other small blue-and-white dishes	5-10-0
2	small enamelled dishes	3-0-0
1	small blue-and-white dish	0-15-0
48	enamelled soup plates	20-0-0
15	blue-and-white soup plates	6-0-0
17	butter saucers	2-0-0
1	coffee and tea china set	5-0-0
1	china jar	1-0-0
3	sugar dishes	3-0-0
1	china mug	1-0-0
3	dishes	1-15-0
7	plates	1-10-0
	"Delf ware"	8-0-0
2	pairs port decanters with ground stoppers	3-0-0
132	jelly and syllabub glasses	5-0-0
96	patty-pans	2-0-0
23	knives and forks	5-0-0
72	pewter plates and 13 dishes	40-0-0
104	wine glasses	10-0-0
	Mustard-pots, salts, cruets, tea-kettle, beer-glasses, etc	14-5-0

There was also much table linen, including one hundred and fourteen napkins and eighteen diaper tablecloths.[51]

[50] Hirsch, *op. cit.*, pp. 247-48.

[51] Singleton, *op. cit.*, p. 125. An equally astonishing number of such articles was found in the home of Philip Ludwell of Virginia later in the century. Here, there were of blue-and-white china seven and a half dozen plates, twenty-two dishes, eleven bowls, and two sets of cups and saucers. Of red-white-and-gilt china, there were thirty-seven plates, eleven dishes, five bowls, and three sets of cups and saucers. There were also a set of white, fourteen chocolate, and eight brown cups and saucers, eight fruit bowls and thirty-nine finger bowls. Glassware included fifteen tumblers, four saltcellars, cider, wine, and strong beer glasses, jelly glasses, and glass salvers. Other tableware included ivory knives and forks, dessert knives and forks, sweet-meat knives and forks, teaspoons, two teapots, tea-boards, tea-chests and canisters, coffee and chocolate pots, a coffee roaster, two mustard pots, butter pots, pickle pots, stone sweet-meat pots, seven decanters, six cruets, pewter plates, pie and cheese

The polite living suggested by these many luxuries was by no means general. Because of their appeal to the imagination and the pleasant glamour they give to the past, the spacious and sumptuous residences of the few have been often regarded as representative of southern colonial homes. Less conspicuous but far more numerous than these magnificent habitations were the modest dwellings of the less well-to-do in the older sections and the rude cabins in the back-woods and on the frontiers. Not so imposing as the dignified Georgian edifices, yet possibly more picturesque, were the small wooden houses with minute dormer windows and the plain rambling cottages which sheltered less prosperous families. Little is known of the homes of the poorer sort. Families of working men in the towns were probably huddled together in mean and bare little houses, and those of the white helpers on the plantations occupied cabins somewhat better than those of the Negro slaves.

As the frontier was extended, evolution from cabin to mansion was repeated in each new settlement. While the older residents of South Carolina on the Ashley and Cooper rivers were surrounding themselves with all the luxuries obtainable in England, those in the Pee Dee Basin were pleased to be emerging from the rude hut stage. In Winyaw Parish in 1729, a newly erected parsonage, apparently representative of the best dwellings in the community, was described as "a wooden building but plaister'd within, a story & half high & 25 foot Square."[52]   According to a letter of the Reverend James Harrison about 1767, the inhabitants of St. Marks Parish, about eight miles from Charles Town, were living in hovels formed of rough unhewn logs which seldom contained more than two rooms.[53] Shortly after this, the vestrymen of St. Marks boasted of providing for their minister "all that was necessary . . . desirable and inviting—a new built house just finished, 36 ft. front, with four good rooms, lobby and staircase—a good kitchen, garden, orchard, stables and necessary out houses."[54] Building restrictions for new towns in North Carolina

plates, plate baskets and hampers, hot-water plates and dishes, a copper cooler, brass chafing dishes, and nut crackers.—*Virginia Magazine*, XXI, 415-16. For lists of furniture, plate, linen, and china of wealthy North Carolinians, see the inventories of Mrs. Jean Corbin, Governor Arthur Dobbs, and Governor Gabriel Johnston, in Grimes, *North Carolina Wills and Inventories*, pp. 482-83, 484-86, 501-6.

[52] Letter of the Rev. Thomas Morritt, in Harvey Toliver Cook, *Rambles in the Pee Dee Basin, South Carolina* (Columbia, S. C., 1926), I, 122.

[53] *Ibid.*, p. 142.   [54] *Ibid.*, pp. 139-40.

suggest the modest demands for dwellings in that colony shortly before the Revolution. Regulations for Charlotte in 1766 required each lot to have "one well framed sawed or hewed Log-House" twenty feet in length, sixteen feet wide, and ten feet "in the clear," with brick or stone chimneys. But as many lot owners could not afford so large a home, the restrictions were later made applicable only to those who owned lots on the front street.[55] While fashionable gentlemen in the eastern counties were importing costly mahogany, silver, and china, pioneer families in the Valley of Virginia were living in one-room cabins equipped no better than the first houses at Jamestown.

In Georgia at the middle of the century the dwellings were still mostly small wooden structures, often with wooden chimneys.[56] Sir Francis Bathurst in 1735 was living in a house twenty feet long and twelve feet wide, divided into two apartments, a bedroom and a dining room, and covered with clapboards. It was declared to be "in some measure water tight," but certainly not "wind tight." The chief building on the plantation of Secretary Stephens was a hut constructed of whole logs. But by the time of the Revolution residences had been improved. Several offered for sale in the *Georgia Gazette* appear to have contained many rooms besides garrets, cellars, and outhouses. One in Savannah advertised by Lewis Johnson in 1764 contained, besides a large store fitted up for dry goods, "four fire rooms and three rooms without fireplaces, a large brick cellar for the use of the store, and a smaller one for the use of the family." Among the outbuildings were two good lodging rooms with fireplaces, a kitchen, washhouse, stable, chair-house, and pigeon house.[57]

A more pretentious town residence advertised by John Graham in 1765 was of two stories with "a handsome balcony in the front." On the first floor were a dining room, two "good bed-chambers," one of which had a fireplace, a passage "eight feet wide, and an easy

<hr/>

[55] *State Records of North Carolina*, XXIII, 772. A visitor in Virginia shortly before the Revolution wrote of the Richmond dwellings: "The houses here are almost all of wood, covered with the same; the roof with shingles, the sides and ends with thin boards, and not always lathed and plaistered within; only those of the better sort are finished in that manner, and painted on the outside. The chimneys are sometimes of brick, but more commonly of wood, coated on the inside with clay. The windows of the best sort have glass in them; the rest have none, and only wooden shutters."—J. F. D. Smyth, *Tour in the United States . . .* , I, 49.

[56] John P. Corry, "The Houses of Colonial Georgia," *Georgia Historical Quarterly*, XIV, 192-93, 197, 198.   [57] *Georgia Gazette*, December 6, 1764.

well finished stair-case," a "kitchen adjoining the house well fitted up," and a piazza the whole length of the house, at one end of which there was a "bed-room lined, plaistered and glazed," and at the other a convenient storeroom. On the second floor were a "large well finished dining-room, a good bed-chamber, both with fire places, and a light closet that will hold a field-bed." There were also a good cellar, and several outbuildings, among which were two good lodging rooms, with a loft over them, a stable and chair-house, and a poultry house. Part of the lot was fenced off for a poultry yard and the other for a garden, and there was a good well in the yard.[58]

The typical backwoods home was a one- or two-room cabin, sometimes with a loft and a "lean-to." The walls were of hewn logs notched so as to fit into one another at the corners and with the cracks between them filled with moss, sticks, straw, and clay. The roof was of clapboards, and the floor, when not simply earthen, was of split puncheons smoothed with the broadaxe. The chimney was made of logs with the back and jamb of stone, in sections where this material was available, and of logs and clay elsewhere. No nails were used in the whole house. The clapboards were hung upon laths with pegs, and the door and windows turned upon wooden hinges and had wooden locks. The furniture usually consisted of a straw mattress on a bedstead constructed by laying boards on forked poles attached to joists in the wall; a table made of a split slab supported by legs set in augur holes; and three-legged stools made the same way. Two small forks attached to a joist held the rifle and shot pouch, and wooden pegs provided a place for hanging clothes. An iron kettle and a frying pan, a few pewter spoons and steel knives brought from the older settlements, and homemade wooden trenchers, bowls, mugs, and tubs completed the furnishings. While most pioneer houses conformed to this general type, they doubtless differed considerably

[58] Corry, *op. cit.*, p. 196. A comfortable plantation home in 1769 was described as follows: "A compleat Dwelling-house newly glazed and painted; in which are two chambers, a dining room and hall, four very good shed rooms, and three fire places; a very good store 30 by 20; a Kitchen of same dimensions; a Smoke, Meat, and Milk House, all framed, and underpinned with brick, and closed with feather edge boards; a compleat Barn 40 by 24, floored flush with two inch planks; a framed Poultry House, and another house under same roof; roomly enough to hold a waggon, cart, and chair; a strong and well framed Stable for six or eight horses; three new Corn Houses made of four inch plank capable of containing 1000 bushels of corn each; an Overseer's House; a very good Garden contiguous to the house of about an acre of ground, and under a good clapboard pailing; an Orchard of eight acres."
—*Georgia Gazette*, April 12, 1769.

in convenience and comfort according to the energy, skill, and ingenuity of their inhabitants. Clapboard shelves, chests, and extra tables and stools made by the father and sons, and feather beds, handwoven blankets, coverlets, and sheets, gay colored quilts, homespun curtains and tablecloths, products of the industry and artistry of the housewife and her daughters, made some houses into homes with more than bare necessities.

Visitors from the settled regions usually wrote very unfavorably of the dwellings on the frontier. Colonel William Byrd, who traveled through the back country while helping survey the boundary between Virginia and North Carolina in 1728, declared that generally the people whom he saw were too lazy to improve their homes, which were often no more than miserable huts. In one wretched hovel, he and his men were "forc't to ly in Bulk upon a very dirty Floor, that was quite alive with Fleas & Chinches," and in another, consisting of "one Dirty Room, with a dragging Door" that would neither open nor shut, he lodged "very Sociably in the Same Apartment with the Family," where, including women and children, they "muster'd in all no less than Nine Persons, who all pigg'd loveingly together." But the most depressing sight was that of a man and his wife and six children who lived in a house with walls but no covering and who in bad weather were forced to take refuge in a fodder stack.[59] Washington, while making a survey in the Shenandoah Valley for Lord Fairfax in 1748, wrote of living among "a parcel of barbarians," where he had not slept on a bed for more than three or four nights, but usually "lay down before the fire upon a little hay, straw, fodder, or bearskin . . . with man, wife, and children, like a parcel of dogs and cats."[60] Daniel Stanton, Quaker preacher in Virginia in 1772, enjoyed the same crude entertainment in the home of a Friend, where he and the family all lay down in one room "like a flock of sheep in a fold, being sixteen in number."[61]

The practice of crowding many persons together to sleep in the same room was not limited to the backwoods. In the best homes in the settled counties, families were so large and guests so numerous

[59] *William Byrd's Histories of the Dividing Line* . . . (ed., William K. Boyd), pp. 40-41, 304-5, 313-15.
[60] *Writings of George Washington* (ed., W. C. Ford), I, 7.
[61] *Journal*, p. 122. For similar descriptions of backwoods homes, see Smyth, *Tour*, I, 74-75, 103, 198, 251; Andrew Burnaby, *Travels*, p. 142; Eddis, *Letters from America*, p. 131; and La Rochefoucauld Liancourt, *Travels*, III, 175-76.

that a person seldom enjoyed the privacy of a separate bedroom. Several beds to a room with two and often three persons to a bed were quite usual. The colonial standard of genteel living, while demanding spacious and magnificent houses equipped with fashionable mahogany, plate, and china, required little privacy. Nor did it require much in the way of convenience. The following comment by the French traveler Chastellux was doubtless true of many Carolinians and Virginians: "Their houses are spacious, and ornamented, but their apartments are not commodious; they make no ceremony of putting three or four persons in the same room; nor do these make any objection to their being heaped together; . . . being in general ignorant of the comforts of reading and writing, they want nothing in the whole house but a bed, a dining-room, and a drawing-room for company. The chief magnificence of the Virginians consists in furniture, linen, and plate; in which they resemble our ancestors, who had neither cabinets nor wardrobes in their castles, but contented themselves with a well-stored cellar, and a handsome buffet."[62]

[62] *Travels in North America in the Years 1780, 1781, and 1782 . . .*, II, 201-2.

CHAPTER III

"IN THE INCREASING WAY"

THE SOCIAL institutions of the colonists, like their houses and furniture, were modeled after those in England. No sooner had the first settlers found themselves shelter and a dependable food supply than they began to attempt to establish homes as much like those they had left as possible, and throughout the period they not only imported from the Mother Country most of their clothing, furniture, and other household articles, but looked to her also for fashions in dress and manners and ideals of social conduct. The education, employments, and general home life of colonial women were according to the same plan as those of their kinswomen across the Atlantic, and their position in the family, the church, and the state was governed largely by English attitudes.

Of particularly great and lasting influence was the English idea of family relations and the domestic duties of women. The English family was a patriarchy. It included, besides father, mother, and children, every other member of the household, from chaplain, tutor, private secretary, and waiting gentlewomen down to the lowest kitchen scullion. At the head was the father—husband and master— whose authority within his home was absolute. Wife, children, and servants were subject to his will, and he in turn was responsible for their physical, moral, and spiritual welfare. He was supposed to exercise his supreme power not for his own pleasure but for the good of his family, but his abuse of his prerogatives did not absolve any member from his or her obligation of submission, respect, and obedience.

The general conception of the father's position was thus expressed by a correspondent to *The Spectator*, one of the most influential periodicals of the day in America as well as in England: "Nothing is more gratifying to the mind of man than power or dominion; and this I think myself amply possessed of, as I am the father of a family. I am perpetually taken up in giving out orders, in prescribing duties, in hearing parties, in administering justice, and in distributing rewards and punishments. To speak in the language of the centurion, I say to one, Go, and he goeth; and to another, Come, and he cometh; and to my servant, Do this, and he doeth it. In short, sir, I look upon my family as a patriarchal sovereignty, in which I am myself both king and priest."[1]

The situation of gentlemen in the southern colonies more nearly resembled the Old Testament characters than did that of fathers of families in England, for they were lords and masters, not only of wives, children, and servants, but likewise of bond servants and slaves. The family of a wealthy planter was in truth a little kingdom. It included, besides his wife and children, his and his wife's dependent relatives living with them, his clerk, the children's tutor, the housekeeper, gardeners, carpenters, and other white employees, and his indentured servants and Negro slaves. He was the head and ruler over all. His word was final in the training of his children, the control over servants, the selection of the home site, the planning and furnishing of the house, and over all other matters inside as well as outside the home. The wife and mother, as mistress of the household, was her husband's agent or second in command.

The status of daughters, sisters, and other women in the home varied with different families. Daughters were usually given a narrower education and inherited a smaller part of their father's estate than sons, but they were apparently regarded with as much affection and respect. After the death of the father, the eldest son, who under the law of primogeniture inherited all his lands, became the head of the family, and, if he were a gentleman of honor, assumed responsibility for his younger brothers and sisters and for dependent relatives, particularly the homeless and poor female kindred. But that many women in necessitous circumstances did not find protection and support under a kinsman's roof is evidenced in the large number of newspaper advertisements of women seeking gainful employment.[2]

The chief occupations of women of all classes were bearing children and attending to household affairs. We have seen that their function in the founding of the colonies was to make comfortable homes for the masculine settlers and to increase the population. Throughout the colonial period and many years after its close, though they were often forced by economic necessity to be breadwinners,

[1] No. 55 (October 3, 1712).
[2] For a description of women in gainful occupations, see below, Chaps. XII, XIII, and XIV.

they were valued chiefly as housewives and mothers. Thomas Jefferson expressed the conventional idea of woman's purpose in life in a letter to his daughter Martha. "Your two last letters," he wrote, "are those which have given me the greatest pleasure of any I ever received from you. The one announced that you were become a notable housewife; the other, a mother."[3]

A large part of the time, strength, and attention of women went into the bearing and rearing of the large families which were the rule and the boast of rich and poor. Men and women prided themselves upon their numerous offspring, not only because of a belief that they were obeying a scriptural command to replenish the earth and a patriotic duty to add new citizens to the Empire, but also because they regarded children as a material investment, a kind of insurance against old age and misfortune. In the seventeenth and eighteenth centuries, when child labor was considered natural and good, and when schooling for the great majority, if any at all, was of brief duration; when a great deal more was said and thought of the filial duties of children than of the responsibilities of parents; and when parents were regarded as entitled to lifelong obedience, respect, and service from their children from the mere fact of having given them birth, children were indeed assets. The larger a man's family the more subjects he had to render him obeisance, the more helpers he had on the farm, and the surer was his support in old age.

In the colonies, even more than in the Mother Country, a numerous progeny was desired. Here there were on the one hand an abundance of food, building materials, firewood, and other raw products, and on the other a small population and a great scarcity of labor. The poorer sort with no great effort could feed many children and receive benefits from their labor. Because of the large land grants, the more prosperous could set up many sons on plantations of their own and thus realize their cherished ambition of founding large, influential families. The isolation of plantation life also contributed to an appreciation of large families because of the companionship they offered; and the loneliness, hardships, and dangers on the frontier made children desirable as defenders as well as producers and companions.

The colonists took a patriotic pride in the fecundity of their women. "Our Land free, our Men honest, and our Women fruit-

[3] Sarah N. Randolph, *Domestic Life of Jefferson. Compiled from Family Letters and Reminiscences* (New York, 1871), p. 192.

ful," was a popular toast drunk at entertainments. Promotion pamphleteers urged the fertility of women in the New World as one of the inducements to emigration, as did John Hammond, who declared that children increased so well there that they would soon sufficiently supply the lack of servants.[4] Travelers were invariably impressed by the early marriages and numerous children in every part of the country. Oldmixon wrote in 1708 that there were ten or twelve children in most of the two hundred and fifty families in Charles Town.[5] Brickell declared of North Carolina: "The Women are very fruitful, most Houses being full of little Ones, and many Women from other Places who have been long Married and without Children, have remov'd to Carolina, and become joyfull Mothers. . . ."[6] Lord Adam Gordon observed of the Virginians that they married early and that their women were "great Breeders."[7]

Family records confirm these reports. Ten or twelve children to one couple were quite common and many families were larger. Among the prominent Virginians who begot a numerous offspring were William Byrd III, with five children by his first wife and ten by his second;[8] Colonel Landon Carter, with four by his first marriage and ten by his second;[9] Major Lewis Burwell, with fifteen;[10] and Warner Washington, with sixteen, by two wives.[11] Robert Carter, called "King Carter," had five children by his first wife and ten by his second; Robert Carter, called "Councillor," of "Nomini Hall," had seventeen children; and Charles Carter of "Shirley," who married twice, had twenty-three.[12] John Page of "Rosewell" had twelve children by his first wife and eight by his second, and his son Mann Page of "Shelby" had fifteen by one wife.[13] John Marshall, the chief justice, was the first of fifteen children,[14] and Mason

[4] "Leah and Rachel," *Narratives of Early Maryland*, p. 296.

[5] "British Empire in America," *Narratives of Early Carolina*, p. 365.

[6] *Natural History of North Carolina*, p. 31.

[7] *Journal*, p. 406.

[8] Glenn, *Some Colonial Mansions*, I, 54-55.

[9] Louise Pecquet du Bellet, *Some Prominent Virginia Families* (4 vols. Lynchburg, Va., 1907), II, 503.

[10] *William and Mary College Quarterly Magazine*, VI, 165. Hereafter cited as *William and Mary Quarterly*.   [11] Du Bellet, *op. cit.*, II, 135-37.

[12] Glenn, *op. cit.*, I, 279, 281; Zella Armstrong, *Notable Southern Families* (Chattanooga, Tenn., 1918), II, 64.

[13] Glenn, *op. cit.*, I, 194, 198.

[14] Allan B. Magruder, *John Marshall* ("American Statesmen Series," Vol. X. Boston and New York, 1898), p. 5.

Locke ["Parson"] Weems was the youngest of nineteen.[15]   Anthony
Alexander of North Carolina mentioned in his will nine sons and
eight daughters.[16]   George Moore of "Moorefields" of the same
colony had twenty-seven children,[17] and Thomas, son of Landgrave
Smith of South Carolina, had twenty, ten by each of his two wives.[18]

The record of the generation of John Thruston of Virginia illustrates the incessant childbearing, hasty remarriage, and large infant
mortality which was apparently not uncommon at the time.   John
Thruston, when twenty-three, married Thomasine, widow and mother
already of three children.   John and Thomasine then had sixteen
children in sixteen years.   Of these one lived to be twenty-six; five
died between the ages of nine and fourteen; four died before they
were two years old; one was stillborn; and the date of the death
of the others is not known.   Thomasine, the wife, died November 30, 1647, thirteen days after the birth of her nineteenth child,
and on January 12, 1648, one month and thirteen days later, her
husband married again.   By his second wife John had eight children, the birth of the last of which he recorded thus: "The first
day of June 1656 about 12 of ye Clocke at noon being Sunday my
wife was delivered of a daughter wch makes my 24th child 12 sons
and 12 daughters."[19]   Of these last children, one died at fifteen and
three died under three years of age.   So of his twenty-four children,
fourteen died under age, one soon after reaching maturity, and it does
not appear how many of the remaining nine survived their father.

While a majority of the large families were the children of more
than one wife, not a few women bore ten or more children.   In the
Bible records of James Maury of Virginia are listed thirteen children born to him and his "dear Molly."[20]   Martha Jefferson Randolph, daughter of Thomas Jefferson, was the mother of twelve,[21]
and Martha Laurens Ramsay, daughter of Henry Laurens, and third

[15] Emily Ellsworth Ford Skeel, *Mason Locke Weems, His Works and Ways*
(New York, 1929), II, xix.

[16] J. Bryan Grimes, *Abstract of North Carolina Wills*, p. 4.

[17] James Sprunt, *Chronicles of the Cape Fear River, 1660-1916* (2d ed. Raleigh,
1916), p. 70.

[18] Elizabeth Anne Poyas, *Our Forefathers, Their Homes and Their Churches*
(Charleston, 1860), p. 148.

[19] *William and Mary Quarterly*, IV, 23-26.

[20] *Ibid.*, X, 123.

[21] Sarah N. Randolph, "Mrs. Thomas Mann Randolph," *Worthy Women of Our
Last Century* (eds., Mrs. O. J. Wister and Miss Agnes Irwin. Philadelphia, 1877),
p. 48.

wife of Dr. David Ramsay, bore eleven in sixteen years.[22]   Betty
Washington Lewis, sister of the first president and second wife of
Fielding Lewis, added eleven children to the three her husband had
by his first wife.[23]   Mary Heathy of South Carolina was also a
"fruitful vine," bearing seven children to her first husband, seven to
her second, and three to her third.   Ramsay, early South Carolina
historian, wrote of a woman of the Greenville District who had
thirty-four children.   From sixteen to twenty-two had been brought
alive into the world by individual mothers in the low country, he
declared, but these instances were rare.   Some women were mothers
at fifteen and a few grandmothers at thirty.   But while the number
of children born was great, he added, the deaths in infancy were also
great, though considerably less than was usual forty years before.[24]
The Reverend Carol August Storch, Lutheran minister in western
North Carolina in 1789, reported that thirteen or fourteen children
were not infrequent in families there.   He himself knew one planter
with twenty-three by one wife, all except two of whom were healthy
and strong.   But frequently, he declared, he found that in families
of such large numbers one was feeble-minded.[25]

Women married so early and bore children so late that they and
their daughters were not infrequently caring for infants at the same
time.   Thus we find Nelly Custis Lewis, herself the mother of several, writing a friend: "My Dear Mother has just recovered from
her confinement with her twentieth Child, it is a very fine Girl, large
and healthy.   Mamma has suffered extremely, and is still weak."[26]
The *South Carolina Gazette*, May 10, 1770, announced the birth of
a son to a woman sixty-nine years old, and Beverley wrote of a
woman in Virginia who had a son at the age of seventy-six.[27]

Men much oftener than women had grandchildren and children
of the same age.   Representative of many of these fathers of double
sets of children was the Reverend Peter Fontaine of Virginia, who,
writing his brothers about his family in 1754, mentioned six grandchildren ranging from an infant to one twelve years old and five

[22] David Ramsay, *Memoirs of the Life of Martha Laurens Ramsay*, pp. 25-26.
[23] Genealogy of Lewis Family, in Rev. Philip Slaughter, *Memoir of Colonel
Joshua Fry, Sometimes Professor in William and Mary College, Virginia . . . 1754
. . .* (Richmond, 1880), pp. 74-75.   [24] *History of South Carolina*, II, 231.
[25] *North Carolina Historical Review*, VII, 244.
[26] Charles Moore, *Family Life of George Washington* (Boston, Cambridge, and
New York, 1926), pp. 166-67.   [27] *Op. cit.*, pp. 91-92.

minor children ranging from four months to twelve years. Though at the time he was past fifty, complaining of his decrepitude and expecting soon to take his departure from the world, two years later he announced the coming of another child. The following year he died, leaving his youngest children to the care of those by his first marriage, who already had growing families of their own.[28] That men and even women suffering the infirmities of age should still be "in the increasing way" does not seem to have been considered extraordinary. In the minutes of the meeting of the President and Assistants for the Colony of Georgia, November 8, 1746, is a petition for relief from Thomas Young with this explanation, "he having a large Family of Children, and both He and his Wife being very infirm thro Age and Sickness. . . ."[29]

The pregnancies of great ladies were sometimes announced in colonial newspapers and the "delicate situation," lying-in, and delivery of ladies were among the most frequently mentioned topics in social correspondence. We find Margaret Calvert, sister-in-law of the fifth Lord Baltimore, writing her niece in Maryland: "I am Extreamly glad to hear ye Ladys are all brought safe to bed but here you are most of you in that way again I am sure I sincerely wish you all a happy minute";[30] and Rebecca Dinwiddie, wife of the governor of Virginia, addressing the wife of the Reverend Thomas Dawson, president of William and Mary: "I do assure you will give me pleasure to hear . . . Mrs. Harrison is well recovered from her lying in: tho by the time you gett this she may be in the way again, if so I sincerely wish her health. . . ."[31] A letter of Andrew Miller to his friend Thomas Burke of Halifax, North Carolina, declares his wife "is now confirmed of her Pregnancy," and another hopes that by the time Mr. and Mrs. Burke can visit him "Mrs. Miller will be in the Straw and restored to her former Temper, which is what she Seldom has during the months of Pregnancy."[32] Among the news related by a Carolina gentlewoman to a gentleman friend and neighbor then in England was this: "Mrs. Thos. Hooper bro't to bed, and

[28] Letters of Peter Fontaine in Ann Maury's *Memoirs of a Huguenot Family*, pp. 333-334, 340, 352, 354, 360, 369, 375.

[29] For his "present Exigence" the board saw fit to allow him four shillings a week.—*Colonial Records of Georgia*, VI, 166.

[30] *Maryland Magazine*, IX, 146.

[31] *William and Mary Quarterly*, III, 314.

[32] *Colonial Records of North Carolina*, IX, 357.

her child dead. . . . Mrs. George—of that name—(Enceinte) again."[33]
The lively letters of Molly Tilghman[34] contain many allusions to
Maryland ladies with "a blessed prospect" or "in that way," and the
many confinements of the Charles Town ladies are recorded faithfully in Mrs. Manigault's journal.[35]

Among well-to-do ladies, lying-in appears to have been treated as
somewhat of a ceremony expected to take place at more or less regular intervals. Every wife had her "child-bed linen," which was
usually as handsome as her circumstances would afford. Shopkeepers
advertised "Suits of Childbed Linen" and "quilted Satin Childbed
Baskets and Pincushions" along with their "elegant" jewelry and
millinery. So valuable was this equipment that it was quite often
bequeathed in wills and sometimes presented as a gift. Frederick
Jones of North Carolina, for example, bequeathed his eldest daughter "all her Mothers Child bede Linnen with white silk Damask
Gown,"[36] and Mary Atkins of Charles Town in South Carolina left
a kinswoman her "best Gowne and petticoate" and all her "childbed
linen and all other Cloaths belongeing to a Child."[37] In a seventeenth-century Maryland letter, we find a gentlewoman writing of
having presented as a wedding present to her cousin "a suett of laced
child bed linnen."[38]

Among the superstitions of the period was the notion that a
pregnant woman was likely to miscarry if denied what she "longed
for." In the minutes of the General Court of Virginia for 1625 is
a case involving a complaint by Elizabeth Hamer against Dr. Pott
for denying her a piece of hog flesh, thus causing her miscarriage.
The judges' opinion was that the doctor's action was not criminal
since he had no way of knowing "she had A longing to it."[39] Whether
this belief was widespread we do not know, but that some women
continued to take advantage of it years later appears in a letter
in *The Spectator*, March 14, 1711/12, in which the writer com-
plains of the extravagant "longings" of his wife. "To trouble you

[33] Letters and Documents Relating to the Early History of the Lower Cape Fear, *James Sprunt Historical Monograph*, No. 4, p. 27.
[34] *Maryland Magazine*, XXI, 20-39, 123-49, 219-41.
[35] *South Carolina Magazine*, XX, 57-63, 128-41; XXI, 10-23, 59-72, 112-20, 204-12, 256-59.
[36] *North Carolina Booklet*, V, 141.
[37] *South Carolina Magazine*, XXVIII, 172-73.
[38] *Maryland Magazine*, IX, 123.
[39] *Minutes of the Council of the General Court of Virginia*, pp. 58-59.

only with a few of them," he writes, "when she was with child of Tom, my eldest son, she came home one day just fainting, and told me she had been visiting a relation, whose husband had made her a present of a chariot and a stately pair of horses; and that she was positive she could not breathe a week longer, unless she took the air in the fellow to it of her own within that time. This, rather than lose an heir, I readily complied with. Then the furniture of her best room must be instantly changed, or she should mark the child with some of the frightful figures in the old-fashioned tapestry. Well, the upholsterer was called, and her longing saved that bout. When she went with Molly she had fixed her mind upon a new set of plate, and as much china as would have furnished an Indian shop: these also I cheerfully granted, for fear of being father to an Indian pagod. . . . What her next sally will be I cannot guess. . . . This exceeds the grievance of pin-money; and I think in every settlement there ought to be a clause inserted, that the father should be answerable for the longings of his daughter."

The wives of the well-to-do as well as of the poorer sort customarily "lay in" at their own homes attended by the neighborhood midwife. Toward the close of the period physicians came more and more to be called in, but many persons still considered the employment of a man-widwife a breach of female modesty.[40] Others felt that while the experienced but unlearned midwife was capable of taking care of the great majority of cases, scientific assistance should be available in case of unusual developments. Thomas Jefferson's advice to his depressed and fearful young daughter illustrates the attitude of the most progressive. "Take care of yourself, my dearest Maria, have good spirits, and know that courage is as essential to triumph in your case as in that of a soldier," he wrote at one time, and a few weeks later advised: "Some female friend of your mamma's (I forgot whom) used to say it was no more than a jog of the elbow. The material thing is to have scientific aid in readiness, that if any thing uncommon takes place it may be redressed on the spot, and not be made serious by delay. It is a case which least of all will wait for doctors to be sent for; therefore with this single precaution nothing is ever to be feared."[41] Despite his reassurance, however, Jefferson was afraid. Well he might be. Not many years before he had been in "perpetual solicitude" about Maria's mother, who, after bearing six children in ten years, had died shortly after the birth of the last. For Maria, too, childbirth was more than a "jog of the elbow," for she never recovered from the ordeal which she had feared so pathetically.

Among rich and poor, mothers frequently died in childbed. Many notices like the following appear in the newspapers:

On the 22d of January, Died in Child-Birth, in the 33d Year of her Age, Mrs. Sarah Carlyle, Wife of Col. John Carlyle, Merchant in *Alexandria*, and Daughter to the late Honourable William Fairfax, Esq: President of Virginia. . . .[42]

Of a Miscarriage of Twins, on the 10th Instant, died here, in the 24th Year of her age, one of the most pious and accomplished young Women in these Parts, in the Person of Mrs. Calhoun, the Wife of Patrick Calhoun, Esq: and Daughter of the Rev. Mr. Alexander Craighead.[43]

Women married young, often suffered continuous ill health thereafter, and all too frequently, before reaching middle age, succumbed to the strain of incessant childbearing. Tombstone inscriptions like the following witness the cruel and fatal strain placed upon the womanhood of the time:

Underneath / lies what was mortal of / Mrs. Margaret Edwards / Wife of Mr. John Edwards, Merchant of this place / Daughter of Mr. Alexander Peronneau, Gent / She Died / in Travail with her tenth Child / Aged 34 years and about 4 months / a Sincere, modest and humble Christian / . . . She committed her Soul to Him whom she ardently loved / and died without fear or a groan / Augt 27th, 1772.[44]

The colonial wife and her husband asked not if these tragedies might be prevented, but accepted them as part of the divine plan to which they must bow uncomplainingly. This attitude is illustrated in the private papers of Henry Laurens, in which he writes of the protracted illness, frequent confinements, and finally the death in childbed of his sincerely beloved wife. Mrs. Laurens' life was not unlike that of many gentlewomen. She married in 1750 at nineteen and during the next twenty years bore twelve children, seven of whom were buried before her. In November, 1764, her husband was writing that it had been a "year of sorrows; a dead eldest daughter, a

[42] *Maryland Gazette*, February 12, 1761.

[43] *South Carolina Gazette*, October 13, 1766.

[44] From the Independent or Congregational Church Yard in Charleston, South Carolina.—*South Carolina Magazine*, XXIX, 238.

sick and dying wife."[45] She continued in a "precarious state," but continued to bear babies for the grave, "suffering extremely," according to one of her husband's letters, "notwithstanding her exemplary patience and meekness." In October, 1768, he wrote that Mrs. Laurens was "confined to her chamber (as usual once in the round of a twelve-month) under the mortifying reflections which arise from the loss of a fine girl." Laurens' biographer suggests that Mr. Laurens ought himself to have felt some mortification at being in a position to write a parenthesis like that. But Laurens, like other colonial husbands, felt no responsibility in such matters. When another eighteen months rolled around, he was writing of the birth of a little girl, adding, "but I have been too deeply affected by the mother's deep distress to take any notice of it." A few weeks later his weary wife finally closed her life, leaving the baby girl who was herself to die in childbed twenty-two years later. Laurens suffered real anguish, but in the spirit of the age submitted to this "stroke of Providence."

Many mothers, like Mrs. Laurens, laid down their lives to bring forth children only for the grave. The rate of infant mortality was shockingly great. Wills of the period show surprisingly few large families, yet other records give evidence of many births. Many small graves in churchyards and burying grounds explain the difference. This tombstone inscription tells a story often repeated:

In memory of
HELEN daughter of EBENEZER and ELIZABETH STOTT, who departed this life . . . aged one year and three weeks. Of another daughter . . . who died three days after her birth, and of five others of their infants still born. . . .[46]

In the Friends' Burying Ground at Charleston, South Carolina, lie seven children of Thomas and Isabella Sikes, all buried between 1751 and 1765,[47] and in the Congregational Churchyard are inscriptions marking the graves of five children of William and Sabina Ellis, all born and buried between 1753 and 1765.[48]

Even among the most intelligent and well-to-do, the loss of a

[45] David Duncan Wallace, *Life of Henry Laurens* (New York and London, 1915), pp. 57-61, 66, 180-81; Letters of Henry Laurens, *South Carolina Magazine*, XXVIII, 162. Laurens' biographer credits him with as many as twelve children certainly and mentions two others as possibly his.—Wallace, *op. cit.*, p. 57, n. 1.
[46] *William and Mary Quarterly*, V (1st ser.), 236.
[47] *South Carolina Magazine*, XXVIII, 104-5.
[48] *Ibid.*, XXIX, 308.

large number of children was expected, and like the death of mothers was accepted as the will of Providence. William Fitzhugh wrote his brother in 1686: "God Almighty hath been pleased to bless me with a very good wife and five pledges of our conjugal affection, three of which he has been pleased to call into the Arms of his Mercy, and lent me two, a hopefull boy and girle, and one other that . . . is preparing to come into the world."[49]   Thomas Chalkley, the famous Quaker preacher, after burying nine of his children, wrote soon after the death of his tenth: "It was some exercise to me thus to bury my children one after another; but this did a little mitigate my sorrow, that I knew . . . it was safer and better for them, and they more out of danger, being taken away in their infancy and innocency. . . ."[50]

Six of Major Lewis Burwell's fifteen children preceded him to the grave,[51] and eight of Colonel James Gordon's fourteen died in infancy.[52]   Only two of Jefferson's six children reached maturity, and only one of these survived him.[53]   All four children of Lawrence Washington, older brother of George Washington, died as infants;[54] Charles Carroll of Carrollton lost four of his seven children;[55] Nathaniel Barnwell of South Carolina lost six of his fourteen in infancy;[56] and Henry Laurens survived all but three of his twelve or fourteen.   The family Bible of the Grimballs of South Carolina tells a story of the distressing waste of womanhood not very uncommon in all the colonies.   Isaac Grimball married in 1734 and had six children, three of whom died in infancy.   His wife died and he married again in 1747 and had three children, only one of whom survived him.   His son John married six wives, three of whom died in childbirth.   Of his nine children, five were stillborn, two died as infants, and of the remaining two it is not known whether they survived their father.[57]

---

[49] *Virginia Magazine*, I, 391.

[50] *The Journal of Thomas Chalkley* . . . , pp. 95-96.

[51] Bishop William Meade, *Old Churches, Ministers, and Families of Virginia* (2 vols.   Philadelphia, 1857), II, 290.

[52] "Gordon Family Bible," *Tyler's Quarterly Historical and Genealogical Magazine*, XI, 41-42.   Hereafter cited as *Tyler's Quarterly Magazine*.

[53] Sarah N. Randolph, *Domestic Life of Jefferson*, p. 49.

[54] Paul Wilstach, *Mount Vernon, Washington's Home and the Nation's Shrine* (Garden City, 1916), pp. 34-35.

[55] Marion Harland, *More Colonial Homesteads and their Stories* (New York, 1899), p. 253.

[56] *South Carolina Magazine*, II, 52-53.

[57] *Ibid.*, XXVIII, 256-58.

Considerably more appears in the records concerning childbearing than child rearing. A rather general notion seems to have been that she was the best mother who bore the greatest number of children. Ladies' books and magazines contained volumes of advice on how to make a pudding or how to treat a husband, but were usually silent on the subject of child training. We find Eliza Pinckney writing a friend in England to send her son, not yet four months old, "the new toy (a description of wch I inclose) to teach him according to Mr. Lock's method (wch I have carefully studied) to play himself into learning," and adding that the baby's father was contriving a set of toys to teach him his letters by the time he could speak. The next year she was writing that the little boy could "tell all his letters in any book without hesitation, and begins to spell before he is two years old."[58] Martha Laurens Ramsay, according to her son's *Memoirs*, studied the outstanding treatises on education in French and in English to learn more about her maternal duties.[59] But Mrs. Pinckney and Mrs. Laurens were exceptional mothers. Their interest in methods of child training was probably as extraordinary as were their other intellectual accomplishments.[60] Mothers generally appear to have depended upon intuition and the principles handed down from their mothers in the management of their children.

Visitors and new arrivals in the colonies sometimes pointed out as harmful the practice of leaving children much in the care of slaves, declaring that their speech, manners, and morals were corrupted by such intimate association with the Negroes.[61] Strangers were particularly shocked at the use of Negro wet nurses. Jonathan Boucher, a young Anglican divine, soon after his coming to Virginia wrote home to an English friend: "I cannot be reconcil'd to hav'g my Bairns nurs'd by a Negro Wench. Seriously, that is a monstrous Fault I find with ye people here, & surely it is the source of many Disadvantages to their Children."[62] John Davis, another Englishman, was also disturbed by this custom. "It may be incredible to some that the children of the most distinguished families in *Carolina*

[58] Ravenel, *Eliza Pinckney*, pp. 113-14.

[59] David Ramsay, *Memoirs of Martha Laurens Ramsay*, pp. 25-26.

[60] For their unusual intellectual interests see below, pp. 206, 230-31, 308-11.

[61] "Observations in Several Voyages and Travels in America" (from the *London Magazine*, July, 1746), *William and Mary Quarterly*, XV, 158; Josiah Quincy, "Journal," Massachusetts Historical Society, *Proceedings*, XLIX, 424-81. Hereafter cited as *Journal*.

[62] *Maryland Magazine*, VII, 6.

are suckled by negro women," he wrote. "Each child has its *Momma*, whose gestures and accent it will necessarily copy, for children, we all know, are imitative beings. It is not unusual to hear an elegant lady say, *Richard always grieves when Quasheehaw is whipped, because she suckled him.*"[63]

The question of the suckling of infants was often discussed. A favorite subject of moralists was the unnatural mother who, to preserve her figure and to have freedom to enjoy amusements, turned her babe over to another. The general excuse used to justify the employment of a wet nurse was the mother's weak constitution. Eliza Pinckney, while on a visit to England, discussed the subject with the Princess of Wales and left this account of their exchange of opinions: "She asked me many little domestick questions as did Princess Augusta among wch if I suckled my children. I told her I had attempted it but my constitution would not bear it. She said she did not know but 'twas as well let alone, as the anxiety a mother was often in on a child's acct might do hurt. I told her we had Nurses in our houses, that it appear^{d} very strange to me to hear of people putting their children out to nurse, we had no such practises in Carolina, at which she seemed vastly pleased; she thought it was a very good thing, the other was unnatural. Princess Augusta was surprized at the suckling blacks; the Princess stroakt Harriott's [Mrs. Pinckney's little daughter] cheek, said it made no alteration in the complexion and paid her the compliment of being very fair and pretty."[64] Fithian recorded in his *Journal* a conversation at the Carters' supper table on nursing children, during which he learned that it was common in Virginia for people of fortune to have their babies suckled by Negresses. Dr. Jones, a guest, informed him that his first and only child was at the time with such a nurse, and Mrs. Carter declared that several of her thirteen children had been suckled by Negro wenches.[65]

Despite the strictures of moralists, the employment of wet nurses was common. If a properly qualified woman was not available among the family slaves, a slave wench or a white woman was hired by the month or year. Many notices like the following appear in the newspapers:

[63] *Travels, 1798-1802*, pp. 93-94.
[64] Ravenel, *Eliza Pinckney*, pp. 151-152.
[65] P. 70.

WANTED,

A NURSE with a good Breast of Milk, of a healthy Constitution, and good Character, that is willing to go into a Gentleman's Family. Such a one may hear a very good Encouragement, by enquiring of the Printer hereof.[66]

Two healthy likely wet nurses with their first children to be hired out by the month. Inquire at the Printers.[67]

Wanted by the Month

A HEALTHY CAREFUL NEGROE WENCH for a WET NURSE. One without a child will be most agreeable, or with a child not above six months old.[68]

Among the most prosperous, children were apparently suckled by slave women and then cared for by Negro nurses until they were old enough to be turned over to tutors and governesses. The amount and kind of attention received from their mothers varied, naturally, with different families. Daughters were more closely supervised by mothers than sons, whose conduct as well as academic education was more often left to their tutors. Quite a number of little boys and a few girls not yet in their teens were sent abroad for their education, leaving their mothers distressed and anxious because of the separation, but free from the responsibility for their education.[69]

Among the less affluent also, children often were separated from their mothers at an early age, but these left home to go to work. The disposition sometimes made of the numerous offspring of parents of narrow means is suggested in this notice from a Maryland paper:

The subscriber, wishing to assist poor, but honest persons, who are afflicted with large families of children, offers himself to take 3 or 4 White Boys, from 8 to 10 years of age, to be bound to him for the *Chimney Sweeping Business*, until they come to the age of *fifteen* years; after that period he will put them to any trade, for which they should incline, in order that they may be able to obtain a further livelihood. . . .[70]

Oldmixon declared that the children in Carolina were set to work at eight years of age,[71] and a Swiss emigrant complained of Carolina: ". . . the children soon go [to work] the one here the other there, and are treated like slaves and brought up in ignorance like the savages."[72]

[66] *Maryland Gazette*, April 4, 1750.
[67] *South Carolina Gazette*, December 31, 1764.
[68] *Georgia Gazette*, October 1, 1766.   [69] See below, pp. 186-87.
[70] *Maryland Magazine*, XII, 317.   [71] *Narratives of Early Carolina*, p. 372.
[72] *South Carolina Magazine*, XXIII, 89-90.

In the colonies as in England, impecunious orphans and children whose parents were living but incapable of maintaining them were bound out for long terms. In many cases women whose husbands had deserted them or were dead found it necessary to apprentice even their very young children. Entries like the following appear in the records:

November, 1702. Martha Plato Binds her daughter Hester Plato to Capt. James Coles and Mary his wife till she comes of age or marries she being now six years of age. . . .[73]

April 10, 1771. Ordered that the widow Brumley be summoned to next court to show cause why her children shall not be bound out according to law.[74]

Nov. 19, 1772. Timothy Ryan being runaway, his children, viz.: Mary, aged 8; Martha, aged 5, and Jeremiah, aged 2, to be bound out.[75]

May 22, 1761. Widow of John Culley summoned to show why she does not provide for her children in a Christianlike manner.[76]

The children thus apprenticed were put to work and in return for their services were maintained by their masters and trained, the boys for a trade and the girls for housewifery.

Mere babies were apprenticed. The vestry of Bristol Parish in Virginia in 1722 bound out Margaret Brannum, not quite two years old.[77] Even younger infants appear in the lists of the records of the court of Augusta County, Virginia. Mary Kenmore, for example, bound her nine-months-old baby to Joseph Culton.[78] John Brush and Lewis Wamanstaff, aged four; William Barnes, Mary Hinds, and Margaret Mooney, aged three; Phoebe Martin, Sarah Curtain, and Jacob Meisner, aged two; and Mary Gold, aged fifteen months, were among the younger apprentices.[79] A large number were between five and ten years of age.

Records like these throw light upon the character of parents and the condition of children among the lower classes. A majority of the children bound out were orphans, but many had one or both parents

[73] *Colonial Records of North Carolina*, I, 566.
[74] Lewis Preston Summers, *Annals of Southwest Virginia, 1769-1800* (Abingdon, Va., 1929), p. 116.
[75] Lyman Chalkley, *Chronicles of the Scotch-Irish Settlement in Virginia*, I, 168.
[76] *Ibid.*, p. 90.
[77] Churchill Gibson Chamberlayne, *Bristol Parish Vestry Book*, p. 11.
[78] Lyman Chalkley, *op. cit.*, p. 436.
[79] *Ibid.*, pp. 287, 167, 284, 114, 274, 285, 266, 287, 282.

living. The large number of these indicates that a feeling of parental responsibility did not accompany the general pride in a numerous offspring. In many cases the father of these children had deserted his family, was physically or mentally unfit to support them, or was idle and worthless. The mother arraigned in court was generally incapable of maintaining her children, though sometimes the implication in the record is that she was also neglectful. Many parents were summoned before the vestry or the county court for not providing for their children "in a Christianlike manner." Unless the parents convinced the justices that they could maintain them properly, their children were apprenticed, on the grounds that otherwise they would become chargeable to the parish. If the master to whom children were thus bound proved cruel or neglectful, they were taken from him and bound to another.

Of the general relations between colonial mothers and their children, evidence is scanty. It was customary for a gentleman in his correspondence to address his mother as "Honour'd Madam," to sign himself, "Your dutifull Son," and to speak of her with respect. Charles Carroll of Carrollton, while a student in Europe, addressed his letters to his father, but usually asked to be remembered to his "dear Mama" in "the most affectionate manner," was solicitous about her health, and assured her of his "love and duty."[80] The letters written to his mother by Peter Manigault while in England for his education, though formal, show a genuine affection and respect for her. He called upon her friends in London, wrote in detail of the people and places he thought would interest her, inquired of her friends and her doings in Carolina, assured her repeatedly of his health and general well-being, sent gifts to her and her acquaintances, and in many other ways sought to please her.[81] The letters of Eliza Pinckney would do credit to a mother of any generation. Those to her two little boys at school in England were affectionate but not sentimental. She sought to save them needless anxiety on her account, made careful arrangements for their comfort and welfare, wrote them sensible advice on practical matters, and gave them repeated assurance of her faith in their intelligence and integrity. When her children grew older, she appears to have been helpful but not interfering and

[80] "Extracts from the Carroll Papers," *Maryland Magazine*, X, 144-59, 220-57, 326-35.
[81] *South Carolina Magazine*, XV, 113-23; XXXI, 179.

to have respected their rights to judge of important matters for themselves.[82]

Other examples might be given of affectionate and sympathetic mothers and dutiful children. But these relations were not always agreeable and happy. There were ungrateful children and foolish, selfish mothers then as in all periods. The letters of Maria Taylor Byrd to her son William Byrd III show that, by indulging and flattering him rather than correcting his faults, by sending him gifts and lending him money, she tried to keep him dependent upon her, and that she even encouraged the estrangement between him and his wife. Her reward was to have this son later record for posterity his dissatisfaction with her in his last will and testament.[83]

George Washington was on many occasions sorely tried and humiliated by his mother. She appears to have been a rather strong-willed person, uncultured and with little regard for appearances, and, in her latter days, she was obsessed with a fear of want. Washington, who after his father's death spent most of his time in the homes of his stepbrothers, who were educated and refined gentlemen, was proud and conventional, ambitious for a genteel mode of life, and painstaking in his efforts to improve himself and his position. When he was a lad, his brothers wished to send him to sea, but his mother by her "trifling objections" prevented his taking what they considered an advantageous offer, and later she strove to prevent his accepting the splendid position on General Braddock's staff.[84] When, after Braddock's defeat, she again sought to keep him from a second campaign, irritated probably by her persistent opposition, he wrote: "It would reflect dishonor upon me to refuse; and *that*, I am sure, must or *ought* to give you greater uneasiness, than my going in an honorable command."[85]

After he established himself and wife at "Mount Vernon," his mother appears not to have visited him, but when he passed through Fredericksburg he always stopped to see her, often spending the night, and frequently answering calls from her for money. At his own expense, he bought her a house and garden of her choosing in Fredericksburg that she might be near her daughter, Mrs. Fielding

[82] Ravenel, *Eliza Pinckney*, pp. 170-72, 180-81, 194, 207-8, 210, 253, 255, 259, 260, 270, 293.

[83] See below, p. 171, n. 33.

[84] Paul Leicester Ford, *The True George Washington*, pp. 17-21.

[85] *Writings of George Washington* (ed., John C. Fitzpatrick), I, 181.

Lewis, and, at a loss to himself, rented her plantation that she might have a fixed income.[86] But he did not wish to have her live at "Mount Vernon," and he told her so, kindly, but definitely. "My house is at your service, and [I] would press you most sincerely and most devoutly to accept it," he wrote, "but I am sure, and candor requires me to say, it will never answer your purposes in any shape whatsoever. For in truth it may be compared to a well resorted tavern, as scarcely any strangers who are going from north to south, or from south to north, do not spend a day or two at it. This would, were you to be an inhabitant of it, oblige you to do one of 3 things: 1st. to be always dressing to appear in company; 2d, to come into (the room) in a dishabille, or 3d to be as it were a prisoner in your own chamber. The first you'ld not like; indeed, for a person at your time of life it would be too fatiguing. The 2d, I should not like, because those who resort here are, as I observed before, strangers and people of the first distinction. And the 3d, more than probably, would not be pleasing to either of us."[87]

While her son was in Philadelphia, Mrs. Washington's complaints that she "never lived so poore" in all her life caused a project to be started in the Virginia Assembly to grant her a pension. When Washington learned of it, mortified and indignant, he wrote a friend to have the proceedings stopped, explaining: ". . . she has not a child that would not divide the last sixpence to relieve her from real distress. This she has been repeatedly assured of by me . . . but in fact she has an ample income of her own."[88] But this was not the end of his humiliation. He discovered that she was complaining of her wants on all occasions and borrowing and accepting gifts from her neighbors, thus putting both herself and her children in an unfavorable light. He wrote a brother to ascertain if there were any basis for her complaints; if there were, to see what was necessary to make her comfortable, and at the same time asked him to make known to her "in delicate terms" the impropriety of her complaints and acceptance of favors.[89] He was so vexed by her conduct that he discontinued renting her plantation, not because he meant to withhold support, he explained, but because, "what I shall then give, I shall have credit for" and not be "viewed as [an] unjust and undutiful son."[90]

[86] *Ibid.*, IX, 183.
[88] *Ibid.*, IX, 183.
[90] *Ibid.*, XI, 115-16.

[87] *Ibid.*, XI, 117.
[89] *Ibid.*, X, 137-39.

With the frequent remarriage which was general at the time, step-mothers and mothers-in-law were numerous. But little appears in the records concerning them. Occasionally in ladies' books the danger of introducing a stepfather into the home was pointed out, but apparently no one questioned the father's right to bring in a succession of stepmothers. Henry Laurens, whose father had married soon after his mother's death, determined not to endanger his children's happiness by introducing a second wife, and Jefferson is said to have kept a death-bed promise to his wife not to put a stepmother over her children.[91] But the interests of children in such matters were rarely considered.

Examples might be given of affection and respect for stepmothers on the one hand and of strained relations on the other. Martha Washington was so attached to her father's second wife that when her daughter Patcy Custis died, Washington, to comfort his wife, invited Mrs. Dandridge to make her home at "Mount Vernon." The letters of Mary Ann Maury of Virginia, telling her sister about different members of their family, describe their brother Peter's second wife as "a lovely, sweet-tempered woman," and declare that she and his first wife's children "have an unusual tenderness for each other." But of her brother Francis she told a different story. The Reverend Francis Fontaine was a professor at William and Mary and had married as a second wife the daughter of a gunsmith, "a mighty housewife," who had "the entire dominion" over him and made him treat his children by his first wife as "castaways." The eldest, Francis, who, according to Mrs. Maury, was "a boy of good parts," was removed from college and bound to a carpenter, and the next son was also apprenticed. "God in His mercy" took the youngest "from under her tyranny." The stepdaughter, Molly, whom the aunt wished to take, was "too serviceable" to her stepmother, who treated her with less indulgence than she did the Negro women. Other members of the family corroborated Mrs. Maury's statements. The following from a letter of Peter Fontaine, informing his brother of the death of "brother Francis," shows that the stepmother maintained her control: "He has left the disposal of all to his wife, who governed him and his with a heavy hand. His eldest son, by this means, will have nothing, and his second son, and his daughter,

[91] Wallace, *op. cit.,* pp. 181-82; Rev. Hamilton W. Pierson, *Jefferson at Monticello: The Private Life of Thomas Jefferson, from Entirely New Materials* (New York, 1862), pp. 106-7.

by his first wife, but what she thinks fit to give them. . . . Frank [the eldest son] has been some years in disgrace, upon account of disobliging his step-dame, and never received one farthing but what his master obliged my brother to do for him by contract. . . . James Maury, his son by his last wife, . . . goes now to the college."[92]

Other examples might be given of cruel stepmothers and difficult mothers, but, generally, colonial women appear to have been regarded as good mothers by their contemporaries. They accepted motherhood as the end of their being and bore multitudes of children, often sacrificing their health and even their lives without question or complaint. They had few interests outside the home and were only seldom accused of neglecting their offspring for amusements and social life. Several visitors left complimentary statements about them in their journals. Burnaby wrote that the Virginia women, though deficient in learning, were as good wives and mothers as any in the world.[93] Janet Schaw commended North Carolina mothers for the excellent manner in which they had trained their daughters,[94] and another visitor observed that "the Girls under such good Mothers, generally have twice the Sense and Discretion of the Boys. . . ."[95]

From the twentieth-century point of view, however, these women seem often to have been poorly qualified for motherhood. Many were girls still in their teens, who, even when naturally intelligent and serious-minded, could hardly have been equal to the responsibilities expected of mothers today. Also, most of them had very little education; many had less learning than their twelve to sixteen-year-old sons. Besides their immaturity and ignorance, they experienced other handicaps in the performance of their maternal duties. Their frequent confinements, protracted illnesses, and sufferings at the loss of their little ones must too often have surrounded their households with fear and gloom and made them unfit to associate with sensitive children, and the great amount of attention demanded by their numerous infants necessarily left them little time and thought for their other children. The observation of the French visitor, Chastellux, that the American women were very fond of their infants but neglectful of their older children[96] was probably true in too many cases.

[92] Ann Maury, *Memoirs of a Huguenot Family*, pp. 325-27, 334-35.
[93] *Travels*, p. 37.   [94] *Journal*, pp. 154-55.
[95] "Observations in Several Voyages and Travels in America" (from the *London Magazine*, July, 1746), *William and Mary Quarterly*, XV, 158.
[96] *Travels*, II, 203-4.

CHAPTER IV

HOUSEWIVES AND THEIR HELPERS

JANET SCHAW, visiting Carolina in 1775, found there much that was not to her liking; but the women she regarded with admiration. Generally, she observed, they were excellent housewives and mothers, carefully instructing their daughters in "the family duties necessary to the sex," and in "other accomplishments and genteel manners."[1] She praised her Carolina-born sister-in-law for her domestic accomplishments, declaring that her dairy and garden were proofs of her industry;[2] and she thought Mrs. Cornelius Harnett a woman of extraordinary good sense. "They tell me," she wrote, "that the Mrs. of this place ["Hilton," seat of Cornelius Harnett] is a pattern of industry. She has (it seems) a garden, from which she supplies the town with what vegetables they use, also with mellons and other fruits. She even descends to make minced pies, cheesecakes, tarts and little biskets, which she sends down to town once or twice a day, besides her eggs, poultry and butter, and she is the only one who continues to have Milk."[3]

The domestic achievements of other women are on record. Colonel William Byrd of Virginia boasted of his daughters to an English friend: "They are every Day up to their Elbows in House-wifery, which will qualify them effectually for useful Wives and if they live long enough, for Notable Women."[4] Fithian praised the wife of Councillor Robert Carter of "Nomini" as "a remarkable Economist," and several times noted her housewifery activities in his journal. On one occasion, she showed him her stock of mutton and fowl for the winter, observing that to live in the country and take no pleasure in cattle and domestic poultry would be to her a manner of life too tedious to endure. Again, returning home at candlelight, he found her "seeing to the Roosting of her Poultry." Several times

[1] *Journal*, pp. 155-56.
[2] *Ibid.*, pp. 160-61. [3] *Ibid.*, pp. 178-79.
[4] "Letter to John Lord Boyle, February 2, 1726-27," *Virginia Magazine*, XXXII, 30.

he walked with her in her kitchen and flower gardens, heard her give directions to the gardeners, and was impressed by her fig and apricot grafts and asparagus beds.[5] Eliza Pinckney of South Carolina, though distinguished herself for intellectual attainments and agricultural experiments rather than household occupations, nevertheless was proud of her daughter's housewifery. Soon after the daughter's marriage, she wrote her son-in-law: "I am glad your little Wife looks well to the ways of her household. . . . The management of a dairy is an amusement she has always been fond of, . . . I find, as you say, she sends her instructions far and near. . . . she has people out gathering simples, different kinds of snake-root, and pink-root, and is distilling herbs and flowers."[6]

There were doubtless many other capable housewives. The home was the only field in which superior women might distinguish themselves. It was by no means a narrow sphere, but one wherein individual initiative and executive ability as well as many other talents might be put to use. But the fact that the care of a family was the only career open to them and that it furnished an opportunity for the expression of broad and varied abilities scarcely justifies a general assumption that all colonial women lived up to or even realized the possibilities of their calling. Their domestic activities, like those of women today, varied in accordance with their personal inclinations and capacities as well as their social and economic position. Wives of large planters and slaveholders, ladies in town mansions, women in frontier cabins, and the poorer sort in town, country, and backwoods naturally had very different employments, and all women of the same class by no means had the same interest, training, and skill in household affairs.

More is known of the life of the mistress on a large plantation than of other classes. She usually had a variety of interesting employments, sufficient help to save her from drudgery, and opportunities to express many-sided abilities. Her chief duties had to do with providing food for her large family and the innumerable guests enjoying her ever-ready hospitality. She had not merely to see to the cooking and serving of food but also to arrange for her supplies, many of which came from her own garden, smokehouse, poultry yard, and dairy. Some idea of the enormous quantity of provisions

[5] Fithian, *Journal*, pp. 61-72, 77, 79, 105, 111, 126.
[6] Ravenel, *Eliza Pinckney*, pp. 243-44.

used in great houses is indicated in Fithian's report of a conversation with the mistress of "Nomini." She informed him that her family consumed annually 27,000 pounds of pork and twenty beeves, 550 bushels of wheat, four hogsheads of rum and 150 gallons of brandy. One hundred pounds of flour were used weekly by the immediate household; white laborers and Negroes ate corn meal.[7]

A feature of social life increasing the responsibilities of the mistress was the custom of inviting into her home all persons needing shelter and refreshment, strangers as well as friends. Beverley wrote that a traveler in Virginia needed no better recommendation to the generosity of the people than that he was a "human creature." If he wanted food or lodging, all he need do was to inquire the way to the nearest gentleman's seat.[8] The other southern colonies had the same reputation for hospitality. Eddis observed that the Maryland mansions were "as well known to the weary, indigent traveller as to the affluent guest."[9] Brickell found the North Carolinians as hospitable as any people in the world and was of the opinion that they gave away more provisions to guests than were consumed by their own families.[10] A visitor in South Carolina in 1751 wrote that the inhabitants kept Negroes at their gates near the public roads to invite travelers in for refreshments.[11]

The mistress had not only to be Lady Bountiful to these strangers within her gates, but had also to be prepared for unexpected visits from friends and relatives. Though they sometimes dined out by special invitation, the colonists considered such formality unnecessary. Whole coach loads of young and old with retinues of servants felt no hesitation in descending without warning upon an unsuspecting matron, and she was supposed to lodge and feed them however great their number might be. It is true, however, that she was not expected to furnish a great deal in the way of comforts. A place at the

[7] *Journal*, p. 121.   [8] *History of Virginia*, p. 258.

[9] Eddis, *Letters from America*, pp. 28-29.

[10] *Op. cit.*, pp. 11, 30.

[11] John Gerard William De Brahm, "Philosophico-Historico-Hydrogeography of South Carolina," Weston, *Documents*, p. 178. See also Hammond, "Leah and Rachel," *Narratives of Early Maryland*, p. 293; Henry Norwood, "Voyage to Virginia," *Force Tracts*, III (No. 10), 48; Francis Louis Michel, "Journey, 1701-1702," *Virginia Magazine*, XXIV, 114-15; Hugh Jones, *op. cit.*, p. 49; John Oldmixon, *British Empire in America*, I, 427-29; Lord Adam Gordon, *Journal*, pp. 397-98, 409; Smyth, *op. cit.*, I, 65, 66, 69, 70, 71; and Thomas Anburey, *Travels*, II, 314.

table and a half or even a third share in a bed was all that any guest expected. A bed to oneself was a rare luxury and a private room unthought of.

According to contemporary accounts, from early days gentle-women loaded their tables with a great variety of foods. A visitor in Jamestown in 1634 found in the better houses "tables fournished with porke, kidd, chickens, turkeys, young geese, Caponetts, and such other fouls . . . besides plentie of milk, cheese, butter, and corne."[12] Beverley wrote in 1700 that the Virginians had a great variety of provisions for their tables, and that the gentry had "their Victuals drest, and serv'd as nicely, as if they were in London."[13] Jones praised the Virginia food, mentioning particularly the hot breads and the bacon and hams.[14] The most ordinary drinks of the Virginians were homemade beer and cider, punch brewed with West Indian rum, apple and peach brandy, and metheglin, a mixture of honey and water. Claret, Fayal, Madeira, and Rhenish were among the wines found usually on gentlemen's tables. A great deal of tea, cof-fee, and chocolate was drunk also. Brickell wrote that the diet of the North Carolinians consisted chiefly of beef, mutton, pork, ven-ison in abundance, wild and tame fowl, fish of several delicate sorts, roots, fruits, several kinds of salads, good bread, butter, milk, cheese, rice, and Indian corn. Liquors in ordinary use were rum, brandy, malt, tea, coffee, and chocolate.[15]

A surprising variety of vegetables appeared on gentlewomen's tables. The colonists paid great attention to their gardens, importing skilled gardeners as well as plants and seeds from the Mother Coun-try, and experimenting extensively with native plants. Dr. Mazzei, who came to Virginia in 1773 to help introduce the cultivation of several agricultural products of Italy and was entertained in many of the best homes, observed that the housewives were very ambitious to place before their guests fruits and vegetables out of season.[16] By

[12] "Extract of a Letter of Captain Thomas Yong to Sir Toby Matthew, 1634," *Narratives of Early Maryland*, p. 60. See also Hammond, "Leah and Rachel," in *ibid.*, p. 291.

[13] *Op. cit.*, pp. 251-54.   [14] *Op. cit.*, pp. 41-42.

[15] *Op. cit.*, pp. 38, 39. The food in South Carolina was similar. See Thomas Nairne, *Letter from South Carolina* (1710), pp. 7-11; Thomas Ash, "Carolina," Samuel Wilson, "Account of Carolina," and Thomas Newe, "Letters," *Narratives of Early Carolina*, pp. 141-49, 171-72, and 181-84; Lord Adam Gordon, *Journal*, p. 400.

[16] *William and Mary Quarterly*, IX (2d ser.), 168.

successive plantings and the use of greenhouses and hotbeds, the energetic matron made her menus varied and attractive. Beverley declared that kitchen gardens throve nowhere better than in Virginia, where they had all the "culinary plants" that grew in England, besides many more.[17] President Blair of William and Mary wrote in his diary of having asparagus on his table in March and green peas in September.[18] In North Carolina gardens, according to Brickell, were parsnips, carrots, turnips, beets, artichokes, radishes, several kinds of potatoes, leeks, onions, shallots, chives, and garlic. Salads commonly grown were curled cabbage, savoy, lettuce, "round prickly Spinage," fennel, endive, succory, mint, rhubarb, cresses of several kinds, sorrel, and purslane. Mushrooms grew all over the fields, asparagus throve without hotbeds, and celery, coleworts, cucumbers, and squash were plentiful.[19]

In the preparation and serving of food, the colonial mistress had for her guidance not only the verbal instructions handed down from her mother and the manuscript directions exchanged with friends, but also a number of printed treatises. *The Compleat Housewife, The British Housewife, Mrs. Glasse's Art of Cookery,* and other "Bookes of cookery" were mentioned in wills and inventories and frequently advertised in newspapers. Some of these manuals have been preserved, and throw light upon the culinary art and the etiquette of serving at the time. The recipes show that dishes were rich, highly seasoned, and often complicated. Meats were usually boiled, roasted, stewed, fried, fricasseed, or made into a ragout or pie, and were invariably served with rich stuffings, sauces, and gravies. A mushroom sauce highly recommended for fowl was made as follows: "Pick a Pint of Mushrooms very clean, wash them, put them into a Saucepan, and put to them one Blade of Mace, a little Nutmeg, and a small Pinch of Bay Salt; add a Pint of Cream and a good Piece of Butter rolled in Flour; set them on a gentle Fire and let broil some little Time, keeping frequently stirring them; when they are enough lay the Fowl in the Dish, pour this Sauce in, and garnish with Lemon."[20] A gravy for veal cutlets was made of white wine, butter, oysters, and sweet breads.[21] The numerous recipes for cakes,

[17] *Op. cit.,* p. 253.

[18] *William and Mary Quarterly,* VII, 137.

[19] *Op. cit.,* p. 18.

[20] Martha Bradley, *The British Housewife,* I, 45. For a description of this and other housewifery books, see below, Chap. X.   [21] *Ibid.,* II, 75.

puddings, creams, syllabubs, and tarts, required lavish use of butter, cream, eggs, and spices. "Common Pancakes" were made with eight "new-laid eggs," "a piece of butter as big as a walnut," a quart of milk, and a glass of brandy. "Rich Pancakes" required a dozen and a half eggs, half a pint each of sack and cream, and several spices; and a "Quaking Pudding" called for a quart of cream and twelve eggs.[22]

Dishes were contrived to please the eye as well as the palate. Among the articles advertised by American shopkeepers just before the Revolution were "shapes, ornaments, and mottoes for Desserts." Recipes often recommended the use of parsley or lemon for a garnish. Eggs were fried in a whirlpool of butter to make them round in shape, and spinach prepared "the French way" was stewed in cream and butter and served with fried bread sticks and poached eggs for decoration. "Much Nicety of Hand" was said to be necessary in "dressing up a Salamagundy," a cold dish of sliced chicken, anchovies, eggs, and onions, arranged in prescribed order on lettuce leaves and served with a dressing of oil and vinegar. "Tansy," an elegant pudding, was made of a quart of cream, twenty eggs, and half a pound of almonds, flavored with orange-flower water and tansy, colored with enough spinach to make it "a lively green," and decorated with blanched almonds, citron, and sliced oranges.[23]

Besides innumerable recipes, the housewifery manuals furnished the mistress with "bills of fare" and engraved "schemes" for the proper arrangement of her dishes on the table and instructions in the etiquette of serving. Dinner menus comprised many dishes, all of which were placed upon the table at once. When on special occasions two courses were served, each consisted of meats, fowl, fish, and vegetables as well as tarts, creams, cakes, pies, and puddings. An especially ornamental dish or "grand conceit" was used as a center-piece and the other dishes arranged, preferably in even numbers, on each side and at the ends. A plan for an everyday dinner in winter suggested by *The Compleat Housewife* had in the first course a giblet pie in the center, gravy soup and chicken and bacon at one end, roast beef surrounded by horse-radish and pickles at the other end, and Scotch collops and a boiled pudding on each side. The second course consisted of a tansy with orange in the middle of the table, woodcocks on toast, and a hare with a savory pudding on each side,

[22] *Ibid.*, 548, 570, 571.   [23] *Ibid.*, I, 360, 565, 671; II, 90-91.

and a roasted turkey and a buttered apple pie at each end. Dishes were more elaborate and more numerous on special occasions.

The mistress presided over the table and carved and served. Carving was one of the accomplishments in which the English lady took great pride. She was instructed in this just as she was taught to dance and play upon the harpsichord. The variety of terms and the complicated directions for carving lead us to wonder if this were not the most difficult of the arts she had to master.[24] We read of Lady Mary Wortley Montagu, who as a girl presided over her father's table, that she not only had to "persuade and provoke his guests to eat voraciously," but had also to carve every dish with her own hands, carefully choosing the right morsel for every man according to his rank. She was instructed by a carving master three times a week, and on days when there was to be company she ate her dinner beforehand.[25]

In the eighteenth century, the lady's duties in "doing the Honours of the Table" were somewhat modified. A housewifery book much used in the colonies just before the Revolution explained that in a former period it had been considered proper for the lady to help her guests, both because she was supposed to understand carving and to know where the best bits lay, and because it gave her an opportunity to show with what satisfaction she waited upon her friends. The French manner, which later became fashionable, was for every person to help himself to the dishes near him and pass his plate to be served by the person sitting near whatever he desired. Under the old English plan, the book pointed out, when there was a large company the mistress had little opportunity to taste any food, while in the French fashion she was only one of the company. The French fashion, the author suggested, was suited to great houses where the dishes and guests were so numerous that the mistress could not serve

[24] According to a popular seventeenth-century treatise, no lady of quality would say "Cut up that chicken or Hen." The correct terms in handling small birds were: "Thigh that Woodcock, Mince that Plover, Wing that Quail or Partridge, Allay that Pheasant, Untack that Curlew, Disfigure that Peacock, Unbrace that Mallard, Spoil that Hen, Lift that Swan, Rear that Goose." The directions for attacking fish were equally exact: "Chine that Salmon, String that Lamprey, Splat that Pike, Sauce that Plaice, Culper that Trout, Tame that Crab, Barb that Lobster."— Hannah Wooley, *The Gentlewoman's Companion, or Guide to the Female Sex* (London, 1675).

[25] Rose M. Bradley, *The English Housewife in the Seventeenth and Eighteenth Centuries* (London, 1912), p. 107.

everybody, but in smaller families and on ordinary occasions, the best form was for the lady to help everybody once and then let each person ask for what he wanted.[26]

Wealthy colonial ladies in the eighteenth century were supplied with the equipment necessary for serving meals in the best English manner. Rich mahogany tables, costly damask tablecloths and napkins, handsome silver plate and china adorned their tables. Yet, there were features unattractive to a twentieth-century diner. Food, prepared in an outdoor kitchen by a Negro cook and a retinue of slave helpers, was carried by slave waiters through all kinds of weather into the mansion house. Despite the use of covered dishes, it must often have been tepid and limp by the time it reached the diners. The slave waiters, too, often uncouth and scantily clad, must have formed a shocking contrast to the sumptuousness of the food and the elegance of the table appointments. A visitor in the southern colonies at the time of the Revolution wrote: "I have frequently seen in Virginia, on visits to gentlemen's houses, young negroes and negresses running about or basking in the court-yard naked as they came into the world, with well characterized marks of perfect puberty; and young negroes from sixteen to twenty years old, with not an article of clothing, but a loose shirt, descending half way down their thighs, waiting at table where were ladies, without any apparent embarrassment on one side, or the slightest attempt at concealment on the other."[27] Timothy Ford, a New Englander in South Carolina, declared that at dinner the slaves surrounded the table like a cohort of black guards, rendering very poor service because of the superfluity of them. No sooner was a call made, he explained, than there was considerable delay, either from all rushing at once, or all waiting for one another.[28] Irregularity in the time of serving meals must also have been trying to punctual persons. William Attmore mentioned in his journal being invited to dine at two o'clock at a gentleman's house in New Bern, North Carolina, and sitting down to dinner at four-thirty.[29] Such laxity was common. The frequent and unexpected arrival of guests, the uncertainties in the mode of travel, and more especially the dependence upon slow and irrespon-

[26] Martha Bradley, *British Housewife*, I, 73-75.
[27] Chastellux, *Travels*, II, 83, note by translator. At "Mount Vernon," "Nomini," and doubtless in many other great houses, the house servants wore liveries.
[28] "Diary," *South Carolina Magazine*, XIII, 142-43.
[29] "Journal of a Tour," *James Sprunt Historical Publications*, XVII (No. 2), 20.

sible Negro servants and the unhurried and easy-going life in general, discouraged any conformity to a strict schedule.

Fithian described the daily schedule at "Nomini," which was probably not unlike that which other orderly families attempted to observe. In summer the children were dressed and in the schoolroom by seven o'clock. The large bell rang at the "Great House" for breakfast at eight, and at nine it rang again for the children to return to their lessons and for the carpenters, gardeners, and other laborers to come to breakfast. At ten it called workmen back to their jobs and at twelve announced the children's play hour. At two it called children and workmen to dinner and at three returned them to study and work. School was dismissed at five-thirty, and late in the afternoon Mrs. Carter served coffee at the "Great House." Supper came between eight and nine. In winter this schedule was moved up an hour; and when there were guests, as was often the case, dinner was served any time between two and four-thirty and lasted longer than the usual hour.[30] Chastellux, visiting in the home of General Nelson shortly after the Revolution, found that "An excellent breakfast at nine in the morning, a sumptuous dinner at two o'clock, tea and punch in the afternoon, and an elegant little supper, divided the day most happily."[31]

In most families supper was ordinarily a light meal, but breakfast was quite substantial, consisting of cold meats, fowl, game, hominy, and hot breads. Dinner was the most considerable meal. Fithian, writing of the everyday fare at "Nomini," noted on the table at one time several kinds of fish and pickled crab, beside a fine ham and an excellent shoulder of mutton, neither of which was touched

---

[30] *Journal*, pp. 60-61, 177-78, 258.

[31] *Travels*, II, 19-23. According to Smyth, the Virginia gentleman of fortune usually rose about nine o'clock, breakfasted between nine and ten on bread, butter, thin slices of venison, ham, or beef, with tea or coffee, and dined between two and three. At dinner, whatever else might be served, ham and greens or cabbage was a standing dish. He did not always drink tea in the afternoon but between nine and ten in the evening ate a light supper, usually of milk and fruit, and retired almost immediately afterward. The middle and lower classes rose about six, breakfasted at ten on cold turkey, fried hominy, toast and cider, bread, butter, tea, coffee, or chocolate, and dined about the same time as those of first rank. But usually they had no supper and the women seldom and the men never drank tea in the afternoon.—*Tour*, I, 41-43. John Harrower, tutor in a Virginia family, wrote that they breakfasted on tea, bread, butter, and cold meat, dined at two, and usually did not drink tea in the afternoon or have supper.—"Diary, 1773-1776," *American Historical Review*, VI, 79.

during the meal. Dining at a neighbor's, he had "an elegant dinner; Beef & Greens; roast-Pig; fine boil'd Rock-Fish, Pudding, Cheese &c.—Drink; good Porter Beer, Cyder, Rum & Brandy Toddy."[32]

Josiah Quincy, who while in Charles Town in 1773 was invited into the homes of the leading families, left interesting notes of the foods and ceremonies at dinners there. He dined with four other gentlemen in the home of David Deis and wrote of the occasion: "Table decent and not inelegant: provisions indifferent, but well dressed: . . . Salt fish brought in small bits in a dish made a corner. The first toast the king: second, a lady: the third, our friends at Boston and your (meaning my) fire-side. The master of the feast then called to the gentleman on his right hand *for a lady:* this was done to every one, except to the ladies at table (Mr. D's daughters about sixteen and eighteen) who were called upon for a *gentleman* and gave one with ease. The ladies withdrew after the first round. . . . Glasses were exchanged every time different wine was filled. A sentiment was given by each gentleman and then we were called to coffee and tea."[33] Later at Colonel Miles Brewton's, he had a dinner of three courses, after which were passed two sorts of nuts, almonds, raisins, three kinds of olives, apples, oranges, and the richest wines he ever tasted. At Roger Smith's the provisions were even better, the wines were good, and there was much festivity. Two ladies being called on for toasts, one gave: "Delicate pleasures to susceptible minds," and the other: "When passions rise may reason be the guide."

The drinking of toasts was as regular a practice in many families as the saying of grace. Colonel Thomas Jones of Williamsburg,

[32] *Journal,* pp. 141-42, 195, 205.

[33] *Journal.* William Black, a Virginian who was on official business in Annapolis in 1744, gave this account of a dinner at the governor's mansion: "We were Received by his Excellency and his Lady in the Hall, where we were an hour Entertain'd by them, with some Glasses of Punch in the intervals of the Discourse; then the Scene was chang'd to a Dining Room, where you saw . . . A Table in the most Splendent manner set out with a Great Variety of Dishes, all serv'd up in the most Elegant way, after which came a Dessert no less Curious; Among the Rarities of which it was compos'd, was some fine Ice Cream which, with the Strawberries and Milk, eat most Deliciously. After this Repast was over, (which, notwithstanding the great Variety,) show'd a face of Plenty and Neatness, more than Luxury or Profuseness, We withdrew to the Room in which we was first Received, where the Glass was push'd briskly round, sparkling with the choicest Wines, of which the Table was Replenished with Variety of Sorts."—"Journal," *Pennsylvania Magazine of History and Biography,* I, 126-27.

Virginia, writing his wife in England about her seven-year-old daughter, Betty Pratt, declared: "She drinks your health very cheerfully every day after dinner."[34] Fithian commented several times upon the toasts given at the Carters' dinner table. It was also the fashion in England and in the colonies for gentlewomen to retire soon after dinner to a separate drawing-room, leaving the gentlemen free to indulge in further drinking and in conversation considered unsuitable for ladies.

The colonial mistress was troubled by no concern for a balanced diet. Abundance and variety were the criteria by which her efforts were judged, and the recurrent bilious complaints of her family were not laid at her door but accepted as afflictions from above. Yet, one of her duties was the practice of "Family Physic." She not only doctored and nursed her patients, but sometimes prepared her own medicines, rivaling the apothecaries in the concoction of salves, balms, ointments, potions, and cordials. Receipts for various nostrums were handed down from mother to daughter and exchanged among gentlewomen like recipes for favorite dishes and were usually given an important place in handbooks on domestic economy.[35] The *British Housewife* gave considerable attention to treatment of "the panes of the gout," cholic, agues, and fevers, the "spleen," the "vapours," the "evil," "hysteric fits," and "hypochondriac complaints," which were among the chief ailments in vogue. "Aqua Mirabilis," one of the cordials doubtless often in demand, was alleged to "be excellent in the Cholick, and against that Sickness and Uneasiness that often follow a full Meal." The mere thought of some of its potions must have been sufficient to frighten the most greedy gourmand into temperance. One highly recommended "Stomachick" was made by boiling garlic in sack. Another was of snails, worms, hartshorn shavings, and wood sorrel stewed in brandy and seasoned with spices and herbs.[36]

Unlike northern and frontier housewives, the southern mistress in the settled counties did not generally spin and weave the clothing of her family. The southern planters had a staple agricultural prod-

[34] Stanard, *op. cit.*, p. 112.

[35] An English lady of 1725 wrote her niece, a young housewife in Maryland: "I have sent hear to in this my Great Book of Receipts and with all the Prescriptions that I have ever had from all the Dockters So that if you or any Friend you have has a head that way they may Set up for Great Praktes and do Good that way."— *Maryland Magazine*, IX, 126.   [36] I, 277, 371-72, 612.

uct, which, while it fluctuated in price, always had a direct market, and, living on navigable streams or harbors, they conveniently exchanged their tobacco for English manufactured goods.[37]   Many had even their plainer garments made in England.   Others imported large quantities of materials at one time, which, as the need arose, were made up by tailors and seamstresses among their indentured servants.   It is true that in many houses there were spinning wheels; Negresses were trained as spinners; and, when the price of tobacco sank below the cost of production or foreign wars obstructed trade, cloth was made for domestic use; but ordinarily clothing, blankets, quilts, and such articles were imported.[38]

As towns grew, an increasing number of shops sprang up, which imported and sold fashionable wearing apparel, and colonial tailors, mantuamakers, and milliners made clothing "after the latest London fashion."   White seamstresses made the simpler garments.   Clothing of slaves, which was sometimes of materials made on the plantation, but oftener of coarse, imported stuffs, was often made by persons employed especially for the purpose.   Wives of overseers, white gardeners, and carpenters were sometimes expected to supervise the cutting and help the Negro women make clothes for the slaves on the plantations where their husbands worked, and many white women earned their living by nursing and sewing for slaves.[39]

With the beginning of the conflict with England, coarse stuffs for Negroes, and occasionally even finer materials for the planters' families, came to be made at home.   Flax was planted, Negresses were taught to spin, and wheels were set in motion on every plantation.

[37] Hugh Jones declared in 1723 that goods made in London or Bristol were delivered at the private landing places of Virginia gentlemen with less trouble and cost than to persons living five miles in the country · in England.—*Present State of Virginia*, p. 34.

[38] Bruce, *Economic History of Virginia*, II, 258-494.   See also Rolla Milton Tryon, *Household Manufactures in the United States, 1640-1860* (Chicago, 1917), pp. 19-20, 37-40, 92-122.   Beverley wrote of the Virginians: "They have their Clothing of all sorts from England, . . . Yet, Flax and Hemp grow no where in the World better than there.   Their Sheep . . . bear good Fleeces; but they shear them only to cool them."—*Op. cit.*, pp. 255-56.   See also Brickell, *op. cit.*, pp. 43, 254.   A list of commodities imported from England into South Carolina made by Governor Glen in 1761 included cloths of all sorts from the finest broadcloth to Negro cloth, cambric to oznabrigs, calicoes and muslins, and ready-made clothes to a great value.—*Historical Collections of South Carolina*, II, 230.

[39] Advertisements appeared like that of Eleanor Chapman, who offered to live on a plantation, raise poultry, attend a dairy, nurse sick slaves and make Negro clothes.—*South Carolina Gazette*, July 23, 1772.

Washington, in response to the urge for homemade goods, hired a white woman to teach his slave girls to spin and built a house especially for spinning and weaving.[40] John Harrower in 1775 wrote in his diary of the activities on another plantation: "This morning 3 men went to work to break, swingle and heckle flax and one woman to spin in order to make course linnen for shirts to the Nigers. This being the first of the kind that was made on the Plantation. An before this year there has been little or no linnen made in the Colony."[41]

Well-to-do housewives were not only generally relieved of the necessity of making the clothing and household linen for their families, but they also had considerable assistance in the procuring of food supplies and the performance of other duties. Unmarried women relatives, who commonly made their homes with their married kin, were expected to aid the mistress. They frequently took over the direction of one or more branches of housewifery, like the dairy or poultry yard, and sometimes assumed the entire responsibility of housekeeper. This extract from a letter of Charles Calvert in Maryland to his father in 1663 suggests the situation of many unmarried gentlewomen: "My Coz Wms sister arrived here & is now att my house, & has the care of my household affaires, as yett noe good Match does present, but I hope in a short time she may fine one to her own content & yr Lopps desire, and I shall further what I can towards it."[42]

Drudgery was done by white indentured servants and Negro slaves, the most intelligent of whom were used as house servants. In the early part of the seventeenth century most of the domestics were white, probably because the newly imported Africans were unfit for housework, but toward the latter part of the century Negro domestics became common. At the time of the Revolution wealthy families had an extraordinarily large number of house servants. Chastellux wrote that the luxury of being served by slaves augmented the natural indolence of the Virginia women, who were always surrounded by a great number of Negroes for their own and their children's service.[43] Timothy Ford declared that the South Carolinians, from the highest to the lowest, required a great deal of attendance. From the multiplicity of servants, he felt, rather than

---

[40] Tryon, *op. cit.*, pp. 110-11.

[41] *American Historical Review*, VI, 103.

[42] "Calvert Papers," Maryland Historical Society, *Fund Publication*, No. 28, p. 244.

[43] *Travels*, II, 203.

the climate, arose the "dronish ease and torpid inactivity so justly attributed to the inhabitants of the southern states.[44] Eliza Pinckney, living very simply and alone in Charles Town after the marriage of her children, wrote of her domestics: "I shall keep young Ebba to do the drudgery part, fetch wood, and water, and scour, and learn as much as she is capable of Cooking and Washing. Mary-Ann Cooks, makes my bed, and makes my punch. Daphne works and makes the bread, old Ebba boils the cow's victuals, raises and fattens the poultry, Moses is imployed from breakfast until 12 o'clock without doors, after that in the house. Pegg washes and milks."[45] Here were six servants for one old lady. And this was a very modest establishment.

Besides bond servants and slaves, the mistress had a surprisingly large number of white helpers who worked for wages. Expert gardeners and experienced housekeepers were common among those in easy circumstances. We find numerous newspaper advertisements like the following:

WANTED IMMEDIATELY,

A DISCREET and capable Woman to officiate as Housekeeper in a Gentleman's Family. Such a Person, upon coming well recommended, will hear of a good Encouragement by Applying to the Post Office, Williamsburg.[46]

Washington apparently considered a housekeeper or steward indispensable at "Mount Vernon" not only after his retirement from the presidency, when the large number of visitors made his home a tavern, but also during the first years after his marriage. We find him at one time writing of the departure of his steward and seeking to hire another to "relieve Mrs. Washington from the drudgery of ordering, and seeing the table properly covered, and things economically used." Later he was advertising in the papers and writing his friends for a good housekeeper, declaring that Mrs. Washington's fatigue and distress for the want of one were so great that the matter of salary would be of no consideration.[47]

In addition to the housekeeper, Mrs. Washington and other matrons of her class generally had the assistance of other white

[44] "Diary," *South Carolina Magazine*, XIII, 142-43.
[45] Ravenel, *Eliza Pinckney*, p. 245.   [46] *Virginia Gazette*, June 2, 1774.
[47] *Writings* (ed., Jared Sparks), XII, Appendix, p. 273; Moncure D. Conway, *Washington and Mount Vernon*, Appendix, pp. 336-39; Sparks, *Letters and Recollections of Washington*, pp. 219, 229, 243.

women. Washington's letters show that he expected the wives of his overseers and white laborers to help supply provisions for his table and make Negro clothes. An agreement in 1762 between him and Edward Violett, an overseer, indicates that Violett's wife was tending a dairy, for which services Washington allowed her one-fourth of the butter she made;[48] and a letter to his manager some-time later declared that he would insist that another overseer's wife attend a dairy and raise fowls for the table at "Mount Vernon."[49] Newspaper advertisements for overseers and white gardeners often stated that the wives of these employees would be expected to take charge of a dairy or poultry yard, and many notices show that single women were commonly employed for wages at this kind of planta-tion work. The following is typical of many notices:

A Right good Overseer, having a Wife that can raise Poultry and man-age a Dairy, may have Employment and Encouragement from
Andrew Rutledge[50]

The colonial planter also had a share in the responsibilities per-taining to domestic economy. A number of women, during the ab-sence or at the death of their husbands, supervised all the plantation business as well as their household affairs. But generally the mis-tress had few cares beyond her immediate household, and the master took responsibility for many domestic matters unthought of by most husbands today. The colonial gentleman, whose office was in the precincts of his home, had opportunity to attend to the education of his children, the entertaining of guests, and the ordering of many household affairs. Though his wife probably informed him of the need of provisions and expressed her preferences in the matter of clothing and furnishings, he commonly kept all household accounts and did the buying, giving careful attention to the selection of fur-niture, draperies, rugs, china, and silverware, as well as to the details of the whole family's wearing apparel. Furthermore, because per-haps of the inadequacy of his wife's education as well as his own sense of domestic responsibility, he took care of the social as well as the business correspondence of the family, writing the notes of invi-tation, acceptance, and regret, and the usual letters to absent friends and relatives.

[48] Worthington C. Ford, *Washington as an Employer and Importer of Labor* (Brooklyn, N. Y., 1889), p. 31.

[49] Conway, *Washington and Mount Vernon*, p. 273.

[50] *South Carolina Gazette*, August 4, 1746.

Many letters of Washington illustrate the surprising amount of attention which men, occupied with extensive public and private business, gave to the minutiae of household economy. He ordered the clothing of his wife and stepchildren from Europe, and it appears that he and not Mrs. Washington ordinarily bought most of the provisions and selected the furniture, carpets, wall paper, and other furnishings for "Mount Vernon." Even after he became president, when confronted with the various duties of setting a new government to work, he still found time to give minute directions for the remodeling of the Morris house, engaged for his Philadelphia residence, and to attend to the distribution of the rooms among his family, the selection of new furniture, the employment of additional servants, and other housekeeping arrangements that one might expect to have been left to his wife's supervision. His letters to Tobias Lear, his secretary, are filled with such details as the placing of furniture and ornaments, the color scheme of the curtains, the exchange of laundry equipment with Mrs. Morris, the choice of housekeeper and steward, the making of servants' uniforms and caps, which washerwomen to bring from "Mount Vernon," and whether the cook should or should not make the desserts and have a hand in planning the meals.[51]

[51] *Letters and Recollections of George Washington being Letters to Tobias Lear*, pp. 3-4, 5, 8, 9, 11, 12, 14, 19, 23, 25-26, 30, 33, 36, 40, 43, 44, 45, and *passim*. Franklin, while on his mission to England before the Revolution, bought household furnishings, gowns and accessories for his wife and daughter, and carefully wrote out instructions for the decoration and furnishing of their new home, which was being completed during his absence. Soon after his arrival in London in 1757 he sent his wife a crimson satin cloak "of the newest fashion" and his daughter a black silk with a scarlet feather, muff, and tippet and a box of fashionable linen for her dress. Among the articles sent later were sixteen yards of "flower'd tissue" for a gown, some "China Melons and Leaves for a Desert of Fruit and Cream," a "little Instrument to core Apples," another "to make little turnips out of great ones," and various materials for bed and window curtains. He informed his wife of the latest fashions and instructed her how to use the articles he sent. The diaper tablecloths, he wrote on one occasion, were to be spread on the tea table, for it was no longer the fashion to breakfast on the naked table, and the blue mohair stuff was for curtains for the "Blue Chamber." "The Fashion is to make one Curtain for each Window," he explained. Even more explicit were his instructions for decorating the "blue room": "I would have you finish it as soon as you can, thus. Paint the Wainscot a dead white; Paper the Walls blue, & tack the gilt Border just above the Surbase and under the Cornish. If the Paper is not equal Coloured when pasted on, let it be brush'd over again with the same Colour:—and let the Papiér machêe musical Figures be tack'd to the middle of the Cieling."—*Writings of Benjamin Franklin* (ed., Albert Henry Smyth), III, 379, 422, 424, 430, 432-34, 435, 439; IV, 359-60, 360, 449-50; V, 33-34.

Not much is known of the life of the less well-to-do. The wives of smaller farmers in the settled sections, like the matrons on larger plantations, doubtless were concerned largely with procuring supplies and serving food to their families. But, while they often had indentured servants and slaves, they did not have efficient housekeepers, skilled gardeners, and other paid white helpers to relieve them of the supervision of the various branches of housewifery. They did, however, often have the help of one or more kinswomen living in the home and of their daughters, whose few weeks of school each year interfered little with their household tasks. With the aid of these women in her family and of her servants, the farmer's wife cared for her dairy, poultry yard, and garden, cured meats, pickled and preserved, cleaned house, and prepared meals for the household.

Some of the more industrious of this class spun and wove materials, of which they made clothing for their children and servants and furnishings for their homes, and sometimes earned pin money selling their cloths. Brickell found that the North Carolina girls were "bred to the Needle and Spinning" as well as to the dairy and other domestic affairs, which, he declared, they managed with a great deal of prudence. Many of the women, he observed, made a great deal of cloth of their own flax, wool, and cotton, and some were so ingenious that they made up all the wearing apparel for husband, sons, and daughters.[52] Governor Fauquier wrote in 1766 that the Virginia women made the cotton of the country into a strong cloth, of which they made gowns for themselves and children and coverlets for beds, and that sometimes they offered some of their cloths for sale in Williamsburg.[53]

The wives of tradesmen in the towns helped in their husbands' shops, which were usually in the home, and, with the aid of a few servants, cared for their children and housekeeping. Unlike the country housewives, they did not produce their food supplies but bought them in local stores or on the streets. Newspaper advertisements show that grocery shops carried many provisions. Fresh vegetables raised on near-by plantations or in local gardens were sold by slaves, who strode up and down the streets crying out their wares. Butter, eggs, chickens, vegetables, and sometimes jellies, pickles, and preserves were bought from farmers' wives. In the larger towns

[52] *Op. cit.*, p. 32.
[53] *William and Mary Quarterly*, XXI, 170.

there were confectionery shops, where pastries, jellies, cakes, tarts, potted meats, and other delicacies were on sale or made to order.[54] For housewives who could afford these services, there were Negro laundresses, cooks, nurses, and chambermaids to be hired by the day, month, or year; tradeswomen to clean and mend their laces, fine linen, and silk hose, quilt their petticoats, stiffen and glaze their chintzes; seamstresses, who would come into the home and sew by the day; and milliners and mantuamakers, who designed and made their best clothes.

It was the housewife of the back settlements who had to depend most upon her own labor and ingenuity. The frontiersman's remoteness from waterways and highways and his lack of a marketable staple crop prevented his trading much with the outside world and made it necessary for him and his wife to produce almost everything consumed in their household. With broadaxe and jackknife, he made his cabin, furniture, and many of the farming implements and kitchen utensils; and with spinning wheel, loom, and dye-pots, she made all the clothing of the family, the household linen, blankets, quilts, coverlets, curtains, rugs, and other such furnishings. She made her own soap and candles, and, to a greater extent than the plantation mistress, had to be doctor and apothecary to her family. From the woods she gathered herbs and roots, from which she made various purges, emetics, syrups, cordials, and poultices. She needed also to understand the use of firearms that she might protect her home from wild beasts and Indians, and kill wild animals for food. William Byrd wrote in 1710 of a well-to-do frontier woman who had entertained him and the other dividing-line commissioners: "She is a very civil woman and shews nothing of ruggedness, or Immodesty in her carriage, yett she will carry a gunn in the woods and kill deer, turkeys, &c., shoot down wild cattle, catch and tye hoggs, knock down beeves with an ax and perform the most manfull Exercises as well as most men in those parts."[55]

The food, clothing, and household comforts of frontier people varied greatly according to the wealth, energy, and skill of the master and mistress of the household. But generally houses were much smaller, furniture and clothing more scanty and crude, and food less varied than in the more populous regions. The backwoods house-

[54] See below, pp. 287-88.
[55] "Boundary Line Proceedings, 1710," *Virginia Magazine*, V, 10.

wife, who had no skilled gardener and no greenhouse where she could raise vegetables out of season and who found it impossible to get the imported delicacies available to the housewives near the coast, supplied her family with a diet which seemed plain and monotonous to refined visitors from older sections. Food in the back country consisted of pork, wild fowl, game, and Indian corn, supplemented in the more industrious families by beef, milk, butter, eggs, domestic fowl, and a few fruits and vegetables. The prevalence of pork was due to the ease with which it was produced. In many sections, hogs roamed about through the woods, feeding on acorns and roots and requiring no attention. Corn, which was raised in little patches near the cabins, was beaten in a hand mortar into coarse hominy or into meal, which was sometimes boiled into a mush and sometimes baked on the hearth as a hoecake. Homemade beer, cider, and brandy were the drinks. William Eddis, who visited the western settlements in Maryland shortly before the Revolution, wrote that Indian corn beaten in a mortar and baked or boiled was the principal subsistence of the poorer inhabitants. When salt beef or bacon was added, he declared, no complaints were made respecting their fare.[56] Another visitor in the backwoods wrote: "The meaner Sort you find little else but Water amongst them, when their Cyder is spent, *Mush* and Milk, or Molasses, *Homine*, Wild Fowl, and Fish are their principal Diet."[57]

The backwoods women had the reputation of being more given to labor than their husbands. Lawson found them the "most industrious sex" in North Carolina.[58] Byrd, writing of the outlying settlements in Virginia and Carolina, declared that the men, like the Indians, imposed all the work upon the women and were themselves "Sloathfull in everything but getting Children."[59] The women, he observed, "all Spin, weave, and knit, whereby they make good Shift

[56] *Letters*, pp. 57-58.

[57] "Observations in Several Voyages and Travels in America" (from the *London Magazine*, July, 1746), *William and Mary Quarterly*, XV, 146. The English officer Anburey, who during the Revolution was stationed near Charlottesville in western Virginia, wrote that the inhabitants of that section, to supply the deficiency of vegetables, sometimes gathered the leaves of the poke plant, which they used as a substitute for spinach. In this back country he found only "poor entertainment," and complained of the food: "[one is] seldom able to procure any other fare than eggs and bacon, with Indian hoe cake . . . the only liquors are peach brandy and whiskey."—*Travels*, pp. 340-41, 376.   [58] *Op. cit.*, p. 142.

[59] *Writings* (ed., John Spencer Bassett), pp. 75-76.

to cloath the whole Family; and to their credit be it recorded, many of them do it very completely."[60]   Oldmixon wrote of the Carolina women: "The ordinary Women take care of Cows, Hogs, and other small Cattle, make Butter and Cheese, spin Cotton and Flax, help to sow and reap Corn, wind Silk from the Worms, gather Fruit, and look after the House."[61]   Brickell also found the wives of the poorer farmers "ready to assist their husbands in any Servile Work, as planting when the Season of the Year requires expedition."[62]

The colonial housewife of tradition was a person of superhuman attainments, a composite of all the virtues and talents of women of every class and type.   Actually, there were different kinds of housewives in colonial days as today, and women's occupations and achievements varied greatly according to their individual abilities and the circumstances of their lives.   Superior women in frontier settlements were strong, daring, and self-reliant, as well as skillful and industrious.   With practically no help from the outside world, they fed, clothed, and physicked their large families, made the household furnishings, and on occasion even defended their homes.   But they were not supposed to possess drawing-room accomplishments or to maintain the refined standards of living expected of matrons in town mansions and on large plantations.   If they had few servants and no markets where they could buy their household necessaries, at the same time they did little entertaining and were expected to supply their families with only the simplest kinds of foods and clothes.   Their houses were small, and they had no costly china, furniture, and silver to keep.   Housewives in settled communities, on the other hand, were not expected to possess the physical courage and strength necessary to protect their families from Indians and wild beasts or to suffer hardships common to pioneers; and when they had the care of large and luxurious establishments they had a great deal of assistance in the performance of their duties.   The plantation mistress of the class to which Martha Washington and Eliza Pinckney belonged was often a person of easy and hospitable manners, industry, and housewifery skill.   She directed a large household and entertained numerous guests.   Without the aid of canned goods, refrigerator, or near-by markets, she loaded her table with a variety of foods prepared and served in the best taste of the time.   She often doctored

[60] *Ibid.*, p. 242.
[61] "British Empire," *Narratives of Early Carolina*, p. 372.
[62] *Op. cit.*, p. 32.

the sick of her household, sometimes making the medicines she administered, and occasionally, when trade with England was obstructed, she helped to direct the making of clothing for her household. But she did not do all this single-handed. The coöperation of her husband, the efforts of women relatives living in the home, the skill of experienced hired housekeepers and expert gardeners, and the labor of many servants and slaves went into the accomplishments with which she alone has generally been credited.

CHAPTER V

PLEASURES AND PASTIMES

AMONG THE CHIEF characteristics of the southern colonists were an extraordinary enjoyment of all kinds of gatherings, a great fondness for display in dress and entertainments, and a most liberal hospitality. Visitors usually described them as easy-going, pleasure-loving, sociable, extravagant, and generous, and, almost without exception, praised their eager readiness to entertain friend and stranger. The seclusion of plantation life made almost any visitor desirable, for he brought news and added to the company. The abundance of food, fuel, and other necessaries made entertaining inexpensive and the large number of servants rendered it comparatively easy.

Considerably less is known of the details of social life during the century following the first settlement than of the fifty years preceding the Revolution. The women of this earlier period doubtless enjoyed fewer diversions outside the home than their granddaughters of the eighteenth century. They were more occupied with the details of housewifery, and there were fewer public amusements available. Still the records show that they prided themselves upon a fine appearance and delighted in social gatherings. The chief opportunity of displaying their finery and associating with their friends was at church. Here, before and after services, they made new acquaintances, renewed old ones, exchanged gossip, issued and accepted invitations. The religious meetings of the different sects of Dissenters were also occasions for social intercourse. George Fox, who went about the colonies holding meetings in 1672 and 1673, wrote in his journal of many large assemblies at which not only Friends but hundreds of "the World's People" and many of "first quality" were present. At a general meeting in Maryland there were as many as a thousand persons, and so many boats were passing up and down the Severn that it was almost like the Thames.[1]

The most popular diversions of men were hunting, fishing, horse-races, and cockfights. Many sought relaxation in drinking and gam-

[1] *Narratives of Early Maryland*, p. 397.

ing at cards and dice. Women attended the races, but they do not appear to have shared in the other sports dear to their husbands. Their favorite amusement was dancing. Though there were a few dancing masters, most seventeenth-century women probably had no professional instruction. Their lack of proficiency, however, did not diminish their enthusiasm. Some carried their fondness so far as to shock their elders and scandalize their neighbors. Several indictments appear in the Virginia county records of persons accused of fiddling and dancing on Sunday.[2]

One of the most splendid public occasions attended by women in Virginia's first century was the celebration on the death of King William III and the proclamation of Queen Anne at Williamsburg. Francis Louis Michel, a Swiss in Virginia at the time, left a graphic account of the elaborate ceremonies. The militia of six counties, two Indian queens with forty warriors, and many other men and women of all classes were present. The first part of the ceremony was one of solemn mourning which lasted until noon and consisted of marching and countermarching of soldiers, a funeral oration, and then the formal announcement of the king's death. The musicians played mournful tunes, the English standards were covered with crape, and the standard bearers were in mourning. The governor also wore mourning and his white horse was draped in black. But immediately after noon, the musicians struck up a lively tune, the governor changed horses and uniforms, and the joyful part of the celebration began in honor of the new queen. There were more marching of soldiers and more speeches, a splendid entertainment given by the governor to the prominent ladies and gentlemen, and at night fireworks more magnificent than any ever seen in the colony before. The next day there was a rifle match with prizes of swords, rifles, saddles, bridles, and money furnished by the governor. The celebration lasted two days. At night most of the people camped under the open sky, as there were not nearly enough houses in the little town to accommodate them.[3]

Among the most frequent occasions for private social gatherings were weddings and funerals. Contrary to English custom, marriage ceremonies and funeral services were both held in private homes, and burials were usually in family graveyards. The tying of the

[2] Philip Alexander Bruce, *Social Life of Virginia in the Seventeenth Century* (Richmond, 1907), pp. 182-83.

[3] "Journey, 1701-1702," *Virginia Magazine*, XXIV, 125-29.

nuptial knot was followed by feasting, dancing, drinking of healths, and general jollity, which usually lasted for several days. A Frenchman in Virginia in 1686 left a description of the wedding of an overseer at which he was present. At least a hundred persons were invited, he wrote, several of good estate, and some ladies "well dressed and good to look upon." Though it was in November, the feast was spread out under the trees. Eighty persons sat down at the first table and were served so abundantly that he was sure there was enough for five hundred men. It was the custom of the country, he observed, to serve the wedding banquet at two in the afternoon. As most of the guests came from afar, they stayed one or several nights. But no beds were provided for the men, as all those available were required for the women and girls.[4]

Funerals, though often sad occasions, furnished opportunities for reunions of friends and relatives and for much feasting and drinking. Invitations were issued as for weddings, and guests came from far and near. In Virginia the price of the funeral sermon was forty shillings, but, according to Hugh Jones, even the middle-class people usually insisted upon having one.[5] The family of the deceased, feeling a solemn obligation to entertain liberally those who had come to pay him their last respects, provided quantities of food and drink, the cost of which was sometimes greatly disproportionate to the value of his estate. Among the provisions consumed at the funeral of Mrs. Frances Eppes of Virginia in 1678, were five gallons of wine, two gallons of brandy, a steer, three sheep, ten pounds of butter, and eight pounds of sugar.[6] The refreshments at the funeral of another Virginian included several bushels of flour, twenty pounds of butter, a pig, turkeys, geese, other domestic poultry, and twelve gallons of different kinds of spirits.[7]

Less ceremonious than weddings and funerals were the harvest festivals. It was customary among the farmers when the grain was ripe to appoint a day for reaping and invite the neighbors to help with the work and participate in the entertainment provided. While the men worked in the fields, their wives prepared a bountiful dinner and made ready for dancing, fun, and frolic. Michel declared that in Virginia sometimes from thirty to fifty people were present at

[4] *A Frenchman in Virginia . . . in 1686*, pp. 33, 34.

[5] *Present State of Virginia*, p. 72.

[6] Bruce, *Social Life of Virginia*, p. 220.

[7] *Ibid.*, pp. 220-21.

these gatherings.[8]   Brickell observed that the North Carolinians frequently came twenty or thirty miles to assist at wheat harvests, partake of the feasts, and enjoy the music, dancing, and general fun of the occasion.   Though these annual revels were very expensive, he declared, they were so much a part of the custom that few planters omitted them.[9]

In the next century we find the same hospitality and sociability which characterized the earlier colonists and more varied and sumptuous entertainments.   The wealth accumulated by planters and merchants in the eighteenth century was displayed in larger and handsomer dwellings designed and equipped for splendid parties, in an increased number of slaves and other household servants, in improved means of travel, and in greater extravagance in dress and amusements.   With the prevailing prosperity among the upper classes, gentlemen had larger opportunity for cultivating the social graces, and their wives and daughters, considerably relieved from housewifery cares, were taught drawing-room accomplishments.

When the seventeenth-century gentlewoman went visiting, attended church or any other social function, she rode horseback or went by water.   Throughout the colonial period rivers and other waterways were the chief highways and each planter had his own private landing place and rowboats.   The more elegant ladies had slaves to row them, but many women paddled their own canoes. George Fox wrote in his journal of being rescued by the wife of a North Carolina official, who went herself in a canoe and brought him to land when she observed that, because of the shallow water, he could not get his boat to shore.[10]   Lawson noted that many of the Carolina women handled their canoes with great dexterity,[11] and Brickell wrote that girls as well as boys were accustomed to managing their canoes from infancy.[12]   The roads during this early period, and on until after the Revolution in the back settlements, were mere bridle paths, distinguishable from cattle paths only by the blazed trees, and both men and women traveled on horseback. Women sometimes rode behind their husbands or sweethearts on pillions, but many had their own horses and sidesaddles.   A French visitor in Virginia in 1686 noted that the women, like the men, rode

[8] "Journey, 1701-1702," *Virginia Magazine*, XXIV, 32.
[9] *Op. cit.*, p. 40.
[10] *A Journal or Historical Account*, II, 162.
[11] *Op. cit.*, p. 143.   [12] *Op. cit.*, p. 32.

always at a canter, and he was astonished to see how well they held themselves on.[13]

During the next century roads were gradually improved and carriages became more and more numerous. In 1723 Jones wrote that most families of any note in Williamsburg had a coach, chariot, berlin, or chaise, and that almost every ordinary person kept a horse.[14] A few years later Brickell observed that in North Carolina carriages like those in England were in use and that the roads were broad enough to accommodate coaches as well as wagons and carts. That from Edenton to Virginia was especially convenient, but in other parts of the colony, though broad enough for carriages, the roads were only blazed trails.[15] By the middle of the century well-to-do families drove a coach and four or six horses, a chariot, or a chaise, and the wealthiest owned several of these pleasure carriages. William Fauntleroy of Virginia in 1741 wrote his London merchant for a "handsome chair to go with two horses abreast" and a whip with his name on it; and in 1752 he ordered a chariot suitable for a large family and engraved with his coat of arms, a whip, and harness for six horses.[16] In 1743 Benjamin Harrison left his wife a coach, a chariot, a chair, and six horses.[17] Francis Jerdonne, a Yorktown merchant, wrote in 1753 that the Virginia gentry were such proud spirits that nothing would do for them but equipages of the best and newest fashions. There were, he declared, sundry chariots in the colony which had cost two hundred guineas and one that cost two hundred and sixty.[18] Lord Adam Gordon noted in 1764 that the Virginians usually drove six horses and traveled from eight to nine miles an hour, going frequently sixty miles to dinner.[19]

At the time of the Revolution, carriages were more luxurious and were sometimes attended by slaves in livery. Fithian noted the arrival at "Nomini" of a new coach costing a hundred and twenty pounds sterling, which he described as "a plain carriage, the upper part black and the lower sage or pea green." Councillor Carter had also another fashionable coach lined with blue morocco, a chariot with six wheels, and a chair. When Mrs. Carter and her daughters "took the air" or went visiting, they were attended by slave waiting

[13] *A Frenchman in Virginia*, p. 117.
[15] *Op. cit.*, p. 262.
[17] *Ibid.*, pp. 98-99.
[18] *William and Mary Quarterly*, XI, 238.
[19] *Journal*, p. 405.
[14] *Present State of Virginia*, p. 32.
[16] *Virginia Magazine*, XXXII, 129.

men in liveries of blue broadcloth and brass buttons.[20]   Abbé Robin
wrote that the "riding machines" of the opulent Annapolis families
were light and handsome and "drawn by the fleetest coursers, managed by slaves richly dressed."[21]   Even in North Carolina, which was
somewhat backward in display, it was said that some gay equipages
might be seen.[22]

Despite the improvement in roads and carriages, however, persons of quality as well as the poorer sort continued to travel a great
deal by water.   When Janet Schaw arrived in North Carolina in
1775, she was conveyed from Brunswick to "Schawfield" in her
brother's phaeton and four, but later when she visited in Wilmington she went in a neighbor's very fine boat, which had an awning
to protect the passengers from the heat and six stout Negroes in
uniform to row her down.[23]   There was, however, still something to
be desired in the means of travel, as appears in the following
description by Molly Tilghman of a country jaunt soon after the
Revolution: ". . . I broil'd 6 Miles by Water, to the Bay Side Church
in such a sun, it was enough to coddle common flesh.   I was then
so stupified with old Gordon's [the Rev. John Gordon's] slow croaking, that I began to dream a dozen times before the Sermon was
over, and finally I got into the Chariot with Aunt Tilghman, who
met me by appointment, and encountered a perpetual Cloud of Dust,
which prevented our seeing the Horses Heads or speaking a Word
lest we shou'd be choak'd.   I came off alive it's true but suffer'd so
much in the battle, that I have made a Vow to say my prayers at
home till it rains, which I begin to think it never will again."[24]

The little capitals of the colonies, though appearing very incon-
sequential to visitors, were social as well as political centers.   Here
planters gathered on court weeks and during assembly meetings and
brought their wives and daughters, who, though taking no part in
political affairs, delighted in the races, balls, and plays arranged for
their pleasure.   Here were celebrated royal anniversaries and the
coming of governors.   On these occasions milliners and mantuamakers
arranged to have on display new importations of the latest fashions,

[20] Glenn, *Some Colonial Mansions*, I, 132-33.   A more detailed description of a
chaise of 1784 is given in the *Virginia Magazine*, VIII, 334.

[21] *New Travels*, pp. 50-51.

[22] "Information concerning the Province of North Carolina, 1773," *Tracts Concerning North Carolina* (ed., William K. Boyd), p. 443.

[23] *Journal*, pp. 146, 177.   [24] *Maryland Magazine*, XXI, 130.

and innkeepers made ready to accommodate large numbers of guests. In South Carolina, and in the other colonies to a smaller extent, some of the planters owned houses in the capitals, to which they repaired during the social season every year, but many stayed at the fashionable inns.

Annapolis was one of the gayest little towns in the South. A visitor there in 1749 wrote: "An universal Mirth and Glee reigns . . . amongst all Ranks of People, and at set Times, nothing but Jollity and Feasting goes forward: Musick and Dancing are the everlasting Delights. . . . You would think all Care was then thrown aside, and that every Misfortune was buried in Oblivion."[25] One of the earliest numbers of the *Maryland Gazette*[26] reported a dinner followed by a ball at the "Stadhouse" given by Governor Benedict Leonard Calvert in honor of Queen Caroline's birthday, and on February 9, 1733, carried this description of a similar celebration: "Last Tuesday being the Birth-Day of the Right Honourable the Lady BALTIMORE, the same was observed here, with all Demonstrations of Joy. The Fort Gun was fired at One of the Clock, which was handsomely returned by the Man of War, and the other Ships lying here. In the Evening His Lordship gave the Ladies a Ball, which concluded suitable to the happy Occasion." The election of the mayor in 1749 was celebrated by a horse race in the afternoon for "the late Mayor's Plate of Twenty Pounds," and a ball in the evening, where there was "a splendid Appearance of Ladies."[27]

Governors seeking to maintain their popularity by giving the people their favorite amusements frequently furnished the purse for horse races and gave public balls. In April, 1754, "his Excellency's gift of twenty pounds" was run for by four horses. According to the newspaper account there were a great number of people present, "upwards of 2000 horses, besides a great Number of Carriages." In the middle of the grounds a large platform was erected for his Excellency and a number of gentlemen and ladies that they might view the horses all the way around the course.[28] Ladies were not always merely spectators at the races. In 1769 they furnished a purse of fifty pounds to be run for,[29] and they probably often had money on the issue of the contests.

[25] "Itinerant Observations in America," Georgia Historical Society, *Collections*, IV, 49.

[26] March 4, 1729.

[27] *Maryland Gazette*, October 4, 1749.

[28] *Ibid.*, April 25, 1754.

[29] *Ibid.*, November 2, 1769.

William Black described in his journal several entertainments he attended in Annapolis while there in 1744 on political business. One was a ball given in honor of the Virginia commissioners, attended by "most of the Ladies of any note in town." They danced in the Council Hall. In an adjoining room were refreshments, many sorts of wines, punch, and sweetmeats. Here those who did not care to dance amused themselves with cards, dice, backgammon, and drinking. The older commissioners stayed at the ball until about ten o'clock and then went to their lodgings, but the Maryland ladies were so very agreeable and seemed so intent upon dancing that the younger Virginians stayed on until one in the morning, when each gentleman waited on his partner to her home.[30]

Annapolis at the time of the Revolution was celebrated for its splendid and hospitable mansions, costly equipages, elegant women, fine horses, and frequent and sumptuous entertainments. Abbé Robin declared that "female luxury" there exceeded that even in France, and added, "A French hair dresser is a man of importance among them, and it is said, a certain dame here hires one of that craft at a thousand crowns a year salary. . . ."[31] Another French visitor pronounced the Marylanders and Virginians the greatest spendthrifts in the world.[32] These reports were probably based on superficial observation and hearsay. But William Eddis, who from 1769 to 1777 lived in Annapolis on very friendly terms with the leading families, though greatly admiring their genuine hospitality and sociability, felt that they too frequently mistook profuseness for generosity and impaired their health and fortunes by splendor of appearance and magnificence of entertainments.[33]

Eddis admired the Maryland ladies. He was persuaded that no town in England of the same size as Annapolis could boast of a greater number of fashionable and handsome women,[34] and he was astonished at the quick importation of fashions from the Mother Country. "I am almost inclined to believe," he wrote, "that a new fashion is adopted earlier by the polished and affluent American, than by many opulent persons in the great metropolis." While the American ladies assiduously cultivated external accomplishments and possessed a natural ease and elegant deportment, they were also attentive to the embellishment of the mind, animated and entertain-

---

[30] *Pennsylvania Magazine*, I, 130-31.   [31] *New Travels*, pp. 50-51.
[32] "French Traveller in the Colonies," *American Historical Review*, XXVII, 74.
[33] *Letters*, p. 112.   [34] *Ibid.*, p. 31.

ing in conversation. "In a word," he continued, "there are throughout these colonies, very lovely women, who have never passed the bounds of their respective provinces, and yet, I am persuaded, might appear to great advantage in the most brilliant circles of gaiety and fashion."[35]

Opportunities were not wanting for Annapolis ladies to display their superior elegance and amuse themselves. There were horse races lasting four or five days, numerous birthday parties, and during the winter assemblies every fortnight. The room where these regular assemblies were held was, Eddis wrote, large and illuminated to great advantage. At each end were apartments for card tables where those so inclined might play without having their attention diverted by the sound of fiddles and "the evolutions of youthful performers."[36] There was also the theatre, where professionals acted the plays then popular on the London stage. During the season of 1760 the American Company put on twenty-seven plays in Annapolis.[37] A ticket for each of these performances was ten shillings for a box and seven shillings and sixpence for the pit. An entertainment began between six and seven in the evening and consisted of a farce, a full-length play, and often singing and dancing between the acts. Shortly before the Revolution a new theatre was built by subscription, an elegant structure, according to Eddis, with commodious and neatly decorated boxes, ample pit and gallery, a stage well adapted for dramatic and pantomimical exhibitions, and well painted scenery. Here fine ladies and gentlemen, as well as ordinary people, assembled to see performances as good as those in the most celebrated provincial theatres in England.[38]

Outside Annapolis, Maryland women of the wealthier classes enjoyed various diversions. The little town of Marlborough had its regular assemblies, horse races, and plays. Burnaby described its theatre as "a neat, convenient tobacco-house well fitted up for the purpose."[39] In country and town there were gay house parties, barbecues, fish feasts, boat races, excursions in pleasure boats on the Bay, private balls and banquets, and much visiting. Representative of the spirit of these frolics is this invitation from the Reverend Thomas Bacon, compiler of the Maryland laws, to his friend, Henry Callister: "You and your Wife are hereby required to appear per-

[35] *Ibid.*, p. 113.   [36] *Ibid.*, pp. 31, 32, 107, 114-15.
[37] *Maryland Gazette*, May 5, 1760.   [38] *Letters*, pp. 94-95, 108.
[39] *Travels through the Middle Settlements of North America* . . . , p. 80.

sonally at my Habitation . . . Choptank on Friday next at or before
the usual [hour for dinner], to assist at demolishing a Sirloin of
[beef], &c., &c., which shall then and there be ready. [We shall]
spend the Evening in Music, Chat, Cards or [whatever] amusements [as] to the Company shall seem In [order]. You are permitted to bring your dancing Pumps, [and prepare for an evening]
of Mirth and good fellowship. . . . Of all which you are not [to
fail to perform] in peril of wanting Tuberose, Eagle Flowers and
Importance for the Decoration of your Garden this [summer]."[40]

Molly Tilghman in her correspondence with her cousin Polly
Pearce gives an entertaining account of the pastimes of Maryland
ladies at the time of the Revolution. Interspersed among her reports of prospective matrimonial alliances, family illnesses, "ladies
in the straw," the costumes of reigning beauties, and the goings and
comings of her numerous family, are lively accounts of long visits
in the homes of her married sisters, of tea drinking, afternoon calls,
weddings, musical concerts, amateur theatricals, balls, and assemblies. This is her description of the manner in which the young and
gay of Chester Town spent the Christmas holidays: "There was a
Ball the night after Christmas, . . . Mrs. Galloway flash'd upon
them in her Muslin dress, attended by her admiring Spouse in his
Rock of Gibralter Coat. They had 16 Couple, and spent a very
agreeable Evening. The play came next night, which afforded a
few unexpected incidents. Some Bucks of true spirit, which was
increas'd by good Liquor, broke open one of the Windows, to the
great dismay of the Ladies. As to the play, it exceeded no one's
expectations. However the Eyes of the Audience were oblig'd by a
vast display of fine cloaths, and Jewels, which more than made up
for any faults in the acting. . . . The Ball gave such a spring to
the Spirit of our Beaux that they have made up a Subscription for
Assemblies, and the first, is to be tomorrow night." Another letter
contains this account of the celebration of a wedding among the
well-to-do: "Betsey Worrell was married last Thursday and so
superb a Wedding was never seen here. A number of most elegant
Cloaths, 6 Brides Men and Maids. . . . Between fifty and sixty
people were present at the Ceremony, who danc'd till 4 o'clock.
Some of the Company retir'd at twelve being afraid (I suppose) of
Injuring their healths by keeping such riotous hours. They kept

up the Ball till Monday, and then went to Middle Neck, accompanied by 6 Carriages well filled. The Bride and Brides groom led the Van in a new Phaeton."[41]

The social life in Virginia towns was very much like that in Maryland. The little capital was throughout the century the scene of many public and private entertainments. Hugh Jones wrote in 1723 that the inhabitants of Williamsburg lived, dressed, and behaved after the same genteel manner as the gentry in London. At the governor's birthnights, balls, and assemblies, he saw as fine appearance of gentlemen and ladies and enjoyed as splendid entertainments as he had anywhere.[42] In 1736 the birthday of the Prince of Wales was celebrated by "firing of guns, displaying of colors and other public demonstrations of joy," followed by a ball and elegant entertainment given by the governor to the ladies and gentlemen. When the King's birthday was celebrated in 1752, the whole city was illuminated and there was a ball attended by a "brilliant appearance of Ladies and Gentlemen."[43] So closely were English customs followed in Williamsburg that in May, 1774, when the Assembly met, a court herald published a code of etiquette for the regulation of the society of the little metropolis.[44]

Besides the governor's entertainments, there were private balls and dinners, amateur and professional theatricals, races, and frequent public assemblies. During the seventeen-thirties, the widows Stagg and Degraffenreidt taught dancing lessons and enlivened the little capital with their balls and assemblies, varied with other attractions. In the *Virginia Gazette*, April 22, 1737, Madame Degraffenreidt announced her intention of giving a ball at her house the following Tuesday and an assembly the next Wednesday, and Mrs. Stagg proposed to have assemblies the following Thursday and Friday at the capitol. As a drawing card, Mrs. Stagg in her advertisement in March, 1738, promised at her assembly "several grotesque dances never yet performed in Virginia" and several valuable goods and "a likely young negro fellow" to be set up and raffled for. Not to be outdone, Madame Degraffenreidt advertised a ball at which would be put up and raffled for "a likely young Virginia negro woman fit for house business and her child."[45] In the seventeen-fifties Mistress Anne Shields, tavern keeper, and Richard Coventon, dancing master,

[41] *Ibid.*, XXI, 125-26, 141.
[42] *Present State of Virginia*, pp. 31, 32. [43] Stanard, *op. cit.*, p. 138.
[44] *William and Mary Quarterly*, XVI, 40. [45] April 7, 1738.

gave balls at the courthouse in Williamsburg, but apparently did not find it necessary to offer special inducements for patronage.

Theatricals were performed in Williamsburg from the beginning of the century.[46] Early in the century a playhouse was erected, which was possibly used for a while by professionals, but in 1736 students at the college and young people of the town were having their plays there. The *Virginia Gazette*, September 10, 1736, announced that on that evening the gentlemen of the college would act the tragedy of *Cato* at the theatre, and on the following Monday, Wednesday, and Friday gentlemen and ladies of the country would act *The Busy-Body, The Recruiting Officer,* and *The Beaux' Stratagem.* Of these amateur productions Colonel Thomas Jones wrote his wife, who was away from home on a visit: "You may tell Betty Pratt [his little step-daughter] there has been but two Plays since she went which is Cato by the Young Gent'm of the College as they call themselves, and the Busy body by the Company on Wednesday Night last, and I believe there will be another to Night, they have been at a great loss for a fine Lady who I think is to be called Dorinda; but that difficulty is now overcome by finding her, which was to be the greatest Secret, and as such 'tis said to be Miss Anderson that came to Town with Mrs. Carter."[47]

Some time after this, the theatre, apparently not being used, was bought and converted into a town hall, but in 1751 a new theatre was built by subscription and opened by a company of comedians at the time of the October court. In 1752 the Hallam Company arrived with "Scenes, Cloaths, and Decorations . . . entirely new, extremely rich, and finished in the highest Taste," and having altered the playhouse to a "regular Theatre, fit for the Reception of Ladies and Gentlemen, and the Execution of their own Performances," advertised that they would open with "a Play, call'd The Merchant of Venice (written by Shakespeare) and a Farce, call'd The Anatomist, or Sham Doctor."[48] Ladies were desired to give timely notice to Mr. Hallam for their places in the boxes and on the day of the performance to send their servants early to keep them and prevent disappointment. In 1768 the "Virginia Company of Comedians" played in Williamsburg for two months, and in 1771 the Hallams returned with the newly organized "American Com-

[46] Lyon Gardiner Tyler, *Williamsburg, the Old Colonial Capital* (Richmond, 1907), p. 228; Stanard, *op. cit.,* p. 234.   [47] *Virginia Magazine,* XXVI, 180.
[48] *Virginia Gazette,* June 12, 1752; August 21, 1752.

pany of Comedians" and popular Sarah Hallam as leading lady. Colonel Hudson Muse, writing his brother of an eleven days' stay in Williamsburg in April, 1771, declared he spent the time very agreeably at the plays every night. Miss Hallam was "super fine," but he was as much impressed by the beauties at the theatre as with the actress. The playhouse was crowded every night and there were "treble the number of fine Ladys that was ever seen in town before."[49]

Petersburg, Norfolk, and Fredericksburg were visited by players, and almost every little town had its racecourse and assemblies. Musical concerts given by local gentlemen of talent were occasionally advertised. In December, 1767, John Schneyder announced a concert to be followed by a ball in Fredericksburg; and in May, 1769, "at the request of several ladies and gentlemen," a concert of instrumental music was given in Hanover by "gentlemen of note, for their own amusement." The ladies, who were probably sponsoring the program, requested that the company "be governed by a becoming silence and decorum, during the performance."[50]

In Alexandria regular annual balls were provided in this manner. Each person attending the ball drew a card out of a hat. The gentleman drawing the king had the honor of giving the ball the following year and the lady drawing the queen made the cake. Nicholas Cresswell wrote of attending one of these entertainments in January, 1775. About thirty-seven ladies were present "dressed and powdered to the life," some very handsome, and all fond of dancing. Between the country dances came "everlasting jigs" to a Negro tune, which the young Englishman thought more like "a Bacchanalian frolic" than a dance for a polite assembly. A cold supper was served, with punch, wine, coffee, and chocolate, but no tea, that being "a forbidden herb." Though these dances usually lasted on into the morning, they were attended by persons of all ages, old women and matrons with children on their laps, as well as young girls.[51]

In North Carolina in the early part of the century population was sparse, and there were less wealth and fewer opportunities for social intercourse than in the older settlements in Virginia. Brickell in 1737 wrote of the hospitality and pleasant life there, but mentioned few public amusements. Horse racing he found very popular. Each town, he noted, had its racecourse, and many inhabitants reg-

[49] *William and Mary Quarterly*, II, 241.

[50] *Virginia Gazette*, December 24, 1767; May 11, 1769.

[51] *Journal*, pp. 52-53.

ularly attended the races in Virginia. The men were much addicted to gaming, especially at cards and dice, and greatly admired cock-fighting, wrestling, leaping, and such activities. Dancing was a favorite amusement with both sexes. They danced to the tune of a fiddle or bagpipe if possible, but if they had no other music they sang for themselves. Music and musical instruments, he observed, were very rare.[52]

By the decade before the Revolution comforts and amusements had increased, though there were still fewer luxuries and splendid entertainments than in the neighboring provinces. New Bern, the little capital, was the scene of festivities on public occasions. Here in December, 1764, the arrival of Lieutenant-Governor Tryon was celebrated with a "very elegant Ball" in the great ballroom of the courthouse. The local newspaper described the entertainment. The courthouse was beautifully illuminated, and there were present, besides the governor and his lady, nearly one hundred ladies and gentlemen. About ten in the evening the company withdrew to the "Long Room" over the ballroom, where was spread "a very elegant Collation." After supper they returned to the ballroom and concluded the evening "with all imaginable Agreeableness and Satisfaction."[53] No record appears of a playhouse at New Bern, but Governor Tryon in 1768 mentioned the presence in the province of a company of comedians,[54] who probably were the players who were in Williamsburg that year. If more newspapers for the period had been preserved, they would probably tell of assemblies, plays, and other diversions similar to those at Williamsburg. At Wilmington and Edenton social life was refined, but without luxury or ostentation. Here, as in other parts of the colony, the chief pleasures in which women shared were private dinners, tea parties, balls, and races.

Charles Town, the capital of South Carolina, to a greater extent than New Bern, Williamsburg, or even Annapolis, was the social center of its community. At the time of the Revolution it was the largest town in the South and its inhabitants were reputed the wealthiest and most polite. Public amusements here, though more varied, were similar to those in the other capitals: birthday entertainments, races, assemblies, concerts, and plays. Milligan wrote of fortnightly

[52] *Op. cit.*, pp. 39-40.

[53] *North Carolina Magazine; or, Universal Intelligencer*, December 28, 1764.

[54] *Colonial Records of North Carolina*, VII, 786-87.

assemblies in Charles Town, where was always a brilliant appearance
of lovely, well dressed women.[55] An exciting account of one of these
balls is given in a letter of Eliza Wilkinson. She and two other
young ladies, she wrote, "must needs go to Town, to play off a few
Airs at the Assemblys." After much powdering, frizzing, curling,
dressing, and admiring of each other's headdresses, they set off in the
carriage at a great rate, and despite the tipsy condition of the postilion,
arrived safe at the hall. It was splendidly illuminated and the music
was so sweet that they could scarcely keep their feet still. But their
joys were all too fleeting. Scarcely had they danced two minuets,
when it was announced that the house was on fire. The assembly
immediately broke up, and powdered beaux and belles scampered
away, leaving the scene of their pleasures to be consumed by the
flames.[56]

Extracts from a journal[57] kept by Ann Manigault, wife of Gabriel
Manigault, from 1754 through 1781 give some idea of the way in
which a wealthy Charles Town matron passed her time. At the time
of the first entries in 1754, Mrs. Manigault had been married twenty-
four years and was probably in her forties or fifties. This abbre-
viated copy of her journal shows that she went to races, balls, and
assemblies occasionally, and went visiting, dined out, had guests to
dinner or to tea, and attended church oftener. She dined at the governor's and entertained him in her home, went once to see a wire
dancer and again to see some experiments in electricity, heard a
Quaker preacher, and attended Whitefield's meetings several times.
But her favorite diversion was the theatre, which she attended frequently each season.

The formal social season in Charles Town was in winter, when
ladies and gentlemen of means moved from the country to their town
houses to enjoy the pleasures of the metropolis. During the "sickly
months" of summer also, when the "country fever" made it almost
impossible for white people to live on many plantations, planters
brought their families to Charles Town, and even those whose
plantations were in healthful situations often migrated to the capital

[55] "A Short Description of . . . South Carolina," *Historical Collections of South
Carolina*, II, 479.

[56] This letter is given in full in George Armstrong Wauchope's *Writers of South
Carolina* . . . (Columbia, 1910), pp. 408-9.

[57] "Extracts from the Journal of Mrs. Ann Manigault," edited by Mabel L.
Webber, *South Carolina Magazine*, XX, 57-63, 128-41, 256-59; XXI, 10-23, 59-72,
112-20. Hereafter cited as *Extracts from Journal*.

for fashion's sake. At these times, though the heat probably did not allow much exertion, there were diversions of a less strenuous sort.

From the third decade of the century Charles Town had its dramatic and musical exhibitions. The *South Carolina Gazette*, February 16, 1733-34, announced "a Consort of Vocal and Instrumental Musick," tickets for which were to be sold at Mrs. Saureau's House for forty shillings. It was to be in the Council Chamber and was to begin at six o'clock. On January 18, 1734-35, it advertised that a tragedy called *The Orphan, or the Unhappy Marriage* would be "attempted" in the courtroom, and the following week announced a second performance of this tragedy. The next month "the Opera of Flora, or Hob in the Well," the first musical play in America, was performed in the courtroom with the "Dance of the two Pierrots, and a new Pantomime Entertainment in Grotesque Characters, called *the Adventures of Harlequin and Scaramouch, with the Burgomaster trick'd.*"[58] In 1736 a playhouse was built at Charles Town. There are records of dramatic performances here in 1746, 1754, 1763, 1766, 1773, and 1774.[59]

Charles Town had also its Vaux Hall, called doubtless from the London pleasure resort of that name, where, in summer, music, dancing, and various amusements and refreshments were to be had for a dollar a ticket. The *South Carolina Gazette*, July 20, 1767, advertised at "New-Vaux-Hall" a concert of vocal and instrumental music, between the parts of which four or five pieces would be exhibited by a person who was confident "very few in Town ever saw" or could "equal his Performance." After these demonstrations there was to be a pantomime followed by a ball, and tea and coffee were included in the price of the ticket.

Charles Town gentlemen, like those in London, had their social clubs and sometimes entertained the ladies, who had no such associations. The St. Cecilia Society was organized in 1762 as a musical association, but from the beginning the balls which followed its concerts were probably more generally enjoyed than the music.[60] Josiah Quincy left an account of a St. Cecilia concert he attended while in

[58] *South Carolina Gazette*, February 15, 1734/35.

[59] A list of the plays given in 1773 and 1774 may be found in the *South Carolina Magazine*, X, 185-86.

[60] Wallace, *Life of Henry Laurens*, pp. 32-33; Edward McCrady, *The History of South Carolina under the Royal Government, 1719-1776* (New York, 1899), pp. 526, 528.

Charles Town in March, 1773. He wrote that the concert hall was "preposterously out of all proportion large." There was no orchestra for the performers, though a kind of loft was provided for fiddlers at the assembly, and, much more to be regretted, there was no organ. But the music was good. The two bass viols and the French horns were "grand," and Abercrombie, the lately arrived Frenchman, played a first fiddle and solo incomparably. This artist had been engaged by the St. Cecilia Society at a salary of five hundred guineas a year. The governor was at the concert and many other persons of the first character, all dressed "with richness and elegance" not usually seen in New England. About two hundred and fifty ladies were present, but he was informed that this was no unusual show. He thought the Charles Town ladies surpassed those of New England in richness of dress and in "taciturnity during the performance," but were inferior to them in loftiness of headdress and in health and countenance. In noise and flirtation after the music, the ladies of North and South were on a par.[61]

Savannah, youngest of the southern capitals, appears to have been the scene of varied social activities in the decade before the Revolution. In December 15, 1763, Sarah Lyon announced a public ball, tickets to which for a lady and gentleman were ten shillings. There is no evidence of a playhouse in Savannah, but "Mr. Lyon's Long-Room," several times mentioned in the papers, apparently served as ballroom, music hall, and theatre. Here on June 4, 1766, was held a concert of music followed by a ball as part of the celebration of the King's birthday. Tickets for the entertainment, which included tea, coffee, and cards, as well as dancing and music, were five shillings.[62] In the same room on June 23, 1768, was performed a farce called *Lethe, or Aesop in the Shades*. According to a newspaper advertisement, there was a variety of entertaining characters, among whom were a fine lady and a fine gentleman, and vocal and instrumental music between the acts.[63]

While the capitals and other principal towns were the centers for public amusements and gave the tone to private entertaining, in the country also social life among the wealthy was easy and pleasant and was characterized by a great deal of entertaining and many diversions. Fithian's account of the everyday doings of the Carters

[61] *Journal*, pp. 424-81.
[62] *Georgia Gazette*, May 28, 1766.   [63] *Ibid.*, June 22, 1768.

at "Nomini Hall" is an excellent description of the manner in which leading country families passed their time just before the Revolution. He wrote of housewarmings, christenings, boat races, horse races, balls, and impromptu dances, and noted almost daily that the Carter ladies had company or had gone visiting. The girls rowed on the river, skated on the frozen millpond, rode horseback, and "went for an airing" with their mother in the chariot. Often the family and their guests, of whom there was usually one or more, spent the evening "in music, chat, and pleasantry." Councillor Carter, who was very fond of music and played several instruments, had at "Nomini" a harpsichord, a harmonica, a pianoforte, a guitar, and German flutes, and at his house in Williamsburg he had a good organ.[64] His daughters were taught by a music master, and they and the other young ladies in the neighborhood frequently performed for the company. On Sundays the family went down the river to Nomini Church in a boat rowed by four men, or the ladies went in the chariot and the gentlemen on horseback. After the service, which with a fashionably brief sermon took only a short time, they strolled about in the churchyard among the crowd of friends and relatives in pleasant talk, and usually went to dinner with friends or brought guests home to dine with them.[65]

One of the most delightful occasions for the young ladies was Mr. Christian's dancing school,[66] which was held in rotation in the homes of the pupils, and usually lasted two or three days. Fithian left an interesting description of the assembly at "Nomini" the week before Christmas in 1773. He dismissed school on Friday morning, he wrote, and before noon several young gentlemen arrived and were given quarters in the schoolhouse. Later arrived three chariots, two chairs, and a number of horses. That evening at the dance were eleven young misses and seven young fellows decked out in the latest fashion. They danced only a short while and by half after nine were dispersed to their several sleeping apartments. The next morning the company breakfasted at ten and then retired to the dance hall. After each pupil had an individual lesson, they all danced several minuets, and then the whole company joined in country dances, moving easily to the sound of well performed music. Dinner came at three-thirty, after which they danced again until dark. In the

[64] *Journal*, pp. 58-59.
[65] *Ibid.*, pp. 58, 296-97.   [66] See below, p. 205.

evening after the candles were lit they played "Button," and, in re-
deeming his pawns, the dignified young tutor confessed, he had several kisses of the young ladies.   A splendid supper was served at
eight-thirty, after which the company formed a semicircle around the
fire and played "break the Pope's neck" until they were dismissed
at ten.   The next morning, which was Sunday, the young folks set
out soon after breakfast for their respective homes.[67]

Balls, like dancing schools, sometimes lasted for several days and
were enjoyed by old as well as young.   One given by Richard Lee
of "Lee Hall" apparently continued from a Monday through the
following Saturday and was attended by about seventy persons.   Mrs.
Carter and her daughters, who were excused from school on the occasion, attended several days, driving over in the afternoon and returning late at night.   Fithian, who was invited to accompany them on
one of the afternoons, described the occasion in his journal.   They set
out at two o'clock, Mrs. Carter and the girls in the chariot, a lady
guest in a chair, and the gentlemen on horseback, and arrived in
plenty of time before dinner.   At four-thirty the ladies dined, and
after them "each nimblest fellow dined first."   The dinner was as
elegant as could be expected for so great an assembly.   At seven in
the evening the dancing began in the ballroom.   First came one
round of minuets; next, jigs; then, reels; and last, country dances,
with several marches now and then.   Two violins and a French horn
furnished the music.   The ladies were in gay and splendid attire, and
when they danced their brocades rustled and trailed behind them.
Those not desiring to dance made up parties in separate rooms, some
at cards, some drinking, and some singing "Liberty Songs."   At
eleven o'clock Mrs. Carter called her family to go, and they set out
for home, leaving many of the guests to spend the night at "Lee
Hall."   The next morning the "Nomini" ladies stayed abed late, and
another holiday from school was declared.[68]

The letters of Eliza Lucas give many glimpses of the pastimes of
a country lady in South Carolina.   With her father absent in the
King's service in Antigua and her mother an invalid, Eliza had unusual responsibilities for a girl in her teens and probably shared less
in public amusements than most girls of her position.   But she was
by no means excluded from society.   To the English lady who had
supervised her education in London and who was apparently uneasy

[67] *Journal*, pp. 62-65.   [68] *Ibid.*, pp. 94-95.

concerning her isolated situation in America, she wrote soon after coming to South Carolina: "I like this part of the World. . . . We have a very good acquaintance from whom we have received much friendship and Civility. Charles Town the principal [town] in this province is a polite agreeable place, the people live very Gentile and very much in the English taste. . . . Wee are 17 mile by land, and 6 by water from Charles Town where wee have about 6 agreeable families around us with whom wee live in great harmony. . . . least you should think I shall be quite moaped with this way of life, I am to inform you there is two worthy Ladies in C^rs Town, Mrs. Pinckney and Mrs Cleland who are partial enough to mee to wish to have mee with them, and insist upon my making their houses my home when in Town, and press mee to relax a little much oftener than 'tis my power to accept of their obliging intreaties, but I am sometimes with one or the other for three weeks or a monthe at a time, and then enjoy all the pleasure C^rs Town affords."[69] Among the pleasures on a visit in Charles Town in 1742 was "a very genteel entertainment and ball" given by the governor on the King's birthnight, at which, she wrote her father, she danced a minuet with an old acquaintance of his.[70]

Her neighborhood offered a pleasing social intercourse. Within walking distance lived Mrs. Chardon, an intimate friend, and not far away on the Ashley stood the stately homes of several of the first families. One of her letters mentions a "festal day" at "Drayton Hall," but gives no details.[71] Another tells of a tour to Goose Creek and St. John's to visit several gentlemen's country seats, at each of which she and her party were entertained with the most friendly politeness. They arrived first at "Crowfield," home of William Middleton, where they spent a most agreeable week, and then moved on to the other places, at each of which they probably stayed a week also.[72]

Not balls and gay house parties, however, but music, gardening, reading, and the informal exchange of friendly visits were her most common pleasures. To a friend in Charles Town wanting to know how she passed her time in the country, she wrote a schedule of her activities. Mornings, after seeing that the servants were at their respective tasks, she read, studied, practiced her music, walked in

[69] Ravenel, *Eliza Pinckney*, pp. 5-6.   [70] *Ibid.*, p. 21.
[71] *Ibid.*, p. 42.   [72] *Ibid.*, p. 53.

the garden or fields, instructed her younger sister, and taught two
little black girls to read. Afternoons and evenings were spent in
music, reading, writing, and needlework. It was the fashion in the
neighborhood, she explained, for ladies to carry their needlework
abroad. Mondays her music master came; Tuesdays she and Mrs.
Chardon were constantly engaged to each other, Mrs. Chardon at
"Wappoo" one Tuesday and Eliza at Mrs. Chardon's house the
next; Thursdays were given to plantation business and writing letters; and Fridays she went "a vizeting."[73]

With other ladies in the country, as with Miss Lucas, visiting
was the most usual diversion. Neighbors frequently dined, drank
tea, or spent the day with one another, and those living at greater
distances made visits lasting from a few days to weeks and months.
Young ladies, and even mistresses of large families, set out on a
series of visits, staying at one house several days or weeks, and moving on to another and then another until they had made the round
of their friends and kindred. We have an interesting record of
such a tour in a journal kept, supposedly, by Lucinda Lee while visiting among the Washingtons, Lees, and other relatives in lower Virginia.[74] This young lady, accompanied by her sister and a maid, set
out some time in the early part of September and was about two
months in completing her circuit of visits. At each place she found
other guests, young people like herself, and older married ones also,
all of whom seemed free to go where and when they chose. Her
journal, supposed to have been written for her friend Polly Brent,
is a delightful record of the carefree, sociable life of young ladies in
wealthy families, who apparently had no responsibilities except to
amuse themselves and be agreeable. It opens at the "Wilderness,"
residence of John Grimes, where the girls stayed over a week, dining
or having tea at near-by houses, reading and weeping over *Lady
Julia Mandeville,* and entertaining beaux and other company. At
"Belleview," home of Thomas Ludwell Lee, they passed the time
in the same manner, "craping" their hair and dressing, playing cards,
and receiving company. The journalist spent one morning "putting
my cloths to rights—a dreadful task." On Sunday, wearing her
"Great-Coat and dress hat," she went in the chariot to church, where
she had the satisfaction of seeing a "beauty" and received a "very

[73] *Ibid.*, pp. 30-31.
[74] *Journal of a Young Lady of Virginia, 1782* (ed., Emily Virginia Mason).

pressing invitation" to go home with Mrs. Fitzhugh and attend the races the next day. But having previously resolved that "no sollid happiness" was to be found in such amusements, she declined, much to the surprise of everyone, who thought it hardly possible for any girl to resist such a fascinating prospect of pleasure. In a few days she departed from "Belleview" for "Chantilly," where she found several guests, among whom was a Mr. Pinkard, who entertained them reading a play, *The Belle's Stratagem*. Besides receiving a great deal of company as usual, the young ladies rode horseback, walked in the garden, and discussed romantic subjects. At "Pecatone," residence of Mrs. Turberville, they found more cousins, a greater number of beaux, a more elegant manner of living, and gayer amusements. Here they "took airings" in the chariot, dressed every day for dinner, and danced every evening. Once, when the fiddler became ill, they diverted themselves very agreeably playing "grind the bottle" and "hide the thimble."

The week at "Pecatone" was followed by a visit to their Washington cousins, who though somewhat rowdy were full of fun and frolic. Here they apparently had no balls, but diverted themselves with practical jokes and other pranks. "About sunset," the journal relates, "Nancy, Milly, and myself took a walk in the Garden (it is a most butifull place.) We were mighty busy cutting thistles to try our sweethearts, when Mr. Washington caught us; and you can't conceive how he plagued us—chased us all over the Garden, and was quite impertinent." At night after they had retired there were more antics: "We took it into our heads to want to eat; well, we had a large dish of bacon and beaf; after that, a bowl of Sago cream; and after that, an apple pye. While we were eating the apple pye in bed—God bless you, making a great noise—in came Mr. Washington, dressed in Hannah's short gown and petticoat, and seazed me and kissed me twenty times, in spite of all the resistance I could make; and then Cousin Molly. Hannah soon followed, dress'd in his Coat. They joined in eating the apple pye, and then went out. After this we took it into our heads to want to eat oysters. We got up, put on our rappers, and went down in the Seller to get them: do you think Mr. Washington did not follow us and scear us just to death. We went up tho, and eat our oysters. We slept in the old Lady's room too, and she sat laughing fit to kill herself at us."[75]

[75] *Ibid.*, pp. 41-43.

The first week in November the girls were at "Blenheim," where were also many other guests including the whole "Bushfield" family and a Mr. Spotswood, Milly Washington's "lately commenced lover." Milly entertained them "on the forti-pianer," "Cousin Washington performed on the Spinnet," and they read Pope's *Eloisa*. The journalist thought the poetry beautiful but disapproved of some of the "sentiments." Those of *Eloisa* were "too Amorous for a female." One morning was spent by the girls discussing the subject, "Regretting the manner in which we have spent our past life." Unfortunately the details of the discourse are not given. The journal ends with a return to "Chantilly." It says that Milly is very angry because Mr. Spotswood, her would-be suitor, has followed her there despite his promise "never to trouble her again on the subject," but leaves us in doubt as to the final results of the young man's persistence.

The pleasures enjoyed by the Carter ladies, Eliza Lucas, and Lucy Lee are representative of those of all southern ladies of their class at the time. Dancing was the darling amusement of young and old, and no social occasion was complete which was not followed by a ball. Balls, however, were by no means always splendid affairs, but varied all the way from an impromptu gathering of a few couples dancing in a small room to the music of a slave fiddler, to the magnificent assemblies at the governor's mansion. After the Revolution dancing came to be almost exclusively the amusement of the young, but in colonial days, ladies of advanced age attended balls, stepped the minuet, and joined in the country dances as gaily as in their youth. Daniel Campbell, writing to Washington June 28, 1754, informed him that his mother was well and added: ". . . very lately I had the honour to dance with her, when your health was not forgot."[76] Mrs. Manigault of South Carolina attended Charles Town assemblies long after she became a grandmother.

Music of a simple kind had come to be an ordinary means of relaxation at the time of the Revolution. Ladies played the spinet, harpsichord, and pianoforte, and gentlemen the flute, French and German horns, and violin. Sometimes they sang ballads and love ditties to their instruments, but vocal music was rarer than instrumental. Reading aloud from popular plays and novels was an agreeable pastime. William Byrd read *The Beggar's Opera* to the ladies of "Tuckahoe,"[77] and James Iredell entertained his friends among

[76] *Letters to Washington* (ed., Hamilton), I, 15.
[77] *Writings* (ed., Bassett), p. 341.

the Edenton ladies with *Tristram Shandy* and *Sir Charles Grand-ison*.[78] The more energetic sometimes acted plays. Cresswell wrote of spending the evening with a Maryland family, when the company amused themselves with several diverting plays, a pastime he thought quite common in the country. From one of Washington's letters it appears that at "Belvoir," residence of his friend, George William Fairfax, they played Addison's *Cato*, with Mrs. Fairfax taking the part of Marcia. Ornamental needlework, which with dancing and music was among the chief accomplishments taught in girls' schools, was a resource for women when left to themselves.

Cards, backgammon, and billiards were pleasures which women shared with men. By the middle of the century whist had come to be very popular in England and America. A kinswoman of William Byrd, writing him from London in 1742, declared that "a Sertain game upon the Cards call'd Whisk (much in vogue these last three or four years)" had "engaged the Men of All ages to keep company with Women more than every thing before."[79] When Eliza Pinckney was in England in 1754, she complained of the perpetual card playing which seemed with many a business of life.[80] Colonial newspapers carried frequent reports of the prodigious sums lost by London ladies at cards and sometimes inserted the strictures of English moralists upon female gaming. Ladies in the colonies liked whist and sometimes played for money. Thomas Jefferson's accounts show that Mrs. Jefferson lost money at cards,[81] and several entries in Washington's ledger are for sums lost to his women friends at whist.[82] But these amounts were small. Though gaming was common among colonial men of all classes, "female gamesters," if existent in the colonies, were rare.

In the decade before the Revolution, although the fashion for female fragility had gained only a small hold in the colonies, ladies were taking less exercise than their grandmothers. Sometimes they walked a mile or so to see their neighbors, but much oftener they

---

[78] Griffith J. McRee, *Life and Correspondence of James Iredell*, I, 142, 158. Hereafter cited as *Iredell*.

[79] *Virginia Magazine*, XXXVII, 112.   [80] Ravenel, *Eliza Pinckney*, pp. 156-57.

[81] William Eleroy Curtis, *Thomas Jefferson* (Philadelphia and London, 1901), p. 317.

[82] John C. Fitzpatrick, *George Washington, Colonial Traveller, 1732-1775* (Indianapolis, 1927), pp. 20, 68-69.

went visiting or "took the air" in carriages. Horseback riding was a fashionable recreation, and jaunty riding habits and sidesaddles were sold in colonial shops, but by no means every girl knew how to ride.

The pursuit of health was a less popular pastime with American women than with ladies of leisure in England, though colonial women sometimes traveled to other colonies for a change of climate and even crossed the Atlantic to consult London physicians and enjoy the benefits of the waters at Bath, Bristol, Epsom, or Tunbridge Wells. Elizabeth, wife of Thomas Jones of Virginia, went abroad for her health in 1728, stayed for a while in London to be treated by a physician, went to Bath to "take the waters," and was away from home nearly two years.[83] In 1773 the *South Carolina Gazette* announced the departure of Mrs. Blakeway, Mrs. Beresford, and Mrs. Peter Delancey, her widowed daughter, for England. The ladies stayed for a while at Bristol Wells, Mrs. Delancey in a futile effort to be cured of a cough, and the others probably to enjoy the diversions there.[84] Many other South Carolina women visited the English watering places, some for their health and many for pleasure. In the seventeen-forties the mineral springs in the Virginia mountains were known for their medicinal properties, and it came to be the fashion for planters in the low country to take their families to drink of and bathe in the healing waters. In 1769 Washington journeyed with his family to the springs, hoping that they might improve the health of his wife's invalid daughter. The accommodations at the Virginia springs were rude, and the amusements not to be compared with the fashionable diversions at the English watering places.

Very little is known of the social life of the wives of the smaller farmers and of the women in the back settlements. For a large number life must have been solitary and dull. Doubtless many who left lively homes in the older counties to follow husbands into sparsely settled communities suffered almost intolerable loneliness. James Iredell, while on his circuit as judge of North Carolina in 1778, wrote his wife of stopping at the home of a lately married couple, who, though wealthy, lived so far from everyone that the young wife had not a single woman with whom she could associate nearer than Hillsborough, eighteen miles away. When Samuel Johnston,

[83] *Virginia Magazine*, XXVI, 163-73.
[84] *South Carolina Magazine*, XXI, 44.

Iredell's companion, told her that he would endeavor to bring Mrs. Johnston to see her, tears flowed from her eyes, and it was with difficulty she could express the great pleasure it would give her.[85]

For women of the poorer classes, life was a continual round of household duties. Their diversions were mostly of the nature of useful work converted into pleasure by coöperative effort, such as spinning matches, candle-dippings, and quilting parties. When a housewife finished sewing together the pieces for a patchwork quilt, she invited her neighbors to spend the day or the afternoon with her and quilt it. Gathered round the quilting frame, while their needles flew, the quilters exchanged gossip of the neighborhood. Sometimes they divided into two teams, working from opposite sides, and had a match to see which would reach the center of the quilt first. The hostess had prepared substantial refreshments, which, with the companionship, the company considered ample reward for their day's work. Log-rollings, house-raisings, corn-shuckings, and harvestings were also social and festive affairs, followed usually by feasting and dancing. The dances on these occasions were not the minuets and country dances enjoyed by more-polite society but three- and four-handed reels and jigs.

Fairs were probably delightful occasions for farmers' wives, for they not only gave the women an opportunity to display their achievements in gardens, poultry yards, and kitchens and to see the latest fashions displayed by milliners and mantuamakers, but they also offered many unusual sights and diversions. Besides the exhibitions of livestock, poultry, preserves, and pickles, there were usually horse races, various other kinds of matches, and music and dancing. The plan of amusements for a holiday celebration of this kind was described in the *Virginia Gazette* in 1737. The advertisement declared there would be a horse race followed by numerous other contests and "comical diversions." A hat valued at twenty shillings would be cudgeled for, a pair of silver buckles wrestled for, and a pair of handsome shoes danced for, and there would be contests in playing the violin and singing. There was also to be a beauty contest with a handsome pair of silk stockings provided for the handsomest country maid appearing on the field that day.

We have several descriptions of the frontier wedding, which, though based largely upon tradition or personal memoirs, are doubt-

[85] McRee, *Iredell*, I, 379.

less reliable as general representations of the kinds of amusements enjoyed by the backwoods people.[86]   In communities where there were no public diversions the wedding was of great interest to young and old and was anticipated with eager delight by the whole neighborhood. Preparations were made for a sumptuous feast and much -merrymaking. The marriage ceremony, according to Doddridge, took place at the bride's home. On the morning of the appointed day the groom's attendants assembled at his home and together they set out on horseback in time to reach the home of the bride by noon, the hour for the ceremony. On the way they observed a rite known as "running for the bottle." When they were a mile or so from their destination, an Indian yell announced the start of the race and the party dashed off, each rider intent on being the first at the bride's door and winning the prize, a bottle of liquor.

After the wedding ceremony the company sat down to a substantial backwoods feast of beef, pork, fowl, and sometimes bear meat and venison, with potatoes, cabbage, and other vegetables. This was often spread on a table made of a large slab hewed out with a broadaxe and supported by four sticks in augur holes, and the food was served in wooden bowls and trenchers. During the dinner the younger members of the company were watchful for any opportunity to steal the bride's shoe, while the bridesmaids and groomsmen were vigilantly on guard to protect her from such theft. If they failed, they had to pay the successful thief a penalty of a bottle of wine or a dollar to redeem the shoe, and the bride was not allowed to dance until after it was restored.

After dinner dancing began and lasted until morning. While the attention of the company was engaged in the frolic, the bridesmaids slipped the bride out and put her to bed upstairs, and shortly afterwards the groomsmen stole off with the groom and placed him snugly by her side. Then the attendants amused themselves in what was known as "throwing the stocking." The maids one after another stood at the foot of the bed with their backs toward it and threw over their shoulders a stocking rolled into a ball. The first

[86] Samuel Kercheval, *A History of the Valley of Virginia* (4th ed., Strasburg, Va., 1925), pp. 60-62; Rev. Dr. Joseph Doddridge, *Notes on the Settlement and Indian Wars of the Western Parts of Virginia and Pennsylvania . . . with a View of the State of Society and Manners of the First Settlers of that Country*, given in Kercheval's *History*, pp. 260-62; John Lewis Peyton, *History of Augusta County, Virginia* (Staunton, Va., 1882), pp. 44-46.

to succeed in touching the bride's head was, they pretended to believe, the next to be married. Then the groomsmen engaged in the same contest, throwing the stocking at the groom's head. In the meantime dancing and the other festivities continued downstairs. The bottle was passed around and this toast drunk to the bridal pair: "Here's health to the groom, not forgetting myself, and here's to the bride, thumping luck and big children."

CHAPTER VI

WARDROBE AND TOILET

With both men and women of the seventeenth and eighteenth centuries, dress was a matter of serious concern. Clothing was important not merely for protection and adornment, but even more as a means of showing social distinctions. The colonists, no less than their kinsmen across the Atlantic, felt called upon to wear clothing of the style and quality belonging to their station; and even in the early years after the first settlements, gentlemen and gentlewomen, unmindful of the inappropriateness of sumptuous attire in their rude surroundings, wore silks, satins, and velvets, costly laces and jewelry. John Pory, secretary of the Virginia Colony, wrote in 1619 that the cowkeeper at James City on Sundays went "accowtered all in freshe flaming silks," and the wife of a former collier in England wore "her rough bever hatt with a faire perle hatband, and a silken suite thereto correspondent."[1] As the planters in each of the southern colonies increased their fortunes, they imported more and more expensive clothing for their families and followed eagerly all the changes of fashion in the Mother Country.

English dress in the seventeenth century was freer from oddities than in the preceding or the succeeding periods and was characterized by simplicity of style and richness of material. Gentlemen wore the picturesque and dashing costume of the Cavalier made familiar by the portraits of Van Dyke, and ladies wore graceful, flowing garments of rich materials. The reign of Charles I saw the abandonment of starched ruff, rigid stomacher, and wheel farthingale for a more natural and beautiful style. The high, stiff ruff was replaced by a soft fichu of light, flexible material; the hard, narrow bodice gave way to a waist that defined but did not cramp the figure; and the gown, no longer stretched out stiffly over the whale-bone wheel, fell gracefully to the ground in soft, full folds. The hair, too, following the mode of studied negligence, was drawn back from the forehead and hung in ringlets on the neck.

[1] *Narratives of Early Virginia*, p. 285.

The chief parts of woman's dress were gown, bodice or waist-coat, and petticoat. The gown, sometimes made in one piece and sometimes a separate bodice and skirt, parted in the middle, display-ing the petticoat, which was not an undergarment, but often the most conspicuous part of the dress. Sleeves, usually elbow length, were finished with wide muslin or lace ruffles, and the neckerchief was also of muslin or lace. A coif or close cap, often of lace or embroi-dered muslin, and a crosscloth or forehead cloth were worn as head-dress. Shoes were of substantial cloth material with high heels and were often decorated with large rosettes. Silk, cotton, or worsted hose, of various colors, were held up by gay garters of ribbons and lace. The outdoor costume included a cape, cloak or mantle, a hat or close-fitting hood, gloves, and usually a mask and muff.[2]

Many materials were available for making ladies' apparel. Taf-feta, heavier than the material of the same name today; ducape, a heavy, corded stuff of plain color; tabby, a watered material; and alamode, sarcenet, tiffany, paduasoy, and lustring, all soft, plain mate-rials, were among the silks most generally used. Damask was a rich fabric woven in elaborate patterns in silk, wool, or linen, and tammy was woolen and glazed like alpaca. Callimanco and prunella were durable stuffs of which shoes as well as gowns and petticoats were made. Calico, originally "calicut" from the town in India from which it was imported, and dimity, a ribbed fabric, were among the most popular cottons, and Holland was a much used linen. Paragon, penistone, fustian, kersey and baize—substantial woolens—and dornex, dowlas, lockram, and oznaburg—cheap, coarse linens—were used for ordinary clothing.[3] Wealthy ladies not only had their gowns made of silk, but used real lace on their caps, neckerchiefs, and sleeve ruffles, and wore earrings, necklaces, rings, and watches set with jewels.

Inventories of the wardrobes of seventeenth-century gentlewomen in the southern colonies include the same kind of apparel as that worn by English ladies—gowns, bodices, and petticoats of the best English stuffs; aprons, scarfs, mantles, and hoods of various mate-

[2] Georgiana Hill, *A History of English Dress from the Saxon Period to the Pres-ent Day* (2 vols. London, 1893), I, 245-67; J. R. Planché, *History of British Cos-tume from the Earliest Period to the Close of the Eighteenth Century* (4th ed. Lon-don, 1913), pp. 310-14, 317-22, 332-33.

[3] Bruce, *Economic History of Virginia*, II, 188-89; Alice Morse Earle, *Costumes of Colonial Times* (New York, 1911), pp. 45, 75, 97, 98, 102, 121, 145, 154, 175, 176, 192, 211, 244.

rials and colors; gold and gilt stomachers; scarlet, black, and green hose and garters of many hues, and laced "headclothes" and neck-wear. In the outfit of a young lady setting out for Virginia from England about 1661 were a white flannel petticoat, a white sarsenet and a ducape hood, two green aprons, a long riding scarf, three pairs of gloves, a mask, and a pair of shoes.[4] The wardrobe of Frances Pritchard of Virginia in the last quarter of the century included a printed calico gown lined with blue silk, petticoats of olive-colored silk, of silver and flowered tabby, and of velvet and white striped dimity, a white striped dimity jacket, a black silk waistcoat, a pair of scarlet sleeves, a pair of Holland sleeves with ruffles, a Flanders lace band, one cambric and three Holland aprons, five cambric handkerchiefs, and several pairs of green stockings.[5] Sarah Willoughby, another Virginia dame, possessed seven petticoats. Four were silk—one red, one blue, one black, and one of India silk. One was of prunella, another of striped linen, and another of calico. Besides these garments she had a black silk gown, a scarlet waistcoat with silver lace, a white knit waistcoat, a striped stuff jacket, a prunella mantle, a sky-colored satin bodice, a pair of red paragon bodices, several Holland aprons, seven handkerchiefs, and two hoods. The handkerchiefs mentioned in these lists were probably for the neck, and not pocket handkerchiefs.[6] An inventory of the possessions of Madam Henrietta Maria Lloyd of Maryland includes the following alluring articles of apparel: "1 satin gown and petticoat, 1 silk gown and petticoat, 1 old silk gown and coat, 1 mourning gown and quilted petticoat, 1 silk mantle, 2 silk petticoats and scarf, a good warm gown, 2 smock coats and 2 waistcoats, a parcel of laces, a pair of bodices, a gauze coat, 1 flowered satin party coat, 4 party coats, 4 pairs of shoes and 1 pair of galoches, silk and worsted stockings, 2 headdresses, a box of handkerchiefs. . . . a parcel of neck lace, 1 diamond ring, 1 mourning ring, 4 stone rings, 3 rings and a pair of earrings. . . . a flowered satin morning gowne, a long scarfe lyned with velvet, a parcel of silver lace and footings, 2 pairs of stays, 1 black scarfe, 1 parcel of beads and silver cross and snuff-box, 1 gowne and party coat, 1 silk petticoat with silver fringe, 1 silk mourning gowne, 1 riding gowne, 1 sable tippet and strings, 2 short aprons, a girdle and mask. . . ."[7]

[4] Bruce, *Economic History of Virginia*, II, 194.
[5] *Ibid.*, p. 194.   [6] *Ibid.*
[7] Hammond, *Colonial Mansions of Maryland and Delaware*, pp. 155-56.

Toward the end of the seventeenth century dress underwent an important change. Following the Restoration in England, the careless grace of the preceding period gave way to exaggeration and affectation, and modes were introduced which were very similar to those abandoned at the beginning of the century. The farthingale was revived as the hoop-petticoat, the tight bodice reappeared, and the elaborately curled and bejeweled coiffure of Queen Elizabeth's day was exceeded in grotesqueness by the towering commode of the eighteenth century. Dress of the period was not altogether unattractive, however, for it was always rich and colorful and sometimes graceful and becoming.

The most characteristic feature of women's costume in the eighteenth century was the hoop-petticoat. This was not an underskirt like the crinoline of later date, but was the outside skirt itself, stiffened with whalebone and often made of costly silks and lavishly embroidered or quilted. At one time fashion called for it to be six feet in diameter, but by the middle of the century it was smaller and spread out in oblong shape. Not only did the hoop require an enormous amount of material to cover it, but it was also very inconvenient. Ladies wearing it found it difficult to enter coaches and sedan chairs and could scarcely sit two in a carriage or walk two abreast on the streets. Special chairs were designed to accommodate the hoop, and in some houses even the staircases were made with balusters curved outward to allow for the voluminous skirts. *The Spectator*, ridiculing the hoop soon after its first appearance, wrote that fashionable churches were "very much straitened" to find seating capacity for their congregations and hoped the new fashion would not drive ordinary women into conventicles.[8] But notwithstanding its absurd cumbersomeness, and despite the denunciations of the pulpit and the ridicule of wits, it held sway throughout three-quarters of a century.

Besides the hoop-petticoat, the dress consisted of a gown opening in front and drawn to the sides in folds and a tight-fitting bodice cut very low in the neck. Attractive stays were worn on the outside, or the bodice itself was laced up over a stomacher. As in seventeenth-century costumes, the short sleeves were finished with muslin ruffles or frills of lace, and often a soft fichu was draped across the shoulders. The French sacque was very fashionable. This was a flowing gown

[8] No. 127.

open in front. At the back broad folds were carried from the neck to the floor without being held in at the waist, while the front and sides were shaped to the person. The negligee, often mentioned, was not a dressing gown, but was worn for full dress, and the night-gown was in the eighteenth century an evening dress. Sleeve-knots and breast-knots of ribbon were usual decorations, and caps and aprons were worn by all classes.

The materials which had to be stretched over the whalebones were less heavy and more flexible than those of which the gowns and petticoats were made in the preceding century, but they were often of beautiful texture and patterns and very costly. The mode called for bright hues and the use of many colors in the same cos-tume. We read of an English lady in Queen Anne's time in "a black silk petticoat with a red and white calico border, cherry-coloured stays trimmed with blue and silver, a red and dove-coloured damask gown flowered with large trees, a yellow satin apron trimmed with white Persian, and muslin head-cloths with crow-foot edging, double ruffles with fine edging, a black silk furbelowed scarf and a spotted hood."[9] Floral patterns were especially popular. This is a contem-porary description of an embroidered white satin gown worn at the English court in 1741: "[at] the bottom of the petticoat [were] brown hills covered with all sorts of weeds, and every breadth had an old stump of a tree that ran up almost to the top of the petticoat, broken and ragged and worked with brown chenille, round which twined nastersians, ivy, honeysuckle, periwinkles, convolvuluses, and all sorts of twining flowers, which spread and covered the petticoat; vines with leaves variegated as you have seen them by the sun, all rather smaller than nature, which makes them look very light; the robings and facings were little green banks with all sorts of weeds; and the sleeves and the rest of the gown loose, twining branches of the same sort as those on the petticoat."[10]

Colonial shopkeepers, who customarily listed latest importations in their newspaper advertisements, offered many alluring dress mate-rials: flowered, striped, figured, and plain modes and satins in all colors; rich China taffetas; English Persians; many colors of dam-ask, sarcenet, paduasoy, and lustring; printed and copperplate linens; "Irish, Princess, and Russia linens"; fine and coarse Hollands; India

[9] Hill, *op. cit.*, II, 73.
[10] G. Woolliscroft Rhead, *Chats on Costume* (London, 1906), p. 142.

and English chintzes and calicoes; flowered, spotted, wrought, and plain lawns; striped, sprigged, and plain muslins; and various colors of plain and striped dimities. The shops advertising these goods usually employed mantuamakers to make them into gowns and petticoats, and milliners to make headgear, neckwear, and other accessories. Also they sold ready-made petticoats, stomachers, handkerchiefs, aprons, and other apparel. Included in their inventories were quilted and puckered silk petticoats of various colors of plain and flowered silks; flowered gauze aprons, worked lawn and muslin aprons, and "Queen's net-work muslin aprons"; silver, ribbon, and lace stomachers, "Blond and Italian Stomachers and Knots," "fine Paste Stomachers and Knots," and "Suits of Ribbons made up in London and Stomachers with Bows"; gauze ruffles, tuckers, and ruffs, "complete suits of fine Minionet Lace Ruffles," and "Honeycomb and other new fashioned Riband Ruffs"; fine lace handkerchiefs; velvet, beaded, and spangled collars; and "Breast Flowers equal to Nature."

As small waists were the fashion, tight lacing was general. Young, growing girls were squeezed in at the waist and stout ladies pinched as far as possible into the shape decreed by fashion. While in England Peter Manigault urged his mother, who had the care of his motherless little girls, not to allow them to wear stays,[11] but his feeling was unusual. Generally, little girls as well as fat ladies wore corsets. Women's and children's stays were advertised regularly by colonial shopkeepers. Some idea of the types worn may be had from the advertisement of a Williamsburg staymaker who offered to make "turn and single stays, Jumps, Half Bone Stays, Stays to buckle before, pin, or button. . . ."[12] "Jumps" were loose stays worn in negligee dress. Fithian complained of the latest importation of stays in Virginia in 1773: "[They] are produced upwards so high that we can have scarce any view at all of the Ladies Snowy Bosoms; and on the contrary, they are extended downwards so low that whenever Ladies who wear them, either young or old, have occasion to walk, the motion necessary for Walking, must, I think, cause a disagreeable Friction of some part of the body against the lower edge of the Stays which is hard and unyielding."[13]

For outdoor wear in winter ladies wore different kinds of capes and cloaks. One oftenest mentioned was the cardinal, a long cloak

[11] *South Carolina Magazine*, XXI, 42-43.
[12] *Virginia Gazette*, March 31, 1774.   [13] *Journal*, pp. 192-93.

with an attached hood, which, though originally scarlet, was sometimes made of black, purple, and other colors. The capuchin was
also a hooded cloak so called from its resemblance to the hooded gar-
ment worn by the Capuchin monks.[14] We find listed in shopkeepers'
inventories dress and undress capes; satin and Persian quilted cloaks;
white and colored silk quilted cloaks; black callimanco cloaks; flowered and spotted mode cardinals and cloaks; white, black, and plaid
satin cardinals; black, purple, crimson, and scarlet cloth cardinals;
capuchins; and "Queen's dress cloaks." Fithian wrote that almost
every lady in Virginia wore a red cloak when abroad and muffled
up her head and neck with a handkerchief, leaving only a narrow
passage for the eyes. He declared that when he first arrived in the
colony, he was distressed, believing every one he met had the mumps
or toothache.[15] Outdoor headgear consisted of hats, bonnets, and
hoods of various shapes and materials. In the decade before the Revolution a fashionable bonnet was the calash, an enormous hood made
on a framework of whalebone hoops resembling the hood of a carriage and pulled over the head by means of strings.

The most conspicuous feature of woman's dress in the beginning
of the century was the tower, or commode. The hair, which under
the Stuarts hung in curls about the face and was decorated with a
single flower or jewel, was now combed up straight from the forehead, piled high in stiff curls and puffs, and surmounted by a wire
frame covered with tiers of lace and ribbons. Hanging down the
sides of the face from the top of the tower were lace pendants called
lappets. Sometime in the second decade the commode disappeared;
the hair was arranged in simple curls close to the head and was surmounted by an ornamental cap. *The Spectator* commented thus
upon the change: "There is not so variable a thing in nature as a
lady's head-dress; within my own memory I have known it rise and
fall above thirty degrees. About ten years ago it shot up to a very
great height, insomuch that the female part of our species were much
taller than the men , . . at present the whole sex is in a manner
dwarfed and shrunk into a race of beauties that seems almost another
species. I remember several ladies who were once very near seven
foot high, that at present want some inches of five."[16]

The headdress varied from time to time in size, shape, and
height. In the seventies the tower of Queen Anne's time reappeared

[14] Earle, *op. cit.*, pp. 79-81.
[15] *Journal*, pp. 58, 296.   [16] No. 98.

in an exaggerated form. The hair was frizzed, piled up in front over wool pads into mountains of curls and puffs, greased with pomatum and powdered, and then covered with a monstrous structure of wire, lace, gauze, ribbon, beads, jewels, and feathers. False curls resembling stuffed sausages hung down on the sides of the face. Ostrich plumes standing upright a yard high were worn by many ladies, and veritable flower gardens appeared atop the heads of others. The "building" of these elaborate edifices naturally required the skill of professional hairdressers and took so much time that ladies often made one dressing serve for weeks and even months, with, it may be imagined, very unsanitary effects.

Naturally, caricatures appeared ridiculing this absurd fashion. A print of the time now in the British Museum is entitled "A Hint to the Ladies to take Care of their Heads." It represents a lady in elaborate costume standing under a chandelier. Though the ceiling is exceptionally high, the towering plumes of her headdress have caught fire from the candles. In another print ridiculing the fashions of the time, the "Friseur" is mounted on a high stepladder frizzing the top of the lady's coiffure. Another caricature pictures a woman with a headdress containing all kinds of vegetables, with carrots especially conspicuous as side curls. The following is from a satirical poem entitled "The Friseur":

> The fair Jesebella what art can adorn,
> Whose cheeks are like roses, that blush in the morn?
> As bright were her locks as in heaven are seen
> Presented for stars by th' Egyptian queen;
> But alas! the sweet nymph they no longer must deck,
> No more shall they flow o'er ivory neck;
> Those tresses, which Venus might take as a favour,
> Fall a victim at once to an outlandish [foreign] shaver;
> Her head has he robb'd with as little remorse,
> As a foxhunter Crops both his dogs and his horse:
> A wretch, that, so far from repenting his theft,
> Makes a boast of tormenting the little that's left:
> And first at her porcupine head he begins
> To fumble and poke with his irons and pins,
> Discharging a steam that the devil would choke,
> From paper, pomatum, from powder and smoke.
> The patient submits, and with due resignation,
> Prepares for her fate in the next operation.
> Is it Taurus's tail, or the *tête de mouton,*
> Or the beard of the goat that he dares to put on?

'Tis a wig en vergette, that from Paris was brought
Une tête comme il faut, that the varlet has bought,
Of a beggar, whose head he has shav'd for a groat;
Now fix'd to her head, does he frizzle and dab it;
'Tis a foretop no more.– 'Tis the skin of a rabbit–
'Tis a muff– 'tis a thing that by all is confess'd
Is in colour and shape like a chaffinch's nest.[17]

In the colonies the headdress never reached the extreme in height or the fantastic shapes worn by London ladies, but it was a very important part of the costume, requiring the services of professional hairdressers and the expenditure of large sums for ornaments. Advertisements of ladies' hairdressers appeared now and then in the papers. In Charles Town Elizabeth Cooper in 1737 and Elizabeth Trueman in 1739 gave notice that they made a business of dressing ladies' heads, and Mary Anne Benoist advertised in 1745 that she dressed heads and made ornaments of silver flowers for young misses' headdresses.[18] Richard Wagstaff offered his services as "Lady's Tate-Maker and Hair Cutter" in Annapolis in 1750,[19] and William Banks Wall advertised in 1761 that he made "Tates and Franzates for Ladies" in any form required so that no one could distinguish them from the lady's own hair.[20] Robert Lyons made wigs, "ladies' locks, Tates, etc.," on order in Williamsburg in 1751,[21] and in 1773 George Lafong, "hair cutter and dresser," informed the ladies and gentlemen of Williamsburg that he had engaged a man from London who dressed hair in the newest and most elegant taste and also made ladies' "headdresses so natural as not to be distinguished by the most curious Eye."[22] Maria Martin, "hairdresser from Paris," offered her services to the ladies of Charles Town in 1772, and two years later was practicing her profession in Savannah.[23]

Fashionable millinery establishments in the colonies carried devices for dressing ladies' hair and various decorations for the headdress. Throughout the period they sold laces, gauzes, ribbons, beads, artificial flowers, and fancy hairpins, and in the seventies they advertised curling tongs, "toupee irons," hair nets, hair rolls, wool packs

[17] Quoted in M. Phillips and W. S. Tomkinson, *English Women in Life and Letters* (Oxford, 1927), p. 120.

[18] *South Carolina Gazette*, March 19, 1737; November 12, 1739; August 19, 1745.

[19] *Maryland Gazette*, January 3, 1750.   [20] *Ibid.*, April 23, 1761.

[21] *Virginia Gazette*, April 4, 1751.   [22] *Ibid.*, January 21, 1773.

[23] *South Carolina Gazette*, August 2, 1772; *Georgia Gazette*, January 12, 1774.

with drop curls, scented hair powder, and pomatum. Egrets, pompons, plumes, and fly caps or "flies," appeared frequently on the lists of imported goods. Egrets were tufts of feathers worn as head decorations, and pompons were ornaments of feathers, lace, beads, tinsel, and similar materials made into various shapes.[24] The fly cap, shaped like a large butterfly, was edged with garnets and brilliants, making a very lustrous setting for the face.[25] Among the "headclothes" often advertised by colonial shopkeepers were the following: "Mock garnet flies," "head, black and white bugle flies," "Italian Caps, egrets, and fillets," "exceeding fine lappet heads," "flower caps and feathers," "crimp'd caps with lappets," "gauze fillets," "neat dressed and puffed caps," "lace and flower caps," "fashionable Lace Caps for a full Dress," "Riband and Shenell Caps," "Mary Scott's Puff and Lappets," and "Paste Hair Sprigs and Pins."

Throughout the colonial period lace was one of the most expensive items of the lady's dress. Often her cap, neckerchief, and sleeve ruffles, and sometimes even her aprons and pocket handkerchiefs, were edged or made of real needlepoint, Mechlin, or Brussels lace. Gauze, bone lace, and "Minionet," resembling modern footing, were also much used. Machine lace was not to be had. In 1677 William Sherwood, a Virginia planter, imported at one time lace valued at over eighteen pounds. Among other items his order included one yard of fine lace for a pinner costing one pound and ten shillings, three yards for "frills and falls" costing two pounds and eight shillings, and three yards of point for a handkerchief worth six shillings and sixpence a yard.[26] A pinner was a headdress with streamers on each side, and "frills and falls" were sleeve ruffles and collars. Washington, soon after his marriage, ordered among other fashionable and expensive apparel for Mrs. Washington a cap, handkerchief, tucker, and ruffles of Brussels lace costing twenty pounds.[27] In 1775 we find Eliza Pinckney writing her daughter: "I send two little panboxes with yr suit of Point. It must be in Taste, for it has not been two months from France; There are two caps to it, the lappited head I think very handsome, I always liked it beyond all other caps."[28] The "lappited head," like the pinner, was a headdress with lappets or streamers.

[24] Earle, op. cit., pp. 105, 191-92.
[25] Hill, op. cit., II, 48.   [26] Virginia Magazine, XI, 60.
[27] Writings of George Washington (ed., Fitzpatrick), II, 331.
[28] Ravenel, Eliza Pinckney, p. 260.

Ladies' shoes, hose, and gloves, like their gowns and headgear, were gay and colorful. Shoes were clumsy in shape and ill adapted to walking or hard wear. The heels, usually of wood, were extremely high and placed far too near the instep to admit of comfort. Colored heels were the mode and red ones were particularly fashionable.[29] Fine shoes were generally imported, but they were occasionally made in the colonies. A Maryland shoemaker advertised in 1761 that he made "all Sorts of Silk or Sattin Shoes for Ladies" and also altered ladies' shoes if too long or too wide. Included among the apparel sold by colonial shopkeepers were brocade, satin, silk, lasting, and callimanco pumps and shoes; women's black stuff shoes; leather, morocco, and white kid shoes; and satin and silk pumps in many different colors.

Hose at the beginning of the century, like those of the preceding period, were of all colors, and often worked with clocks of gold, silver, or silk, but in the thirties white stockings became the rage and continued to be worn almost to the end of the century.[30] They were of thread, cotton, worsted, and silk, and were held up by fancy garters. The attention given to the latter is indicated in a newspaper notice in which a woman offers to weave for gentlemen and ladies garters with their names or any "posy" on them.[31] Shopkeepers advertised white and colored worsted, thread, silk, and cotton hose, "superfine *China* silk and *India* cotton hose," "fine Irish garters," "Paste and Shoe-Knots," and women's "double-gilt shoe Buckles."

Gloves were worn on almost every occasion. There were long gloves reaching to the elbow, gauntlets, shorter gloves, mittens, and mitts, all made of thread, cotton, silk, kid, lambskin, and leather. Oftener than not they were white or black, but various colors were popular. Purple and white kid gloves, crimson and purple leather gloves, white and colored lamb gloves, white gloves "glazed in grain," colored French silk gloves, colored lamb mitts, black and white patent mitts, and wash leather gloves and mitts were among the kinds advertised.

Ladies' shoes and gloves must have been much less durable than today, for surprisingly large numbers were imported for the same person at one time. In 1737 John Lewis ordered for his ward, a young schoolgirl, one pair of laced silk shoes, one pair of morocco,

[29] Iris Brooke and James Laver, *English Costume of the Eighteenth Century* (London, 1931), pp. 26, 44.   [30] *Ibid.*, p. 36.
[31] *South Carolina Gazette*, January 15, 1763.

four pairs of plain Spanish leather, and two pairs of calf shoes, and
eight pairs of white and two pairs of colored kid gloves.[32]   Washington in 1759 ordered for Mrs. Washington one pair of black satin,
one pair of white satin, and four pairs of callimanco shoes, and six
pairs of gloves and eight pairs of mitts, both to be of the best kid.[33]
At the same time he ordered for Patcy Custis, his little stepdaughter,
four pairs of leather pumps, two pairs of silk and four of callimanco
shoes, eight pairs of kid mitts and four of kid gloves.   Two years
later he ordered for the same little girl four pairs of callimanco, six
pairs of leather, and two pairs of satin shoes, twelve pairs of mitts,
and six pairs of white kid gloves.[34]   In 1768, when Miss Patcy was
in her teens, ten pairs of pumps were bought for her at one time.
Four pairs were leather, six were of black callimanco, one was of
black and another of white satin.[35]

An indispensable part of the colonial lady's dress was her fan.
This was not merely an ornament, but was also a means of expressing
her moods and emotions, and was an important part of the coquette's
equipment for subduing her admirers.   To know how to flutter her
fan properly was as necessary an accomplishment as to know how to
curtsy.[36]   Every lady of fashion had many fans, each suited to a
particular function, and in dressing she had to be careful to choose the
right one for the occasion.   Many colonial shops made a specialty of
mounting and mending fans and carried regularly "complete assort-
ments" of fans for various occasions.   Among the articles advertised
in the decade before the Revolution were "Mecklenburgh Fans,"
carved and painted ivory fan sticks, and "Wedding, Mourning, Second Mourning and other Fans in the latest Fashion."

Other accessories advertised by colonial shops were feather muffs
and tippets, "silver-mounted Morocco leather Pocket Books with
Instruments," "Prussion blue, leaf gold, ivory-leaved Pocket-Books,"
"gold and velvet Pocket-Books," and various colored silk purses;
lawn, cambric, and silk pocket handkerchiefs; "silver, paste, and jet
Stay Hooks"; engraved smelling bottles in carved and plain cases;
ivory and bone toothpicks in silver mounted tortoise-shell cases;
tortoise-shell pocket combs in cases; "genteel snuffboxes"; silver and

[32] Earle, *op. cit.*, p. 11.
[33] *Writings of George Washington* (ed., Fitzpatrick), II, 331.
[34] *Ibid.*, II, 334-35.
[35] *Diaries of George Washington* (ed., Fitzpatrick), I, 273.
[36] For discussions on "the exercise of the fan," see *The Spectator*, Nos. 102, 134.

morocco etuis and housewives with instruments; and "India umbrellas." Muffs varied in size from time to time and were of velvet, satin, and other cloths as well as of feathers and fur. The tippet was a narrow covering for the neck often made to match the muff. Sometimes the muff and tippet were merely ornamental, as when worn with evening gowns, but they were often of fur or fur-trimmed and used for warmth in winter. The stay-hook was an ornamental hook fastened into the edge of the bodice upon which the lady hung her watch and etui or housewife. The etui was a case in which small personal belongings, probably toilet articles, were carried, and the housewife, a similar case, held scissors, thimble, and needles. Handsome smelling bottles, toothpicks and cases, and costly snuffboxes were important items in the accoutrement of fine ladies and gentlemen.

Colonial women were fond of jewelry. The wealthy wore costly watches, necklaces, rings, and earrings set with precious stones, and those not so well off decked themselves in pinchbeck ornaments set with gems of marcasite and paste. Mrs. Susanna Moseley of Virginia had a valuable collection of jewels. In 1650 she sold to Mrs. Frances Yeardley a gold hatband set with diamonds, which had been bought in Holland for five hundred gelders, a "jewel" enamelled and set with diamonds worth thirty gelders, and a diamond ring. She explained that she would not have parted with her jewels but for her great want of cattle, but generously added that she would rather have Mrs. Yeardley wear them than any other gentlewoman in Virginia. Mrs. Moseley had other costly jewelry, a ruby, a sapphire, and an emerald ring, and at least one diamond necklace. In her will she directed that her "best diamond necklace and jewel" be sent to England to be sold and that the money they brought be used to buy diamond rings for six of her friends and for two marble tombstones, one to be placed over her own grave and the other over the grave of the second of her three husbands.[37]

In 1687 Thomas Pitt left to his wife her wedding rings, two diamond rings, an enamelled ring, and a necklace of pearls, and in 1669 Colonel John Carter left his wife her necklace of pearls and diamonds and gave his son his mother's hoop ring and crystal necklace.[38] It was customary for the husband to bequeath his wife her wearing apparel and jewelry, since by marriage all her personal

[37] Stanard, *op. cit.*, pp. 208-9.   [38] *Ibid.*, p. 209.

property was vested in him. Robert, called "King Carter," provided in his will that thirty pounds be paid for a gold watch and twenty-five for a pearl necklace for his daughter Mary when she should arrive at the age of sixteen and that diamond earrings to cost fifty pounds be imported for his daughter Elizabeth.[39] In 1742/43 William Randolph of "Tuckahoe" bequeathed his daughter Judith her mother's trinkets and provided that two hundred pounds sterling be spent for trinkets for his younger daughter.[40] The jewelry of Penelope, daughter of Governor Gabriel Johnston of North Carolina, included five gold lockets, one garnet necklace set in silver, one "Bristol stone necklace set in silver," a "gold repeating watch and chain," a set of gold tweezers, a Mother of Pearl snuffbox set in gold, a small picture set in gold, a gold girdle buckle, and a "Bristol stone buckle set in silver."[41] Among the ornaments advertised by colonial shopkeepers were paste pins, necklaces, and earrings; "Mother of pearl Collars and Earrings"; plain gold and paste lockets and brooches; "Lockets set in Gold to preserve Lover's hair"; "Gold Bobs for Earrings"; marcasite hoops, lockets, pins, and crosses; plain gold, pinchbeck, silver, and marcasite lockets; gold rings with garnets; paste hairpins; and silver and paste shoebuckles.

Not only jewelry but also gowns, petticoats, and other apparel were commonly bequeathed or given away. The comparatively slow changes in fashion, the high cost of materials, and the intricate sewing on articles of attire made them valuable possessions, and no one seems to have objected to wearing secondhand clothing. A woman's garments were, at her death, usually given to her daughters, and, if she had no daughters, were distributed among her relatives and friends. Mary Atkins of South Carolina in her will in 1694 left to her cousin Hannah her "best Gowne and petticoate," to her uncle's three oldest daughters her "Three next best Gownes and petticoates" and all her "wearing linnen," to Ann Seaver, probably a friend, her "black Crape Gowne and petticoats" and her "Stuffe Gowne with the petticoats I usually weare," and to Elizabeth Ams "a Gray Silke Gowne and a serge petticoate with Silver lace."[42] Robert Pringle in his journal notes the death of his "dear wife Jane" and then writes of distributing her apparel among her friends.[43] Sometimes the hus-

[39] Ibid., p. 210.   [40] Ibid.
[41] Grimes, North Carolina Wills and Inventories, p. 505.
[42] South Carolina Magazine, XXVIII, 172-73.
[43] Ibid., XXVI, 94, 105.

band sold his deceased wife's clothing. In the *Virginia Gazette*, January 2, 1752, an advertisement appears in which the subscriber explains that having had the misfortune to lose his wife, he offers for sale "sundry Sorts of Household Goods, and also Womans wearing Apparel."

A catalogue of the ornaments and devices used by a "fantastical lady of fashion" appears in an English dramatic pastoral of the seventeenth century. This is a part of the list:

> Chains, coronets, pendants, bracelets, and ear-rings;
> Pins, girdles, spangles, embroyderies, and rings;
> Shadowes, rebatoes, ribbands, ruffs, cuffs, falls,
> Scarfes, feathers, fans, maskes, muffs, laces, cauls,
> Thin tiffanies, cobweb lawn, and fardingals,
> Sweet fals, vayles, wimples, glasses, crisping-pins,
> Pots of ointment, combes, with poking sticks, and bodkines,
> Coyfes, gorgets, fringes, rowles, fillets, and hair-laces,
> Silks, damasks, velvets, tinsels, cloth of gold,
> Of tissues with colours of a hundred fold;
>
> . . .
> Nor in her weeds alone is she so nice,
> But rich perfumes she buys at any price;
>
> . . .
> Waters she hath to make her face to shine,
> Confections eke to clarify her skin:
> Lip-salves, and clothes of a rich scarlet dye
> She hath which to her cheeks she doth apply;
> Ointment, wherewith she pargets o'er her face,
> And lustrifies her beauty's dying grace.[44]

Colonial ladies had many aids to beauty. Despite the pronouncements of moralists against "the woman who weneth to make her more faire than god hath made her," they prepared in their own stillrooms various concoctions for preserving the bloom of youth and imported scented waters, powders, paints, and lip salves. Housewifery books commonly contained formulas for cosmetics as well as cookery receipts. The patience and time required for making many of these beauty preparations indicate the zeal women brought to the task of improving their persons. This is one formula for a Balsamic Water to prevent wrinkles: "Take barley water, strain it through a piece of linen cloth, and drop therein a few drops of balm of Gilead; shake the bottle incessantly for ten or twelve hours together, until

---

[44] Quoted from the anonymous *Rhodon and Iris* in Planché, *op. cit.*, pp. 318-19.

the balsam is entirely incorporated with the water, which is known
by the turbid milky appearance of the water. . . . Before this precious
fluid is used, the face should be washed clean with rainwater."[45] A
receipt for "removing Worms in the Face" called for "the distilled
waters of whites of eggs, bean-flowers, water-lilies, white lilies, melon-
seeds, iris-roots, Solomon's seal, white roses, or crumb of wheaten
bread, either mixed together, or separately, with the addition of the
whites of a new laid egg."[46] For whitening the teeth these instructions were given: "Take dried leaves of hyssop, wild thyme and mint,
of each half of an ounce; rock-allum, prepared hartshorn, and salt,
of each a drachm; calcine these ingredients together in a pot placed
on burning coals; when sufficiently calcined, add thereto pepper and
mastic, of each a drachm; myrrh a scruple; reduce the whole into a
very fine powder, and mix into a consistence of an opiate with florax
dissolved in rose-water. Rub the teeth with a small bit of this opiate
every morning, and afterwards wash the mouth with warm water."[47]
"Aqua vitae," a common base used in making many beautifying
waters, contained, according to one receipt in use, no less than thirty
ingredients and required two months for its preparation.[48]

Besides their homemade preparations, English ladies had cosmetics from many different lands. There were paints from China,
a lip salve from India, a marvelous mixture enabling ladies of fifty
to retain the bloom of twenty-one, soaps and perfumed waters from
several countries.[49] From Greece came "Jerusalem Washballs" and
the "Bloom of Circassia." This "Liquid Bloom" claimed a superiority over all others in that it "instantly gave to the cheek a rose
hue not to be distinguished from the animated bloom of rural
beauty" and would not come off with perspiration.[50] Ladies generally wore gloves to keep their hands white and smooth, masks to
preserve their complexions, and black patches, possibly to emphasize
the whiteness of their skins. Colonial shopkeepers advertised patches
and patch boxes, sweet powders and powder boxes, "Swan Skin and
Silk Powder Puffs," eyewaters, lip salves, waters to prevent tanning,
almond paste for the hands and face, cold cream for sunburn, tooth
brushes and dentifrices, and lavender, honey, and Hungary waters.

[45] *The Lady's Magazine*, August, 1772, pp. 367-68.
[46] *Ibid.*   [47] *Ibid.*
[48] This receipt is given in full in Rose M. Bradley, *English Housewife*, pp. 126-27.
[49] Hill, *op. cit.*, II, 80-86.
[50] Phillips and Tomkinson, *op. cit.*, p. 123.

From the variety of articles mentioned in newspaper advertisements it would seem that the most elegant lady might have outfitted
herself in the shops of her nearest town, but the wives of the larger
planters imported much of their apparel.   It was probably considered more polite to purchase one's clothes directly from London
merchants than from provincial shopkeepers.   Not until shortly before the Revolution were fashion plates in use, but dressed dolls
were sent from fashion centers to the provinces to illustrate the
latest modes.   Friends and kinswomen in England also helped colonial ladies keep up with the change in styles, as appears in the following from a letter written from London in 1731 by Mrs. Margaret
Calvert to her niece in Maryland: ". . . and now for English fashing
ye french heads are little wore mostly English ye hoops very small
upper petycoats of but 4 yards ye gowns unlind and ye Sleeves . . .
very little and short and . . . [their hair?] very full at ye sides. . . ."[51]
The Lady's Magazine, which appeared first in 1770, described the
changing modes and carried full-page engraved illustrations of the
latest styles, and other periodicals helped keep colonial ladies abreast
of the times.   The *Virginia Gazette*, February 11, 1773, quoting from
a London paper, printed this description:

LADIES

The Toupees are apparently decreasing and Jewels partly supply the Place
of Front Curls; the back Part of the Head *en chenouille*, with the Side
Curls pretty much the same: the Height of Stays on a Par, with sharp
pointed Peaks; the Projection in Front rather on the Increase; Stomachers,
three Rows of Plaits upwards; a single Breastknot and Sleeveknots of the
same Silk; triple Flounces to the Sleeves, twelve, nine, and five Inches;
triple Ruffles on the Outside, eighteen, fifteen, and eleven inches; Inside,
six, four, and two Inches.

On the Petticoat of the Negligee a Frill comes all round, plaited next the
Tail; six Inches above that is a Flounce a Quarter of a Yard deep only
in the Front; close over that is another Frill as on the Bottom, all of the
same Silk, Trains nine Inches and a Half; full Dress as usual, with larger
Trains.

Despite the fashion notes in magazines and in private letters,
however, ladies in the colonies could not be very particular in their
requisitions but usually had to leave much to the discretion of their
husbands' agents.   The planter, who commonly wrote the orders for
his wife's as well as his own apparel, sometimes sent measurements

[51] "Some Old English Letters," *Maryland Magazine*, IX, 140.

for gowns, petticoats, and shoes and stated within certain limits what the more expensive articles should cost, but he ordinarily gave no exact size for hats, gloves, and hose, and frequently left the choice of color, material, and style of all garments to his London merchant. He usually stated, however, that garments were to be "of the latest fashion." Representative of the more explicit orders was one sent by Dr. Charles Carroll of Annapolis to his merchant in 1744. He wrote for a flowered silk nightgown of salmon color made to enclosed measurements and costing about ten shillings a yard, two hoop-petticoats of the same size, a girdle, a fashionable tippet and neck-lace not exceeding a guinea in cost, a nosegay of artificial flowers of six shillings value and a "Sprigg Jessamine" costing about half a crown. With the order was this request: "As You or some in Your Family are Acquainted with the Genteelest Fashion I request the favor that the Gown &c being for a Young Lady may be agreeable thereto and good in its kind."[52]

The wives of English merchants were often called upon to shop for colonial ladies. In 1737 Elizabeth Perry, wife of Micajah Perry, London merchant, wrote to Mrs. Thomas Jones in Williamsburg: "I am very glad what I do for my friends in Virginia pleases them. I have done my best endeavors that Misses things should be what she likes, for a walking gown I have bought a Turkey Burdet for I thought Cery dery had too mean a look and tho' what I have sent is something dearer it will answer it in the wear, as for the piece of sprigged muslin you wish for there is no such thing for the money you allow. I have been, or sent, all over the town and there is none to be got under double the price, so have not sent you any."[53] Rebecca Chamberlayne of New Kent, Virginia, writing to John Norton, London merchant, July 28, 1770, declared that her goods had arrived safely and thanked Mrs. Norton for "her trouble in the choice of a Petticoat." Sometime later, when acknowledging the arrival of other goods, she expressed her appreciation of Mrs. Norton's "selection of work'd muslin."[54] William Byrd wrote one of his merchants in the seventeen-thirties: "Mrs. Byrd wishes you marryed, God forgive her, because then she fancys you would be able to manage Female commissions something better."[55]

[52] "Account and Letter Books of Dr. Charles Carroll," *Maryland Magazine*, XXI, 249.

[53] Stanard, *op. cit.*, p. 215.   [54] MS, Norton Papers.

[55] "Letters," *Virginia Magazine*, XXXVI, 213.

Ladies, and gentlemen too, when abroad were requested to shop for their friends at home. When Mrs. Thomas Jones was in England in 1728, Mrs. Mary Stith wrote her from Virginia: "When you come to London pray favour me in your choice of a suit of pinners suitably dressed with a cross-knot or whatever the fashion requires, with suitable ruffles and handkerchief. I like a lace of some breadth, and of a beautiful pattern, that may be plainly seen, fine enough to look well, but not a superfine costly lace. And likewise beg your choice of a genteel fan."[56]   In 1752, when Lady Gooch, wife of Governor Sir William Gooch, went home, she was requested by the Reverend Thomas Dawson, rector of Bruton Church in Williamsburg, to purchase these articles for his wife: a fashionable laced cap, handkerchief, ruffles, and tuckers; a fashionable brocade suit; a pair of stays; a blue satin petticoat; a scarlet cloth under-petticoat; a pair of blue satin shoes; a hoop; a pair of blue silk stockings; a fashionable silver girdle; and a fan.[57]

Whether they imported their clothing directly from Europe or had it made at home, well-to-do colonial ladies appear to have dressed in the best English fashion. Visitors and newcomers frequently expressed surprise at the elegance and modishness of the American women. Representative of the observations of many is the following written by the Reverend Jonathan Boucher to one of his English friends soon after his arrival in Virginia: "I assure you Mrs. James, the common Planter's Daughters here go every Day in finer Cloaths than I have seen content you for a Summer's Sunday. . . . Nay, so much does their Taste run after dress that they tell me I may see in Virginia more brilliant Assemblies than I ever c'd in the North of Engl'd, and except Royal Ones p'rhaps in any Part of it."[58]

Representative of the wardrobes of wealthy gentlewomen shortly before the Revolution was that described in the inventory of the estate of Madam Ann le Brasseur, widow of a prominent Charles Town merchant and planter. Besides ordinary calico, muslin, and linen garments, the list included the following: a brown "grograin gown" trimmed with gold lace valued at fifteen pounds, a flowered brocaded nightgown, a striped lustring gown and coat valued at fifteen pounds, and a "Gold Brocaded Night Gown with a blew silk Tail" worth thirty-five pounds; a white Persian quilted petticoat valued at seven pounds and a white paduasoy petticoat valued at twenty-five pounds; "old red damask cloggs," gold laced brocaded shoes, white damask silver laced shoes, and two pairs of new green callimanco shoes; a black headdress with ruffles and handkerchief of very fine lace worth forty pounds, another handkerchief "laced around" valued at fifteen pounds, and a double bordered headdress with ruffles and fringes worth two pounds. There were two pairs of silk and eight of worsted stockings; a pair of mittens and fourteen pairs of gloves; lace, plain, and fringed aprons; net and gauze hoods; silk tippets; girdles; a "Fustian stomacher" appraised at fifteen pounds; and twenty-two pocket handkerchiefs, six of which were trimmed with expensive lace. Among the ornaments and accessories were one new ivory fan and five other fans, masks, a gold thimble, a pearl necklace, silver buckles worth five pounds, a diamond ring valued at sixty pounds, and a gold watch and appurtenances appraised at ninety pounds.[59]

Fithian was impressed by the splendid apparel of the ladies he saw at "Nomini." This is his description of Miss Betsy Lee, a young lady of family and fortune visiting in the neighborhood: "She is a well set maid, of a proper Height, neither high nor low. . . . she sits very erect, places her feet with great propriety, her Hands She lays carelessly in her lap, & never moves them but when she has occasion to adjust some article of her dress, or to perform some exercise of the *Fan*. . . . When She has a Bonnet on & Walks, She is truly elegant; her carriage neat & graceful, & her Presence soft & beautiful—Her hair is a dark Brown, which was crap'd up very high, & in it she had a Ribbon interwoven with an artificial Flower—At each of her ears dangled a brilliant Jewel; She was pinched up rather too near in a long pair of new fashioned Stays. . . . I imputed the Flush which was visible in her Face to her being swathed up *Body* & *Soul* & *limbs* together—She wore a light Chintz Gown, very fine, with a blue stamp, elegantly made, & which set well upon her—She wore a blue silk Quilt [petticoat]—In one word Her Dress was rich & fashionable."[60]

The young ladies attending dancing school at "Nomini" also sported the latest fashions. "Miss Washington," a well proportioned though not handsome miss of seventeen, appeared in a chintz cotton

[59] Hirsch, *Huguenots of South Carolina*, pp. 248-49.
[60] *Journal*, pp. 192-93.

gown with an elegant blue stamp, a sky-blue silk quilt, and spotted apron. Her light brown hair was craped up with rolls at each side and she wore a small cap of beautiful gauze and rich lace interwoven with an artificial flower. "Miss Hale," a "slim, puny, silent Virgin" of fourteen, with black eyes and hair, wore a white Holland gown, fine diaper quilt, and a lawn apron, and on top of her hair, which was also craped up, she wore a small tuft of ribbon for a cap. "Miss Lee," a tall, slim, genteel girl of about thirteen, was dressed in a neat shell calico gown and had her hair done up with a feather.[61]

Little girls generally wore the same kind of clothes as their mothers. In voluminous hoop-petticoats, stiff stays, and high-heeled shoes, they appeared miniature ladies, and while still in the nursery, they were made to wear masks and long gloves to protect their complexions. Washington's order for Patcy Custis in 1759 gives some idea of the wardrobe of a miss only four years old. Besides the gloves and shoes already mentioned, the list included six pairs of fine thread and four of worsted stockings, two caps, two pairs of ruffles, two tuckers, bibs, and aprons; two fans, two masks, two bonnets, and six pocket handkerchiefs; one cloth cloak and one stiffened coat of fashionable silk made to packthread stays; six yards of ribbons, two necklaces, and one pair of silver sleeve buttons with stones.[62] When Patcy was six, he ordered the following apparel for her: a stiffened coat of fashionable silk, four fashionable dresses to be made of long lawn, two fine cambric frocks, a satin "Capuchin hat and neckatees," a Persian quilted coat, a pair of packthread stays, a fashionable cap or fillet, laced aprons, ruffles, and tuckers, six handsome egrets of different sorts, six yards of ribbons, one pair of silver shoe buckles and one pair of neat sleeve buttons.[63]

Women of the poorer classes naturally could not afford the costly clothing worn by the wealthy. Their petticoats, gowns, and caps were of cheap, coarse materials and their shoes country-made. The clothing allowed to indentured women servants as part of their freedom dues suggests what was considered a proper outfit for an ordinary woman. A Maryland act of 1715 provided that a servant be given at the expiration of her term a waistcoat and petticoat of "new half tick or penistone," a new shift of white linen, a pair of

[61] Ibid., pp. 184-86.
[62] Writings of George Washington (ed., Fitzpatrick), II, 334-35.
[63] Ibid., pp. 369-70.

shoes and stockings, a blue apron, and two white linen caps.[64]   A county court in Virginia in 1734 required a master to give his servant a calico gown and apron, a fine shift, a handkerchief, a pinner, and a pair of shoes.[65]   In South Carolina the legal allowance was a waistcoat and petticoat of "new half tick or coarse plains," two new shifts of white linen, a blue apron, two caps of white linen, and a new pair of shoes and stockings.[66]

Advertisements of runaway servants sometimes describe them as wearing gowns and petticoats of "Virginia cloth" or "country cloth" and country-made shoes, but oftener they appear to have been wearing the cast-off clothing of women in better circumstances.   Hannah Daylies, for instance, wore a light colored petticoat, a blue striped satin gown, and a pair of pale blue callimanco shoes,[67] and another Virginia servant wore gold bobs set with stones, black callimanco shoes with plated buckles, white cotton stockings, an old calico gown, and a scarlet cloak.[68]   Mary Lambert, who ran away from James Davis in North Carolina, wore a checked woolen petticoat, calico gown, red stockings, and old callimanco shoes, and took with her a dark calico gown, a lawn apron, and a white satin hat with red ribbon.[69]   Many notices state that the runaway carried off clothing not her own.   Mary Holland, described by her Georgia master as "much conceited in her beauty," wore a reddish stuff gown, green petticoat, white flowered bonnet, and a large roll under her hair, and carried a fine lawn apron and flowered handkerchief stolen from her mistress.[70]   Sarah Taylor, a Maryland servant, carried off a straw hat with black ribbon and strings, a new Holland cap, a yellow petticoat, a pair of white yarn stockings, and a pair of women's pumps,[71] and Anne Barret of Virginia took a striped Holland gown, a quilted callimanco petticoat, several headdresses, ruffles, and aprons, and new pumps with red heels.[72]

These advertisements suggest a love of finery common among all classes and found among men as well as women.   But, though gentlemen were no less eager to be in fashion than their wives and though

[64] *Laws of Maryland* (ed., Maxcy), I, 112.
[65] MS, Northumberland County Order Book, No. 7, p. 148.
[66] *Public Laws of South Carolina* (ed., Grimké), p. 197.
[67] *Virginia Gazette*, March 26, 1767.   [68] *Ibid.*, September 27, 1770.
[69] (Newbern) *North Carolina Gazette*, April 15, 1757.
[70] *Georgia Gazette*, June 29, 1774.
[71] *Maryland Gazette*, December 1, 1730.
[72] *Virginia Gazette*, February 20, 1752.

their costume was no less extravagant, the passion for dress was ordinarily treated as a "female foible." Woman's absorption in personal adornment and the absurdities of her dress were perennial subjects for the pens of wits and moralists. *The Spectator*, the most popular commentator on social customs and one of the gentler critics, described woman as "an animal that delights in finery," scolded the ladies of the day repeatedly for the excessive care given to adorning their persons, and poked fun at their headdresses, their petticoats, their "borrowed complexions," and their "equestrian costumes."[73] Books of advice to women devoted many pages to the discussion of dress, emphasizing the general notion that women's clothing should be by all means feminine and suited to their station in society, pointing out the transiency of beauty, and admonishing them that a virtuous heart and an amiable disposition were more to be desired than a beautiful face and a fashionable figure. But women were not thus to be persuaded to forego their modish apparel and their salves, waters, and powders. Concerning beauty they agreed with sprightly Molly Tilghman, who wrote to her cousin Polly Pearce: "Wisdom says it is a fading flower, but fading as it is, it attracts more admiration than wit, goodness, or anything else in the world."[74]

[73] See Nos. 15, 41, 98, 104, 127, 265, 435.
[74] *Maryland Magazine*, XXI, 34.

CHAPTER VII

COURTSHIP AND MARRIAGE-MAKING

A SEVENTEENTH-CENTURY writer on domestic conduct defined marriage as a "covenant of God, whereby all sorts of people may, of two, bee made one flesh; for multiplying of an holy seed, avoiding of fornication, and mutuall comforting of each other."[1] This was the prevailing English conception of the institution. Orthodox divines, who during the sixteenth century regarded marriage as a necessary evil justifiable only as a means of continuing the species, later came to extol it as a more honorable state than celibacy, and pulpit and press urged it as both a blessing and a duty. Popular works like *The Spectator* commonly represented the man who undertook the responsibilities of wedlock as benefiting himself, his church, and his country. The colonists held marriage in the same high favor. They praised it as a helpful companionship, frequently pointed out its advantages over libertinism, and even oftener stressed its service in increasing the population. Furthermore, they gave proof of their strong belief in the desirability of entering the matrimonial state by actively and persistently putting their convictions into practice.

A part of this enthusiasm for the "holy institution" was the feeling that while marriage was for man a pleasant duty, it was woman's reason for existence, and that since the end of her creation was to continue the species and be a helpmate to man, the chief ambition of every woman should be to get a husband. This attitude, stated explicitly in treatises on marriage, was often implied elsewhere. Chief among the inducements offered women to emigrate to America were promises of desirable matches, and the glowing accounts by the colonists of the good fortunes befalling them in the New World often mentioned the "disposal" of their single females as not the least of their blessings. Representative of many letters was the following

[1] Matthew Griffith, *Bethel: or Forme for Families.* Quoted in Chilton Latham Powell, *English Domestic Relations, 1487-1653. A Study of Matrimony and Family Life in Theory and Practice as Revealed in the Literature, Law, and History of the Period* (New York, 1917), p. 239.

from an emigrant to South Carolina to his brother in Switzerland: "We have provided well for our single women, who consisted of 13 persons. They have all been favorably married. In the old country they would not have had such good fortune. . . . poor females who are of scanty means should come to America if they are virtuous and sensible. They will get along nicely inasmuch as all can make their fortune, for here men do not care for money as they do in Switzerland."[2] Colonel William Byrd, boasting of Virginia's advantages, declared that matrimony "thrives so excellently" that "an Old Maid or an Old Bachelor are as scarce among us and reckoned as ominous as a Blazing Star."[3] In like manner an English visitor praised Maryland as "a paradise on Earth for women," explaining: "That great curiosity, an Old Maid is seldom seen in this country. They generally marry before they are twenty-two, often before they are sixteen."[4]

Unmarried persons were regarded as pitiable encumbrances. The tax imposed upon bachelors in Maryland[5] indicates the widespread feeling that the man without a family was evading a civic duty, and numerous expressions of commiseration reveal the prevailing notion that the husbandless woman had no purpose in life. It is true that thinking persons sometimes voiced the opinion that a single life was preferable to a union with an unworthy person; yet even these held out very little hope of happiness to her who was denied the blessing of a husband save the consolation to be derived from the consciousness of having been piously resigned to her unhappy fate and of having lived a life of complete self-sacrifice.

Newspaper caricatures of "old virgins," announcements of matrimonial lotteries for "ancient maids of desperate expectations," and fictitious petitions of spinsters for aid in securing husbands reflect

[2] *South Carolina Magazine*, XXIII, 86-88. John Hammond advised women coming to Maryland or Virginia to "sojourn in a house of honest repute," explaining, "for by their good carriage, they may advance themselves in marriage."—"Leah and Rachel," *Narratives of Early Maryland*, p. 293. George Alsop thus encouraged women emigrants to Maryland: "The Women that go over into this Province as Servants, have the best luck here as in any place of the world besides; for they are no sooner on shoar, but they are courted into a Copulative Matrimony, which some of them (for aught I know) had 'they not come to such a Market with their Virginity, might have kept it by them untill it had been mouldy. . . ."—"Character of Province of Maryland," *Narratives of Early Maryland*, p. 358.

[3] *Virginia Magazine*, XXXII, 30.

[4] Nicholas Cresswell, *Journal*, pp. 271-72.

[5] *Archives of Maryland*, XXXII, 95.

the popular contempt for the unmarried woman. Ordinarily she was represented as homely in appearance, fault-finding and disagreeable in disposition, critical of the innocent amusements of youth, envious of her married sisters, mendacious regarding her age, and, though pretending to hate men, desirous of nothing more in life than a husband. Thus the *Virginia Gazette* printed what it entitled "The Picture of an Old Maid": "Mrs. Mary Morgan has lived to the Age of fifty-five unmarried, but she merits no Blame on Account of her Virginity, for she certainly would have entered into the Marriage State if any Man had thought proper to make his Addresses to her. Nature has bestowed on her no Beauty, and not much Sweetness of Temper; the Sight of every pretty Woman, therefore, is very offensive to her, the Sight of a married One hardly supportable. . . . Inwardly tortured with her own ill Nature, she is incapable of any Satisfaction but what arises from teasing others. . . . She has read just enough to render her distinguishingly pedantick, but too little to furnish her Mind with any useful Knowledge. . . ."[6] With the same derision the *South Carolina Gazette* printed an alleged petition of maids in which the "humble petitioners," declaring themselves to be "in a very melancholy Disposition of mind, considering how all the Bachelors are blindly captivated by Widows," requested the governor to come to their aid and prevent any widow from presuming to marry any young man until all the maids were provided for.[7] The *Georgia Gazette* published, apparently with a great deal of amusement, the account of the death of an "old-virgin," who though having reached her one-hundred-and-ninth year, had not abandoned hope of getting a husband.[8]

The prejudice against the spinster was due probably not merely to the prevailing notion that it was the duty of all to marry and help swell the population, but even more to the fact that she was often a dependent and unwanted guest in the home of a married brother or sister. Unmarried women of independent fortune and character like

[6] November 19, 1772.   [7] March 2, 1733/34.

[8] March 22, 1764. A North Carolina paper printed this diatribe: "An old maid is one of the most cranky, ill-natured, maggotty, peevish, conceited, disagreeable, hypocritical, fretful, noisy, gibing, canting, censorious, out-of-the-way, never-to-be-pleased, good for nothing creatures . . . she pretends to be very religious, and visits the churches, in order to watch what *signs*—what *tokens of love* may be going on. . . . Of all things on earth she says she hates a man, because every man hates her. . . . In short, an old maid enters the world to take up room, not to make room for others. . . ."—*State Gazette of North Carolina*, January 16, 1790.

Margaret Brent of Maryland[9] were apparently treated with the greatest respect. It is also true that in many households the unmarried sister or aunt was recognized as a useful and beloved member. But considered generally, the old maid was looked upon as "the most calamitous creature in nature."[10]

This disrespect for spinsters, together with the custom which pointed to wifehood as the end of a woman's education and the object of all her endeavours, aroused young girls to begin thinking of matrimony almost before they left the nursery and to be ambitious to enter the desirable state as soon as they had barely reached their teens.   Thus we find twelve-year-old Alice Lee of "Stratford" in Virginia expressing her regard for "the holy sacred institution" and protesting against her kinswoman's "retarding her success in the Matrimonial Way";[11] and fifteen-year-old Rebecca Dulany writing a younger sister about an attachment manifested by the latter's sweetheart for another young lady: "I would have you provide another string to your bow, for I am certain you stand not the slightest chance with him."[12]

Girls usually married before twenty, and she who was still outside the charmed circle of matrons at twenty-five was reckoned an old maid.   Lawson wrote of North Carolina: "They marry very young; some at thirteen or fourteen; and she that stays till twenty is reckoned a stale maid, which is a very indifferent character in that warm country."[13]   William Byrd declared in 1727 that the most "antique Virgin" he knew was his own daughter Evelyn, who was then about twenty.[14]   It was customary for a father when making a gift or bequest to his daughter to state that the property was to be hers at her coming of age or marriage, which latter event it was usually presumed would precede.   The marriage of girls who had still to celebrate their seventeenth birthday was not uncommon, and some undertook the responsibilities of wifehood at an even earlier age.   Ursula Byrd, daughter of William Byrd I,[15] and Sally Cary,

[9] See below, pp. 236-41.   [10] *The Ladies Calling*, II, p. 3.

[11] Edmund Jennings Lee, *Lee of Virginia, 1642-1892. Biographical and Genealogical Sketches of the Descendants of Colonel Richard Lee* (Philadelphia, 1895), p. 288.

[12] Letter in Elizabeth H. Murray, *One Hundred Years Ago, or the Life and Times of the Rev. Walter Dulany Addison, 1769-1848, compiled from Original Papers . . .* (Philadelphia, 1895), pp. 8-9.

[13] *Op. cit.*, pp. 142-43.   [14] *Virginia Magazine*, XXXII, 30.

[15] *Writings of William Byrd* (ed., John Spencer Bassett), p. lxxxvii.

daughter of another distinguished Virginian,[16] both married at sixteen and died a year later in childbed. Elizabeth Carter, first wife
of William Byrd III, was sixteen and a half at her marriage;[17]
Elizabeth Haynie married at sixteen, had eight children, and died
at thirty-two;[18] and Sarah Hext was the wife of Dr. John Rutledge
at fourteen and the mother of seven children at twenty-five.[19] A
visitor in Virginia wrote of a woman there, a gentleman's lady, who,
though said to have just attained her twenty-first year, was the
mother of seven children. The women in general, he asserted, arrived at maturity very early and were marriageable at fourteen or
fifteen.[20] In genealogies may be found many cases of girls who
married at fourteen or fifteen.[21]

Instances appear in the records of the clandestine marriage of
wealthy little girls not yet in their teens. A letter to the Council of
Maryland from a Colonel Coursey, June 22, 1688, tells of his com-
mitting to jail one Archibald Burnett for marrying Sarah Vanhart,
eleven-year-old heiress, to Stephen Coleman, a tailor, without the
consent of her guardian. The justices, it seems, were inclined to
deliver the child to the would-be husband, but Colonel Coursey insisted that she should not be removed from her aunt, who had
brought her up, and to keep Coleman from getting possession of the
child, had kept her in his own home until he could be advised what
to do. It is gratifying to read that the Council approved his action.[22]
In Virginia in 1662, Elizabeth Charlton, twelve-year-old heiress of
one of the best families on the Eastern Shore, was stolen from
school by John Severne, a prominent citizen, carried to the other
side of the bay where she was unknown, and secretly married.
Whether the marriage was annulled does not appear, but Severne
was condemned and severely reprimanded by the county justices.[23]

For the prevention of such clandestine or other irregular marriages, laws were enacted providing for the punishment of ministers

[16] Wilson Miles Cary, *Sally Cary—A Long Hidden Romance of Washington's
Life* (New York, 1916), p. 91.
[17] *William and Mary Quarterly*, VIII, 42.
[18] *South Carolina Magazine*, XXXI, 11.
[19] *Ibid.*   [20] Burnaby, *Travels*, pp. 61-62.
[21] For example, *William and Mary Quarterly*, V, 5; VI, 121; IX, 55; XVI, 287;
XVII, 119; *Virginia Magazine*, XXVI, 418; Armstrong, *Notable Southern Families*,
IV, 141.   [22] *Archives of Maryland*, VIII, 32-34.
[23] Philip Alexander Bruce, *Institutional History of Virginia in the Seventeenth
Century* . . . (2 vols., New York and London, 1910), I, 325-26.

or others marrying couples without publication of banns or a license. If the couple were under age, they had to have the consent of their parents before the license could be obtained.[24] Also the bridegroom was required to give bond with good securities to pay a certain sum should the intended marriage be unlawful in any respect.[25] As an added precaution against the secret marriage of heiresses, severe punishment was prescribed for those "taking away maids that be inheritors" or marrying them without the consent of their parents or guardians, and provision was made for the forfeiture of her estate to her next of kin by any girl between twelve and sixteen who should contract matrimony contrary to the will of her parents or guardians.[26] This act was intended to defeat the fortune-hunter rather than to punish the heiress, for it provided that at the death of her husband her inheritance should revert to her, or, in case she did not survive her husband, to her heirs. Virginia, which was troubled by runaway couples slipping across the boundary into Maryland and marrying there contrary to the laws of their own colony, passed an act providing that if any minister went out of the colony and married persons resident thereof without a license or publication of banns, he was to suffer the same penalty as if the offense had been committed within the province.[27]

The English act forbidding the marriage of persons related by consanguinity or affinity was also in force in the colonies. The following table,[28] established by the Church of England, was required to be set up in every parish church, that the inhabitants might not be ignorant of the degrees within which marriage was forbidden:

A man shall not marry his	A woman shall not marry her
Grandmother	Grandfather
Grandfather's wife	Grandmother's husband
Wife's grandmother	Husband's grandfather
Father's sister	Father's brother
Mother's sister	Mother's brother

[24] W. W. Hening, *Statutes . . . of Virginia*, I, 156, 181, 241, 332, 433; VI, 83; *Archives of Maryland*, I, 374; XXXIII, 114-15; *Colonial Records of North Carolina*, II, 213.
[25] *Archives of Maryland*, IV, 25, 51, 66; *William and Mary Quarterly*, II, 74; *South Carolina Magazine*, XIX, 95-100.
[26] Hening, *Statutes*, III, 149-51, 443, 444; VI, 83; *A Collection of the Statutes of the Parliament of England in Force in the State of North Carolina* (ed., Francois-Xavier Martin), pp. 159, 287; *Public Laws of South Carolina* (ed., Grimké), pp. 60-61.   [27] Hening, *Statutes*, III, 441, 442.
[28] *Laws of Maryland* (ed., Maxcy), I, 332-36.

A man shall not marry his	A woman shall not marry her
Father's brother's wife	Father's sister's husband
Mother's brother's wife	Mother's sister's husband
Wife's father's sister	Husband's father's brother
Wife's mother's sister	Husband's mother's brother
Mother	Father
Step-mother	Step-father
Wife's mother	Son
Daughter	Husband's son
Wife's daughter	Daughter's husband
Son's wife	Brother
Sister	Husband's brother
Wife's sister	Sister's husband
Brother's wife	Son's son
Son's daughter	Daughter's son
Daughter's daughter	Son's daughter's husband
Son's son's wife	Daughter's daughter's husband
Wife's son's daughter	Husband's son's son
Wife's daughter's daughter	Husband's daughter's son
Brother's daughter	Brother's son
Sister's daughter	Sister's son
Brother's son's wife	Brother's daughter's husband
Sister's son's wife	Sister's daughter's husband
Wife's brother's daughter	Husband's brother's son
Wife's sister's daughter	Husband's sister's son

Marriages within these forbidden degrees were voidable and the persons entering such unions and the ministers solemnizing them were subject to severe penalties. A people among whom it was not so very rare for one's grandfather's wife to be a tempting girl in her teens and with whom it was common for dependent relatives, young and old, to live in the homes of their married kin, probably found such restrictions beneficial.[29]

[29] Apparently few "incestuous marriages" were brought to the attention of the legal authorities. An instance of the voluntary separation of persons married within forbidden degrees appears in the Virginia records. Mathrom Wright married Ruth Griggs, his uncle's widow. No action appears to have been started against them, but at least ten years after they had entered the marriage, her conscience began to raise objections, and, according to a record in Lancaster County of a bond dated October 2, 1684, he agreed to separate from her paying her alimony and schooling their daughter. In St. John's Parish in Baltimore County, Maryland, in 1744 Jacob Jackson and his wife, who was niece of his deceased wife, were bound over to the county court when they could furnish no legal defense for marrying contrary to the established tables. In 1752 the vestry of the same parish, having summoned John Giles for marrying his deceased wife's sister and admonished him to put her away, upon his refusing, had him presented to the grand jury. It does not appear whether

More effective than these legal restrictions in regulating marriage was the social convention which insisted upon parental consent to a match. A word of instruction seldom omitted in ladies' guides to morality was that a girl should never listen to any proposal of marriage made by one who had not first secured the permission of her parents to address her. "Children are so much the goods, the possessions of their Parents," declared *The Whole Duty of Man,* the most generally accepted authority on domestic conduct, "that they cannot, without a kind of theft, give away themselves without the allowance of those that have the right in them."[30] Also it was usually held by moral preceptors that maids, who were likely to be governed by "amorous inclinations," could not be trusted to judge of the character and suitability of their lovers. Another reason sometimes given for leaving the selection of the husband to parents was that this sort of procedure was "most agreeable to the Virgin Modesty, which would make Marriage an act rather of their obedience than their Choice."[31] The same persons, however, who thus upheld parental authority, usually maintained that parents should not force their children to marry against their own inclinations.

Marriage was regarded as a family matter, and a prudent couple did not venture to enter it without first being assured of the approval of both his and her relatives. A letter of Henry Laurens of South Carolina reproving a middle-aged, fortune-hunting Frenchman for paying unauthorized addresses to his daughter describes the general idea of propriety in courtship. Answering the Frenchman's plea that he remember his own courtship, Laurens replied: "When I paid my addresses to the lady my daughter's mother, I was in the vigour of youth and there was little disparity between our ages. That lady was also under guardianship, and altho' my life and conversation, my connections and prospects were intimately known to her guardians, to her father and brothers, I scorned to attempt an attachment of her affections, 'till I had obtained the consent and approbation of

these cases were tried according to the law. In 1724 cases were sent to England from Virginia and Carolina for legal opinion regarding marriage between a man and his deceased wife's sister. The questions asked on these occasions indicate that the colonial courts were unaccustomed to dealing with such cases.—*Tyler's Quarterly Magazine,* XI, 166; Edward Ingle, *Parish Institutions of Maryland, with Illustrations from Parish Records* ("Johns Hopkins University Studies in Historical and Political Science," Vol. I, No. 6), p. 38; R. T. Barton, ed., *Virginia Colonial Decisions,* Barradall's Reports, B18-B20.

[30] See below, p. 208.   [31] *The Ladies Calling,* Pt. II, p. 20.

the other parties so nearly interested. I should have deemed a contrary conduct a species of dishonourable fraud."[32]

Custom required that the parents of the young man as well as those of the young lady consent to a marriage. James Iredell, though of age and permanently settled in North Carolina three thousand miles away from his parents in England, and contributing to their support, felt obliged to apologize to his father for presuming to offer addresses to a young lady without first getting his approval.[33] Peter Manigault, writing from England to his mother in South Carolina, who was fearful that he might marry while abroad, took care to assure her that he "would never harbour a thought of that kind" without her approbation;[34] and twenty-three-year-old Charles Carroll, while in Europe for his education, expressed the same respect for his father's rights, assuring him: "I here solemnly promise as long as you live, which I hope will be long, never to marry without your full & free consent & approbation."[35]

Representative of the respectful manner with which dutiful girls acknowledged their filial obligation is a letter of Eliza Lucas to her father, who, desirous of arranging a suitable match, had proposed two gentlemen for her choice. Thanking him for his "paternal tenderness," which, she admitted, claimed all her obedience, she prayed his "indulgence" in requiring her to accept neither suitor. Toward one of the gentlemen proposed, who, it appears in her letter, was old and rich, she declared she could not have "Sentiments favourable enough" to make him her husband, and of the other she had too slight knowledge to form any judgment. She "respectfully requested" him to put aside thought of her marrying for two or three years, assuring him: "You are so good as to say you have too great an opinion of my prudence to think I would entertain an indiscreet passion for any one, and I hope Heaven will direct me that I may never disappoint you, and what indeed could induce me to make a Secret of my Inclination to my best friend, as I am well assured you would not disprove it to make me a Sacrifice to wealth, and I am certain I would indulge no passion that had not your approbation. . . ."[36] Colonel Lucas apparently made no further attempt to

[32] Wallace, *Life of Henry Laurens*, p. 29.

[33] McRee, *Iredell*, I, 126.

[34] *South Carolina Magazine*, XXXI, 282.

[35] *Maryland Magazine*, XI, 327-28.   [36] Ravenel, *Eliza Pinckney*, pp. 55-57.

get a husband for his daughter, and several years later she formed a matrimonial connection agreeable to them both.

The undutiful maid and youth who married in defiance of their parents ran the risk of suffering not only the general disapprobation of their friends and the everlasting unforgiveness of parents, but also the loss of her marriage portion and his inheritance. Elizabeth Duke, wife of the rebel, Nathaniel Bacon, was disinherited by her father, Sir Edward Duke, who in his will gave her a legacy of £2,000 with this proviso, "but if she marry Bacon, void." When after the death of both her father and her husband, she brought an unsuccessful suit in England for her portion of her father's estate, the Lord Chancellor voiced his opinion of her disrespectful marriage: "such an example of presumptuous disobedience highly meriting [merited] such a punishment, she being only prohibited to marry with one man, by name; and nothing in the whole fair Garden of Eden would serve her turn, but this forbidden fruit."[37]

Fathers in the colonies also left wills depriving their children of inheritance should they marry against parental wishes. Andrew Percival of South Carolina left a sum of £3,000 to his daughter Mary to be paid when she was twenty-one or married with the consent of his wife, but providing that in case of her marrying without such consent her portion was to be divided between the wife and other children.[38] Thomas Hubbard of the same colony bequeathed his daughter £100 on condition she did not marry Thomas Martin.[39] Charles Carroll I of Maryland left legacies to his daughters providing that should they not "prove dutiful to their mother and my trustees hereafter named and marry according to the directions of them," the disposal of their portions was to be left to the mother and trustees.[40] It is related of another father, John Thompson of Virginia, that he was so offended by his daughter's elopement that he not only refused to see her and declared that her husband need never expect a penny from him, but in retaliation married his housekeeper that he might have other children to inherit his property.[41]

[37] Edward D. Neill, *Virginia Carolorum: The Colony under the Rule of Charles the First and Second A. D. 1625-A. D. 1685, based upon Manuscripts and Documents of the Period* (Albany, 1886), p. 393.

[38] *South Carolina Magazine*, XII, 150-51. [39] *Ibid.*, p. 85.

[40] Kate Mason Rowland, *The Life of Charles Carroll of Carrollton, 1737-1832, with his Correspondence and Public Papers.* (2 vols. New York and London, 1898), II, 377.

[41] *William and Mary Quarterly*, XI, 160.

The young couple who dared risk being disinherited were usually condemned as guilty not only of filial disobedience but also of selfish and foolish disregard for the material welfare of each other and their children.

The custom which gave parents such control over the marriages of their children made the conventional courtship often a tedious and matter-of-fact affair. The young lover who was properly observant of the proprieties did not declare himself at once to the object of his affections but first sought the consent of his father, who, if in sympathy with the proposed union, gave him a letter to the father of the young lady telling him of his son's hopes and informing him what property he would settle on his son should the marriage take place. If the girl's father approved the match, in his reply he stated what he expected to give his daughter as her marriage portion. When the suitor was thus made certain of parental coöperation and an adequate provision, he paid his addresses to his beloved, who, it was assumed, was up until the time of his declaration entirely innocent of his intentions. Typical of the letters usually written on these occasions is the following from Thomas Walker to Colonel Bernard Moore, both of Virginia:

DEAR SIR:

My son, Mr. John Walker, having informed me of his intention to pay his addresses to your daughter Elizabeth, if he should (be) agreeable to yourself, lady and daughter, it may not be amiss to inform you what I feel myself able to afford for their support, in case of an union. My affairs are in an uncertain state, but I will promise one thousand pounds, to be paid in 1766, and the further sum of two thousand pounds I promise to give him; but the uncertainty of my present affairs prevents my fixing on a time of payment. The above sums are all to be in money or lands and other effects, at the option of my son, John Walker.

The answer was equally business-like:

DEAR SIR:

Your son, Mr. John Walker, applied to me for leave to make his addresses to my daughter, Elizabeth. I gave him leave, and told him at the same time that my affairs were in such a state it was not in my power to pay him all the money this year that I intended to give my daughter, provided he succeeded; but I would give him five hundred pounds more as soon after as I could raise or get the money, which sums you may depend I will most punctually pay to him.[42]

[42] Stanard, *op. cit.*, pp. 172-73.

The lovers sometimes wrote their own letters, which were naturally more feeling than those penned by practical parents. Thus Thomas Addison, Jr., of Maryland addressed the father of Rebecca Dulany, seventeen-year-old daughter of Walter Dulany:

MOST KIND SIR:

Permit me with gratitude and sincerity to return you thanks for your candid and compassionate letter in answer to mine—wrote you when I was in Annapolis—where you generously expressed your sentiments and acquainted me with your objections. Your remarks are very just and show the tender parent. But though your daughter is young, she may have as much prudence as one of more years; however I could wait with the greatest pleasure in hopes of a future reward. If you have, however, other objections, I must desist and submit to my ill fortune. . . .

If I thought it would disturb the peace of mind and contentment she enjoys, I would rather submit to the present load of affliction that now hangs upon me, and labor under it through life than to interrupt her happiness.[43]

The disconsolate lover did not have to submit to his "load of affliction" for life. In the *Maryland Gazette*, December, 1767, we find the announcement of the marriage of Thomas Addison to Rebecca Dulany.

It is not to be imagined that formalities like these preceded all colonial marriages, or that all lovers of the period were so restrained in their wooing. Among those who expected to inherit little either of family prestige or property, courtship was probably more spontaneous and free and the wishes of parents of less weight. Also it appears that, even among the most wealthy, young lovers sometimes made their avowals and had secret understandings between themselves before confiding in their parents. In many instances, doubtless, the business arrangement between the parents was merely a formal acknowledgment of an agreement already made between the lovers.

Such was the case of Jackie Custis, stepson of George Washington. While pursuing his studies under the Reverend Jonathan Boucher in Annapolis, Jackie, without consulting his parents or teacher, courted and engaged himself to Nelly Calvert, daughter of Benedict Calvert, who, while of distinguished family, had not the handsome portion which young Custis' large fortune entitled him to expect with a wife. Washington, though regretting his ward's unadvised engagement, nevertheless wrote a letter to Nelly's father,

[43] Elizabeth H. Murray, *op. cit.*, pp. 10-11.

praising her "amiable qualities" and asserting that "an alliance with her family would be agreeable to his," but suggesting that the marriage be deferred until Custis had completed his education. Calvert agreed that the young man was too inexperienced to enter the "matrimonial state," but the young lovers had their way and in less than a year Jackie had left school and they were married.[44]

Thomas Jefferson, while a law student in Williamsburg, sought to win assurance of the regard of Betsy Burwell, the "Belinda" of his letters, without "proceeding in form." Resolved to go to England and hence postpone matrimony, yet unable to endure the suspense of not knowing how he stood in the lady's affections, he solicited his friend, John Page, to broach to her the subject of a private understanding until his return. Later he wrote Page of a "confab" with "Belinda" herself, in which he opened his mind freely, explaining his intention of going abroad and the consequent delays, and asking "no question which would admit of a categorical answer" but assuring her that "such questions would one day be asked." But Miss Betsy evidently did not relish the idea of waiting for a formal proposal at her suitor's convenience and promptly married his rival.[45]

A less egoistic lover was James Iredell, who likewise divided his attention between the law and tender reflections of his lady, Hannah Johnston. He wrote in his diary of pleasing himself with a look at the smoke of the chimney of the room where she stayed, of waiting all the morning for the happiness of seeing her in the street, and of being "ineffably happy" in her "lovely and endearing company."[46] Because of his youth and uncertain circumstances, for a while he paid her only indirect addresses, but when he learned that she had rejected Sir Nathaniel Dukinfield, his friend and rival, he threw caution to the winds, proposed, and was promptly accepted.

Hannah Johnston, it appears in the Iredell correspondence, did not keep her suitors long on their knees. Her refusal of the gallant baronet, though courteous, had been as unhesitating and final as her acceptance of the youthful Iredell. Many others among the more sensible women doubtless dealt with their lovers in the same frank and straightforward manner. But this was not the fashion. The polite code of courtship required the lady to affect not only surprise

[44] *Writings of Washington* (ed., W. C. Ford), II, 376-78; *Letters to Washington* (ed., S. M. Hamilton), IV, 188-90.
[45] *Writings of Thomas Jefferson* (ed., P. L. Ford), I, 348-49, 353, 354-55, 357.
[46] McRee, *Iredell*, I, 130.

but even disapproval of her suitor's first declaration. As stated by *The Lady's Magazine,* "the acknowledgment of a mutual flame in the female breast . . . the confession which fills the lover with unalterable ecstasy, and covers the fair with amiable confusion" was "not to be given unsolicited for," but was to "be obtained by importunity, and granted with deliberation."[47]   Washington, advising Nelly Custis on the subject of love and marriage, assured her earnestly that delicacy precluded all advances on the woman's part, explaining: "The declaration, without the *most indirect* invitation of yours, must proceed from the man to render it permanent and valuable."[48]   A successful belle needed infinite tact to judge precisely how long to keep her lover waiting.   Discussing the question of "demurrage," *The Spectator* suggested that while the modesty of the sex rendered "a retreat from the first approaches of a lover both fashionable and graceful," a lady should "demur only out of form and so far as decency requires," adding, "a virtuous woman should reject the first offer of marriage, as a good man does that of a bishoprick; but I would advise neither the one nor the other to persist in refusing what they secretly approve."[49]

Allusions to their tactics and wiles in letters and newspapers show that colonial belles knew their game.   Molly Tilghman wrote of a Maryland beauty who finally accepted her suitor after keeping him dancing attendance for three years: "Her reign has been brilliant, and she has clos'd it in very good time, while her train was undiminish'd.   It is a nice point for a Belle to know when to marry, and one in which they are very apt.   She understood the matter."[50] Another gossipy letter tells of the fashionably prolonged wooing of a "Squire of high degree": "The world . . . have determin'd that his next visit to the Maid of the Mill, will be a conclusive one, and they say also, that after so long a Siege, the Lady may Capitulate without any offense to decorum."[51]

A lively epistle of Anne Blair describes the politely disdainful manner in which a Virginia fair one received a proposal from one of her suitors: "She was in a little Pett, but it was a very becoming one, let me tell you.   A growing blush suffus'd o'er her face attended with a trembling, insomuch that in extending her arm to

---

[47] November, 1772, pp. 514-15.

[48] George Washington Parke Custis, *Recollections and Private Memoirs of Washington* (New York, 1860), pp. 43-44.   [49] No. 89 (June 12, 1711).

[50] *Maryland Magazine,* XXI, 235.   [51] *Ibid.,* p. 38.

reach me *the creature's insolence* I thought ye Paper would have fallen from her Hand. The emotions I saw her in did not fail of exciting ye curiosity in me natural to all our Sex, so that a dog would not have caught more eagerly at a bone he was likely to lose than I did at the fulsome stuff (as she call'd it) tho' must own on perusal was charmed with ye elegance of his stile; I dare say he might with truth declare his Love for her to equal that of Mark Anthony's for Cleopatra. She thought proper to turn his letter back again with just a line or two signifying ye disagreeableness &c, &c, of ye subject. . . ."[52]

A striking contrast to these fastidious belles was Betsy Hansford, another Virginia lady, who, defying decorum, resorted to direct methods to obtain the man of her choice. According to a tradition of the colony, an unsuccessful suitor of the independent miss, discouraged at his own vain efforts, prevailed upon the Reverend John Camm to use his influence with the lady. The parson had in the early days of his rectorship baptized Betsy and now as rector of the parish was her spiritual adviser. He called upon his hard-hearted parishioner and, quoting from the Scriptures, urged upon her the duty of marrying. But she remained resolute. Finally, when his eloquence proved of no avail and he was about to retire in failure, she suggested that he would find in the Bible, 2 Samuel xii.7 the reason for her refusal. When upon returning home he looked up this reference, he was amazed to find these significant words staring him in the face: ". . . *thou art the man.*" But that he was not displeased with his young charge's audacity appears in a notice in the *Virginia Gazette* announcing the marriage of the Reverend Mr. John Camm and Miss Betsy Hansford.[53]

The coquetry and inconstancy of women were often complained of by disappointed lovers, some of whom even sought the aid of the law in holding their mistresses to their promises. In 1623 Virginia had an exciting breach-of-promise case featuring Mistress Cicely Jor-

---

[52] Frederick A. Horner, *Blair, Banister, and Braxton Families* (Philadelphia, 1898), p. 51.

[53] *William and Mary Quarterly*, X, 11; XIX, 29; Tyler, *Williamsburg, the Old Colonial Capital*, p. 156. Martha Goosley wrote a friend in London on this occasion, "Mr. Camms Marriage has made a great Noise here but Pray why may not an old Man afflicted with the Gout have the Pleasure of a fine hand to rub his feet and warm his flannells comfortable amusement you will say for a Girl of fifteen but She is to have a Chariot and there is to be no Padlock but upon her Mind."— *John Norton and Sons . . .* (ed., Frances Norton Mason), p. 102.

dan, a young and wealthy widow with variable affections. A few days after the death of Captain Samuel Jordan, the Reverend Greville Pooley, mindful of the desirability of his widow and fearful lest a rival precede him, persuaded his friend Captain Isaac Madison to broach for him a proposal of marriage. Madison, reluctant to "meddle in such business," nevertheless approached the widow and returned with the answer that she would as soon marry Pooley as anyone but intimating that she thought such haste not quite decent. Thus encouraged, Pooley visited her and secured a promise of marriage, but with the understanding that he would not reveal their engagement until she thought "the time fitting." But the parson, evidently too elated over his success to keep it to himself, and possibly, too, hoping to bind the widow more firmly, told it. Whereupon the high-spirited lady, angered by his exposing her unseemly haste, and finding another suitor more to her liking, engaged herself to him, declaring of the discarded parson that he "had fared better had he talked less." Pooley sued the widow for breach of promise, but he not only lost his case but had to give bond in the sum of five hundred pounds "never to have any claim, right or title to her." Still, the governor and council, seeing in the high-handed action of Mistress Jordan an evil precedent dangerous to the peace and harmony of the colony, issued a solemn proclamation against its recurrence.[54]

This prohibition was ineffective, however, in keeping women faithful to their promises. A year after its publication another fickle lady, Eleanor Spragg, was required to stand before the congregation in church and, acknowledging "her offence in contracting herself to two several men at one time," ask "God's and the Congregation's forgiveness." The court in an attempt to prevent another such offence ordered that every minister give warning in his church that "what man or woman soever shall use words amounting to a contract (or engagement) of marriage to several persons, shall be whipped or fined according to the quality of the persons offending."[55]

Some years later a Virginia gentleman, William Roscow, evidently doubtful of his betrothed yet eager to secure her, had from her the following written contract:

[54] Bruce, *Social Life of Virginia*, pp. 224-26.
[55] *Virginia Magazine*, XIX, 231, 234; XXI, 142-45; *Journal of the House of Burgesses*, I, Appendix, p. 121.

These are to Certifye all persons in Ye World that I, Sarah Harrison, Daughter of Mr. Benja. Harrison, do & am fully resolved & by these present do oblige myself (& cordially promise) to Wm. Roscow never to marry or contract marriage with any man (during his life) orlly himself. To confirm these presents, I the above said Sarah Harrison do call the Almighty God to witness & so help me God.   Amen.

(Signed) Sarah Harrison.[56]

This paper was duly recorded April 28, 1687.   But his extraordinary precautions did not save the lover from disappointment, for two months later the capricious Sarah renounced her solemn agreement and married Dr. James Blair, afterward founder of William and Mary College.   If, however, the rejected suitor was present at the wedding, he must have found consolation in what took place.   When during the service the minister instructed the bride to repeat the promise to obey, she replied, "No obey."   When a second and a third time he repeated this part of the ritual, she replied each time more emphatically than before, "No obey."   Then the minister, realizing the uselessness of further insistence, with the acquiescence of the bridegroom, went on with the rest of the ceremony.[57]

In later years, while lovers did not attempt to bind their mistresses by legal restraints, they continued to complain of their caprice. Thus William Reynolds of Yorktown, Virginia, wrote a London friend of a recent, and his second, disappointment: ". . . my Suit with a certain young Lady was yesterday ended, after the greatest Encouragement for four weeks she denied me without giving me any reason whatever, you must think I have had a luckey Escape for I am convinced a Coquette can never make a tolerable Wife, this behaviour has almost determined me to swear revenge against the Sex, & never will I put it in the power of a *third* to deny me."[58]   One rejected suitor, explaining that it was his purpose to save other "credulous gentlemen" from "falling a sacrifice to the artifice of a vain coquette," calling his mistress by name, described her fickle character in a signed letter in the *Virginia Gazette*.   When a knightly gentleman calling himself "Juvenis" undertook to defend the lady, a lively literary combat ensued, during which, amidst much calling of names, the former suitor gave "Juvenis" this word of warning: "You will have, no doubt, in the course of your commerce with the fair, observed, that, in spite of our boasted superiority, woman, frail woman!

[56] *Virginia Magazine*, VII, 278.
[57] *Ibid.*, XXXI, 84.   [58] MS, William Reynolds' Letter Books.

is still our master-piece in intrigue,—still vanquishes, paradox as it may seem, by pretending to be conquered. . . . The betrayer, under whose standard you have so lately enlisted . . . will, the moment she fancies herself secure of your affections, and that you are no longer your own, by seeming to yield, rank you in the number of her victims, and treat you as lawful spoil; while your folly, from being warned, will be without excuse, and your destruction without alleviation."[59]

In newspaper poems and essays women also complained of the faithlessness of their lovers, and some brought suits against them in the courts. One of the earliest court actions was that of the General Court of Virginia which in 1631 issued this order: "Because Edw. Grymes lay with Alice West he gives secur not to marry any wom. till further ordr from the Govr & Council."[60] Elizabeth Elliott, a South Carolina spinster, in 1768 entered a caveat in the Court of Ordinary against Uz. Rogers' being "joined in the Holy State of Matrimony" to any other woman until she could be heard.[61] A Boutetourt County court in Virginia in March, 1773, awarded Elizabeth Leatherdale twenty-five pounds in a breach-of-promise suit and Rebecca Roods one hundred pounds in a suit for breach of marriage contract and seduction.[62] Several similar cases were reported in the Virginia, Maryland, and Georgia papers, in each of which damages were awarded the plaintiff.[63]

The considerations which the colonists regarded most important in marriage were of the practical kind, and gentlemen were as hard-headed in arranging matrimonial alliances as in any business transactions. It was generally asserted that those matches were happiest which were made on rational grounds such as suitableness of character, rank, and fortune, rather than on mere personal liking or passion. Girls were advised to prefer the "man of sense" to the "cox-comb," "fop," and "rake," and were urged to be guided by the recommendations of their friends. Representative of the questions a sensible young lady was supposed to ask regarding her suitor were those suggested by Washington to Nelly Custis: "Is he a man of

[59] July 6, 1776; September 27, 1776.
[60] *Minutes of the Council and General Court of Colonial Virginia*, p. 480.
[61] *South Carolina Magazine*, XXVII, 94.
[62] Summers, *Annals of Southwest Virginia*, pp. 181-82.
[63] *Virginia Gazette*, July 10, 1752; *Maryland Gazette*, April 11, 1754; *Georgia Gazette*, May 16, 1765.

good character; a man of sense? . . . what has been his walk of life? Is he a gambler, a spendthrift, or drunkard? Is his fortune sufficient to maintain me in the manner I have been accustomed to live, and my sisters live, and is he one to whom my friends can have no reason[able] objection?"[64]

Young men were warned against being too greatly influenced by beauty of person and advised to choose for a wife one who was agreeable, sensible, and of "equal" family and fortune. Charles Carroll of Annapolis, writing his son Charles, then in England, suggested that the woman he took as wife should be virtuous, sensible, goodnatured, complaisant, neat, and cheerful in disposition; of good size, well proportioned, and free from hereditary disorders; and of the same social rank and religion as he. The matter of her fortune, which "in Prudence should not be overlooked," was not to overweigh that of her character. Yet, he advised, "if you should condescend to take the woman unequal to you in Point of fortune I hope the inequality will be Compensated in Point of Family, by her virtue & the other good qualities of her mind & person."[65]

Of the qualities contributing to a woman's success in the matrimonial market worldly goods were by no means least important. In the colonies the large surplus of males gave women advantages, increasing the importance of their persons as compared with their possessions; yet a bride was expected to bring a dowry proportionate to her husband's estate, and money was frankly accepted as a highly significant matter in marriage-making. A lover, when asking his father's permission to address a young lady, was very particular about informing him of her estate, and, in praising his betrothed to his friends, felt no indelicacy in mentioning her fortune along with her personal charms. Newspaper announcements of marriages commonly described the bride as "possessed of an amiable disposition and a handsome fortune," with the assertion or implication that these qualifications were the requisites of "connubial bliss." They sometimes stated the amount of the bride's estate. Elizabeth Stith of Virginia, for instance, was described as "a very amiable Lady with a fortune of 1000£ sterling," and Susannah Seabrook of South Carolina as "endowed with all agreeable Accomplishments and a Fortune of £15000."[66]

[64] G. W. P. Custis, *op. cit.*, pp. 43-44.   [65] *Maryland Magazine*, XI, 272-74.
[66] *South Carolina Gazette*, November 6, 1749.

Men discussed marriage as a means of obtaining pecuniary advantages, with surprising frankness. John Gibbon of Virginia, for instance, regretted leaving the colony because there he had been offered land and made "generous proffers of marriage."[67] Governor Charles Calvert, without any implication of reproach, wrote of a Maryland gentleman who had separated from an Indian woman whom he had married for her money: ". . . your Lopp [Lordship] needs not to fear any ill Consequence from that Match, butt what has already happened to the poore Man who unadvisedly threw himselfe away upon her in hopes of a great portion, which now is come to Little."[68] The same frank acceptance of mercenary marriage as a part of the social order is reflected in Governor Nicholson's explanation of the decrease in the number of capable men coming to the colonies. "Formerly," he wrote the Lords of Trade, "there was good convenient land to be taken up and there were widows [who] had pretty good fortunes which were encouragement for men of good parts to come but now all or most of these good lands are taken up and if there be any widdows or maid of any fortune the natives for the most part get them."[69]

A most impudent fortune-hunter was Captain John Posey, neighbor and debtor of Washington, to whom he wrote soon after the death of his wife: "I could [have] been able to [have] Satisfied all my old Arrears, Some months Agoe, by marrying [an] old widow woman in this County, She has Large soms [of] cash by her, and Pritty good Est. [Estate]—She is as thick, as she is high—And gits drunk at Least three or foure [times] a weak—which is Dis[a]grable to me—has Viliant Sperrit when Drunk—its been [a] Great Dispute in my mind what to Doe,—I belieave I shu'd Run all Resk's—if my Last wife had been [an] Even temper'd woman, but her Sperrit, has Given me such [a] Shock—that I am afraid to Run the Resk Again. . . ."[70] The shameless captain evidently did not take the risk, or the old woman changed her mind, for some time later he was lodged in jail, presumably for debt.

Another feature of colonial marriages somewhat shocking to

[67] *Virginia Magazine*, XXXVII, 68.

[68] "Calvert Papers," Maryland Historical Society, *Fund Publication*, No. 28, p. 264.

[69] James Curtis Ballagh, "White Servitude in the Colony of Maryland," Johns Hopkins University *Studies*, XIII, 73-74.

[70] *Letters to Washington* (ed., Hamilton), IV, 64.

twentieth-century sensibility was the number of unions made by the same person and the quickness with which a deceased husband or wife was succeeded by another. Women assuming the cares of mother-hood at an immature age often became broken in health and sank into an early grave, resigning their husbands to a succession of other wives. Men worn out by the harshness of pioneer life, exposed to disease by insanitation, and too often weakened by intemperance, were swept away before their prime, leaving their widows to enter one or several more unions. Three marriages by one person were not at all unusual; some made four, five, and even six ventures. Colonel John Carter, the first of his family to come to Virginia, had five wives.[71] George Washington's brother Samuel, by whom he was called upon so frequently for financial aid, married five times before he was forty-seven.[72] Colonel Thomas Ferguson, who rose from overseer to Carolina planter, made five financially advantageous matches and had twenty-seven children;[73] James Postell of the same colony, who according to his local gazette died much regretted at the age of fifty, had buried four wives and left a fifth;[74] and John Grim-ball had occasion to record in his Bible the "taking away" of five wives and his marriage to a sixth.[75]

So great was the haste with which a widower consoled himself with a new partner that sometimes he was condoled upon the death of a former wife and congratulated upon his choice of a second at the same time. A letter to Joseph Morton, twice governor of South Carolina, for instance, declares: "I am sorry to hear of the death of your good wife and wish you success in the dach [Dutch] widow you had thought of."[76] With the same apparent insensitiveness, a London friend writing to Roger Pinckney expressed regret at the death of Mrs. Pinckney and added: "I have now only to hope that when your grief has subsided, you will look out for yourself a good rich planter, and make up your fortune with her assistance for life."[77]

Many examples may be given of marriage within only a few months or even days after the burial of a deceased partner. John

[71] Glenn, *Some Colonial Mansions*, I, 220.

[72] Sparks, *Life of Washington*, p. 550.

[73] Ulrich B. Phillips, *Life and Labor in the Old South* (Boston, 1929), p. 308.

[74] *South Carolina Gazette*, April 12, 1773.

[75] *South Carolina Magazine*, XXVIII, 256-58.

[76] *Ibid.*, XXX, 2.

[77] "Letters of Richard Cumberland, Esq. to Roger Pinckney, Esq.," *Documents Connected with South Carolina* (ed., Weston), p. 144.

Laurens, father of Henry Laurens of Revolutionary fame, married Elizabeth Wicking exactly three months after burying his children's mother.   Possibly dissatisfaction at this prompt introduction of a stepmother into the family was responsible for the unexplained estrangement of John Laurens' daughter Mary, and for the expressed determination of Henry Laurens later, when his own wife died, not to jeopardize his affectionate relations with his children by a second marriage.[78]   But whether or not it was disapproved by his own family, John Laurens' hasty remarriage was entirely in keeping with the custom of the time.   His neighbor, Benjamin d'Harriette, also married a widow three months after the death of his first wife.[79] Colonel Harry Willis of Virginia waited only two months to repair the loss of his wife;[80] Dr. George Gilmer, two months and ten days,[81] and John Thruston courted and won a second wife one month and thirteen days after the death of a wife who had borne him sixteen children.[82]

When, in the third month of his widowhood, Colonel Charles Pinckney of South Carolina, aged forty-five, married Eliza Lucas, a young girl who had been a frequent visitor in his home, apparently some unfavorable comment was made, for a person going from Charles Town told the first Mrs. Pinckney's relatives in London that she had been neglected during her last illness.   Upon getting news of this gossip, the young bride wrote to her predecessor's sister protesting that the tale was a vicious falsehood, adding: "had I not known him [Mr. Pinckney] to have been the best of husbands, I had not been in the relation I now am to him."[83]   This assurance evidently removed the doubts of the English relations, for a friendly correspondence ensued between them and the new Mrs. Pinckney.

Other hasty remarriages were complained of now and then by relatives of the deceased husbands and wives and were probably regarded as unseemly by many in the community.   The religious denomination of Friends objected as a group to their associates remarrying too shortly after the passing of a husband or wife.   George

[78] Wallace, *Life of Henry Laurens*, p. 11.

[79] Hirsch, *op. cit.*, p. 221.

[80] Slaughter, *Memoir of Colonel Joshua Fry*, p. 73.

[81] Extract from the Family Bible of Dr. George Gilmer, in George R. Gilmer, *Sketches of Some of the First Settlers of Upper Georgia, of the Cherokees, and the Author* (New York and London, 1855), p. 12.

[82] *William and Mary Quarterly*, IV, 23-26.

[83] Ravenel, *Eliza Pinckney*, p. 96.

Fox, founder of the Society of Friends, admonished them to show respect to the memory of their deceased companions by allowing a sufficient time to elapse between the death of one partner and the taking of another.[84]   Remarriage in less than a year was thought too hasty.   In the Minute Book of the Quakers of Albemarle in North Carolina for the years 1702-1727 is this "paper of self-condemnation" read by Edward Mayo as a public apology for his excessive haste: "Dear Friends:—Through the instigation of the enemy, and for want of watchfulness, I did let out my mind and make suit to the widow Gormack by way of courtship, contrary to the good and wholesome order settled among Friends; it being too soon after the death of her husband and the death of my wife.   Therefore I am heartily sorry I should cause the blessed truth to be evilly spoken of by evil-minded people, and do condemn this my forward action and indecent procedure in this matter."[85]

Other religious groups and people in general had not such strict ideas.   Usually neither widows nor widowers were expected to mourn their loss for long.   Though some ladies' books advised against the remarriage of widows, their counsel was often unheeded, for widows as well as widowers were not slow in exchanging their weeds for wedding garments.   Jane Sparrow of Virginia buried her husband, Major Charles Sparrow, member of the House of Burgesses, on Tuesday, September 11, 1660, and on the following Sunday became the bride of William Rollinson, merchant.[86]   Anne Fairfax Washington, widow of Lawrence Washington, bestowed her hand and goods upon Colonel George Lee only five months after the death of her husband, and when George Washington came into possession of the person and fortune of the wealthy Martha Custis, his predecessor, Daniel Parke Custis, had been in his grave just seven months.   So

[84] "Memoir of George Fox," *Friends' Library*, I, 70, 73-74, 79.   According to the discipline of the Society of Friends, a couple desiring to marry acquainted the women's and the men's meetings with their intention.   A committee of men and one of women Friends was then appointed to "see that the relations of those who proceeded to marriage were satisfied, that the parties were clear from all others; and that widows had made provision for their first husband's children, before they married again, and what else was needful to be inquired into. . . ."   If the committee reported no objections to the union, the couple then designated a meeting at which they would take each other for husband and wife.   No priest or magistrate officiated, but at least twelve Friends had to be present as witnesses and the marriage was to be recorded.—"Institution of the Discipline," *Friends' Library*, I, 128-29.

[85] Francis L. Hawks, *History of North Carolina* (2 vols. Fayetteville, N. C., 1857-1858), II, 322.   [86] *Virginia Magazine*, XLI, 191.

quickly did women surrender their independence and possessions to a new master that many instances may be found in court records of a second husband's being granted the probate of the will of the first. In many cases the woman bringing in an inventory of her deceased husband's estate or petitioning for her dower had already remarried. Thus when the widow of Richard Wood of North Carolina asked a Tyrrell County court for a division of his estate, she had already become Elizabeth Fitzpatrick,[87] and when Richard Newcome's widow brought into court an account of his goods, she gave her name as "Hannah Townsend (late Newcome.)"[88] Bruce tells of a case in Essex County in Virginia in which a minister, the Reverend Boulware, brought suit and obtained a judgment against one Edward Danneline for fees due him not only for performing the marriage ceremony for Danneline and his wife but also for preaching the funeral service for Mrs. Danneline's former husband.[89]

The wife who lost her second or third husband sometimes took a fourth or even a fifth. The woman having the most husbands to her credit was one Elizabeth, whose maiden name is unknown, but who married successively Thomas Stevens, Raleigh Travers, Robert Beckingham, Thomas Wilks, and George Spencer, all prominent gentlemen, and is supposed to have taken William Mann later as a sixth husband.[90] Mary Sisson, whose name had been changed to Pope, then to Bridges, and again to Nichols, married a fourth husband, David Whitliffe, by whom she had three children.[91] Frances Gerrard, also thrice a widow, was led to the altar a fourth time by Colonel John Washington.[92] Penelope Galland, Governor Eden's stepdaughter, had had three husbands before she married Governor Johnston sometime between 1737 and 1741.[93] Hannah Barkersdale of Georgia, who died in her forty-eighth year, was four times married, twice to Baptist ministers.[94] Anne Barnwell of South Carolina had four husbands, having married her third and fourth after she was forty-five,[95] and Lady Mary Mackenzie is known to have had

[87] MS, Tyrrell County Court Minutes, 1761-1770.
[88] MS, Henrico County Court Orders, 1707-1709.
[89] Social Life of Virginia, p. 229.   [90] Stanard, op. cit., pp. 171-72.
[91] William and Mary Quarterly, XII, 193.
[92] Ibid., IV, 35.
[93] North Carolina Historical and Genealogical Register, I, 54.
[94] David Benedict, General History of the Baptist Denomination in America, and Other Parts of the World (2 vols., Boston, 1813), II, 183-184.
[95] South Carolina Magazine, II, 50.

four husbands and evidence points to a fifth.[96]   Many examples are found of thrice-married ladies, but Dame Frances Berkeley enjoyed the unique distinction of having won three governors successively. As the widow of Governor Stevens, she married Sir William Berkeley, then governor of Virginia, and at his death became the wife of Governor Ludwell of North Carolina, though she was known for the rest of her life as "Lady Berkeley."[97]

As may be imagined, persons who made so many trips to the altar often embarked upon their last ventures somewhat late in life. No person, it would seem, whether man or woman, was too old to marry.   Captain Michael Cresap of Maryland took a second wife at eighty.[98]   Colonel Miles Brewton, a conspicuous South Carolina leader, at seventy married as his third wife the widow Paine, who had been twice married before;[99] Michael Mackenzies, aged seventy-three, married Susannah Molloson, aged fifty-one;[100] and John Strahan at seventy married the widow Painter of sixty.[101]   Rachel Russ, a South Carolina widow possessed of large estate and unusual ability as a planter, at the advanced age of sixty-eight, took as her third husband the Reverend Bartholomew Henry Himili.   It would be natural to assume that the Reverend Himili in taking such an antique bride had dreams of a considerable monetary reward, but a marriage agreement drawn up at the time, reserving her entire property for her sole use and disposal during her life and the right to dispose of half by will, indicates that the old lady had no notion of handing over all her worldly goods as a price for companionship.[102]

In a letter to his niece, Judge James Iredell of North Carolina told of the marriage in that colony of a "hearty Methuselah" about seventy to an "antiquated widow" of about forty-five, who was "old-fashioned, ugly, and horribly formal," but an excellent nurse, for which last qualification the practical-minded bridegroom stated frankly he wished her for a wife.   Iredell's comment that "the old fellow" was "more fitted for his grave than matrimony"[103] indicates that the

[96] *Ibid.*, XX, 140.

[97] *Colonial Records of North Carolina*, I, xvii.

[98] Brantz Mayer, *Tah-Gah-Jute or Logan and Captain Michael Cresap* . . . (Baltimore, 1851), p. 22.

[99] *South Carolina Magazine*, II, 129.

[100] *South Carolina Gazette and Country Journal*, April 30, 1771.

[101] *South Carolina Gazette*, March 17, 1732.

[102] *South Carolina Magazine*, XXVII, 159-60.

[103] McRee, *Iredell*, I, 470.

North Carolina justice had little sympathy with these ancient lovers. Others evidently shared his disapproval. Thus Colonel Carter of Virginia commented in his diary: "I heard Nat Harrison was courting Sam Gordon's widow. I do not know anything more demonstrative of weakness than an old man's turning a lover."[104]

More distasteful to men like Judge Iredell and Colonel Carter, probably, were the unions between the very old and the young. The proverb about winter mating with spring, though frequently on the lips of the colonists, was many times disregarded. Hoary-haired gentlemen courted and won girls still in their teens, and, what is more surprising, young men sometimes took as wives women far on the other side of fifty. One of the most shocking of these unequal marriages was announced as follows in the *Virginia Gazette*, March 15, 1771: "Yesterday was married, in Henrico, Mr. William Carter, third son of Mr. John Carter, aged twenty-three, to Mrs. Sarah Ellyson, Relict of Mr. Gerard Ellyson, deceased, aged eighty five, a sprightly old Tit, with three Thousand Pounds Fortune." The same paper shortly afterward gave notice of a marriage between Benjamin Rhodes, aged twenty, and Elizabeth Adams, "a Maiden Lady, in her sixty-second year."[105] The *South Carolina Gazette* announced the marriage of John Wilson aged twenty to Mary Rake, a widow of seventy-nine,[106] and published an account of the wedding of Elizabeth Street of Ashley Ferry, aged sixty-four and John Goodwin, forty-eight, declaring that it was "attended by most of the Neighbours of Distinction, with Musical Instruments of Joy on that Occasion."[107]

The advertisement of the respective ages of these couples indicates that the unions between young gentlemen and such ancient ladies were not commonplace. The marriage of old men to girls young enough to be their daughters, or even granddaughters, was more ordinary and thus was mentioned less frequently by newspapers. One, however, extreme enough to be interesting as news was between Robert Fergus, a widower of eighty-three, and Anne Jones, a girl between fourteen and fifteen.[108] Governor Dobbs of North Carolina when seventy-eight was said to have become enamoured of a Miss Davis, a lady of "sprightly fifteen," of good family and some fortune, who, though in love with a young man near her own age, was per-

[104] *William and Mary Quarterly*, XVI, 152.
[105] April 15, 1775.
[106] September 19, 1774.
[107] September 5, 1743.
[108] *Virginia Gazette*, March 12, 1767.

suaded by her parents to become a governor's lady. The day was
fixed and the nuptial feast provided. But when it was discovered
that the wily old governor had conveyed all his property to his son,
the indignant parents of the young lady, without informing the governor, immediately sent for her young suitor and the true lovers were
married.[109]

Colonel Thomas Mann Randolph, a widower of distinguished
Virginia family and large possessions, when much advanced in age
and the father of thirteen children, married a girl under twenty.
In this case the parents were careful to secure a handsome provision
for their daughter, for by a marriage contract the old gentleman
settled on his young bride and her issue most of his large estate to
the exclusion of his children and grandchildren by a previous marriage. Thomas Jefferson, writing to his daughter Martha, who had
married the son of the old Colonel, though admitting that the marriage settlement might be imprudent, nevertheless urged her to try
to prevent any "diminution of affection" between her husband and
his father and to endeavor to be the "link of love, union, and peace
for the whole family."[110] Whether Martha was able to adhere to
this advice does not appear. To do so certainly was not easy, especially later when at her father's death his estate was swallowed up
by debts, and she and her twelve children were without any means of
support. Colonel Randolph did not long survive his second marriage, and, as was to be expected, his young widow soon bestowed her
hand and fortune upon a second husband.

[109] *Colonial Records of North Carolina*, VI, 738.
[110] Sarah N. Randolph, *Domestic Life of Jefferson*, pp. 187-88.

CHAPTER VIII

"CONJUGAL FELICITY" AND DOMESTIC DISCORD

KEEPING IN MIND the prosaic, businesslike manner in which marriages were often made in colonial days, and considering the immature age of many persons undertaking marital responsibilities, the haste with which a deceased mate was frequently replaced by another, and the numerous ventures often made by the same person, one wonders what was the sequel to this kind of marriage-making. Unfortunately the matrimonial histories of individual couples have not been preserved. But abundant materials at hand reflect the prevailing conception of proper conjugal conduct and throw light upon the general state of marriage.

The subject treated in most detail by seventeenth-century family books was the mutual duties of husbands and wives. Generally it was stated that the husband should guide, defend, and provide for the wife, while she was to serve him in subjection, be modest in speech and dress, and be a good housewife. "A wise husband," declared *A Godly Form of Household Government*, "and one that seeketh to live in quiet with his wife, must observe three rules. Often to admonish: Seldom to reprove: and never to smite her."[1] The commonly accepted idea of the proper treatment of a husband was described by a "well-spoken" wife in *A Looking Glasse for Maried Folks:* "When he lookt at any time very sad, & there were not fit time to speak to him, I would not the laugh & daily with him, and play the tom-boy . . . but I put upon me a sad countenance, and lookt heavily. . . . So it beseemes an honest wife to frame herselfe to her husbands affections. . . . And if at any time he were stired, I would either pacify him, with a gentle speech, or give way to his wrath. . . . This course also I tooke: if he came drunken home, I would not then for anything have him a foule word, but I would cause his bed to be made very soft and easie, that he might sleepe the better, and by faire speeches get him to it."[2]

[1] Chilton Latham Powell, *English Domestic Relations*, p. 133.
[2] *Ibid.*, p. 141. Sir Thomas Overbury in his *Characters* (1614), describes "A Good Woman" as one "whose husband's welfare is the business of her actions." Her

These views somewhat elaborated were embodied in ladies' books and treatises on marriage throughout the next century, though later writings usually gave more attention to the wife's duties and less to the husband's. She was supposed to exist for her husband, be an agreeable and obedient companion to him, a tender mother of his children, a capable and industrious manager of his house, and a gracious and attractive hostess to his guests. This feeling expressed by an exemplary matron in *The Spectator* was that of the true wife: "I am married, and I have no other concern but to please the man I love; he is the end of every care I have; if I dress, it is for him; if I read a poem, or a play, it is to qualify myself for a conversation agreeable to his taste; he is almost the end of my devotions; half my prayers are for his happiness."[3]

The *Virginia Gazette* offered the "fair sex" these "Rules for the Advancement of Matrimonial Felicity": "Never dispute with him [your husband] whatever be the Occasion . . . And if any Altercations or Jars happen, don't separate the bed, whereby the Animosity will cease . . . by no Means disclose his imperfections, or let the most intimate Friend know your Grievances; otherways you expose yourself to be laugh'd at. . . . Read often the Matrimonial Service, and overlook not the important word OBEY."[4] One "Receipt for the Ladies to retain the Affections of their Husbands" emphasized good humor and discretion as most desirable wifely qualities, and another described the "Good Wife" as one "humble and modest from Reason and Conviction, submissive from Choice, and obedient from Inclination."[5] A North Carolina paper urging upon wives the importance of neatness in dress and a sweet temper, concluded with this advice:

> . . . her Wit must never be display'd,
> Where it the husband's province might invade:
> Be she content sole *Mistress* to remain,
> Nor poorly strive for the *Mastership* t' obtain.
> This would occasion Jars, intestine Strife,
> Imbitter all the sweets of nuptial Life:

chief virtue is that "Shee is Hee." William Habington in *Castara* (1634), describes the ideal wife's attitude toward her husband: "Shee is inquisitive onely of new wayes to please him, and her wit sayles by no other compass then that of his direction. Shee lookes upon him as Conjurers upon the Circle, beyond which there is nothing but Death and Hell; and in him shee beleeves Paradice circumscrib'd."—Quoted in Myra Reynolds, *The Learned Lady in England, 1650-1760* (Boston and New York, 1920), pp. 24, 32.   [3] No. 254.

[4] May 20, 1737.   [5] *Ibid.*, March 19, 1772; January 21, 1773.

Then let her not for Government contend,
But use this Policy to gain her end - -
Make him *believe* he holds the Sov'reign Sway,
And she may *rule*, by seeming to *obey*.[6]

To what extent colonial wives subscribed to these rules and attempted to put them into practice does not appear. Nor is it known whether husbands generally took advantage of their position as "lords of creation." The records show on the one hand a great deal of conjugal affection, loyalty, and happiness, and on the other discord and discontent. As evidence of mutual confidence and devotion, one might point to many wills in which the testator made careful provision for his "beloved wife," to affectionate letters, and to occasional glimpses of happy married life in private papers. Governor William Berkeley of Virginia left his "deare and most virtuous wife" all his estate with this declaration, "if God had blest me with a far greater estate, I would have given it all to my most Dearly beloved wife."[7] Likewise John Smithson of Maryland, in a nuncupative will, declared of his wife, "All I have I leave her, and if I had more she should enjoy it."[8] Some wills included a verbal tribute besides a generous bequest as did that of Benjamin Harrison, who gave his wife handsome legacies besides her thirds and added this explanation, "she hath at all times behaved in a most dutiful and affectionate manner to me and all-ways been assisting through my whole affairs."[9] John Rutledge explained that because of his wife's "good understanding" and tenderness to his seven young children, he was leaving her his entire estate with the right to use or dispose of it according to her discretion.[10] John Randolph made large provision in different kinds of property, jewelry, and money for his "dear and most beloved wife," stating that it was for "her ffaithfulness affection and prudence."[11]

Scattered through the records are many declarations of tender sympathy and expressions of anxiety at the suffering or grief at the decease of a beloved mate. In 1716 Mann Page of "Roswell" in Virginia wrote in his Bible: "On the 12th day of December (the most unfortunate day that ever befell me) about 7 of the clock in the morning, the better half of me, my dearest wife, was taken from

[6] *North Carolina Gazette*, July 14, 1775. For other discussions of the wife's duty, see below, Chap. X.
[7] *Minutes of the Council and General Court of Virginia*, p. 535.
[8] *Archives of Maryland*, IV, 45-46.   [9] *Virginia Magazine*, XXXII, 98.
[10] *South Carolina Magazine*, XXXI, 10-11.
[11] *Virginia Magazine*, XXXVI, 376-79.

me." At about the same time, grief-stricken William Byrd informed a relative of his "dear Lucy's" death, exclaiming: "Alas! how proud was I of her and how severely I am punished for it."[12]   Louis Henry de Rosset of North Carolina declared of his "dear best friend" that her many virtues had so endeared her to him that he "fully enjoyed every conjugal felicity for thirty years."[13]   William Stephens of Georgia mourned for a wife with whom he had lived for nearly forty-four years, during the whole of which time, he declared, "a mutual tender affection" had remained between them.[14]   Henry Laurens was overwhelmed at the passing of his "bosom friend," whom he praised as "ever loving, cherishing and ready to obey— who never once,—no, not *once*—during the course of twenty years' most intimate connection threw the stumbling block of opposition" in his way.[15]

More convincing evidence of conjugal affection and mutual help-fulness appears in sympathetic and affectionate letters like the following written by General William Campbell of Virginia in 1776:

My Dearest Betsy:

      . . .
I received your sweet and most affectionate letter of the 9th inst. by Col. Meredith.   The fear you there express for my going to the north-ward, or against the Cherokees, you may entirely lay aside. . . . If the horse you mentioned please you right well, by all means buy him, though inquire . . . if he is given to stumbling or starting. . . .

I most heartily thank you, dear, for your attention, for providing me such necessaries as I stand in need of.   I fear you are too solicitous and give yourself too much trouble.   You bring to my mind Solomon's excel-lent description of a good wife. . . . Such is my dearest Betsy.   Her worth I esteem far above rubies.

I have now lived about a week in the house where I was first blessed with a sight of my dear Betsy.   Little did I at that time think that such superlative happiness was destined for me.   From that happy moment I date the hour of all my bliss.   I love the place on your account.

      . . .
Will see you as soon as I possibly can. . . .
Your most affectionate
      WM. Campbell[16]

[12] Stanard, *op. cit.*, p. 107.

[13] "The de Rosset Papers."   Letters and Documents relating to the Early History of the Lower Cape Fear. *James Sprunt Historical Monograph*, No. 4, p. 18.

[14] *Colonial Records of Georgia*, XXII (Pt. II), 424.

[15] Wallace, *Life of Henry Laurens*, pp. 180-81.

[16] Thomas Lewis Preston, *A Sketch of Mrs. Elizabeth Russell, Wife of General William Campbell, and Sister of Patrick Henry* (Nashville, Tenn., 1888), pp. 11-13.

Letters of James Iredell to his "dear Hannah" reveal a similar affection and esteem. When obliged to be away from home holding court, he wrote her frequently, giving interesting details of his travels, and always lamenting their separation, imploring her to be careful of her health, urging her to write him by every opportunity, and assuring her of his lasting devotion. "O! how long every hour seems to me," he exclaimed while on one circuit. "Never did I feel more anxiety to see you. . . . I will apply day and night to the business at Hillsborough, in order to shorten the time of my further absence from you."[17]

Mutual confidence, loyalty, and devotion were doubtless enjoyed by many other couples. But there were also unhappy marriages. Those who point to the colonial period as a golden age of family relations can hardly be acquainted with the eighteenth-century discussions lamenting the decadence of the domestic virtues, with the suspicion and distrust reflected in private papers, with the large number of public notices of absconding wives and voluntary separations, and with the many complaints by husbands and wives in court records.

"Reflections on unhappy marriages" was a favorite subject of journalists. Among the reasons usually given for the "degeneration of the Married state" were "female extravagance," excessive fondness for dress and display, and neglect of domestic duties. A correspondent to the *Virginia Gazette*, declaring one of the greatest "unhappinesses" of the time was that matrimony was so much discountenanced, suggested as causes of the "interruption of domestic peace" the fact that ladies gave themselves up too generally to an idle and expensive life, and that men, for the sake of beauty or wealth, ran the "desperate hazard" of taking to their bosoms a "fury" or an "ideot."[18] A note familiar to every generation was sounded by a contributor to the *Lady's Magazine:* "If women would recover that empire which they seem in a great measure to have lost . . . they must change their present fashionable method of living, and do what their grandmothers did before them, go often to church, and be well acquainted with their own houses."[19]

Misunderstanding and dissension were reflected now and then in colonial wills, as in this provision made by Willie Jones, prominent North Carolina patriot: "Now, as it is possible and indeed probable that my wife will not be satisfied with the provisions which I have

[17] McRee, *Iredell*, I, 380.
[18] February 4, 1773.   [19] May, 1773, p. 238.

hereinbefore made for her, and consequently could refuse to be bound by this very will. . . . I leave to my wife to do better for herself if she can."[20] Hendrick Sluyter of Bohemia Manor in Maryland left posterity a hint of his domestic problem in this clause, "As my wife, to my sorrow, has always some difference with my friends, it is my desire that she retire to her former home in Philadelphia or elsewhere."[21] A more shameless testator was Colonel John Custis of Virginia, who ordered the following vindictive inscription placed upon his tombstone:

> Beneath this Marble Tomb lies ye Body
> of the *Hon. John Custis, Esq.*
>
> . . .
>
> Aged 71 Years, and yet lived but seven years,
> which was the space of time he kept
> a bachelor's home at Arlington
> on the Eastern Shore of Virginia.[22]

The seven years which he counted were those after the death of his wife, Frances Parke, with whom he had lived in a turbulent marriage.

Gossip of this eccentric couple must have provided conversation for many Virginia dinner parties. For weeks at a time, it was said, they would not speak to each other, communicating when necessary through the servants. She would say, for instance, "Pompey, ask your master if he will have coffee or tea, and sugar and cream," and he would reply, "Tell your mistress I will have coffee as usual, with no cream." During one of their periods of ominous silence, to her surprise he asked her to go for a drive, and she accepted. Heading his horse into Chesapeake Bay, he drove out into the water. "Where are you going, Mr. Custis?" she asked after a time. "To hell, Madam," he replied. "Drive on," she answered, not the least disconcerted, "any place is better than Arlington." On and on out into the water he drove until the horse was forced to swim, and still the undaunted lady uttered no protest. "I believe you would as lief meet the Devil himself, if I should drive to hell," he announced as he turned again toward the shore. "Quite true, Sir," she retorted,

---

[20] W. C. Allen, *History of Halifax County* (Boston, 1919), p. 156.

[21] Rev. Charles Payson Mallery, *Ancient Families of Bohemia Manor; their Homes and their Graves.* "Papers of the Historical Society of Delaware," VII, 35-36. The lady here disparaged later married a second, a third, and a fourth husband.   [22] *Virginia Magazine*, XXXII, 239.

"I know you so well I would not be afraid to go anywhere you would go."[23]

A contract drawn up between this spirited pair now on file in Northampton County suggests that disagreement over financial matters was at the root of their strife. Having brought her husband a large estate at marriage, Frances probably felt entitled to some say as to how it should be used and did not always express her feelings with proper amiability. The immediate bone of contention was some silver plate and damask linen inherited by Frances, which she had removed from the house. She demanded a "more plentiful maintenance" for herself and family and a more businesslike management by him of the estate that was to descend to her children. The text of the contract is revealing as a statement of what were considered proper marital rights in such cases. Frances promised to return the linen and plate and never to take anything else of value from the house without his consent, and John covenanted not to dispose of these articles during her life and to give them to her children immediately after her death. Each agreed to "forbear" to call each other "vile names," to "live lovingly together" and to "behave themselves to each other as a good husband & wife ought to do." She was to avoid meddling with his business matters, and he was to permit her sole control over her domestic affairs. He was to render annually to a third person a true account of his estate, and of the clear profits was to allow her one half for clothing herself and children, for the children's education, and for housekeeping articles from England. Also he promised to contribute certain provisions made on the plantation such as wheat, Indian corn, meats, wool, and flax. All of this was promised on condition that Frances did not exceed her allowance, run him into debt, or break any part of her agreement. Whether she or he or both violated the contract is not known, but it evidently did not, as they had hoped, "end all animositys and unkindness" between them.[24]

Somewhat similar to this covenant was one signed by the Reverend Caspar Stoever, Lutheran minister of the German congregation in Virginia, and his second wife, Maria Magdalena. In their articles of agreement drawn up in 1734, they promised to "totally forget and bury in oblivion" all differences between them. He agreed to

---

[23] Charles Moore, *op. cit.*, pp. 65-66; Paul Wilstach, *Tidewater Virginia* (Indianapolis, 1929), pp. 194-96.   [24] *Virginia Magazine*, IV, 64-66.

provide her with maintenance and clothes according to his station and means, and she to "obey his lawful commandments as a Christian wife ought to do." Also he agreed that if he should travel to some other place and, against her wishes, leave her there, half of his estate would fall to her share, provided she were not the cause of his so leaving her. Provision for her mother and for his children by a former marriage was another cause of dispute. He stipulated to give certain property to his children by a former wife and then leave those by Maria Magdalena his sole heirs, and promised to maintain his mother-in-law and to "shew her all love and faithfulness due from a child." In return, the mother was to be "careful of not giving offense . . . especially to leave off all evil speaking, back-biting & slandering" and to "admonish her Daughter to beware of offending." This provision, inserted "to the end the congregation may not be offended," was duly signed by the mother-in-law as well as the husband and wife. Furthermore, it was written into the contract that, if the husband wished it, the mother-in-law was to reside in some place other than with him.[25]

Another marriage possibly more poignantly unhappy than that of the Stoevers or the Custises was the union between Colonel William Byrd III and his first wife, Elizabeth Hill Carter, daughter of Secretary John Carter of "Shirley." The cause of their differences is unknown, but his mother, Maria Taylor Byrd, evidently encouraged her son's dissatisfaction with his wife. Forsaken by her husband then serving in the French wars, deprived of her three oldest boys, who were in England at school, and disparaged by her mother-in-law, young Elizabeth Byrd must have led a melancholy existence at "Belvidere." The older Mrs. Byrd disliked both her daughter-in-law and the girl's mother. She spoiled her son, gave him money, and wrote him flattering letters, in which she insinuated animadversions upon his wife. At one time she complained to him that "the Lady," meaning Elizabeth, had not once been to see her though she had offered her her chariot for the purpose.[26] Again, writing him affectionately of money she had placed with her London agent for his use, she added: "That may help to pay for Mrs. Byrd's [Elizabeth Byrd] Invoice for I hear She has writ one which orders her underclothes to be made & Ruffled in England. I cant but think, She had better make them herself. It would be some employment for her.   I am sure it is the most extravagant Fashion in the world to have them made in that manner."[27]

In her letters Elizabeth Byrd appears fond though somewhat afraid of her husband.[28]   To his command that she send her sick baby to her mother-in-law at "Westover," where the air was supposed to be more wholesome than at "Belvidere," she replied dutifully: "I am very sorry you have limited Poor, sweet Otway, so that he has but a short time to stay with me.   Poor dear babe. . . . But Sir, your Orders must be obeyed whatever reluctance I find thereby."[29] After the surrender of the French at Quebec, Elizabeth hoped her husband would return to her in Virginia, but at the end of the war he deliberately went into garrison at Pittsburgh, evidently not desiring to return home.[30]   A letter from John Kirkpatrick to George Washington declared: "Colo. Bird I am told has repudiated his Wife, who is now in a Delirium for his Behaviour, and is resolved to make a Campaign under Lord Loudon—he has committed his Estate to the Charge of some Friends, & Settled all w[ith] a design never to return to Virginia."[31]   The unhappy wife died at the age of twenty-nine in July, 1760, from anxiety and distress, it was asserted by one supposed to have accurate family information.[32]   Before news of her death reached her husband, her mother-in-law ordered her children sent at once to "Westover," demanded the keys of "Belvidere" from the deceased wife's own mother, and wrote her son advising that he require a "righteous account" of articles there.[33]

[27] *Ibid.*, pp. 249-50.
[28] *Ibid.*, pp. 242-43, 246-47, 247-48, 349-50.
[29] *Ibid.*, pp. 246-47.   [30] *Ibid.*, p. 349.
[31] *Letters to Washington* (ed., Hamilton), I, 335-36.
[32] *Virginia Magazine*, XXXVIII, 52-53.
[33] *Ibid.*, pp. 155-56, 347, 350.   Six months later Colonel Byrd married Mary Willing of Philadelphia, who was apparently better able to cope with a spoiled husband and a meddlesome mother-in-law, for, though he wasted a large part of his estate gambling, their marriage seems to have been happy.   His affectionate confidence in this wife, and also his later dissatisfaction with his mother and children appear in his will.   He appointed his wife executrix, directed that his son Otway be disinherited if he quit the navy, and that his son Thomas Taylor be disinherited if he should marry Susannah Randolph.   In distributing his estate among his children, he ordered that there should be deducted from the share of those of the first marriage "such sums as they may claim under the wills of my deluded & superannuated Mother & my ungrateful son, William."—*Ibid.*, pp. 59-61.   This harsh reference to his deceased mother indicates that, despite her dislike for Elizabeth Byrd, the old lady left the larger part of her property to Elizabeth's children rather than to those of her son's second wife.

Other domestic troubles are found scattered through private papers. William Fitzhugh of Virginia, consulting the Maryland attorney general in 1681 for some legal remedy for an unhappy relative, explained: "The cruelty of Mr Blackstone towards my sister in Law is grown so notorious and cruel that there is no possibility of keeping it any longer in private, with the preservation of her life his cruelty having already occasioned her to make two or three attempts to destroy herself which if not timely prevented will inevitably follow."[34]   Some time later, writing his mother of the death of his own sister, he expressed a belief that her husband's "unkindness and foolery shortened her days."[35]   A more flagrant case of abuse was that of a clergyman, who, according to a letter of Governor Dinwiddie to the Bishop of London, had "very near perpetrated" murder on his wife by "ty'g her up by the Leggs to the Bed Post and cut'g her in a cruel Man'r with Knives."[36]   Colonel James Gordon noted in his diary at one time that Robert Edmonds had deserted his wife and at another that Captain Glascock, a family connection, had run away with a young woman, leaving his wife. Again he wrote that the death of a Mrs. Chin, probably a neighbor, was laid to her husband, who was reported to have beaten and abused her.[37]   Timothy Ford, a New Englander in South Carolina, wrote of many family troubles there, "especially of the conjugal kind." "I every day hear of unhappy marriages both in time past and present," he declared. He attributed the extraordinary amount of domestic unhappiness to the "sinister views" of the people, who "plumed themselves on rank & fortune, in the making of matches," and to their "confirmed habits of idleness and dissipation."[38]

A cause of much wretchedness of wives must have been the unfaithfulness of husbands, which, though not considered serious by courts or society in general, could hardly have been borne with the equanimity advised in ladies' morality books. These writings usually upheld a different morality for men and women and advised the wife to conceal from everyone her knowledge of her husband's infidelities.[39]   A husband might have a practical motive in verifying his

[34] *Ibid.*, I, 40-41.   [35] *Ibid.*, IV, 418-19.

[36] "The Official Records of Robert Dinwiddie," Virginia Historical Society, *Collections*, IV, 696.

[37] *William and Mary Quarterly*, XI, 217; XII, 2, 9.

[38] "Diary, 1785-1786," *South Carolina Magazine*, XIII, 192.

[39] This explanation by a correspondent to the *Lady's Magazine*, August, 1771, was representative of many: "A licentious commerce between the sexes . . . may be

suspicion, it was explained, namely, that he might cast off an unfaithful wife. But as a wife could not cast off an offending husband or get any redress, she should not desire to find proof of her suspicions. The inquisitive matron who attempted to pry into her mate's left-handed connections was held far more contemptible than her philandering husband, so long as he kept his amours private. This attitude is illustrated in a little play in *The Lady's Magazine,* a summary of which follows. *Honoria,* wife of *Morosus,* informed by a friend of her husband's intrigue, laid a plot to detect him with his mistress at their rendezvous, the house of a celebrated milliner. She surprised the lovers at breakfast by rushing into the apartment adjoining their bedchamber, and this dialogue ensued:

Morosus (in confusion) Honoria, Madam, what brings you here?

Honoria That is a question which ought to be put to you. — I came in pursuit of an ungrateful, too much beloved husband; — you to indulge a lawless flame for an abandoned prostitute.

Morosus Madam, — Madam, this does not become you.

Honoria Does it become you, sir, to leave your honest home and wife, — make pitiful excuses for your absence, and skulk in corners with a wretch like this, — this abject hireling of licentious wishes. . . . (Starting toward the mistress).

Morosus Hold, Madam, hold — this Lady has put herself under my protection, and I will take care to defend her from all insults whatever. (Turning to Honoria) As for you, Madam — you have only exposed me and undone yourself; — I will never see you more.

Then taking his "trembling mistress" by the hand, he led her down the stairs, while *Honoria* followed, catching hold of his arm, and

---

carried on by the men without contaminating the mind, so as to render them unworthy of the marriage bed, and incapable of discharging the virtuous and honorable duties of husband, father, friend. . . . [But] the contamination of the female mind is the necessary and inseparable consequence of an illicit intercourse with men . . . women are universally virtuous, or utterly undone." The most common argument for a double standard, however, was that of Dr. Johnson: "Confusion of progeny constitutes the essence of the crime; and therefore a woman who breaks her marriage vows is much more criminal than a man who does it. A man, to be sure, is criminal in the sight of God: but he does not do his wife a very material injury, if he does not insult her; if, for instance, from mere wantonness of appetite, he steals privately to her chambermaid. Sir, a wife ought not greatly to resent this. I would not receive home a daughter who had run away from her husband on that account. A wife should study to reclaim her husband by more attention to please him."—James Boswell, *Life of Samuel Johnson* (text of 3rd ed., printed in 1927), I, 372. See also II, 205.

begging him to let the woman go. But throwing his wife aside "with
the utmost contempt," he was out of the house and gone. Next day
Honoria received a letter saying he would never return. "In fine,
an eternal disunion must be the consequence of your behaviour," he
wrote, "nor should the tongues of the angels dissuade me from this
resolution;—you will do well to bear it with patience, as the misfortune . . . which has happened entirely through your own fault."
Honoria begged forgiveness, pleading with him to remember their
seven years of happy married life and their children. But he continued determined upon a separation, reminding her thus of the in-
excusability of her crime: "During the whole course of the years we
lived together, you never had the least shadow of a cause to complain of my want either of respect or tenderness. If I indulged any
pleasures, which I imagined would give you disquiet, I took care to
be very private in them;—Why then did you suffer yourself to be
led by an idle curiosity to pry into secrets, which the discovery of
must give you pain. . . ?" So, poor *Honoria*, finding her husband
inflexible, retired into the country, where she lived "a melancholy
example of the ill effects of the officiousness of female friendship and
female jealousy."[40]

In the colonies as in the Mother Country, a gentleman's illicit
affairs did not prevent his moving in the best society. A South
Carolina journalist, lamenting the tendency of parents to accept as
proper matches for their daughters men of notorious profligacy, declared that unless a young fellow had killed his man and debauched
his woman, he was considered "a spiritless, ignorant milksop."[41]
Another correspondent wrote that even "professed Friends to Religion and Virtue" did not hesitate to "make Choice of an abandon'd
Fellow, who has been often over-run with a polite Disorder, debauched two or three innocent Virgins or kept half a dozen Negro
Wenches in the Face of the Sun."[42]

Men prominent in the history of the colonies were guilty of
flagrant immoralities. Thomas, second Lord Culpepper, a conspicuous figure in Virginia affairs, offended even the lax standards of
his day by his outrageous conduct,[43] and the records of the Calvert

---

[40] *The Lady's Magazine*, September, 1771.

[41] *South Carolina and American General Gazette*, April 8, 1768.

[42] *South Carolina Gazette*, January 26, 1738.

[43] Leaving his wife, who had brought him a large fortune, and his daughter, he
spent most of his revenue upon Susanna Willis, a mistress with whom he lived openly

family, the proprietors of Maryland, disclose shocking indecencies—liaisons, illegitimate children, debauchery, and even rape.[44] Colonel Daniel Parke, an outstanding personage in Virginia, was famed for his amorous intrigues as well as his gallantry in war.[45] In Georgia it was reported that General Oglethorpe was living openly with a pretty married woman of bad reputation, and that several office-holders had left their wives for mistresses.[46] Governor Johnston of North Carolina was known to have two natural children,[47] and Henry E. McCulloch, member of the council, kept a mistress by whom he had a son and about whom he wrote quite shamelessly to his young nephew, James Iredell.[48] Cornelius Harnett, Robert Halton, Francis Nash, and Matthew Rowan, all prominent North Carolina gentlemen, acknowledged illegitimate children.[49] A South Carolina law limiting the amount of his estate a husband and father of lawful children might leave to his mistress and bastards indicates that these extra-marital unions were not uncommon in that colony.[50]

Freedom in sex relations was not just a fashionable vice of the well-to-do, but was also found among other classes. Disagreement as to who was entitled to perform the marriage ceremony, the lack

for many years and by whom he had two daughters. Some months before his death, he settled his estate upon these natural daughters and later by his will confirmed the settlement, leaving the lands acquired with his wife's fortune charged with his debts, a large part of which was contracted for rich household furnishings, plate, and jewels for Susanna.—*Virginia Magazine*, XXXIII, 250-53, 261-62, 266.

[44] Benedict Leonard Calvert, who died in 1715 the fourth Lord Baltimore, not only kept as mistress a Mrs. Grove, but treated his wife with barbarous cruelty. Charles, fifth Lord Baltimore, kept the same Mrs. Grove.—*Maryland Magazine*, X, 372-73. Benedict Calvert of Annapolis, whose daughter Eleanor married Jackie Custis, George Washington's stepson, was the illegitimate son of this Lord Baltimore, who recognized him as his son, bestowed lands upon him, and made him a member of the Maryland Council.—Moore, *op. cit.*, pp. 93-94. The colonial newspapers for the year 1768 carried shocking accounts of the atrocious conduct of Frederick, sixth Lord Baltimore, who carefully planned and executed a rape upon a young girl of recognized reputation. Dying without legitimate children in 1771, this last Lord Baltimore made his natural son proprietor of Maryland, giving a reversion to the boy's sister and giving legacies to his own sisters on condition that they assent to the will.—*Letters to Washington* (ed., Hamilton), IV, 113-16; Thomas W. Griffith, *Sketches of the Early History of Maryland* (Baltimore, 1821), p. 63.

[45] Moore, *op. cit.*, pp. 61, 62, 67-68; G. W. P. Custis, *op. cit.*, p. 26; *Writings of William Byrd* (ed., Bassett), pp. l-li.

[46] *Colonial Records of Georgia*, IV, 344-45, 482, 499; V, 344, 399, 573.

[47] [Janet Schaw], *Journal*, Appendix, p. 293.

[48] McRee, *Iredell*, I, 42, 43, 51.   [49] [Janet Schaw], *Journal*, p. 173.

[50] *Digest of the Laws of South Carolina* (ed., James), p. 66.

of churches in which banns could be published, and often the long distances to be traveled to reach a minister or justice, as well as the excessive freedom of frontier society and the presence of servile women, encouraged the formation of loose unions. Brickell wrote that the "generality" of the Carolinians lived "after a loose and lascivious Manner."[51] An Anglican missionary declared that in North Carolina polygamy was very common, bastardy no disrepute, and concubinage general.[52] A similar situation was described in a complaint before the South Carolina Assembly in 1767 by a group of inhabitants of the upper part of the province. Through the want of churches and ministers, they declared, many persons had been married by itinerant preachers of various denominations, and supposing these unions only temporary had separated and formed new ones whenever they desired, ". . . Swapping away their Wives and Children, as they would Horses or Cattle."[53]

More evidence of lax morality is found in court records, which abound with grand jury presentments of both men and women for adultery and with bastardy cases. These offenders were usually not persons of high social standing, but those without sufficient pride or wealth to make private compensation for their lapses. The justices, who were concerned more with saving the community from charges of dependent mothers and children than with the suppression of immorality, apparently did not trouble themselves with apprehending and punishing the person who voluntarily undertook the responsibility of providing for his reputed child and its mother.[54]

A form of immorality often noted by visitors was the cohabitation of white men with women of colored races. All the southern colonies found it necessary to pass laws against intermarriage or cohabitation between the whites and blacks, and many men and a number of women were brought into court for forming such unnatural unions. These offenders were often servants and almost always of the lowest class. The paternity of a mulatto child was probably not inquired into if there were no danger of his becoming a charge on the community. But though seldom indicted for such crimes, the well-to-do appear to have been partly responsible for the widespread admixture

[51] *Natural History of Carolina*, pp. 36-37.

[52] *Colonial Records of North Carolina*, VII, 288. See also, I, 767.

[53] Fulham MS. North Carolina, South Carolina, Georgia, No. 72. A copy of the petition is given in Harvey Tolivar Cook, *Rambles in the Pee Dee Basin*, pp. 203-5.   [54] See below, Chap. XV.

of races. An early Virginia annalist tells of a member of the House of Burgesses in 1676, "a Parson not meanly acquainted with . . . learning," who enjoyed the "darke imbraces of a Blackamoore, his slave."[55] Brickell found a venereal disorder common among the Carolinians, who, he asserted, got it by cohabitation with their Negro servants.[56] Janet Schaw declared that the planters often "honour their black wenches with their attention," chiefly, she believed, to increase the number of their slaves.[57] Josiah Quincy wrote: "The enjoyment of a negro or mulatto woman is spoken of as quite a common thing: no reluctance, delicacy or shame is made about the matter. It is far from being uncommon to see a gentleman at dinner, and his reputed offspring a slave to the master of the table. I myself saw two instances of this, and the company very facetiously would trace the lines, lineaments and features of the father and mother in the child, and very accurately point out the more characteristick resemblance. The fathers neither of them blushed or seem[ed] disconcerted. They were called men of worth, politeness and humanity."[58] To what extent these unions between masters and their female servants were formed is not known, but the many mulattoes mentioned in newspapers and other records indicate that, despite the stringent laws against miscegenation, there was considerable intercourse between Negroes and whites.

Though Indian women, who did not live in such proximity to the whites, were less tempting generally than the Negroes, they were commonly kept as concubines by visitors in the Indian territory. Some white traders remained constant to their temporary wives for several years and helped rear their half-breed offspring, but they usually left these children with their Indian mothers when they returned to their white families. Itinerants formed more transient connections, leaving a half-breed progeny strewn all through the Indian territories. One South Carolinian boasted that he had upwards of seventy children and grandchildren among the Indians.[59] Lawson wrote that traders ordinarily took Indian wives, "whereby they soon learn the Indian tongue, keep a friendship with the savages; and,

---

[55] "A Narrative of the Indian and Civil Wars in Virginia," *Force Tracts*, I (No. 11), 46.
[56] *Op. cit.*, p. 48.   [57] *Journal*, p. 154.
[58] *Journal*, p. 464. For similar reports, see Anburey, *Travels*, II, 386; Davis, *Travels*, pp. 56, 250, 400, 414; Bernard, *Retrospections of America*, p. 147.
[59] Arthur Wallace Calhoun, *Social History of the American Family*, I, 325.

besides the satisfaction [of] a she bed fellow, they find these Indian girls very serviceable to them, on account of dressing their victuals and instructing them in the affairs and customs of the country."[60] Other journalists observed that it was customary for Indians to offer strangers their young women as bedfellows for the night, which hospitality the white guests apparently had few scruples about accepting.[61]   Nicholas Cresswell found it not merely convenient but necessary to take an Indian wife, and wrote quite frankly of his own and other alliances of the kind.[62]

Colonial newspapers furnish abundant evidence of marital friction.   Suspicion, anger, and distrust appear in numerous advertisements of their wives by husbands, and in announcements of voluntary separations.   In many notices the subscriber stated merely that he would not be responsible for his wife's debts, but in numerous others he sought to justify himself and condemn her publicly.   Usually he declared she had been so imprudent as to contract debts without his knowledge, had run him unnecessarily into debt, or threatened to ruin him by her debts.   Charges besides extravagance were made. George Jones justified posting his wife on the grounds that he and she could not agree in the management of their affairs.[63]   John Brown declared that as his Catharine had "behaved in a very imprudent manner," he felt "justifiable in advertising her to the world as an unworthy person."[64]   One wife was discredited for behaving "unseemly" to her husband; another for being "highly undutiful and disaffectionate"; and another for being "fond of other men's company."[65]   Mary Face refused to "cohabit as a wife"; Martha Beasley

[60] Op. cit., p. 301.   For similar accounts see Brickell, op. cit., pp. 294-301; Smyth, Tour, pp. 190-91; William Bartram, Travels, pp. 194-95, 449; Benjamin Hawkins, Letters, pp. 18-21, 35-36, 39-40, 44, 45, 47, 54, 56, 57, 83-85, 188, 252, 253, 430.

[61] Writings of William Byrd (ed., Bassett), pp. 96-97; Cresswell, Journal, pp. 105-6.

[62] Ibid., pp. 107-8, 109-10, 113-14, 115-17, 121, 122.   Byrd attributed the war of the Indians upon the Carolinians in 1713 largely to the abuse of the Indian women by white traders.—Op. cit., pp. 239-40.   The Reverend Peter Fontaine declared that many of the colonists' Indian troubles were due to the mistreatment of their Indian concubines by white traders.—Ann Maury, Memoirs of a Huguenot Family, pp. 349-51.

[63] Virginia Gazette, January 30, 1772.

[64] Maryland Journal and Baltimore Advertiser, November 2, 1779.

[65] Virginia Gazette, July 26, 1770; ibid., March 28, 1771; Maryland Journal and Baltimore Advertiser, September 10, 1782.

went about "scandalizing her husband"; and Delphia Coldwell was a "naughty furious Housewife."[66]

Several husbands renounced their wives in the press. Seth Yeomans advertised "ANNE YEOMANS, who says she is my wife, but with whom I do not cohabit." James Conaway stated that Margaret who went by his name and pretended to be his wife was only his "bought Servant." Another notice declared: "Penelope, who stiles herself the wife of the subscriber . . . hath behaved so indiscreet, that he cannot live with her."[67] These public repudiations usually went unchallenged, but Mary McLaughlin answered her husband's denial of her at once, declaring: "His assertion is false; and altho' I do not think he is worthy the name of husband, yet he is certainly mine; as may be seen by the Registry Book of St. Anne's Parish."[68]

In many notices the subscriber stated that his wife had "eloped from his bed and board," "clandestinely left his home," or "voluntarily separated herself from him." To those believing that marital disunion was a rare occurrence in colonial days, the large number of such advertisements is astonishing. Inserted between notices of stray horses and fugitive slaves, they are almost as numerous as advertisements of runaway servants. The ostensible purpose of the husband was to protect himself from debts with which his absconding wife might charge him, but actually in many cases his evident motive was to vent his exasperation, elicit public sympathy, and wreak vengeance upon his offending spouse.

Besides warning the public against crediting his wife, the deserted husband often cautioned all persons against "harbouring or entertaining" her, threatening that they would do so "at their peril" or "on Pain of incurring the utmost Rigour of the Law." Many also forbade masters of vessels from carrying off the fugitive, and several offered a reward for information of her whereabouts. Like the runaway servant, an eloping wife was sometimes described for identification as in the following notice:

Whereas my wife Mary Oxendine, hath eloped from me, this is to forewarn all persons from Harbouring or entertaining her, day or night,

[66] *Virginia Gazette*, March 22, 1770; *ibid.*, August 24, 1751; *ibid.*, January 21, 1775.

[67] *Dunlap's Maryland Gazette; or the Baltimore General Advertiser*, February 20, 1776; *Maryland Gazette*, August 15, 1765; *Maryland Journal*, August 2, 1775.

[68] *Maryland Gazette*, July 13, 1748.

or crediting her in my name, as I am determined not to pay any debts by her contracted. All masters of vessels or others, are hereby cautioned against carrying her off the province, as they may expect to be prosecuted with the utmost severity.– She is of fair complexion, with light colour'd hair, and has a mark over one of her eyes.[69]

One subscriber advertised his fugitive wife as "a short, thick Woman, of dark Complexion, with black Hair, black Eyes, aged about fifty Years, and has lost one of her fore Teeth."[70]

The subscriber frequently stated that his departing wife had carried off "sundry of his effects," mentioning such valuables as slaves, horses, household furniture, silver plate, his own and her apparel. Elizabeth Sully was advertised as having taken with her eight hundred pounds worth of money, plate, and rings.[71] Elizabeth Homewood took ten pounds in cash, a new shirt, four silver spoons, a new calico counterpane, new sheets, and some china.[72] Anne Campbell "robbed" her husband of "all her Wearing Apparel, a fine Pair of English Cotton Curtains, a Chintz Counterpane . . . two Pillow Cases, three Diaper Napkins, a large Diaper Table-Cloth . . . and a Side Saddle."[73]

Subscribers to these advertisements apparently felt no indecency in thus exposing their matrimonial partners. Other husbands published the infidelity of their mates in scandalous notices like the following:

CATHERINE TREEN, the wife of the subscriber, having, in violation of her solemn vow, behaved herself in the most disgraceful manner, by leaving her own place of abode, and living in a criminal state with a certain *William Collins*, a plaisterer, under whose bed she was last night, discovered, endeavoring to conceal herself, her much injured husband, therefore, in justice to himself, thinks it absolutely necessary to forewarn all persons from trusting her on his account, being determined, after such flagrant proof of her prostitution, to pay no debts of her contracting.[74]

One announced shamelessly that his bosom companion had brought into his family "an adulterous Child,"[75] and others accused their wives of improper relations with Negro men.[76]

[69] *South Carolina Gazette*, May 25, 1765.
[70] *Virginia Gazette*, October 31, 1751.
[71] *South Carolina Gazette*, January 3, 1743.
[72] *Maryland Gazette*, February 2, 1758.   [73] *Ibid.*, March 16, 1758.
[74] *Maryland Journal*, January 20, 1774.
[75] *Maryland Gazette*, March 29, 1759.
[76] Henry Pratt, *Maryland Gazette*, April 22, 1773, and Walter Skinner, *ibid.*, October 12, 1769.

A number of wives eloped with other men, probably for practical as well as romantic reasons. Elizabeth Sellman went away with William Freeman, taking many of her husband's clothes.[77]   Mary, wife of Robert Taylor, set out with a man named Cuttings, intending to go to England for some money which she had just inherited.[78] Susanna, wife of Robert Grier, was supposed to have been accompanied in her flight by a former convict who had been freed and entertained by her husband.   She took with her her fourteen-year-old son, two Negro children, some silver spoons, chinaware, and other household furniture.   Her companion, described as a person with good education, fluent in conversation, and "as genteel in person as insinuating in address," took a horse and valuable books. The husband offered ten pounds reward for their apprehension.[79]

Robert Grier was apparently a man of some means and cultural interests.   A few other husbands who advertised their wives appear to have been well-to-do, but a majority were probably of the poorer classes.   Those whose professions were given were planters, merchants, apothecaries, silversmiths, overseers, barbers, butchers, tailors, bricklayers, and marines.   Quite a number were apparently fathers of grown sons, as they signed their names with a "Sen."   Several runaway wives, like Sarah Page, mentioned in her husband's advertisement as "late Sarah Eden,"[80] were evidently brides.

The advertisements as a rule give no clue to the reasons for the wife's leaving home.   The husband sometimes stated that she had gone "without any lawful reason," "without any just cause," or "without any Fault in me."   John M'Adooe's Anne had eloped "after the most tender treatment of upwards of twenty years."[81]   Prudence Cockney was advertised as having deserted her family upon the advice of her friends.[82]   Isaac Simmons' Mary left to work in the playhouse at Charles Town.[83]   Mark Edwards suspected his Margaret had been "seduced by bad company,"[84] and William Wheat's Amy was supposed to be "disorder'd in her mind."[85]

Occasionally a high-spirited wife published her grievances in answer to her husband's advertisement, as in the following statement by Sarah Cantwell:

[77] *Ibid.*, September 5, 1750.
[78] *Virginia Gazette*, July 6, 1769.
[79] *Ibid.*, December 14, 1769.
[80] *South Carolina Gazette*, May 9, 1768.
[81] *Virginia Gazette*, June 21, 1770.
[82] *Maryland Journal*, October 26, 1774.
[83] *South Carolina Gazette*, February 5, 1737.
[84] *Virginia Gazette*, April 27, 1769.
[85] *Maryland Gazette*, April 3, 1755.

John Cantwell has the impudence to advertise me in the Papers, cautioning all Persons against crediting me; he never had any Credit till he married me: As for his Bed and Board mention'd, he had neither Bed nor Board when he married me; I never eloped, I went away before his Face when he beat me.[86]

Margaret Franks gave the public this "true state" of her "supposed elopement" from her husband: "My now being absent from him was occasioned by his most cruel and inhuman Treatment to me, . . . by his severe Threats, Blows, and turning me out of Doors, in the Dead of Night, leaving me, and a poor helpless infant, whom I had by a former Husband, naked, and exposed to the inclemency of the Weather."[87]   Mary Myers explained that her husband had driven her away by "inhumanity and preferring an old negro wench for a bedfellow."[88]   Elizabeth Moore's husband had "publickly said his Mother would sooner live in a hollow Tree" than with her, and had himself removed her to her father's house and left her there.[89]

The subsequent history of these absconding wives is not known. Many probably continued to live separate from their husbands, supporting themselves by whatever employment they could find.   Those less capable possibly made their homes with relatives.   Others, by court order or voluntary agreement with their husbands, secured separate maintenance.   Many dissatisfied wives, after a rest from the monotony of domesticity and a bit of adventure, probably returned home and were welcomed with open arms.   Running away seems to have been Susanna Starr's means of getting vacations, for a postscript to her husband's advertisement stated that this was her fourth elopement.[90]   Edward Day's Anne absconded in 1757, evidently returned, and ten years later eloped again.[91]   Sometimes the husband in his newspaper notice requested his truant mate to return, promising she would be kindly received and supported according to his ability.   Samuel Gaither publicly apologized for posting his "beloved Anne," revoked his order against giving her credit, and explained that "all Contentions and Misunderstandings" between them were at at end.[92]   John Baker, Charles Town merchant, tried a more lordly

[86] *South Carolina and American General Gazette,* March 27, 1776.

[87] *South Carolina Gazette,* July 12, 1770.

[88] *Ibid.,* November 14, 1768.

[89] *Virginia Gazette,* May 9, 1771.

[90] *Maryland Gazette,* January 29, 1756.

[91] *Ibid.,* July 7, 1757; August 20, 1767.

[92] *Ibid.,* March 31, 1757.

method, commanding his Unice-Mary to return at once to his habitation.[93]

In a number of advertisements the husband stated that as he and his wife had separated by mutual consent and he had agreed to allow her separate maintenance, he would no longer be responsible for her debts. Thomas Barkley notified the Maryland public that he and his wife Isabella had agreed to live apart and that, as she had in her possession free from his intermeddling, her own and her children's share in her former husband's estate, he would not be responsible for her debts.[94] Articles of separation like the following were also published:

COLEMAN THEEDS and ELIZABETH, his Wife, having this Day parted by mutual Consent, and given Bond each to the other, the Subscribers being Witnesses to their Agreement, that they will not interfere with any Estate which shall hereafter accrue to either Party, this Notice is given to the Gazette, that no Person, after this Date, may credit the Wife on the Husband's Account, or the Husband upon that of the Wife's. Given under our Hands, this 12th Day of June, 1773.

RICHARD BEASLEY
JOHN JAMES[95]

A most extraordinary notice was a contract between Joseph and Mary M'Gehe signed by both and published in the [New Bern] *North Carolina Gazette*, April 7, 1775. Mary admitted having eloped with another man, by whom she was then with child, acknowledged her intention never to live with her husband again, and, in consideration of his having delivered to her "effects" to the value of one hundred and twenty pounds, covenanted never to claim further support from him. Joseph promised to allow her full and free use of these "effects," and agreed never to claim her as his wife, but to allow her to go wherever she chose. By these articles, they declared, they "solemnly agreed before God and the World, to be no longer Man and Wife, but for ever hereafter, be as if we had never been married." This agreement would probably not have been considered binding by the courts, but, according to reports of Anglican missionaries, such divorces were followed by remarriage and were not uncommon.[96]

Occasionally more serious domestic tragedies appeared in the

[93] *South Carolina Gazette*, May 27, 1766.
[94] *Maryland Gazette*, April 7, 1747.   [95] *Virginia Gazette*, February 10, 1774.
[96] *Colonial Records of North Carolina*, I, 767; VII, 288.

press. The *South Carolina Gazette* in 1736 published news of a husband, who, having been imprisoned for refusing maintenance to his estranged wife, shot himself and died instantly, and later reported the case of another, who, "living unhappy with his wife," committed suicide.[97]   In 1751 John Steadman, fifty-four years old, was executed for the murder of his wife, who was found dead in bed with bruises on her body and the marks of a man's fingers on her throat.[98]   Two years later, John Barret acknowledged the barbarous murder of his wife, and the death of a prominent gentlewoman, Mrs. Alethia Cook, was laid to her husband, a clergyman, whose "horrid Usage and un-paralell'd Barbarity" was, according to the report, "such as Decency forbids us to relate."[99]   Another husband, maddened by jealousy, shot his wife as she lay asleep in bed.[100]   John Frentz, a Georgia barber, some time after his wife's elopement, went to the house where she was lodged, asked her to make up their differences and go home with him, and upon her refusal shot her, killing her instantly. He was apprehended by neighbors, tried, and executed.[101]

Court records, like newspapers, reveal a surprisingly large amount of general domestic dissatisfaction.[102]   While the husband usually proclaimed his grievance in the press, the wife was oftener the complainant in court.   There was no tribunal in the South empowered to grant absolute divorces, but courts frequently heard cases of domestic trouble, sometimes ordering a separate maintenance for the wife, but oftener merely requiring the husband to give bond for good behavior to her.   Charges usually brought were cruelty, desertion, and nonsupport, probably because these were offences for which justices were most ready to grant a remedy.   Many pages of court minutes are filled with altercations, scandalous accusations and recriminations, and patched-up agreements between husbands and wives, which indicate a state of matrimony somewhat out of keeping with the ideals set up by domestic conduct books and other guides to conjugal felicity.

[97] May 29, 1736; *ibid.*, January 1, 1737.
[98] *Maryland Gazette*, April 17, 1751.
[99] *Ibid.*, November 8, 15, December 6, 1753; *ibid.*, February 1, April 26, 1753.
[100] *Ibid.*, August 20, 1759.
[101] *Georgia Gazette*, August 5, July 20, 1768; January 11, 1769.
[102] For court action in matrimonial cases, see below, Chap. XVI.

CHAPTER IX

THE SCHOOLING OF GIRLS

BRUCE, WRITING of Virginia in the seventeenth century, declares that while the plantation system made impractical the establishment of a public school system similar to that in New England, it did not prevent the establishment of schools by the voluntary action of individuals or small groups. In addition to the many little schools taught by private tutors in the homes of the wealthier planters, there were what later came to be called "Old Field Schools," established at some place convenient to every boy and girl in the neighborhood, and occasional free schools resting on private foundations. Concrete evidence of the interest in education appears in numerous instances in deeds and wills in which parents took care to provide for the tuition of their children, as well as in the efforts made by county justices to secure the education of orphans bound out under articles of indenture or placed in the care of guardians.[1]

Records of seventeenth-century Virginia show that the schooling of girls, though usually more limited than that of boys, was not entirely neglected. While parents were ordinarily more careful to provide in their last testaments for sons, they sometimes left orders for the tuition of daughters also. In 1657 Clement Thrash directed that his entire estate be responsible for the schooling of his thirteen-year-old stepdaughter for three years, the instruction to be given by a Mrs. Peacock, probably the mistress of a small neighborhood school. Sarah Pigot made her whole estate liable for her granddaughter's tuition; Nicholas Granger set aside a definite number of cattle to provide for the expenses of his daughter's tuition, and Francis Page directed his executor to give his daughter "the best education which this country could afford."[2] John Russell provided that his daughter's education continue "so long as she keeps herself without a husband."[3]

Laws governing the management of orphans' estates and the

[1] *Institutional History*, I, 293-361.   [2] *Ibid.*, pp. 209, 297, 304, 305.
[3] *William and Mary Quarterly*, III, 154.

binding out of poor children required guardians and masters to provide girls under their care, as well as boys, with the rudiments of learning. The York County Court in 1668 directed the guardian of Dorothy Tucker to spend for her maintenance and tuition an amount in due proportion to the value of her estate; and ten years later the stepfather and guardian of Elizabeth Longe, who had probably been brought into court for neglecting her education, promised the justices of Northampton to send her to school the next two years.[4] Indentures of apprentices usually stated that the boys be taught some trade while the girls were to be instructed in housewifery, and both were to be taught at least to read.[5]

To what extent girls shared in the other educational facilities of the colony is not known. It is not clear whether they were admitted to the Syms, Eaton, and similar free schools, but they probably attended the "parsons' schools," and records show that daughters of prosperous planters were sometimes taught by private tutors and neighborhood schoolmasters. An agreement between Richard Burkland and Richard Kellam, for instance, states that Kellam was to give Burkland's daughter lessons in reading, writing, and casting accounts and board her, and a similar arrangement was made between the father of Martha Willett and Mary Coar, who agreed to teach Martha for a term of one year for one thousand pounds of tobacco.[6]

A few girls were sent home to the Mother Country for their education. Peter Hopegood provided in his will that his daughter remain at school in Virginia until 1680, when she was to be taken to

[4] Bruce, *Institutional History*, pp. 309, 310.

[5] Upon the petition of Charles Edwards that Grace Griswold, an orphan, might live with him until she was eighteen years old or married, the court ordered him to "oblige himself" to maintain her decently and see that she be taught to read, sew, spin, and knit. Robert Mangon and his wife, to whom Rebecca Francis was apprenticed, were directed to furnish her with sufficient clothing and take care that she "be virtuously brought up" and given "a Compleat yeares schooling, to be Educated in Reading ye vulgar tongue." Ann Chandler, an orphan bound to Philemon Miller, was to be taught "to read a chapter in the Bible, ye Lord's prayer, and ten commandments, and semptress work."—Lyon G. Tyler, "Education in Virginia," *William and Mary Quarterly*, V, 219-22. The indentures of Anne Matthewes required her master to see that she be taught not only to sew and "such things as were fitt for women to know" but also to read, and, apparently to write.—Bruce, *op. cit.*, p. 311. The master of Elizabeth Perry was ordered to have her taught "to reade distinctly in the Bible, and to sowe, soe as Shee may be capable to make all her wearing Linnen."—MS, Northumberland County Record, 1652-1665, Bk. I, p. 94.   [6] Bruce, *Institutional History*, p. 326.

England and there continue her education under the guardianship of an uncle.[7] Susan and Ursula, daughters of William Byrd, were sent to school at Hackney in England. Susan and a son Will were already in England when in 1685 Byrd wrote his father-in-law regarding his younger daughter: "My wife hath all this year urged me to send little Nutty [Ursula] home to you, to which I have at last condescended, & hope you'll be pleased to excuse the trouble. I must confess she could learne nothing good here in a great family of Negroes. She comes in the Ship Culpepper where the master promised she shall want nothing that's necessary for her. I write to Mr. North & Mr. Coe [his English agents] to supply her with what necessary's she wants. I pray God send her safe to you."[8]

Although a few daughters of the favored classes were educated abroad and others were taught in private or neighborhood schools, and though justices were strict in requiring orphans and apprentices to be given some instruction, a large majority of seventeenth-century women in Virginia were totally illiterate, and those who had any schooling were generally taught only the most elementary subjects. Many belonging to prominent families were unable to write their names. Many men also could not read and write, but, according to Bruce, illiteracy prevailed to a much greater extent among women than men. His tables illustrating the extent of literacy among the whole population of the colony show that only one woman of every three was able to sign her name, as compared with at least three of every five men.[9]

The women in the other southern colonies were no better educated. In Maryland before 1700, religious differences, which brought about frequent disagreement and often led to disturbances,

[7] *Ibid.*, p. 320.

[8] As she was not quite seventeen when she died thirteen years later in 1698, Ursula must have been only four years old when she went to England. After she and Susan had completed their education, because of the war between England and France, Byrd felt it unsafe for them to risk capture on a voyage, and kept them in England in charge of a brother-in-law. Upon his complaint, however, regarding his nieces, Byrd had them removed and wrote his agent in London to "put out the Girls for their most advantage without any unnecessary charge." Where they then lived is not known. As Susan married John Brayne of London, she probably did not return to Virginia. Ursula returned, married Robert Beverley, the historian, and died in 1698, leaving one son.—*Writings of William Byrd* (ed., Bassett), Preface, pp. xxxii-xxxiv, xlii-xliii.

[9] Bruce, *Institutional History*, pp. 454-57.

checked the setting up of parsonage schools, and the isolation of plantations discouraged popular education.[10]   Except the unsuccessful attempt to found free schools, few references are found to education of any kind.[11]   In Carolina several fathers provided in their wills for the tuition of daughters, but no record appears of any school or professional schoolmaster there before 1700.[12]

After the colonies were better established, schoolmasters became more numerous, and new and different kinds of schools were founded. The most effective interest manifested in the education of the poor appeared in the apprenticeship regulations.   Virginia's custom of in- sisting that the apprentice be given the rudiments of learning along with vocational training continued throughout the next century. Many justices demanded that girl apprentices be taught only to "reade the Bible thoroughly."   Others required instruction in house- hold occupations as well as reading.   A court of Northumberland County ordered that Ann Walker be given "A Christian education" and taught reading, sewing, spinning, and "such like womanish im- ployments," that Eliza Tignor be taught "to read the Bible per- fectly" and educated "in Christian duties as well as household employments," and that Rebecca Husk be taught "to read the Byble thoroughly to sow & doo other suitable & necessary household im- ployment & Christian education."[13]   A similar order by a Lancaster County court required the master of Mary Collins to "cause her to be taught to reade the Bible well and . . . to be learned such house- wifely exercises as may tend to her future advantage."[14]   The dis- tinction usually made between girls and boys appears in the inden- tures of Susanna and Isaac Atkins, which stated that she was to be

[10] Governor Charles Calvert wrote the proprietor in 1673 regarding a school- master he had sent to Maryland: "I entertaine [him] at my owne house, and Employ him to teach my Children and shall give him all Encouragement that lyes in my power, shall Endeavour the promoting of a schoole here, . . . but doubt he will not finde the people here so desirous of that benefit of Educating their Children in that nature as he might p[rob]ably Expect, for the Remoteness of the habitations of one p[er]son from another, wilbe a greate obstacle to a schoole. . . ."—"Calvert Papers," Maryland Historical Society, *Fund Publication*, No. 28, p. 286.

[11] Records for Kent County and Kent Island, 1656-1662, show a much higher percentage of illiteracy among women than men.—*Maryland Magazine*, VIII, 7.

[12] *South Carolina Magazine*, XII, 147-48, 150-51.

[13] MS, Northumberland County Order Book, No. 4A (1699-1713), Pt. II, p. 763; Book No. 5 (1713-1719), p. 184; Book No. 4A, Pt. II, p. 837.   Many orders required the apprentice to be taught to read, sew, knit, and spin.—*Ibid.*, Book No. 6 (1720-1729), pp. 296, 333; Book No. 7, pp. 223, 224, 233.

[14] *William and Mary Quarterly*, VIII, 82.

taught "to read the Bible thoroughly Sew and household work" and that he should be taught "to Read write & cypher as far as the Rule of Three & the Trade of a Carpenter."[15]

The North Carolina law for apprentices was like that in Virginia,[16] but the provision regarding education appears not to have been so generally observed. Upon the petition of John Swain, praying that his sister, an orphan bound to John Worley, be taught to read by her master, a precinct court of Chowan ordered that the girl be taught to read.[17] A Pasquotank County court in April, 1752, when binding Ann Stewart, ordered that her master "learn her to read and write."[18] The justices of Craven County on March 20, 1740, ordered William Carlton, to whom a young girl had been bound, to "do his endeavour to teach her . . . to read the Bible," and later ordered an orphan girl to be taught to read and write.[19] Not all justices, however, were so strict. Those of Edgecombe County ordered girl apprentices taught only "the art and mystery of Carding and Spinning,"[20] and the Chatham Court required instruction merely in the "business of housewifery."[21] Maryland and South Carolina directed apprentices to be taught trades, but apparently did not require any schooling.[22] A Georgia law of 1799 ordered that apprentices be taught to read and write and "the usual rules of arithmetic,"[23] but it does not appear whether this custom was observed before the Revolution.

Besides the apprenticeship practices, other means of forwarding the training of poorer children were the founding of free schools and scholarships by private grants and legacies. Virginia had a number

[15] MS, Northumberland County Court Orders, Book No. 4A, Pt. II, p. 650.

[16] *Colonial Records of North Carolina*, XXIII, 581.

[17] *Ibid.*, II, 266.

[18] MS, Pasquotank County Court Minutes, April 14, 1752.

[19] MS, Craven County Apprenticeship Papers, 1748-1779. A Hyde County court, when binding out Elizabeth Anderson, fourteen years old, and Ann Rorork, twelve, ordered that they be taught to read and write.—MS, Hyde County Court Minutes, 1744-1760.

[20] Orders regarding Sally Gay, January, 1765; Sarah Dorman, April, 1765; Aidwith Allen, July, 1765; Lucretia Johnson, 1767. MS, Edgecombe County Court Minutes, 1764-1772.

[21] Orders regarding Mary Drake, May, 1774; Sarah Wood, August, 1774; Ann White, February, 1775; Mary Griffin, May, 1775. MS, Chatham County Court Minutes, 1774-1779.

[22] Edgar Wallace Knight, *Public Education in the South* (New York, 1922), p. 62.

[23] *Digest of the Laws of the State of Georgia* (ed., Prince), p. 161.

of such institutions besides those set up by Syms and Eaton in the preceding century,[24] and South Carolina had several free schools and a number of scholarships founded by philanthropic societies. Girls probably did not share in all these charitable undertakings, but the South Carolina Society, established about 1737, paid the salary of a schoolmistress and a schoolmaster for instructing children of both sexes. Girls were admitted between the ages of eight and twelve, while boys attended until they were fourteen.[25] The deed providing for the founding of a free school by Mary Smith at Smithfield, Virginia, stated that the boys were to attend for three years and were to be taught reading, writing, and arithmetic; girls were to be taught only reading and writing and for a shorter term of two years.[26]

In Maryland several attempts were made to found free schools, but although in 1701 one was opened in Annapolis and in 1723 an act was passed providing for one in each county, the rivalry between the residents of the eastern and western shores and between Protestants and Catholics, together with the general public indifference, rendered these efforts of little effect.[27] The records of the meetings of the visitors of the free school in Queen Anne's County, founded in 1724, give some idea of the meagre qualifications expected of teachers and the limited course of study in these institutions. The schoolmaster was to be a member of the Church of England, of "pious and exemplary life," and "capable of teaching well the grammar, good writing and the mathematics," if such a person could "conveniently be got." He was paid twenty pounds current money for teaching ten pupils chosen by the visitors and was permitted to teach other children whose parents paid him for their tuition. Evidently this school was free only for a limited number of children designated by the visitors as "foundation scholars." Girls apparently were selected now and then, though the name of only one girl appears in the two surviving lists of foundation scholars.[28]

[24] Tyler, "Education in Colonial Virginia," *William and Mary Quarterly*, VI, 71-85.

[25] Edward McCrady, "Education in South Carolina Prior to and during the Revolution. A paper read before the Historical Society of South Carolina 6th of August, 1883."

[26] *William and Mary Quarterly*, VII, 266-67.

[27] Newton D. Mereness, *Maryland as a Proprietary Province* (New York and London, 1901), pp. 137-44.

[28] Edwin H. Brown, Jr., "First Free School in Queen Anne's County," *Maryland Magazine*, VI, 1-15.

In 1751 a scheme was advertised for erecting a "Charity-working School" in Talbot County, Maryland, where poor children of both sexes were to be fed, clothed, lodged, and taught. The children, "after being brought up in the Knowledge and Fear of GOD, and inured to useful Labour, as well as fitted for Business by their School-learning," were to be "put out to Apprenticeships or Service, as may best tend to the Good of the Public and Benefits of the Children."[29] Gifts for carrying out the design were later announced,[30] but it does not appear whether the plan was successful.

More opportunities for education at public expense seem to have been provided by Georgia than by the other southern colonies. The common council in 1743 provided for the opening of a school free to all children and the employment of a teacher at a salary of twenty pounds a year.[31] After the Crown took over the colony in 1752, it enjoyed the unusual advantage of having an item for the support of schools included in the annual budget of the House of Commons.[32] Philanthropic societies also aided in the education of the poor. The Union Society announced in the *Georgia Gazette*, November 9, 1768, that it would pay for the schooling of ten children and advertised for a person to undertake the tuition of these pupils. The following year the members of St. Andrew's Society notified the public that they had appropriated a part of their fund for the education of ten children and requested any person desirous of having his children educated on this bounty to make it known to the treasurer.[33]

The outstanding charitable institution in Georgia was the Orphan House at Bethesda, established by the Reverend George Whitefield for the care and education of orphan girls and boys. Whitefield's idea was to have these unfortunate children brought up piously and taught to labor so that they could make their own living.[34] A visitor in 1745-46 left this picture of the pupils: "They were at Dinner

[29] *Virginia Gazette*, July 25, 1751.

[30] *Ibid.*, October 24, 1751. See also *William and Mary Quarterly*, VII, 142-43; XII, 156-57.

[31] "Minutes of the Council, April 18, 1743," *Colonial Records of Georgia*, II, 408-17.

[32] Martha Gallaudet Waring, "Savannah's Earliest Private Schools, 1733 to 1800," *Georgia Historical Quarterly*, XIV, 324-34.

[33] *Georgia Gazette*, February 8, 1769.

[34] *A Continuation of the Reverend Mr. Whitefield's Journal after His Arrival at Georgia, 1741*, pp. 3-4. Before building the house at Bethesda, Whitefield opened a school for girls in Savannah and employed a woman to teach children how to spin.— Rev. George Whitefield, *Journal*, p. 5.

when we arrived, the whole Family at one Table, and sure never was a more orderly, pretty Sight: ... besides Mr. Barber, the schoolmaster, and some Women, there were near 40 young Persons of both Sexes, dress'd very neatly and decently. After Dinner they retir'd, the Boys to School, and the Girls to their Spinning and Knitting."[35] The following is a description by one of the inmates of the schedule regularly observed at the Orphan House:

They rise about five o'clock and each is seen to kneel down by himself for a Quarter of an Hour, to offer up their private Prayers from their own Hearts; during which Time they are often exhorted what to pray for, particularly that Jesus Christ would convert them, and change their Hearts.

At Six, all the Family goes to Church, where a Psalm is sung, and the second Lesson is expounded. ...

At our Return Home about Seven, we sing Bishop Ken's Morning Hymn; and whoever is President of the House, uses Family Prayer as the Spirit gives him Utterance, varying it according to the Circumstances we are in. ...

Between seven and eight we go to Breakfast in the same Room with the Children, who sometimes sing a Hymn before, sometimes after, and sometimes both before and after every Meal, as well as say Grace. During Breakfast the Business of the Day is talked of, and each appointed his Station, and perhaps some useful Questions are asked the Children, or Exhortations given them.

From eight to ten, the Children go to their respective Employs, as carding, spinning, picking Cotton or Wool, sewing, knitting. One serves the Apothecary who lives in the House, others serve in the Store or Kitchen; others clean the House, fetch Water, or cut Wood. Some are placed under the Taylor, who lives in the House; and we expect other Tradesmen, as a Shoemaker, Carpenter, etc. to which others are to be bound. As the Grace of God appears in any, together with suitable Abilities, they are to be bred to the Ministry. ...

At Ten they go to School, some to writing, some to reading. At present there are two Masters and one Mistress, who in teaching them to read the Scripture, at the same Time explain it to them. ...

At Noon we go to Dinner all in the same Room, and between that and two o'clock every one is employed in something useful, but no Time is allowed for Idleness or Play, which are Satan's darling Hours to tempt Children to all Manner of Wickedness. ... So that tho' we are about seventy in Family, yet we hear no more Noise than if it was a private House.

From Two till Four they go to School as in the Morning, and from four to Six Work in their respective Stations, as before mentioned.

At Six the Children go to Supper, when the Masters and Mistresses attend to help them, and sing with them, and watch over their Words and Actions.

At Seven the Family all goes to Church, where is a Psalm and Exposition after the second Lesson, as in the Morning Service. And at our Return about Eight, many of the Parishioners come in to hear Mr. Whitefield examine and instruct the Children by way of Question and answer. . . . His main Business is to ground the Children in their Belief of Original Sin, and to make them sensible of their damnable State by Nature, and the absolute Necessity of a Change to be wrought on their Souls by the Power of God, before they can be in a salvable State. . . . for this Purpose they are ordered to get by Heart our excellent Church Articles of Original Sin, of Free-Will, and of Justification.

At Nine o'clock we go to Supper, and the Children up to their Bed-room, where some Person commonly sings and prays again with them. . . .

On the Lord's Day we all dine on cold Meat, prepared the Day before because all may attend the Worship of God, which we have that Day four Times at Church, which fills up those Hours employed at Work on the other Days; and thus is our Time all laid out in the Service of God, the Variety of which is a sufficient Relaxation to a well-disposed Mind, and obviates those idle Pretences for what is called innocent (tho' in Reality damnable) Recreations.[36]

Instruction in reading—and sometimes writing—with training in sewing, spinning, and knitting, constituted the utmost of poor girls' education. Girls at the Orphan House and apprentices generally had greater advantages than the poor who lived with their parents, a majority of whom probably had no schooling whatever.

Daughters of the well-to-do were taught in their own homes by private tutors, attended little private schools in the neighborhood, or were sent to boarding schools in town. It was customary for a planter to employ a tutor for his own children and, in addition to furnishing him with board, lodging, and a schoolroom, and paying him a stipulated salary, to permit him to supplement his income by teaching other pupils. John Harrower, for example, engaged by

[36] "The Manner of the Children's Spending their Time at the Orphan House in Georgia. A Collection of Papers lately published in the Daily Advertiser."—Published with Whitefield's *Journal*.

Colonel William Daingerfield to teach his three children, went about the neighborhood teaching other children in the afternoons, evenings, and on Sundays.[37] Sometimes the tutor kept a regular school at the home of his employer, to which children in the neighborhood were sent back and forth every day. Colonel James Gordon of Lancaster County, Virginia, sent his daughter Judith to a little school at a neighbor's, where five children were taught by a Mr. Chiswell.[38] Children who lived too far to walk or ride were boarded as well as instructed in the home where the teacher lived.

These home schools were kept sometimes in a part of the "Great House," but often an outbuilding was used for a schoolroom and for sleeping quarters for the tutor and the boys of the family. Philip Fithian, tutor in the family of Councillor Robert Carter in Virginia, left an account of the little school at "Nomini," which was perhaps very much like many others in the colonies. There were eight pupils, two of Councillor Carter's sons, a nephew, and five daughters. Ben, the oldest and the only pupil expected to learn the classics, was reading Sallust and studying Latin and Greek Grammar. Priscilla, the oldest daughter, "just turned of fifteen," was reading *The Spectator* and studying addition, division, and multiplication. Nancy, the second daughter, was "reading out of a spelling book" and beginning *The Compleat Letter Writer;* Fanny and Betsy, next in age, were learning to read, and Harriott, the youngest, was beginning her letters. Fithian thus describes the regular winter routine: "In the morning so soon as it is light a Boy knocks at my Door to make a fire; . . . By the time I am drest the Children commonly enter the School-Room, which is under the Room I sleep in: I hear them round one lesson, when the Bell rings for eight o'clock . . . the Children then go out; and at half after eight the Bell rings for Breakfast . . . after Breakfast, which is generally about half after nine, we go into School, and sit til twelve, when the Bell rings and they go out for noon. . . . After dinner is o'er, which . . . when we have no Company is about half after three we go into School, and sit til the Bell rings at five, when they separate til the next morning."[39]

This was a very flexible program accommodating itself to various interruptions occasioned by company, visiting, music lessons, and

[37] "Diary of John Harrower, 1773-177 ," *American Historical Review,* VI, 96, 102-3, 106-7.
[38] "Journal of Col. James Gordon, of Lancaster County, Virginia," *William and Mary Quarterly,* XI, 100.   [39] *Journal,* pp. 295-96.

dancing school. Councillor Carter, a musician himself, stressed music in the education of his children. He had a music master attend regularly to instruct his daughters on the piano and harpsichord and taught them himself to play the guitar. He assigned them music lessons and allowed them to be absent from school every Tuesday and Thursday to practice. Dancing was also a very important part of education. Fithian notes frequently the fact that some of the children are away taking dancing lessons and gives one instance of the flogging of one of the boys for skipping dancing school.[40]

Occasional letters penned by little girls themselves throw light upon their education. The following is from eleven-year-old Betty Pratt of Virginia to her brother at school in England in 1732: "I find you have got the start of me in learning very much, for you write better already than I can expect to do as long as I live; and you are got as far as the Rule of three in Arithmetick, but I can't cast up a sum in addition cleverly, but I am striving to do better every day. I can perform a great many dances and am now learning the Sibell, but I cannot speak a word of French."[41] Accompanying this missive was one from Betty's grandmother declaring the little girl had made a pocket handkerchief very "prettily" and was then hemming a neck handkerchief. Maria Carter of "Sabine Hall" in Virginia, addressing her cousin Maria Carter of "Cleve" in 1756, explained that she was able to write nothing of "how the World goes on" because of her close confinement at school, and thus described her daily schedule: "I am awakened out of a sound Sleep with some croaking voice either Patty's, Milly's, or some other of our Domestics with Miss Polly Miss Polly get up, tis time to rise, Mr. Price is down Stairs, & tho' I hear them I lie quite snugg till my Grandmamma uses her Voice, then up I get, huddle on my cloaths & down to Book, then to Breakfast, then to School again, & may be I have an Hour to my self before Dinner, then the Same Story over again till twilight & then a small portion of time before I go to rest, and so you must expect nothing from me. . . ."[42]

Another glimpse of the everyday life and education of a little girl a few years before the Revolution appears in the following letter written by Anne Blair of Williamsburg to her sister regarding the latter's little daughter: "Betsey is at work for you. I suppose she

[40] For a description of one of the dancing schools see above, pp. 102-3.
[41] "Jones Papers," *Virginia Magazine*, XXVI, 288.
[42] *Virginia Magazine*, XV, 432-33.

will tell you to-morrow is Dancing day, for it is in her thought by Day & her dreams by night. Mr. Fearon (dancing master) was surprised to find she knew much of the Minuet step, and could not help asking if Miss had never been taught, so you find she is likely to make some progress that way. . . . her Reading I hear her twice a day, and when I go out she is consign'd over to my Sister Blair: we have had some few quarrels, and one Battle; Betsey & her Cousin Jenny had been fighting for several days successively, and was threaten'd to be whip'd for it as often, but as they did not regard us - - her Mama & self thought it necessary to let them see we were in earnest - - if they have fought since have never heard of it - - she has finished her work & Tucker, but the weather is so warm, what with all ye pains I can take with clean hands, and so forth she cannot help dirtying it a little. I do not observe her to be fond of Negroes Company now nor have I heard lately of any bad Words; chief of our Quarrel's is for eating of those Green apples in our Garden & not keeping the Head smooth."[43]

Daughters of small planters and successful tradesmen probably attended the subscription schools. These were organized by the joint effort of several parents who together undertook the responsibility of providing a schoolhouse and hiring a schoolmaster. A number of citizens in North Carolina, for instance, established the New Bern Academy and later built a schoolhouse by private subscriptions.[44] A group of parents at Port Royal in Virginia advertised for a schoolmaster for youth of both sexes and offered him a "commodious School House" and "a genteel Living."[45] These schools usually did not undertake to teach more than reading, writing, and ciphering, though the more ambitious sometimes offered Latin for boys. They were ordinarily in charge of one schoolmaster, who taught ten to twenty-five children of both sexes and all ages, but occasionally they were larger. Subscribers at Cabin Point in Virginia in 1773 advertised for two masters, one who understood Latin and mathematics to

---

[43] *William and Mary Quarterly*, XVI, 177. That other little girls in the best families also resorted to physical combat appears in the following note in Fithian's journal: "Before breakfast Nancy & Fanny had a Fight about a Shoe Brush which they both wanted - - Fanny pull'd off her Shoe & threw it at Nancy, which missed her and broke a pane of glass of our School Room. They then enter'd upon close scratching &c. . . . Harry happen'd to be present & afraid lest he should be brought in, ran and informed me - - I made peace, but with many threats."—*Journal*, p. 105.

[44] *North Carolina Magazine; or Universal Intelligencer*, July 6, 1764; *Colonial Records of North Carolina*, IX, 239, 281. [45] *Virginia Gazette*, January 14, 1770.

teach fifteen or more "scholars," and another qualified to teach English, writing, and arithmetic to about thirty.[46]

Elementary schools founded by the different religious denominations also admitted girls. The Society for the Propagation of the Gospel was instrumental in setting up many small schools for instructing children in the established religion, and the dissenters were also active in providing instruction according to their own beliefs. The Presbyterians, particularly, insisted that all their children learn to read, but, though zealous in establishing institutions for the higher education of boys, they regarded girls sufficiently learned if they could read the Bible, repeat the catechism, and write a legible hand.[47] Though the Moravians had separate schools for boys and girls, they made less distinction between their academic training than did the Anglicans and Presbyterians.[48] The Friends also provided equal learning for girls and boys.[49]

In the towns were many private schools for girls. These varied all the way from the little day schools, at which small girls were taught to read and sew, to the fashionable boarding schools, at which young ladies acquired all the branches of a polite education. More than fifty of these institutions were advertised in Charles Town during the forty years preceding the Revolution. Many were very simple, offering merely reading in English, plain needlework, and occasionally ciphering. The more fashionable "French Schools" taught French and ornamental needlework. One of the first school-mistresses to advertise in the papers was the Widow Varnod, who gave notice in the *South Carolina Gazette*, May 11, 1734, that she had "set up a French-School for young ladies" in the house of a Mr. Deuxant, where she would teach all sorts of embroidery. Some years later, Jane Voyer offered to teach "any young Ladies that have a Mind to learn Embroidery, Lace-work, Tapistry or any other Needlework, Drawing and French."[50]

Little girls living in the country as well as those in Charles Town attended these schools, for many teachers boarded and lodged their

<hr/>

[46] *Ibid.*, December 23, 1773.

[47] Rev. William Henry Foote, *Sketches of North Carolina, Historical and Biographical, Illustrative of the Principles of a Portion of her Early Settlers* (New York, 1846), pp. 518, 523-24.

[48] Adelaide L. Fries, *Records of the Moravians in North Carolina*, I, 203-4, 241.

[49] Zora Klain, *Quaker Contributions to Education in North Carolina* (Philadelphia, 1925), pp. 284-96.

[50] *South Carolina Gazette*, July 28, 1739.

pupils and other women made a business of caring for country children attending school in town. Three "young French ladies just arrived from Rotterdam" opened a school in 1746, where they furnished their pupils with board and lodging,[51] and Abigail Diamond kept a school where young ladies could board or attend by the day.[52] Elizabeth Cassens announced in 1755 that she would teach children to read and "do plain work" and would take two or three as boarders. Twelve years later she advertised that she could take in her school six more young ladies as "constant boarders" and six as "day boarders" and promised "close attention to their education and improvement."[53]

Mistress Cassens' notices indicate the manner in which small dame schools developed into the fashionable boarding schools which became so popular in the last half of the century. Like the earlier institutions, these more elaborate ones were usually held in the homes of the schoolmistresses, but in addition to reading and needlework often taught by the mistress herself, they offered more ornamental subjects, which were given by special masters. One of the first was advertised by Mary Hext, who in 1741 announced that she would board "young misses," teach them fashionable needlework, and engage well qualified masters in writing, arithmetic, dancing, and music to give "due attendance."[54] Elizabeth Anderson boarded eight young ladies and engaged masters to teach them music, dancing, and drawing "as they inclined"; M. Harward taught girls to read, embroider, and "flourish," and employed masters for writing and ciphering; and Anna Maria Hoyland taught reading and needlework and engaged masters for writing, arithmetic, dancing, music, and French.[55]

In the next decade, Rebecca Woodin advertised that she had moved from Meeting Street into "a healthful and convenient house" on White Point, where she would continue to have young ladies taught "in the different branches of Polite Education, viz. Reading English and French, Writing and Arithmetic, Needlework; and Music and Dancing, by proper masters."[56] Elizabeth Girardeau advertised her "boarding and day school," where the same subjects

[51] *Ibid.*, July 7, 1746.   [52] *Ibid.*, February 26, 1750.
[53] *Ibid.*, December 11, 1755; February 24, 1767.
[54] *Ibid.*, August 6, 1741.
[55] *Ibid.*, May 8, 1749; April 17, 1736; January 6, 1757.
[56] *Ibid.*, June 29, 1767.

were taught, and promised the parents of her pupils to "take the utmost care of their behaviour."[57] The most pretentious advertisement was that of a Mrs. Duneau, gentlewoman from England, who claimed to have kept "one of the genteelest Boarding-Schools about London" and brought up many young ladies of rank. She offered to teach "the French and English Languages grammatically–Geography–History–and many instructing Amusements to improve the Mind–with all Sorts of fashionable Needle Work," and to engage proper masters to "attend the young Ladies for their Dancing, Music, and Drawing; Writing and Arithmetic."[58]

Similar schools were found in the larger towns of the other colonies, though in smaller numbers than in Charles Town. Mary Anne March of Annapolis announced in the *Maryland Gazette*, March 27, 1751, that she and her daughter would "teach young Misses, all Sorts of Embroidery, Turkey Work, and all Sorts of rich Stitches learnt in Sampler Work" at ten shillings a quarter, and would teach children to read and spell at thirty shillings a year. Three years later, Mary Salisbury announced her intention of opening a school in Annapolis, where she would board young ladies and teach French, "Tapestry, Embroidery with Gold and Silver, and every other Curious Work which can be performed with a Needle, and all Education fit for young Ladies, except Dancing."[59] John and Mary Rivers taught and boarded children in Annapolis for thirty pounds a year. Their course of study included dancing, singing, French, and fancy needlework.[60] For "the amusement and improvement of young ladies," a Mrs. Polk kept a "morning school," where she taught "embroidery, tambour, dresden, point, netting, and all other kinds of needlework, at the moderate price of one dollar entrance, and twenty shillings per quarter." The hours of her school were from eight until one. She offered to "wait upon" any ladies in their homes who were "inclined to encourage the above undertaking" and did not "chuse" to attend the school.[61]

One of the first private schools advertised in the Virginia papers was kept by John Walker and his wife, who arrived from London and opened a school in Williamsburg in 1752. He taught boys read-

[57] *Ibid.*, August 29, 1761; February 23, 1765.

[58] *Ibid.*, May 17, 1770. See facsimile facing next page.

[59] *Maryland Gazette*, February 21, 1754.

[60] *Ibid.*, November 6, 1755; May 22, 1760.

[61] *Ibid.*, July 28, 1774.

ing, writing, arithmetic, and "the most material branches of classical learning and ancient and modern geography and history," while his wife gave young ladies lessons in needlework.[62]   E. Gardner in 1766 advertised that she had taken a house in Norfolk where she would board young ladies and teach them French and the latest fashions in needlework.   Six years later as E. Armston, she announced she was continuing her school at Point Pleasant and offered a more elaborate course of study, including "Petit Point in Flowers, Fruit, Landscapes, and Sculpture, Nuns Work, Embroidery in Silk, Gold, Silver, Pearls, or embossed, Shading of all Kinds, in the various Works in Vogue, Dresden Point Work, Lace Ditto, Catgut in different Modes, flourishing Muslin after the newest Taste, and most elegant Pattern, Waxwork in Figure, Fruit, or Flowers, Shell Ditto, or grotesque, Painting in, Water Colours and Mezzo tinto; also the Art of taking off Foliage, with several other Embellishments for the Amusement of Persons of Fortune who have Taste."   Reading was her "peculiar Care" and writing and arithmetic were taught by special masters. Also she offered, if her patrons desired, to "engage Proficients in Musick and Dancing."[63]   In 1776 a Mrs. Neill, who had for some time been governess in a prominent Virginia family, advertised her intention of opening a boarding school for young ladies in Williamsburg on the plan of the English schools.   She offered to instruct them in reading, tambour, and other needlework, and furnish them board, lodging, and washing for one guinea entrance and thirty pounds a year.   Dancing and writing, taught by special masters, were to be paid for separately.   "Day Scholars" were taken at one guinea entrance and four shillings a year.[64]

In Georgia a Mrs. Stedman had under her care and tuition the children of prominent families in Savannah sometime before 1767. In 1769 Elizabeth Bedon announced her intention of opening a school in Savannah if she could secure sufficient pupils, and offered reading, writing, arithmetic, and needlework upon these terms: "Day Boarders," twelve pounds a year; "Night Boarders," twenty-five pounds; "Day Scholars," five pounds.   Drawing for needlework would be given for the extra sum of twenty shillings entrance fee and twenty shillings a quarter.   Some years later, Mary Garrety advertised her

[62] *Virginia Gazette*, November 17, 1752.
[63] *Ibid.*, March 21, 1766; February 27, 1772.
[64] *Ibid.*, December 27, 1776.

school, where children were taught arithmetic, geography, and "most kinds of needle work."[65]

In the few North Carolina papers preserved, no advertisements of girls' schools appear before the Revolution. As there were no large towns in the province, it is probable that fashionable boarding schools were less numerous than in the neighboring colonies. But the provision for the tuition of daughters in many wills and the sums spent for education, as found in guardians' accounts of orphan girls, indicate the existence of girls' schools of some kind.[66]

Though private schools were generally not coeducational, there were a few which, like the neighborhood and subscription schools, admitted both sexes. In Savannah Peter Gandy kept a school for boys and girls, and James Whitefield not only taught but also boarded and lodged "young masters and misses."[67] These institutions generally offered a more solid education than the girls' schools. One advertised by William Johnson of Charles Town in 1767 offered, apparently for both sexes, instruction in reading, writing, arithmetic, English grammar, geography, and natural philosophy.[68] Another at Jacksonburgh advertised reading, writing, arithmetic, dancing, geography, French, Latin, mathematics, mechanics, and fencing.[69] Girls doubtless were not admitted to the last two courses and most probably did not take mathematics or Latin. Usually they did not

[65] Georgia Gazette, June 3, 1767; August 9, 1769; July 18, 1775.

[66] The guardian of Elizabeth Murdens paid in 1752 four shillings for a month's schooling and two shillings and eight pence for a spelling book for her. Six years later, when she was probably attending boarding school, he paid £7.11s.8d. The account of Miriam Pritchards shows that her guardian paid someone named "Chancey" ten pounds for her board one year and £2.16s.8d. for "5 months schooling her." Elizabeth Pritchards, her sister, went to school five months in 1769 at a cost of 16s.8d. and nine months the following year for £2.5s. Martha Markham had three months schooling in 1768 for ten shillings, nine months in 1769 for £1.20s., and seven months in 1770 for £1.3s. Sarah Stamp's account showed nine months tuition in 1767, one year in 1768, and one year in 1769 at two pounds a year. One sister, Miriam, had six months schooling in 1767, and another sister, Deborah, had four months in 1767 and one year in 1769 at the same rate. Deborah and Miriam were probably later sent to boarding school, for their guardian's account for 1771 showed £4.12s.8d. for board, clothing, and schooling of each of them.—MS, Pasquotank Orphans Court Minutes, 1757-1785. The guardian of Abigail Terrell of Bute County in 1772 paid £3.11s. for her dancing lessons, £1.6s. for one year of schooling for her, and £6 for her board, and the guardian of Pheeby Hudson paid £3 for lessons in psalmody for her.—MS, Bute County Guardian Accounts, 1770-1795.

[67] Georgia Gazette, May 25, 1768; April 8, 1767.

[68] South Carolina Gazette, July 6, 1767.   [69] Ibid., June 10, 1766.

attend classes with boys, but were taught in a separate "ladies' department." A Mr. Walston advertised at his academy a room for young ladies "distinct from that in which the young Gentlemen are to be," and another Charles Town schoolmaster advertised for young ladies "a convenient separate Room (from the young men)."[70]

Special textbooks were prepared for girls, who were expected to acquire only a superficial knowledge of subjects which their brothers studied for longer periods and more seriously. On booksellers' lists advertised in newspapers appear *Newton's Ladies Philosophy*, *The Lady's Geography*, *The Female Academy*, *The Ladies Compleat Letter Writer*, and *The Female Miscellany*. The last work, according to the advertisements, was divided into two parts, the first including "a Sketch of English Grammar, an Abridgement of the Holy History, a small Collection of Fables, etc.," and the second being "a Series of Letters addressed to a young Lady who had made some progress in Reading." Another popular book, *An Accidence to the English Tongue*, was a simplified grammar prepared for boys who did not know Latin and "for the benefit of the Female Sex."

Other opportunities for improvement were offered by special masters in writing, dancing, music, or drawing, who attended young ladies in their own homes or set up schools devoted exclusively to one of these ornamental branches. Writing was among the most polite accomplishments and several different "hands" were taught. Thomas Lyttleton gave lessons in the Italian hand,[71] and Daniel Thomas advertised lessons "in the Italian, round, or any other hand" and also offered to instruct them in "that useful Part of Education, corresponding by Letter in a polite, familiar, Style."[72]

During the last quarter of the colonial period, many masters advertised lessons on the different musical instruments, several taught singing, and a few offered theory and composition. In 1739 "a person lately arrived" in Charles Town offered instruction in the "art of Psalmody, according to the exact rule of the Gamut in all the various measures both of the old or new version," and in 1753 another singing teacher announced her intention of opening "an evening school for instructing Persons in plain Psalmody."[73] Edmund Larkin, organist from England, advertised lessons on the harpsichord and

[70] *Ibid.*, August 24, 1769; December 19, 1741.
[71] *South Carolina Gazette*, December 19, 1741.
[72] *Ibid.*, February 4, 1774. Supplement.
[73] *South Carolina Gazette*, February 15, 1739; November 16, 1753.

spinnet and also in singing. Pupils taught at home were to pay twelve shillings entrance fee and the same for each month of eight lessons; those taking lessons at his house were charged eight shillings entrance fee and twelve shillings a month.[74] John Tompkins taught "a true Method of singing Psalms" for "a Dollar entrance and a Pistole when Attendance is given."[75] Elizabeth Smith opened a singing school in Annapolis in 1764, and in 1775 James Digins, "Vocal-Master from Boston," proposed to open a school in Baltimore. His terms were thirty shillings a year, seven shillings and six pence of which were to be paid at entrance, and he promised to use "his utmost endeavours" to make his pupils "perfect in that excellent and harmonious art."[76]

Teachers of instrumental music were more numerous. Frederick Grundzweig taught the harpsichord, guitar, viol, and German flute.[77] P. A. Van Hagen, Jr., formerly "Organist and Director of the City's Concert in Rotterdam," proposed to teach young ladies and gentlemen to play the organ, harpsichord, pianoforte, violin, violincello, and viola, and also composition.[78] A Mr. Singleton taught the violin; Francis Russworm, the violin and "the German and common flutes"; and "Mr. Wall, Comedian," gave lessons on the mandolin and the guitar.[79] John Stevens announced his intention of opening a school for teaching "the Theory as well as Practical Parts of Musick." Pupils were to attend two days in the week for ten pounds a year and a guinea entrance fee. Those who chose to be instructed in their own homes were "waited on at fourteen pounds per annum."[80]

Occasionally drawing and painting, and even riding, were taught by special masters. An advertisement in the *South Carolina Gazette,* April 3, 1736, announced that children would be "taught to draw on their Dancing Days at Mr. Holt's School." Lewis Turtaz, "Limner and miniature painter from Lausanne, Switzerland," advertised a school for miniature painting and drawing, and offered to teach ladies in their own homes,[81] and a Mr. Lessly also advertised lessons in drawing and painting.[82] Thomas Griffith, "Riding Master from

---

[74] *Ibid.,* November 13, 1751. [75] *Virginia Gazette,* November 3, 1752.

[76] *Maryland Gazette,* April 5, 1764; *Maryland Journal,* May 10, 1775.

[77] *South Carolina Gazette,* April 6, 1747.

[78] *South Carolina and American General Gazette,* November 4, 1774.

[79] *Virginia Gazette,* June 25, 1752; *ibid.,* May 16, 1771; *Maryland Gazette,* September 3, 1773. [80] *Georgia Gazette,* May 27, 1767.

[81] *South Carolina Gazette,* March 30, 1767.

[82] *South Carolina and American General Gazette,* April 14, 1775.

London," offered to teach young ladies and gentlemen "to ride with the same safety, ease, and gentility as is now practiced in the best Riding-Schools in London."[83]

Dancing, a favorite amusement for young and old, was by far the most necessary accomplishment. The most celebrated of the Virginia dancing teachers was Sarah Hallam, the popular actress, who, after retiring from the stage, opened a dancing school for the daughters of the well-to-do.[84] In Maryland, Martha Rogers opened a dancing school in 1755, and two years later John Ormsby was giving dancing lessons in Annapolis on Fridays and Saturdays and in Upper Marlborough on Tuesdays and Wednesdays. His terms were six pounds a year and a pistole entrance fee.[85] Adalbert B. Ebert gave lessons three days a week at four dollars entrance and four dollars a quarter.[86] Many masters advertised dancing lessons in the South Carolina papers.[87] In Georgia John Revear offered to take "all imaginable care" in instructing children in "all the celebrated dances that are used in polite assemblies." His hours were from ten to twelve and from three to five on Thursdays and Fridays, and he also kept an evening school for adults and offered to teach any lady at her own house.[88] Medley D'Arcy Dawes taught gentlemen on Monday, Wednesday, and Friday evenings, and children and young ladies on Thursday and Saturday afternoons.[89]

The dancing master was a familiar figure not only in the towns but also in the country, where he went about from plantation to

---

[83] *South Carolina Gazette*, April 11, 1771.

[84] *Virginia Gazette, August* 17, 1775. In 1716 William Levingston was given permission to use a room in William and Mary College for teaching students and others to dance until his own dancing school was finished. A short time later Charles Stagg and his wife were teaching dancing and holding balls in Williamsburg, and Madame la Baronne de Graffenreidt was giving lessons and enlivening the town with her assemblies.—Stanard, *op. cit.*, pp. 142-43. In 1751 Richard Coventon announced his intention of having a ball for his "scholars" at the courthouse in Williamsburg, and in 1771 Francis Russworm offered to wait upon young ladies in their homes to teach them to dance a minuet "after the newest and most fashionable Method."—*Virginia Gazette*, October 24, 1751; May 23, 1771.

[85] *Maryland Gazette*, November 13, 1755; *ibid.*, August 4 and October 20, 1757.

[86] *Ibid.*, July 24, 1766.

[87] In the *South Carolina Gazette* are advertisements of William Brawn (August 12, 1732), William Dering (December 11, 1749), Nicholas Scanlon (June 18, 1750), Andrew Rutledge (February 7, 1761). A Mr. Pike conducted a dancing school and gave annual balls to display the achievements of his pupils during the decade before the Revolution.—*South Carolina and American General Gazette*, November 14, 1766; *South Carolina Gazette and Country Journal*, January 12, 1768.

[88] *Georgia Gazette*, September 26, 1765. [89] *Ibid.*, August 31, 1768.

plantation holding classes in the homes of his pupils. The best known of these itinerant teachers was a Mr. Christian, who organized and taught dancing schools in country neighborhoods in Virginia from sometime about the middle of the century until the Revolution. Washington wrote in his diary, April 18, 1770, that Patcy Custis, his stepdaughter, and Milley Posey, a neighbor's daughter, had gone to Colonel Mason's to attend dancing school, and at the same time noted in his ledger a payment of two pounds to Mr. Christian for the entrance fee of the two girls. In the same diary we learn that the dancing school was held at "Mount Vernon" the following May, July, and September, and on each of these occasions the teacher and his pupils were guests of the Washingtons for two or more days and nights.[90] In 1773 Christian was holding classes at "Nomini," "Stratford," and other houses in the vicinity. Fithian noted in his journal, several times, the fact that the Carter children were absent attending dancing school at a neighbor's or that "Mr. Christian the Dancing Master Came home with the young Ladies."

In addition to the advantages afforded by private tutors and schools and special masters, daughters of the wealthier classes sometimes enjoyed the benefit of travel and a few attended school in the northern colonies, in England, or on the continent. A Mrs. Taylor of Philadelphia sought patronage for her boarding school in the southern papers. Besides the ornamental subjects taught in southern schools, she offered to teach young ladies "to crown childrens caps, make up baby linen, mark letters, to pickle, preserve, and to clearstarch."[91] Following the precedent set by his father, Colonel William Byrd II sent his daughters, Evelyn and Wilhemina, to be educated in the Mother Country, and Colonel John Baylor of Virginia in 1762 placed his four daughters in boarding school at Croyden in England.[92] Frances, daughter of John Rutherford of North Carolina, was, with her two brothers, sent to England to be educated after the death of her mother in 1768.[93] Thomas Jefferson put his daughters, Martha and Marie, in a convent in France for their education. In the Carroll family of Maryland, daughters as well as sons were educated abroad. The sisters of Charles Carroll II were sent to Europe under the care of their "Uncle Darnell" for their schooling.

[90] *Diaries* (ed., Fitzpatrick), I, 373.
[91] *Maryland Gazette*, September 12, 1775.
[92] Stanard, *op. cit.*, pp. 221, 289-90.
[93] [Janet Schaw], *Journal*, Appendices, pp. 299-300.

This Charles Carroll had no daughter, but his granddaughter Catherine, daughter of Charles Carroll of Carrollton, at eleven years of age was sent to an English convent at Liége, and in turn her daughter, Mary Harper, was sent to France, where it was said she would be "more piously educated than at the very best boarding-school in Philadelphia."[94]

A number of women and girls went to England for long visits. William Beverley of "Blandfield" in Virginia took his wife, son Robert, and daughter Anna to England in 1750. In his diary he recorded the details of what must have been an enjoyable stay, the meeting of relatives and friends, dining out, attending plays at Covent Garden, and other similar pleasures.[95] In 1752 Eliza Lucas Pinckney, with her two sons and little daughter Harriott, accompanied her husband, Charles Pinckney, to England, where Colonel Pinckney held the position of commissioner of the colony in London. They were presented to the royal family, spent a season at Bath, and traveled over seven hundred miles visiting around among relatives and friends in several counties. Then they settled down in a furnished house in London and spent the time until their return in 1758 in visiting, attending plays, and other social entertainments.[96] Martha Laurens, with her younger sister, aunt, and uncle, sailed for England in June, 1775, and sojourned there and in France until the end of the Revolution.[97]

The cultural advantages of daughters in the Laurens, Byrd, and Carroll families were very exceptional. In considering the opportunities of girls in general, we find that while much was said and written about their education, they were given only the most elementary instruction. Although many apprentices were required under the laws to be taught to read and less often to write and other girls were sometimes given tuition at the expense of benevolent individuals or philanthropic societies, the more fortunate of the poor seldom had more than an introduction to reading and writing and a majority had no schooling. Girls able to attend the subscription, denominational, and other little community schools received instruction generally for not more than two or three years, and often for only a few months,

[94] Rowland, op. cit., I, 17; II, 106-7.   [95] Virginia Magazine, XXXVI, 161-69.
[96] Ravenel, Eliza Pinckney, pp. 134-66. Eliza Lucas married Colonel Charles Pinckney in 1744.
[97] South Carolina and American General Gazette, June 2, 1775; South Carolina Magazine, XXIV, 5; Wallace, Life of Henry Laurens, p. 226.

in reading, writing, and sometimes arithmetic, but usually did not study grammar, languages, and other subjects offered boys. Those of the most prosperous classes, who had private tutors and special masters or attended fashionable boarding schools, acquired little beyond drawing-room accomplishments and the three R's. A small number studied history, geography, and natural philosophy at the more advanced institutions, and a few with intellectual interests continued to acquire knowledge from books by independent reading after finishing school, but the formal schooling of the most well-to-do lasted only a few years and embraced little beyond the rudiments of learning. The general attitude of the colonists regarding women's educational needs was that expressed in the last will and testament of John Baptista Ashe, North Carolina gentleman, who, after giving detailed directions for the liberal education of his sons in Latin, Greek, French, and Mathematics, made this provision for his daughter: "I will that my daughter be taught to write and read & some feminine accomplishments which may render her agreeable; And that she be not kept ignorant as to what appertains to a good house wife in the management of household affairs."[98]

[98] Grimes, *North Carolina Wills and Inventories*, p. 16.

Engraved for the Lady's Magazine.

Two Ladies in the newest Dress.

From Drawings taken at Ranelagh May 1775.

Published by G. Robinson June 1 1775.

Often inserted between notices of stray horses and fugitive slaves, advertisements of runaway wives were numerous.—Facsimile of a *Supplement to the South-Carolina Gazette*, Saturday, September 18, 1762

A Young Ladies Boarding School.

From *The Lady's Magazine*, September, 1771

A Boarding-School,

FOR THE

EDUCATION OF YOUNG LADIES,

Will be opened the approaching WHITMONDAY, *at the Houfe oppofite the Rev. Mr.* COOPER's *in* NEW CHURCH-STREET,

By Mrs. DUNEAU,

A Gentlewoman come from ENGLAND,

WHO has brought up many Ladies of Rank and Diftinction, having herfelf kept one of the genteeleft Boarding-Schools about London.

Teaches the French and Englifh Languages grammatically—Geography—Hiftory—and many inftructing Amufements to improve the Mind—with all Sorts of fafhionable Needle Work.—Proper Mafters will attend the young Ladies, for their Dancing, Mufic, and Drawing; Writing and Arithmetic.

Agreeable Indulgence will be allowed for the Amufement and Encouragement of the young Ladies.—Mrs. DUNEAU will be much obliged to the Gentlemen and Ladies, who pleafe to Favour her with the Care of their Daughters Education; and has the Honour to fubfcribe herfelf,

Their moft obedient humble Servant,
ELIZABETH DUNEAU.

BOSTON, April 23.

ON Tuefday laft the Houfe of Reprefentatives, by a majority of 70 out of 74 votes, made choice of JOHN HANCOCK, Efq; to be Speaker, pro temp re, for the prefent feffion, and during the bodily in difpofition of THOMAS CUSHING, Efq; and having prefented him to the Lieutenant-Governor for his approbation, his Honour was pleafed to fend to the houfe the following meffage, *viz.*

Gentlemen of the Houfe of Reprefentatives,

YOU having fignified to me by a meffage, that Thomas Cufhing, Efq; your fpeaker, is neceffarily abfent, by reafon of ficknefs, and that you have made choice of John Hancock, Efq; to be fpeaker pro tempore, for the prefent feffion, and during the

The advertisement of Mrs. Duneau's boarding school in the
South-Carolina Gazette, May 17, 1770

Plate I.   Frontispiece to the Compleat English Cook.

Jaques Le Fore Inv.   Behold, ye Fair, united in this Book B. Cole sc.
The Frugal Housewife, and experienc'd Cook.

Mr. Norton

Sir

Mr. Norton from York called on me the other
Morning and Informed me he had sent home my former Letters &
Orders and that I might Expect both them and every thing Else
I wanted bought in the best & Cheapest Manner, And with all the
Speed Posible, you May rely on My being Exact & Punctual in My
payments, And when I fail in this, I shall Expect to be used Accordingly

You will Sir Oblige me very Much by sending me the
Contents of the Inclosed Invoyce by the very first Opportunity
as I am quite Out of every Sort of Article I have Now Wrote
for, And you will Sir Infinately serve

Ayour Most Obeyd: Humt Servt
Cath. Rathell

Williamsburg
Decr 29.th 1771
I have Ordered some Goods from Messrs. Flight & Co. and from
one or two more, but all not to Exceed £60, beg youll receive
and send them

A Letter of Catherine Rathell, Williamsburg shopkeeper, to John Norton
and Sons, London, December, 1771. The original is in the archives
office of Colonial Williamsburg, Incorporated, Williamsburg, Virginia

One of the most persistent advertisers among the Charles Town shopkeepers was Agnes Lind. This advertisement appeared in the *South-
Carolina Gazette*, August 21, 1762

1. Trial by water to see whether a woman be a witch.

2. A ducking stool for babbling women.

3. Whipping at the cart tail.

4. The pillory for perjurers and petty thieves.

5. On the gallows.

6. Burning at the stake.

Instruments of Punishment for Women Criminals

Drawings by Lucia Porcher Johnson, based upon contemporary prints

CHAPTER X

THE LADY'S LIBRARY

COLONIAL WOMEN, who were more expert with the needle than with the pen and skilled in the "mysteries of cookerie" rather than in the art of composition, were not accustomed to airing their ideas in print or even to confiding them to diaries or private letters. Therefore, they left few personal records of themselves. If, however, little information regarding them is to be had from what they wrote, revealing evidence is available in the books they read. Occasionally in the private correspondence, journals, wills, and inventories of colonial gentlemen, and frequently in newspaper advertisements of colonial booksellers, one finds the names of writings designed for the "fair sex." These ladies' books, many of which have been preserved, throw considerable light upon the woman of colonial days and make known to us, if not what she was, at least what she was supposed to be.

In accordance with the English tradition that though a woman should not be learned she should have "knowinge of the law of God" sufficient to "withstonde the perilles of the sowle," the colonial lady generally had for her use a Bible and Prayer Book and often owned *The Whole Duty of Man*,[1] which afforded her private devotions for various occasions and careful directions, corroborated by the Scriptures, for the conduct of the different members of her household. A library typical of the collections of devout gentlewomen of the early part of the eighteenth century was that of Mistress Mary Degge, a wealthy spinster, who in 1716 bequeathed her nieces these volumes: *The Whole Duty of Man, The Practice of Piety, Meditations on Eternity*, the *Book of Common Prayer*, a Church Catechism, *The Art of Contentment, The Ladies Calling*, Lord Halifax's *The Lady's New Year's Gift, or, Advice to a Daughter*, and William

---

[1] *The Whole Duty of Man, laid down in a plain and familiar way for the Use of All, but especially the Meanest Reader. Divided into Seventeen Chapters; One whereof being read every Lord's Day, the Whole may be read over Thrice in the Year. Necessary for all Families. With Private Devotions for several Occasions.* London, 1684.

Sherlock's *Practical Discourse concerning Death*.[2] In the decade preceding the Revolution, pious ladies fortified their souls with Dr. Watts's *Psalms and Hymns*, the Reverend James Hervey's *Meditations and Contemplations*, Elizabeth Burnet's *A Method of Devotion*, Elizabeth Rowe's *Devout Exercises of the Heart*, a Mrs. Stewart's *Meditations upon Several Texts of Scriptures*, and the sermons of Archbishop Tillotson and the Reverend George Whitefield.

The works which constituted the greater part of the library of seventeenth-century gentlewomen and held an important place on the shelves of ladies throughout the following century were handbooks on domestic economy, many of which were printed in England and imported into the colonies. These furnished the lady with complete instructions pertaining to her position as housewife; or, as claimed in the title of one manual, they contained all "the inward and outward virtues which ought to be in a compleate woman."[3] *The Cook's New Years Gift, Cookery refined, or The Lady, Gentlewoman and Servant-Maid's Companion* (1697), advertised as written by "Mrs. A. M. a long practiser of this curious Art," offered directions in the "Art of dressing all sorts of Flesh, Fish, and Fowl, various ways, after the newest Mode; with their proper seasonings, sauces, Garnishes, serving up and carving, etc."[4] Another work very popular in England and probably often included among the "Bookes of Cookerie" mentioned in colonial inventories was Hannah Woolley's *The Queenlike Closet, or a rich Cabinet stored with all manner of rare Receipts for preserving, Candying, and Cookery*, the eleventh edition of which appeared in 1696.[5] *The Gentlewoman's Companion or Guide to the Female Sex*, also by Mrs. Woolley, gave many practical suggestions to the housewife, among which was the following regarding the treatment of servants: "If you have a bad or unfaithful servant (as nowadays there are too many, more than ever) whom you cannot either by fair means or foul, reclaim, vex not nor fret at what you see is remediless, but first making her thoroughly sensible of her errors, give her fair warning to provide for herself, and convenient

[2] *William and Mary Quarterly*, XXI, 194-97.

[3] [Gervaise Markham], *The English House-wife, containing the inward and outward Vertues which ought to be in a compleate Woman. As her Skill in Physick, Surgery, Cookery, Extraction of Oyles, Banqueting stuffe, Ordering of Great Feasts, Preserving of all Sorts of Wines, Conceited Secrets, Distillations, Perfumes, ordering of Wooll, Hempe, Flax, making Cloth, and Dying. . . . By G. M.* 5th ed., 1657.

[4] Myra Reynolds, *The Learned Lady in England, 1650-1760*, pp. 91-92.

[5] *Ibid.*, p. 91.

for your own affairs, and do not, as a great many much to blame, give too ill a character of her, which will raise you little benefit, although it may lay a basis of her utter ruin; but rather be silent if you cannot speak good. . . . Though a bad servant, detain not the wages, nor any part that is justly due, for the labourer is worthy of his hire."[6]   Other recommendations to the housewife were to have everything kept clean in the chambers, the beds turned often, the furniture well brushed in the sun, and once every month to take account of all expenses of the household.

Works like William Lawson's *New Orchard and Garden* aided the gentlewoman in the arrangement and care of her flower garden, and treatises like John Gerard's *Herbinal*[7] instructed her not only in the cultivation of her "Physick Garden" but also in gathering, drying, and distilling herbs for remedies for the maladies in fashion and for pomades and beauty washes.   A more comprehensive book, *The Accomplished Lady's Delight in Preserving, Physick, Beautifying, Cookery, and Gardening*,[8] gave instructions in all the various branches of housewifery.   Part I described the art of preserving and candying fruits and flowers and of making conserves, syrups, jellies, and pickles. Part II, called "The Physical Cabinet," contained receipts in "Physick and Chyrurgery" and "Beautifying Waters."   This part must have been particularly interesting to colonial ladies living on isolated plantations, for it gave them detailed instructions for making in their own homes all kinds of "Oyles, Oynments and Powders to Adorn and add Loveliness to the Face and Body," numerous formulas for making the teeth white and sound and the breath sweet, and other receipts to "prevent the marks of smallpox," to make the nails grow, to make the hair curl, and one "to make the Body fat and comely." Part III, entitled "The Complete Cook's Guide," included directions for dressing all kinds of flesh, fowl, and fish, both in the English and

[6] Rose M. Bradley, *The English Housewife in the Seventeenth and Eighteenth Centuries*, pp. 144-45.   [7] *Ibid.*, pp. 111, 115.

[8] 9th ed., 1706.   Other seventeenth-century housewifery manuals were: T. Dawson's *The Good huswife's jewell . . . most excellent and rare devises for conceits in cookery* (1596); *a Closet for ladies and gentlewomen, or, the art of preserving, conserving, and candying* (1608); H. Platt's *Delights for ladies, to adorne their persons, tables, closets, and distillatories.   With beauties, bouquets, perfumes and waters* (1602); J. Murell's *A Delightful daily exercise for ladies and gentlewomen. Whereby is set forth the secrete misteries of the purest preservings in glasses and other confectionaries* (1630), and *A new book of cookerie, with the newest art of carving and serving.—Cambridge History of English Literature*, IV, 543.

the French mode, with their proper sauces and "sallads" and "the
making of Pyes, Pasties, Tarts and Custards, with many of their forms
and Shapes." Part IV, "The Lady's Diversion in her Garden," contained, besides "choice Curiosities relating to Plants and Flowers,"
instructions for the "nice adorning of Balconies, Turrets, and Windows, with Flowers, or Greens, every month in the Year."

The manual advertised most often in colonial newspapers was E.
Smith's *The Compleat Housewife; or Accomplished Gentlewoman's
Companion*.[9] From its full title we learn that it was a "Collection
of upwards of Five Hundred of the Most Approved Receipts in
Cookery, Pastry, Confectionary, Preserving, Pickles, Cakes, Creams,
Jellies, Made Wines, Cordials," and that it included nearly two hundred family receipts for drinks, syrups, salves, ointments, and "many
other things of Sovereign and approved Efficacy in most Distempers,
Pains, Achs, Wounds, and Sores," which were intended both for the
use of private families and for "such Publick-Spirited Gentlewomen
as would be beneficent to their Poor Neighbors." Fortunate was the
lady who possessed this comprehensive volume, for, besides these
numerous receipts, it contained "a scheme engraven on copper plate"
for the proper arrangement of her dishes on the table, "Bills of fare"
for every month in the year, and instructions in other very practical
matters such as "An excellent way of washing, to save soap and
whiten cloaths," a method "To boil Plate," and directions for
"destroying Buggs."

Almost as popular as *The Compleat Housewife* was *The Art of
Cookery Made Plain and Easy* advertised as written by Hannah
Glasse.[10] It claimed to exceed all other cookery books published
before and to be written not in a "high polite stile" but in language
simple enough to be understood by the "lower Sort." Martha Bradley's *British Housewife: or, the Cook, Housekeeper's, and Gardiner's
Companion*, also frequently advertised by colonial booksellers, gave

[9] An American edition was printed in Williamsburg by William Parks in 1742
and another by William Hunter in 1752.—Virginia State Library, *Trial Bibliography
of Colonial Virginia*, p. 131.

[10] *The Art of Cookery Made Plain and Easy, which Far Exceeds Anything of the
Kind Yet Published*. 9th ed., London, 1759. This famous book, which was widely
used in England and in America, is said to have been a clever fraud, as "Mrs.
Glasse," the supposed author, never existed, and its real author, instead of being "a
Lady," as is set forth on the title-page of the first edition, was a man named Hill,
who made money on this cook book to finance his less successful, though more literary
writings.—Bradley, *op. cit.*, pp. 235-36.

copious information on every subject connected with domestic economy.   Besides instructions in all the branches of cookery, preserving
and pickling, brewing and distilling, it contained discussions of the
"Art of Marketing"; the "Nature of all Kinds of Foods and the
Method of suiting them to different Constitutions"; the "polite and
easy Manner of doing the Honours of the Table"; the "Conduct of
a Family in Respect of Health, the Disorders to which they are
every Month liable, and the most approved Remedies for each";
the breeding and feeding of beasts and fowls; and the "Management of the pleasant, profitable, and useful Garden."   The whole
was "embellished" with curious copper plates illustrating the manner
of trussing game and fowls and the order of setting tables so that,
explained the author, those unable to read might instruct themselves.
Similar works evidently much in use were *The Lady's Companion*,[11]
The Accomplished Housewife or Gentlewoman's Companion,[12] *Mrs.
Brooke's Cookery* and *Mrs. Harrison's Housekeeper's Pocket Book,
and Complete Family Cook.*

Though works on domestic economy continued important, as the
century advanced they gave way somewhat to instructions in social
conduct and books of more general improvement and entertainment.
In England in the eighteenth century, and to a lesser extent in
America, housewifery declined as the all-absorbing interest of gentlewomen and their attention came to be called more to the "embellishment" of their minds.   A very popular subject in the periodicals of
the day was the means of "improving the fair sex," and numerous
articles appeared describing the type of reading suitable to the "female character."   A correspondent to the *Maryland Gazette*,[13] for
instance, observing that generally the ladies knew "little more than
their Work, a small Share of *Housewifery*; and a great deal of *Gossiping*," proposed to "divert their Minds from useless Trifles" and
"furnish their Breasts with valuable Knowledge."   As the literature
usually available to them was either "too loose" or "too serious," he
promised to "intice them to reading" with writings "more agreeable
to their modesty" and pleasing to their taste.

[11] *The Lady's Companion.   Containing upwards of Three Thousand different
Receipts in every Kind of Cookery; and those the best and most fashionable; being
four times the Quantity of any Book of this Sort. . . .* 6th ed., 2 vols., London, 1753.

[12] *The Accomplished Housewife, or Gentlewoman's Companion; to which are
prefixed Some Serious Instructions for the Conduct of the Fair Sex with Regard to
their Duty towards God and towards their Neighbours.*   Date not known.

[13] December 10, 1728.

More descriptive of the prevailing attitude was the proposal of Sir Richard Steele, who, as a means of furnishing the sex with "reflections and sentiments proper for the companions of reasonable men," recommended a "Female Library," which would "consist of such authors as do not corrupt while they divert, but shall tend more immediately to improve them as they are women." His collection of books, he promised, would be "such as shall not hurt a feature by the austerity of their reflections, nor cause one impertinent glance by the wantonness of them. They shall all tend to advance the value of their innocence as virgins, improve their understanding as wives, and regulate their tenderness as parents . . . but the whole shall be so digested for the use of my students, that they shall not go out of character for their inquiries, but their knowledge appear only a cultivated innocence."[14]

The ladies' books most widely circulated in the southern colonies conformed admirably to Steele's ideal. They were unquestionably designed for members of the female sex, and by no means could they be said to cause ladies to wrinkle their brows or spoil their features by undue mental activity. On the contrary, they furnished their readers no necessity whatever for reflection or inquiry, but gave them definite and final instructions on all matters with which they were supposed to be concerned.

Of the guides to female morality and decorum the most outstanding was *The Ladies Calling*,[15] which for over a century was accepted in England and America as final authority on the nature and duties of women. The views it set forth were approved by almost every writer on woman's education, and whole passages from its text were paraphrased or incorporated verbatim in many publications which followed it. It may be accepted as truly expressive of the prevailing colonial conception of woman and as representative of the best of the ladies' books of the period. The first part was an exaltation of the virtues which, according to the divine command, were the proper "Ornaments of Women"; the second described the duties of the sex in each of "their several estates, virginity, marriage, and widowhood." Underlying its whole conception of woman's responsibilities was the idea that women have "peculiar aptnesses" toward goodness and that "the All-wise Creator" has "drawn a distinction"

[14] *Tatler*, Vol. IV, No. 248 (November 9, 1710).

[15] *The Ladies Calling, In Two Parts, By the Author of the Whole Duty of Man.* "Second Impression," 1673. See facsimile facing p. 214.

between masculine and feminine virtues, making that "comely for the one Sex, which often is not (at least in the same degree) for the other."

The virtues described as peculiarly feminine were modesty, meekness, compassion, affability, and piety. Modesty, it declared, was evident "in the face in calm and meek looks, where it so impresses it self, that it seems thence to have acquir'd the name of shamefacedness." A "breach of modesty" appeared in "indecency of loquacity," "Unhandsome earnestness or loudness of discourse," and in "virile boldness" or "daring manliness" in speech, manner, or dress. Modesty as opposed to wantonness was presented as "the most indispensable requisite of a woman; a thing so essential and natural to the sex, that every the least declination from it, is proportionate receding from Womanhood." Meekness was enjoined of women especially because they were placed by God and nature in a position of inferiority to the other sex. Compassion, affability, and piety were also deemed particularly appropriate for women not only because of their "native tenderness" but also because of their exemption from public employments, which required austerity in men. Men, the author explained, had many cares, both private and public, to distract them from pious reflections, while the most that was usually required of women was but "a little easy inspection within their own walls" and "the oversight of a few children."

Quite in keeping with these ideas of the character of women were the views of their duties. The young maid was reminded that modesty and obedience were "the two grand Elements essential to the Virgin State," that her look, speech, and behavior should "own an humble distrust of herself," and that she should beware of "mischievous curiosity" and, regarding "Indecent Things," affect ignorance. She was told not to read romances, which aroused "amorous Passions," and was admonished to spend her time on "the offices of Piety," "Household Managery," and "ornamental improvements" like writing, needlework, and music. A fundamental rule laid down for virgins was that they should never listen to any proposal of marriage made to them directly, but should direct all such overtures from themselves to their parents, not only because parents had such a "native right" in them that it would be unjust as well as disobedient to dispose of themselves without their consent, but also because such procedure was most agreeable to the virgin modesty, which would make marriage an act rather of their obedience than of their choice. "Superannuated Virgins" were consoled with the suggestion that if they would behave with gravity and "reservedness" and "addict themselves to the strictest virtue and piety," they would give the world cause to believe that it was not their necessity but their choice that kept them unmarried.

The chief duty of the wife was obedience to her husband, which was required of her both because she promised it in her marriage vow and because subjection was the punishment laid upon all wives by the first woman's disobedience. In addition to submitting to the will of her husband, she was admonished to guard his reputation by "setting his Worth in the clearest light" and "putting his infirmities in the shade." She was warned to guard against jealousy and to "put the most candid construction upon any doubtful action" of her husband. If the proof of his infidelity were thrust upon her, she had the consolation of being no longer in doubt and might find comfort in patient submission. Not "virulence or recrimination," but a "wise dissimulation" or "very calm notice" was suggested as the most likely means of reclaiming him. If a virtuous wife were to suffer from the causeless jealousy of her husband, she was to accept this traducing of her innocence as God's punishment for some other sin she might have committed, and contrive to relieve her husband of the torture of jealousy by denying herself even the most innocent liberties which might cause him uneasiness.

The wife's duty did not end with the death of her husband. As a widow she was instructed to revive the memory of all that was praiseworthy in him, to vindicate him from calumny, and to be careful to do nothing unworthy of his name. She was to retreat from the world, "put on a more retir'd temper of mind, a more strict behaviour," and "abound in works of Piety and Charity." Although admitting that the remarriage of widows was not forbidden by the Scriptures, the author argued against it, declaring that she who had had a good husband might reasonably doubt that in "this common dearth of Vertue" two good husbands would fall to any woman's lot, and, on the other hand, she who had had a bad one should find caution enough against a new venture in the memory of what she had suffered. Yet experience showed, the author declared, that women, though the weaker sex, had fortitude enough to "baffle all these considerations."

Another little book which dictated the rules of conduct to ladies for well over a century was Lord Halifax's *The Lady's New Year's Gift, or, Advice to a Daughter*,[16] which, though less religious in character, was very similar to *The Ladies Calling* in its conception of woman's nature and mission. So popular was it in England that between 1688 and 1765 it ran through fifteen editions and in the colonies it was frequently listed in inventories and newspaper advertisements. Though it described the proper female virtues and discussed general behavior, it concerned itself chiefly with the subject of "How to live with a husband." Underlying the whole discussion was the view of the difference between the sexes: "You must first lay it down for a Foundation in general, That there is *Inequality* in the *Sexes*, and that for the better Oeconomy of the World, the *Men*, who were to be the Law Givers, had the better share of *Reason* bestow'd upon them; by which means your Sex is the better prepar'd for the *Compliance* that is necessary for the better performance of those *Duties* which seem to be most properly assign'd to it. . . . We are made of differing *Tempers*, that our Defects may the better be Mutually Supplied: Your *Sex* wanteth our *Reason* for your *Conduct*, and our *Strength* for your *Protection*; Ours wanteth your *Gentleness* to soften and to entertain us." Although this distribution of powers might at first glance seem unjust, it explained, really women have the advantage, for they have it in their power to subdue their masters, and without violence throw both their natural and legal authority at their feet. "You have more strength in your *Looks*," the daughter was assured, "than we have in our Laws, and more power by your *Tears*, than we have by our *Arguments*."

Since it was settled by law and custom that woman was to be subject to masculine authority, and since one of the disadvantages of her sex was that she seldom might choose the man she married, it was most necessary that she be instructed how to make the best of whatever might fall to her lot. Therefore, for her direction, hints were given of the most ordinary causes of dissatisfaction between man and wife with suggestions as to how she might cure, or at least endure, whatever frailties her husband might have. If he should prove to be a philanderer, she was to "affect ignorance" of his infidelities. Should he be a drunkard, she was to be thankful that he had some

[16] Lord Halifax (George Savile, first marquis of Halifax), *The Lady's New Year's Gift: or, Advice to a Daughter*. 1688.

faults, which would most likely soften the arrogance of his nature and throw a veil over her own weaknesses. If he proved "Cholerick and Ill-humour'd," she was to "take care of increasing the Storm by an unwary Word," and seek to reclaim him by smiles and flattery. Even the most difficult type of husband, "a close-handed Wretch," was not an "incurable grievance," for no man was so addicted to avarice that he would not at some time become prodigal, and an appeal to his vanity or ambition at these "Critical Moments," or sometimes a dose of wine, would "work upon his tough Humour." If he should be weak-minded, she was to take consolation in the thought that "a wife often made a better Figure, for her Husband's making no great one," and that his incompetence gave her dominion if she made the right use of it. But, while governing, she was advised by all means to let it appear to him and to the world that he still held the reins.

A much more pretentious work was *The Ladies Library*,[17] which, though advertised as "written by a Lady and published by Richard Steele," was really a compilation of passages appropriated from several seventeenth-century writers. Like the other women's morality books, it was a discussion of the qualities of character peculiarly desirable or objectionable in the sex and of the particular duties in the different states through which, it was assumed, every normal woman would pass. Volume I discussed these topics: Employment, Wit and Delicacy, Recreation, Dress, Chastity, Modesty, Meekness, Charity, Envy, Detraction, Censure and Reproof, Ignorance, and Pride. Volume II described the duties of the lady in each of her relations as daughter, wife, mother, widow, and mistress. Made up of whole sections engrafted, often without abridgment, from such different works as *The Ladies Calling*, Lord Halifax's *Advice*, and Mary Astell's *Serious Proposal*,[18] it was repetitious and inconsistent. To the colonial girl it must have been more confusing than enlightening, for one section enjoined her to be modest to the point of "shamefacedness,"

---

[17] *The Ladies Library. Written by a Lady and Published by Sir Richard Steele.* 3 vols. London, 1714. 3d ed., 1722. Many later editions.

[18] *A Serious Proposal to the Ladies, for the Advancement of their True and Greatest Interest.* London, 1697. Other works from which passages were taken were Taylor's *Holy Living;* Fleetwood's *Relative Duties of Parents and Children; The Whole Duty of Man; The Government of the Tongue;* Locke's *Treatise on Education;* Lucas's *Practical Christianity and Enquiry after Happiness;* Scott's *Christian Life;* Tillotson's *Sermons;* and Hickes's *Education of a Daughter.*— Reynolds, *op. cit.,* p. 332.

while another warned her against affected modesty. One chapter admonished her to be always sincere and frank and another advised her at times to "affect ignorance" and practice dissimulation; one part upbraided her for her lack of intellectual ambition and informed her that women have "as good Talents as Men," while many other passages reminded her of her mental inferiority and the divinely ordained limitations of her sphere. For the most part, however, the book was conservative. It was generally accepted in England and America as a collection of the most authoritative sources on the subject of woman's character and education, and was so popular that between 1714 and 1772 it ran into eight editions. Representative of the general approval with which it was held in the colonies was this suggestion in a letter from Benjamin Franklin to his wife regarding the education of their daughter Sally: "I hope she continues to love going to Church, and would have her read over and over again *The Whole Duty of Man* and *The Ladies Library*."[19]

Another book often recommended for young ladies was advertised repeatedly in colonial newspapers as *The Gentleman and Lady Instructed*.[20] The part devoted to ladies was a graphic and witty picture of the common foibles of the sex, followed by instructions for their proper conduct. Thus it described the morning occupation of a lady of fashion: "She chuckles together a whole Covy of Essences and Perfumes, she commands Combs to their Posts, Pomatums to theirs, Washes a-la-mode to theirs . . . And now her Ladyship brandishes the Combs, and the Powders raise Clouds in the Apartment. She trims up the Commode, she places it ten times. . . . At length she comes to patches; Here is Plea for Fancy, and Room for Inventions, no wonder then if the Operation takes up Time, and calls for Study and Reflection; its hard to resolve upon the Number, harder upon the Size, and much more easy to billet an Army, than to assign each Patch its proper Station. Twelve strikes before her Cheeks are inlaid, and her face be checker'd a-la-mode." A chapter entitled "Regulation of their Daily Actions" described the proper employments of the gentlewoman. She was to rise early, and after "discharging her duty to God," spend her time in the management

[19] *Writings of Benjamin Franklin* (ed., Albert Henry Smyth), III, 435.
[20] William Darrell, *The Gentleman Instructed, in the Conduct of a Virtuous and Happy Life, in Three Parts. Written for the Instruction of a Young Nobleman. To which is added a Word to the Ladies, by Way of Supplement to the First Part.* 8th ed., 1723.

of her household. After dinner she might embroider, or even read, for, it explained, "though Women should not pretend to commence Doctors," they should not "forswear knowledge nor make a vow of Stupidity."   She was cautioned, however, not to "Rival the Knowledge of the Sybils, nor the Science of the Muses," nor "wade too deep into Controversy, nor soar so high as Divinity," for these studies "lie out of a Lady's Way: They fly up to the Head, and not only intoxicate weak Brains, but turn them."   As a diversion, she might return visits or receive them, but she was admonished to avoid long conversations as "Women seldom have Materials to furnish a long Discourse, unless they comment upon their Neighbour's failures." She was not to display her wit in company, for "Women seldom appear more foolish, than when they aspire to the Glory of being thought wise," and was warned against discoursing of love intrigues, as "the Laws of *Decorum* are so severe in regard of Women, that it's almost a Fault to pronounce the Word Love."

During the decade preceding the Revolution, two new books appearing regularly in the announcements of booksellers were Dr. Gregory's *A Father's Legacy to his Daughters*,[21] and Dr. Fordyce's *Sermons to Young Women.*[22]   In these writings, which exalted the passive and negative qualities of character and held up masculinity as the most displeasing characteristic ladies could possess, one finds some explanation of the exaggerated sex consciousness and unnatural manners of many women of the period.   *The Legacy,* advertised as written by "a tender Father, in a declining state of health," was intended, the author explained, to inform his daughters regarding the "many nameless delicacies in female manners" and to point out those "virtues and accomplishments" which rendered women "most amiable in the eyes" of his own sex.   It emphasized a "soft delicacy" and an "exquisite sensibility" as among the chief excellencies of women and considered piety peculiarly necessary for them not only because of their "natural softness and sensibility," the sheltered condition of their lives, and their particular need of both the restraints and supports of religion, but more so because men—even those who were

[21] Dr. John Gregory, *A Father's Legacy to his Daughters. By the Late Dr. Gregory of Edinburgh.* London, 1774. Reprinted in Annapolis in 1775, and in Boston in 1779. Many other editions also.

[22] James Fordyce, D.D., *Sermons to Young Women.* 3rd American ed., from the 12th London ed., Philadelphia, 1809. Many other editions. A similar, though apparently less popular, work was Dr. Fordyce's *Character and Conduct of the Female Sex. . . .* London, 1776.

unbelievers themselves—regarded irreligion as "odious in women," as "proof of that hard and masculine spirit," which of all feminine faults they disliked most.

The book gave advice on such subjects as dress, amusements and recreations, general conduct in society, and marriage, reminding the reader always that a "modest reserve" and a "retiring delicacy" were her most attractive characteristics. It declared that wit, seldom found with "softness and delicacy," was the most dangerous talent a girl could possess, thus admonishing her: "Be even careful in displaying your *good sense*. It will be thought you assume a superiority over the rest of the company. But if you happen to have any learning, keep it a profound secret, especially from the men, who generally look with a jealous and malignant eye on a woman of great parts and a cultivated understanding." Bodily vigor, also unfeminine, was likewise to be concealed. "Though good health be one of the greatest blessings of life," it cautioned, "never make a boast of it; but enjoy it in grateful silence. We [men] so naturally associate the idea of female softness and delicacy with a correspondent delicacy of constitution, that when a woman speaks of her great strength, her extraordinary appetite, her ability to bear excessive fatigue, we recoil at the description, in a way she is little aware of."

The same nicety was advised in courtship and marriage. For a woman to admit she was in love was not "consistent with the perfection of female delicacy." Even after marriage she should not declare the full extent of her affection for her husband, for it would produce in him "satiety and disgust." In matters of marriage, it explained, women have little choice, since it is a maxim that love is not to begin on their part; but though they have not the privilege of choosing whom they may love, they have been endowed by nature with a "greater flexibility of taste" which makes it possible for them to love whatever person prefers them. Thus it described the regular and proper course of woman's love: "Some agreeable qualities recommend a gentleman to your good liking and friendship. In the course of his acquaintance he contracts an attachment to you. When you perceive it, it excites your gratitude; this gratitude rises into preference; and this preference, perhaps, at least advances to some degree of attachment, especially if it meets with crosses and difficulties. . . . If attachment was not excited in your sex in this manner, there is not one of a million of you that could ever marry with any degree of love."

Dr. Fordyce's *Sermons to Young Women* was saturated with the same sentimentality as that which pervaded Dr. Gregory's *Legacy*. The author extolled the "submissive dependence," "timidity of temper," "lovely meekness," "modest pliancy," and "complacent deportment" of the sex, and in a manner similar to that of Lord Halifax thus laid out the province of women: "Nature appears to have formed the faculties of your sex, for the most part, with less vigor than those of ours, observing the same distinction here, as in the more delicate frame of your bodies. . . . But you yourselves, I think, will allow that war, commerce, politics, exercises of strength and dexterity, abstract philosophy, and all the abstrusser sciences, are most properly the province of men . . . those masculine women that would plead for your sharing any part of this province equally with us, do not understand your true interests. There is an influence, there is an empire which belongs to you, and which I wish you ever to possess: I mean that which has the heart for its object and is secured by meekness, by soft attraction, and virtuous love."

In spite of their exaggerated notions of feminine delicacy and unnatural standards of conduct, these books were exceedingly popular. No lady's library was complete without them, and they were sometimes used as required readings in girls' schools. They were welcomed in the colonies as expressing a "new and more refined" attitude toward the "softer sex" and not only dictated the rules of female decorum during the period just before the Revolution, but, handed down from generation to generation, they had an incalculable influence in fixing the conception of the proper nature of women throughout the following century.

Other books considered as helpful in the education of colonial young ladies were Lady Pennington's *A Mother's Advice to Her Absent Daughters*,[23] Mrs. Chapone's *Letters on the Improvement of the Mind*,[24] *The Polite Lady*[25] of unknown authorship, and *The*

[23] Lady Sarah Pennington, *An Unfortunate Mother's Advice to her Absent Daughters; in a Letter to Miss Pennington.* London, 1761.

[24] Mrs. Hester Mulso Chapone, *Letters on the Improvement of the Mind Addressed to a Young Lady.* 2 vols. London, 1772. Several later editions.

[25] *The Polite Lady; or, a Course of Female Education. In a Series of Letters from a Mother to her Daughter.* 3rd ed., London, 1775.

Lady's Preceptor.[26]   Lady Pennington gave definite instructions to young ladies regarding such important matters as their education, everyday employments, dress, choice of a husband, and conduct as wives.   She stressed religious training as being of greater consequence than a "polite education," and, while insisting that the management of domestic affairs was certainly the proper business of women, maintained that learning did not make them poorer wives and mothers or less efficient housewives.   Discussing the manner in which ladies should spend their time with "innocence and propriety," she suggested that they devote the morning to household occupations and mental improvements and the afternoon to diversions, such as "company, books of the amusing kind, and entertaining productions of the needle, as well as plays, balls, cards, &c."   Representative of much of her advice was this counsel concerning the paying of visits and behavior in company: "When the conversation is only insignificant, join in it with an apparent satisfaction; talk of the elegance of a birthday suit, the pattern of a lace, the judicious assortment of jewels, the cut of a ruffle, or the set of a sleeve, with an unaffected ease; not according to the rank they hold in your estimation, but proportioned to the consequence they may be of in the opinion of those you are conversing with.   The great art of pleasing is to appear pleased with others: suffer not then an ill-bred absence of thought, or a contemptuous sneer, ever to betray a conscious superiority of understanding, always product of ill-nature and dislike;— suit yourself to the capacity and to the taste of your company, when that taste is confined to harmless trifles. . . ."   Mrs. Chapone's work consisted of ten letters addressed to her niece.   The first was a discussion of "the first principles of religion," and the next two were designed as a guide to the study of the Scriptures.   Letters IV, V, and VI were concerned with moral virtues; Number VIII, entitled "On Politeness and Accomplishments," described the proper behavior of young ladies in society and the subjects which should be included in their education; and Numbers IX and X were abstracts

---

[26] *The Lady's Preceptor, or, a Letter to a Young Lady of Distinction upon Politeness. Taken from the French of the Abbé D'Ancourt, and Adapted to the Religion, Customs, and Manners of the English Nation. By a Gentleman of Cambridge.* London, 1743. Another manual was *The Whole Duty of a Woman; or, a Guide to the Female Sex, from the Age of Sixteen to Sixty. . . . Written by a Lady.* London, 1735.

for the study of geography and history. *The Polite Lady,* a more pretentious work, discussed in detail the studies which should be included in a "Course of Female Education" and the virtues accepted as "the glory and ornament of the female sex," and gave advice on such subjects as dress, amusements and recreations, and general female decorum.

The Lady's Preceptor, while discussing the proper behavior of the young lady at church and her duties to her parents and other superiors, was concerned more with manners than with morality. It reminded her that it was not the business of her sex to concern herself about the rites and ceremonies of the church or to pass judgment upon the sermon, but to listen to the minister with gravity and attention and manifest respect and a desire for information. Regarding her demeanor in company, it admonished her to avoid appearing absent-minded and to evince interest in what her superiors had at heart by asking them questions; to abstain from gossip and a spirit of contradiction, which, while disagreeable in everyone, was especially so in the "fair sex"; to be careful not to be too quick and passionate in conversation or too inquisitive; and to "endeavour that Cheerfullness, Sweetness, and Modesty be always blended in your Countenance and Air." It gave special directions for her conduct when with men, warning her never to be alone in their company, especially with only one, and advising: "Be careful of maintaining that strict Watch over your Eyes, Words and Heart, that they may not in the least perceive you have any particular Regard for them." Men, it warned, took great pleasure in being thought irresistible lovers and in gaining victories over "the most rigid virtue"; therefore, the young lady should put little confidence in what they promised, and when fine things were said to her, should "acquit yourself by a gentle Smile accompanied with a Blush to shew that you are neither a Prude or a Coquette." When questioned on the subject of matrimony, without betraying any inclination, she should reply that she was not the person to be consulted "upon such a Head," but her father and mother, whose will she would always make her own.

Besides all these writings on general conduct, every one of which gave copious advice on the proper treatment of husbands, there were several specific guides to "conjugal felicity," the most frequently mentioned of which were Dean Swift's *A Letter to a Very Young Lady on her Marriage*[27] and Mrs. Chapone's *Letter to a New-Married Lady*.[28] Swift's letter, while contemptuous of women generally, was a sincere attempt to give helpful advice to a young friend. It was said that the lady to whom it was addressed did not appreciate it as a compliment either to herself or her sex, but it was so favorably regarded by the public that it was printed in America as well as in England. Summarized briefly, its suggestions to the bride were as follows: to keep her modest and reserved behavior rather than assume the bold and forward manner too often found in wives; to avoid displaying affection for her husband in public, affecting uneasiness during his absence, or demanding letters from him by every post while he was abroad; to be careful of her dress; to take into her confidence no "she-companions" but to let her company be of the masculine sex and chosen by her husband; and to keep herself informed of her husband's income and manage her household affairs so that they would come within her allowance rather than be like "those politic ladies, who think they gain a great point when they have teased their husbands to buy them a new equipage, a laced head, or a fine petticoat, without once considering what long scores remain unpaid to the butcher." Swift's primary advice, however, and the part, probably, to which the young bride objected, was an explanation of the way in which she might improve her mind and thus "become a reasonable and agreeable companion" for her husband.

Mrs. Chapone did not accept Dr. Gregory's opinion that a wife should conceal the extent of her affection from her husband, and disagreed also with Swift and the other male writers on marriage, almost every one of whom, she declared, held that the passion of love in man was infallibly destroyed by possession and could subsist but a short time after marriage. Admitting, however, an inevitable abatement, she urged the bride to cultivate the habit of affection and build the solid foundation of friendship while passion was subsiding, and offered suggestions as to how she might make herself agreeable to her husband. Her recommendations were the usual kind given to brides of every generation: "Avoid everything that can create a moment's disgust toward either your person or your mind. . . . Do

---

[27] *The Prose Works of Jonathan Swift* (ed., Temple Scott), XI, 124.

[28] Mrs. Hester Mulso Chapone, *A Letter to a New-Married Lady*. London, 1828. Earlier editions were advertised in newspapers in the southern colonies.

not disturb him with the detail of your grievances from servants or tradespeople, nor with methods of family management. . . . But when he returns to his own house, let him there find everything serene and peaceful, and let your cheerful complacency restore his good humour, and quiet every uneasy passion. . . . Endeavour to enter into his pursuits, catch his taste, improve his knowledge; nor let anything that is interesting to him appear a matter of indifference to you . . . next to displeasing or disgusting him, you should of all things dread his growing dull and weary in your company." Unlike the masculine advisers on marriage, Mrs. Chapone recognized the bride's difficulties in adjusting herself to her "In-laws" and, while advising her to strive to adopt her husband's sentiments regarding his relations and to be careful that no dispute ever arise between his mother and herself, she approved of the husband who declined to have his mother live with him after his marriage and advised the young wife thus to deal with her mother-in-law: "If she should desire to control your actions, or to intermeddle in the affairs of your family, more than you think is reasonable, hear her advice with patience, and answer with respect, but in a manner that may let her see you mean to judge of your own duties for yourself."[29]

The ladies' books so far discussed were written as sermons or lectures and made no attempt to conceal the fact that their purpose was instruction rather than entertainment. Others sought to make their teaching more palatable by presenting it in such a disguised form that the reader would scarcely be conscious of being improved while she was being amused. Such a work found in colonial inventories and advertised often in colonial newspapers was *Sophronia, or Letters to the Ladies*,[30] which gave instruction, not in "a dry bead-roll of precepts," it claimed, but in the form of animated letters written by a happy matron, who advised her correspondents out of her own experience on the subject of domestic relations. In one letter to an unhappy wife, *Amoret*, she explained that the very instant her own husband put the wedding ring on her finger, she considered herself completely "in the power of another" and re-

---

[29] Other guides to matrimonial happiness often advertised in the colonies were *The Matrimonial Preceptor, The School for Wives in a Series of Letters, Letters to Married Women*, and *Reflections on Courtship and Marriage; in two Letters to a Friend; wherein a practicable Plan is laid down for obtaining and securing Conjugal Felicity.* [30] 2d ed., London, 1775.

solved to part with her own will, and that she had since "made it an inviolable law to myself to study to oblige the man from whom I am to derive all my happiness, in this life." Later she gave a neglected wife a broad hint regarding her conjugal duties by relating for her benefit the "romantic instances of philandering" of a duke who had confessed to her that he had been a "follower of the ladies" only since he and his wife had "parted beds," and concluded with the opinion of the aggrieved duchess that "parting of beds is a terrible thing." *Fables for the Ladies*[31] presented the rules of female decorum in amusing little morality tales told in verse. One poem warned wives not to be careless of their dress; another illustrated the oft-repeated maxim that a woman can never regain her honor after it is once lost. Still another, called "The Owl and the Nightingale," in which the domestic nightingale who "minds the duties of her nest" enjoys the approval of man and bird, while the pedantic owl is held up to scorn, made clear the prevailing disapproval of the learned lady.

The Female Spectator,[32] also designed to entertain while it furnished instruction, was quite popular in the colonies. Besides discussions of the usual subjects deemed of special interest to ladies, it presented romantic little episodes each inculcating a moral. The adventures of *Martesin,* who, though beloved by her husband, fell in love with another, lost her reputation, and came to a tragic end, brought home the idea that a young lady should not marry until she was "well assured of her own heart." The unhappy *Seomanthe,* who, having been brought up by a prudish aunt, eloped with a worthless adventurer, illustrated the danger of confining girls too closely; and the ruin of the unfortunate *Erminia,* an innocent girl, trapped and seduced by a man disguised as her brother, demonstrated the danger of masquerades. The story of *Alithea, Doriman, and Melissa* showed how a wife might reclaim her unfaithful husband. Instead of displaying jealousy, the discreet *Alithea* feigned ignorance of *Doriman's* philandering, and when his mistress, *Melissa,* had a child, went to the midwife to whom it had been given, brought it

[31] Edward Moore, *Fables for the Ladies* (1744), in *The Works of the English Poets* (ed., Alexander Chalmers), XIV, 217. A third edition, illustrated, appeared in 1766.
[32] [Mrs. Eliza Haywood], *The Female Spectator.* Originally issued in monthly parts, April, 1744-May, 1746. 2d ed., 4 vols., London, 1748. Mrs. Haywood's *Epistles for the Ladies* (London, 1749-1750), was also popular.

home and cared for it as her own. *Doriman*, conscience-smitten at her prudence and generosity, cast off his heartless and wicked mistress, and returned to his faithful and forgiving wife. Similar stories were included to illustrate the dire effects of vanity, immodest behavior, and gaming, and of a woman's attempting to overstep her preordained sphere or to govern her husband. These little "histories," the author explained, were intended to "reform the morals, and improve the manners of an age, by all confessed degenerate and sunk," and to "enforce *precepts* by *example*, and make the *beauty of virtue* and the *deformity of vice*, sink deeper into the reader's mind."

Books designed to improve the ladies by praising their sex or presenting for their emulation examples of worthy women in the past were popular. *A Present for the Ladies*,[33] found frequently in inventories and newspaper advertisements, was a defense of the sex against the charges usually brought against them and a description of their virtues and contributions to mankind. Some of its ideas were so unconventional that one is surprised to find it often in the libraries of colonial gentlemen. Its version of the creation, for instance, exalting woman as "the Consummation of the Works of God," was radically opposed to the usual interpretation of the account in Genesis. Woman, it maintained, was of "more delicate Composition" since she was "built" after the "divine Artifice" had first been practised upon inferior animals and man. The author's suggestions that husbands would do well to consult their wives in important business matters may have met the secret approval of colonial ladies, but his assertion that women were as capable as men, not only of learning, but even of governing, was probably received by them as a ridiculous piece of nonsense. Of the works describing the "memorable actions" of illustrious ladies in the past, the most popular was George Ballad's *Memoirs of British Ladies*,[34] a presentation of sixty biographies of accomplished women in an attempt to remove "that vulgar prejudice of the supposed incapacity of the female sex." *The Female Excellency, or the Ladies Glory*, praising the general worth of the sex, presented for emulation "the Worthy

[33] N. Tate, *A Present for the Ladies: being an Historical Account of Several Illustrious Persons of the Female Sex. To which is added, The Character of an Accomplish'd Virgin, Wife, and Widow in Verse.* 2d ed., 1693.

[34] *Memoirs of Several Ladies of Great Britain, who have been Celebrated for their Writings or Skill in the Learned Languages, Arts, and Sciences.* Oxford, 1752. 2d ed., 1775.

Lives and memorable Actions of Nine Famous Women, who have been renowned either for Virtue or Valour in several Ages of the World."[35]

A publication providing intellectual stimulus and diversion was *The Ladies Diary*, a new edition of which seems to have been printed with the Virginia Almanac each year. The *Virginia Gazette*, June 30, 1768, advertised the forthcoming number for the year 1769 as containing a "Variety of improving and entertaining Particulars, such as Enigmas, Acrosticks, Rebusses, Queries, Paradoxes, Nosegays of Flowers, Plates of Fruit, Mathematical Questions, &c. &c.," and the following February announced the winner of the award offered for the best answer in verse to the prize enigma. The successful lady, who signed her name as *Isabella*, was desired to send to the printer for the ten copies of *The Ladies Diary* offered as prize, or, if she preferred, to wait and have ten of those printed the following year.[36]

Besides these various ladies' books there was on sale in the colonies a London periodical called *The Lady's Magazine*,[37] which was evidently intended to be for women what *The Gentleman's Magazine* was for their husbands. No available record furnishes more revealing evidence than this monthly, not only of the literary taste

[35] Richard Burton [Nathaniel Crouch], *Female Excellency or the Ladies Glory*. . . . London, 1688. Similar works were: William Alexander: *The History of Women from the Earliest Antiquity; giving Some Account of Almost Every Interesting Particular concerning the Sex, among All Nations, Ancient and Modern*. 2 vols. 3d ed., London, 1782; James Bland, *Essay in Praise of Women; or, A Looking-glass for Ladies to See their Perfections in, shewing how they Behav'd in all Ages*. . . . 2d ed., London, 1735; M. Jacques Du Boscq, *The Accomplished Woman, written in French by M. Du Boscq, A Franciscan, Counsellor and Preacher in Ordinary to the King in the Year MDCXXX in two volumes. Translated by a Gentleman of Cambridge*. London, 1753; *The Female Worthies; or Memoirs of the Most Illustrious Ladies, of All Ages and Nations, who have been Eminently Distinguished for their Magnanimity, Learning, Genius, Virtue, Piety, and Other Excellent Endowments, conspicuous in all the various Stations and Relations of Life, public and private*. . . . n. d.; William Russell, *Essay on the Character, Manners, and Genius of Women in Different Ages. Enlarged from the French of M. Antoine Leonard Thomas*. 2 vols. London, 1773.

[36] *Virginia Gazette*, February 13, 1769. *The Ladies Diary* published in Virginia was evidently an imitation of *The Ladies Diary: or, The Woman's Almanack, Containing many Delightful and Entertaining Particulars, peculiarly adapted for the Use and Diversion of the Fair-Sex* published in England from 1703 to 1726, which contained enigmas, paradoxes, and arithmetical questions, for the best answers to which it offered prizes. For a description of the English *Ladies Diary* see Reynolds, *op. cit.*, pp. 327-29.

[37] *The Lady's Magazine; or, Entertaining Companion for the Fair Sex, Appropriated solely to their Use and Amusement*. 28 vols. London, 1770-1797.

of ladies of the period but also of the prevailing attitude regarding their intellectual and social status. In the prefatory address of the first number the editor gave a forecast of his publication, by means of which, he declared, he proposed to "render the minds of the sex not less amiable than their persons." The persons were not to be neglected, however, for, he explained, "as external appearance is the first inlet to the treasures of the heart," he intended to present ladies with "most elegant patterns for Tambour, Embroidery, or every kind of Needlework" and with illustrations of all the "fluctuations of fashions." Those living in the country were to be kept informed of "every innovation made in the female dress, whether it respects the covering of the head, or the cloathing of the body." For the instruction of their minds he promised to ransack every branch of literature to find interesting stories that would "confirm chastity and recommend virtue."

The magazine was not very different from ladies' magazines of today. Each number carried a travel story entitled "A Sentimental Journey by a Lady"; a life story of some contemporary woman and an historical account of some famous woman of antiquity under the heading "The Lady's Biography"; a collection of maxims on woman's conduct called "The Oeconomy of Female Life"; an article called "The Female Rambler," which was a discussion of some subject considered of particular interest to women; and a section entitled "The Lady's Housemaid; or Housekeeper's Calendar," which was a collection of menus and recipes "embellished" with a full-page engraving of the arrangement of dishes for a first and second course for the month. Besides these feature articles there were miscellaneous essays on subjects like love, courtship, and marriage, and morality tales, enigmatical questions, confectionery recipes, patterns, charts, and directions for embroidery, netting, and other needlework, and full-page illustrations of the latest fashions.

Of even greater interest to ladies, perhaps than this periodical, were the romances, large numbers of which poured into the colonies during the last half of the century. In England the reading of novels was so widespread that every writer on woman's education took occasion to condemn it. The newly established circulating libraries, which dealt largely in these "fictitious stories," were denounced as "evergreen trees of diabolical knowledge," and the novel-reading girl with her fanciful ideas, affected manners, and general preciosity, became a comic type in the literature of the day.   In the colonies, also, journalists pointed out the evils in "these damn'd story-books," but the same papers which published their remonstrances carried announcements of circulating libraries appealing to ladies for patronage and bookseller's advertisements of long lists of the objectionable writings.   These lists included, besides the works of Richardson, Fielding, Smollett and Sterne, which apparently were not generally condemned by the preceptors of young ladies, numerous "Tales," "Memoirs," "Histories," and "Adventures" which are now generally unknown.[38]

It is not to be imagined that all colonial ladies restricted their reading to the works specially prepared for their sex.   Those who had real interest in books probably became acquainted with standard works in history, travel, science, philosophy, and English literature, many of which were sometimes found in colonial libraries.   The wife of Councillor Carter of "Nomini Hall" in Virginia was said to read more habitually than the parson of the parish.[39]   Mrs. William Hooper, wife of the signer of the Declaration of Independence from North Carolina, was described as possessing a great knowledge of history, conversational ability "equal to high subjects," and such other "accomplishments of mind" as to completely efface the first impression made by her lack of beauty and "very ordinary appearance."[40] Martha Laurens of South Carolina, according to memoirs written by her son, was acquainted with the best in English literature, and was

---

[38] The following were often advertised in colonial newspapers: *The History of Lady Julia Mandeville*; *Eliza Musgrove, her history, in a series of letters*; *The Female Cavalier, a Story Founded on Facts*; *The Nunnery of Coquettes*; *The History of Miss Betsey Thoughtless*; *The History of Lucy Wellers*; *Female Quixote*; *Female Foundling*; *The Cloister, or Amours of a Jesuit and a Nun*; *Betsey, or the Caprices of Fortune*; *The History of Charlotte Manners*; *La Belle Philosophe, or the Fair Philosopher*; *History of Emily Montague*; *The False Step, or the History of Miss Bradenwell*; *The Maid of Quality, or the History of Lady Lucy Layton*; *Harriot, or the Innocent Adulteress*; *The Old Maid, or the History of Miss Ravensworth*; *Maidenhood well Lost*, by "Miss Vansitort," *The Virtuous Wife*, by Mrs. Bailey, *The Vestal Nun, or true History*, by "Lady Harrington," *Wives Excuse, or Cuckolds make themselves*, by "Lord Grosvenor," *The Rival Milliners*, by "Mrs. Rheda and Miss S- in Bow Street," *Wife to be Let*, by "Mr. Bailey," *All for Love*, by "Miss Hunter," *Wife's Revenge*, by "Lady Percy," *Platonick Love*, by "Mrs. Cornewell and Mr. Bradshaw," *The Petticoat Plotter*, by "the Princess Dowager of Wales," *Fashionable Lady*, by "Mrs. Lessingham," *The Clandestine Marriage*, by "Lady Waldegrave and the Duke of Gloucester," *The Forsaken Shepherdess*, by "Lady Waldegrave."

[39] Fithian, *Journal*, p. 108.   [40] McRee, *Iredell*, I, 393-94.

known to have read the New Testament in Greek with her sons and in French with her daughters.[41]   Eliza Lucas of the same colony, who wrote of spending much time in the well furnished library of her home and of borrowing books from her neighbors, found pleasure in the works of Plutarch, Virgil, and Locke, and even delved into the study of law.[42]   But these women were conspicuous as exceptions to the general rule.   Colonial women ordinarily read very little.   Intellectual attainments were not expected of "the weaker sex."   Works like *The Ladies Calling* and *The Compleat Housewife* contained all that the most exemplary gentlewoman was expected to know.

[41] David Ramsay, *Memoirs of the Life of Martha Ramsay*, pp. 11-24.
[42] Ravenel, *Eliza Pinckney*, pp. 28-32, 51.

CHAPTER XI

PARTICIPATION IN PUBLIC AFFAIRS

Wifehood and motherhood, it has been shown in preceding chapters, were held before the colonial woman as the purpose of her being, and home as the sphere of all her actions. Her mission in life was, first, to get a husband and then to keep him pleased, and her duties were bearing and rearing children and caring for her household. Her education, directed to these ends, consisted of instructions in morality, training in household occupations, and, among the upper classes, the acquirement of the social amenities. But while homemaking was the one occupation for which women were trained and was probably the sole business of a large majority, it did not absorb all the energies of some women and was by no means the only employment required of others. Quite a few gentlewomen interested themselves in affairs beyond their households, and a much larger number than is generally known were forced by necessity into performing services outside their own families.

Women, it will be remembered, had an active part in founding the southern colonies. Not only did wives accompany their husbands to the New World and share with them the hardships and responsibilities of subduing the wilderness, but single women came on their own ventures, bringing in new settlers, and establishing plantations.[1] It is true that women were desired as colonists chiefly to provide comfortable homes for the masculine settlers and to bear children to increase the population, but while performing these functions the more energetic were active also in public affairs. In the early records appear the names of a number who distinguished themselves in matters of common concern and of some who, while not deliberately championing the principle of political rights for their sex, were drawn into the public arena by their exertions in behalf of friends or relatives or in the protection of their own private estates.

Among the "women of figure" at Jamestown at an early date was the wife of Thomas Nuice, whose strenuous efforts in relieving the

[1] See above, p. 11.

needs of the poor and suffering inhabitants of the little colony during
the war and famine of 1622 were commended to the Virginia Company in London and inscribed in the public documents.[2]   Another
notable Virginia dame was remembered for her courage and independence during the same evil times.   The historian Stith relates
that during the fearful days following the Indian massacre the
authorities, "much frightened at this lamentable and unexpected
Disaster," decided to abandon the outlying plantations and assemble
all the inhabitants into five or six of the most defensible places.   It
was impossible, naturally, on sudden notice for the planters to trans-
fer their cattle and other goods, and several of the most daring, unwilling to leave their plantations to be pillaged by the Indians, refused
to move themselves and their people.   Among them was Mistress
Alice Proctor, a widow, described as "a proper, civil, and modest
Gentlewoman," who "with an heroic spirit" defended her plantation
against the assaults of the Indians for over a month.   Later she continued in her refusal to obey the order of the council to abandon
her house for a safer place at Jamestown until the officers threatened
to burn it down.[3]

A Virginia matron who at an early period left her housekeeping
to interfere in political matters was Elizabeth Pott, wife of John Pott,
one of Virginia's earliest physicians.   Dr. Pott was acting governor
of Virginia in 1629 and was later chief agitator against unpopular
Governor Harvey.   Soon after the arrival of Harvey in Virginia,
Dr. Pott was charged with cattle stealing and tried before the general court.   He was found guilty, but the question of his punishment
was referred to the king of England.   Mistress Pott, in defiance of
authorities, boarded a vessel and traveled all the way to London to
defend her husband before the king.   There she pleaded his cause
so earnestly that she secured a pardon for him.[4]

A few decades later, women were among the most zealous participants in the popular uprising known as Bacon's Rebellion.   The
wife of Anthony Haviland, one of the first to help gather the people
together, was sent posthaste up and down the country as Bacon's
emissary to carry his "declaration papers."   Sarah Drummond, wife
of William Drummond, Bacon's leading adviser, by her fiery speeches
denouncing and defying Governor Berkeley, spurred the wavering to

[2] *Records of the Virginia Company of London*, II, 383.
[3] William Stith, *History of Virginia*, pp. 235-36; *William and Mary Quarterly*,
XV, 39.   [4] *Ibid.*, XIV, 99.

action. Sarah Grendon, wife of Colonel Thomas Grendon, was charged
with being "a great encourager and assister in the late horrid Rebellion" and was the only woman excepted from the pardon in the act
of indemnity and free pardon passed by the Assembly in February,
1677.[5]

Another instigator of rebellion was Lydia, wife of Major Edmund
Chiesman, an insurgent who after Bacon's death was condemned to
death by Berkeley. One of the chroniclers of the time gives this
dramatic account of Mistress Chiesman's gallant defence of her husband: "When that the Major was brought into the Governours presence, and by him demanded, what made him to ingage in Bacon's
designes? Before that the Major could frame an answer to the Governours demand; his Wife steps in and tould his honour that it was
her provocations that made her husband joyne in the case that Bacon
contended for; ading; that if he had not bin enfluenced by her in-
stigations, he had never don that which he had done. Therefore
(upon her bended knees) she desired of his honour, that since what
her husband had done, was by her meanes, and so, by consequence,
she most guilty, that she might be hanged and he pardoned. Though
the Governour did know, that what she had saide, was neare to the
truth, yet he said little to her request. . . ."[6] Mistress Chiesman's
courageous shouldering of responsibility did not save her husband,
for he escaped the gallows only by dying in prison before the governor's vengeance could be executed.

Other gentlewomen, wives of Berkeley's supporters, were impressed by the rebels into service in a unique manner. An Cotton,
one of the leading chroniclers of the rebellion, gives this account
of Bacon's extraordinary tactics: "He was no sooner arrived at Towne
[Jamestown] but by several small partyes of Horse (2 or 3 in a
party, for more he could not spare) he fetcheth into his little League,
all the prime mens wives, whose Husbands were with the Governour,
(as coll. Bacon's Lady, Madm. Bray, Madm. Page. Mdm. Ballard,
and others) which the next morning he presents to the view of their
husbands and ffriends in towne, upon the top of the small worke hee
had cast up in the night; where he caused them to tarey till hee had
finished his defence against his enemies shott. . . ."[7] Another annalist

[5] *Ibid.*, XV, 41.

[6] "Narrative of the Indian and Civil Wars in Virginia, in the Years 1675 and
1676." *Force Tracts*, I (No. 11), 34.

[7] "An Account of Our Late Troubles in Virginia," *Force Tracts*, I (No. 9), 8.

wrote of Bacon's placing the gentlewomen atop his breastworks: "The poor Gent:women were mightily astonished at this project; neither were their husbands voide of amazements at this subtill invention. If Mr. Fuller thought it strange, that the Divells black guard should be enrouled Gods shoulders, they made it no less wonderful, that their innocent and harmless wives should thus be entred a white garde to the Devill. This action was a method in war, that they were not well acquainted with (no not those the best inform'd in military affaires) that before they could com to pearce their enemies sides, they must be obliged to dart their weapons through their wives brest."[8] Naturally Berkeley's supporters refused to fire upon their wives. So, concluded the narrator, "these Ladyes white Aprons" proved to be of greater protection to Bacon and his men than all his fortifications.

Lady Berkeley was not among the "white aprons." Neither was she at home attending to household occupations. According to a letter written by Mistress Bacon to her sister, June 29, 1676, the governor had sent his lady to England with "great complaints" against Bacon, relying upon her, apparently, to represent to those in authority his side of the troublous events.[9]

Though the complaints carried by Dame Berkeley were first to reach the ears of the king, those of Bacon's female followers later also crossed the Atlantic and helped to bring royal censure and reproof upon the governor. When, after Bacon's sudden death and the subsequent disorganization of his supporters Berkeley regained power, he charged the chief of his opponents with treason, confiscated their estates, and had twenty-three hanged. Among these was William Drummond, husband of the spirited Sarah. Mistress Drummond did not bow in calm resignation to the governor's orders. Determined to justify her husband and proclaim Berkeley's harshness as well as to regain her property, she sent a petition to the Lords for Trade and Plantations, explaining that her husband had been sentenced to die by martial law and executed, though he had never borne arms or any military office, and that the governor had seized his plantation and goods and forced her and her five children to fly from their habitation. Her case was reported to the king, who or-

<hr>

[8] "Narrative of the Indian and Civil Wars in Virginia," *Force Tracts*, I, (No. 11), 22.

[9] *William and Mary Quarterly*, IX, 5.

dered that her property be restored and announced that her husband had been put to death contrary to the laws of the kingdom.[10]

In Maryland as in Virginia, women took part in political and religious struggles and were active in other public matters. An account of the quarrel and battle between Governor Stone and the Puritan Party in 1655 mentions women among the participants. It tells of the Puritans' capture of the governor and all his company and relates that the victors condemned ten to death, executed four, and would have executed all had it not been for the incessant pleading of some good women, which saved some, and the petitions of the soldiers, which saved others.[11] The Puritans, endeavoring to prevent stories of their brutality from getting abroad and determined to have only favorable accounts of their actions presented before Cromwell, immediately sent dispatches to England and attempted to keep their prisoners incommunicado. But the governor's wife, Virlinda, who had not been allowed to see her wounded husband, was determined that he and his followers should not suffer from the misrepresentation of Puritan messengers. She wrote at once to Lord Baltimore, describing the armed conflict and explaining the issues from the governor's point of view. Her letter shows not merely a keen interest in her husband's predicament but also an understanding of the whole political situation.[12] Another Maryland matron to plead her husband's cause before his enemies could "make their owne tale" in England was Barbara Smith, wife of Captain Richard Smith of Calvert County. During the Revolution of 1689, when her husband was imprisoned for refusing to take part with the insurgents, Mistress Smith hurried to England to lay his case before the authorities there.[13]

The outstanding woman in early Maryland, however, was not a devoted wife, but, as she appears repeatedly in the records, "Mistresse Margarett Brent, Spinster." This remarkable woman was not only the most conspicuous of her sex, but was one of the most prominent personages in the colony, whose business and public activities fill many pages of court records and suggest a career which the most ambitious of modern feminists might envy. Margaret Brent was of

---

[10] *Virginia Magazine*, XXII, 235-36; Neill, *Virginia Carolorum*, p. 380.

[11] John Langford, "Refutation of Babylon's Fall," *Narratives of Early Maryland*, p. 264.

[12] The whole of her letter is given in the *Narratives of Maryland*, pp. 265-67.

[13] *Archives of Maryland*, VIII, 153; *Maryland Magazine*, II, 374.

distinguished family and apparently a person of means, but as a Catholic she suffered persecution in England. Dissatisfied, probably, with the disabilities of her family under the English laws and encouraged by Lord Baltimore's extraordinary offers of land and privileges in Maryland, she decided to emigrate, and, with her brothers Giles and Fulke and her sister Mary, arrived in the province in November, 1638.

Though accompanied by their brothers, the Mistresses Brent came on their own ventures, bringing in servants, patenting large tracts of land in their own rights, and establishing plantations. As owners of manorial estates, they had the right to hold courts-baron, where controversies relating to manor lands were tried and tenants did fealty for their lands, and courts-leet, where residents on their manors were tried for criminal offences. One of the few surviving records of a court-baron is of that held at St. Gabriel's Manor by the steward of Mistress Mary Brent, where the tenant appeared, "did fealty to the Lady," and took possession of thirty-seven acres according to the custom of the manor.[14] Whether Mistress Margaret exercised such feudal rights over her tenants does not appear, but the many references to her in the minutes of the provincial court bear witness to her diligence and perseverance in prosecuting her debtors. Between the years 1642 and 1650 her name occurs no less than one hundred and thirty-four times in the court records, and during these eight years there was hardly a court at which she did not have at least one case. Occasionally she appeared as defendant, but oftener as plaintiff, and, it is interesting to know, a majority of these cases were decided in her favor.

Her successful handling of her own affairs probably accounts for her being called upon often to act on behalf of her friends and members of her family. When her brother Fulke returned to England, he gave her a power of attorney to conduct his affairs, and on several occasions she acted for her other brother, Giles.[15] As guardian of the little Indian princess, Mary Kittamaquund, daughter of the Piscataway Emperor, she brought suits and collected debts due her, and she also acted as agent for other gentlewomen.[16] Because she so frequently transacted business for others by power of attorney, it has been mistakenly assumed that she was an attorney at law, but no

[14] *Archives of Maryland*, IV, 417.
[15] *Ibid.*, IV, 192, 228, 357, 477, 481; X, 28, 49.
[16] *Ibid.*, IV, 259, 264, 265, 487-88.

evidence appears to show that she made any claim to membership in the legal profession.

During the first eight years of her residence in Maryland, Mistress Brent's energies were exerted largely in the conduct of private business, but rapidly moving events following the civil wars thrust her into a position of great public responsibility and for a time placed in her hands the destiny of the whole colony. Leonard Calvert, the governor, went to England in April, 1643, to consult with his brother, Lord Baltimore, about affairs in the province and, on his return in September, 1644, found the colony on the verge of an insurrection. Led by William Claiborne and Richard Ingle, a band of rebels soon took possession of Kent Island, invaded the western shore, and established themselves at St. Mary's. Governor Calvert with a large number of the councillors fled to Virginia, leaving Maryland in a state of anarchy. Toward the end of 1646 he returned with a small force of Virginians and Maryland refugees, entered St. Mary's, and established his authority over the province. But he had hardly restored order when on June 9, 1647, he died, leaving Maryland once more without a strong hand to direct her affairs.[17] On his deathbed, by a nuncupative will, he named Thomas Greene to succeed him as governor and appointed Margaret Brent his executrix with the enigmatical instruction, "Take all and pay all."[18]

With her appointment as executrix of Governor Calvert, Margaret Brent's public career began. She was summoned into court to answer numerous suits for his debts and found it necesary to start legal proceedings for sums due his estate. The most urgent matter before her was the satisfaction of debts due the soldiers of Fort Inigoes. Governor Calvert had brought these volunteers from Virginia to help regain the government from the rebels, and, in order to secure their much needed services, had pledged his entire estate and that of the Lord Proprietor to pay them. Before his executrix could complete her inventory, the captain of the fort, on behalf of the soldiers, demanded their back wages and secured an attachment upon the whole Calvert estate.[19]

Mistress Brent now found herself confronted by a grave and critical situation. Leonard Calvert's estate was inadequate to meet the demands upon it. The price of corn was soaring higher and

[17] William Hand Browne, *Maryland: A History of a Palatinate* (Boston and New York, 1884), pp. 58-64.
[18] *Archives of Maryland*, IV, 314.   [19] *Ibid.*, p. 338.

higher and famine threatened. Enemies of the existing government were just outside the borders of the province, awaiting an opportunity for a new invasion, and the hungry soldiers in the fort, frightened by the rise in prices and the scarcity of food, became unruly and threatened mutiny. Realizing the necessity for prompt and decisive measures, she demanded and obtained a power to act as attorney for the Lord Proprietor and quieted the clamorous soldiers by promising to send to Virginia for corn and by selling enough of the proprietary's cattle to pay them. Thus she rescued the struggling little colony from certain disaster and very probably saved it from all the evils of another civil war.

One of Maryland's historians, commenting upon her courageous handling of the situation, suggests that Leonard Calvert might have done better had he reversed his testamentary dispositions and made Margaret Brent governor and Thomas Greene executor.[20] But it was not a day of political rights for women, as Mistress Margaret soon discovered. On January 21, 1647, probably in order to be in a better position to look after the Calvert interests, she went before the assembly and demanded a seat, thereby unconsciously distinguishing herself as the first woman in America to claim the right to vote. The minutes of the proceedings for the day state: "Came Mrs Margarett Brent and requested to have vote in the howse for herselfe and voyce also for that att the last Court 3d: Jan: it was ordered that the said Mrs. Brent was to be looked upon and received as his Lordships Attorney. The Governor denyed that the sd Mrs Brent should have any vote in the howse."[21] She did not submit quietly to this decision, however, for, according to the record, she protested against all the proceedings in the assembly unless she might be present and vote.

The members of the assembly, while unwilling to allow a woman within the sacred precincts of their ordained sphere, nevertheless appreciated her public services and commended her to the Lord Proprietor. Lord Baltimore, ignorant of the succession of disturbances in his colony and hearing of the bold manner in which Margaret Brent had taken matters into her own hands and disposed of his cattle, wrote to the assembly, complaining of her highhandedness. In answer, the assembly wrote him a long letter describing the calamities and disorders they had suffered and concluding with this

[20] Browne, *op. cit.*, p. 64. [21] *Archives of Maryland*, I, 215.

earnest justification of their countrywoman: ". . . as for Mrs Brents undertaking and medling with your Lordships Estate here (whether she procured it with her own and others importunity or no) we do Verily Believe and in Conscience report that it was better for the Collonys safety at that time in her hands than in any mans else in the whole Province after your Brothers death for the Soldiers would never have treated any other with that Civility and respect and though they were even ready at times to run into mutiny yet she still pacified them till at the last things were brought to that straight that she must be admitted and declared your Lordships Attorney by an order of Court (the Copy whereof is herewith inclosed) or else all must go to ruin Again and then the second mischief had been doubtless far greater than the former so that if there hath not been any sinister use made of your Lordships Estate by her from what it was intended and engaged for by Mr Calvert before his death, as we verily Believe she hath not, then we conceive from that time she rather deserved favour and thanks from your Honour for her so much Concurring to the Public Safety then to be liable to all those bitter invectives you have been pleased to express against her."[22]   Lord Baltimore was not moved by this spirited defence to withdraw his accusations or to express any appreciation of Mistress Brent's services, but continued distrustful and hostile.

Margaret Brent's fall from grace, however, was not due altogether to her selling the proprietary cattle. She and her family were the victims of a new policy which the proprietor was observing in order to meet the change in English politics. A shrewd politician, Lord Baltimore warily watched the undercurrents of popular feeling in England, determined to gain the good will of those in power and thereby save his proprietary estates by whatever means he found expedient. Perceiving the rise of the Puritans to power in Parliament, he sought to conciliate them by showing disfavor to prominent Catholics and granting concessions to Protestants in Maryland.[23] Deprived of the Maryland proprietor's favor, the Brents moved down to Westmoreland County in Virginia, where they patented land and established a plantation, giving it the significant name "Peace." Though Mistress Margaret continued active in the conduct of business for other people and for herself, she was no longer prominent in political

[22] *Ibid.*, I, 216-17.
[23] Matthew Page Andrews, *History of Maryland: Province and State* (New York, 1929), p. 93.

affairs and after about 1650 her name disappears from the public records.

The idea of a woman's conducting business enterprises and having a hand in public matters was not new to the early colonists. It was customary for English women of the aristocracy to be interested in national affairs and for those of the lower classes to be engaged in what today we call gainful occupations. Family letters and other records present gentlewomen as active participants on both sides of the political and religious struggles of the first half of the seventeenth century.[24] Among the nobility, the management of the family estate was often left to the care of the wife while the husband was detained at court, was devoting himself to politics, science or religion, or was abroad for business or pleasure. The wife of the English husbandman looked after the farm during his absence and at his death frequently took over its entire management. Poorer women labored for wages in the fields at almost every kind of farm work. Women of means sometimes carried on enterprises requiring considerable capital, and wives of shopkeepers and tradesmen, whose places of business were ordinarily in the home, commonly assisted their husbands in their shops. Women also practiced medicine and surgery and had almost a complete monopoly in the field of obstetrics.[25]

But with the advance of the seventeenth century, English women of the upper classes came to be less concerned with business and other affairs. The great increase in wealth and the vogue for frivolous entertainments following the Restoration discouraged the exercise of initiative, energy, and independence in the conduct of practical affairs and brought about a rapid deterioration in the physique, the morale, and the general efficiency of upper-class women.[26] Their whole education in the eighteenth century stressed sex differences, encouraged the development of passive rather than active qualities, opposed robustness of mind and body as vulgar, and emphasized the importance of ornamental rather than utilitarian accomplishments. In the southern colonies also the eighteenth century saw a decline in the vigor and self-reliance of women in wealthier families and a lessening of their influence in public matters. Because of the rural character of their lives and the general influence of the frontier, American

[24] Alice Clark, *Working Life of Women in the Seventeenth Century* (London and New York, 1919), pp. 23-28.

[25] *Ibid.*, pp. 14-23, 29-35, 44-92, 150-289.

[26] *Ibid.*, pp. 35-41.

ladies were less idle and artificial than those in England, but compared with the daring and independent matrons of the preceding century, they appear somewhat effeminate and timid.

In the back settlements and on the frontier, women continued to be valued for their strength and valor, and though their exploits seldom got into the records, they were probably busy with many matters beyond their cabins. The early records of Georgia tell of the important part played by Mary Musgrove [later Matthews], daughter of an Indian mother and an English father, and wife of a Carolina trader.[27] Finding that she could speak the Creek language as well as English and that she had a great influence over the Indians and was a skillful diplomat, Oglethorpe secured her services as interpreter and adviser on Indian affairs, agreeing to allow her an annual stipend of one hundred pounds. That he relied upon her advice is evident in many references to her like the following in the secretary's journal: "Matthews Wife has always been in great Esteem with the General, and not without good Reason; for being half Indian by Extract, she has a very great influence upon many of them, particularly the Creek Nation, our next neighbours . . . and the General would advise with her in many Things, for his better dealing with the Indians; taking her generally for his Interpreter, and using her very kindly on all Occasions."[28]

Mary was a person of means as well as influence. She owned broad acres of valuable land and had many Indian traders under her command. When food was scarce, she supplied the hungry colonists with provisions and at her own expense furnished Indian warriors to serve Oglethorpe. When trouble threatened with the neighboring Spanish colony of Florida, Oglethorpe sent her to the border to establish a trading post on the Altamaha River, from which she could watch the Spaniards and acquaint him with their movements and at the same time treat with the Indians and keep them on friendly terms with the Georgia colonists. When hostilities began, she rallied her war Indians to Oglethorpe's side and sent her traders to the conflict. Until her marriage with Thomas Bosomworth, an avaricious and unscrupulous English clergyman, who attempted to use her influence over the Indians and in the colony to acquire wealth and

[27] After Musgrove's death, Mary married Jacob Matthews, and as a third husband married Rev. Thomas Bosomworth.
[28] *Colonial Records of Georgia*, IV, 518.

power for himself, she continued to be of incalculable help to Ogle-thorpe and the colonists.[29] One of Georgia's historians writes of her services: "Her assistance was invaluable, and her aid, not only in concluding treaties but also in securing warriors from the Creek con-federacy during the conflict between Georgia and Florida, indispen-sable. Promptly did she respond on all occasions to any request made of her. . . . She was certainly of great use to him [Oglethorpe] and to the colony."[30]

Other women in pioneer communities probably played important rôles which were not committed to record, and, as will be shown in following chapters, many throughout the colonies were occupied with making a living. But those who enjoyed the advantages of wealth and refinement came more and more to be content to be "shining ornaments" in their families. A comparison of petitions presented by the undaunted dames of the first years of the colonies with the requests of the more modest ladies of the next century reveals a con-sciousness of sex and an unnatural prudishness in the latter not observ-able in their pioneer grandmothers. Sarah Drummond, Virlinda Stone, and Margaret Brent stated their requests confidently and boldly, professed no ignorance of politics, and made no attempt to excuse their interference in public matters. Their petitions disclose no doubts regarding their ability to understand and explain the polit-ical issues of the time or their right to interpose in matters of public concern. The women of the later period appear disinclined to admit any interest in public policy and anxious lest their private requests be mistaken for an unwomanly meddling in politics. One petitioner, for instance, soliciting Governor Martin of North Carolina regard-ing some requirements made of her husband, was very careful to preface her entreaty with this modest declaration: "It is not for me, unacquainted as I am with the politics and laws, to say with what propriety this was done."[31] A petition of some ladies of Wilming-ton, North Carolina, asking the governor to rescind an order regard-ing the removal of the wives and children of Tories from the state, declares apologetically, "It is not the province of our sex to reason

[29] Merton Coulter, "Mary Musgrove, Queen of the Creeks," *Georgia Historical Quarterly*, XI, 1-30.

[30] Charles C. Jones, *History of Georgia* (2 vols. Boston and New York, 1883), I, 384.

[31] *State Records of North Carolina*, XVI, 389-90.

deeply upon the policy of the order," and justifies their "earnest supplication" on the grounds that it was prompted by the distress of the innocent and helpless.[32]

These petitioners had evidently been carefully educated in the eighteenth-century ideals of female character. They had doubtless read in their *Spectators* that participating in politics was "repugnant to the softness, the modesty, and those other endearing qualities . . . natural to the fair sex," and agreed that gentlewomen should "distinguish themselves as tender mothers and faithful wives rather than as furious partisans."[33]   In many admonitions like the following from one of their textbooks on behavior, they had been warned against presuming to understand political matters: "It [politics] is a subject entirely above your sphere.   I would not willingly resign any of the privileges that properly belong to our sex; but, I hope, I shall have all the sensible part of it on my side, when I affirm that the conduct and management of state affairs is a thing with which we have no concern. Perhaps our natural abilities are not equal to such an arduous task; at any rate, our education, as it is now conducted, is too slight and superficial to render us competent judges of these matters; and I have always thought it as ridiculous for a woman to put herself in a passion about political disputes, as it would be for a man to spend his time haranguing upon the colour of a silk, or the water of a diamond."[34]

During the Revolution, women emerged for a time from their circumscribed sphere.   Moralists who had maintained that woman's interests should be confined to her family, as soon as serious national difficulties threatened, sought to arouse her patriotism and began to apprise her of her public duty.   Journalists who previously had commended the sex for their retiring modesty, now praised the more daring female patriots for their display of zeal.   Women who joined themselves into associations and gave public demonstrations of their patriotism were applauded loudly and even had their names printed in the papers.[35]   The lively protests of the ladies of the famous Edenton tea party, which provoked the customary ridicule from male wits

[32] *Ibid.*, pp. 467-79.
[33] Nos. 57, 81, 342.   [34] *The Polite Lady*, pp. 266-67.
[35] Articles of this type appear in the *Virginia Gazette*, December 24, 1767, February 18, 1768, July 27, 1769, January 20 and 27, 1774, June 9 and November 3, 1774; *South Carolina Gazette*, April 3, 1775; *South Carolina Gazette and Country Journal*, January 7, 1766, August 2, 1774; *Georgia Gazette*, January 6, 1768; (Fayetteville) *North Carolina Gazette*, September 14, 1789.

in England, were commended by neighboring journalists.[36] The voluntary association of "the young ladies of the best families of Mecklenburg County" in North Carolina and their public declarations not to receive the addresses of any gentleman who had failed to do his military duty were acclaimed by the newspapers as significant and exemplary proceedings,[37] and similar resolutions adopted by the ladies of Rowan County were entered into the minutes of the Committee of Safety as "worthy the imitation of every young lady in Ameria."[38] Enthusiastic matrons plunged into the conflict and wrote fiery articles for the newspapers inciting their countrywomen to action. One of these ardent patriots wrote that when she reflected on the American grievances she was ready to start up with sword in hand to fight by the side of her husband.[39] Other correspondents urged their countrywomen not to be "tame spectators" and reminded them that "much, very much depends on the public virtue the ladies will exert at this critical juncture."[40]

But the Revolution had no permanent effect on the status of women. The author of the Declaration of Independence believed that woman's place was the home and hoped that American women would be "too wise to wrinkle their foreheads with politics."[41] The popular phrases, "rights of man," and "all men are created free and equal," so often on the lips of men and women of the period, were generally applied to men only. Glancing into the future, we find the founders of the republic no more ready to permit their wives and daughters to have a hand in public affairs than were the founders of the colonies.

In church affairs as in those of government, while women were generally supposed to be meek and quiet onlookers, they were sometimes persons of influence. The Anglican Church, the established form of worship in all the southern colonies, held strictly to the Pauline doctrine regarding woman, maintaining her inferiority and subjection in the creation and her exclusion from all church offices. Representative of the views of orthodox divines, were those of the author of *The Ladies Calling*. While regarding woman as the

[36] *Virginia Gazette*, November 3, 1774. Postscript.
[37] *South Carolina and American General Gazette*, February 9, 1776.
[38] *Colonial Records of North Carolina*, X, 594.
[39] *Virginia Gazette*, September 21, 1776.
[40] *Ibid.*, September 15, 1774.
[41] *Writings of Thomas Jefferson* (ed., Ford), V, 390-91. Also Randolph, *Domestic Life of Thomas Jefferson*, p. 158.

"weaker vessel," he allowed her a soul "of as Divine an Original" and as "endless a Duration" as that of man. Indeed, "in respect to their eternal well-being," he believed God gave women advantages over men, for he implanted in them "some native propensions" toward virtue and "closelier fenced them in" from temptations and "those wider excursions, for which the customary liberties of the other Sex afford a more open way." Piety was a virtue enjoined especially on woman and irreligion was more odious in her than in man. But, though possessing "peculiar aptness" toward piety, she should not presume to lift her voice in the church. The silence enjoined upon the sex by the apostle, he declared, was based "not only on the inferiority of the Woman in regard of the creation and first sin . . . but also on the presumption that they needed instruction."[42] Nonconformists, though holding somewhat different views of her natural tendency toward virtue, agreed that woman should not presume to understand theology, pass judgment on the sermons, or teach in the church. But they all expected her to understand the fundamental principles of religion well enough to teach them to her children and servants, and, if her husband were an unbeliever, to reclaim him by persuasive arguments as well as by her good example. Also, though she had no voice in church business, it was taken for granted that she was a more faithful attendant at divine services than her husband, and a generous contributor.

Women were stanch upholders and liberal benefactors of the church. A letter from the Jesuit missionaries in Maryland in 1618 told of the death of a noble Catholic matron, who "with more than woman's courage bore all difficulties and inconveniences," and added: "She was given to much prayer, and most anxious for the salvation of her neighbors—a perfect example of right management as well in her self as in her domestic concerns—she was fond of our society while living, and a benefactor to it when dying—of blessed memory with all, for her notable examples, especially of charity to the sick, as well as of other virtues."[43] Some years later Mary Taney, wife of the sheriff of Calvert County, was active in behalf of the Protestant population of Maryland. Distressed by the want of a church and ministers, in 1685 she wrote the Archbishop of Canterbury, calling his attention to the "sad condition" of his "stray flock" and re-

[42] (2d ed., 1673), pp. 8-9, 81, 101.
[43] *Narratives of Early Maryland*, p. 123.

questing five or six hundred pounds for a church and "some small encouragement for a minister." A church settled according to her plan, she pointed out, would "prove a nursery of religion and loyalty through the whole Province." When her proposal reached the ears of the king, he appropriated from his private purse the amount necessary to establish a Church of England in Maryland.[44]

Mary Robinson, a wealthy London widow, by her will in 1618 left the sum of two hundred pounds toward the founding of a church in Virginia, which was known as Mary Robinson's church.[45] Among the early benefactors of Bruton Church at Williamsburg were Catherine Besouth, who left ten pounds for a piece of plate, and Alice Page, who in 1698 gave "one pulpit cloath and cushion of Best Velvett."[46] Affra Coming, "a lady of eminent piety and liberality," in 1698 gave seventeen acres of land adjoining Charles Town for the use of the minister as a parish lot. This grant was the beginning of parsonage property in South Carolina.[47] Mistress Blake, wife of Governor Blake, contributed generously to the adornment of St. Philip's, the English Church in Charles Town, and Frances Simonds, a widow, in 1704 gave the lot on which the old White Meeting House was built, and three years later added another lot.[48]

Among some of the newer sects, women were leaders as well as conscientious supporters. The "New Light" or "Separate" Baptists, who won large numbers of converts among the southern colonists during the decade before the Revolution, had great faith in the immediate teaching of the spirit and permitted women to speak at their public meetings. Because of this unusual practice, however, and other irregularities, they were disclaimed by the "Regular" Baptists, who believed in allowing only ordained ministers to preach.[49]

Women were among the most active leaders among the early

[44] Anna Sioussat, "Colonial Women of Maryland," *Maryland Magazine*, II, 225-26.

[45] Brown, *The First Republic*, p. 275.

[46] Tyler, *Williamsburg, the Old Colonial Capital*, p. 98.

[47] Frederick Dalcho, *An Historical Account of the Protestant Episcopal Church in South Carolina, from the First Settlement of the Province, to the War of the Revolution.* . . . (Charleston, 1820), p. 34. Her will is given in the *South Carolina Magazine*, XII, 75.

[48] McCrady, *South Carolina under the Proprietary Government*, pp. 697-98.

[49] Robert B. Semple, *A History of the Rise and Progress of the Baptists in Virginia* (Richmond, 1910), p. 5; Samuel Bownas, *An Account of the Life, Travels, and Christian Experiences in the Work of the Ministry* (1759), pp. 102-3.

Methodists. In England, Wesley's female converts went about the country speaking in cottages and in the open air, organizing societies, and sometimes addressing large assemblies of men and women.[50] The distinction of founding Methodism in America belongs to Barbara Heck, who came to New York in 1760 with her cousin Philip Embury, a lay minister, and several other Methodists. Mistress Barbara apparently did not preach herself, but was responsible for the first Methodist meetings and erection of the first Methodist church in this country.[51] We find no women preachers among the Methodists in the southern colonies, probably because the movement was already well established in England before it began to take root here. Wesley had encouraged the ministry of women in the early years, explaining that the extraordinary circumstances attending the whole Methodist movement justified an exception to St. Paul's injunction, but after his followers were better organized and a sufficient number of masculine preachers became available, women were discouraged from ascending the pulpit.[52] They were, nevertheless, the most ardent converts to Methodism. The Reverend Francis Asbury found here many "heroines for Christ," who opened their houses for preaching, entertained itinerant ministers, gave testimonies at love feasts, and, as class leaders, traveled about the country conducting prayer meetings and teaching and exhorting members of their own sex.[53]

The Society of Friends or Quakers from its beginning recognized the spiritual equality of men and women and the right of women to be teachers of religious truth. George Fox, its founder, believed that the operation of the Spirit was in no way limited as to individual, time, or place and admitted the ministry of women not as an exception to a rule but as a permanent principle. He felt that women's help was needed in the conduct of church affairs, and set up women's meetings coördinate in scope and influence with the men's meetings.[54]

[50] Abel Stevens, *The History of the Religious Movement of the Eighteenth Century called Methodism.* . . . (3 vols. New York and London, 1858-61), III, 101-2, 114-19, 224-26.

[51] *Ibid.,* I, 427; H. K. Carroll, *The Makers and Making of American Methodism. The Customs, Morals, and Social Conditions of the Pioneer Days drawn from the best Historical Sources.* . . . (New York and Cincinnati, 1916), pp. 15-18.

[52] Stevens, *op. cit.,* II, 268-69; III, 135-136; Thomas Jackson, *Recollections of My Life and Times,* pp. 42-48.

[53] Frances Asbury, *Journal,* Vols. I-III, *passim.*

[54] George Fox, *Journal,* II, 173-74.

Called upon frequently to defend their policy of allowing women to preach, Friends argued that there was no evidence in the Scriptures to prove that the gifts of prophecy and teaching were confined to one sex, quoted texts to prove the contrary, and pointed to examples of female prophets and teachers in the Bible. They regarded Paul's injunction as for particular women in special circumstances and held that the prohibition of women's preaching was a relic of the seclusion of women which was customary in the countries where Christianity had its beginning.[55]

Quaker ministers were not appointed but "acknowledged" and they were paid no salaries. Those undertaking missionary voyages to distant countries, however, apparently had their expenses paid by their societies. Among these were single women, wives, and mothers, who traveled far and wide spreading the Quaker gospel. The itinerant minister carried with her a certificate from the society of which she was a member, signifying the soundness of her faith and her husband's consent to her leaving him. Apparently, a man also had to have the consent of his wife before the society would approve his undertaking a missionary journey.[56]

Sometime in 1656, Elizabeth Harris of London came on a religious visit to Maryland, where, according to a letter to Fox in 1657, she was gladly received and made many "convincements." At about the same time Mary Fisher, "a religious maiden," and Anne Austin, mother of five children, attempted to carry the message to Massachusetts. But they found the colonists unreceptive and, after having been whipped and flung out of Boston, they sailed for Barbadoes, where they were more successful.[57] These women were the first Friends known to have visited America.

At the time of this visit, Mary Fisher was an unmarried woman of about twenty-two. She had been a servant in England, but sometime after joining the Quakers, she became a minister, and, on account of her religion, spent two terms of imprisonment in York

[55] Ibid.; Robert Barclay, A Catechism and Confession of Faith for Quakers, pp. 65-66; John Helton, Reasons for Quitting the Methodist Society; being a Defence of Barclay's Apology (1784), pp. 15-20; Daniel Phillips, Vindiciae Veritatis: or An Occasional Defence of the Principles and Practices of the People Called Quakers (1703), pp. 141-49; Sophia Hume, An Exhortation to the Inhabitants of South-Carolina (1747), pp. 3-9; Thomas Chalkley, Journal and Works, pp. 44-45, 266-67; "Institution of the Discipline," Friends' Library, I, 117-18.
[56] Rufus M. Jones, The Quakers in the American Colonies (London, 1911), p. 310. [57] Ibid., pp. 264-68.

Castle. In 1660 she made an extraordinary missionary journey to the Turks. She visited the sultan in his camp near Adrianople, where she was kindly treated and offered a guard to escort her to Constantinople. She declined this, however, and went on her way unattended. The interesting circumstances of her visit and her courteous reception by the Turk were celebrated in prose and poetry. Soon after her return from the East in 1662, she married William Bayley, a minister, and three years after his death in 1675 she married John Crosse of London. Sometime before 1685, Mary and John Crosse emigrated to South Carolina, acquired land, and settled on Ashley River, where she apparently spent her remaining days. By William Bayley she had three children, the daughter of one of whom became a renowned Quaker preacher.[58]

Among the other women who traveled through the southern colonies were Mary Tomkins and Alice Ambrose. In 1662 they visited Virginia, where, they wrote Fox later, they "had good service for the Lord," but their travels were hard and their labors sore. By an act in 1660, Virginia had provided for the imprisonment and expulsion of Quaker missionaries and made it unlawful for masters of vessels to bring them into the colony or for the inhabitants to entertain them or permit them to hold meetings in their houses.[59] Mary Tomkins and Alice Ambrose were pilloried, given thirty-two lashes each with a nine-corded whip, and after having their goods seized, were expelled from the colony.[60] In the autumn of 1663, the persecuted missionaries were at the Cliffs of the Chesapeake in Calvert County, Maryland, where they were apparently more cordially received.[61]

Women disciples of the Quaker missionaries also suffered persecution by the Virginia authorities. A letter from Governor Berkeley to the sheriff of Lower Norfolk County, August 8, 1660, ordered him to stop "ye frequent meetings of this most pestilent Sect of ye

[58] James Bowden, *History of the Society of Friends in America* (2 vols. London, 1854), I, 40-41; *South Carolina Magazine*, XII, 106-8.

[59] Hening, *Statutes*, I, 532-33.

[60] Bowden, *op. cit.*, I, 349; Jones, *op. cit.*, p. 276; Samuel M. Janney, *History of the Religious Society of Friends, from its Rise to the Year 1828* (4 vols. Philadelphia, 1860), II, 97.

[61] Charles Evans, *Friends in the Seventeenth Century* (Philadelphia, 1875), pp. 172-74; Neill, *Virginia Carolorum*, p. 299; Neill, *The Founders of Maryland as Portrayed in Manuscripts, Provincial Records and Early Documents* (Albany and New York, 1876), pp. 143, 148.

quakers" and charged him if any should "bee refractory" to "send them up prisoners to James Citty."[62]   For abusing the officer who came to her house to suppress a Quaker meeting, Isabel Spring was in August, 1661, ordered to be given twenty lashes on her bare back and to be kept in the sheriff's custody until she begged forgiveness.[63] Female converts were the most refractory.   So Berkeley instructed his justices that all women who, after the reading of the royal proclamation regarding Quakers, should attend Quaker assemblies and publicly declare "their schismatical and heretical doctrines," should be tendered the oath of allegiance and supremacy.   Those who refused were to be imprisoned.   Seven women were among the persons who defied this act and were arrested in Lower Norfolk County, December 15, 1662.[64]   In 1663 Mary Emperor was sentenced to be sent out of the colony as punishment for her third offence in attending Quaker meetings, and Ann Godby was fined five hundred pounds of tobacco for her second offence.   The sentence against Mistress Emperor, however, who was a person of influence, seems not to have been carried out.[65]   Elizabeth Watkins, a sixteen-year-old Quakeress, was in 1685 sentenced to imprisonment by a Henrico County Court for refusing to take an oath.   But later when she was brought again to the bar, "persisting in ye same obstinacy as she pretends out of conscience sake," the court, "out of their clemency in consideration of her young years," remitted her offence and released her from confinement.[66]

In the next century, Quakers fared better at the hands of the authorities, but itinerant women ministers suffered many hardships in their travels and often met with ridicule or denunciation for presuming to preach.   Yet many journeyed through the colonies,[67] often

[62] William and Mary Quarterly, II, 178.

[63] Edward W. James, ed., Lower Norfolk County Virginia Antiquary, III, 105.

[64] Bruce, Institutional History, I, 236.

[65] [J. P. Bell], Our Quaker Friends of Ye Olden Time, pp. 178-79.

[66] William and Mary Quarterly, XXV, 55.

[67] One of the outstanding missionaries was Jane Fenn [later Hoskens], who, accompanied by Elizabeth Lewis, traveled through Maryland, Virginia, and North Carolina in 1722-1725, then to the Barbadoes, from where she sailed for New England. She visited the southern colonies again with Abigail Bowles in 1726, and came a third time with Margaret Churchman in 1744.—"Life of that Faithful Servant of Christ, Jane Hoskens, a Minister of the Gospel," Friends' Library, I, 460-473. Mary Hayes from Antigua, accompanied apparently by her husband, was in Albemarle on a religious visit in 1713, and Susanna Morris and Ann Roberts from Pennsylvania were there in 1723.—F. L. Hawks, History of North Carolina,

making their way on horseback through the wilderness, carrying their provisions, and sometimes spending the night in the woods with no roof but the sky.   They visited the indigent inhabitants of the back settlements as well as those in the towns, sharing their mean provisions and the discomforts of their houses.

The best known woman preacher among the southern Friends was Sophia Hume, granddaughter of the famous Mary Fisher. Sophia was the daughter of Susannah Bayley and Henry Wigington, who was for many years a public official of South Carolina, and the wife of Robert Hume, a well-to-do Charlestonian.   Though her mother belonged to the Quaker Society in Charles Town, Sophia, according to her own testimony, was brought up in the ways of the world, wearing gay apparel, taking music lessons, and attending fashionable amusements.   Sometime after the death of her husband in 1737, she joined the Quakers and parted with "superfluity of apparel" and other luxuries to which she had been accustomed.   Thus she came to be considered "singular and despicable" to her children and acquaintances, who were concerned that she should appear "in so contemptible a Manner."[68]   But, convinced of the rightness of her course, she took up her cross and devoted the rest of her life to spreading the Quaker gospel.   After an absence of six years, she returned to Charles Town in 1747 and published her *Exhortation to the Inhabitants of South-Carolina,* a sermon which was several times printed.   For the next twenty years or more, she traveled in the colonies and abroad, distributing tracts, writing, and preaching.   That she was regarded as a notable personage appears in the manner in which her arrivals and departures were noted in the papers.   On June 9, 1767, the Charles Town gazettes announced the arrival from London of "several Passengers, particularly Mrs. Sophia Hume, well known for her Writings in Favour of the Quakers."   Later, not only the South Carolina papers but also those outside the colony carried

---

II, 328.   The Charles Town records show that Elizabeth Nixon of North Carolina and Mary Weston of London were there in 1750, Mary Peisley [later Neale] from Ireland and Catherine Payton from England in 1753, Susannah Hatton from Ireland and Phoebe Trimble from Pennsylvania in 1761, Mary Stedham and Rachel Wright from Bush River in South Carolina in 1768, Sarah and Mehitabel Jenkins from New England in 1773, and Elizabeth Robinson from England and Ruth Holland of Maryland in 1774.—"Records of the Quakers in Charles Town, South Carolina" (ed., Mabel S. Webber), *South Carolina Magazine,* XXXVIII, 22-43; 94-107, 176-97.

[68] *An Exhortation to the Inhabitants of South Carolina,* 1747.

this announcement: "Yesterday Mrs. HUME (the celebrated writer and preacher lately arrived from England) delivered an exhortation to a numerous body of people, of all professions, at the Quaker meeting house."[69] Though advanced in years, Mrs. Hume continued her ministerial labors. This note from the minutes of the Charles Town Society, April 1, 1768, is the last record we have of her in the colonies: "This Day our Antient and Worthy Friend Sophia Hume sailed from hence . . . Bound for London after Labouring in ye Ministrey Amongst us Neare Eight Months, and we are sensibly convinced that nothing Less Could induce her to this Service but the strongest perswasion of her Love and Duty to Mankind, in becoming an Instrument in Publishing the Glad Tidings of the Gospel of Life and Salvation by Jesus Christ."[70]

In the early part of 1769, the southern newspapers were announcing the coming and going of Rachel Wilson, a famous Quaker preacher from England, who, setting out from Philadelphia, made a missionary journey through Maryland, Virginia, and Carolina. Accompanied by Sary Janney, she arrived at Charles Town in February with certificates from English Friends signifying her unity with them and her husband's willingness to give her up to the service.[71] She preached several times in the Quaker meeting house, which soon became too small for her congregations. On Sunday, according to the local gazette, she preached at the old Baptist meetinghouse "to crowded audiences of all denominations."[72] She was evidently well received. Henry Laurens, writing William Fisher of Philadelphia, who had recommended the eminent Quakeress to his Charles Town correspondent, wrote that she and her companion were "attended both in private & Public by many of the best Inhabitants," adding: "I have not known strangers at any time amongst us, meet a more Cordial Reception, nor do I remember to have parted from any with more Regret."[73]

The courtesy shown Mistress Wilson and her companion does not indicate that the Charlestonians were inclined to countenance women's preaching. It was their universal hospitality and politeness and their desire to please their Quaker friends who had recommended

[69] July 6, 1767; *Virginia Gazette*, August 6, 1767.
[70] *South Carolina Magazine*, XXVIII, 178.
[71] *Ibid.*, p. 179, 181.
[72] *South Carolina Gazette and Country Journal*, February 7, 1769.
[73] *South Carolina Magazine*, XXVIII, 259-60.

CHAPTER XII

PROFESSIONAL OCCUPATIONS

DURING THE seventeenth century and on into the eighteenth, many occupations considered today as professions were carried on by persons who had little education or special training. Even teachers, physicians, and surgeons often had few qualifications beyond disposition and inclination, and journalists, printers, nurses, and midwives learned only in the school of experience. As long as they required no formal education and no technical knowledge, these vocations were open to women as well as men. Except among the sects that did not ordain and pay their preachers, women were excluded from the ministry, and they evidently did not practice law or aspire to military and political offices, but they were engaged in performing services for pay in many other professions.

A Mrs. Peacock, apparently mistress of a small school in Rappahannock County in Virginia in 1657, is the first school dame we find mentioned in the records. Mary Coar was teaching in Northumberland County in 1663 and Katharine Shrewsbury was employed sometime about 1693 in teaching the son of a Richmond County planter.[1] Elizabeth Wetherick was mentioned in 1707 in the will of William Adams of Charles Town, South Carolina, who directed that his daughter be "put to school to learn" under her instruction.[2] But schoolmistresses were rare in the first century of the colonies. Private tutors and other teachers were usually men.

During the fifty years preceding the Revolution, more women came to be employed as private tutors and schoolmistresses, and a larger number set up schools on their own initiative. Parents advertised frequently for teachers for their children, and though they usually wanted "a single, sober ·man," they sometimes preferred a woman. A South Carolinian desired one who "could be well recommended as to her Morals and manner of having been educated."[3]

[1] Bruce, *Institutional History*, I, 299, 326, 327.
[2] *South Carolina Magazine*, XIII, 58-59.
[3] *South Carolina Gazette*, November 28, 1771.

Another specified "a Prudent Woman" to manage children and teach them to read.[4]   A Virginia father preferred an elderly woman capable of "educating and bringing up" children, and offered "good Encouragement" to one who could come well recommended.[5]

Teachers also sought positions by advertising in the newspapers. "A young Woman of unblemished Character, and Liberal Education" desired to undertake the instruction of young ladies in a gentleman's family.[6]   Another, describing herself as "A Middle aged Woman, who can be well recommended, and understands Musick, dancing, and all sorts of Needlework, and can speak Four different Languages," declared she would "be glad to engage as a Tutoress to Children, or, if encouraged would keep a School."[7]   By no means all governesses were able to speak four languages.   Usually if they could teach English, French, and ornamental needlework, they were considered well qualified.   The following is representative of several advertisements: "A young lady well acquainted with the French language—having resided several years in France—wishes a place in a genteel family to instruct young ladies in French and other useful and ornamental work."[8]

It seems that neither the very young nor the old were desired as governesses.   One subscriber added this postscript to his advertisement: "N. B.   None under 20, or that has passed her grand climacteric need apply."[9]   One teacher, recognizing apparently the importance of coming within the proper age limits and at the same time unwilling to be too explicit, inserted this notice: "An English woman between 20 and 40 who has a good education and understands most branches of needlework, tambour, embroidery, etc. writes a good hand and is well acquainted with arithmetic, wants a place as teacher of children.   No objection to living in the country."[10]

Very little is known of these teachers.   Fithian left in his journal a few references to two young women employed as tutors in the neighborhood of "Nomini Hall."   One was the English governess of the daughters of Colonel Tayloe, a Miss Garrot, whom he described as "chatty, satirical, neat, civil," and as making "many merry remarks at Dinner."   The other was Sally Panton, a young girl also

[4] *Ibid.*, April 28, 1757.   [5] *Virginia Gazette*, March 8, 1770.
[6] *Maryland Gazette*, June 14, 1764.   [7] *Ibid.*, December 24, 1772.
[8] *South Carolina and American General Gazette*, October 2, 1776.
[9] *South Carolina Gazette*, September 11, 1755.
[10] *South Carolina and American General Gazette*, October 28, 1774.

from England, who taught French, writing, and English to Miss Turburville, a friend of the young ladies at "Nomini." Miss Panton appears to have been homesick and unhappy, and Fithian wondered why she had come to Virginia when she had an estate of fifty pounds sterling a year in England. Because of her "huge stays, low headdress, enormous waist, a dress entirely contrary to the liking of the Virginia ladies," he declared, she was considered "not handsome," and he observed that one of the young ladies of the neighborhood had "with a Sneer, & with ill-nature enough, swore She would not think of imitating such a thing as her."[11]

As shown above,[12] a large number of women established schools of their own. Many supplemented their incomes by taking little girls into their homes and teaching them to read and do plain sewing. Sometimes they taught their pupils only a few hours a day, but often they engaged to board and lodge them and attend to their morals and manners as well as their studies. A large number whose business ability was probably superior to their academic education set up and conducted boarding schools for young ladies. Usually they undertook very little of the actual instruction of the pupils beyond reading and needlework, but they attended to their physical and moral needs and employed special masters for teaching the various accomplishments.

Keeping school was for many persons only one of several vocations. Martha Logan, for instance, managed a plantation, sold garden seeds and plants, and boarded and taught children at her home about ten miles from Charles Town.[13] Magdalene Hamilton kept a little school, took in drawing and "plain work," and laundered ladies' headclothes.[14] Anna Maria Hoyland ran a fashionable boarding school and did braziery and tin work.[15] Mary Ann Valois, mistress of a French school, did clearstarching, washed laces and gauzes, and was "a perfect Sack and Negligee-Maker, in the true Parisian Taste."[16] Sarah Singleton made baby linen for sale, took in draw-

[11] *Journal*, pp. 142, 146, 225. Miss Panton evidently returned to England in 1778, for in January of that year Richard Henry Lee wrote his brother in London for two or three pounds sterling, explaining that he needed it to pay the wages of Miss Panton, tutoress to his children, who was returning to England and, therefore, could not use our paper money.—*Letters of Richard Henry Lee* (ed., James Curtis Ballagh), I, 384. [12] Chap. IX.

[13] *South Carolina Gazette*, March 6, 1742.

[14] *Ibid.*, April 27, 1748. [15] *Ibid.*, November 13, 1751.

[16] *Ibid.*, December 1, 1759.

ing, and rented rooms, besides teaching.[17] Frances Swallow ran a fashionable boarding school and a popular millinery shop and later kept a tavern.[18] Mary Anne March, an Annapolis teacher, took in quilting and needlework, and a Mrs. Polk kept a morning school, painted ribbons, drew patterns, and worked gowns, shoes, ribbons, men's waistcoats, and ruffles in tambour.[19]

Many of these schoolmistresses were married. Frances Swallow was the wife of Newman Swallow, a merchant. Mrs. Adams, another Charles Town teacher, was the wife of William Adams, a writing master. Often a man and his wife were both teachers. Kate and James Brownlow kept a school for years at Lexington, Virginia, and later taught together at Abington.[20] John and Mary Rivers advertised a school in Annapolis,[21] and John Walker and his wife instructed young ladies and gentlemen at their home in Williamsburg.[22] Nathaniel and Mary Gittens gave lessons in reading, writing, arithmetic, and needlework, and Martha and Mark Anthony Besseleu taught a French and English day school.[23] Rebecca Woodin, who boarded young ladies and had them taught all the branches of a polite education, was the wife of Thomas Woodin, a cabinetmaker and drawing teacher.[24] Her husband probably gave drawing lessons to her pupils. In the advertisement of her school, a Mrs. Lessly of Charles Town announced that she had engaged a young lady from England to teach French and that Mr. Lessly would teach drawing and painting as usual.[25] Whether Mr. Lessly had other employment besides assisting his wife does not appear. Occasionally a wife was an assistant to her husband. Ann Winsor, for instance, gave lessons on the harpsichord to the pupils of her husband's school. But ordinarily women appear to have been better qualified for attending to the business end of the school than for teaching, probably because they had more natural ability than formal education.

Though many women with husbands were employed as teachers, marriage was for some a happy escape from the schoolroom. Ann Imer, widow of the Reverend Abraham Imer, who after her hus-

[17] *South Carolina Gazette and Country Journal*, October 11, 1774.
[18] *South Carolina Gazette*, June 17, 1766; *ibid.*, May 11, 1773, June 20, 1774.
[19] *Maryland Gazette*, March 27, 1751; *ibid.*, July 28, 1774.
[20] Armstrong, *Notable Southern Families*, I, 39.
[21] *Maryland Gazette*, November 6, 1755.
[22] *Virginia Gazette*, November 17, 1752.
[23] *South Carolina Gazette*, August 27, 1744; November 23, 1747.
[24] *Ibid.*, June 29, 1767.   [25] *Ibid.*, August 10, 1767.

band's death had kept school in Charles Town, stopped her advertisement after her second marriage. Mary Stedman advertised in
the *Georgia Gazette* that she had discontinued her school, thanked
her patrons for "entrusting her with the care of their children," and
explained: "[She] can only plead in excuse for abruptly leaving
them a change of circumstances, such as she flatters herself their
candour will not condemn her for embracing."[26] Her patrons were
not left in doubt as to the nature of her "change of circumstances,"
for the same paper carried this announcement: "On Sunday the 31st.
ult. was married, Henry Yonge, Esq. Surveyor-General of this
Province, to Mrs. Mary Stedman."

It has been observed that generally women were qualified to
teach only the elementary subjects, leaving the higher branches of
learning and the polite accomplishments to special masters. There
were, however, a few women dancing teachers and several professional musicians and painters. Elizabeth Smith taught singing in
Annapolis.[27] A Mrs. Neill gave lessons on the guitar in Williamsburg,[28] and Ann Winsor taught Charles Town ladies to play the
harpsichord. Mistress Winsor apparently did more than teach. The
South Carolina Gazette, June 11, 1772, announced that she was on
trial as a candidate for organist of St. Michael's Church, but it is
not known whether she or her masculine competitor was chosen.
Several women painters sought patronage in the papers. Mary
Roberts, widow of Bishop Roberts, and apparently an artist, advertised in 1734 that she had several pictures to dispose of and offered
to do "Face Painting."[29] The *South Carolina Gazette*, December
31, 1772, announced the arrival of a lady who was a niece and pupil
of "her Majesty's Portrait Painter, the celebrated Miss Reid," and
reported her intention of following "the Art of Painting Portraits
in Crayons" in Charles Town. The following April it advertised a
Mrs. Bambridge, wife of Mr. Bambridge, portrait painter, as "a
very ingenious Miniature paintress."[30]

Actresses appear more numerous than female musicians and
painters and seem to have shared equally with men the honors of
the stage. According to a Virginia historian, the earliest leading
lady in the colonies was Mary Stagg. By a contract recorded at

[26] June 3, 1767.
[27] *Maryland Gazette*, April 5, 1764.   [28] *Virginia Gazette*, July 11, 1777.
[29] *South Carolina Gazette*, February 9, 1734.
[30] *Ibid.*, April 5, 1773.

Yorktown, July 11, 1716, William Levingston, merchant, agreed with Charles Stagg and his wife, Mary, described as "actors," to build a theatre for them in Williamsburg and to provide players, scenery, and music "for the enactment of comedies and tragedies." This enterprise, however, seems to have proved unsuccessful, and after her husband's death in 1735 Mistress Stagg made her living teaching dancing and giving "assemblies" at the Virginia capital.[31]

A theatre was erected at Charles Town early in the century and theatricals were performed there, but nothing is known of the players. Among the first actresses mentioned in the southern newspapers was a Mrs. Osborne, who was playing principal parts in Annapolis in 1752. She was evidently the same Mrs. Osborne who was the leading lady with the Virginia Company of Comedians at Norfolk and Williamsburg in the season of 1767-68 and with the New American Company in Annapolis in 1769.[32]

In 1752 Lewis Hallam's American Company arrived in this country with Mrs. Hallam, wife of the manager, as leading lady. They presented *The Merchant of Venice* at Williamsburg, September 5, 1752, and played before Virginia audiences with "universal applause" for nine months, during which time they gave twenty-four full plays and eleven shorter pieces. When they left for New York in 1753, Governor Dinwiddie gave them a letter endorsing their dramatic ability and personal conduct.[33] In April, 1754, they began the season with *The Fair Penitent* in Philadelphia, where they played through June, and the following October they opened with the same play in Charles Town.[34] While in Jamaica between 1754 and 1758, Lewis Hallam died and his widow married David Douglas, who reorganized the company in 1758. Mrs. Douglas continued to be the star, and her son, young Lewis Hallam, was the leading man. A historian of the theatre describes Mrs. Douglas as "the acknowledged star of the American stage from 1752 to 1766," and declares that in considering all the actors and actresses who made the theatrical epoch previous to the Revolution, the first place should undoubtedly be accorded this talented woman. Among the better-

[31] Stanard, *op. cit.*, pp. 230-31.
[32] *Virginia Gazette*, February 4, 1768; George O. Seilhamer, *History of the American Theatre* (3 vols. Philadelphia, 1888-91), I, 4, 8-10, 235, 258.
[33] *Ibid.*, p. 45.
[34] Eola Willis, *The Charleston Stage in the Eighteenth Century* (Columbia, S. C., 1924), p. 42.

known parts played by her were the queen in *Hamlet*, Jane Shore in the play *Jane Shore*, Cordelia in *King Lear*, Lady Macbeth and also Lady Macduff in *Macbeth*, Portia in *The Merchant of Venice*, Desdemona in *Othello*, Queen Elizabeth in *Richard III*, Arpasia in *Tamerlane*, and Juliet in *Romeo and Juliet*.[35]

Another outstanding leading lady was Margaret Cheer, who, having already won a reputation as an actress, made her first appearance before the American public as Violante in the first American production of Mrs. Centlivre's comedy, *A Wonder: A Woman Keeps a Secret*, at the New Theatre in Charles Town, April 25, 1764.[36] As Mrs. Douglas advanced in age, Miss Cheer gradually assumed the rôles she had played, and, like her predecessor, was given the choice of parts. During her short stay of only two years on the stage, she is known to have played fifty of the leading characters of the drama of the time, besides parts in pantomime and farce. Miss Cheer is the first American actress known to have captured a nobleman for a husband. In 1768 her marriage was announced to Lord Rosehill, youthful son of an Earl in the Scottish peerage, who was apparently in Maryland on a visit. She did not immediately withdraw from the stage, but continued to play for nearly a year after her marriage. It is possible that she did not return to Scotland with her husband, for after her retirement she played in *Richard III* in New York for Mrs. Douglas' benefit as late as 1773.[37]

A Miss Wainwright joined the American Company at the same time as Miss Cheer and was considered next to her in importance. She was said to be "a pupil of the celebrated Dr. Arne," and an accomplished actress and talented singer, playing such parts as Polly in *The Beggar's Opera* and Rosetta in *Love in a Village*. For some reason not known, she did not remain long on the stage, but left the American Company and lived in retirement for many years in Philadelphia.[38]

Other players often mentioned in the papers were the Storer sisters, who, with John Henry, an actor, came from Jamaica to this country in 1767. Ann Storer was the eldest and at first the most prominent. The second sister, Fanny, later Mrs. Mechlar, was on the stage for only a short time. Maria, the youngest, was a child

[35] Seilhamer, *op. cit.*, I, 338-40.
[36] Willis, *op. cit.*, p. 47.   [37] Seilhamer, *op. cit.*, pp. 204-8.
[38] *Ibid.*, pp. 158, 254-55. The "celebrated Dr. Arne" was probably Thomas Augustine Arne (1710-1778), English musical composer.

when they made their American début, but under the guidance of Henry she developed into a more brilliant actress than either of her sisters. She is described as "slight, girlish, blue-eyed . . . the ideal Ariel of our early drama."[39] She appears to have been an exquisitely beautiful person, but capricious and sometimes so disobliging as to win the disapproval of her audience and incur uncomplimentary criticism from newspaper correspondents.

Sarah Hallam, niece of Mrs. Douglas, won greater acclaim and more lasting popularity than either Margaret Cheer or Maria Storer. She is said to have made her musical début in Charles Town, November 13, 1765, and her first appearance on the stage the following January. A dramatic critic wrote of her in a Charles Town paper at the time: "I am much deceived, if Miss Hallam in *Cinthia* . . . does not discover a greater force of Genius, than the Audiences hitherto, notwithstanding the applause she has received, have imagined her to possess."[40] This prophecy came true. As the leading lady of the American Company, Sarah Hallam was adored by her audiences. The Marylanders were rapturous over her portrayal of Imogene in *Cymbeline*. One delighted theatre-goer wrote of her: "On finding that the part of Imogen was to be played by Miss Hallam, I instantly formed to myself, from my Predilection for her, the most sanguine hopes of Entertainment. But how was I ravished on Experiment. She exceeded my utmost idea. Such delicacy of manner. Such classical strictness of expression. The music of her tongue—the vox liquida, how melting . . . methought I heard once more the warbling of Cibber in my ear."[41] A Maryland poet exclaimed at her beauty, "Ye Gods, 'Tis Cytherea's face," and with glowing enthusiasm accorded her every dramatic talent.[42] Charles Wilson Peale, sharing the general enthusiasm, was inspired to paint her in the part in which the Marylanders liked best to see her.

Sarah Hallam was apparently as charming in private life as on the stage. After the Continental Congress resolved to discountenance theatrical entertainments in 1774, she returned to Williamsburg, where she made a living by conducting a fashionable boarding school for girls. It is related that "the personal charm to which she held fast, even in old age," is still among the traditions of the little town.[43]

[39] *Ibid.*, p. 352.
[40] *South Carolina Gazette and Country Journal*, March 4, 1766.
[41] *Maryland Gazette*, September 6, 1770.   [42] Seilhamer, *op. cit.*, I, 280.
[43] *William and Mary Quarterly*, XII, 236-37; Stanard, *op. cit.*, p. 250.

It is not very surprising to find women making their living on the stage and in the schoolroom, since it has for a long time been assumed that teaching and acting were professions for which they were naturally qualified. But the discovery of women running printing presses and publishing newspapers is more unexpected. The first female printer of whom we have record was Dinah Nuthead, wife of William Nuthead, who had in 1686 started a printing establishment at St. Mary's in Maryland. Inheriting her husband's press at his death sometime about 1694-95, Mistress Nuthead carried it to Annapolis, the newly established seat of the government. In May, 1696, she petitioned the assembly for a license to "print blanks, bills, bonds, writs, warrants of attorney, letters of administration and other necessary blanks useful for the public offices of this Province," and promised to forfeit her license and go out of business if she should print anything other than specified. The assembly voted to grant her request, but required her to give security to keep her promise. She gave bond for one hundred pounds, and two neighbors acted as her sureties. An astonishing fact about this bond is that Mistress Nuthead signed it with her mark. Incredible as it may seem, she must have directed the business herself while depending upon a journeyman printer to do the typesetting.[44]

Dinah Nuthead did not publish a newspaper. The pioneer woman journalist in the colonies was Elizabeth Timothy, wife of Louis Timothy, a French Huguenot. Timothy had in 1734 reëstablished the *South Carolina Gazette*, begun in 1732 by Thomas Whitmarsh. In December, 1738, he was fatally injured in an accident, and his widow, Elizabeth, took over the publication of his paper. In the issue for January 11, 1739, she published this appeal to her husband's patrons for a continuation of their "Favours":

Whereas the late Printer of this Gazette hath been deprived of his life by an unhappy Accident, I take this opportunity of informing the Publick, that I shall continue the said Paper as usual, and hope by the assistance of my Friends to make it as entertaining and correct as may be reasonably expected. Wherefore I flatter myself, that all those Persons, who, by

[44] *Archives of Maryland*, XIX, 306, 370; Lawrence C. Wroth, *History of Printing in Colonial Maryland* (Baltimore, 1922), pp. 12-15. Sarah Packe, widow, was a partner in the printing establishment of William Parks at Williamsburg in 1749, but she apparently was only a silent partner. Parks died at sea April 1, 1750. His will, proved the following June, directed that his wife, Eleanor Parks, and his son-in-law complete the printing of the laws of Virginia, which he had undertaken.— *William and Mary Quarterly*, VII, 11.

Subscriptions or otherwise, assisted my late Husband, in the Prosecution of the said undertaking, will be kindly pleased to continue their Favours and good Offices to his poor afflicted Widow with six small Children and another hourly expected.

The public evidently responded to this naïve solicitation and sent in subscriptions, for Mistress Timothy continued to publish the paper until her son Peter came of age and took possession in 1741. After Peter's death, his widow, Ann Timothy, following in the footsteps of her mother-in-law, published the *Gazette* and became state printer, a position which she held until her death in 1792.[45]

The second southern paper to be published by a woman was the *Maryland Gazette*, which on April 16, 1767, announced the death of Jonas Green, its publisher, and carried this notice to the public signed by his widow, Anne Catherine Green:

I presume to address You for your Countenance to Myself and numerous Family, left, without your Favour, almost destitute of Support, by the Decease of my Husband, who, long abed, I have the Satisfaction to say, faithfully served You in the Business of Provincial Printer; and, I flatter myself, that, with your kind Indulgence and Encouragement, MYSELF and SON, will be enabled to continue it on the same Footing. On this Expectation, I shall venture to supply my late Husband's Customers with News-Papers, on the same Terms he did, until I receive Orders to the Contrary, and shall be ready to publish from Time to Time, the Advertisements that shall be sent to the Printing-Office.

At this time Mistress Green was probably about forty-five years old. She had borne six sons and eight daughters and had buried eight of her children. Yet, while other women in her circumstances might have felt that their work was finished, she undertook the support of her family and the performance of important public service. She assumed responsibility for the publication of her husband's paper and succeeded him as printer to the colony. In 1768 the assembly voted her "nine hundred and forty-eight dollars and one half dollar" for her services, and thereafter allowed her forty-eight thousand pounds of tobacco annually when the assembly was in session and something over thirty-six thousand pounds for other years until her death in 1775. This was the same amount as that paid her husband. Besides the *Gazette* and the public work, she printed an annual almanac, political pamphlets, and a few satirical pieces. It is written that under

[45] Isaiah Thomas, *History of Printing in America* (2 vols. Worcester, 1810), II, 158, 255.

her management neither the *Gazette* nor the public printing suffered retrenchment or deterioration.[46] The *Maryland Gazette,* March 30, 1775, announced her passing and printed this tribute to her character: "She was of a mild and benevolent disposition, and for Conjugal Affection, and Parental Tenderness, an Example to her Sex."

Two years before the death of Mrs. Green, Clementina Rind, widow of a Virginia newspaper publisher, explained that she was "unhappily forced to enter business on her own account," announced her intention of continuing her husband's paper, and appealed to the public for support of her undertaking. Like Elizabeth Timothy and Mistress Green, she had a numerous family of children dependent upon this business for a living. In her first notice she urged her patrons to be punctual in sending cash with their advertisements, explaining that her business could not be carried on "with that Spirit which is necessary, without sufficient Funds to support it."[47]

Soon after entering upon her editorial duties, Mistress Rind was involuntarily forced into a controversy by a correspondent of a rival gazette, who, signing himself as "An Attentive Observer," accused her of departing from the motto of her paper[48] and the principles of freedom upon which it was founded, because she had refused to publish a libelous article sent in by an anonymous writer. The article in question was an exposé of the misconduct of one of "the guilty great," who, the "Attentive Observer" declared, were above the law and "amenable to the Publick" only through the medium of the press. Mrs. Rind replied that she could not publish indiscriminately everything that might be offered and that the article she was accused of suppressing related to an affair "cognizable in a court of law, where it must be more fully determined in the injured party's favour than by any publication in a newspaper." She added that she did not think herself authorized to publish "an anonymous piece" pointing at private persons, but that, if the author of the article would disclose his name, she would publish his writing, though it would be "repugnant to her inclination."[49] Thus she upheld the dignity of her pro-

[46] Wroth, *op. cit.,* pp. 90-93.   [47] *Virginia Gazette,* September 2, 1773.
[48] The motto of Rind's *Virginia Gazette* was: "Open to all Parties, but influenced by none." The criticism of the "Attentive Observer" was printed in Purdie and Dixon's *Virginia Gazette,* December 23, 1773. It is said that because the other Virginia papers refused to publish anything against the governor, Rind had been induced in 1766 to come from Maryland to publish "a free paper" in Virginia.— *Virginia Colonial Decisions* (ed., R. T. Barton), I, 146.
[49] *Virginia Gazette,* December 30, 1773.

fession against those who would use the press as a vehicle for private wrangles and detraction.

In May, 1774, Mrs. Rind and the publishers of a rival *Virginia Gazette*, Alexander Purdie and John Dixon, each petitioned the House of Burgesses for the right to succeed the late William Rind as public printer. The members determined their election by ballot, and when the tickets were read, it was found that sixty had voted for Mrs. Rind alone, twenty-five for Mrs. Rind and Mr. Purdie to act jointly, and two for Mrs. Rind and Mr. Dixon.[50] Quite evidently, every member was in favor of her having, if not all, at least a part of the public business. As this position paid four hundred and fifty pounds annually, it must have helped considerably in maintaining her "dear infants." While thus engaged in making a living for her family, Mrs. Rind was suffering from a lingering and distressing illness, which resulted in her death only a year after she assumed control of her husband's paper. Her courage and ability were apparently appreciated by the public. Her competitors, Purdie and Dixon, praised her as "a Lady of singular Merit, and universally esteemed,"[51] and a correspondent to another gazette eulogized her thus in verse:

> .   .   .   .
> To her, blest shade, a plaintive verse is due,
> Lov'd by the muses, and fair science too;
> And sure a happy proof of this remains,
> In her soft numbers, and harmonious strains.
> With manly sense, and fortitude of mind,
> The softer graces of her sex combin'd,
> To form a bright example in her life,
> Of friend, of mistress, daughter, mother, wife.[52]
> .   .   .   .

The only other woman journalist in the southern colonies of whom we have record, was Mary Katharine Goddard, who in February, 1774, took over the publication of the Baltimore *Maryland Journal*. This paper was formerly edited by her brother, William Goddard, who left it in her hands when he was appointed surveyor of the post roads by congress. When after the first year he did not return, she assumed full control, published the paper in her own name, and carried it successfully through the trying times of the war.

[50] *Journals of the House of Burgesses*, XIII, 77, 125.
[51] *Virginia Gazette*, September 29, 1774.
[52] (Pinckney's) *Virginia Gazette*, October 6, 1774.

She was described as "an expert and correct compositor of types," and her journal "second to none in the colonies in interest." While publishing her paper, she was postmistress at Annapolis, did job printing, and kept a bookstore. At the end of the war in 1784, she turned the journal back over to her brother, but kept her job as postmistress until the establishment of the federal government in 1789. After that she apparently devoted her whole attention to her book shop.[53]

One of the professions which nineteenth century women found most difficult to enter was that of medicine. Yet in the period before the Revolution, they were apparently allowed unlimited freedom in practicing "physick" and "chirurgery." The reason for this difference of attitude lies, of course, in the fact that in the early days no special training was required, and women were regarded as having as great natural ability for the healing arts as men. Amateur doctors did not always attend the sick gratuitously, and women as well as men were paid for their treatments. Katharine, wife of Thomas Hebden, a carpenter, was evidently a physician of some note in the colony of Maryland. Several suits were instituted by her and her husband in the provincial court for payment due for her services. In 1644 Thomas prosecuted Edward Hall, declaring that Katharine "did chirurgery upon the legg of John Greenwell," Hall's man-servant, and "did diett him for 7 weeks . . . for wch said chirurgery & diett the said Edw. Hall agreed to pay 190 tob: beyond 20 received in hand." The justices evidently appreciated the value of Katharine's services, for they granted her husband the amount claimed.[54] A few years later Hebden demanded of the administrator of John Cole fifty weight of tobacco for curing his ague and fever, twenty-five for a purge, and twenty-five for stopping his blood, and recovered payment. About the same time Katharine brought suit in her own name against George Manner's estate for one hundred and forty pounds of tobacco due her for medicine, and was paid nineteen hundred weight out of the public levy for "Physick Charges bestowed by her upon Richard Lawrence," probably a soldier.[55]

Mary, wife of Thomas Bradnox, was another Maryland doctress. In 1648 she demanded from the estate of William Cox "that cow calf whereby his hand was occasioned to be hurt, which said calf the said William Cox gave unto the said Mary . . . for her pains taken

[53] Wroth, *op. cit.*, pp. 144-46.
[54] *Archives of Maryland*, IV, 268.　　　[55] *Ibid.*, X, 97, 122, 415.

in endeavoring the cure of his hand," and also "a yearling heifer which, Francis, the wife of the aforesaid William Cox, also deceased, gave unto the said Mary . . . for her pains likewise taken in curing her child's mouth and tending her in her last sickness."[56] On October 30, 1661, the wife of Oliver Spry brought suit in a court of Kent County, Maryland, against a man named Hambleton for curing his wife of "some Distemper" and received six hundred pounds of tobacco in payment.[57] Mary Vanderdonck, daughter of the Reverend Francis Doughtie, Anglican minister, had a regular practice as a physician in Charles County, Maryland. She also demanded fees for her services and arraigned her debtors in court when they were slow about paying. Sometime in 1662 she married Hugh O'Neal, a planter, who afterwards joined her in her suits for the collection of her pay.[58]

John Clayton, in his "Observables in Virginia" in 1688, wrote of a female practitioner in that colony: "A Gentlewoman, that was a notable female Doctress, told me, that a Neighbour being bit by a Rattle-Snake swelled excessively; some days afterwards she was sent for, who found him swelled beyond what she thought it had been possible for the Skin to contain, and very thirsty. She gave him *oriental benzoar* shaved, with a strong Decoction of the aforesaid Ditanny, whereby she recovered the Person."[59] Katharine Shrewsbury, the school dame mentioned above, apparently made some pretention to the practice of physic, for in 1693 she brought suit against Peter Foxson, stating she had restored him to health. The court, however, did not sustain her claim.[60] Sometime later, Colonel William Byrd described a Mrs. Fleming as "a notable quack," and in mentioning the important inhabitants of the town of Fredericksburg, declared, "I must not forget Mrs. Levistone, who Acts here in the double Capacity of a Doctress and Coffee Woman."[61]

Colonial housewives were fond of experimenting with herbs and took pride in their pills, potions, and salves, but usually they prescribed these remedies only for members of their own households or gave them to their neighbors. A few, however, ambitious for pecuniary reward for their successful experiments, offered to sell their formulas or to cure various disorders then prevalent. In November, 1748, Mary Johnson petitioned the Virginia Assembly, declaring

[56] *Ibid.*, IV, 446.
[58] *Ibid.*, XXIII, 161, 357, 361.
[60] Bruce, *Institutional History*, I, 327.
[57] *Maryland Magazine*, VIII, 23.
[59] *Force Tracts*, III (No. 12), 44.
[61] *Writings* (ed., Bassett), p. 341.

that she had for several years been very successful in curing cancer and was willing to communicate her method to the public and rely upon the assembly for such reward as they should think reasonable. The matter was referred to a committee, who heard several testimonials of cures she had effected and recommended that she be rewarded. Thereupon, the assembly voted her the sum of one hundred pounds.[62] In 1754 her cure was published in the Virginia almanac. In October, 1766, a testimonial of the cure of several cases of cancer by Constant Woodson appeared in the *Virginia Gazette*, and the next month Mistress Woodson petitioned the House of Burgesses, offering to communicate her remedy for "a Valuable consideration." The assembly voted to allow her a hundred pounds and to print her formula in the local gazette.[63] Not everyone was satisfied with Mistress Woodson's method, however, for the irate husband of one of her patients denounced her in a newspaper notice, declaring that her endeavors to cure his wife had not only proved ineffectual but had made her much worse than she had been before.[64] This bad publicity evidently did not discredit the doctress, for the *Virginia Gazette*, announcing the death of a prominent citizen two years later, declared that he had gone "unhappily too late" to Mrs. Woodson, "famous for the cures she has made."[65]

Women advertised remedies for other ailments. Mary Adams offered to cure "the blind and all disorders in the eyes."[66] A Mrs. Kayser declared she was "possessed of an infallible remedy for the ague," adding: "It effects a cure in three days. Her charge for the cure is only *Five Shillings*."[67] A Mrs. Hughes offered to cure "Ringworms, Scald Heads, Sore Eyes, the Piles, Worms in Children, and several other Disorders," promising, *"No Cure, No Pay."*[68] Julia Wheatley proposed to cure "the most inveterate ringworms, scald heads, sore eyes," and sold a remedy for "the worms, gravel, and many other disorders incident to both sexes."[69]

Nursing, like the practice of medicine and the making of curative remedies, was largely a domestic art applied by housewives in their own families. A number of women, however, earned their living

[62] *Journals of the House of Burgesses*, VII, 303, 329.
[63] *Ibid.*, XI, 42, 124-25.
[64] *Virginia Gazette*, June 16, 1768.   [65] *Ibid.*, December 13, 1770.
[66] *South Carolina Gazette*, March 21, 1764.
[67] *Maryland Journal*, October 16, 1773.
[68] *Virginia Gazette*, December 16, 1773.   [69] *Ibid.*, January 20, 1776.

by taking care of the sick and disabled.   In parish and county records, frequent entries are found of payments to women for nursing the poor.   The Maryland provincial court in 1659 ordered the commissioners of Calvert County to pay Mary Gillford for her attention to a sick boy.[70]   Mary Blount was in 1708 allowed forty shillings by the vestry of St. Paul's Parish in Chowan Precinct for taking care of an indigent man in his sickness and burying him at her charge.[71]   The vestry of Christ Church Parish in Middlesex County, Virginia, in 1685 ordered that Thomas Wilson, "a poor, decrepid man," be kept by a Mrs. Robinson, who was to be paid monthly one hundred pounds of tobacco.   If she should cure him, she was to be allowed what seemed "meete and Fitting."   In 1715 John Rose was paid one thousand pounds of tobacco for keeping John Purton, and three hundred pounds for "his wives dressing his Sores."   Some years later Elizabeth Morgan was allowed three hundred pounds for "keeping Susannah Middleton 3 months & curing her of A Sore legg."[72] The vestry of Bristol Parish, Virginia, in 1727/28 ordered that Mary Hall take care of Peter Plantine, a poor man "much hurt by an accident," and "Do her Endeavour to Cure him," adding that she was to bring in her account at the next parish levy.   Between 1727 and 1756 Mistress Hall's name appeared frequently in the vestry book as the recipient of payments for caring for the sick and disabled.[73]

All during the period, women found employment in attending disabled soldiers.   In an account of the military expenses for early Maryland, we find that Elizabeth Black and Eleanor Felton were paid each two pounds for nursing sick soldiers.[74]   In the French and Indian wars, women nurses accompanied the armies and apparently cooked and washed for them.   Mrs. Browne, a gentlewoman who was with Braddock's expeditionary force on its march to Fort Cumberland in 1754, noted several times in her diary that the nurses were baking bread, boiling beef, and washing.[75]   A letter from Colonel Bouquet to George Washington from Reas Town Camp, September 4, 1758, commanded him to leave his disabled men in the fort and

[70] *Archives of Maryland*, XLI, 332.

[71] *Colonial Records of North Carolina*, I, 670.

[72] C. G. Chamberlayne, ed., *Vestry Book of Christ Church Parish, Middlesex County, Virginia*, pp. 48, 151, 175.

[73] C. G. Chamberlayne, ed., *Bristol Parish Vestry Book*, pp. 37, 75, 100, 107, 120, 124, 131, 163-164.   [74] *Archives of Maryland*, XLIV, 427.

[75] "Mrs. Browne's Diary in Virginia and Maryland (1754)," *Virginia Magazine*, XXXII, 313, 315.

to order a sufficient number of women to attend as nurses, adding, "They will be paid."[76]

At the beginning of the Revolution, notices like the following appeared in the papers: "WANTED for the Continental Hospital in Williamsburg, some NURSES to attend the sick. Any such coming well recommended, will have good encouragement by applying to the Director of the hospital."[77] Other records like the following entry from the orderly book of Major William Heth show that women were employed as nurses at these military hospitals: "A proportionate Number of Women to the Sick of each regim't to be Sent to the Hospital at Mendham & Black River, to attend the Sick as Nurses."[78] The Maryland Council of Safety in 1776 ordered the treasurer to make payments to a number of women for nursing the sick at the hospital.[79] That caring for sick soldiers was not an easy or a lucrative occupation appears in this appeal to the governor and council of Maryland from one of the hospital nurses:

... you[r] petitioner has been a nurse at the hospital for about a year she has been deligent and carefull in her office, [for] which she your petitioner humbly beg[s] for an augmentation to her pay as she only is allowed two dollars a month she has at this present time sixteen men for to cook and take care off . . . she is oblige[d] to be up day and night with some of the patients and never has been allowed so much as a little Tea, or Coffee which she your Petitioner hopes your honours will take . . . into your consideration and your Petitioner in duty Bound will ever Pray.

Alice Redman

P. S. She your petitioner out of that two dollars pr month is oblig[d] to buy brooms and the soap we wash with. . . .[80]

Private persons sometimes employed nurses. John Nunne, by a deed recorded, April 19, 1649, delivered to Mary Sheircliffe a "Cowe Calfe," which, he declared, was "for the paynes and care that her mother tooke with mee when I was sicke and could not help myself."[81] An entry in the records of Accomac County, Virginia, for 1682 states that Agnes Williams testified that "Maudlin, wife of John Major, did bargain with Susan Helline, widdowe, for to keep her while she lay in child bed and did promise to give her 12 hens."[82]

[76] *Letters to Washington* (ed., Hamilton), III, 83.

[77] *Virginia Gazette*, July 26, 1776.

[78] Virginia Historical Society, *Collections*, XI (new ser.), 362.

[79] *Archives of Maryland*, XII, 245, 257, 298.

[80] *Maryland Magazine*, XVII, 379.   [81] *Archives of Maryland*, IV, 483.

[82] J. C. Wise, *Ye Kingdom of Accawmacke or the Eastern Shore of Virginia in the Seventeenth Century*, p. 320.

Years later, entries in the account book of Washington show that on several occasions he paid for the services of a nurse. An entry for July 2, 1755, states: "By 8 days attendance of a Nurse in my Sickness 8/," and another for March 25, 1756: "By Cash to my Nurse £1.0.0."[83]

Nurses occasionally advertised their services in the papers. Rebecca Pollard informed her Charles Town patrons that she had just returned from the country and was "ready to wait on any sick Persons or Lying-in Women." Also, she declared she had been quite successful with smallpox cases.[84] Smallpox was a much dreaded disease. Inoculation was comparatively new, having been brought by Lady Mary Wortley Montagu from Turkey in the first half of the eighteenth century, and was quite the fashion in the colonies. In order to confine the risks of contagion to one house and also to alleviate the tedium of isolation, often several persons took the virus at the same time and were shut up together to go through all the stages in company. The patients were occasionally quite ill and a few died, but ordinarily they appear to have been kept in bed only three or four days of the six to eight weeks of confinement. Some women made a business of opening their houses to persons who had been inoculated and attending them while they had the smallpox. Advertisements like this appeared in the press: "Elizabeth Girardeau gives this public notice that she takes in persons to have the Small-Pox at her house next to the Orange Garden, where the best attendance will be given, nurses, and every necessary found at Ten pounds per week."[85]

Some few women probably maintained themselves entirely by attending the sick, but generally nursing and the practice of medicine were only side lines by which the poor supplemented their meagre incomes and those better off earned pin money. Midwifery, on the other hand, was usually carried on by persons who considered it their chief business and depended upon it for a living. Furthermore, it was a profession which for centuries had been regarded as inviolably reserved for women. Though in the eighteenth century men physicians began to include obstetrical cases in their practice, midwives maintained almost exclusive control over the field throughout the colonial period.

The midwife was an important personage in every community,

[83] Fitzpatrick, *Washington, Colonial Traveller*, pp. 77, 95.
[84] *South Carolina Gazette*, April 3, 1742.   [85] *Ibid.*, June 11, 1763.

and at all times, during peace or war, plenty or famine, she did not lack employment. Because of the peculiar opportunities she had for obtaining information of a private nature, she was frequently summoned into court as a witness. Eliza Waterton, for instance, was called upon to give evidence before the general court of Virginia concerning the age of Ann Hudson. As she had been midwife to Ann's mother, her testimony was accepted as sufficient evidence.[86] In bastardy cases, great consideration was given to the midwife's testimony, since it was generally believed that a woman in labor would, when questioned on oath, disclose the father of her child, and there was usually at least one reputable midwife on every jury of women summoned in cases of infanticide.

Occasionally the names and achievements of notable midwives were given in the newspapers. A South Carolina notice in 1738 requested all persons who had "demands on the Estate of Mrs. Mary Harris late of Charleston Midwife" to bring in their accounts,[87] and the *Maryland Gazette*, March 26, 1761, announced the death of Mrs. Mary Callahan, "for many Years an eminent Midwife." A Virginia paper, in mentioning prominent persons who had died, included "Mrs. Catharine Blaikley, of this City [Williamsburg], in the seventy-sixth year of her Age; an eminent Midwife, and who, in the course of her Practice, brought upwards of three Thousand Children into the World."[88] Mistress Blaikley's record was equaled by that of Elizabeth Phillips, on whose tombstone at Charles Town it is stated that she assisted at the birth of three thousand children,[89] and it was surpassed by that of another South Carolina matron whose accomplishments were published in the following newspaper notice:

Tuesday last died, greatly lamented, aged 73 years, Mrs. Elizabeth Hunt, a native of this province, and practising midwife.—It is said to appear, by an account regularly kept by her, that she had been present at the birth of near 4000 children.[90]

Ordinarily midwives did not advertise their services in the papers, but they sometimes announced a change of address and, when moving into a new community, informed the public of their quali-

---

[86] *Minutes of the Council and General Court of Virginia*, p. 312.

[87] *South Carolina Gazette*, September 21, 1738.

[88] *Virginia Gazette*, October 24, 1771.

[89] Richardson Wright, *Hawkers and Walkers in Early America*. . . . (Philadelphia, 1927), p. 120.

[90] *South Carolina Gazette*, December 22, 1766.

fications. A woman just arrived in Charles Town in 1745 advertised
in the local gazette that she had for several years "followed the
Business of a Midwife" and intended to follow the same business
in Charles Town.[91] Mary Kelsey announced in the *South Carolina
Gazette*, January 31, 1771, that she had had thirteen years' experience
"in the capacity of a midwife," and "having had Success, and given
great Satisfaction," she hoped, with the recommendation of those she
had attended, to "meet with Encouragement." Jane Creighton, another Charles Town midwife, declared in a public notice that she had
been "maliciously accused" of cruelty to a woman who had died at
childbirth, but that this charge was only an attempt to "ruin her
reputation in her profession," and that she was "ready to answer the
allegations."[92] Julia Wheatley, a Virginia midwife, announced that
she had moved from Norfolk to Richmond, where she proposed to
"carry on her business as heretofore."[93] A Mrs. Hughes, "Midwife
late from the West Indies," informed the Norfolk ladies that she
was ready to receive the commands of those who might employ her.[94]

A very large majority of the colonial midwives were trained only
by experience. But in the decade before the Revolution, a few advertised that they had received special instruction in their profession
and offered to produce credentials showing their proficiency. A Mrs.
Grant, in offering her services as midwife, declared she had "studied
that art regularly and practised it afterwards, with success, at Edinburgh," and could produce certificates from "the Gentlemen whose
Lectures she attended, and likewise from the professors of Anatomy
and Practice of Physick in that City." She added this postscript,
which, we imagine, brought her more patronage than all her learning:
"N. B. She will, with the greatest chearfulness assist the poor,
Gratis."[95] The following similar advertisement appeared in the
Virginia Gazette, November 28, 1771:

The Subscriber having studied and practised MIDWIFERY for some
Time past, with Success, under the Direction, and with the Approbation
of Doctors *Pasteur* and *Gale*, flatters herself she will meet with Encouragement, as Nothing will be spared to complete her in the Knowledge of an
Art so eminently necessary to the Good of Mankind. Ladies, and others,
are therefore desired to take Notice that they will be waited upon on the
Shortest Warning, by their humble Servant,

MARY ROSE

[91] *Ibid.*, October 28, 1745.   [92] *Ibid.*, April 28, 1759.
[93] *Virginia Gazette*, January 20, 1776.   [94] *Ibid.*, December 16, 1773.
[95] *South Carolina Gazette*, December 29, 1768.

Midwives were probably led to seek training for their profession because of the increasing competition with men practitioners. In the *Maryland Gazette*, September 30, 1747, a Dr. Thomson offered to attend "those who desire his assistance as a physician, chirurgeon, or man-midwife." Some years later, Doctor Hulse advertised that he practiced "Physic, Surgery, and Midwifery" in Baltimore County.[96] Doctor Gilmer of Virginia announced his intention of "pursuing, with the Practice of Medicine, the art of Midwifery" in the *Virginia Gazette*, December 11, 1766, and three years later, John Minson Galt, "just arrived from London," notified the public that he proposed settling in Williamsburg, where he intended practicing as "a Surgeon, Apothecary, and Man-Midwife."[97]

The employment of men as midwives, however, was vehemently denounced as a pernicious fashion, dangerous to the life of mother and child and destructive of female modesty. A "LETTER on the present State of MIDWIFERY" printed in the *Virginia Gazette*, October 1, 1772, expressed what appears to have been a rather general feeling. The writer argued that since "Labour is Nature's Work," no more art is necessary in assisting women than is taught by experience, and asked, "If Men-Midwives were requisite to bring Children into the World, what would become of the Wilds of America, the Plains of Africa?" Furthermore, he declared, "Women are infinitely safer than men," and continued: "It is a notorious fact that more Children have been lost since Women were so scandalously indecent as to employ Men than for Ages before that Practice became so general. . . . [Women midwives] never dream of having recourse to Force; the barbarous, bloody Crochet, never stained their Hands with Murder. . . . A long unimpassioned Practice, early commenced, and calmly pursued is absolutely requisite to give Men by Art, what Women attain by Nature." Finally, he argued, the familiarities taken by men in attending pregnant women and those in labor are "sufficient to taint the Purity, and sully the Chastity, of any Woman breathing," and concluded with this pronouncement, "True Modesty is incompatible with the Idea of employing a MAN-MIDWIFE."[98]

[96] *Maryland Gazette*, February 5, 1767.

[97] *Virginia Gazette*, February 2, 1769.

[98] This same idea is presented at great length by Francis Foster in his book entitled *Thoughts on the Times, but Chiefly on the Profligacy of Our Women . . . Shewing . . . the Absurdity of our Female Education—the Folly and Bad Tendency of Fashionable Life—and the Evils that Arise from French Refinement, and . . . How Seldom Men-Midwives are Necessary. . . . That it is Repugnant to Modesty. . . .* (2d ed., London, 1779).

CHAPTER XIII

SHOPKEEPERS AND ARTISANS

Because of the limitations of their education, colonial women were better fitted for occupations requiring general intelligence and social tact than for those demanding specialized knowledge and formal training. Therefore, they were generally more at home in business than in the professions. It was customary in the colonies, as in England, for the wife of a shopkeeper or tradesman to work as her husband's partner in his shop and thus become acquainted with the business, which at his death she was able to continue alone. Many advertisements like the following appear in the newspapers:

This is to give Notice that Hannah Lade Widow and Administratrix of Mr. Nathaniel Lade deceased, continues in the House and Shop and keeps on the Business of her said late deceased Husband . . . and hath to sell very cheap for ready Money, all sorts of Goods lately advertised by the said Mr. Nathaniel Lade, with sundry other sorts of Goods since imported and fit for the Season.[1]

In many cases, however, the tradeswoman did not inherit her business, but established it by her own initiative.

Though they engaged in many kinds of enterprises, women were particularly successful as retail dealers, and they almost monopolized the millinery and dressmaking trades. Dealers in foodstuffs were the first lady shopkeepers to solicit patronage through the newspapers. In Charles Town a number of women were advertising groceries in the thirties. Mrs. Bell had "Good Anchovies to be sold at reasonable Rates." Mrs. Hammerton sold "the best Bohea and green tea as cheap by the half or quarter pound as by the pound." The "Widow Fisher" advertised "brown, middling, and milk Bisket, Gammons, Coffee, Teas, and Sugar."[2] Later, Anne Forrester had pickled herrings and coffee for sale "in Bedon's Alley," and Sarah Saxby offered "the best Vinegar at 10s. per gallon, fine Pickles of different sorts done after the English manner, in large or small

---

[1] *South Carolina Gazette*, April 9, 1741.
[2] *Ibid.*, August 5, 1732; May 12, 1733; August 17, 1738.

quantities, very good Kitchop, and Mushrooms."[3]   Merchants informed their customers of newly imported goods in notices like the following:

Just imported in the Charles-Town, Capt. Schermerhorn, from New York, Flour, Milk, and Butter Bisket, Starch and Blue, cut Tobacco, good Vinegar, and all sorts of Garden Seeds, to be sold next Door to Mrs. Trusler on the Bay by
Catherine Seurlock[4]

Margaret Warden advertised "choice brown and middling bread, with flour in barrels imported from Philadelphia," and Catharine Smart offered flour, butter, and milk from New York.[5]   Just before the Revolution, Ann Ball kept a store on Motte's Wharf, where she sold "exceeding fine Potatoes . . . likewise Jamaica and West Indian Rum, Muscovado Sugar, red Port Wine by the Dozen . . . superfine Flour in Kegs, Coffee, Burlington Hams."[6]   In Annapolis, Elizabeth Marriott advertised "Choice Cheshire Cheese, and good fresh Lisbon lemons at the Sign of the Ship"; Rebecca Irvin offered "Choice fresh limes"; and Anne Catharine Green sold "Choice good Coffee" and "very good Chocolate" at the postoffice.[7]

Women had no scruples, apparently, about selling intoxicating drinks.   Catharine Pritchard advertised at her house in Annapolis "Very good West-India Rum, at 7s. and 6d. *per* Gallon."[8]   Ann Cunningham and her partner sold sugar, molasses, and spirituous liquors in Savannah.[9]   Susannah Gates informed the customers of her deceased husband in Charles Town that she continued to sell wine and rum at the shop "in Thomas Elliott's Alley,"[10] and another retailer of alcoholic beverages gave the public this notice:

To be sold, on Thursday the 23d instant, at 3 o'clock in the afternoon, at the house of Mrs. Morand, in Broad Street, near the Watchhouse; about Fifty or Sixty dozen of claret, in lots without reserve.

As the said Mrs. Morand intends to leave off shop-keeping, and retire into the country, she will dispose of what goods she has on hand at very low prices.[11]

[3] *Ibid.*, March 11, 1766; December 16, 1745.

[4] *Ibid.*, October 31, 1751.

[5] *Ibid.*, July 3, 1749.   [6] *Ibid.*, January 2, 1775.

[7] *Maryland Gazette*, May 8, 1751; June 19, 1760; July 1, 1746; March 22, 1749.

[8] *Ibid.*, May 27, 1746.   [9] *Georgia Gazette*, January 12, 1764.

[10] *South Carolina Gazette*, December 19, 1741.

[11] *Ibid.*, June 6, 1768.

The gazettes contain many notices signed by women whose businesses are not known. Anne Milner, for instance, advertised lime for sale; Mary Frost, "very good Hay and Corn Blades," Mrs. Fillion, "very good fresh Cabbage Seed," and Mary Owens, "family medicines."[12] Several Charles Town women appear to have been stationers. Elizabeth Wicking, whose shop was mentioned incidentally in 1735, several years later announced that she had just imported for sale "a choice Collection of Books."[13] Elizabeth Timothy, who had just a few years before turned over her editorial and printing responsibilities to her son, in 1746 advertised for sale next door to the printing office "Pocket Bibles, Primmers, Hornbooks . . . Reflections on Courtship and Marriage . . . Pamela."[14] The next year Anne Timothy, probably her daughter-in-law, was advertising ink, paper, and all writing materials along with fans, necklaces, handkerchiefs, gloves, and other accessories.[15]

Martha Logan, daughter of Governor Daniel, last of the proprietary governors, appears to have been a dealer in nursery plants and a horticulturist of some note. She was "the Lady of South Carolina" whom the *South Carolina Gazette* in 1752 mentioned as having printed a gardener's calendar "esteemed a very good one."[16] Her calendar was reprinted several times, and she is said to have written a treatise on gardening when she was seventy years of age.[17] Mrs. Manigault, Charles Town gentlewoman, wrote in her diary in 1763 of having been to Mrs. Logan's to buy roots.[18] As gardening was a fashionable hobby of the time and wealthy ladies and gentlemen were very much interested in planting their extensive grounds with rare plants and shrubs, Mistress Logan's nursery was probably a profitable enterprise. She advertised garden seeds, roots, and shrubs for sale at different times in notices like the following:

Just imported in Capt. Lloyd from London and to be sold very reasonably by Martha Logan at her house in Meeting-street, three doors without the gate:

A fresh assortment of very good garden seeds and flower roots; also many other sorts of flowering shrubs and box edging beds, now growing in her garden.[19]

[12] *Ibid.*, August 2, 1742; August 6, 1750; September 21, 1738; June 10, 1751.
[13] *Ibid.*, April 19, 1735; August 8, 1740.
[14] *Ibid.*, October 18, 1746.
[15] *Ibid.*, September 14, 1747.   [16] January 1, 1752.
[17] *South Carolina Magazine*, XX, 205.   [18] *Ibid.*
[19] *South Carolina Gazette*, February 15, 1768.

Catharine Joor sold dry goods in Charles Town for many years. Though she did not advertise her wares, her shop was mentioned in the papers in 1732, and eight years later she informed her customers that she had moved from her former place of business to Tradd Street.[20] Sarah and Lucy Weaver were the first dealers in dry goods to use the press for advertising. In 1735 they announced they had for sale in the shop formerly kept by Mrs. Owen in Broad Street "all sorts of Millinery Ware, and other European Goods, at reasonable Prices." Mrs. Owens, their predecessor, apparently did not solicit business through the press. In 1737 Lucy Weaver advertised:

Just imported in the William, . . . Baker from London, and to be sold by Lucy Weaver in Broad street, china pentes, cups, sawcers, glass decanters, wine and water glasses, bohea tea, double refin'd sugar, fine lace and edgings . . . hoop-petticoats, womens and childrens stays, toys, and many other sorts of European Goods at reasonable rates.[21]

In the same year Sarah Packe in Williamsburg advertised "Bombazeens, Crapes, and other Sorts of Mourning, for Ladies: also Hatbands, and Gloves, for Gentlemen."[22]

Charles Town shopkeepers appeared frequently in the papers from this time on throughout the period, but in the other southern colonies business women did not advertise to any great extent until sometime after the middle of the century. Ann Dalrymple, milliner, mantuamaker, and shopkeeper, gave notice in the *South Carolina Gazette*, April 30, 1737, that she would attend Ashley Ferry and Strawberry Fairs and carry along an assortment of millinery and other wares such as "cambricks, hollands, farlix, edgings, ribbons, fans, powder." Some years later Judith Miller, another itinerant dealer, advertised that she would attend Ashley River Fair and carry "a variety of goods to be raffled for."[23] In the forties Catharine Dalbiac announced her intention of continuing her husband's dry goods business; Hannah Lade offered for sale "for ready money" all kinds of goods recently imported and "fit for the season"; and Elizabeth Carne announced the arrival of "an assortment of Lawns, spotted and plain, cambricks . . . Leghorn hats . . . a Variety of Ribbons, and sundry other Articles."[24]

[20] *Ibid.*, September 2, 1732; November 27, 1740.

[21] *Ibid.*, September 7, 1735; January 29, 1737.

[22] *Virginia Gazette*, March 1, 1737. Besides this store, Mistress Packe owned half interest in the printing establishment run by William Parks.—*Virginia Magazine*, XXXII, 17-18.   [23] *Ibid.*, April 26, 1740.

[24] *Ibid.*, October 9, 1740; April 9, 1741; June 8, 1748.

Anne Waller kept a shop in Charles Town intermittently from 1749 through 1770. She inserted her first public notice in the paper, March 1, 1749, and the following July announced her intention of leaving the province and selling her whole stock of goods. Twelve years later, she was again advertising European goods for sale. On August 23, 1770, she once more announced her intention of disposing of her business, but the next year she was advertising a new importation of goods from London as usual.[25]

Mary Cooper and Anne Matthews were the most assiduous advertisers during the fifties. The former kept shop from sometime before 1755 until May, 1774, when she announced she was leaving the province and declared that every bond or note due her and not settled would be left in the hands of an attorney to be sued for immediately.[26] Anne Matthews, who had inherited her husband's establishment at his death in 1755, continued to import goods from England and gradually enlarged her stock.[27] She seems to have been quite successful until just before the Revolution, when the Continental Congress took active measures against the importation of European goods. A newspaper article stated that she and her son, who evidently had become her partner a short time before, had signed the resolutions not to import articles from London and agreed to store what they already had on hand until the hated English acts were removed, but a committee of inspection had found that their European stock had been opened and sold. The son claimed that his mother had disposed of the merchandise during his absence, but Anne and Benjamin Matthews were both advertised as "Violaters of the Resolutions" and the public was cautioned against having any dealings with them.[28]

Advertisements of millinery and dry goods establishments increased greatly in number and in length during the period preceding the Revolution. Between 1760 and 1775, no less than thirty-six women advertised shops in the Charles Town papers,[29] and at least thirteen advertised in the *Virginia Gazette*. Seven of these were in

[25] *Ibid.*, January 10, 1761; August 1, 1771.

[26] *Ibid.*, October 31, 1755; April 15, 1766; May 30, 1774.

[27] *Ibid.*, November 27, 1755; July 1, 1756; June 30, 1759; January 6, 1761; August 20, 1762; February 19, 1763; October 31, 1765; June 10, 1766; February 9, 1767.

[28] *South Carolina Gazette and Country Journal*, June 5, 1770; June 28, 1770.

[29] Those whose names appeared most frequently were Eleanor Dryden, Agnes Lind, Anne Baron, Frances Swallow, and Katharine Lind.

Williamsburg,[30] while the others had shops in Fredericksburg,[31] Petersburg,[32] and Richmond.[33] Six in Annapolis,[34] one in North Carolina,[35] and two in Georgia,[36] published notices in the papers. As advertising in the newspapers was by no means general during this period, it may be supposed that this list includes only a small proportion of the women who sold dry goods at the time.

These shopkeepers did not run a card in the papers regularly describing the general type of merchandise with which they dealt, but at intervals of several months or more, inserted their names, addresses, and a long, detailed list of the various articles they had for sale with the name of the boat and the captain bringing the goods from Europe. The following is a typical notice:

KATHARINE BOWER,

Has just imported, and has for SALE, at her STORE the fourth
corner of *Tradd-street* next the Bay,

A very neat ASSORTMENT of

MILLINARY GOODS

Consisting of the followings ARTICLES,

A NEAT assortment of fashionable CAPS, stomachers, shoe-knots, Italian sprigs, a variety of white and black blond lace, thread lace and edgings, white spotted satin, black and white laced ditto, crimson ditto, black peelongs, figures and plain modes, English persians, of all colours, a great variety of sash and other RIBBONS, fashionable FANS, women and girls white and coloured GLOVES, mens buckskin and *real* beaver ditto, plain and figured GAUZE, ditto handkerchiefs, womens black stuff shoes, pound and paper PINS, needles, cap wire, printed linens, small French wax beeds, black and coloured collars, sewing silks, black and white laced satin cloaks and bonnets, purple and white ditto; all which she will dispose of on the *lowest* TERMS.

N.B. At the above-mentioned store, she carries on the MILLINARY BUSINESS in all its branches, and will be much obliged to her FRIENDS for a continuance of their favours.[37]

[30] Catherine Rathell, Sarah Pitt, Jane Hunter, Margaret Hunter, Mary Dickinson, Jane Charlton, Mary Davenport.

[31] Catherine Rathell had a shop in Fredericksburg before she moved to Williamsburg.

[32] Mary Hill, Elizabeth Mathias, and Ellis Williams.

[33] Mary, Anne, and Eliza Strachan.

[34] Elizabeth Marriott, Clementina Grierson, Catherine Rathell, Elizabeth Moulding, Jane and Anne Nelson.

[35] Mrs. Batchelor at New Bern.

[36] Mary Hughes and Lucretia Triboudet.

[37] *South Carolina Gazette and Country Journal*, February 16, 1773.

Shopkeepers often took advantage of special occasions to advertise, such as court weeks or the meetings of the assemblies. Mary Dickinson of Williamsburg, for instance, on May 7, 1772, notified her customers that she expected a cargo of European goods by the following June court. Catherine Rathell, while keeping store in Fredericksburg, announced that her "present Scarcity of Cash" induced her to "attend a few Days at Williamsburg, during the Sitting of the next Assembly, from whence it will be more convenient for many Ladies and Gentlemen to furnish themselves than from this Town." Later she notified her customers that she intended going to England after the June court, "to purchase a cargo against the October court."[38]

These advertisements must have sorely tempted colonial ladies, for they declared that the goods were of the latest fashion, just from Europe, and to be sold cheap. Then they described such alluring objects as "crooked tortoise shell combs set with paste," fancy hair pins, rolls [for the hair] and "drop curls," French pearl and wax necklaces and earrings, carved and painted ivory fan sticks, and fan-mounts "of newest fashion, of various Colours and most beautiful Patterns." They dangled before feminine imaginations such irresistible finery as brocades, English Persians, "a-la-mode," lutestring, paduasoy, flowered lawns, "fashionable ribands, figured and plain," gold and silver lace, Italian egrets, imported serges, Irish linens, "suits of Ribbons made up in London and stomachers with Bows," white and colored feathers, satin and callimanco shoes, white and colored silk stockings, colored French silk gloves, and Barcelona handkerchiefs.

Most shopkeepers carried a curious collection of wares. Elizabeth Holliday sold hoop-petticoats, women's stays and jumps, "sundry calicoes and chintz" and all sorts of haberdashery with spices, coffee, tea, sugar, capers, biscuit, flour, and toys.[39] Elizabeth Carne offered leghorn hats, lawns, and "all sorts of Cordial Waters," and Mary Cranmer advertised millinery, dry goods, a face wash, snuff, school books, pictures, maps, and bird cages.[40] Anne Waller's stock included various dry goods, guns, pistols, and gold watches.[41]

[38] *Virginia Gazette*, February 19, 1767; April 13, 1769.
[39] *Ibid.*, August 4, 1739.
[40] *Ibid.*, June 8, 1748; September 30, 1756.
[41] *Ibid.*, March 1, 1749.

Susann ʼh Crockatt sold Italian chairs, silk shoes, medicines, stationery, draperies, wine, tea, and sugars.[42] Frances Swallow advertised tea, olives, spices, walnuts, capers, sweet oil, and china along with satins and brocades.[43] Anne Matthews carried gunpowder and gunflint, loaf sugar, fiddles, spices, teapots, chafing dishes, and pudding pans, as well as the most fashionable millinery goods.[44] Agnes Lind, another Charles Town importer of "the most genteel" millinery goods, sold "high and low toasted snuff" and "Rogers best cut tobacco."[45] Owners of fashionable millinery establishments in Williamsburg advertised along with their elaborate brocades, satins, and laces, such articles as printing types, ink, ledgers, and memorandum books, teaspoons, salt shovels, and sugar tongs, walking sticks, canes, and rattans, "chased and plain silver nutmeg graters," smelling bottles, silver toothpicks and tortoise shell toothpick cases, toothbrushes, violins, dolls, marbles and other toys, music for the harpsichord, flute, and violin, "neat Paper Snuff Boxes," "Weston's Scotch and Rappee Snuff," "fine Shag Tobacco," and "genuine Dr. Anderson's pills."

Most shopkeepers carried cosmetics. With her "neat assortment of millinery goods," Sarah Sanders advertised "king's honey water, hungary water, double distilled lavender water." Sarah Watson offered "an excellent eye water" that would "take off specks, cataracts, and strengthen weak eyes," lip salve, tooth powder, almond paste for the hands and face, and perfumed wash balls. Anne Maurouet advertised "a very good water to prevent ladies faces from tanning and to keep them smooth and white," and "the very best powder for preserving the teeth and gums."[46] Almost every new assortment of goods included "scented wash balls," pomatum, tooth powder, cold cream, powder boxes, and powder puffs.

Shopkeepers frequently not only sold a variety of merchandise but conducted other activities likewise. Marie Hume, an Annapolis merchant, made all sorts of millinery work, ladies' headdresses, hats, and bonnets "in the newest fashion," and cloaks, slips, and frocks for young ladies. She also washed laces, blond, gauzes, and silk stockings "to look equal to new."[47] Catherine Rathell, Williamsburg shop-

[42] *Ibid.*, May 12 and June 23, 1759. [43] *Ibid.*, June 16, 1766.
[44] *Ibid.*, June 10, 1766. [45] *Ibid.*
[46] *Ibid.*, December 16, 1760; March 5, 1763.
[47] *Maryland Gazette*, July 21, 1774.

keeper, made all sorts of millinery and washed laces, and Mary Martin in Savannah dressed ladies' hair, made fashionable caps and bonnets, and washed laces and silk stockings.[48]

Most proprietors of dry goods shops were either trained milliners and mantuamakers themselves or they employed assistants who had served an apprenticeship in these branches. If the business were large, the owner often took young girls as apprentices, who helped in the shop while they acquired their training. Jane Hunter employed her sister Margaret, a trained milliner, as an assistant, and later, when she had to return to England, turned over to her the management of the business.[49] Sarah Pitt, another Williamsburg shopkeeper, informed the ladies of Virginia that she had an assistant just arrived from London to make bonnets and cardinals, and to mount fans.[50] Jane Thomson of Charles Town advertised several times for young girls to serve as apprentices to the millinery business.[51] These assistants and apprentices, after completing their period of training, sometimes began businesses of their own. Margaret Freeman, formerly assistant to Mrs. Webley, announced to the Charles Town ladies that she had left Mrs. Webley, and proposed setting up a millinery establishment of her own. Hannah Coleman advertised that she had been an apprentice to Mrs. Wish, prominent shopkeeper then deceased, and intended carrying on the mantuamaking business in all its branches.[52]

European travelers in the colonies often expressed surprise at finding the ladies at Annapolis, Williamsburg, and Charles Town always dressed in the latest mode. The provincial milliners and mantuamakers knew their jobs. They bought in Europe "the most fashionable, new, and genteel goods," and they sometimes went to London themselves to get new ideas and purchase merchandise. Many notices appear in the papers of milliners and mantuamakers just arrived from London. Frances Swallow, for instance, proprietor of a fashionable shop in Charles Town, sailed for London in October, 1766, and returned in December, 1767, with a variety of the latest goods and new ideas about how to teach the tambour work.[53]

[48] Virginia Gazette, April 18, 1766; Georgia Gazette, January 12, 1774.

[49] Virginia Gazette, October 1, 1767; April 27, 1769.

[50] Ibid., December 21, 1769.

[51] South Carolina Gazette, May 30, 1771; South Carolina and American General Gazette, January 28, 1774.

[52] South Carolina Gazette and Country Journal, February 27, 1770.

[53] Ibid., October 7, 1766; December 8, 15, 1767.

Shopkeepers and tradeswomen usually advertised that they sold for "ready money only," but numerous notices requesting their debtors to settle their accounts suggest many exceptions to this rule. Some asked for payment as a special favor. Jane Hunter explained in a public notice that her ill state of health made it necessary for her to go to England and added this polite request: "I flatter myself that my obliging customers indebted will see the necessity of my receiving payment before my departure. I cannot therefore doubt but that they will, on this earnest request, pay me this April court."[54] Agnes Lind, evidently less confident of the obliging disposition of her debtors, prodded them in the following less flattering but probably more forceful notice: ". . . all persons indebted to her are desired to pay off their accounts, especially those of two or three years standing, otherwise they may expect to find them in the hands of an attorney at law."[55]

While many milliners and mantuamakers were proprietors of dry goods establishments, others devoted their attention entirely to the making of hats, gowns, cloaks, and such articles. Elizabeth Cooper made mantuas, mantulets, riding habits, new fashioned silk hats, and velvet capes, and dressed heads "after the newest and best fashion"; Katharine Willis, "lately arrived from England," made mantuas, "hanging sleev'd coats," short and long coats, and mantulets, and Mary Anne Benoist dressed ladies' heads, and made bonnets, mantulets, and ornaments of silver flowers for young misses' headdresses.[56] A Mrs. Parker in Savannah made "sacks and coats, gowns, Brunswicks, Fiscuits, and Corsicans, Hats and Bonnets," and in Annapolis, Verlinda Clements carried on the mantuamaking business "in all its branches" and "after the newest and most genteel Modes and Fashions."[57]

Some of these mantuamakers were perhaps seamstresses who took in sewing which they did alone in their own homes, but others appear to have been proprietors of important mantuamaking and tailoring establishments, employing assistants and taking apprentices to aid them. Ann Nichols, for example, informing her customers of a change of address, announced that, being provided with more hands than formerly, she could assure her customers that their orders

[54] *Virginia Gazette*, April 27, 1769.
[55] *South Carolina Gazette*, February 16, 1765.
[56] *Ibid.*, March 19, 1737.
[57] *Georgia Gazette*, March 9, 1774; *Maryland Journal*, May 17, 1775.

would be executed with greater dispatch and in all respects to their satisfaction.[58] Mary Minskie advertised that she had two excellent workmen and carried on the staymaking business in all its branches. She made all sorts of women's apparel, and women's quilted petticoats "to a very great nicety," and likewise made men's apparel, both coarse and fine, and would be proud to serve ladies and gentlemen in any of these branches.[59] Sarah Callahan, widow of James Callahan, tailor, announced that "having hands to perform the same," she continued to carry on "the TAYLOR'S BUSINESS" at the same place where her late husband lived, and hoped for the continuance of his customers.[60] Barbara Bence, apparently the proprietress of an establishment, advertised for "a sober industrious person" to aid her in the tailor's business.[61] Sarah Quash, Elizabeth Harvey, Eleanor Porter, Isabella Wish, and Mary Turpin carried on the stay-making business in Charles Town,[62] and Elizabeth Ferguson in Annapolis.[63]

Anne Wilson of Charles Town mounted fans and sold fan mounts; Mrs. Grenier quilted petticoats and corselets; and Mary Baker did pinking and made handkerchiefs and ruffles.[64] Anne Griffith of Annapolis advertised "Quilting, Plain or Figur'd, coarse or fine . . . performed in the best and cheapest manner." Penelope House, having served an apprenticeship to the business in London, mended hoop-petticoats of any fashion. A Mrs. Williamson offered to make, mend, or alter hoop-petticoats, and Sarah Munro to quilt gowns, petticoats, or bed quilts.[65]

Fine laundering, clearstarching, dyeing, and glazing were among the other occupations advertised by women. Elizabeth Hall informed the ladies of Charles Town that she did clearstarching of gauze or suits of lace in the best manner. Mary Griffith cleaned blonds and gauzes by the French method, and Elizabeth Ash and Magdalene Hamilton washed and ironed ladies "head-Cloaths." Mary Drysdell proposed "to follow the business of Clear-Starching, washing Gauze, scouring and grafting Silk Stockings, and Cleaning Silks from any

[58] *South Carolina Gazette*, April 4, 1768.

[59] *Maryland Gazette*, July 28, 1768.

[60] *Ibid.*, April 26, 1759.   [61] *Ibid.*, June 30, 1774.

[62] *South Carolina Gazette*, August 7, 1762; March 17, 1752; August 28, 1762; October 11, 1774; November 1, 1773.

[63] *Maryland Gazette*, October 25, 1770; July 7, 1774.

[64] *South Carolina Gazette*, August 11, 1746; May 31, 1735; March 6, 1762.

[65] *Maryland Gazette*, December 27, 1749; June 6, 1754; July 16, 1752.

spots of Grease."[66] "M. Evans" mended and washed lace and silk stockings for the ladies of Williamsburg.[67] Elizabeth Harramond "stiffened and glazed" chintz, and another Charles Town woman inserted this notice: "Dyeing in all Colours, and Scowering of all Sorts, is performed as usual by *Mrs. Bartram*. N. B. Chints's and Callicoes are cleaned and glazed after the best Manner."[68] A Mrs. McClellan advertised that she had lately filled up a calender and would glaze all silks, linens, damasks, calicoes, bed and window curtains, women's gowns and petticoats, men's night gowns, and silk and thread stockings.[69]

A fashionable lady of any of the larger towns was able not only to have her dresses and hats made "after the newest fashion" and her fans mounted, her petticoats altered, mended, and quilted, her laces and silk stockings mended and cleaned by the French method, but could likewise purchase delicacies for her table at a genteel pastry shop. In 1738 Mistress Stagg of Williamsburg advertised "Hartshorn and Calvesfoot jellies fresh every Tuesday" and other confectioneries including "mackaroons, Savoy biscuits and Barbadoes sweetmeats."[70] In Charles Town Margaret Cresswell, "pastry cook from London," made all kinds of pastry and jellies "in the best manner," and Elinor Bolton, also an imported confectioner, advertised dainties that must have appealed to the most fastidious lady.[71] Margaret Nelson at first made all kinds of delicacies at home "when bespoke," but later she opened a pastry shop and advertised the following: "Rich plumb cake at 10s. per pound, biscuit and seed ditto, syllybubs and jelleys, 20s. per dozen, white custards in glasses at 15s. per dozen, lemon and orange cream blomage, 20s. per plate, rice cups, at 12s. 6d. per plate, lemon, orange, citron, and almond pudding, 20s. a piece, orange pye, 30s., snow cheese, 30s., apple tarts, curd, and apple cheese cakes, 24s. per dozen, almond and lemon ditto, 30s. per dozen, minced pies, 3s. 9d. a piece, preserved oranges, 7s. 6d. a piece, apples 15s. per

[66] *South Carolina Gazette*, November 20, 1762; April 11, 1771; April 4, 1748; August 17, 1769.

[67] *Virginia Gazette*, November 28, 1771.

[68] *South Carolina Gazette*, November 10, 1746.

[69] *Ibid.*, December 15, 1737.

[70] *Virginia Gazette*, October 13, 1738.

[71] *South Carolina Gazette*, December 17, 1763; April 11, 1761. In Savannah Elizabeth Anderson announced that she was continuing the baking business formerly owned by Mrs. Pagey.—*Georgia Gazette*, December 21, 1768.

plate, orange and apple marmalade, collard and potted beef, and many other articles too tedious to enumerate."[72]

A number of colonial women were engaged in businesses quite different from such womanly employments as millinery and mantuamaking, baking, quilting, and mounting fans, or cleaning and mending ladies' finery. Rebecca Weyman was an upholsterer. In 1762 she was offering to make all kinds of bed or window curtains, either festoon or otherwise, and easy-chair cases for washing, and engaged "to work well and with despatch."[73]   Ann Fowler was also in the upholstery business and sold paper hangings, "bed furniture, bed lace, feathers, jean for gentlemen's wear," looking glasses, and tea trays.[74] Mary Stevenson, widow of John Stevenson, a glazier and painter, announced that she would continue her husband's business.[75]   Jane Inch advertised herself as a silversmith, and Mary Willet, as executrix of her husband, notified the public that she would carry on the pewterer's business in the same manner and at the same rates as charged during her husband's lifetime.[76]   Anna Maria Hoyland did "any kind of braziery and tinwork as her mother used to do."[77] Maria Warwell offered "to mend china, viz. beakers, tureens, jars, vases, busts, statues, either in china, glass, plaster, bronze, or marble," and announced that "should a piece be wanting she will substitute a composition in its room and copy the pattern as nigh as possible."[78]

Cassandra Ducker owned and ran a fulling mill. She announced in the *Maryland Gazette*, September 12, 1776, that it had been reported about the country that her mill did not go, much to her prejudice, but that it was then in good order and those who favored her with their custom might depend upon having their cloth done in the neatest and best manner. Mary Wilson of Norfolk advertised that she carried on the shoemaking business in all its branches,[79] and Elizabeth Russell of South Carolina, after the death of her husband, continued his trade as a shipwright.[80]   Catherine Park of Vir-

[72] *South Carolina Gazette*, April 11, 1769.
[73] *Ibid.*, September 18, 1762.
[74] *South Carolina Gazette and Country Journal*, January 24, 1775.
[75] *South Carolina Gazette*, October 11, 1735.
[76] *Maryland Gazette*, April 28, 1763; February 25, 1773.
[77] *South Carolina Gazette*, November 13, 1751.
[78] *South Carolina Gazette and Country Journal*, July 21, 1767.
[79] *Virginia Gazette*, August 20, 1772.
[80] *South Carolina and American General Gazette*, April 24, 1771.

ginia owned and managed a tan yard,[81] and Mary Robinson, widow of Thomas Robinson, tanner and leather dresser of Charles Town, announced that she still carried on his business and had for sale "ready made Buck and Doe skin Breeches." She "dressed deer skins with or without the hairs, and dyed, washed, and mended Buck skin breeches."[82]

Jane Massey inherited a gunsmith shop from her husband, and with the help of an assistant, continued his trade for several years.[83] Jane Burgess, a Maryland widow, added this postscript to her notice as executrix of her husband: "N. B. I still carry on the Blacksmith Business, and shall be obliged to my Friends for the continuance of their Favours."[84] Mary Butler, also of Maryland, announced that she had several good blockmakers and would supply customers with all sorts of blocks for ships or other vessels made in the best and cheapest manner. She likewise made pumps for ships and wells "with the greatest expedition."[85] Elizabeth Butler of Charles Town advertised her services as a barber, and Margaret Oliver and her mother were both butchers.[86] Elizabeth Kelly sold and repaired whips in Annapolis,[87] and Martha Clifford kept a livery stable in Charles Town.[88]

The woman who advertised her tannery, shipwright, or shoemaking business or sought patronage for her gunsmith or blacksmith shop did not, as a rule, initiate such a business but at the death of her husband, continued his trade in order to maintain herself and family. In many cases the shop was a part of the home, and the wife, having served as her husband's assistant, was able to take his place and carry on his business without any interruption. Occasionally women merchants also inherited their establishments, but apparently the proprietors of millinery and dry goods stores, pastry shops and similar concerns usually started these enterprises on their own initiative.

While a majority of colonial women in business were widows, some had husbands living. Sarah Pitt, who kept a fashionable shop

[81] Letter from Richmond, March 30, 1781, in *Calendar of Virginia State Papers*, I, 608-609.

[82] *South Carolina Gazette*, August 10, 1738.

[83] *Ibid.*, August 25, 1739; January 19, 1740; April 23, 1741.

[84] *Maryland Gazette*, April 1, 1773.   [85] *Ibid.*, May 27, 1756.

[86] *South Carolina Gazette*, March 23, 1765.

[87] *Maryland Gazette*, July 7, 1747.

[88] *South Carolina Gazette*, December 8, 1766.

in Williamsburg for several years, was the wife of Dr. George Pitt. Her obituary, published in the *Virginia Gazette*, described her as "a lady whose many virtues through every varied scene of private life did honour to the principles she professed," whose "bosom was tremblingly alive to every tender sentiment of connubial and maternal affection," and who "discharged the duties of wife and mother in such a distinguished manner as must make her revered, and her loss forever regretted, by each of those relations."[89]

Frequently husbands and wives offered their services to the public in the same advertisement like the following:

> George Charleton, Taylor, lately arriv'd from London, now lives in Williamsburg, at the House next to Col. Gryme's, (late Mr. Clayton's), by whom Gentlemen may have Cloaths made, after the newest and most fashionable Manner.
>
> N. B. His Wife is a mantua-maker, and offers her Service, in that way of Business, to the Ladies, whom she will undertake to oblige, with the newest and genteelest Fashions now wore in England, and at reasonable Rates.[90]

Charles Walker Fortescue, in his notice of his school for young gentlemen, added this postscript: "N. B. All Gentlewomen who may be pleased to employ the above Subscriber's Wife, in the Business of Mantua-making, etc. shall be served in the most elegant, new and modish manner."[91] William Trueman offered to write deeds, settle accounts, and sell goods on commission, while his wife, Elizabeth Trueman, made mantuas, mantulets, velvet hoods, caps, and hats.[92] John Thompson advertised himself as an umbrella-maker and his wife as a milliner and mantuamaker,[93] and John Gow and his wife offered their services together as stay and mantuamakers.[94]

A wife's notice usually appeared as a subscript to her husband's advertisement, but these relative positions were reversed in the case of the Swallow family. Frances Swallow's name appeared in large type at the head of a long, detailed list of goods on sale at her shop, while her husband's less pretentious notice was added as an appendage.[95] Apparently her enterprises were more successful than his, for her advertisements ran regularly while little appeared regarding him.

[89] *Virginia Gazette*, November 19, 1772.   [90] *Ibid.*, September 1, 1738.
[91] *South Carolina Gazette*, December 14, 1747.
[92] *Ibid.*, November 12, 1739; August 23, 1742.
[93] *South Carolina Gazette and Country Journal*, August 29, 1769.
[94] *South Carolina and American General Gazette*, September 26, 1766.
[95] *South Carolina Gazette*, June 17, 1766.

On August 30, 1768, she advertised herself as "a sole dealer," probably to protect her business against her husband's debts. Two years later she announced she was opening a boarding school and would still continue her millinery business.[96] In 1772 the papers announced the death of Newman Swallow, merchant, declaring that it was supposed he had died from a broken heart.[97] His obituary notice also stated that he had left a widow and six little children. Evidently Mistress Swallow had not failed in her duty to add to the population of the colony while pursuing her many activities. Soon after her husband's death, she moved to a suitable house, advertised for "waiting boys," and in addition to her other business activities began to keep tavern.[98] Two years later she married again.[99] But she apparently did not expect this husband, any more than her first, to support her and her six children, for without any interruption she continued her tavern under her new name.[100]

Marriage and remarriage affected little the business activities of several other prominent shopkeepers. Ann Nichols advertised as "formerly Ann M'Gaw" and assured her former customers that she would continue the mantua-making business.[101] Eleanor Dryden, whose public notices appeared frequently in the Charles Town papers, was the wife of James Dryden, a staymaker. When, after his death, she married David Bruce, a printer, she still kept her shop, advertising as "Eleanor Bruce, late Eleanor Dryden."[102] Elizabeth Roffe also continued her business as a merchant after her marriage to George Blakey.[103]

One of the most persistent advertisers among the Charles Town shopkeepers was Agnes Lind, whose husband, Thomas Lind, was a factor. A few weeks after her death in October, 1766, a newspaper notice stated that Thomas Lind had procured Miss Katherine Smith to carry on the millinery business of the late Agnes Lind at the same shop on Tradd Street,[104] and the following month the marriage of Thomas Lind to Katherine Smith was announced.[105] For several

[96] Ibid., October 30, 1770. [97] Ibid., October 8, 1772.
[98] Ibid., May 11, 1773; June 20, 1774.
[99] South Carolina and American General Gazette, July 8, 1774.
[100] Ibid., July 15, 1774. [101] Ibid., April 4, 1768.
[102] Ibid., December 8, 1759; April 13, 1765.
[103] South Carolina Gazette and Country Journal, November 17, 1767; August 30, 1768; May 14, 1771.
[104] South Carolina Gazette, November 10, 1766.
[105] South Carolina and American General Gazette, December 29, 1766.

years thereafter advertisements of Katherine Lind appeared similar
to those of her predecessor.   Thomas Lind died in 1771,[106] and nine
months later his widow married William Bower, a watch-maker.[107]
The business begun by Agnes Lind, however, continued uninter-
rupted, undergoing no change, apparently, except in name, for Katherine Bower assured her friends that she still carried on the millinery
business at the shop on Tradd Street.

[106] *South Carolina Gazette*, November 7, 1771.
[107] *South Carolina Gazette and Country Journal*, October 20, 1772.

CHAPTER XIV

TAVERN HOSTESSES AND PLANTERS

THE TAVERN hostess was as familiar in colonial days as the lady merchant. She was found in backwoods and country districts as well as in the towns, and appears to have shared largely in the innkeeping business, which in the days of stagecoach and horseback travel was an important occupation. Though it was customary for planters to invite into their homes all strangers who came their way, their residences were often so far apart and the means of transportation so slow that travelers going any distance depended largely upon public houses for accommodations for themselves and horses. In the larger towns, which were also the capitals, inns were much used, during court sittings and sessions of the assembly, by gentlemen from the country; and at all times they were a kind of community center as well as the resort of persons stopping in town for amusement, shopping, or other business.

For the widow who inherited the mansion house and a few slaves from her husband's estate, entertaining strangers was a ready means of support. Her home was often already equipped to take care of many persons besides her family, and her experience as mistress of a large household and as frequent hostess to numerous guests was an invaluable asset. Particularly fortunate was she if her place were on a highway, near a ferry, or convenient to the courthouse. She found an immediate income by renting rooms and taking private boarders; or, if she desired a larger business, she purchased extra beds and chairs, stored her cellar with barrels of wine and kegs of beer, set up a bar, shuffle-board, and billiard table, applied for a license, hung out a sign, and advertised for customers for her tavern.

Numerous advertisements appeared in the papers of "lodgings to let" and "boarders taken in." Mary Paine, "living near the Scotch Meeting-House" in Charles Town, had lodgings by the year, quarter, or week. Ann Imer advertised "room for a few lodgers, who may be accommodated with breakfast."[1] Susanna Colleton of-

[1] *South Carolina Gazette*, January 25, 1768.

fered "Private lodgings for gentlemen and ladies, and good Stabling for horses," and declared she would take "a few contract boarders."[2] Mary Stevens had "taken a commodious house . . . on the Bay" and proposed keeping a private boarding house for eight gentlemen.[3] The "widow Flynn" in Annapolis offered "everything necessary for the Accommodation of such gentlemen and ladies as choose private lodgings."[4] This notice in the *Virginia Gazette* describes what was considered a commodious and convenient lodging house:

THE subscriber begs leave to inform the publick in general, and her friends in particular, that she has removed from *Lester's* ferry, and rented Dr. Carter's large brick house, on the main street in *Williamsburg*, where she proposes to accomodate Ladies and Gentlemen with private lodgings. She has 12 or 14 very good lodging rooms, with fireplaces to most of them, which will hold two or three beds each. She is willing to rent out some of them yearly, to such as may incline to find their own beds and furniture. The rooms above are convenient for Gentlemen, those below for Ladies; the house consisting of two parts, and divided lengthwise by a brick partition. She has also another house on the lot, separate from the first, with two rooms and fireplaces below, very suitable for a family. Her terms will be entirely regulated by her friends. She is *now* tolerably prepared for the reception of lodgers and horses, but hopes to be more completely so by the ensuing *April* court.

MARY DAVIS

N. B.   Any Ladies that may choose to spend a few weeks in private times, whether for pleasure or education, may do it here both reasonably and with convenience.[5]

Many of these notices sought the custom of the subscriber's "country friends" whenever they were in town. Others solicited the patronage of regular guests as well as transients, offering rooms and board by the year, quarter, or month as well as by the day. A number of subscribers offered to take care of country children in town for their education. Ann Imer announced that her house "being convenient to the provincial free school," she would take "a select number of youth" to board and lodge.[6] Esther Copp had taken a commodious house in Broad Street near the schools and would be obliged to her friends who would favor her with their children to board and lodge.[7] Mary Somers advertised for six children to board and lodge at her house in Savannah, and Mary Burdus of Annapolis

[2] *Ibid.,* October 22, 1764.   [3] *Ibid.,* July 11, 1768.
[4] *Maryland Gazette,* April 7, 1774.   [5] March 22, 1770.
[6] *South Carolina Gazette,* July 11, 1768.
[7] *Ibid.,* April 10, 1762.

boarded young gentlemen and ladies by the year "at a reasonable price."[8]   Quite a large amount, we imagine, would not have been unreasonable pay for Mary Baker, who advertised accommodations in Charles Town for "about half a dozen young masters," and promised to "keep them clean and neat" and see that they observed "due attendance at school."[9]

Entries like the following from the Northumberland County Records for 1652-1655, show that women were licensed innkeepers at an early date: "Upon the Petition of Mrs Ann Moore It is ordered that she hereby [be granted license?] to keepe an Ordinary at the house where shee now liveth; Wine, Drames, & Beer to sell according to Act of Assembly."[10]   Later, as roads and means of transportation improved, innkeepers increased.   County records for the eighteenth century show numerous instances of the granting of licenses to women to keep ordinaries.   These licenses usually included the right to sell intoxicating drinks as well as food and lodging.   An order of a Hyde County court in North Carolina, for instance, in 1758 granted Elizabeth Sinclair permission "to sell liquors and victuals, etc. as a tavern keeper."[11]   The applicant for a license had to give security to conduct her house according to law.   When in 1741 Elizabeth Slaughter obtained from the Chowan County court permission to keep ordinary at her dwelling in Edenton, she gave bond, promising to provide "wholesome and cleanly Lodging and Dyet for Travaillers—stable, corn, pasturage for horses," and to prevent all unlawful gaming and tippling.   Like many of her countrywomen in the same business, Mistress Slaughter signed this bond with her mark.[12]

Rival innkeepers could compete for the patronage of their locality only by means of the quality of their services, for charges were fixed by law.   The following schedule of rates was established by the Chowan County Court in North Carolina, April, 1746:[13]

	£ s. d.
Madeira, Vidonia (?), and other Wines by the Quart & in proportion	10-15-0
A quart of flip with half pint of Rum in it.................	0- 4-0
Carolina Cyder per Quart.............................	0- 1-0

[8] *Georgia Gazette*, February 25, 1767; *Maryland Gazette*, July 22, 1756.
[9] *South Carolina and American General Gazette*, May 5, 1775.
[10] MS, Northumberland County Records, 1652-65. Order Book No. I, p. 58.
[11] MS, Hyde County Order Book, No. 1, p. 58.
[12] MS, Chowan County Papers, 1738-1741.
[13] MS, Chowan County Papers, vol. IV (1745-48).

Northern Cyder per Quart............................	0- 2-0
Strong Malt Beer of America per Quart or Bottle..........	0- 5-0
A Diet of fresh Meat, Wheat Bread, & Small Beer..........	0- 6-0
Lodging per Night.................................	0- 2-6
A Gallon of Oats or Corn............................	?- ?-?
Pasturage for a horse for 24 hours.....................	0- 1-3
Claret per Bottle.................................	1- 5-0
A Breakfast......................................	0- 5-0
Rum per gallon & in proportion.......................	2-10-0
Strong malt Beer, or porter of Great Britain per qt or Bottle...	0- 7-6
A Quart of Punch with Loaf Sugar, Lime Juice, and half pint of rum	0- 5-0
British Ale, or Beer Bottled & Wired in Great Britain........	0-10-0

A Boutetourt County court in Virginia, February 14, 1770, established similar rates for drinks and added: "for a warm diet with small beer, nine pence; for cold diet with small Beer, six pence; for lodging in clean sheets, one in a bed, six pence; if two in a bed, three pence and three farthings; if more than two, nothing."[14]

Names of tavern hostesses appeared in the earliest newspapers. In the *South Carolina Gazette*, September 2, 1732, a Mrs. Peach notified the public that she kept the New Tavern in Church Street, Charles Town, and the same paper advertised a cockfight "at the house of Mrs. Eldridge on the Green." About the same time, the houses of Mrs. Saureau, Mrs. Delamare and Mrs. Flavel in Broad Street, and Mrs. Ramsay "on the Bay" were mentioned in the gazette.[15] Mary Bedon advertised in 1740 that she had taken the house where Mr. Carr lately kept tavern and assured all gentlemen who would be so kind as to be her customers that they would meet with the best reception and entertainment in her power.[16] In 1748 Anne Shepheard announced her intention of opening a tavern at her dwelling, "Brampton-Bryan," about a mile from Charles Town, where those who pleased to "favour her with their Custom" might "depend on having the best Entertainment and the civilest Usage."[17]

With the advance of the century, advertisements of tavern hostesses increased. The following was representative of many notices:

The Subscriber hereby informs the friends and customers of her late husband, deceased, that she continues to keep the same house of entertain-

[14] Summers, *Annals of Southwest Virginia*, p. 65.
[15] *South Carolina Gazette*, May 19, 1733.
[16] *Ibid.*, November 27, 1740.   [17] *Ibid.*, February 22, 1748.

ment as usual, with good lodgings and attendance for country Gentlemen, or others, who please to favour her with their custom. . . . The Billiard Table is also new levelled, and fit for use; and a continuance of her customers favours will greatly oblige their humble servant,

Anne Neilson[18]

Elizabeth Carne in Broad Street offered "entertainment for Man & Horse."[19]   Ann Hawes "at the Sign of the Bacchus" advertised "good Stabling for Horses, and Lodging for their Grooms," and "the best Liquors and Relishes."[20]   Jane Stewart advertised "a genteel Ordinary," where "any gentleman bespeaking a Dinner or Supper" might be assured of having it sent to his apartments at the hour appointed.[21]

Several hostesses advertised services somewhat similar to those offered by the fashionable coffee-house in England.   Mary Brickwell announced she was continuing the coffee-house kept by her husband and would take care of all the mail sent there.[22]   Mrs. MacGregor advertised "A Genteel Coffee-House" at the Orange Garden, and stated that the gardens would be kept in the best order to amuse ladies and gentlemen who might be pleased to honor her with their company.[23]   Martha Wallis entertained ladies and gentlemen with coffee and tea at her house pleasantly situated on Ashley River about four miles "up the Path."[24]

The houses of Mary Frazier "at the Sign of the Indian King" and of Sarah Warfield were mentioned often in the Maryland papers of 1747 and 1748.   Elizabeth Kelly, also of Maryland, advertised in 1748 that she had "left off ordinary keeping" and had for sale "a Parcel of Household Furniture, such as beds, tables, glasses, etc."[25]   Catharine Jennings kept a public house in Annapolis sometime before 1756, when she announced she was discontinuing the business and had for sale "an exceeding good BILLIARD-TABLE."[26]   The most renowned of the early Annapolis hostesses, however, and apparently one of the most successful, was Elizabeth Marriott "at the Sign of the Ship."   The announcement of her death in 1755 declared she had left an estate "worth upwards of 3000 pounds."[27]   The inn was in-

[18] Ibid., January 30, 1762.
[19] South Carolina Gazette and Country Journal, April 22, 1766.
[20] Ibid., October 23, 1770.   [21] Ibid., March 19, 1771.
[22] South Carolina Gazette, January 13, 1757.
[25] Maryland Gazette, August 24, 1748.   [24] Ibid., April 18, 1771.
[26] Ibid., November 26, 1763.   [20] Ibid., May 27, 1756.
[27] Ibid., March 6, 1755.

herited by her daughter, who sometime later inserted this notice in
the gazette:

ANNE HOWARD, (Living at the Sign of the SHIP where her Mother
formerly kept Tavern, in *Annapolis*, and) having a Number of very good
spare Beds and Bedding, and a convenient House for Entertainment, will
take in Gentlemen of the Assembly, at the ensuing Session, at THREE SHIL-
LINGS *per* Day.

N. B.   She keeps a House of Entertainment, for Strangers, as usual.[28]

It was at the house of Mistress Howard that George Washington
stopped when he was in Annapolis, October 29, 1774, paying a pound
and twopence for his accommodations.[29]   Anne Howard had several
rivals.   Mary Fonnereau advertised in 1755 that she had taken out
license to keep tavern "over against the church," where all gentlemen might "have good entertainment, for themselves, servants, or
horses."   She had good wines and other liquors, and her house was
"large and very well contrived, with a good number of rooms for
different companies."[30]   A Mrs. Baldwin kept tavern near the courthouse,[31] and Margaret Jane M'Mordie advertised her house of entertainment "at the Sign of the Blue-Ball."[32]

Innkeepers outside the capital also advertised in the Annapolis
papers.   Sarah Chilton announced that she had opened tavern in a
large and commodious house in Baltimore, where she was provided
with "a stock of excellent liquors and other necessaries . . . good
stables and provender for horses."[33]   Sarah Flynn notified "all
Gentlemen, Ladies and Others, that have Occasion to travel the
Road from the Southward, on the Eastern Shore of Maryland," that
she had opened her house in Frederick-Town at Sassafras Ferry and
offered her customers "genteel Entertainment and good Usage."[34]
Anne Allingham advertised her house "at the Sign of the Indian
King in Bladensburg," and Janet Kinsman kept tavern "at the Sign
of the Ship in Port Tobacco."[35]

Williamsburg was an especially desirable location for the innkeeper, for it was the seat of William and Mary College as well as
the capital and metropolis.   The most celebrated of the hostesses

[28] *Ibid.*, August 25, 1757.

[29] Fitzpatrick, *Washington, Colonial Traveller*, p. 368.

[30] *Maryland Gazette*, November 13, 1755.

[31] *Ibid.*, June 18, 1761.   [32] *Ibid.*, March 23, 1769.

[33] *Ibid.*, August 20, 1772.   [34] *Ibid.*, August 16, 1759.

[35] *Ibid.*, April 2, 1761; January 7, 1762.

here was Jane Vobe, who conducted a much frequented public house
from 1752 to 1784.[36] She did not advertise for customers, but her
house, the King's Arms Tavern, was often mentioned as the place
where lost and found articles were to be returned, tickets for plays
and concerts bought, and meetings and public vendues held.   A
French traveler in Williamsburg in 1765 wrote of lodging at Mrs.
Vobe's, "where all the best people resorted."   Here he met a number
of Virginia gentlemen, among whom were Colonel William Byrd
and other "professed gamesters."[37]   Washington stopped frequently
at Mrs. Vobe's, usually dividing his custom between her house and
that of a Mrs. Campbell.   Martha Washington seems to have preferred a private boarding house kept by Elizabeth Dawson.   When
in Alexandria, Washington stopped occasionally at the house of a
Mrs. Hawkins, and frequently with a Mrs. Chew.   In Hampton, he
stayed at a Mrs. Brough's.[38]

Though they did not advertise in the papers, many North Carolina women made a living entertaining strangers.   The county records contain many instances of the granting of ordinary licenses to
women.[39]   Between 1741 and 1753, eight women were granted the
right to keep ordinaries in the little town of Edenton, and another
kept a public house on the road from Edenton to Virginia.[40]   A Mrs.
Warburton of Onslow County was described in the newspaper account
of her death as "a Lady well known to the Public, for the very elegant
and genteel House of Entertainment she has for many Years kept."[41]

[36] Other hostesses mentioned in the *Virginia Gazette* were Sarah Coke (October
15, 1767), Mary Page (September 24, 1767), Sarah Crawley (September 20, 1769),
a Mrs. Julian (July 9, 1772), and a Mrs. Camp (September 7, 1776).

[37] "French Traveller in the Colonies, 1765," *American Historical Review*, XXVI,
741-42.

[38] Fitzpatrick, *Washington, Colonial Traveller*, pp. 109, 130, 138, 141, 161, 162,
167, 173, 175, 193, 197, 200, 210, 238, 254.

[39] Martha Riding was granted right to keep tavern in Pasquotank in 1742.—MS,
Pasquotank County Court Minutes, 1742-1744.   Mourning Blin renewed her license
in 1756.—MS, Beaufort County Court Minutes, 1756-1761.   Elizabeth Cotton was
granted "leave to keep an ordinary & victualling house" at her dwelling in Edgecombe in 1765.—MS, Edgecombe County Court Minutes, July, 1765.   Mary Jones,
Mary Brown, and Catherine Thornton kept ordinaries in Cumberland County between
1755 and 1765.—MS, Cumberland County Court Minutes, 1755-59, 1759-65.

[40] Elizabeth Slaughter (MS, Chowan County Papers, July 16, 1741), Mary
Richards (*ibid.*, April 15, 1742), Dorothy Sherwin (*ibid.*, July 29, 1744), Frances
Oliver (*ibid.*, July, 1748, October 19, 1752), Rebecca Stokes (*ibid.*, July, 1748),
Mary Butler (*ibid.*, July 19, 1751), Rebecca Yeals (*ibid.*, July 19, 1753), Rachel
Farlee (*ibid.*, April 19, 1753).

[41] *North Carolina Gazette*, January 30, 1778.

A Mrs. Austin ran a fashionable inn at Wilmington just before the Revolution. In March, 1775, the Committee of Safety, informed of a ball to be given there by the gentlemen of the town, warned her against permitting such entertainments, declaring they were contrary to the resolves of the Continental Congress.[42]

Among the six persons granted permission to keep public house in Savannah in 1766 were two women, Mary O'Neal and Abigail Minis. The treasurer's notice naming these licensed tavern keepers reminded the public that no one else could "sell any wine, cyder, beer, brandy, rum, or other strong liquors whatsoever, in less quantities than three gallons, or keep a skittle alley, shuffle-board, or biliard-table, or any gaming place whatsoever."[43] Jane Stutz advertised board for gentlemen and stabling for horses in Savannah in 1775, and Florence Mahoney was mentioned as "a victualer and vintner."[44] Lucy Tondee was proprietress of a tavern in Savannah made famous as a meeting place of the Council of Safety during the Revolution.[45]

Like the shopkeeper, the tavern hostess often found it necessary to urge her debtors to pay, sometimes with entreaty and often with threats. To avoid this difficulty, perhaps, Jane Blythe advertised for the patronage only of those with "ready money" except "her constant good customers."[46] Mary Stevens thanked the gentlemen who frequented her house for their custom and added that she would "esteem it additional favour" if they would pay her so that she could pay her "very urgent creditors."[47] Less complaisant and long-suffering were Mary Saureau, Elizabeth Hammerton, Mary Frazier, and Jane Vobe, who warned all persons owing them that if payment were not forthcoming immediately, they were resolved to begin legal proceedings.[48] This notice inserted by Ann Tilley was probably somewhat disturbing to her politician customers:

All Persons who had of the Subscriber, living at *South-River* Ferry, Liquors and Provision, for themselves, and Provender and Stabling for their Horses, at the last General Election in *December* 1767, are desired

[42] *Colonial Records of North Carolina*, IX, 1136.

[43] *Georgia Gazette*, January 7, 1767.

[44] *Ibid.*, November 22, 1775; October 25, 1775.

[45] *Georgia Historical Quarterly*, X, 314.

[46] *South Carolina Gazette*, July 3, 1749.

[47] *South Carolina and American General Gazette*, August 18, 1775.

[48] *South Carolina Gazette*, April 14, 1733; *ibid.*, September 19, 1743; *Maryland Gazette*, February 3, 1748; *Virginia Gazette*, September 12, 1771.

immediately to discharge the same, as the Gentlemen who stood as Candidates at that Election, have refused to pay me.[49]

Colonial inns were of many kinds, varying all the way from the wretched shanty kept by a miserable slattern to the genteel house of entertainment presided over by an artist in hospitality as well as in the culinary arts. Representative of many on the less frequented roads, was an ordinary at which William Attmore stopped on his way from Greenville to Tarboro in North Carolina. The house consisted of two apartments. One, the sitting room, had only a dirt floor and contained one bed. The other was floored with boards and contained four beds. The landlady, though eighty-four years old, was brisk and lively. She waited on travelers herself, even going to the stable and taking care of their horses.[50]

In contrast with this backwoods hostess, was the accomplished and cultured gentlewoman dispensing hospitality in what was once a beautiful private home. A number of innkeepers were women who had seen better days. Mary Luke, the most prominent tavern keeper in Williamsburg in 1710, was the widow of John Luke, who had been collector of the customs.[51] Elizabeth Dawson, at whose house the Washingtons and their friends often stayed, was the widow of Commissary William Dawson, at one time president of William and Mary.[52] Catherine Poinsett, Charles Town hostess, was the widow of Elisha Poinsett, who held many important offices in South Carolina.[53] Chastellux wrote of stopping at a public house kept by a gentlewoman at Petersburg, Virginia. The landlady and her daughter were both elegant in appearance and polite and easy in conversation. They were such entertaining company that at first he had misgivings as to what kind of supper he might expect. But their service was as excellent as their conversation. Scarcely had he had time to admire the neatness and beauty of the tablecloth before it was covered with many good dishes.[54]

The hostess of a genteel house of entertainment needed to be a versatile and accomplished person, trained in the social amenities as

[49] *Maryland Gazette*, October 27, 1768.
[50] "Journal of a Tour," p. 32.
[51] Tyler, *Williamsburg, the Old Colonial Capital*, p. 24.
[52] Fitzpatrick, *Washington, Colonial Traveller*, p. 210.
[53] *South Carolina Gazette*, February 28, 1771.
[54] *Travels*, II, 129.

well as in housewifery arts, for much was expected of her. Her duties were not only to provide travelers with comfortable lodgings, savory food, and refreshing drinks, and furnish accommodations for their servants and horses, but included many other services. Her house was often a combination hotel, tavern, coffee-house, and community club. It was the resort of townspeople as well as travelers, a gathering place of merchants and planters, statesmen and politicians, society belles and fashionable young beaux. Lodge meetings and socials, musical concerts and shows, receptions and suppers, public balls and assemblies, vendues and the drawing of lotteries, cockfights and even duels were sometimes staged there. Jane Eldridge's house "at the Bowling Green" was the center of much of the business and social life of Charles Town in the thirties. It was advertised as the scene of a cockfight, a lottery for raffling coach horses, a meeting place of the tax collectors, and a social entertainment for guests at the funeral of the governor.[55] The houses of Catherine Poinsett in Charles Town, Abigail Minis in Savannah, Jane Vobe in Williamsburg, Elizabeth Marriott in Annapolis, and Sarah Chilton in Baltimore were often mentioned in the gazettes as places where various articles were to be sold, societies to meet, lost articles were to be returned, and certain persons were "to be spoke with."

Sometimes the hostess furnished transportation for her guests. A Mrs. Hammerton, Charles Town tavern keeper, kept a sedan for hire, charging ten shillings for the first hour and five for each additional hour.[56] Sarah Flynn kept "a chaise and pair" and saddle horses to let to persons stopping at her tavern in Frederick-Town, Maryland.[57] Many innkeepers maintained ferries for the use of their customers and other travelers. Bridget Arthur and her husband kept a public house at New Bern and ran a ferry across Neuse River.[58] Sarah Raymer ran boats regularly between Annapolis and her tavern at Broad Creek on Kent Island, and Anne Middleton also ran ferry boats across the bay from her inn at Annapolis to Kent Island.[59]

Numerous inlets, rivers, and creeks made it necessary for travelers to make frequent use of the ferry. To facilitate transportation, county authorities appointed dependable persons living near impor-

[55] *South Carolina Gazette*, September 2, 1732; February 9, 1734; April 30, 1737; December 8, 1737.   [56] *Ibid.*, February 5, 1757.

[57] *Maryland Gazette*, November 17, 1757.

[58] *Colonial Records of North Carolina*, IV, 1190.

[59] *Maryland Gazette*, April 7, 1763; *ibid.*, September 6, 1770.

tant crossings to maintain boats and hands, allowing them a monopoly of the business and sometimes paying them a fixed sum out of the public treasury. From early times, women had a share in this business. In 1657 the Maryland Assembly voted to pay a Mrs. Fenwick five hundred pounds of tobacco for "her trouble and charge in entertaining and setting people over the river," and about the same time the widow Beasley was keeping a public ferry in the same colony.[60] Anne Bankes complained to the council in Maryland sometime about 1685 that the commissioners of Calvert County had contracted with her to keep the ferry and then, after she had hired a fit person to manage it, they had given the concession to another person. The council ordered the commissioners to confirm the order giving her the keeping of the ferry.[61] The Virginia House of Burgesses in 1684 ordered that Sara Clayborne be paid "for ferrying in the Countries service."[62]

County records contain many later appointments of women to keep ferry. Ann Lynes of Charles County, Maryland, was in 1710 granted the right to run a ferry from her plantation to Virginia.[63] In 1715 the North Carolina Council appointed Annie Wilson to keep "a good and sufficient ferry" over Perquimans River from her plantation to that of James Thickpenn, declaring that no other persons were "to presume to ferry over any horse or man within at least five miles either above or below that place."[64] Elizabeth Kennon was appointed by the Bristol Parish Vestry in Virginia to keep ferry sometime before 1720 and was paid twenty-five hundred pounds of tobacco annually for the next fifteen years.[65] In 1756 a court in Beaufort County, North Carolina, appointed Elizabeth Hill to keep ferry from her dwelling across the river to Richard Ellgood's plantation, allowing her to charge one shilling and four pence for man and horse and eight pence for foot passengers.[66] A court in Talbot County, Maryland, in 1760 agreed to pay Elizabeth Skinner forty-nine hundred pounds of tobacco annually if she would "keep a good boat fit for such use and transport the inhabitants of the County, their horses and carriages, over Oxford ferry . . . as often as they

[60] *Archives of Maryland*, I, 365. [61] *Ibid.*, XVII, 375-76.
[62] *Journals of the House of Burgesses*, II, 257.
[63] *Archives of Maryland*, XXVII, 498.
[64] *Colonial Records of North Carolina*, II, 184.
[65] C. G. Chamberlayne, ed., *Bristol Parish Vestry Book*, pp. 2, 6, 11, 12, 19, 30, 36, 39, 47, 57, 63, 67, 71, 78.
[66] MS, Beaufort County Court Minutes, 1756-1761.

shall have occasion." Persons living outside the county were to pay
her at these rates: "man and horse, 9d; foot, 4d; horse and chaise
and persons riding therein, 2s, and any persons enlisted in his majesty's service without fee or reward."[67] At the same time, Deborah
Nichols was warned that if she did not give better attendance at her
ferry between Barker's Landing and Hog Island, her allowance
would be reduced. According to her advertisement in the *Maryland
Gazette*, Flora Dorsey had an allowance from Anne Arundel County
for twenty-five years for keeping the Lower Ferry on Patapsco
River.[68]

Women were sometimes given appointments to positions in the
public service which were more surprising than those for keeping
ferry. The president and assistants of the county of Savannah in
1742 appointed the Widow Fitzwalter to succeed her husband in
the office of wharfinger.[69] Several women kept jails. Records of
Augusta County for August, 1768, contain an "Order on Mrs. Gault,
jailer at Williamsburg."[70] The *Virginia Gazette* carried notices
signed by "Mary Lindsey, Gaoler" of Henrico County, and "Elizabeth Daniels, jailer," of Middlesex, informing the public of runaway
slaves committed to their care.[71] The woman sexton was not at all
unusual. In 1757 Susanna Woodlief was appointed by Bristol Parish
Vestry in Virginia to replace Thomas Bonner as sexton of Jones Hole
Church and was paid four hundred pounds of tobacco yearly. Sarah
Williams was paid two hundred and fifty pounds for her services as
sexton at the Sappony Church. Mary Alley received a regular salary
from 1741 through 1760 for "washing the surplice and performing
the other duties of the Brick Church."[72] These other duties were not

[67] Oswald Tilghman, *History of Talbot County, Maryland, 1661-1861. . . .* (2
vols. Baltimore, 1915), I, 11.
[68] March 25, 1773. Ferries kept by Elizabeth Wilson at Annapolis, Anne
Conner "at Pig-Point on Patuxent River," and Mary Anne Noble on Potomac
River were advertised in the *Maryland Gazette*, December 9, 1746; March 11,
1762; September 6, 1764. Janet Mitchell and Mary Gibbons notified the public
regarding their ferry at York Town in the *Virginia Gazette*, April 28, 1774. Ferries
kept by "Madam Parker," Elizabeth Hazelwood, and Katharine Welshuysen were
mentioned in the *South Carolina Gazette*, December 5, 1741; September 24, 1744;
July 4, 1754.
[69] *Colonial Records of Georgia*, VI, 51.
[70] Lyman Chalkley, *Chronicles of the Scotch-Irish in Virginia*, I, 356.
[71] July 1, 1775; July 8, 1775; February 24, 1774.
[72] Chamberlayne, ed., *Bristol Parish Vestry Book*, pp. 99, 104, 107, 143, 168, 172,
174, 180.

described, but were probably the usual ones of keeping the church and grounds, ringing the bell, and attending to burials. Eleanor Williams was sexton of "the Chappel" in Henrico County from 1731 through 1768, and Agnes Holmes served Curl's Church in the same parish from 1757 through 1771.[73] In Maryland, Mary Munroe was paid five pounds currency by the vestry of St. Ann's Parish annually for serving as sexton and "washer of the Church Linnen,"[74] and Hannah Ingram performed the same services in St. John's Parish.[75]

Though many women were engaged in trade and performed public services, a larger number made their living as planters or small farmers. Among the first settlers in the colonies were a number of spirited dames who came on their own initiative, brought over servants, patented lands, cleared forests, and established plantations. Also many women were left in charge of plantations at the death of their husbands. It was customary for the widow to be made executor or administrator of her husband's estate and to be allowed the use during her life of one-third of his lands. In many cases, she continued to live at the mansion house and cultivated her own and her children's lands for their support. The early records contain the names of many of these women planters, who came into court to patent lands, register cattle marks, draw up indentures for servants, and to bring suits for debts due them or answer suits of their creditors.

The wealthiest gentlewoman planter in seventeenth-century Virginia was Elizabeth Digges, widow of Edward Digges, at one time governor of Virginia. She owned one hundred and eight slaves, the largest number held by anyone in the colony, and her personal property, valued at eleven hundred and two pounds, was the largest in York County. According to the inventory of her estate in 1699, her residence was large for the standards of the time, handsomely furnished, and well equipped with damask and silverware.[76] Lady Rebecca Axtell, widow of Daniel Axtell, a landgrave of South Carolina, was among the notable planters of the early days. Her hus-

---

[73] "Vestry Book of Henrico Parish, Virginia, 1730-1733," with notes by R. A. Brock, in *Annals of Henrico Parish* (ed., J. Staunton Moore), pp. 8, 107, 143, 144.

[74] "Vestry Proceedings, St. Ann's Parish, Annapolis, Maryland," *Maryland Magazine*, VIII, 270, 284.

[75] Edward Ingle, *Parish Institutions of Maryland*, p. 42. Seven women sextons were mentioned in the Vestry Book of Christ Church Parish, Middlesex County, Virginia, and seven in Kingston Parish.

[76] Bruce, *Economic History*, II, 88, 155, 167, 168, 172, 174, 182-84, 195, 249.

band died a year or two after their arrival in the province, but she continued to reside at his plantation, managed the estate, and in 1705 was granted a thousand acres on the north side of the Ashley River.[77] Besides her large tracts of land, Mistress Margaret Brent of Maryland possessed houses and cattle of considerable value and owned and operated a mill, which apparently brought in a dependable income.[78] Mary and Margaret Brent, Mary Tranton, Frances White, Jane Cockshott, and Winifred Seaborne had cases frequently in the Maryland provincial court involving their business transactions,[79] and Diana Foster and Susanna Hartley appeared often in the North Carolina courts in the conduct of their affairs.[80]

Captain John Smith wrote, probably with exaggeration, of the remarkable achievements of a Virginia planter of about 1629: "Mistress *Pearce*, a honest industrious woman, hath beene there [in Virginia] neere twentie yeares, and now returned, saith, shee hath a garden at *James* towne containing three or four acres, where in one yeare shee hath gathered neere an hundred bushels of excellent figges, and that of her owne provision she can keepe a better house in *Virginia*, than here in *London*, for 3. or 400 pounds a yeare, yet [she] went thither with little or nothing."[81] John Clayton wrote in 1688 of Virginia matrons who drained swamps, cultivated thriving tobacco plantations, raised cattle, and bought slaves. The gentlewoman at whose home he lived he described as "a very acute, ingenious Lady."[82] He admired her probably because she listened to his advice regarding the conduct of her plantation affairs, draining her swamp lands, and having her cows milked in winter according to his recommendations.

Newspaper advertisements throw light upon the property holdings of women in the eighteenth century, and indicate to some extent their problems and the activities they conducted. All the gazettes carried notices signed by women advertising lands, houses, and Negroes for sale or to be leased, offering rewards for runaway servants and slaves, and urging their debtors to pay. Henrietta Maria Dulany, a landed proprietress of Maryland, offered for sale three "parcels of

[77] *South Carolina Magazine*, VI, 175.   [78] *Archives of Maryland*, IV, 417.
[79] *Ibid.*, index.
[80] *Colonial Records of North Carolina*, I, 392, 398, 399, 405, 410, 413, 414, 427-28, 430.
[81] *General History of Virginia* (London ed., 1727), II, 259.
[82] "Observables in Virginia, 1688," *Force Tracts*, III (No. 12), 21-22.

land" in Queen Anne's County and four tracts in Dorchester, the seven tracts totaling 2,750 acres.[83]   Justina Moore, daughter of Landgrave Smith, advertised in the *South Carolina Gazette* that she had just arrived "from her Settlements at Cape Fear," and proposed selling a thousand acres of land fronting Winyau River.[84]   "Lady" Houston of Savannah desired to sell "a Valuable Tract of Land" containing a thousand acres upon a navigable creek leading from the Altamaha River; Elizabeth Yates, Virginia landowner, advertised a tract of four hundred and thirty acres with a dwelling house and all the necessary outhouses; and Sarah Allen of North Carolina offered for sale several plantations and town lots, declaring that two of the plantations had very good brick dwelling houses and convenient outhouses.[85]

Sarah Blakeway was apparently a planter of considerable wealth and importance, for her name appears frequently in the *South Carolina Gazette*, advertising slaves for hire, dwelling houses to let, Indian corn for sale, and large tracts of land and slaves to be disposed of.[86]   On September 5, 1741, she gave notice that she intended leaving the province and had for sale houses and lots, lands and Negroes, a handsome spinet, a set of mahogany chairs, several beds, and some books, and offered to reward well any person who would undertake a journey to Cape Fear to attend to business for her.   A Mrs. Nichols of Stono, South Carolina, evidently had the management of several plantations, for at one time she advertised that she needed two overseers.[87]   Elizabeth Hill, Catherine Cattell, Elizabeth Bellinger, Martha Logan, and Ann Drayton used the newspapers frequently in conducting their plantation affairs, advertising lands and slaves to be let or sold, and threatening to prosecute their debtors.

Mary Willing Byrd, widow of the third William Byrd, appears to have been a capable business woman and manager of plantation affairs. Her husband inherited an immense estate, but was a spendthrift and gambler and at his death left his affairs in great disorder. Mistress Byrd undertook the responsibility of supporting and educating her eight children and preserving for them what property

<hr />

[83] *Maryland Gazette*, July 17, 1755.   [84] May 25, 1734.

[85] *Georgia Gazette*, September 29, 1763; (New Bern) *North Carolina Gazette*, November 15, 1751.

[86] February 7, 1736; October 30, 1736; November 13, 1740; January 1, 1741; September 5, 1741.

[87] *South Carolina Gazette*, April 12, 1760.

she could from the wreck of their father's princely fortune. Visitors at "Westover" were impressed by her prudent management and remarkable success. Chastellux wrote of her: "She has preserved his beautiful house, situated on James-River, a large personal property, a considerable number of slaves, and some plantations which she has rendered valuable. She is about two-and-forty, with an agreeable countenance and great sense. . . . Her care and activity have in some measure repaired the effects of her husband's dissipation and her house is still the most celebrated, and the most agreeable of the neighborhood. . . . She takes great care of her negroes, makes them as happy as their situation will admit, and serves them herself as a doctor in time of sickness. She has even made some interesting discoveries on the disorders incident to them, and discovered a very salutary method of treating a sort of putrid fever which carried them off commonly in a few days, and against which the physicians of the country have exerted themselves without success."[88]

The outstanding woman planter in the colonies was Eliza Lucas, an ingenious agriculturist as well as an able manager of plantation business. She was the daughter of Colonel George Lucas, a British army officer stationed in the West Indies, who had in 1737 or 1738 brought his family to South Carolina, hoping the climate there would be beneficial to his delicate wife. His military duty soon called him back to Antigua and, as his wife's health prevented her from undertaking any responsibility, he left his seventeen-year-old daughter Eliza in charge of his Carolina affairs.

Colonel Lucas was interested in experimental agriculture and frequently sent his daughter new plants and seeds, encouraging her to try them and discover what crops best suited the soil and climate of South Carolina. Eliza also professed to "love the vegitable world extremely," and, in addition to transacting the business of three plantations, spent much of her time conducting experiments. Extracts from her letters and memoranda indicate her many interests and activities. This entry appears in her notes made in July, 1739: "I wrote my father a very long letter on his plantation affairs . . . on the pains I had taken to bring the Indigo, Ginger, Cotton, Lucern, and Cassada to perfection, and had greater hopes from the Indigo— if I could have the seed earlier the next year from the East Indies,—

---

[88] *Travels*, II, 162-68. For a similar account of Mistress Byrd see Anburey, *Travels*, II, 369.

than any of ye rest of ye things I had tryd, . . . also concerning pitch
and tarr and lime and other plantation affairs."[89] Some years later
she was writing that the cotton, "Guiney corn," and most of the
ginger had been cut off by the frost, the lucern was "but dwindling,"
and though she had had a fine crop of indigo seed upon the ground,
the frost took it before it was dry.[90] She kept her father informed
of the various details of plantation business and frequently asked his
advice regarding new projects. She wrote in 1742: "The crop at
Garden Hill turned out ill, but a hundred and sixty bar^ls [of rice]
and at Wappoo only forty-three, the price is so low as thirty shillings
pr hundred, we have sent very little to town yet, for that reason. . . .
In my letter of February 3rd. I desired to know if you approved of
setting a plantation to the North near Major Pawly. Please let me
know in your next if it has your approbation and it shall be done in
the Fall."[91]

Eliza's friends declared she had "a fertile brain at schemeing"
and smiled at her various projects. One of these schemes she described to "Miss Bartlett," a friend in Charles Town: "I have planted
a large figg orchard, with design to dry them, and export them. I
have reckoned my expence and the prophets to arise from those figgs,
but was I to tell you how great an Estate I am to make this way,
and how 'tis to be laid out, you would think me far gone in romance."[92] Later she was very busy "providing for posterity" by
"making a large plantation of oaks." These, she expected, would
bring considerable returns "when oaks are more valueable than they
are now, wch you know they will be when we come to build fleets."[93]

Whether posterity enjoyed benefits from her fig orchards and oak
groves does not appear, but her neighbors and the whole province
profited greatly by her introduction of indigo. The making of indigo
was a long and complicated process. The cultivation of the plant
required careful preparation of the soil and considerable attention
during growth. The leaves had to be cut at exactly the right time and
then soaked in vats until they had fermented just long enough to get
the proper color. The liquid was then drawn off into a second vat
and beaten until it began to thicken, then led into a third vat and
allowed to settle. The clear water was drawn off and the sediment

[89] Ravenel, *Eliza Pinckney*, p. 7.
[90] *Ibid.*, p. 9.
[91] *Ibid.*, p. 14.
[92] *Ibid.*, pp. 31-32.
[93] *Ibid.*, p. 38.

formed into lumps or cakes, which, after being carefully dried in the shade, were finally ready for market. After several unsuccessful attempts, Eliza succeeded in bringing the plant to perfection, and Colonel Lucas sent an overseer from the West Indies to superintend the soaking and fermenting of the leaves. But the indigo lumps he produced were almost worthless. Watching him closely, Eliza discovered that he was purposely spoiling them, probably to save his native island from competition with the Carolina product. Colonel Lucas then sent a Negro from one of the French islands, with whose help she at last succeeded in making a product fit for market.

One of her chief difficulties in raising indigo had been in getting seed in time for the crop to ripen before frost. To make it easier for others to cultivate the new plant, in 1744 she devoted her whole crop to making seed, which she distributed freely among her neighbors. Three years later, these planters were making enough indigo to make it worth while to export it for sale. To protect the South Carolina product against French indigo, Great Britain offered a bounty of six pence a pound, which, with its market value, enabled many planters to double their capital in three or four years. Thus indigo came to be the chief staple of the highland part of South Carolina and continued a very valuable commodity until the Revolution.[94]

In the same year in which her indigo experiments proved successful, Eliza, then only twenty-one years old, married Colonel Charles Pinckney, a childless widower over twice her age, and went to live at "Belmont," his place about five miles from Charles Town. Here two sons and a daughter were born, to whose education she gave the same intelligent attention bestowed upon her agricultural projects. But agriculture was not neglected. She continued her supervision of her father's plantations and tried out many new schemes, one of which was the cultivation of silk. She sent for eggs, gave careful attention to the proper drying of the cocoons, and had the Negro children gather the leaves and feed the worms. She and her maids reeled the silk. Thus she produced enough raw silk for three dresses, which she had made when she went to England in 1753.[95]

[94] *Ibid.*, pp. 102-7.

[95] *Ibid.*, pp. 130-31. In Virginia in the seventeenth century, several women were publicly praised for their efforts in behalf of silk culture.—Bruce, *Economic History*, I, 366. Later, many women in Georgia were gainfully employed in raising silkworms and reeling off the silk.—*Colonial Records of Georgia*, I, 314, 528; II,

Soon after Colonel and Mistress Pinckney returned from England in 1758, he died, leaving her grief-stricken and confronted by serious responsibilities. His estate was large, consisting chiefly of lands and Negroes in various localities; and during his five years' absence the plantations had suffered greatly from neglect. The uncertainties of colonial affairs, ignorant and dishonest overseers, and an unprecedented drought made her situation so difficult that she had to write her agent in London: "All that we make from ye planting interest will hardly defray ye charges of ye plantations." Prospects for the future were better, however, for she had "prevailed upon a conspicuous good man" who was an excellent planter to undertake the direction and inspection of the overseers. With his aid, she hoped "to Clear all [due upon the estate] next year." She wrote: "I find it requires great care and attention to attend to a Carolina Estate, tho' but a moderate one, and to do one's duty, and make all turn to acc[oun]t."[96] But she was equal to the task and discharged her new duties with the same success that had characterized all her former undertakings.

Eliza Pinckney was of course an exceptional person. Few women were so keenly interested in agriculture as she and few so capable in the conduct of affairs. But, like her, many were left with plantations to manage and children to maintain. A majority probably took new husbands to whom they gladly turned over their business responsibilities, but a number of wealthy widows directed extensive plantations and many others among the less well-to-do earned a livelihood cultivating small farms.

Women without lands or other means of support sometimes maintained themselves by doing various kinds of plantation work. In the colonies, they did not usually work for wages in the fields, but they were often employed to take care of poultry yards and dairies, make Negro clothes, and nurse sick slaves. Notices like the following appeared in the papers: "A single woman, with a child, would be glad of a place on a plantation, to take charge of a dairy, raise poultry, etc."[97] One stated, "A Dairy Woman who can make negro clothes wants work.[98] A "single elderly woman experienced

487; IV, Part II, 134-35, 136, 230-32, 248-49; VI, 95, 190, 206-7, 310-11; XXIV, 343-44.   [96] Ravenel, *Eliza Pinckney*, pp. 192-93.
[97] *South Carolina Gazette*, November 5, 1764.
[98] *Ibid.*, September 12, 1774.

in the business" desired a place to look after a dairy and attend to poultry raising,[99] and another wanted work as housekeeper, caring for sick Negroes, or raising poultry and managing a dairy.[100] A South Carolina planter offered "Perquisites equal to a £100 a year" to a single woman who would manage a dairy and raise poultry.[101]

The wife of an overseer was often expected to keep a dairy and poultry yard on the plantation which her husband directed. Charles Carroll, writing his son Charles Carroll of Carrollton regarding plantation affairs, declared he was well pleased with a new overseer because his wife was "a neat Housewifely woman," who would manage the dairies and raise all sorts of fowls on all the plantations under her husband's care, and would make linens and woolens sufficient to clothe her family.[102] Washington, about to engage a gardener, declared that if he had a wife, she would be expected "to be a Spinner, dairy Woman, or something of that usefulness."[103] Many advertisements for overseers stated a preference for a single man, but added that if a man had a wife who understood dairying, poultry raising, and other "country business," she would be no objection.

Another employee found often in plantation homes, and also in the larger houses in town, was the housekeeper. Newspapers contain many advertisements for housekeepers and notices of women desiring work of this kind. From the qualifications demanded, it appears that the position and duties of the housekeeper varied greatly with different families. A Marylander desired "a Person of good Character, that is qualified to be Housekeeper, and more Particularly to take Care of a Kitchen."[104] Another specified "a Sober careful Woman, who can sew and iron Linnen."[105] A well-to-do subscriber wanted "A Genteel well-bred Woman, of a good Character and capable of undertaking the Management of a Gentleman's Family."[106] The housekeeper was often expected to be a versatile person, performing various offices. Thomas Hanson Marshall of Maryland advertised for "a Woman that is qualified for managing Household Affairs and bringing up Girls, in a Genteel Way."[107] A South Car-

[99] *South Carolina and American General Gazette,* January 16, 1769.
[100] *South Carolina Gazette and Country Journal,* January 24, 1775.
[101] *South Carolina Gazette,* October 12, 1769.
[102] *Maryland Magazine,* XIII, 73.
[103] *Diaries* (ed., Fitzpatrick), III, 444-45.
[104] *Maryland Gazette,* November 2, 1748.
[105] *Ibid.,* September 20, 1753.
[106] *Ibid.,* July 9, 1767.   [107] *Ibid.,* February 21, 1771.

olinian desired "a Woman to care for children and manage a large family."[108]   Another wanted "a young woman industriously brought up to wait upon young ladies, be housekeeper, and look after negroes."[109]   A woman offering her services as housekeeper declared she had no objection to caring for children and understood making pastry, jellies, pickling, and preserving.[110]   Another described herself as "a *sober, industrious, honest Woman,* that understands all sorts of Family work."[111]   Single, sedate, sober, and discreet were adjectives commonly used in describing the person desired.

In some houses the housekeeper was regarded as a member of the family, while in others her status was that of an upper servant. John Harrower, tutor in the home of Colonel William Daingerfield of "Belvidere" in Virginia, wrote that the colonel, his lady, the children, the housekeeper, and he, all ate at the same table.[112]   At "Mount Vernon" it was different.   Washington wrote regarding a housekeeper whom he had just engaged: "Mrs. Forbes will have a warm, decent and comfortable room to herself, to lodge in, and will eat of the Victuals of our Table, but not set at it, at any time *with us,* be her appearance what it may; for if this was *once admitted,* no line satisfactory to either party, perhaps, could be drawn thereafter."[113]   This arrangement apparently proved quite satisfactory to Mrs. Forbes, for she continued as housekeeper at "Mount Vernon" until after Washington's death.

[108] *South Carolina Gazette,* December 6, 1773.
[109] *South Carolina Gazette and Country Journal,* November 25, 1766.
[110] *Ibid.,* August 18, 1767.
[111] *South Carolina Gazette,* October 1, 1772.
[112] "Diary," *American Historical Review,* VI, 79.
[113] Conway, *Washington and Mount Vernon,* pp. 336-39.

CHAPTER XV

CRIMES AND PUNISHMENTS

ONE OF THE most familiar figures in the colonial court records was the unmarried woman arraigned before the justices for the crime of bastardy. Many of these women came from the most profligate classes in England, and upon their arrival in this country found conditions which did not help in their reformation. Those who were indentured were prevented by law from marrying without the consent of their masters, who naturally were reluctant to approve their entering a relation which was almost certain to result in childbearing and, consequently, numerous interruptions in their work and possibly the total loss of their services by death or permanent disability. Thus denied the restraining influence of husband, family, and home, they were often led to form unconventional unions and to bear children outside of wedlock. Also their work and recreations brought them into intimate association with the most dissolute type of men, and the menial duties of their domestic service exposed them to the advances of licentious masters, who often did not hesitate to take advantage of their power.

If multiplicity of restrictive laws could assure righteousness, all the women of easy virtue who came to the colonies would soon have been converted into models of continence, for from the time the first Englishman set foot at Jamestown they were assiduous in enacting legislation for the preservation of morality. Sir Thomas Dale made adultery punishable with death and provided severe punishment for fornication.[1] The first assembly in 1619 passed a measure instructing ministers and churchwardens to present the "comitters" of all "ungodly disorders" and give them "goode admonitions and milde reproof," and directed that if any person after two warnings did not "forbeare the said skandalous offenses" and "amende his or her life in point of evident suspicion of Incontinency," he should be suspended from church. Then if he did not humbly submit himself to the

[1] "Articles, Lawes, and Orders, Diuine, Politique, and Martiall for the Colony in Virginia . . . 1612," *Force Tracts*, III (No. 2), 11.

church, he should be excommunicated and his person apprehended and his goods seized.[2]

Evidently neither the "goode admonitions" nor the prescribed punishments induced the early colonists to "amende," for the records show that they continued to commit "enormous sinnes" in a manner most grievous to the authorities. The question of the suppression of immorality was a perennial problem before the Virginia House of Burgesses and was also often a subject for discussion in the assemblies of the other colonies. They passed numerous acts for the punishments of fornication and adultery and gave detailed instructions regarding proceedings to be taken in bastardy cases.[3]

Provisions of the bastardy acts indicate that while the lawmakers may have been interested in maintaining virtue, they were more intent upon saving their parishes from the upkeep of numerous bastards than concerned with the preservation of morality for its own sake. Fatherless children whose mothers were incapable of providing for them were cared for at the expense of the parish in which they were born and therefore added to the already large burdens borne by the taxpayers in caring for the poor and aged. These taxpayers quite naturally urged their representatives to take measures for reducing the burdens arising from such causes. Colonel Lawrence Smith of Gloucester County, Virginia, for instance, in 1696 sent a proposition to the House of Burgesses "for Easeing of parishes in that Excessive

[2] *Journals of the House of Burgesses,* I, 13-14.

[3] A Virginia act of 1691 fixed a fine of ten pounds sterling for fornication, twenty pounds for adultery, and directed that the offender receive thirty lashes or be imprisoned three months if unable to pay the fine. Later acts of 1705 and 1727 provided for a fine of one thousand pounds of tobacco for adultery and five hundred for fornication, and instructed that, if unable to pay the fine, the offender should be given twenty-five lashes at the public whipping post well laid on her bare back.— Hening, *Statutes,* III, 74, 213, 361, 453. The Maryland Assembly in 1715 fixed the fine for adultery at three pounds current money or twelve hundred pounds of tobacco and for fornication thirty shillings or six hundred pounds of tobacco. Offenders unable to pay these fines were to be whipped upon their bare bodies until the blood appeared, with as many stripes, not exceeding thirty-nine, as the justices should order.—*Archives of Maryland,* XXX, 233-34; *Laws of Maryland* (ed., Bacon), Act of 1715, Chap. 27. A later Maryland act of 1749 provided these same fines, but placed more responsibility upon the woman, directing that if she refused to disclose the person guilty with her, she was to pay an additional fine of thirty shillings, evidently his fine as well as her own.—*Ibid.,* Act of 1749, Chap. 12. In North Carolina the penalty for the first act of fornication was fifty shillings or a whipping not exceeding twenty-one lashes at the court's discretion, and for adultery a fine of five pounds or a similar whipping.—*State Records of North Carolina,* XXIII, 174.

Charge that lyes upon them by meanes of Bastard Children born of Servant Women."[4] The preamble of the bastardy act of each of the colonies explained that the act was passed not only to discourage "a lewd life" but also to relieve the parish from excessive burdens arising from bastard children.[5]

The usual steps in bastardy cases were for the mother to be brought first before the justices and examined regarding the paternity of her child, and then the man whom she named as the father was summoned and required to give security to maintain the child or to appear at thé next court to answer the charges against him. If the mother refused to expose the father, she was compelled to give security to "save the parish harmlesse" from any charges arising from her child.[6] A Maryland act of 1715 provided that if a mother refused to disclose her bastard's father, she was to be fined or sentenced to corporal punishment according to the discretion of the court.[7] A later act abolished corporal punishment of women having "base born children" but provided that if a mother refused to disclose the father of her bastard, she should pay double the fine for fornication and give good security for preventing the child from becoming a charge upon the county.[8] Under the North Carolina law any two justices of the peace, upon their own knowledge or on information made to them, might summon before them any single woman that was pregnant or had been delivered of a child and examine her concerning the father. If she disclosed the begetter of her child, he was ordered to stand charged with its maintenance and required to give security to perform the court's order; if she refused to tell who the father was, she was made to pay the fines for fornication and to give security to keep the child from being chargeable to the parish, or was committed to prison.[9] The South Carolina act

[4] *Journals of the House of Burgesses*, III, 64, 67. See also *ibid.*, II, 894, 895; III, 1335, 1421, 1423; XI, 259, 302; XII, 103.

[5] Hening, *Statutes*, VIII, 374; Martin, *Statutes of England in Force in North Carolina*, p. 403; *Public Laws of South Carolina* (ed., Grimké), pp. 5-7.

[6] Hening, *Statutes*, I, 438-39; II, 168; III, 453; VI, 361; VIII, 376-77; *Archives of Maryland*, XXX, 233-34; *Laws of Maryland* (ed., Maxcy), I, 110, 230; *State Records of North Carolina*, XXIII, 64-65; *Statutes of South Carolina* (ed., Cooper), II, 224-27; *Public Laws of South Carolina* (ed., Grimké) 5-7; *Digest of Georgia Laws* (ed., Watkins), 519-20.

[7] *Archives of Maryland*, XXX, 233-34.

[8] *Laws of Maryland* (ed., Bacon), Act of 1715, Chap. 12; *Laws of Maryland* (ed., Maxcy), I, 230.

[9] *State Records of North Carolina*, XXIII, 173-75.

of 1703 allowed any justice of the peace who suspected a woman of being pregnant with a bastard child to summon her before him and examine her concerning the father, require her to give bond in the sum of twenty pounds to appear at the next general court sessions, and, for want of such security, commit her to prison. If at the next court after her delivery, she was found guilty of having borne a bastard, she was fined an amount not exceeding ten pounds, and upon failure of payment was publicly whipped on her bare back with not more than thirty-one stripes. For a second offense she was fined or publicly whipped with not more than thirty-nine lashes, and for the third was tied to the tail of a cart and publicly whipped through as many streets of Charles Town as should be ordered by the chief justice. The person whom she accused as the begetter of her bastard was required to give bond to appear at the next court after the child was born. If he were then adjudged the reputed father, he was fined a sum not more than ten pounds or less than five or publicly whipped with a number of stripes not exceeding thirty-one, and was required to support the child until it reached the age of ten years. The mother and the reputed father jointly were required to give security to indemnify the parish of any charges whatever concerning the child. The care and custody of a bastard child, unlike one born in lawful wedlock, was given to its mother rather than to its father.[10]

If an indentured servant were "got with child" during the time of her servitude, her crime was considered not only a "great dishonor of God" and an injury to the community, but was also a great damage to her master. A servant woman guilty of bastardy was therefore compelled not only to pay the fines and charges usually exacted from free unmarried mothers, but in addition was obliged to indemnify her master for the loss of service he suffered by her pregnancy and lying-in. As a servant generally had no money with which to pay her fine and compensate her master, she was usually required to make satisfaction by extra service.

Some colonies placed part of the responsibility of indemnifying the master upon the father of the bastard; others placed the whole burden entirely upon the mother. In Maryland, if the mother could prove that a certain person was the begetter of her child, he was required, if a freeman, to pay the whole damage to her master

---

[10] *Statutes of South Carolina* (ed., Cooper), pp. 224-27; *Public Laws of South Carolina* (ed., Grimké), pp. 5-7.

for her loss of service. If he were a servant, he was obliged to pay only half.[11] The Virginia statute of 1657-58 compelled the reputed father to pay the master fifteen hundred pounds of tobacco or serve him one year, besides giving security to defray the charges of the child,[12] but later Virginia acts required the father to give bond for the maintenance of the child only and placed the responsibility of recompensing the master wholly upon the mother.[13] The North Carolina law was like that of Virginia.[14] South Carolina placed the responsibility of requiting the master upon the reputed father, directing that he pay the master five pounds of current money or serve him double the time the mother had to serve at the time the offense was committed, provided this doubled time did not exceed one year.[15]

The statutes were not always definite regarding the evidence necessary to prove a man the father of a bastard. Generally they left the question of the validity of the proof largely to the discretion of the justices before whom the case was tried. An early Maryland act declared that if the mother were able to prove her charge by "sufficient Testimony of witnesses," confession of the person accused, or "pregnant Circumstances agreeing with her Declaration in the Extremity of her paines and Throes of Travell" and her oath taken by the magistrates, the person accused should be adjudged the father.[16] The Virginia statute left the court free to judge according to the circumstances of the case.[17] The North Carolina acts stated that if the mother accused any person of being the father of her

[11] *Archives of Maryland*, II, 396-97; *Laws of Maryland* (ed., Maxcy), I, 110.

[12] Hening, *Statutes*, I, 438-39.

[13] The act of 1661-62 provided that if a white servant committed the crime of fornication, her master could pay her fine of five hundred pounds of tobacco and that she should serve him in return an extra half year. If she had a child, she should, for the "losse and trouble" sustained by her master, serve him two years after the expiration of her term by indenture or pay him two thousand pounds of tobacco in addition to the amount of her fine. The reputed father was obliged only to give bond to maintain the child and "save the parish harmlesse." If he were a servant, the parish supported the child until the end of his indenture, at which time he was required to make satisfaction. The statutes of 1696, 1705, and 1753 reduced the amount of damages to which a master was entitled for his loss of service from two years or two thousand pounds of tobacco to one year's service or one thousand pounds of tobacco.—*Ibid.*, II, 115, 168; III, 139-40, 453; VI, 361.

[14] *State Records of North Carolina*, XXIII, 64-65, 195.

[15] *Statutes of South Carolina* (ed., Cooper), II, 226-27; *Public Laws of South Carolina* (ed., Grimké), pp. 5-7.

[16] *Archives of Maryland*, II, 396-97.   [17] Hening, *Statutes*, VIII, 374-77.

bastard, he should be adjudged the reputed father, but made no provision in case the accused should deny the charge.[18] The South Carolina law declared that if a woman accused a person of being the father of her bastard when examined under oath by the magistrates, and remained constant in her accusation during her travail, the person accused should be adjudged the reputed father, notwithstanding his denial, unless his pleas and proofs and other circumstances were such as the chief justice should consider sufficient to judge him innocent.[19]

In imposing penalties judges did not always adhere exactly to the provisions of the bastardy acts. Instead of ordering corporal punishment or the payment of a fine, they sometimes merely admonished offenders, required them to do public penance, or gave them some lighter punishment. Often, too, they did not take the trouble to apprehend the reputed father, but followed the way of least resistance, requiring the mother to pay all the charges of the bastard and allowing the father to escape without any responsibility. One court before whom Henry Kinge and the wife of John Jackson were presented "on suspicion of incontinency . . . they lyinge together in her husband's absence," merely ordered that Kinge should "remove his habitation from her, and not to use her company until her husband's retorne."[20] John Hassell of North Carolina, indicted in 1716 for living in adultery with Sarah, wife of William Wilkinson, was required merely to give security that he would not cohabit with her again. When, several years later, he was presented a second time for the same offense, he was fined five pounds and was again required to give security that he would not cohabit with Sarah Wilkinson for twelve months.[21]

In the early days persons guilty of sex immorality were sometimes required to confess their sins publicly and beg for forgiveness. A Virginia couple were sentenced in March, 1643, to stand draped in white sheets in the church, acknowledge their sin of adultery and ask forgiveness in these words:

I B. H. and J. V. do here acknowledge and confess in the presence of this whole congregation that I have grievously sinned and offended against the Divine Majesty of Almighty God and all Christian people in commit-

[18] *State Records of North Carolina*, XXIII, 173-75.
[19] *Statutes of South Carolina* (ed., Cooper), II, 224-27; *Public Laws of South Carolina* (ed., Grimké), 5-7.   [20] Hening, *Statutes*, I, 145.
[21] *Colonial Records of North Carolina*, II, 262, 437.

ting the foul and detestable sin of Adultery and am heartily sorry and truly penitent for the same and do unfeignedly beseech Almighty God of his infinite goodness to be merciful unto me and forgive this my heinous offense and I do heartily desire this congregation and all good people likewise to forgive me and pray for me.[22]

Edith Tooker was robed in a white sheet and led into the parish church after the worshipers had taken their seats and urged by the minister to repent of her "foul sin." But instead of beseeching forgiveness, she "did, like a most obstinate and graceless person, cut and mangle the sheet wherein she did penance." For her contemptuous behavior she was ordered to receive thirty lashes and appear in the same church clothed in a sheet the following Sabbath fortnight.[23]

Occasionally the court ordered the same punishment for the man and woman found guilty of immoral conduct, but oftener it demanded some kind of payment from the man and sentenced the woman to be whipped. A Lower Norfolk County court in 1649 ordered a man who was presented for fornication to pay half the charges towards building a bridge over a creek in the neighborhood, and sentenced the woman guilty with him to receive fourteen lashes on her bare back.[24] In Maryland, John Nevill and Susan Attcheson, for their "notorious and Scandalous Course of Life," were each sentenced to receive twenty lashes, but upon the presentation of a petition by Nevill's friends requesting that his punishment be remitted, the court ordered that if he or his friends would pay a fine of five hundred pounds of tobacco, he would be exempted from corporal punishment. No commutation of the woman's sentence was requested.[25] In Accomac County, Virginia, the mother of a bastard, was sentenced to be whipped with thirty lashes on her bare back, while the father was required merely to confess his sin before the congregation in his parish church.[26] Jane Pauldin, brought before the Maryland Provincial court in 1657 for having a bastard, declared that John Norton, a planter, was the father, that "on a Certaine time when his wife was abroad [he] Came and Importuned" her "to be dishonest with him." The court ordered that she be given thirty lashes upon her bare back with a whip and that he give security for keeping the child and for his good behavior.[27]

[22] Lower Norfolk County Virginia Antiquary, I, 145-46.
[23] Bruce, Institutional History, I, 47-48.   [24] Ibid., p. 48.
[25] Archives of Maryland, X, 558, 560.   [26] Bruce, Institutional History, I, 47.
[27] Archives of Maryland, X, 516; XLI, 14.

Orders like the following are common in the county court minutes: "Kath Davis having committed ye sin of fornication & having lately had a bastard child it is order'd yt ye Sher:f take ye sd Katharine into Safe Custody & give her 20 stripes on her bare back until ye blood come."[28] In many cases, however, corporal punishment was remitted upon payment by the woman of a fine. The fines of servants, who constituted a large majority of the offenders in bastardy cases, were usually paid by their masters, who were repaid by extra service.

In trying servant women the court very often did not take the trouble to discover the reputed father, but ordered the master to pay the various charges and required the servant to compensate him by extra service. The following order is typical of numerous others found in the county court minutes: "Whereas Ann Servt to John Motley hath had a Bastard Child in ye tyme of her Service, It is ordered yt she make her sd Master satisfaction for his trouble, Charge, & loss of tyme, & for her fine according to Act Mr John Motley ingageth to pay ye fine of five hundred pounds of tobacco & Cash in ye behalf of ye Delinquent."[29] In Maryland, where the burden of indemnifying the master was placed upon the father of the bastard rather than upon the mother, the court seems to have made greater effort to apprehend the guilty man. John Hambleton, for instance, accused by Robert Taylor's servant as the father of the child of which she was pregnant, although the matter of its paternity could not be determined until after her delivery, inasmuch as he had "been caught Suspiciously and uncivilly with her," had his goods taken into custody as security for indemnifying the woman's master.[30] Roger Scott, the alleged father of Roger Groce's maid's child, was required to give security for maintaining the child and for paying Groce the damages he should sustain by his maid's having been "got with child."[31]

A Virginia statute of 1672, pointing out that under an existing law a master who was himself the begetter of his servant woman's child could demand compensation from her for her bastardy in the form of extra service, attempted to remedy this evil. Declaring that "late experiments shew that some dissolute masters have gotten their maides with child, and yet claime the benefitt of their service," it provided that a master who was himself the father of his servant's

[28] MS, Northumberland County Order Book, 1666-1678, p. 19.
[29] Ibid., p. 31.
[30] Archives of Maryland, X, 337.   [31] Ibid., pp. 526-27.

bastard could not claim any extra service from her, but that after the term of her indenture expired she should be sold by the church-wardens for the use of the parish for two years.[32] Governor Nicholson of Virginia also called attention to the getting of women servants with child by their masters as a serious grievance.[33] But the court records contain only a few instances of a servant woman's laying her bastard child to her master. The scarcity of such cases may be accounted for partly by the fact that in a large number of bastardy reports the name of the reputed father was not given. It is possible that in many of these cases the unrecorded father was the woman's master, who was rewarding her for her silence or was threatening to make her remaining years in his service intolerable should she expose him. Also, women having bastards by their masters were probably not often brought into court. It was the master who usually reported his servant's delinquency that he might be compensated for his loss of service. When he was the begetter of her child, naturally he did not have her arrested, but, instead, attempted to conceal her crime.

In a few cases in which servant women having bastards by their masters were brought into court, the justices sentenced the master to pay a fine,[34] but much oftener they appear to have required him only to give security to maintain the child. A Virginia court, for instance, ordered Elizabeth Phillips to be sold after the expiration of the term of her indenture for the use of the parish because she had a child by her master, but gave the master no punishment. A year later, the justices ordered her to serve this same master an extra year for having

[32] Hening, *Statutes*, II, 167. Later acts of 1705 and 1753 also provided that a master whose woman servant had a bastard by him could not claim any extra service from her, but that the woman should be sold for one year after the end of her indenture.—*Ibid.*, III, 453; VI, 361. The North Carolina acts of 1715 and 1741 contained provisions similar to these.—*State Records of North Carolina*, XXIII, 64-65, 195. None of these acts deprived the master of any of the woman's full time of service, however, or provided any punishment for him other than giving security for maintaining the child.

[33] *Executive Journals of the Council of Colonial Virginia*, II, 35.

[34] A Virginia court sentenced Mathew Rolles, who had a bastard by her master, Richard Cox, to be whipped and then sold to serve the parish for two years after her term of servitude expired and ordered her master to give security for his good behavior and to pay a fine of five hundred pounds of tobacco.—MS, Northumberland County Order Book, 1678-1698, p. 5. Another court ordered Randolph Chamblett, father of a bastard born of Mary Bennett, his servant, to give security for bringing up the child until he was twelve years old and to forfeit one thousand pounds of tobacco for freeing the woman from corporal punishment and for his own crime of fornication.—MS, Lancaster County Order Book, 1655-1666, p. 66.

another bastard in the time of her service.[35] Mary Rogers was jailed for concealing the name of the father of her child, but when the court discovered that her master was the guilty man, it ordered her to be sold for the use of the parish and apparently exacted no penalty from him.[36]

The court usually dealt severely with the woman who accused a man falsely of being the father of her bastard. A county court in Virginia in 1678 ordered Mary Greene, a servant who had accused William Gordon, apparently a gentleman, of begetting her child, to be taken to the public whipping post and be given thirty-nine lashes on her bare back "well laid on."[37] Anne Thornton was given twenty stripes for charging Daniel Bigsby with being the father of her child and "not proving the accusation to the satisfaction of the court."[38] Elizabeth James charged John Haskins with being father to her bastard, but when it was pointed out to the court that the child was born in September and that he did not "keep company with her" until January, he was vindicated and she was declared to be "a common and notorious strumpet," and was sentenced to receive thirty lashes on her bare back.[39]

Fear of punishment does not seem to have decreased the amount of bastardy; on the other hand, it often led mothers of illegitimate children to commit the greater crime of infanticide. Many cases of child murder were reported similar to the following, all three of which appeared in the *Maryland Gazette*, February 19, 1761:

One Morning last Month, a young Infant was found Dead in a Well at Chester-Town in Kent County. It was drawn up by the Bucket, and had lain there for some Time. It had a String round it's Neck, was cramn'd into Part of a Stocking, and is suppos'd to have been tied to a Pair of Pot-Hooks which was found at the Bottom to sink it. The suppos'd Mother is taken up and committed to Prison there.

Last Week a Woman in Baltimore County, who had lived near *Deer-Creek*, was committed to Prison at *Joppa*, for the Murder of a Bastard Child. She was often tax'd with being with Child, but always denied it; and at the Time of her Travail, went to the Creek Side, and was delivered by herself, and flung the Child in. A few Days after, the dead Child being found by the Children of the House, and she being charg'd, confess'd the Fact.

[35] MS, Northumberland County Order Book, 1720-1729, p. 75.
[36] *Ibid.*, 1699-1713, p. 223.
[37] MS, Middlesex County Order Book, 1673-1680, p. 138.
[38] MS, Northumberland County Record, 1652-65, p. 133.
[39] *Ibid.*, p. 152.

And on Tuesday Afternoon last, a Dead Female Child was found float-
ing in a Pond in this Town, sew'd up in a Linen Bag, supposed to have
been not above 4 or 5 Days since the Birth. A large Pin was stuck in the
Hip of it, and some other marks of violence. The Mother (if Wretches
of her Stamp may be call'd by that Appellation) is not yet discovered;
but it is to be hop'd she will soon.

Because it was impossible usually for courts to determine whether
a bastard born and buried privately were born dead or had been maliciously destroyed, acts were passed providing that any woman who
should conceal the death of her bastard, whether it were born alive
or dead, should suffer death as in case of murder, unless she could
prove by one witness at least that the child was born dead.[40] Some of
the authorities appear to have been inclined to mitigate the harsh provisions of these statutes. In 1714 Governor Spotswood wrote this
letter to England requesting the queen's pardon for a poor woman
condemned by a Virginia court for concealing the death of her bastard:

I take the liberty to represent to y'r Lord'p, (as I have formerly to my
L'd Dartmouth) ye Case of Jane Ham, who was condemned here for
concealing the death of her bastard Child, upon a late Act of Assembly,
which the penalty of such concealment ye same as for willful murder. The
Judges who passed the Sentence, recommended her to me as an Object of
mercy, in regard there was not any proof of the least Violence offered to
ye Child to occasion its death, and that it also appeared that ye Act of
Assembly had never been read in ye parish Church where she lived . . .
but as I am restrain'd by my Instructions from pardoning murder without
her Maj't's espress Command, I beg y'r Lo'p will be pleas'd to move her
Maj'tie to extend her Royal mercy to this unfortunate Woman, (who has
now lain upwards of fifteen months in prison) and is the more deserving
of compassion in regard that being a Servant, by the laws of this Country,
her having a Bastard Child would have entailed upon her a Longer Servitude; the fear of which, probably, was the reason why she conseal'd her
Delivery and the Death of the Child.[41]

The Maryland Council in 1692 reprieved Rebecca Saunders, condemned for murdering her bastard, and wrote a letter to the king
representing her case as follows: " . . . the tender Care she took of the
Child in wrapping it in Clean Linen, nothing of Violence offered appearing about it, with other Circumstances induces this Board to think
it was shame more than Guilt caused her to conceal the matter, and

[40] Hening, *Statutes*, III, 516; *State Records of North Carolina*, XXIII, 324; *Statutes of South Carolina* (ed., Cooper), II, 513.
[41] Virginia Historical Society, *Publications*, II, 74.

therefore this Board humbly recommend her to his Majesty's Mercy.[42]

Other women were not treated so sympathetically. Catherine McCarty, arrested before a Virginia county court on the charge of infanticide, gave a straightforward account of the circumstances of the birth of her child. She declared she had left her master's house and in climbing over a fence had fallen and hurt herself. Being with child, she was in great pain and took a path that led to the side of a branch, where she fell in travail and was delivered of a dead child. She had then raked a hole in the ground with her hands and buried it. Her mistress and a woman companion testified that she had confessed to them she was with child before her delivery, that she had provided "childbed linen," a matter usually regarded as important in cases of this kind, and that before her arrest she had told them of the manner of her delivery. The county justices, nevertheless, declared she could not be discharged and remanded her to the county jail to await trial at the general court at Williamsburg.[43] It is not known whether she was there convicted or acquitted. Many instances appear of the execution of women for child murder or for concealing the death of a bastard.[44]

Though infanticide was the means by which unwelcome children were most often destroyed, abortion was not unknown. In 1652 Captain Mitchell, a prominent citizen of Maryland, was accused of a number of crimes, among which was attempted abortion. Susanna Warren testified that when Captain Mitchell perceived "she bred Child by Him," he prepared a "potion of Phisick," put it in an egg,

[42] *Archives of Maryland*, VIII, 331.

[43] MS, Northumberland County Order Book, 1713-1719, pp. 109-10.

[44] Margaret Hatch was found guilty of infanticide and sentenced to be hanged, June 24, 1633.—Hening, *Statutes*, I, 209; *Virginia Magazine*, XIII, 390. Mary Axell was sentenced to die for destroying her child, but as she was pregnant at the time of her trial, she was reprieved; immediately after her delivery, however, the Council ordered the sheriff to put her to death.—*Archives of Maryland*, XVII, 439. The Governor of Virginia in 1702 signed a warrant for the execution of Ann Tandy, who had been condemned by the General Court for concealing the death of her bastard.—*Executive Journal of the Council of Colonial Virginia*, II, 236. Martha Sharp of Virginia was executed for infanticide in 1767 although she denied the crime until her death and declared that it was the child's father who was guilty.—*Virginia Gazette*, June 11, 1767. Magdalen Collar, a poor woman of North Carolina, was sentenced to be hanged for child murder in 1720.—*Colonial Records of North Carolina*, II, 398-400. Mary Arnett of Maryland confessed to having flung her child into a pond, where it drowned, but she died before she could be brought to trial.—*Maryland Gazette*, February 26, 1761,

and forced her to take it, and that two or three days afterward he had told her that if she were with child "he would warrant that he had frighted it away."[45] Elizabeth Robins, a married woman, was accused of adultery and of taking medicine to destroy her child. A jury of women appointed to examine her made this report: "We found the Said Elizabeth in a very Sad Condition, . . . & [she] Confessed that She had twice taken Savin; once boyled in milk and the other time strayned through a Cloath, and at the takeing thereof not Supposing her self with a Child as She sayeth, takeing it for wormes not knowing the Vertue thereof any other wayes, farther Confessed She Supposed her Self to have a dead Child within her, and if a Child, that the true begetter of it was her husband Robert Robins."[46]

The jury of matrons was frequently summoned in cases of infanticide, abortion, and witchcraft, and in trials in which women accused of capital crimes pleaded pregnancy to save themselves from immediate punishment. The matrons were not supposed to make final decisions regarding the guilt of the accused, but were expected to discover and report information needed by the masculine jurors in forming their verdict. In the colonies as in England, pregnant women were not executed, but, if convicted of a capital offence, were reprieved until after they were delivered. To prevent female culprits from taking advantage of this possible moratorium, it was often necessary to summon a jury of matrons, usually including at least one reputable midwife, to ascertain whether a woman were actually with child or only pretending. In 1633 Margaret Hatch of Virginia, sentenced to be hanged for infanticide, pleaded pregnancy, but a jury of matrons summoned to examine her reported that she was not with child.[47] Jane Parker, a Maryland spinster, was convicted of stealing goods above the value of forty shillings and sentenced to die, but a jury of matrons summoned on her plea of pregnancy declared that she was with child. Thereupon the council advised that she be pardoned.[48] The *Maryland Gazette* reported a similar case: "A Woman was tried for Felony, found Guilty, and received Sentence of Death. She pleaded her Belly, on which a Jury of Matrons were summoned, who found her Quick with Child." A later issue added this information: "The poor woman who was sentenced to Die for Felony, and pleaded her Belly, has since obtain'd his Excellency's Pardon."[49]

[45] *Archives of Maryland*, X, 176. [46] *Ibid.*, XLI, 20.
[47] Hening, *Statutes*, I, 209. [48] *Archives of Maryland*, XVIII, 524.
[49] September 25, 1751; October 30, 1751.

Women accused of infanticide were often examined by a jury of matrons to discover whether they had been delivered of a child within the time covered by the accusation. Judith Catchpole, summoned before a Maryland court upon suspicion of having murdered her bastard, denied she had ever had a child. Then the court ordered that a jury of "able women" be impanelled. They reported: "We the Jury of Women . . . having according to our Charge and Oath Searched the body of Judith Catchpole doe give in our Verdict that according to our best Judgment that the said Judith hath not had any Child within the time Charged."[50]

Occasionally a woman was accused of witchcraft and a jury of matrons was called to search her body for witch marks. But, though county magistrates when given their commissions were directed "to inquire, among other things, respecting witchcraft, enchantment, sorceries and magic arts,"[51] they apparently did not consider charges of witchcraft very seriously. One of the first persons accused of practicing the black art in the southern colonies was Goodwife Wright. Robert Thresher swore before the General Court of Virginia in 1626 that Goodwife Wright came to him and requested him to give her some plants. He had answered her that when he had served his own purpose, she should have them. She had then gone away and that night all his plants were drowned. Elizabeth Gates, examined at the same time, declared that Goodwife Wright had come to a Mr. Moore's to buy some chickens, but he would sell her none, and shortly afterwards all his chickens died. This, she admitted, "she had hearde from others."[52]

Three women on ships bound for Maryland and Virginia were executed for witchcraft on the high seas,[53] but no instance appears of any severe punishment having been imposed for witchcraft in the southern colonies. Barbara Winbrow was accused of witchcraft before the general court of Virginia in 1657, but was acquitted.[54] Alice Stephens was charged with being intimate with evil spirits in 1665,[55] and in

[50] *Archives of Maryland*, X, 456-57.
[51] John B. Dillon, *Oddities of Colonial Legislation.* . . . (Indianapolis, 1879), p. 33; Bruce, *Institutional History*, I, 283; E. H. Nutler, *History of Maryland*, pp. 38-39; Hawks, *History of North Carolina*, II, 116-17.
[52] *Minutes of the Council and General Court of Virginia*, p. 114.
[53] Mary Lee, 1654 (*Narratives of Early Maryland*, pp. 117, 141; *Archives of Maryland*, III, 306-308); Elizabeth Richardson, 1658 (*Archives of Maryland*, XLI, 328); and Katharine Grady, 1659 (*Minutes of the Council and General Court of Virginia*, p. 504).
[54] *Ibid.*, p. 506. [55] *Virginia Magazine*, VIII, 237.

1671 a Mrs. Neale was accused by Edward Cole of having said "a kind of prayer" that "neither he nor any of his family might ever prosper," after which utterance all the people on his plantation became ill.[56] These stories, however, were evidently regarded by the justices as tittle-tattle. In 1679 John Salmon accused Alice, wife of Thomas Cartwrite, of bewitching his child, who had died. But the jury of women summoned to search her reported that they could "find noe Suspitious marke whereby they can Judg her to bee a witch," and the court ordered her acquittal.[57] A jury of Currituck Precinct in Albemarle County, North Carolina, in 1697 reported that Susannah Evans, "not having the fear of God before her eyes, but being led by the instigation of the devil, did . . . the body of Deborah Bourthier . . . devilishly and maliciously bewitch, and by assistance of the devil, afflict, with mortal pains, the body of the said Deborah Bourthier, whereby the said Deborah departed this life. And also did diabolically and maliciously bewitch several other of her majesty's liege subjects."[58] The matter ended, however, with this presentment.

The most famous of the southern witches was Grace, wife of James Sherwood of Princess Anne County, Virginia. She seems to have had the reputation of being a witch several years before she was charged with the crime and brought to trial. In September, 1698, James Sherwood and Grace, his wife, brought suit against John Gisburne and Jane, his wife, for slander, complaining that they had defamed and abused Grace by saying that she had bewitched their cotton, and asked for judgment in the sum of one hundred pounds, sterling. On the same day, they sued Anthony and Elizabeth Barnes, claiming that Elizabeth had said that Grace came to her one night, rode her, and went out of the keyhole or a crack of the door like a black cat. The court, possibly regarding the defamation as trivial, awarded no damages in either case.[59]

James Sherwood died sometime in 1701 and thereafter Grace had to defend her reputation alone. In 1705 she brought suit against Luke Hill and his wife in an action of assault and battery, setting forth that the defendant's wife had "assaulted, bruised, maimed and barbarously beaten her," and recovered damages in the sum of twenty

[56] Bruce, *Institutional History*, I, 282.
[57] *William and Mary Quarterly*, I, 127-29.
[58] Hawks, *History of North Carolina*, II, 116-17.
[59] *Lower Norfolk County Virginia Antiquary*, II, 92-94.

shillings sterling.[60] Probably in retaliation, Luke Hill had her summoned to appear before the court to answer the charge of witchcraft.

Although the Hills were persistent in maintaining their charges, the court appears to have made but a half-hearted attempt to prosecute the alleged witch, putting off her trial from court to court and finally leaving the matter unsettled. In March, 1705-06, they had the sheriff impanel a jury of women to search her and "make due inquiry and inspection into all circumstances." Elizabeth Barnes, the forewoman, very probably the same Elizabeth Barnes whom Grace had sued for defamation in 1698, reported that the jury had found "two things like titts with several other spots."[61] Luke Hill then brought the matter before the Council, who referred his petition to the attorney general. This officer was of opinion that the charges were too general and that the county court ought to make a further examination of the matters of fact. Thereupon, the county court, May 2, 1706, ordered that the sheriff take Grace into safe custody and search her house and "all Suspicious places carefully for all Images and Such like things as may anyway Strengthen The Suspicion," and that another jury of women be summoned to examine her.[62] The following June, Grace appeared in court according to order, but the jury of matrons were all absent. The court then ordered that a new jury of women be summoned to appear at the next court and allowed Grace to give security for her appearance.

The justices, evidently tired of the way the matter was dragging on from month to month and eager either to acquit her or "give more strength to the suspicion" against her, ordered that Grace be tried in the water by ducking.[63] But, the record declares, when the time for the trial came "the weather being very rainy and bad, so that possibly it might endanger her health," the court ordered a postponement of the test until the following Wednesday. On July 10, 1706, the sheriff was directed to get all the assistance in boats and men he should think fit and meet at John Harper's plantation, where he should put

[60] *Ibid.*, p. 140.
[61] *Ibid.*, p. 141.   [62] *Ibid.*, p. 34.
[63] The ordeal by water was based on the theory that because of her unclean nature, the witch would not sink in the pure element water, or that by her connection with Satan, she was rendered preternaturally light. When a woman suspected of witchcraft was subjected to trial by water, she was stripped naked and cross bound, the right thumb to the left toe, and the left thumb to the right toe, and cast into some deep water. It was believed that she would sink if innocent.— *Ibid.*, III, 52.

Grace into the water above man's depth and see whether she swam. He was instructed particularly to have a "care of her life to preserve her from drowning." He was to have as many "ancient and knowing women as possible he could get" to examine her as soon as she came out of the water and search her carefully, and also to request some other women to search her before she went into the water to be sure that she carried nothing about her to cause any further suspicion.[64]

According to the record, Grace made no excuses and said nothing in her own behalf, but relied on what the court should do, consenting to be tried in the water and likewise to be searched again by a jury of women. These "experants" were finally tried and when bound and put into the water, she swam, "contrary to custom and the judgment of all the spectators." Also she was declared by this second jury of women not "like them nor no other woman that they knew of." But the court, still not convinced of her guilt, ordered the sheriff to take her again into his custody, commit her to the county jail, and there secure her in irons to await further trial.[65]

It is not known whether she was ever convicted. As no record of a later trial appears, she probably was neither condemned nor exonerated, but passed the remainder of her days under suspicion and subject to the petty persecutions of her enemies in the community. She apparently died in this same county in which she was tried for witchcraft, for her will, dated August 20, 1733, was presented in a Princess Anne Court by her executor and on December 3, 1740, an inventory of her estate was ordered to be recorded.[66]

Next to bastardy, slander was the most common offense of colonial women. Gossiping was a favorite amusement and a besetting sin. A form of punishment often used for these "double-tongued and naughty women" was that of ducking. The wetting seems to have been considered efficacious in cooling their hot tempers, and the mortification of being publicly drenched was thought to humble their pride. A machine especially made for this purpose was a part of the necessary equipment of county courthouses, along with branding irons, stocks, pillory, and whipping post. A Virginia act of 1662 ordered

[64] *Ibid.*, p. 36.   [65] *Ibid.*, pp. 53-54.
[66] *Ibid.*, p. 57. Other women accused of witchcraft were Phyllis Money (Bruce, *Institutional History*, p. 284), Elizabeth Dunkin (*ibid.*, pp. 284-85), Anne Byrd (*Lower Norfolk County Virginia Antiquary*, I, 56-57, and *William and Mary Quarterly*, II, 59-60), and the wife of Richard Manship (*Archives of Maryland*, X, 399).

each county to erect at public expense a pillory, stocks, a whipping post, and a ducking stool. Declaring that "brabling women often slander and scandalize their neighbors for which their poore husbands are often brought into chargeable and vexatious suites, and cast in greate damages," it provided that in actions of slander occasioned by the wife, if the husband refused to pay the damages, the wife was to be punished by ducking. If the slander were so "enormous" as to call for greater damages than five hundred pounds of tobacco, the wife was to be ducked one time for every five hundred pounds adjudged against her husband.[67] A Maryland act of assembly of 1663 required every county, except Talbot and Baltimore, which were thought not sufficiently settled, to erect a pillory, stocks, and a ducking stool,[68] and sometime later, at a court-baron of St. Clement's Manor, the lord of the manor was indicted for not having these "instruments of justice" and was ordered to provide them before the next court.[69] Later acts of the Virginia and Maryland assemblies made it compulsory for counties to build ducking stools, and county court minutes show many court orders for the erection of such apparatus.[70]

An old letter said to have been written by Thomas Hartley from Hungar's Parish in Virginia in 1634, gives the following graphic description of a ducking stool and of a ducking he had just witnessed:

The day afore yesterday at two of ye clock in ye afternoon I saw this punishment given to one Betsey wife of John Tucker, who by ye violence of her tongue had made his house and ye neighborhood uncomfortable. She was taken to ye pond where I am sojourning by ye officer who was joyned by ye magistrate and ye Minister Mr. Cotton, who had frequently admonished her and a large number of people. They had a machine for ye purpose yt belongs to ye Parish, and which I was told had been so used three times this Summer. It is a platform with 4 small rollers or wheels and two upright posts between which works a Lever by a Rope fastened to its shorter or heavier end. At the end of ye longer arm is fixed a stool upon which sd Betsey was fastened by cords, her gown tied fast around her feete. The Machine was then moved up to ye edge of ye pond, ye Rope was slackened by ye officer and ye woman was allowed to go down under ye water for ye space of half a minute. Betsey had a

[67] Hening, *Statutes*, II, 166-67.

[68] *Archives of Maryland*, I, 473, 475, 490-91.

[69] Hester Dorsey Richardson, *Side-Lights on Maryland History, with Sketches of Early Maryland Families* (2 vols. Baltimore, 1913), I, 71; John H. Johnson, "Old Maryland Manors with the Records of a Court Leet and a Court Baron," Johns Hopkins University, *Studies*, I, 38.

[70] *Journals of the House of Burgesses*, I, 196, 203, 461; II, 462; IV, 145, 161, 203; *Archives of Maryland*, II, 67.

stout stomach, and would not yield until she had allowed herself to be ducked 5 severall times.   At length she cried piteously Let me go Let me go, by Gods help I'll sin no more.   Then they drew back ye machine, untied ye Ropes and let her walk home in her wetted clothes a hopefully penitent woman.[71]

A Virginia court in 1627, informed of the "unquiett life" which the people of Archer's Hope were suffering because of the "scoldings railings & fallings out" and the "abominable contentions" between Amy, wife of Christopher Hall, and the wife of William Harman, ordered the quarrelsome Amy to be "toughed round aboard the *Margaret and John*" and ducked three times.[72]   Anne Wension and Anne Stephens of Accomac County were sentenced to be ducked for having uttered "most vyle and scandalous speeches" to the discredit of John Waltham and his wife.[73]

Lacking a specially constructed contrivance, the officers accomplished the ducking by other means.   A court held at James City in 1626 charged Margaret Jones with beating John Butterfield, making a clamor, and railing against her husband, and ordered that she be "toughed or dragged at a boates Starne in ye River from ye shoare unto the *Margaret & John* and thence unto the shoare againe."[74]   Joane Butler of Northampton County was, for slander, sentenced to be drawn over King's Creek at the stern of a boat,[75] and a "limber-tongued sister" of Accomac was given her choice as to whether she should publicly ask forgiveness or be drawn across King's Creek at the stern of a canoe.[76]

The courts frequently required gossipers and scandal mongers to do public penance.   This form of punishment, though less dampening to the body, must have been as depressing to the spirit of a "scolding quean" or a meddlesome tattler as a public ducking.   Mrs. Thomas Causon, having cast aspersion on the memory of the deceased Adam Thoroughgood by reporting that "he had paid slowly or paid not at all," was, upon the complaint of the colonel's widow, ordered to apologize to Mistress Thoroughgood on her knees in the court room

[71] Alice Morse Earle, *Colonial Dames and Goodwives* (Boston and New York, 1895), pp. 93-94.

[72] *Minutes of the Council and General Court of Colonial Virginia*, p. 153.

[73] Bruce, *Institutional History*, pp. 629-30.

[74] *Minutes of the Council and General Court of Colonial Virginia*, p. 119.

[75] "Extracts from the Records of Northampton County, Virginia," Massachusetts Historical Society, *Publications*, June, 1886.

[76] Bruce, *Institutional History*, p. 269.

and also in the parish church before all the congregation.[77] Elizabeth Large, for writing and singing a scandalous song "much touching ye reputation and Creditt of Walter Dune and Mary his wife," was required to acknowledge her fault in open court, and, upon her knees, to beg pardon.[78] Mary White, of Accomac, having abused her aunt, Goody Hait, was ordered to ask forgiveness three times, once in open court and once at each church in the county "in the face of the congregation."[79] Joane Wardley, having spoken words to the disparagement of Colonel Beale and his wife, was ordered to be present at the next county court held for York and on her knees "acknowledge her hearty sorrow and repentance" and wear a paper on her breast describing her fault, or suffer imprisonment.[80] She refused, however, to appear. It is not known whether she continued unhumbled and endured the longer but less humiliating punishment of imprisonment or finally submitted to the mortifying ordeal of publicly asking forgiveness. Husbands sometimes encouraged wives in their contumacy. When the wife of John Williams was ordered to apologize for a wrong she had done, he exclaimed that she should be hanged before she should be made to go down on her knees, "without it bee to God."[81]

A few women were brought into court for drunkenness, swearing, and fighting. A deponent in the General Court of Virginia, September 25, 1626, stated that as he was walking behind Goodwife Fisher and a Mr. Southern, he saw Goodwife Fisher reel and stagger as she went and then stumble and fall upon a cow, and that Mr. Southern had to lead her by the arm. He said that his companion at the time had remarked that it was a great shame to see a man drunk but more shame to see a woman in that case, and that a man would be set in the stocks or "lye neck and heeles" for such an offense.[82] The record does not say whether Goodwife Fisher was punished like a man for her delinquency. The grand jury of Henrico County, Virginia, presented Thomas Wells and his wife for swearing "in a most horrible nature," and indicted Ann Stop for profanity, charging her with having been guilty of that crime at least sixty-five times.[83] For beating Anne

[77] *Ibid.*, p. 52.
[78] MS, Northumberland County Order Book, No. 3, 1678-1698, Pt. I, p. 348.
[79] *Virginia Magazine*, VI, 103.
[80] *Minutes of the Council and General Court of Virginia*, pp. 262, 267.
[81] MS, Northampton County Records, Vol. for 1654-55, p. 15.
[82] *Minutes of the Council and General Court of Virginia*, p. 115.
[83] MS, Henrico County Records, Vol. for 1677-92, p. 336.

Snoade, Alice Thornbury was given forty stripes at the whipping post, and both Alice and Anne were warned that if they broke their good behavior they would be whipped three times.[84]   Margaret Briggs of North Carolina was arraigned for an assault on James Warden. The presentment states: "she with force & arms . . . did make and him beat wounded & evilly intreated and other Enormities to him."[85] Mary McDonald of Virginia was bound by the court to keep the peace for putting John Cunningham in fear of his life,[86] and Anne Brown was also bound to good behavior for coming into court and calling Justice William Wilson a "rogue" and declaring that on his coming off the bench she would "give it to him with the Devil."[87]   The *Maryland Gazette,* June 16, 1747, carried a lively bit of news to the effect that at a recent meeting of the court a Mrs. "S. C." of Patapsco was fined the sum of one penny for whipping the "Reverend Mr. N———l W———r" with a hickory switch, "it being imagined by the court that he well deserved it."

Women were not usually sentenced to sit in the stocks, which instrument of punishment was evidently reserved for men as the ducking stool was for women, but the whipping post and the pillory claimed their victims from both sexes. The pillory was a device consisting of a frame of adjustable boards erected on a post and having holes through which the head and hands of the offender were thrust; its purpose was to expose criminals to public scorn and abuse. It was often employed in connection with whipping or some other form of punishment and was generally used for persons convicted of perjury. The perjurer, if unable to pay his fine, was required to stand in the pillory one hour with his ears nailed during the whole time, and at the expiration of the hour to have both ears severed from the head, leaving them nailed on the pillory until the setting of the sun.[88] For giving false testimony regarding the ownership of a cow, Blanch Howell, a Maryland matron, was condemned to stand in the pillory and to lose both her ears.[89] Anne Howard of South Carolina, convicted of receiving stolen goods, was sentenced to suffer five lashes on

[84] *Minutes of the Council and General Court of Virginia,* p. 150.

[85] MS, Chowan County Papers, Vol. V (1748-51).

[86] Oren Frederic Morton, *History of Rockbridge County, Virginia* (Staunton, Va., 1920), p. 56.

[87] Lyman Chalkley, *Chronicles of the Scotch-Irish in Virginia,* I, 64.

[88] *State Records of North Carolina,* XXIV, 13-14; *Laws of Maryland* (ed., Bacon), Act of 1692, Chap. 16, Sec. 4.   [89] *Archives of Maryland,* IV, 445.

her bare back and then stand in the pillory from eleven until twelve o'clock,[90] and Ann Chapman was condemned to suffer the same punishment and in addition pay a fine of five pounds currency.[91] Mary Bond, a runaway servant, was required to stand in the pillory two hours for having forged a pass,[92] and a white woman of Maryland was pilloried for swearing to a white man a child which turned out to be a mulatto.[93]

The colonists apparently had no feeling against the hanging of women. Courts frequently condemned them to this punishment and newspapers described the execution of female felons at the gallows without comment.[94] In a few rare cases women were sentenced to a more horrible punishment than hanging. Under the English law the wife who murdered her husband and the slave who killed her master were guilty of petit treason, a crime punishable by burning at the stake. In 1746 a slave named Eve was convicted of poisoning her master and was burned alive by order of the court at a place near the Orange County courthouse in Virginia. The county paid her master's estate fifty pounds for her loss.[95] In 1769 a Negro woman belonging to James Sands, Charles Town merchant, and a Negro man were burned alive on the workhouse green for administering poison to Sands, his wife, and child.[96] No instance appears of a wife's having been burned at the stake for the murder of her husband, but the following extracts from the *Maryland Gazette* record what appears to have been the burning alive of a white woman:[97]

[90] *South Carolina Gazette*, December 5, 1771.

[91] *South Carolina Gazette and Country Journal*, February 11, 1772.

[92] MS, Northumberland County Order Book, No. 7. Orders August 8, 1737.

[93] *Maryland Gazette*, August 19, 1746.

[94] John Williams, Mary Williams, and Mary Clocker, who were convicted of felony by a Maryland court in 1658-1662, were all sentenced to be hanged "by the neck till they bee dead."—*Archives of Maryland*, XLI, 255. The record of the hanging of another woman is found in a gruesome petition read before the Virginia House of Burgesses in 1712 in which William Timson asked to be allowed compensation for hanging Elizabeth Gordon.—*Journals of the House of Burgesses*, V, 8. Susannah Brasier was executed for murder at the gallows near Williamsburg, Virginia, in 1775, and three women were sentenced to be hanged by a Virginia court in 1739, two for felony and one for murder.—*Virginia Gazette*, January 14, 1775; *ibid.*, November 2, 1739. In 1752 Martha Bassett and Mary Powell were hanged at Joppa in Baltimore County, Maryland, for the murder of a Mrs. Clark.—*Maryland Gazette*, January 2, 16, 23, 1752.

[95] *Virginia Magazine*, III, 308; IV, 341; *Tyler's Quarterly Magazine*, IV, 109-10.

[96] *Virginia Magazine*, IV, 341.   [97] May 6, 20, 1746.

Friday last was held, at Chester in Kent County, a special Court of Oyer and Terminer, for trying the murderers of Richard Waters; when the two Men and the Woman were found guilty of the Indictment, and received Sentence of Death; Grant and Horney are to be hang'd and the Woman (Esther Anderson) is to be burnt.

On Friday last, Hector Grant, James Horney, and Esther Anderson, were executed at Chester in Kent County, pursuant to their Sentence, for the Murder of their late Master. The Men were Hang'd, the Woman Burn'd. They died penitent, acknowledging their Crimes.

No information appears to show why the woman was burned while the men were hanged.

In England, men convicted of certain capital offenses could plead benefit of clergy and thereby suffer burning in the hand and imprisonment rather than death. This dispensation arose from the immunity of the clergy from the jurisdiction of the civil courts, and came to be allowed to any man who could read. As a woman could not, even by a fiction, be of the clergy, she was not allowed to claim this benefit. But in the reign of William and Mary a statute was passed allowing women convicted of felonies to claim the same privileges as men.[98] Male criminals in the colonies were often granted the benefit of clergy, but the privilege was apparently not extended to women until the eighteenth century. In 1712 South Carolina adopted as a part of her law the English statute regarding women convicted of small felonies. This act declared that, as by law the benefit of clergy was not allowed to women convicted of felony, "by reason whereof many women do suffer death for small causes," thereafter, any woman convicted of stealing money or goods above the value of twelve pence and under ten shillings, the offense not being burglary or robbery near the highway or stealing from the person of a man or woman, but only such an offense as in a like case a man might have his clergy, should for the first offense be branded with the letter "T" on the left thumb, and then be further punished by imprisonment, "stocking," or sending to the house of correction as the justices should think fit.[99] The same statute was adopted by the

[98] Arthur Lyon Cross, "The English Criminal Law and Benefit of Clergy during the Eighteenth and Early Nineteenth Centuries," *American Historical Review*, XXII, 554-55; Cross, "Benefit of Clergy in American Criminal Law," Massachusetts Historical Society, *Proceedings*, LXI, 166-77.

[99] *Public Laws of South Carolina* (ed., Grimké), p. 86; *Statutes of South Carolina* (ed., Cooper), II, 512.

North Carolina Assembly in 1749, and a similar one by the Virginia House of Burgesses in 1732.[100]

These acts suggest that in earlier times the female criminal suffered a harsher punishment than the male malefactor. Court records do not furnish sufficient evidence to show whether women generally did suffer death for crimes for which men, by pleading the benefit of clergy, were sentenced to milder punishment. Many women were executed for stealing and other felonies, but information regarding the circumstances of their crimes is too scant to enable one to judge whether a man guilty of the same offense would have had the benefit of clergy. After the enactment of measures allowing them the privileges accorded men by the benefit of clergy, women convicted of felony were often branded and imprisoned. Usually they suffered the same punishment as men for their offenses. Bridget Rogers and James Conner of Virginia, for instance, were at the same time found guilty of grand larceny and were both sentenced to be burned in the hand.[101] Jane Sewell, for stealing sundry goods; John Hart, for stealing bacon; and "J. W.," for stealing rum were all branded and punished alike.[102]

Under the English law a husband was held liable for felonies committed by his wife in his presence. A doctrine of the common law which, according to Blackstone, was at least a thousand years old, was that in some cases the command or authority of the husband, express or implied, would privilege the wife from punishment. If a married woman were to commit theft, burglary, or other civil offense by the coercion of her husband, or even in his company, in which case the law would construe a coercion, she would not be held guilty of any crime, as she would be considered as acting by compulsion and not of her own will. This practice of exempting the wife was explained on the grounds that under the ancient law the husband could plead benefit of clergy while the wife had no such right. In cases in which a husband and wife committed felony together, the judges felt it would have been an odious proceeding to sentence the wife to die and dismiss the husband with only a slight punishment. So, to avoid such injustice, they excused the wife altogether.[103] The husband was not responsible, however, for his wife's misdemeanors, or for her felonies committed without his company.

[100] Martin, *Statutes of England in Force in North Carolina*, p. 366; Hening, *Statutes*, V, 546. [101] *Virginia Gazette*, April 23, 1772.
[102] *Maryland Gazette*, April 17, 1751. [103] Blackstone, *Commentaries*, IV, 28-29.

338   WOMEN IN THE SOUTHERN COLONIES

Governor Horatio Sharpe in 1755 explained his reasons for pardoning a woman accused of forgery on the grounds that he presumed
she had committed the crime by the compulsion of her husband.[104]
But whether colonial courts were inclined to excuse married women
on this basis does not appear. In several cases of crimes not punishable with death, they held both husband and wife responsible for
offenses committed by them together. A Virginia court before whom
Thomas Mould and his wife were convicted of entertaining felons
and receiving stolen goods, for instance, ordered the husband and
wife each to be given thirty stripes.[105] When in 1661-62 John Alford
and his wife were found guilty of wounding the sheriff, though acting with her husband, she was punished with twenty lashes and he
with thirty.[106] In a number of cases the husband was indicted because of his wife's misconduct, but upon proof of his lack of responsibility each time he was discharged. William Barnes of North
Carolina was arraigned in court in 1753 for his wife's retailing liquor
unlawfully, but when he proved he was absent at the time the liquors
were sold, he was excused.[107] Jacob Smith of Virginia was indicted
for his wife's entertaining felons and protecting them by keeping the
constable out of the house, but as it did not appear that he was at
home or had anything to do with aiding the criminals, he was
discharged.[108]

As the husband under the law came into possession of all his
wife's personal estate at the marriage and was entitled to the income
from her property and her services, he was naturally expected to pay
her fines and damages. The following entry from the records of
Cambridge, Maryland, August 6, 1690, is typical of numerous others
in the court minutes: "This day the Court ordered that James Nowells be fined five hundred pounds of tobacco for his wife Margaret
Nowells abusing Mr Wm. Hill and our Burgesses biding them 'be
damned'."[109] When Ann Godby of Lower Norfolk County, Virginia, was found guilty of slandering Nicholas Robinson's wife, the
court ordered her husband to pay a fine and the costs of the suit.[110]
Often, it seems, the husband had the choice between paying his wife's

[104] *Maryland Gazette*, July 10, 1755.
[105] MS, Northumberland County Order Book, No. 2 (1666-1678), p. 117.
[106] *Journals of the House of Burgesses*, II, 19.
[107] *Colonial Records of North Carolina*, V, 34.
[108] *Virginia Magazine*, XXIII, 76-77.
[109] Elias Jones, *Revised History of Dorchester County, Maryland* (Baltimore, 1925), p. 52. [110] *William and Mary Quarterly*, II, 59.

fine and allowing her to suffer corporal punishment for her offense. When Sarah, wife of Jeoffrey Bow, was in 1672 convicted of uttering scandalous words against a neighbor, the court ordered that he pay one thousand pounds of tobacco for her defamation or that she be ducked.[111]

The awkward situation in which justices sometimes found themselves because of the husband's legal responsibility for his wife's fines is illustrated by a case which came before the North Carolina General Court in 1722. Mary Haughton was summoned to appear before this court to answer an indictment for adultery. Her husband, William Haughton, appeared and was ordered to forfeit five pounds for her offense. The judges, however, recognizing the injustice of compelling a husband to make compensation for his wife's unfaithfulness to him, allowed the payment of the fine to be suspended during his lifetime.[112]

Although a few married women possibly escaped punishment for their felonies on the legal presumption of coercion by their husbands and a larger number whose husbands were able and willing to pay their fines and damages escaped corporal punishment, women generally paid the full penalty for their crimes. They did public penance, sat in the ducking stool, and stood in the pillory. No special regard for their sex diminished the number of stripes they received on their bare backs at the public whipping post or saved them from the branding irons and the gallows. Female offenders against morality usually fared worse than male delinquents. While the statutes called for equal punishment for them, the courts frequently ordered the man to pay for his offense with a sum of tobacco while it sentenced the woman to be whipped, not because they considered her more blameable, probably, but because she had no means with which to pay a fine. In dealing with bastardy cases, justices were governed largely by expediency and were usually less careful to apportion punishment according to the culpability of the offender than they were to save the parish from the charges of a child born as a result of the crime. Therefore, because the mother was more easily discovered and apprehended than the father, she was often sentenced to pay a fine or to be whipped and in addition give security to maintain the child, while the father, who was difficult to find, was allowed to escape punishment altogether.

[111] MS, Northumberland County Records, Book No. 1 (1652-65), p. 224.
[112] Colonial Records of North Carolina, II, 472.

CHAPTER XVI

UNDER THE LAW

THE LEGAL position of English women in the seventeenth century was thus summarized by the author of *The Lawes Resolutions of Womens Rights:*

In this consolidation which we call wedlock is a locking together. It is true, that man and wife are one person; but understand in what manner. When a small brooke or little river incorporateth with Rhodanus, Humber, or the Thames, the poor rivulet looseth her name; it is carried and recarried with the new associate; it beareth no sway; it possesseth nothing during coverture. A woman as soon as she is married, is called *covert;* in Latine *nupta,* that is, "veiled"; as it were, clouded and overshadowed; she hath lost her streame. I may more truly, farre away, say to a married woman, Her new self is her superior; her companion, her master . . . Eve, because she had helped to seduce her husband, had inflicted upon her a special bane. See here the reason of that which I touched before,—that women have no voice in Parliament. They make no laws, they consent to none, they abrogate none. All of them are understood either married, or to be married, and their desires are to their husbands. I know no remedy, that some can shift it well enough. The common laws here shaketh hand with divinitye.[1]

This idea of the unity of husband and wife was a fundamental principle of the law in the southern colonies. Here, as in England, all women were without political rights, and generally wives were legal nonentities.[2] Single women, however, were considered as fully com-

---

[1] *The Lawes Resolutions of Womens Rights: Or, the Lawes Provision for Women.* London, 1632.

[2] In the early days of the colonies, when frontier conditions prevailed and there were few trained lawyers and legal textbooks here, the technicalities of the English common law were sometimes dispensed with and occasionally married women brought suit in their own names and were allowed other privileges in court which would have been denied them by the more learned English jurists. But with the increase of population and wealth, colonial attorneys came more and more to get their training in England and to rely upon English legal treatises and cases. In the colonies of the South, particularly, which from the beginning were more orthodox in legal, as well as religious, matters than Puritan New England, there was general acceptance of the principles of the English laws governing women. An examination of numerous files of county court records and other legal records in the southern

petent persons for all the purposes of private law. They brought
suit in court and were sued, made contracts, executed deeds, disposed
of their estates by last will and testament, administered the estates
of deceased husbands or relatives, and served as guardians of minors.
The records contain the names of a few spinsters and of numerous
widows in court in the exercise of their rights as citizens.

But as soon as a woman married her legal existence was suspended or incorporated into that of her husband, who was regarded
as her head and lord. She could have no will or property of her
own. The acceptance of the common law doctrine of the dominion
of the husband over the person of his wife is indicated in the texts
of numerous advertisements by colonial husbands of their runaway
wives. These notices usually state that the wife has "eloped" or
"absented herself" from her husband's bed and board, and threaten
any person who "harbours or entertains" her with "the utmost rigour
of the law." The implication throughout is that the husband had a
vested right in the company and services of his wife and that anyone
giving assistance to an absconding wife was acting to deprive the husband of a legal possession just as much as if he were aiding a runaway
slave or a servant.

How far colonial judges would have gone in upholding the claims
of these husbands does not appear, for few cases involving fugitive
wives were brought before them. Not many justices, probably, would
have concurred with a court of Northumberland County, Virginia,
who, upon complaint by a husband against his absconding wife, issued
this order: "Whereas it appears to this Co:rt yt Sarah ye Wife of Paul
Littlefield hath demeaned herself very scandalously, and refuseth to
live with her husband; It is ordered yt Wm. Flowery Constable for
ye South side of Wororomake take ye sd Sarah into safe Custody &
convey her unto ye next Constable for so to be carryd from Constable
to Constable untill she be deliv'd unto her sd Husband Paul Littlefield at ye Plantation of Mr. Robt King in Stafford County."[3] A
recognition by other justices of the husband's proprietary interest in
the person of his wife is indicated in an order by an Augusta County

---

colonies has disclosed very few departures from these principles. For a discussion
of the theories of the extent to which the English law was transplanted to America
and the peculiar rights enjoyed by women under early American law, see Richard
B. Morris, *Studies in the History of American Law* (New York and London, 1930),
particularly, Chaps. I and III.

[3] MS, Northumberland County Order Book, No. 2 (1666-1678), p. 14.

court against Joseph Collet, who was charged by Henry Brown with "robing him of his wife and sundry Goods."[4]

The husband's control over the wife's person extended to the right of giving her chastisement. "Her will ought to become his will," declared an early commentator, and "to make her obedient thereunto, the Common-law doth seem to allow him to give her lawfull and reasonable chastisement."[5] But he was not entitled to inflict permanent injury or death on his wife, and if he exceeded his legal prerogatives, she could have him bound to keep the peace. Many instances appear in the colonial records of a wife's appealing to the court for protection against the ill-usage of her husband. The justices usually ordered the offending husband to appear in court and give security for his good behavior, but occasionally they fined or gave him corporal punishment.[6] Judges recognized the husband's right to give his wife corporal punishment, however. An order of a Maryland court in 1681 expresses what appears to have been an orthodox opinion. This order was to the sheriff of Charles County and explained that Jane, wife of John Bread, had made supplication to the court complaining that she had been "grievously and manifestly threatened" by her husband of her life and of "mutilation of her members." It instructed the sheriff to summon the husband and have him give bond not to do "any damage or evil" to his wife "otherwise than what to a husband, by cause of government and chastisement of his own wife, lawfully and reasonably belongeth."[7]

In a number of cases when the court was convinced that a woman's life was endangered by the abuse of her husband, it allowed her to live away from him and required him to furnish her a separate maintenance. Mary Taylor in 1699 complained that her husband was "so cross and cruel" that she could not live with him and asked for

[4] Lyman Chalkley, *Chronicles of the Scotch-Irish in Virginia*, I, 74.

[5] Edmund Wingate, *Maximes of Reason . . .*, p. 771.

[6] Joseph Johnson of Virginia, arraigned in 1625 for "ye Contynuall squabbling and misusinge" of his wife, was required only to give bond for his behavior, but Thomas Wilson was set in the stocks and fined for the same offense.—*Minutes of the Council and General Court of Colonial Virginia*, pp. 62-63, 70. Upon proof by Sarah Gibson that her husband had beat her violently so that she was wounded "in a Lamentable Condicon," a Virginia court ordered that she be at liberty to go to England as she desired.—*Ibid.*, p. 452. Ezekiel Adams of South Carolina was given thirty-five lashes for abusing his wife and absenting himself from tatoo.—*South Carolina Magazine*, V, 88. John Mason was fined ten pounds for assaulting his wife.—*South Carolina Gazette and Country Journal*, May 31, 1774.

[7] Bread's Case, 2 Bland's Chancery *Reports*, 562.

separate maintenance in a home of her own where she would be "secure from danger." The court ordered her husband to deliver up her furniture and wearing apparel and to allow her twelve hundred pounds of tobacco or six pounds sterling annually for her support.[8] Elizabeth, wife of William Wildy, a landholder and officer of Northumberland County, Virginia, in 1700 charged her husband with gross cruelties, claiming that he beat and maimed her, put her into the fire and held her there until her clothes burned, and many times had threatened to shoot her. She declared that she was forced to depend upon her mother's charity and asked that her husband be compelled to allow her an "annual pension" suitable to her condition. The justices ordered that Wildy be summoned to appear before the next court to answer this complaint and if he failed to appear, that his wife be allowed relief out of his estate.[9] Becknell Alverson, charged with abusing his wife and refusing to entertain her, was in 1723 ordered to deliver to her her wearing apparel and pay her four hundred and fifty pounds of tobacco yearly until they should agree to cohabit again.[10]

In other cases of marital differences courts sometimes allowed the wife a separate maintenance. The amount of alimony was usually proportionate to the social status of the wife and the estate she brought her husband at the marriage. Robert and Elizabeth Leshley declared before the council of Maryland in 1676-1678 that they had resolved never to live together again. She desired an allowance commensurate with the estate she had at her marriage, and he agreed to allow her whatever the governor and council decided was fit.[11] Elizabeth Tennisson complained in 1680 that she could not live with her husband without danger to her person and prayed for a competent maintenance. John Tennisson denied her allegation of cruelty, but confessed he could not love her or afford her the countenance in his house properly due a wife. The council ordered that he deliver

[8] Bruce, *Social Life of Virginia*, p. 243.

[9] MS, Northumberland County Order Book, No. 4 (1699-1713), Pt. I, pp. 119-20.

[10] In 1707 Margaret, wife of Thomas Macnamara, complained before a Maryland court of brutal cruelties and other outrageous treatment by her husband. When summoned to answer the complaint, Thomas refused to appear, claiming that the court had no jurisdiction in the matter. But the chancellor, convinced by his own knowledge as well as "undeniable testimonies" of Macnamara's barbarity, ordered that he deliver to his wife her clothes and pay her yearly fifteen pounds sterling.—Macnamara's Case (1707), 2 Bland's Chancery *Reports*, 566-67; *Archives of Maryland*, XXV, 229-30.   [11] *Ibid.*, XV, 206-7.

to her one good bed and furniture, her wearing apparel, and allow her yearly three hundred pounds of meat, three barrels of corn, and one thousand pounds of tobacco.[12]

In all these cases only a separation from bed and board was granted. In the southern colonies there was no tribunal empowered to decree an absolute divorce. There seems to have been considerable uncertainty in the minds of the justices as to whether they had the right to decree a separate maintenance. In England separations were ordered only by the ecclesiastical courts. Here there were neither church courts nor statutes giving existing courts jurisdiction in such matters. Moreover, under the English law alimony could not be allowed in an independent action, but only as incident to a divorce.[13] So colonial justices, dubious of their authority to force an unwilling husband to pay alimony to his wife, probably entertained petitions for such relief only as necessary remedies in extreme circumstances.

In these separations no question seems to have arisen regarding the custody of the children. The father's rights were probably considered as indisputable under every circumstance. The English law gave the father authority over his children even after his death, for he might by his will or deed dispose of the custody not only of living children but also of one unborn. According to Blackstone, a mother had no legal right over her children, but was entitled only to reverence and respect.[14] Colonial fathers were insured these same

[12] Ibid., XV, 321-22. See also the case of Cannady v. Cannady, ibid., X, 471. The Grand Council of South Carolina in 1692 ordered Peter La Salle to cohabit with his wife, Jan La Salle, and maintain her as his wife or pay her six pounds sterling annually and allow her the Negro woman she had at her marriage.— Journal of the Grand Council of South Carolina, April 11, 1692-September 26, 1692, p. 17. Outstanding cases of separate maintenance in Maryland were Galwith v. Galwith, 1689, 4 Harris and McHenry Reports, p. 477; Codd v. Codd, 1727, 1 Bland's Chancery Reports, 101, Sarah Wright's Case, 1730, ibid., pp. 101-2; Lynthecumb's Case, 1738, Scott's Case, 1746, Govanne's Case, 1750, 2 Bland's Chancery Reports, 568-74. Virginia cases were Fulcher v. Fulcher, Calendar of Virginia State Papers, I, 20; Brown v. Brown, 1765, "Augusta County Records," in Chalkley's Chronicles of the Scotch-Irish, I, 122, 334, 341; Archer v. Archer, 1772, ibid., p. 365; Purcell v. Purcell, 4 Hening and Munford's Reports, 506; and Almond v. Almond, 4 Randolph Reports, 662.

[13] George E. Howard, History of Matrimonial Institutions Chiefly in England and the United States (3 vols. Chicago, 1904), II, 366-76.

[14] Commentaries (ed., Judge Christian), I, 438, 452, 462. Judges before whom cases involving the custody of children were brought after the Revolution declared that there had been no precedent for depriving a father of the custody of his child even in cases in which his brutal treatment and licentious conduct had made it necessary for the child's mother to separate from him.—Case of Jennett Prather, 1809,

rights by the statutes which had been passed in the colonies.[15]

The general idea of the father's supreme control in the education of his children is illustrated in an opinion of a Virginia council in a case which came before it in 1708. George Walker was a Quaker and Ann, his wife, a member of the Church of England. Ann objected to having her children brought up as Quakers and complained to the council. Recalling the hostility of the Virginia authorities toward Quakers, we should expect the councillors to have decided in favor of the orthodox disputant. But respect for a husband's authority was greater even than prejudice against heretics, and the rights of the Quaker husband were maintained against those of the Anglican wife. The councillors declared that the husband was only exercising his lawful rights in insisting upon having his children brought up in his own religion. No person, whatever, they insisted, should undertake to persuade any man's children against the instructions of the father. They pointed out to Ann her husband's generosity in permitting her the liberty of enjoying her own religion and declared that she should leave the children's religious instruction to him and "forbare" to interpret or expound to them any portion of Scripture without his "leave or advice."[16]

Colonial fathers, by their last wills and testaments, frequently appointed guardians for the estates of their children, but only in rare cases did they assign their custody and tuition to anyone other than their mothers. Sometimes the husband appointed his wife guardian only so long as she remained a widow, and provided that if she married again certain persons whom he named were to have the care of the children. The husband wrote of his and his wife's children as if they were his alone. One testator, for example, declared in his

---

4 Desaus, 33. S. C. *Rep.*, Book 21, pp. 14-17; Threewits *v.* Threewits, 4 Desaus, 560, S. C. *Rep.*, Book 21, pp. 225-31. See also *Ex parte* Oliver Hewitt, 11 Rich. 326, S. C. *Rep.*, Book 18, pp. 110-11; Helms *v.* Franciscus, 2 Bland's Chancery *Reports* (Maryland), 217-20; and Perkins *v.* Dyer, 6 Ga. *Rep.*, 401-4.

[15] A Virginia act of 1748 provided that a father, by deed or will, might dispose of the custody of all his unmarried infant children, including those not born at his death.—Hening, *Statutes*, V, 449. Similar acts were passed in the Carolinas.— Cooper, *Statutes of South Carolina*, III, 708; *State Records of North Carolina*, XXIII, 577. A Maryland act of 1729 provided that if a man being a Protestant should die and leave a widow with a child and his widow should marry a Catholic or be herself of that faith, it should be lawful for the governor and council, upon application made to them, to remove such child out of the custody of the mother and place him where he would be educated in the Protestant religion.—*Archives of Maryland*, XXV, 496. [16] *Virginia Magazine*, XVI, 79-81.

will: "In consideration of the entire confidence reposed in my ever dear and affectionate wife I do will and appoint that she shall have the sole guardianship and tuition of all my children so long as she continues single and in case of her death or marriage during the minority of any of my children then I will and appoint that my much esteemed and sincere friends Thomas Blackburn and William Alexander Esqrs shall have the guardianship and tuition of them during their minority."[17]   His wife was the mother of these children. Captain Joseph Ball of Virginia provided in 1720 that his brothers have the tuition of his children and the management of their estates, but added: "Notwithstanding it is my desire that they do not take my children from their dear mother, upon any account than as they shall think reasonable for the better educating them, nor their estate without she marry again, and that her husband should prove unkind to my children, and not take provident care of them and their estate, that then my desire is that my said brothers take upon them the whole care of my children and the management of their estate."[18]

The custom of appointing a guardian other than the mother was not usually due to lack of confidence in the ability or affection of the mother, but was a means of protecting a child and his estate from a possible unscrupulous stepfather. As under the law a wife and all she possessed became subject to her husband's authority, a mother, however capable and desirous she might be of looking after the interests of her children, would not be in a position to protect them from the abuse of her second husband. If anyone else were guardian, he could sue the stepfather for waste of the orphan's estate or bring him into court for mistreatment of the ward, but the mother would be disqualified from suing her husband or giving testimony against him.

The married woman in the southern colonies was under the same general disabilities as in England, though in a few instances she was apparently allowed greater freedom. As a rule she could not make a valid contract, bring suit or be sued in court, execute a deed, administer an estate, or make a will. A case before a county court in Virginia sometime about 1678 illustrates the manner in which courts occasionally attempted to administer justice and at the same time do lip service to the English law. Elizabeth Jones complained that John Courtney had failed to perform the conditions of an agreement made with her concerning the occupation of her son's plantation, and asked

[17] Hayden, *Virginia Genealogies*, pp. 603-4.   [18] *Ibid.*, p. 66.

for his ejection. The court declared that as the plaintiff was under
coverture and therefore incapable of making any contract, the agreement was void. But, at the same time, they ordered that Courtney
be ejected from the plantation.[19] A case came before a Maryland
court involving an agreement between the wife of Walter Pakes and
John Trussell by which Mistress Pakes had covenanted to cure
Trussell's servant for one hundred pounds of tobacco. The doctress
was questioned as to what power she, a married woman, had to make
a contract, but she answered that she had a letter of attorney from
her husband "to doe any business whatsoever."[20]

A number of married women appeared in the courts to conduct
business as agents of their husbands. Frances Kitching, wife and attorney of Robert Kitching, answered a suit brought against him in a
North Carolina court in 1695,[21] and Mary Jennings had a power
from her husband to "get in his debts," let his plantation, and sell
his sheep, mares, and other stock.[22] Restituta Hallowes and Ann
Dandy acted as attorneys for their husbands in the Maryland courts.[23]
Anne, wife of John Hammond, had a letter from him authorizing
her to "act, doe, Say, Implead, buy, sell, order & dispose of" anything belonging to him whatsoever, "in as full and ample power as
may or can be Exprest, and as if my Self were personally present."
Armed with this power, Mistress Anne appeared frequently in court
in the management of business affairs.[24] But the governor and council of Maryland apparently did not approve of allowing married
women such freedom, for in 1658 they forbade husbands to appoint
their wives as attorneys for them, and requested that in their absence
they appoint other persons instead.[25]

In a few rare cases a wife brought suit in her own name for debts
due her before her marriage,[26] but usually suits of this kind were
brought by the husband alone or in the name of both husband and

[19] MS, Northumberland County Order Book, No. 3 (1678-1698), Pt. I, p. 115.
[20] Archives of Maryland, X, 15-16.
[21] Colonial Records of North Carolina, I, 443.
[22] William and Mary Quarterly, VII, 231.
[23] Archives of Maryland, X, 100, 443.
[24] Ibid., X, 449, 463, 467, 472, 492, 494, 526, 527, 528.
[25] Ibid., XLI, 233. For a wife to act as attorney for her husband was in keeping with the common law.—Blackstone, Commentaries, I, 443.
[26] Diana (Foster) White (Colonial Records of North Carolina, I, 478, 488);
Katharine Hebden (Archives of Maryland, X, 122, 415); and Elizabeth Smith
(ibid., p. 422).

wife. To prevent a married woman's claims from elapsing because of her inability to bring action for them and her husband's neglecting to sue for her, so-called "saving clauses" were incorporated within the various statutes of limitations. A Virginia act of 1657-58, for example, provided that suits for lands were to be commenced within five years or the claimant would be forever barred, but stated that orphans, "feme coverts," and those "non compos mentis" should be allowed five years in which to bring suit after the removal of their disabilities.[27] A Maryland act of 1729 declared: "All actions upon administration and testamentary bonds shall be commenced within twelve years after passing the bond, and not after. Saving to infants, Femme Covert, Non Compos, imprisoned, or beyond sea, a right of bringing such actions within five years after disability removed."[28]

The case of Susannah Cooper, who in 1744 presented a petition to the Virginia House of Burgesses, illustrates some of the disabilities of married women under the law. She stated that at her marriage with Isles Cooper in 1717 she had possessed a considerable personal estate, but that he had been without property. In less than three years after the marriage he had deserted her, after having first spent most of the estate she brought him and contracted debts for which his creditors had taken the remainder after his departure. She had been reduced to the utmost misery and was obliged for a time to depend upon the charity of her friends and relatives for support. A short time after leaving her, her husband had married another wife, and at her death shortly after, had married a third wife, by whom he had several children. She had not heard from him in twenty years, during which time she had by her industry purchased a few slaves and acquired a small estate. But she was at a great disadvantage in not being able to dispose of any of her property, as no purchaser would treat with her on account of her coverture. In her situation she was exposed to many injuries. Some people committed

---

[27] Hening, *Statutes*, I, 451.

[28] *Laws of Maryland* (ed., Maxcy), I, 202-4. A Georgia act of 1767 provided that actions of ejectments be limited to seven years after the action accrued, except in cases of "feme-coverts, non compos mentis, imprisoned, or beyond seas."—*Digest of Georgia Laws* (ed., Oliver H. Prince), p. 315. South Carolina had an act providing that unclaimed lands be advertised and, if not claimed within a year, that they escheat to the state, but with this proviso: "That nothing herein contained shall prejudice the rights of individuals having legal title, who may be under the disabilities of infancy, coverture, lunacy, or beyond the limits of the United States."— *Statutes at Large of South Carolina* (ed., D. J. McCord), VI, 48.

trespasses on her tenements and others refused to perform their contracts with her, from which wrongs she could maintain no action because of her coverture. Also she desired to make provision for her son and leave him her estate, but could not make a will so long as her husband was living. In compliance with her request, the burgesses passed an act enabling her to make contracts, sue and be sued, and to dispose of her estate, and directing that none of her property be liable to the debts, control, or disposition of Isles Cooper, provided that she did not claim any part of his estate.[29]

The general features of the English laws regarding woman's inheritance and ownership of property were in force in the colonies. These rules showed a preference for sons over daughters in the distribution of intestate estates and conferred upon husbands enormous powers over the property of their wives. Under the law of primogeniture, the eldest son inherited all the real estate of which his father died seized to the exclusion of all female and younger male descendants. In the absence of sons, daughters inherited as coparceners, that is, as joint heirs.[30] This law was in force in all the southern colonies until after the Revolution.

In the division of the personal estates of intestates, females were admitted with males. Statutes provided that if a husband died without a will and left not more than two children, one-third of his personalty passed to his widow and the other two-thirds was divided equally between his children. If there were more than two children, the widow received only a child's part; that is, for example, if there were a widow and five children, the widow and each of the five children received a sixth of the estate. If there were no widow, the estate was divided equally among the children or their legal representatives. The heir at law, notwithstanding any lands he might have received by descent or otherwise, had equal share with the other children in the distribution of the personal estate. If there were no children or legal representatives of children, the widow was entitled to one-half the estate and the other half was divided among the husband's next of kin or their legal representatives, but no represent-

[29] Hening, *Statutes*, V, 294-96.
[30] Blackstone, *Commentaries*, II, 213-15. Males were also preferred in the matter of lineal inheritances, that is, kindred derived from the blood of male ancestors however remote were admitted before those from the blood of the female however near, except in those cases in which the lands had in fact descended from the female.— *Ibid.*, 235.

atives were admitted among collaterals after brothers and sisters. If there were no legal representative, the widow was entitled to the whole of the personal estate after the debts were paid.[31]

In making provision for their wives and children in their last wills and testaments, the colonists often followed the direction of the law. The most common type of will was that in which the testator bequeathed a third of his personalty and a life interest in a third of his realty to his wife and divided the rest among his children. Sometimes the testator whose children were still infants left his wife the use of all his property during her lifetime, but directed that at her death the remainder should go to his children. Occasionally the husband who had neither children nor grandchildren living gave his entire estate, real and personal, to his wife, but oftener he left her a life estate and gave the remainder to his collateral relatives. Lawrence Washington, for example, devised to his wife, Anne Fairfax Washington, the use of his "Mount Vernon" estate for her lifetime, but gave the estate in fee to his brother, George Washington.[32]

In many wills in which the husband gave his wife more of his estate than the law required, he bequeathed it to her on condition that she did not remarry. John Godfrey of South Carolina, for instance, devised his whole estate to his wife during her life, but directed that if she should marry again she should have only her thirds as the law required.[33] Rowland Burnham of Virginia distributed his estate among his wife and several children and directed: "My will is that my wife shall enjoy the third part of the house & clear ground for the imployment of her servants during her widowhood & no longer but then [after her remarriage] to depart without injureing the houses or drawing a naile about [out] or in any of them."[34]

Augustine Washington, father of George Washington, left his best plantation with the cattle and stock on it to his oldest son, Law-

---

[31] *Laws of Maryland* (ed., Bacon), Act of 1715, Chap. 39; Hening, *Statutes*, III, 373-74; *Colonial Records of North Carolina*, II, 282; *Public Laws of South Carolina* (ed., Grimké), p. 81; *Colonial Records of Georgia*, III, 378-79.

[32] Anne soon married as a second husband Colonel George Lee, who made an arrangement with Washington whereby Washington was to take immediate possession of "Mount Vernon" and pay him annually fifteen thousand pounds of tobacco. This amount Colonel Lee received from Washington until Anne's death terminated his interest in the property and gave Washington a clear title.—Charles Moore, *Family Life of Washington*, p. 38.

[33] *South Carolina Magazine*, XVI, 134-36.

[34] MS, Lancaster County Order Book, No. II, p. 46.

rence, and his next best to his other son by his first wife. He gave each of his sons by his second wife small plantations and made little provision for his second wife. He provided that the estates of his sons by his second wife be left in their mother's hands until they should come of age, but instructed that if she should remarry and her second husband refused to give security for the sons' estates, his executors should take these sons and their property out of the custody and tuition of their mother.[35] The Reverend John Scott of Virginia evidently sought to restrain his wife from a second matrimonial venture by this provision in his will: "I give and bequeath to my dear and loved wife Elizabeth during her widowhood one half of all my estate above mentioned on condition that she accept the same in lieu of all marriage settlements and dower but if (contrary to my present hopes and opinion of her respect to my memory and tenderness for the welfare and happiness of her infant children) she should marry, then it is my will that this bequest be wholly void and that she have only such part of my estate as the law will give her."[36] A rare exception to the type of husband represented by the Reverend Scott was John Ball of North Carolina, who, after giving all his personal estate to his wife with the direction that she was to have the free disposal of it "how & to whom she pleases," added this extraordinary instruction: "Also my Will and Desire is that in Case my Loving Wife Do marry that then her husband and She Do Remain upon my now Dwelling Plantation During her Naturall Life and Injoy the Same with all the Rights and Privileges in as Large and ample manner as She did in my Life Time."[37]

Usually a part of the property which a testator disposed of in his will had come to him by marriage. So in many cases a wife was given property which was formerly hers on condition that she did not marry, and in others she received only a part of what had been hers at the marriage. Thomas Hebden apparently acquired his estate from Katharine, his wife, at marriage, and during the marriage collected and appropriated compensation for her services as a surgeon. At one time he made a will giving her the whole of his estate, but later he revoked it and by a deed of gift made over all his property to three friends in trust. He gave Katharine a life interest in the whole estate and the right to dispose of a third part, but provided

[35] *Letters to Washington* (ed., Hamilton), III, Appendix, 394.
[36] Hayden, *Virginia Genealogies*, pp. 602-4.
[37] MS, Chowan County Papers, 1685-1738.

that the other two-thirds be disposed of by the trustees. She complained to him of his unkindness in disposing thus of the estate he had acquired with her at marriage and he assured her that the will he first made would stand. But after his death the court upheld the deed of gift rather than the will and she took only a life estate in what had been her own property.[38]

Occasionally the husband bequeathed to his wife the property which had come to him through her. Charles Carroll of Annapolis left his wife certain properties in place of her dower, and in addition made the following provision for her: "In case any gift or legacy be made to my wife during my life, or that any devisional part of the estate of any parent or Relation fall to her in that time, my will is that it be reckoned no part of my Estate, but [I] do hereby give the same to my said Wife, to be disposed of as she shall think fitt."[39] Governor Arthur Dobbs of North Carolina bequeathed his wife and any child she might have by him all the slaves and other chattels which had been or thereafter should be given her by her father.[40] Peter Gourdin of South Carolina was one of the very rare husbands who devised the property that came to him from his wife to her relatives rather than his own. He bequeathed all his estate to his son, Peter, but instructed that if Peter died before coming to the age of nineteen, the estate which came to him from his first wife, Esther Sullivan, should be given to his brother-in-law, John Sullivan, and his sister-in-law, Margaret (Sullivan) Richbourgh, and that all that came to him with his last wife, Ann Lester, should return to her brother and sister.[41]

Provisions which seem strange today are those in which a husband bequeathed his wife her own clothing, jewels, and other intimate personal articles. Persons of all classes in colonial times included wearing apparel and jewelry in their estates and disposed of them along with lands and Negroes. It was customary for a husband to bequeath his wife her own clothing and jewelry, if she survived him, and if she died before him to give these personal possessions to her daughters. James Hughes of Virginia gave most of his estate to his

---

[38] *Archives of Maryland*, IV, 511-12, 519, 548; X, 418.

[39] Rowland, *Life of Charles Carroll*, II, 378.

[40] *State Records of North Carolina*, XXII, 301.

[41] William W. Boddie, *History of Williamsburg, Something about the People of Williamsburg County, South Carolina, from the First Settlement by Europeans about 1705 until 1923* (Columbia, S. C., 1923), pp. 77-78.

second wife during her life, but bequeathed to his daughter by his first wife her mother's wearing apparel and sidesaddle.[42] Wilson Cary of "Celeys" in Virginia left his wife, along with other property, "her cabinet gold watch and rings."[43] John Custis bequeathed his wife "all her Wearing Apparel both Linen and Woollen of what nature soever they be, and Silks with all her Rings, Jewells, and a Gold chain, or locket."[44] All husbands were not so generous, however. The Reverend Caspar Stoever, Sr., minister of the Evangelical German Lutheran Congregation in Virginia, made a bequest to his wife with this proviso, "That during my absence she behaved herself as a good wife and that she did not slander my office and honor with her wicked tongue and thereby gave offense. In such case everything shall be taken from her from the greatest to the least, even including the clothes on her body, since they all came from me, and shall be added to the share of the children."[45]

A wife was not bound to accept a will in which her husband bequeathed her less than a third of his personal property and a life interest in a third of his lands, but was entitled to a choice between a devise and her legal thirds. Many entries like the following appear in the county court records: "Sarah Day the late wife of William Herbert Deceased came into Court and objected to the will of her said late husband & Claimed her thirds of the said William Herberts Estate. Whereupon William Preston, James McCorkle . . . [and others] are appointed to allot of the said Sarah's Dower of the said Estate agreeable to Law."[46]

In making provision for children by last will and testament, fathers sometimes followed the principle of the law of primogeniture and entail. John Daniel of Virginia, for instance, in 1685 divided his personal estate among his wife and all his children without regard to sex and devised his real property to his eldest son with the direction that should he die without heirs, it should pass to the second son. If he too should die without heirs, it should descend to the third son,

[42] Lyman Chalkley, *Chronicles of the Scotch-Irish*, III, 96.
[43] Fairfax Harrison, *The Virginia Carys* (New York, 1919), p. 175.
[44] *Letters to Washington* (ed., Hamilton), III, 383.
[45] *Virginia Magazine*, XIV, 163.
[46] MS, Fincastle County Minutes, 1773-1777, p. 222. One very rare case was found of a wife's objecting to her husband's will on the grounds of his insanity. Elizabeth Black contested the will of her husband, David Black, maintaining that he was insane at the time of making it, but her objections were overruled and the will was recorded.—Lyman Chalkley, *Chronicles of the Scotch-Irish*, I, 160.

and if the third and last son should die without heirs, it should go to the eldest daughter, and then to the second and youngest daughter in case of the death of the oldest without heirs.[47] Oftener the testator gave the home place and best plantation to his first-born, divided the remaining realty among his other sons, and gave his daughters legacies in money, household goods, and other personalty. In a few wills lands as well as personal property were divided equally among all the sons and daughters, but these were exceptional. Many testamentary provisions indicate a strong prejudice in favor of lands descending only to sons. Thomas Lawson of Virginia provided, for example: "To ye Child my Wife now goes with if it be a Boy ye planta[tion] where I formerly Lived . . . & to his heires for Ever but If it Should be a Girle then ye sd Land to goe to ye heire."[48] Colonel William Burgess of Maryland left large tracts of land to each of his sons, but bequeathed to each of his daughters only three hundred pounds in money, plate, and other personal property.[49] Thomas Smithson of North Carolina devised to his son, Joshua, his plantation on which he lived, explaining that it was to go "to him and his ears [heirs], and so from eair to eair so long as there is a Smithson to be found." To his other sons he left lands, and to each of his daughters he bequeathed one Negro.[50] David Maybank, a South Carolina carpenter, bequeathed to each of his three daughters a Negro and a small sum of money and devised his plantation and a hundred pounds in money to his son.[51]

So strong was the feeling that lands should descend to male members of a family that testators sometimes devised them to brothers or nephews rather than to daughters. Francis Lightfoot of Virginia, possessor of a large real and personal estate, bequeathed to his daughter one thousand pounds sterling to be placed at interest until she should be of age or marry and devised all the rest of his estate, real and personal, to his son, Francis. To insure the continuance of the lands in the male line, he inserted this clause: "But in Case my s'd Son dies with'd such Male Issue or there be any Failure thereafter in the Male line, then I give all my Estate Real and Personal to

[47] Bruce, *Social Life of Virginia*, p. 125.

[48] *Lower Norfolk County Virginia Antiquary*, I, 48.

[49] Joshua Dorsey Warfield, *Founders of Anne Arundel and Howard Counties, Maryland* (Baltimore, 1905), p. 52.

[50] Grimes, *Abstract of North Carolina Wills*, p. 349.

[51] *South Carolina Magazine*, V, 101-2.

my well beloved Brother Phillip Lightfoot and his Heirs forever he or they paying to the Daughters of my s'd Son, or in Case there be none such, to my Daughter Elizabeth 2500 £ Current money of Virginia in full Compensation of the same."[52]   Colonel William Churchill left his lands to his sons with this provision: "If son Thomas should die without an heir, then my land shall be equally divided between the sons of my brothers, John and Armistead Churchill, they paying my daughters, each of them, 2,000 pounds, and if they do not choose to take the land on these terms, then if my son should die, the land must be equally divided between all my daughters."[53]

Sometimes the oldest son who was given all the lands of his father inherited liabilities in proportion. Out of the income from these lands he was expected to educate younger brothers and pay his sisters' marriage portions, and assume responsibility for all the dependent members of the family. Occasional advertisements like the following, signed by Nelson Berkeley, show how estates descending to the eldest son were sometimes encumbered: "To discharge my Sisters Fortunes, I will sell at private Sale 15 or 20 valuable Slaves (in Families) among them is a good Blacksmith, an excellent Laundry Servant, several good Spinners, Boys and Girls of different Ages."[54]   The petition of Ralph Wormley to the Virginia House of Burgesses in 1738, requesting that the entail of some of his lands be docked so that he might be enabled to pay his sisters' portions, also suggests the responsibilities sometimes borne by the heir. Out of the profits of the estate, he was expected to maintain three sisters and a younger brother, who was to be educated in England. At their coming of age or marriage, he was to give a portion of eight hundred pounds sterling to one sister and five hundred pounds to each of the other two, and was to pay an annuity of one hundred pounds sterling to the younger brother on his coming of age. He stated in his petition that he had maintained the younger brother and sisters, but was unable to pay his sisters' portions without disposing of some of the entailed lands.[55]   Only a few elder brothers, however, inherited such great responsibilities. Usually the heir was favored by his father's will as well as the law.

[52] Lightfoot v. Lightfoot, *Virginia Colonial Decisions* (ed., R. T. Barton), I, 84.

[53] Du Bellet, *Some Prominent Virginia Families*, II, 508.

[54] *Virginia Gazette*, December 26, 1777.

[55] *Journals of the House of Burgesses*, VI, 334.

The colonial law regarding the rights of husband and wife in the property of each other was like that in England. At marriage the husband came into immediate and absolute possession of all his wife's personal property and during the marriage was entitled to take into his possession any personalty to which she became entitled, such as debts due her, arrears of rent, loans, or any bequest of personalty. What he thus obtained by marriage could be disposed of to anyone or in any way he chose during his life or by his last will and testament, and also could be taken by his creditors to pay his debts contracted either before or during the marriage. The husband did not acquire absolute possession of his wife's lands, but became entitled to the use of all her real estate with the right to collect the rents and profits and use them as his own.[56] If he had issue by her born alive and capable of inheriting her estate, he held her lands upon her death as tenant for life by the curtesy of England. This right endured even in cases in which the wife died leaving no living children and the inheritance fell to her collateral kinsmen and in cases in which the husband married a second time.[57]

Besides absolute possession of his wife's personal property and a life estate in her lands, the husband took any other income that might be hers. He collected wages earned by her labor and could without her assent give a discharge for any demand arising from her services. Naturally it followed that the proceeds of the joint labor of husband and wife belonged to the husband. Damages allowed by the court for injuries suffered by the wife were also the property of the husband. If as the next of kin a wife were entitled to administer an estate, her husband was given the administration in her place. At the death of the wife, the husband had the exclusive right to administer her estate. She could not by a will appoint another as executor; nor had the court the power to refuse the husband letters of administration.

[56] Sir Frederick Pollock and Frederic William Maitland, *History of the English Law before the Time of Edward I* (2 vols. 2d ed., Cambridge, 1898), II, 401-3, 414-17.

[57] It has been observed that the origin of the name of this privilege is found in the peculiarly favorable light in which English husbands were regarded by the law, that the husband claimed a life estate in the lands of his wife, not according to Norman law, which deprived him of this right when he married again, nor according to the Scottish law, which allowed him the use of those lands which his wife inherited and not in those given her, but by the special "curtesy of England."— *Ibid.*, pp. 414-17.

Colonial husbands appear to have claimed and enjoyed all of these marital privileges allowed by the common law. Numerous court orders like the following illustrate the general acceptance of the husband's rights: "It appeareing to this Honoble Court by oath that *Bennett Marjorum* Did Bequeath his Estate vnto Mrs. Agnes Marble wife of Mr. Geo: marble It is therefore ordered by this Court that James Alsapp deliver vnto the said Mr. Marble in Rt of his wife the said marjorums Estate Vppon his Oath, and that the said Mr. Marble enjoy the Same he paying his just Debts."[58] Typical of many other entries is one from a North Carolina record stating that upon the petition of Henry Bonner, praying that the estate of Deborah Whitby, his "now wife," be taken out of the hands of her guardian, Dennis Macclennon, it was ordered that the guardian deliver unto the petitioner all the estate of Deborah his wife.

Husbands frequently brought suit and received payment for debts due their wives before marriage and for wages and other compensation for their services. Suits for damages are more rare. In 1704 Colonel Phillip Lightfoot petitioned the Council of Virginia asking that a fine of five pounds sterling adjudged against John Geddes for an assault and battery on Alice Lightfoot, his wife, be paid to him, but it does not appear whether he received this compensation.[59] Many instances appear in the court records of the appointment of a husband to administer in the place of his wife, similar to the following extract from a North Carolina Council Journal: "Upon Petition of Richard Corp showing that Eliza Deane Widd [widow] is dead and hath made noe will and that he marry [married] ye only Daughter of ye said Deane therefor prays Administration on ye said Deane's Estate in right of his wife as nearest of Kin Ordered that Admtion [administration] be granted to ye said Richard Corpe as prayd."[60] Newspaper advertisements also furnish many examples of the assumption by husbands of these rights. Frequently, as stated in another connection, the account of the death of a husband was soon followed by the announcement of the marriage of the widow and a public notice by the second husband as administrator of his predecessor's estate.[61]

[58] *Minutes of the Council and General Court of Colonial Virginia*, p. 403.

[59] *Executive Journals of the Council of Colonial Virginia*, II, 398.

[60] *Colonial Records of North Carolina*, II, 71.

[61] Occasionally a husband and wife were appointed to act jointly as administrators or executors when the right fell to the wife. William Booth petitioned the General Court of North Carolina, July 28, 1713, explaining that he had married Hester,

A husband acquired by marriage whatever right his wife had in
the estate of her deceased husband. The case of George Washington,
who when a young man of small estate acquired a fortune by marriage with Martha Custis, illustrates some of the privileges conferred
upon husbands by the law. Daniel Parke Custis died intestate, leaving a son and a daughter. As heir-at-law the son inherited all his
father's lands and slaves, which were accounted real estate at the time.
The widow received as her dower the use for her lifetime of a third
of the lands and slaves. The personal estate, which was very large,
was divided equally among the widow and the children, each receiving about thirty-three thousand dollars. When, about seven months
after her husband's decease, Martha Custis married George Washington, her part of the personal property vested absolutely in her
new husband, and her dower right became his also. As second husband of the widow, Washington administered the Custis estate, and
as guardian of the Custis children, he managed their part of the
property. When the daughter died some years later, her part of the
estate was divided equally between her mother and her brother, and
the mother's part passed immediately to Washington as his own.[62]
Thomas Jefferson, who also married a rich widow, received as his
wife's dower in the lands of her former husband property worth
forty thousand dollars. About a year after his marriage, the death
of his wife's father brought him forty thousand acres more of land
and one hundred and thirty-five slaves, a fortune which he declared
was about equal to his own patrimony.[63]

Husbands also demanded compensation for the unpaid labors of
their predecessors. David Minetrie petitioned the Virginia House of
Burgesses asking that, as he had married the widow and administratrix of John Juce, he might be paid what was due to the deceased
Juce for salary and fees for keeping the public jail. The House
ordered his petition referred to the consideration of the committee for
public claims.[64] In the following letter from a Savannah citizen to

the "widow and relict" of Adam Lewis, deceased, and praying that he might have
administration of "ye Goods & Chattles" of the said Lewis. The court ordered that
Williams and Hester have administration "equally granted to them both."—*Colonial Records of North Carolina*, II, 102. See also *ibid.*, I, 452; II, 95.
   [62] Eugene E. Prussing, *The Estate of George Washington, Deceased* (Boston,
1927), pp. 93-98.
   [63] Curtis, *Thomas Jefferson*, pp. 33, 51-52.
   [64] *Journals of the House of Burgesses*, IV, 254.

the Georgia trustees, the writer excuses his failure to pay a debt on
the grounds that the colony had not paid him for services performed
by his wife's first husband:

I do assure Your Honors. [I] wou'd pay it with a great deal of pleasure
were it in my power, it being very just, but [I] have a considerable sume
of Mony due me from the Collony on Account of Mr. Roger Lacy deceased (I having married his Widow) but cannot receive a Shilling. I
believe your Honours may have heard of the Services of Mr. Lacey hath
done for the Collony by going as Agent to the Indian Nation twice, likewise settling a Town and building a Fort at Augusta Imploying Ten of his
own Men for a great many Months . . . Mr. Lacy hath Expended above
£500 in this Colony . . . nor did any Man take more pains in the province then himself, considering he went entirely upon his own Substance,
and I am very sorry to Acquaint your Honrs, that his Successor is undone
by it.[65]

The marital rights of wives were few compared with those of
husbands. The husband was liable for debts of his wife unpaid at
the marriage and for her contracts for necessaries during the marriage.
But if she displeased him, he could by giving public notice relieve
himself of responsibility for her contracts. Numerous advertisements appeared in the papers of husbands declaring they would not
be responsible for debts made by their wives. But the courts upheld
the wife's right to support from her husband, and, as has been observed, occasionally even granted her a separate maintenance. The
husband was also liable for the unpaid debts of his wife's former
husband. Secretary Stephens, in his relation of Georgia affairs in
1741, told of the disillusioning experience of one John Slack, who
had courted a widow assiduously and finally become engaged to her:
"But all this at last comes to nothing: Slack got Information, that
there were some Debts of her former Husband yet standing out
unpaid, and that there had been no Administration, wherefore he
would become liable to satisfy such Creditors which he stumbled at,
and his Interest outweighing his Love, thought it too great a Price
to pay for a wife."[66]

The most important proprietary right of the widow in her husband's estate was her dower. This was guarded so carefully that a
husband could not alienate his lands so as to bar his wife's right
without her concurrence. To protect her from coercion, the law re-

[65] *Colonial Records of Georgia*, XXII (Pt. II), 277-78.
[66] *Ibid.*, IV, Supplement, 100-1.

quired that before she could effectually relinquish her right of dower or convey her real estate she must be privately examined apart from her husband that the court might know whether she "made her acknowledgment willingly and freely, and without being induced thereto by fear of threats of, or ill usage by her husband, or fear of his displeasure."[67]   A South Carolina statute allowed the widow to renounce a jointure and claim dower, but forbade her having both jointure and dower.[68]   A Maryland act gave the widow the privilege of choosing between a devise and her thirds, but provided that she could not have both.   It also provided that any estate settled by jointure upon her by her husband before marriage would be a bar to her dower, but not to any devise in his will.[69]   Though the law gave the widow no absolute right to administer her husband's estate, the court usually preferred her claim to that of her husband's creditors or next of kin.   But it ordinarily required her to give security for her "faithful administration."

Besides her dower and share in her husband's personalty, the widow was entitled to her paraphernalia.   According to the common law, the wearing apparel and ornaments of a married woman which she had at the time of the marriage or which came to her during the marriage remained her husband's property, which he might dispose of during his life; but those which remained undisposed of at his death belonged thenceforth to her.[70]   In awarding the widow her paraphernalia, the court took into consideration her rank and the property she brought her husband at the marriage.   A court order of 1641 allowed the widow of Captain Thoroughgood of Virginia the following articles: one bed with its furnishings, two pairs of sheets and pillow cases, one table with carpet [tablecover], a tablecloth and some napkins, a cupboard and cupboard cloth, six chairs, six stools, six cushions, six pictures, a pewter basin and ewer, a warming pan, a pair of andirons, tongs, and a fire shovel, a child's wicker chair, a salt cellar, a bowl, a tankard, a wine cup, a dozen spoons, and some knives and forks.[71]   Elizabeth Green was allotted her bed, a chest, a pot,

[67] *Laws of Maryland* (ed., Maxcy), I, 127, 242; Hening, *Statutes*, II, 317; III, 319; V, 410-11; *Public Laws of South Carolina* (ed., Grimké), pp. 132, 292; *Digest of Georgia Laws* (ed., Prince), pp. 109-11.

[68] *Public Laws of South Carolina* (ed., Grimké), pp. 50-52.

[69] *Archives of Maryland*, XXXVIII, 41-42.

[70] Pollock and Maitland, *op. cit.*, II, 405.

[71] *Virginia Magazine*, II, 416-17.

two pewter dishes, and six spoons;[72] and Hannah Horner was allowed her wearing apparel, jewelry, a horse and sidesaddle, and one bed with its furnishings.[73] Widows in less well-to-do families naturally were awarded less. Ann Hales, for example, received only her wearing apparel and three barrels of corn, and Bridgett Prisbett was allowed to keep her clothes, a bed, and a pot.[74]

While the marital rights of husbands were jealously guarded by the courts, in extraordinary circumstances wives sometimes were allowed certain rights over their own property. Upon complaint by Joanne Sheapard that her husband had departed from the country "much ingaged," a Virginia court ordered that what she should earn by her own labor should be used by her "according to her disposition . . . without being lyable therewith to discharge her Husbands debts."[75] Rachell Price explained to a county court in 1707 that her husband had become a servant and incapable of supporting her and her children. She asked that she be allowed the privilege of using her own plantation and labor to maintain herself and children and that her husband be "barred from violently comeing & takeing away of her Goods, as also from turning her out of her sd plantation." The court granted her the benefit of her own and her children's labor and the use of her plantation free from molestation by her husband.[76] Justices were not always so ready to allow this benefit. Elizabeth Hall complained to a county court in 1709 stating that at the time of her marriage to Edward Hall she possessed "a plentiful estate," which he had squandered. He had later absconded and she had nothing but her labor for support. She prayed that she might have the benefit of her labor for her own use free from the claims of her husband's creditors. The court declared it thought "fitt that the said Pet[ition] Shall Lye untill such time as ye sd Elisabeth is troubled or molested in or about the Premises."[77]

Legislatures sometimes passed special measures enabling married women to control or dispose of their own property. Susannah Tracy petitioned the Maryland Assembly in 1709 declaring that Thomas Tracy, her husband, had deserted her and her several children and

---

[72] MS, Northumberland County Order Book, No. 2 (1666-1678), p. 165.

[73] *Ibid.*, Book No. 4 (1699-1713), p. 397.

[74] *Ibid.*, Book No. 1 (1652-1665), pp. 92, 93.

[75] *Ibid.*, Book, No. 2 (1666-1678), p. 48.

[76] MS, Henrico County Court Orders, 1707-1709, p. 165.

[77] *Ibid.*, p. 165.

had left the province. She wished to sell a tract of land left her by a former husband, but could not execute a deed because of her coverture. The assembly passed an act allowing her to lease the lands and declaring that the tobacco she received in payment could not be liable for any debts of her husband.[78]   In 1752 the Virginia House of Burgesses passed a bill enabling Frances Greenhill to dispose of her estate in the same manner as she could if she were unmarried. Her husband had apparently deserted her and had not lived with her for over twenty years. But a committee of the Board of Trade in England disallowed the act, on the grounds that: "this is the first Instance wherein the Legislature in any of the Colonys Abroad have taken upon them to alter the Law in so Settled and known a point as giving a power to a Feme Covert to sell or dispose of her Real and Personal Estate in the Supposed life time of her Husband and as it may not be advisable to countenance any attempts of this kind."[79]

The married woman who desired to carry on business on her own responsibility could be made a sole trader and thereafter make contracts, sue and recover debts due her, and be sued just as if she were single. The business of a married woman who was a sole trader was not subject to attachment for her husband's debts and he was in no way liable for the debts of the business.[80]   Advertisements of married women as sole traders appeared now and then in the Charles Town papers and less often in the other colonies.

Several means were available for securing certain property rights to married women without legislative or court action. Occasionally a gift was made to a daughter or other female relative with the direction that it was for "her sole and separate use." Henry Peyton of Virginia, for example, bequeathed his sister-in-law one hundred pounds sterling with this instruction: "Her husband to have nothing to do with it."[81]   John Barber of North Carolina devised his estate

[78] *Archives of Maryland,* XXVII, 470-72.

[79] *Journals of the House of Burgesses,* pp. 21, 24, 27, 34, 60, 61, 70.

[80] A South Carolina statute of 1744 thus explained her responsibilities and privileges: "Any feme covert being a sole trader, notwithstanding her husband may be absent from this state, shall be liable to any suit or action to be brought against her for any debt contracted as a sole trader; and shall, also, have full power and authority to sue for an recover, naming her husband for conformity, from any person whomsoever, all such debts, as have been, or shall be contracted with her, as a sole trader, and all proceedings to judgment and execution by, or against, such feme covert, being a sole trader, shall be, as if such woman was sole, and not under coverture."—*Digest of South Carolina Laws* (ed., Benjamin James), p. 139.

[81] Hayden, *Virginia Genealogies,* p. 481.

to Ann Boyce, wife of William Boyce, and directed that Boyce be debarred from any claim to the property,[82] and Matthew Rowan left a sum of money from which an annuity was to be paid to his stepdaughter "for her sole use free from the power of her husband Archibald Maclaine nor in any wise subject to his debts."[83] Edward Text of Charles Town left fifteen hundred pounds in currency in trust for his niece and specified that it was to be for the maintenance of her and her children, and "without the control of her husband."[84] Christopher Wright of Virginia bequeathed to his daughter Penelope Reed ten pounds annually "to be delivered into her own hands every fall of the year by some trusty person whom my Executors can confide in, for the sole purpose of furnishing her with provisions while she stands in need, but no part, nor the whole thereof to be delivered to her husband, Thomas Reed, nor any person in his behalf."[85]

In these wills it is obvious that the desire of the testator was to exclude a particular husband. Christopher Wright, for example, left money to married daughters other than Penelope Reed, but he did not secure it in any way from the control of their husbands. In a few wills, however, it is clear that the testator desired not so much to deprive a son-in-law of the enjoyment of his marital rights as to provide his daughter with an independent estate subject to her own control and disposition. Charles Carroll of Carrollton left real and personal property in trust for his daughter Mary Caton "for her sole and separate use free from the controul or power of her present or any future husband," and directed that she receive the rents and profits for her "sole and separate use." For each of his granddaughters he also created a separate estate, declaring that they "may at all times hold their said respective interests free from the controul of their present or future husbands, and be able and capable notwithstanding their Coverture, to use or dispose of the same . . . by deed, will, or otherwise, as absolutely and freely as if they were sole and unmarried."[86] John Mann of Gloucester County, Virginia, directed in his will dated 1694/5 that Matthew Page, his son-in-law, allow his daughter, Mary, twenty pounds a year "for her owne proper use" out of the estate he was leaving her.[87] By a deed of gift, Judith

[82] Grimes, *Abstract of North Carolina Wills*, p. 17.
[83] *State Records of North Carolina*, XXII, 298-99.
[84] *South Carolina Magazine*, VI, 31.
[85] *Lower Norfolk County Virginia Antiquary*, I, 130.
[86] Rowland, *op. cit.*, I, Appendix C, 397-423.
[87] *William and Mary Quarterly*, VI, 137.

Daly of Georgia gave five Negroes in trust for her daughter with careful instructions that they were to be free from "any molestation, let, or hindrance . . . of any person who may hereafter marry and become the husband of the said Martha Daly."[88]

Antenuptial agreements by which the husband settled a part of his wife's property upon her were more generally favored than separate estates created for her by her relatives. Marriage settlements were fairly common among the wealthiest class. A large number of agreements providing for a settlement appear in the court records, and in many wills there is reference to "my wife's settlement" or to her jointure. Before the marriage of a young man and woman of well-to-do families, their parents drew up a marriage contract whereby hers agreed to give her a stipulated sum as a marriage portion and his contracted to settle certain property upon her. On the eve of the marriage of Rebecca Blake, daughter of Lady Blake of South Carolina, and George Smith, son of Landgrave Smith, for instance, an indenture was drawn in which Lady Blake agreed to give a certain sum as her daughter's portion and Landgrave Smith assented to the settlement of certain lands upon Rebecca as her jointure.[89]

The purpose of these settlements was not so much to give the wife money for her own use as to keep property in the family from which it descended. Many antenuptial agreements gave the wife no control over the property settled on her during her life, but provided merely that after her death it should go to her heirs. A principle usually regarded in making marriage contracts was that the amount settled on a wife should be in proportion to the marriage portion she brought her husband. Also there was a widespread feeling that if a man's lands were entailed or otherwise involved so as to bar his wife's dower, he should before the marriage make a settlement upon her of a part of her fortune.[90] Sometimes when a wife inherited entailed lands, she and her husband petitioned the assembly to have the entail docked so that they might be able to dispose of the lands. When docking these entails, the assembly often provided for the settlement upon the wife of other property.[91]

[88] *Georgia Gazette,* July 18, 1765.

[89] *South Carolina Magazine,* I, 157.

[90] For a discussion of this principle, see particularly a conversation reported in the diary of Colonel Landon Carter of Virginia between him and a son-in-law, whose lands were entailed.—*William and Mary Quarterly,* XV, 12-17.

[91] *Journals of the House of Burgesses,* IX, 87, 92; XI, 262, 296, 310, 316-17, 320; XIII, 83; *Laws of Maryland* (ed., Kilty), Vol. I, Chap. 21.

The purpose of marriage settlements was not always to protect the interests of the wife. Sometimes an agreement was made whereby a small amount was settled on the wife to prevent her from claiming dower. Charles Carroll of Carrollton, in order to debar his future wife's dower rights in his estate, very unromantically postponed his marriage from October until June so that the assembly could pass an act enabling his fiancée, who was under age, to renounce her dower and accept a settlement. So cool and calculating was he that he wrote a friend that if the assembly terminated without passing the desired act he would have to put off the marriage two years longer until the future bride came of age. The reason "inducing the settlement and strongly justifying it," he explained, was that the lady to whom he was engaged, "altho blessed in every good quality," had not been favored by fortune with respect to money, and as by the laws of the colony widows were entitled to absolute possession of one-third of the personal estate of their husbands, in the case of his death a very large proportion of his estate would probably be carried into another family.[92] It did not prove necessary, however, to postpone the marriage further, for the assembly passed a private act in June, 1768, entitled "An Act to enable Mary Darnall, an infant, to enter into and accept of a marriage settlement and agreement," and a few days later the contract was drawn and the marriage took place.[93]

Some marriage contracts made no settlement upon the wife, but provided that she was to have certain powers over her own property. James Glen and Sarah Barrow of North Carolina entered into articles agreeing that Glen was to have the entire disposal of any property he then had or might thereafter acquire in his own right and also all the property that Sarah then owned except six Negroes and their future increase, which Negroes were to be at her disposal to give, sell, hire, or in any way dispose of at her own discretion as freely as if the marriage had never been solemnized.[94] Peter Godson of Maryland, about to marry Jane, widow of Richard Moore, signed an agreement promising "not to lay any Clayme to or Intermeddle with all or any part of the Estate late of Richard Moore . . . menconed in the written Deed of Conveyance to be by the said Jane disposed of to her Childrens use."[95] An agreement between John

[92] Rowland, *op. cit.*, I, 86-87.
[93] *Laws of Maryland* (ed., Kilty), Vol. I, Chap. 2.
[94] *North Carolina Historical Review*, II, 238.
[95] *Archives of Maryland*, X, 396.

Hurst and Elizabeth Alford of Virginia in 1675 stated that he should not "meddle" with his wife's property, and that she should be fully authorized not only to manage but also to sell it, should she so desire, as if she were still unmarried. In addition, she was to be allowed the power to convert to her own use the bills of exchange, tobacco, and other merchandise which she should at any time send out of the colony, and to distribute her estate by last will and testament in such manner as she chose.[96]

Marriage contracts were made more frequently before a second or later marriage than in the case of a first venture. A widow with children often before entering a second alliance secured to these children and herself a part or the whole of the property left her by her former husband. Elizabeth Turgis of South Carolina, for instance, before her marriage with Joseph Blake, entered into an agreement with him in which he contracted to pay to each of her two daughters a certain sum at her coming of age or marriage, and to maintain these daughters and educate them in a manner deemed "requisite" by their mother.[97] The widow of Theodorick Bland of Virginia, before contracting a new marriage, entered into articles securing to her "after the same intended marriage shall have taken effect, the same unlimited and uncontrolled estate in and power over the said lands, slaves, and moveable chattels as she now hath and as she would or could have exercised, had she remained sole and discovert."[98]

Although marriage contracts were fairly numerous among the wealthy and separate estates were sometimes created for married women, they were the exception and not the rule. A large majority of colonial women probably never knew what it was to have actual control over property at any time except possibly during a few months of widowhood. As girls married very early, the estates to which they were entitled passed immediately from their parents or guardians to their husbands without ever coming into their own possession. Colonial lawmakers, like those in England, were partial to the marital rights of husbands and the colonists generally agreed with *The Spectator* (No. 295) that "separate purses between man and wife" were "as unnatural as separate beds."

[96] Bruce, *Social History of Virginia*, p. 236.
[97] *South Carolina Magazine*, I, 156-57.
[98] *Virginia Magazine*, IV, 280.

BIBLIOGRAPHY

NOTE: Secondary works treating of this subject directly are few. Arthur Wallace Calhoun's *A Social History of the American Family* (2 vols., New York, 1917) and Thomas Woody's *A History of Women's Education in the United States* (2 vols., New York, 1929) deal with southern women before the Revolution. Elisabeth Anthony Dexter's *Colonial Women of Affairs* (second edition, Boston and New York, 1931) and Alice Morse Earle's works, though dealing chiefly with women in the northern colonies, include a few southern women also. Mary Sumner Benson's *Women in Eighteenth Century America* (New York, 1935) describes preachment writings found in all the colonies. Mary Newton Stanard's *Colonial Virginia, its People and Customs* (Philadelphia and London, 1917) and Philip Alexander Bruce's histories of seventeenth-century Virginia contain much material throwing light upon the everyday life of women in that colony. Of the more general secondary sources, there are many. A list of these would include histories of the colonial period and of the separate colonies of Maryland, Virginia, the Carolinas, and Georgia; county and town histories; family histories and biographies; histories of education, of printing, and of the theater; historical accounts of the different religious denominations; works describing the life of English women of the period; descriptions of houses and furniture and other works dealing with the social life, dress, manners, and customs in England and in America in the seventeenth and eighteenth centuries. Limitations of space, however, forbid the printing of this comprehensive secondary list. Wherever data from secondary sources have been used in this study, reference is given to them in the footnotes. Also because of space limitations, housewifery manuals and other contemporary ladies' books, which are described in the text and footnotes and listed in the index, are omitted from this bibliography; and, with few exceptions, general collections of both primary and secondary publications are given only in connection with specific articles taken from them. The following bibliography is thus limited to the primary sources found most useful for the present study.

I. MANUSCRIPTS

Albemarle County, North Carolina. Papers, 1678-1739. 2 vols.[1]
Antrim Parish, Halifax County, Virginia. Vestry Book, 1752-1817.
Augusta Parish, Augusta County, Virginia. Vestry Book, 1746-1779.
Beaufort County, North Carolina. Court Minutes, 1756-1761.

[1] The North Carolina county records given in this list are in the library of the North Carolina Historical Commission at Raleigh, and the Virginia county records are in the Virginia State Library at Richmond.

368   BIBLIOGRAPHY OF PRIMARY SOURCES

———— Miscellaneous Material, 1750-1832.
Bertie County, North Carolina. Court Minutes, Vol. I (1767-1772); Vol. II (1772-1777).
———— Inventories of Estates, 1728-1744; 1762-1768; 1770-1777; 1776-1786.
Blissland Parish, New Kent County, Virginia. Vestry Book, 1721-1786.
Bute County, North Carolina. Court Minutes, 1767-1776, 1774-1778.
———— Court Papers, 1765-1779.
———— Guardians' Accounts, 1770-1795.
———— Inventories of Estates, 1764-1779.
———— Wills, 1765-1779.
Carteret County, North Carolina. Court Minutes, Vol. I (1723-1747); Vol. II (1747-1764); Vol. III (1764-1777).
Chatham County, North Carolina. Court Minutes, 1774-1779.
Chowan County, North Carolina. Court Papers, District of Edenton, 1751-1787.
———— Customs House Papers, Port of Roanoke, Vols. I-II, 1682-1775.
———— General Court Papers, Vols. I-II, 1690-1754.
———— Papers, 1685-1805.
———— Wills, 1733-1752.
Craven County, North Carolina. Apprenticeship Papers, 1748-1779.
———— Court Minutes, 1712-1715; 1730-1746; 1747-1756; 1749-1750; 1757-1762; 1762-1766; 1767-1772; 1772-1784.
———— Guardians' Bonds, 1766-1856.
———— Miscellaneous Court Papers, 1742-1836.
———— Wills and Inventories, 1749-1766; 1755-1764.
Cumberland County, North Carolina. Court Minutes, 1755-1759; 1759-1765; 1765-1772.
———— Wills and Inventories of Estates, 1759-1792.
Currituck County, North Carolina. Orphans' Docket and Guardians' Bonds, 1772-1827.
Edgecombe County, North Carolina. Court Minutes, 1757-1759; 1759-1764; 1764-1772; 1772-1776.
Fairfax County, Virginia. Order Book, 1772-1774.
Fincastle County, Virginia. Court Minutes 1773-1777. Typescript.
General Court. North Carolina. Minutes, 1747-1751; 1752-1761.
Henrico County, Virginia. Court Minutes, 1719-1724; 1755-1762.
———— Court Orders, 1678-1693; 1694-1701; 1710-1714; 1737-1746; 1763-1767; 1767-1769.
———— Court Records, 1677-1692; 1706-1709.
———— Deeds, wills, 1688-1697; 1725-1737; 1750-1767.
———— Miscellaneous Documents, wills, deeds, executions, etc., 1755-1762.
———— Wills, 1714-1718.
Hyde County, North Carolina. Court Minutes, 1744-1760; 1764-1767; 1767-1784.

Kingston Parish, Mathews County, Virginia. Vestry Book, 1679-1796.

Lancaster County, Virginia. Court Orders, 1655-1666.

Lynnhaven Parish, Princess Anne County, Virginia. Vestry Book, 1728-1892.

Middlesex County, Virginia. Order Books, 1673-1680; 1680-1694; 1694-1705; 1705-1710; 1710-1720; 1721-1726; 1732-1737; 1740-1744; 1745-1752; 1752-1758; 1758-1767; 1765-1767; 1769-1772; 1772-1782; 1783-1784; 1784-1786.

———— Will Books, 1698-1713; 1713-1734; 1740-1748; 1748-1760; 1760-1772; 1772-1787; 1787-1793.

Nelson Letter Book, July 25, 1766-August 18, 1775. Virginia State Library.

Newport Parish, Isle of Wight County, Virginia. Vestry Book, 1724-1772.

Northampton County, North Carolina. Wills, 1762-1791.

Northumberland County, Virginia. Order Books, 1652-1665; 1658-1666; 1666-1678; 1678-1698; 1699-1713; 1713-1719; 1720-1729; 1729-1737; 1737-1743; 1743-1749; 1749-1753.

———— Record Books, 1652-1658; 1666-1672; 1706-1720; 1710-1713; 1718-1726; 1726-1729; 1738-1743.

Norton Papers. Colonial Williamsburg, Incorporated, Williamsburg, Virginia.

Onslow County, North Carolina. Court Papers, 1772; 1774-1775.

Pasquotank County, North Carolina. Account Book, 1746.

———— Court Minutes, 1737-1738; 1739-1741; 1742-1744; 1746-1747; 1748-1751; 1751-1752; 1752-1753; 1754-1755.

———— Inventories of Estates, 1749-1783.

———— Orphans' Court Minutes, 1757-1785.

Petsworth Parish, Gloucester County, Virginia. Vestry Book, 1677-1793.

St. Andrew's Parish, Brunswick County, Virginia. Vestry Book, 1732-1797.

St. George's Parish, Northampton County, North Carolina. Records, 1773-1814.

St. John's Parish Records, 1742-1841. Two Vestry Books of St. Paul's Church at Beaufort, North Carolina.

St. Paul's Parish, Hanover County, Virginia. Vestry Book, 1705-1785.

Tryon County, North Carolina. Court Minutes, 1768-1782. 1 vol.

Tyrrell County, North Carolina. Court Minutes, 1761-1770; 1770-1782.

———— Inventories of Estates and Administrators' Accounts, 1750-1775. 1 vol.

Wicomico Parish, Northumberland County, Virginia. Vestry Book, 1703-1795.

William Reynolds' Letter Books. Typescript. Colonial National Monument, Yorktown, Virginia.

II. PRINTED SOURCES

A. Newspapers

Maryland Gazette (William Parks, at Annapolis), 1728-1734.

Maryland Gazette (Jonas Green, Anne Catherine Green, and William Green, at Annapolis), 1745-1776.

The Maryland Journal and the Baltimore Advertiser (William Goddard, Mary Katherine Goddard, at Baltimore), 1773-1783.

Dunlap's Maryland Gazette: or, the Baltimore General Advertiser (John Dunlap, at Baltimore), 1775-1776.

The Georgia Gazette (James Johnston, at Savannah), 1768-1776.

The North Carolina Magazine: or, Universal Intelligencer (James Davis, at New Bern), 1764-1765.

North Carolina Gazette (Andrew Steuart, at Wilmington), 1764-1767.

The Cape Fear Mercury (Adam Boyd, at Wilmington), 1769-1775.

The South-Carolina Gazette (Thomas Whitmarsh, Lewis Timothy, Elizabeth Timothy, Peter Timothy, at Charles Town), 1732-1775.

The South-Carolina and American General Gazette (Robert Wells, at Charles Town), 1764-1775.

The South-Carolina Gazette; and Country Journal (Charles Crouch, at Charles Town), 1765-1775.

The Virginia Gazette (William Parks, at Williamsburg), 1736-1746.

The Virginia Gazette (Hunter, Royle, Purdie and Dixon, Dixon and Hunter, at Williamsburg), 1751-1776.

The Virginia Gazette (William Rind, Clementina Rind, John Pinckney, at Williamsburg), 1766-1776.

B. Official Documents

1. *Georgia*

The Colonial Records of the State of Georgia. Compiled under the authority of the legislature by Allen D. Candler. 25 vols. Atlanta, 1904-1916.

Digest of the Laws of the State of Georgia. Eds. R. and G. Watkins. Philadelphia, 1800.

Digest of the Laws of the State of Georgia, from its Settlement as a British Province, in 1755, to the Session of the General Assembly in 1800, inclusive. . . . Eds. Horatio Marbury, William H. Crawford. Savannah, 1802.

Digest of the laws of the State of Georgia. . . . Ed. Oliver H. Prince. Milledgeville, Georgia, 1822.

Revolutionary Records of the State of Georgia (1769-1784). Compiled by A. D. Candler. 3 vols. Atlanta, 1908.

Statutes of Georgia (1754-1805). Ed. A. D. Candler. Atlanta, 1910-1911.

2. *Great Britain*

Board of Trade. *Journal of the Commissioners for Trade and Planta-tions, 1704-1758.* Vols. I-X. London, 1920—.
Privy Council. *Acts of the Privy Council of England, Colonial Series. 1613-1783.* 6 vols. London, 1908-1912.
Public Record Office. *Calendar of State Papers, Colonial Series, America and West Indies, 1574-1715.* 33 vols. London, 1860-1928.

3. *Maryland*

Abridgment and Collection of the Acts of Assembly of the Province of Maryland. . . . Ed. James Bisset. Philadelphia, 1759.
Archives of Maryland. Published under the direction of the Maryland Historical Society. 51 vols. to date. Vols. I-XVII, XIX-XXXII, ed. William Hand Browne; XXXIII-XXXV, ed. Clayton Colman Hall; XVIII, XXXVI-XLV, ed. Bernard Christian Steiner; and XLVI-LI, ed. J. Hall Pleasants. Baltimore, 1883-1934. In progress.
A Compleat Collection of the Laws of Maryland with an Index, and Marginal Notes. . . . Annapolis, 1727.
A Digest of the Laws of Maryland, being an Abridgment of all the Public Acts . . . from the First Settlement of the State, to the end of Novem-ber Session, 1797, inclusive. . . . Ed. Thomas Herty. Baltimore, 1799.
Laws of Maryland at Large, [*1637-1763*] . . . *Now First Collected into One Compleat Body, and Published from the Original Acts and Records.* . . . Ed. Thomas Bacon. Annapolis, 1765.
The Laws of Maryland . . . [*1692-1799*]. Ed. William Kilty. 2 vols. Annapolis, 1799.
The Laws of Maryland . . . [*1704-1809*]. Ed. Virgil Maxcy. 3 vols. Baltimore, 1811.

4. *North Carolina*

A Collection of the Private Acts of the General Assembly of the State of North Carolina from the Year 1715, to the Year 1790, inclusive, now in Force and Use. Compiled by Francois-Xavier Martin. New Bern, 1794.
A Collection of the Statutes of the Parliament of England in Force in the State of North Carolina. Compiled by Francis-Xavier Martin. New Bern, 1792.
Colonial and State Records of North Carolina. 26 vols. Goldsboro and Raleigh, 1886-1890. Vols. I-X, ed. William L. Saunders, entitled *Colonial Records of North Carolina.* Vols. XI-XXVI, ed. Walter Clark, are *State Records of North Carolina.*
Laws of the State of North Carolina, 1715-1790. Ed. James Iredell. Edenton, 1791.

5. South Carolina

Alphabetical Digest of the Public Statute Law of South Carolina. Comp. Joseph Brevard. 3 vols. Charleston, 1814.

A Digest of the Laws of South-Carolina, containing the Public Statute Law of the State, down to the Year 1822. . . . Ed. Benjamin James. Columbia, S. C., 1822.

Journals of the Commons House of Assembly of South Carolina for the Session beginning September 20, 1692 and ending October 15, 1692 and for the Four Sessions of 1693. Ed. Alexander Samuel Salley, Jr. Columbia, 1907.

Journal of the Commons House of Assembly of South Carolina for the Session beginning January 30, 1696 and ending March 17, 1696. Ed. A. S. Salley, Jr. Columbia, 1908.

Journal of the Commons House of Assembly of South Carolina for the Session beginning November 24, 1696, and ending December 5, 1696. Ed. A. S. Salley, Jr. Columbia, 1912.

Journals of the Commons House of Assembly of South Carolina for the Two Sessions of 1697. Ed. A. S. Salley, Jr. Columbia, 1913.

Journals of the Commons House of Assembly of South Carolina for the Two Sessions of 1698. Ed. A. S. Salley, Jr. Columbia, 1914.

Journal of the General Assembly of South Carolina, March 26, 1776-April 11, 1776. Ed. A. S. Salley, Jr. Columbia, 1906.

Journal of the General Assembly of South Carolina, September 17, 1776-October 20, 1776. Ed. A. S. Salley, Jr. Columbia, 1909.

Journal of the Grand Council of South Carolina, August 25, 1671-June 24, 1680. Ed. A. S. Salley, Jr. Columbia, 1907.

Journal of the Grand Council of South Carolina, April 11, 1692-September 26, 1692. Ed. A. S. Salley. Columbia, 1907.

The Public Laws of the State of South Carolina, from its First Establishment as a British Province down to the Year 1790, in which is Comprehended such of the Statutes of Great Britain as were Made of Force by the Act of Assembly of 1712. . . . Ed. John Faucheraud Grimké. Philadelphia, 1790.

The Statutes at Large of South Carolina. 10 vols. Vols. I-IV, ed., Thomas Cooper; Vols. VI-X, ed., D. J. McCord. Columbia, S. C., 1836-1841.

6. Virginia

Abstracts of the Proceedings of the Virginia Company of London, 1619-1624. Prepared from the Records in the Library of Congress by Conway Robinson, ed. R. A. Brock. Pts. I-II. Virginia Historical Society, *Collections,* new series, vols. VII-VIII. Richmond, 1888-1889.

Abstracts of Virginia Land Patents. Prepared by W. G. Stanard. *Virginia Magazine of History and Biography,* I-VIII, *passim.*

Acts of the General Assembly, January 6, 1639-1640. William and Mary College Quarterly Magazine, second series, IV, *passim.*

Calendar of Virginia State Papers and Other Manuscripts. Preserved . . . at Richmond (1652-1869). Eds. W. P. Palmer and others. 11 vols. Richmond, 1875-1893.

Colonial Records of Virginia (1619-1680). Eds. Thomas H. Wynne and W. S. Gilman. Richmond, 1874.

Council Papers (1698-1701). From the Original Volume in the Virginia State Library. *Virginia Magazine of History and Biography*, XXI-XXV, *passim*.

Council Proceedings, 1716-1717. *Virginia Magazine of History and Biography*, IV, 364-76.

Council Journals, 1726-1753. From the Transcripts in the Public Record Office, London. *Virginia Magazine of History and Biography*, XXXII-XXXIX, *passim*.

Journals of the Council of Virginia. Executive Sessions, 1737-1767. *Virginia Magazine of History and Biography*, XIV-XVI, *passim*.

Executive Journals of the Council of Virginia (1680-1705). Ed. H. R. McIlwaine. 4 vols. Richmond, 1925-1930.

Legislative Journals of the Council of Colonial Virginia. Ed. H. R. McIlwaine. 3 vols. Richmond, 1918-1919.

County Records: County Court Proceedings in Virginia, 1734. *Virginia Magazine of History and Biography*, XXIII, 72-78; Extracts from the County Records, *ibid.*, VIII, 171-94; Lower Norfolk County Records (1636-1646), *ibid.*, XXXIX, XL, *passim*; Northampton County Records in the Seventeenth Century, *ibid.*, IV, V, *passim*; Prince George County Records, *ibid.*, IV, 272-92; Isle of Wight County Records, *William and Mary College Quarterly Magazine*, VII, 205-315.

Journals of the House of Burgesses of Virginia, 1619-1776. Ed. H. R. McIlwaine. 13 vols. Richmond, 1905-1915.

Lower Norfolk County Virginia Antiquary. Ed. E. W. James. 5 vols. Richmond and Baltimore, 1895-1906.

Minutes of the Council and General Court of Colonial Virginia, 1622-1632, 1670-1676, with Notes and Excerpts from Original Council and General Court Records, into 1683, Now Lost. Ed. H. R. McIlwaine. Richmond, 1924.

Minutes of the Council and General Court (1622-1632). From the Originals in the Library of Congress. Copied and contributed by Lathrop Withington. *Virginia Magazine of History and Biography*, XIX-XXXI, *passim*.

Miscellaneous Colonial Documents. From the Originals in the Virginia State Archives. *Virginia Magazine of History and Biography*, XVI-XX, *passim*.

The Randolph Manuscript. Virginia Seventeenth Century Records. *Virginia Magazine of History and Biography*, XV-XXII, *passim*.

The Records of the Virginia Company of London; the Court Book (1619-1624) from the Manuscript in the Library of Congress. Ed. Susan Myra Kingsbury. 2 vols. Washington, D. C., 1906

Reports of Cases determined in the General Court of Virginia (1730↓ 1740, 1768-1772). Comp. Thomas Jefferson. Charlottesville, Va., 1829.

Robinson Transcripts. Virginia Historical Society Manuscript Collection: Decisions of Virginia General Court (1626-1670), *Virginia Magazine of History and Biography*, III-V, *passim;* and Notes from Council and General Court Records (1641-1682), *ibid.*, VIII, IX, XI, XIII, XIV, *passim.*

The Statutes at Large; Being a Collection of all the Laws of Virginia from the First Session of the Legislature in the Year 1619. . . . Ed. William Waller Hening. 13 vols. Richmond, 1809-1823.

Virginia Colonial Decisions. The Reports by Sir John Randolph and by Edward Barradall of Decisions of the General Court of Virginia, 1728-1741. Ed. R. T. Barton. 2 vols. Boston, 1909.

Virginia Legislative Papers. From Originals in the Virginia State Library. *Virginia Magazine of History and Biography*, IX, XII-XVIII, *passim.*

C. LETTERS, JOURNALS, AND OTHER SOURCE MATERIALS

Abridgement of the Laws in Force and Use in her Majesty's Plantations; viz, of Virginia, Jamaica, Barbadoes, Maryland, New-England, New-York, Carolina, &c. Digested under proper Heads in the Method of Mr. Wingate and Mr. Washington's Abridgements. London, 1704.

Abstract of the Sufferings of the People called Quakers for the Testimony of Good Conscience, from the Times of their being first distinguished by that Name, taken from Original Records, and other Authentick Accounts. 3 vols. London, 1733, 1738.

Abstracts from the Records of the Court of Ordinary of the Province of South Carolina, 1692-1700, 1700-1711. Ed. Alexander S. Salley, Jr. *South Carolina Historical and Genealogical Magazine*, VIII-XIII, *passim.*

Account of the Colony of the Lord Baron of Baltimore, 1633. *Narratives of Early Maryland.* Ed. Clayton Colman Hall. Pp. 1-10.

Account of the Doctrine and Discipline of Mr. Richard Davis, of Rothwell, in the County of Northampton, and those of his Separation. With the Canons of George Fox, appointed to be Read in all the Quakers Meetings. London, 1700.

Adams, Richard. Letters of Richard Adams to Thomas Adams. From the Originals in the Collection of the Virginia Historical Society. *Virginia Magazine of History and Biography*, XX, 379-95.

Adams, Thomas. Letters to Thomas Adams, 1769-1771. *Virginia Magazine of History and Biography*, V, VI, *passim.*

Alsop, George. A Character of the Province of Maryland. 1666. Maryland Historical Society, *Fund Publication*, No. 15. Also in *Narratives of Early Maryland*, pp. 335-87.

Anburey, Thomas. *Travels through the Interior Parts of America. In a Series of Letters. By an Officer.* 2 vols. London, 1789.

Archdale, John. *A New Description of that Fertile and Pleasant Province of Carolina.* . . . London, 1707. Reprinted in *Historical Collections of South Carolina.* Ed. B. R. Carroll. II, 85-120.

Archives of Maryland as Illustrating the Spirit of the Times of the Early Colonists. Maryland Historical Society, *Fund Publication*, No. 22.

Articles, Lawes, and Orders, Divine, Politique, and Martiall for the Colony in Virginia: first established by Sir Thomas Gates. . . . Againe exemplified and enlarged by Sir Thomas Dale. . . . London, 1612. Reprinted in Peter Force (comp.), *Tracts and Other Papers*, Vol. III, No. 2.

Asbury, Francis. *Journal.* 3 vols. New York, 1852.

[Ash, Thomas]. Carolina; or a Description of the Present State of that Country. . . . London, 1682. Reprinted in *Historical Collections of South Carolina.* Ed. B. R. Carroll. II, 59-84; and in *Narratives of Early Carolina.* Ed. A. S. Salley, Jr. Pp. 135-59.

Atkinson, Roger. Letters of Roger Atkinson, 1769-1776. Ed. A. J. Morrison. *Virginia Magazine of History and Biography*, XV, 345-59.

Attmore, William. Journal of a Tour to North Carolina, 1787. Ed. Lida Tunstall Rodman. *James Sprunt Historical Publications.* Chapel Hill, 1922. Vol. XVII, No. 2.

Auld, James. Journal, 1765-1770. Southern History Association. *Publications*, VIII, 255-56.

[Ball, Colonel Burgess]. Old Letters of Revolutionary Date. *Virginia Magazine of History and Biography*, V, 387-91.

Baltimore, Lord. Instructions to the Colonists, 1633. *Narratives of Early Maryland*, pp. 11-23.

Barclay, Robert. *A Catechism and Confession . . . which containeth a true . . . Account of the Principles . . . of the Churches of Christ . . . reproachfully called Quakers.* . . . Philadelphia, 1788.

Bartram, William. *Travels through North & South Carolina, Georgia, East & West Florida, the Cherokee country . . . containing an account of the soil and natural productions . . . together with observations on the manners of the Indians.* Philadelphia, 1791.

[Bell, J. P.]. *Our Quaker Friends of Ye Olden Times. Being in Part a Transcript of the Minute Books of Cedar Creek Meeting, Hanover County, and the South River Meeting Campbell County, Va.* Lynchburg, Va., 1905.

Bennett, Thomas. *A Confutation of Quakerism.* . . . 2d ed. Cambridge, 1709.

[Berkeley, Sir William]. *A Discourse and Views of Virginia.* London, 1663.

———— A Perfect Description of Virginia. . . . Being sent from Virginia, at the request of a Gentleman of worthy note. . . . London, 1649. Force, *Tracts*, Vol. II, No. 8.

Berkeley Manuscripts. *William and Mary College Quarterly Magazine*, VI, *passim*.

Bernard, John. *Retrospections of America, 1797-1811.* Edited from the Manuscript by Mrs. Bayle Bernard. . . . New York, 1887.

[Beverley, Robert]. *The History and Present State of Virginia. In Four Parts.* 1705. 2d ed. London, 1722.

Beverley, William. Diary of William Beverley of "Blandfield," during a Visit to England, 1750. *Virginia Magazine of History and Biography*, XXXVI, 161-69.

———— Some Letters of William Beverley. *William and Mary College Quarterly Magazine.* First Series, III, 223-39.

Black, William. Journal, 1744. Ed. R. Alonzo Brock. *Pennsylvania Magazine of History and Biography*, I, II, *passim.*

Blackstone, Sir William. *Commentaries on the Laws of England. From the last London Edition . . . with Notes and Additions by Edward Christian.* . . . 4 vols. Philadelphia, 1818. *See also* Tucker, St. George.

Blair, John. Diary of John Blair. Copied from an Almanac for 1751, preserved in Virginia Historical Society. Verified by Lyon G. Tyler. *William and Mary College Quarterly*, VII, VIII, *passim.*

Blome, Richard. *The Present State of his Majestie's Isles and Territories in America, from the year 1686-1700.* London, n.d.

Boucher, Reverend Jonathan. Letters. *Maryland Historical Magazine*, VII-X, *passim.*

Boundary Line Proceedings, 1710. A Journall of the Proceedings of Philip Ludwell and Nathaniel Harrison Commissioners Appointed for seteling ye Limits betwixt Virginia & Carolina Begun July ye 18th 1710 by P. L. *Virginia Magazine of History and Biography*, IV, V, *passim.*

Bowman, William. *The Imposture of Methodism Display'd; in a Letter to the Inhabitants of Dewsbury.* . . . London, 1740.

Bownas, Samuel. *An Account of the Life, Travels, and Christian Experiences in the Work of the Ministry.* London, 1759.

Boyd, William K. (ed.). *Some Eighteenth Century Tracts concerning North Carolina.* Publication of the North Carolina Historical Commission. Raleigh, 1929.

———— *See also* Byrd, William, II.

Brailsford, Edmund. Correspondence between Edmund Brailsford and his Father. *South Carolina Historical and Genealogical Magazine*, VIII, 151-63.

Brickell, John. *The Natural History of North Carolina. With an Account of the Trade, Manners and Customs of the Christian and Indian inhabitants.* . . . Dublin, 1737.

Brief Account of the People called Quakers; their Doctrines and Discipline; taken from a Dictionary of Arts and Sciences lately Published at Edinburgh. Leeds, 1791.

Briefe Declaration of the Plantation of Virginia during the First Twelve Years, . . . and Downe to this Present Tyme. By the Ancient Planters nowe Remaining Alive in Virginia. 1624. Reprinted in *Colonial Records of Virginia*. Richmond, 1874.

Briggs, Isaac. Three Isaac Briggs Letters. *Georgia Historical Quarterly*, XII, 177, 184.

Brissot de Warville, Jacques Pierre. *New Travels in the United States of America Performed 1788*. Translated from the French edition. Dublin, 1792.

Brock, R. A. (ed.). Records of the Parish of Henrico in their Entirety, with their Quaint and Antique Language and Entries, from the Original Vestry Book, from 1730 to 1773, with Notes. In J. Staunton Moore, *History of Henrico Parish and Old St. John's Church, Richmond, Virginia*, 1611-1904. Richmond, 1904.

Broughton Letters. Copied and Annotated by D. E. Huger Smith. *South Carolina Historical and Genealogical Magazine*, XV, 171-96.

Brown, Alexander (ed.). *The Genesis of the United States*. 2 vols. Boston and New York, 1890.

Browne, Mrs. Diary in Virginia and Maryland. From a Photostat copy of a manuscript entitled "Journal of a Voyage from London to Virginia, 1754." Ed. Fairfax Harrison. *Virginia Magazine of History and Biography*, XXXII, 305-20.

[Bull, Maria Lucia]. A Woman's Letters in 1779 and 1782. *South Carolina Historical and Genealogical Magazine*, X, 125-28.

Bullock, William. *Virginia, Impartially Examined . . . under which Title, is Comprehended . . . the Now Plantations of Virginia and Maryland etc.* London, 1649.

Burnaby, Andrew. *Travels through the Middle Settlements in North America in the years of 1759 and 1760; with Observations upon the State of the Colonies.* London, 1798.

Byrd, William. Letters (1683-1685). *Virginia Historical Register*, I, II, *passim*.

———— Letters of William Byrd, First (1683-1691). *Virginia Magazine of History and Biography*, XXIV-XXVIII, *passim*.

Byrd, William, II. *History of the Dividing Line and Other Tracts from the Papers of William Byrd of Westover, in Virginia, Esquire*. Ed. T. H. Wynne. 2 vols. Richmond, 1866.

———— Letters of Colonel William Byrd of Westover, 1736-1739. *American Historical Review*, I, 88-90.

———— Letters of William Byrd, 2d. of Westover. *Virginia Magazine of History and Biography*, IX, *passim*.

———— *William Byrd's Histories of the Dividing Line betwixt Virginia and North Carolina*. Ed. W. K. Boyd. Publication of the North Carolina Historical Commission. Raleigh, 1929.

———— *The Writings of Colonel William Byrd of Westover in Virginia Esqr.* Ed. John Spencer Bassett. New York, 1901.

Byrd Family. Letters of the Byrd Family. Contributed, chiefly, by Mr. William Byrd of New York City. *Virginia Magazine of History and Biography*, XXXV-XXXIX, *passim*.

Calvert Papers, Nos. I-III. Maryland Historical Society, *Fund Publications*, Nos. 28, 34-35. Baltimore, 1889, 1894, 1899.

Camm, John. Original Letters of John Camm and Hudson Muse (1766, 1771). *William and Mary College Quarterly Magazine*, II, 237-41.

[Campbell, G. L.]. Itinerant Observations in America. Reprinted from the *London Magazine*, in the Georgia Historical Society, *Collections*, IV, Pt. II. See also *William and Mary College Quarterly Magazine*, XV, *passim*.

Carolina in 1710. A Letter from a Swiss Gentleman in South Carolina to a Friend in Bern. *University of North Carolina Magazine*, IV (1855), 289-305.

Carroll, Dr. Charles. Extracts from Account and Letter Books of Dr. Charles Carroll of Annapolis. *Maryland Historical Magazine*, XVIII-XXVII, *passim*.

Carroll, Charles. Extracts from the Carroll Papers. *Maryland Historical Magazine*, X-XVI, *passim*.

Carter, Landon. Extracts from the Diary of Landon Carter, 1770-1776. *William and Mary College Quarterly Magazine*, First Series, XIII-XVIII, XX, XXI, *passim*.

Carter Papers. *Virginia Magazine of History and Biography*, V-VII, *passim*.

Carver, Jonathan. *Three Years Travels throughout the Interior Parts of North America*. Boston, 1797.

Cawley, Henry H. (ed.). Tombstone Inscriptions, Richardson Cemetery. Located in Old St. Mark's Parish; four Miles Southeast of Remini, Clarendon County, South Carolina. *South Carolina Historical and Genealogical Magazine*, XXVIII, 55-68.

Chalkley, Lyman (comp.). *Chronicles of the Scotch-Irish Settlement in Virginia; extracted from the Original Records of Augusta County, 1745-1800*. 3 vols. Rosslyn, Virginia, 1912.

Chalkley, Thomas. *A Collection of the Works of Thomas Chalkley. In Two Parts.*. Philadelphia, 1749.

——— *The Journal of Thomas Chalkley. To which is annexed a Collection of his Works*. New York and Philadelphia, 1808.

Chamberlayne, Churchill Gibson (ed.). Old Blandford Tombstones. An Exact Transcript of the Epitaphs on all the Tombstones now existing within the Original Enclosure of old Blandford Churchyard, near Petersburg, Virginia. *William and Mary College Quarterly Magazine*, V, 230; VI, 18.

——— *The Vestry Book and Register of Bristol Parish, Virginia, 1720-1789*. Richmond, 1898.

——— *The Vestry Book of Christ Church Parish, Middlesex County, Virginia, 1663-1767*. Richmond, 1927.

——— *The Vestry Book of Kingston Parish, Mathews County, Virginia (until May 1, 1791, Gloucester County), 1679-1796*. Richmond, 1929.

Chapman, Richard. Letters from the Letter Book of Richard Chapman, 1739. *William and Mary College Quarterly*, First Series, XXI, 90-100.

Chastellux, Francois Jean, Marquis de. *Travels in North America in the Years, 1780, 1781, and 1782. . . . Translated from the French by an English Gentleman who Resided in America at that Period.* 2 vols. London, 1787.

Clayton, John. A Letter from Mr. John Clayton, Rector of Crofton at Wakefield in Yorkshire, to the Royal Society, May 12, 1688. Giving an Account of several Observables in Virginia. . . . Force, *Tracts*, Vol. III, No. 12. *See* Force, Peter.

Collection of Memorials concerning Divers deceased Ministers and others of the People called Quakers, in Pennsylvania, New Jersey, and Parts adjacent, from nearly the first Settlement there to the Year 1787. Philadelphia, 1787.

Confession of Faith, put Forth by the Elders and Brethren of Many Congregations of Christians, Baptized upon Profession of their Faith, in London and the Country. Adopted by the Baptist Association of Philadelphia, September 25, 1742. And by the Charleston, in 1767. Second Charleston Edition. . . . Charleston, S. C., 1813.

Conway, Moncure Daniel. *George Washington and Mount Vernon. A Collection of Washington's unpublished Agricultural and Personal Letters edited with Historical and Genealogical Introduction.* Memoirs of the Long Island Historical Society, Vol. IV. Brooklyn, N. Y., 1889.

Cook, Ebenezer. The Sot-Weed Factor: or a Voyage to Maryland, 1708. Maryland Historical Society, *Fund Publication*, No. 36, pp. 9-31.

—— Sotweed Redivivus: Or the Planters Looking-Glass. 1730. Maryland Historical Society, *Fund Publication*, No. 36, pp. 35-52.

Cotton, Mrs. An. An Account of our Late Troubles in Virginia, written in 1676 by Mrs. An Cotton of Q. Creek. Force, *Tracts*, Vol. I, No. 9, pp. 1-10.

Cox, Samuel Hanson. *Quakerism not Christianity: or Reasons for Renouncing the Doctrine of Friends.* Boston, 1833.

Coxe, Daniel. *A Description of the English Province of Carolina.* London, 1741.

Cresswell, Nicholas. *Journal, 1774-1777.* New York, 1924.

Crouch, Nathaniel. *The English Empire in America.* . . . London, 1685. 7th ed., 1729.

Crozier, William Armstrong. *Virginia County Records. Spotsylvania County, 1721-1800. Being Transcriptions from the Original Files at the County Court House, of Wills, Deeds, Administrators' and Guardians' Bonds, Marriage Licenses.* . . . New York, 1905.

Cumberland, Richard. Letters from Richard Cumberland, Esq. to Roger Pinckney, Esq. . . . 1764-1775. *Documents Connected with the History of South Carolina* (ed. P. C. J. Weston), pp. 102-54.

Dankers, Jaspar, and Peter Sluyter. *Journal of a Voyage to New York and a Tour in Several of the American Colonies in 1679-80.* Translated from the Original Manuscript in Dutch for the Long Island Historical Society, and edited by Henry C. Murphy. Brooklyn, 1867.

Davis, John. *Travels of Four Years and a Half in the United States of America during 1798, 1799, 1800, 1801, and 1802.* New York, 1909.

De Brahm, John Gerard William. Philosophico-Historico-Hydrogeography of South Carolina, Georgia, and East Florida. *Documents Connected with the History of South Carolina* (ed., P. C. J. Weston. London, 1856), pp. 155-227.

Declaration of the State of the Colonie and Affaires in Virginia: with the Names of the Adventurors, and Summes adventured in that Action. By his Majesties Counseil for Virginia. Force, *Tracts,* Vol. III, No. 5.

De Rossett. Extracts from the Papers of the De Rossett Family, of Wilmington. . . . *James Sprunt Historical Monograph,* No. 4, pp. 9-53. Chapel Hill, N. C., 1903.

Description of Georgia, by a Gentleman who has Resided there Upwards of Seven Years, and was One of the First Settlers. London, 1741. Force, *Tracts,* Vol. II, No. 12.

Diary of a Journey of Moravians from Bethlehem, Pennsylvania, to Bethabara, North Carolina, 1753. *Travels in the American Colonies.* Ed. Newton D. Mereness, pp. 325-56. *See* Mereness.

Diary of a Little Colonial Girl. *Virginia Magazine of History and Biography,* XI, 211-14.

Dickinson, James. Journal ... 1745. *The Friends' Library,* XII, 52-145. *See* Friends' Library.

Dinwiddie, Robert. The Official Records of Robert Dinwiddie, Lieutenant-Governor of the Colony of Virginia, 1751-1758. Virginia Historical Society, *Collections,* New Series, Vols III and IV.

Documents Connected with the History of South Carolina. Ed. P. C. G. Weston. London, 1856.

Drayton, John. *A View of South Carolina, as Respects her Natural and Civil Concerns.* Charleston, 1802.

Dulany. Extracts from the Dulany Papers. *Maryland Historical Magazine,* XIV, XVI, passim.

Durand of Dauphiné. *A Frenchman in Virginia being the Memoirs of a Huguenot Refugee in 1686.* Translated by a Virginian [Fairfax Harrison]. Privately printed. 1923.

Early Description of Georgia. From the *Gentleman's Magazine,* January, 1756. Reprinted in the *Georgia Historical Quarterly,* II, 37-42.

Eddis, William. *Letters from America, Historical and Descriptive; Comprising Occurrences from 1769, to 1777, Inclusive.* London, 1792.

Eden, Governor. Correspondence. *Maryland Historical Magazine,* II, passim.

Elfe, Thomas. The Thomas Elfe Account Book, 1768-1775. *South Carolina Historical and Genealogical Magazine,* XXXV, 153-65.

Extracts from the Annual Letters of the English Province of the Society of Jesus, 1634, 1638, 1639, 1640, 1642, 1654, 1656, 1681. *Narratives of Early Maryland*, pp. 113-44.

Extracts from the Minutes and Advices of the Yearly Meeting of Friends Held in London, from its First Institution. 2d ed. London, 1802.

Fithian, Philip Vickers. *Journal and Letters, 1767-1774.* Edited for the Princeton Historical Association by John Rogers Williams. Princeton, N. J., 1900.

Fitzhugh, William. Letters. *Virginia Magazine of History and Biography*, I-VI, *passim*.

———— Will of William Fitzhugh and Other Extracts from the Records of Stafford County. *Virginia Magazine of History and Biography*, II, 276-80.

Fontaine, Jacques. *See* Maury, Ann. *Memoirs of a Huguenot Family.*

Force, Peter (comp.). *Tracts and Other Papers, relating Principally to the Origin, Settlement, and Progress of the Colonies in North America. . . .* 4 vols. Washington, 1836-1846.

Ford, Timothy. Diary . . . 1785-1786, with Notes by Joseph Barnwell. *South Carolina Historical and Genealogical Magazine*, XIII, *passim*.

Fothergill, John. *An Account of the Life and Travels in the Work of the Ministry of John Fothergill. . . .* 2d ed. London, 1773.

Fox, George. Extracts from the Journal of George Fox, 1672, 1673. *Narratives of Early Maryland*, pp. 389-405.

———— A Journal or Historical Account of the Life, Travels, Sufferings . . . of . . . George Fox. London, 1694, 1709, 1765. New York, 1800.

Frenchman in Virginia. *See* Durand of Dauphiné.

Friends' Library, Comprising Journals, Doctrinal Treatises, and Other Writings of Members of the Religious Society of Friends. Eds. William Evans and Thomas Evans. 14 vols. Philadelphia, 1837-1850.

Fries, Adelaide. *Records of the Moravians in North Carolina.* 2 vols. Publication of the North Carolina Historical Commission. Raleigh, 1922.

Gamble, Captain Robert. Orderly Book. Virginia Historical Society, *Collections*, New Series, XI, 231-72.

[Glen, Governor]. A Description of South-Carolina: containing Many Curious and Interesting Particulars relating to the Civil, Natural, and Commercial History of that Colony. . . . London, 1761. *Historical Collections of South Carolina*, II, 193-272.

Glover, Thomas. An Account of Virginia, its Situation, Temperature, Productions, Inhabitants . . . Communicated by Mr. Thomas Glover an ingenious Chirurgion that hath lived some years in that Country. Reprinted from the *Philosophical Transactions* of the Royal Society, June 20, 1676.

Gordon, Lord Adam. Journal of An Officer who Travelled in America and the West Indies in 1764 and 1765. *Travels in the American Colonies* (ed. N. D. Mereness), pp. 365-453.

Gordon, Colonel James. Journal of Colonel James Gordon of Lancaster County, Virginia, 1758-1763. *William and Mary College Quarterly Magazine*, First Series, XI, XII, *passim*.

Griffith, John. *Journal of Life, Travels, and Labours in the Work of the Ministry*. Philadelphia, 1780.

Grimes, J. Bryan. *Abstract of North Carolina Wills compiled from Original and Recorded Wills in the Office of the Secretary of State*. Published under authority of the trustees of the Public Libraries. Raleigh, 1910.

——— *North Carolina Wills and Inventories Copied from Original and Recorded Wills and Inventories in the Office of the Secretary of State*. Raleigh, 1912.

Habersham, Honorable James. Letters . . . 1756-1775. Georgia Historical Society, *Collections*, Vol. VI. Savannah, 1905.

Habersham, Joseph. Some Letters of Joseph Habersham. Ed. Ulrich B. Phillips. *Georgia Historical Quarterly*, X, 144-63.

Hall, J. L. Ancient Epitaphs and Inscriptions in York and James City Counties. Virginia Historical Society, *Collections*, New Series, XI, 63-111.

Hamilton [Dr. Alexander]. *Hamilton's Itinerarium being a Narrative of a Journey from Annapolis, Maryland, through Delaware, Pennsylvania, New York, New Jersey, Connecticut, Rhode Island, Massachusetts, and New Hampshire from May to September, 1744*. Ed. Albert Bushnell Hart. St. Louis, Missouri, n.d.

Hammond, John. Leah and Rachel, or, the Two Fruitful Sisters, Virginia, and Maryland. . . . London, 1656. Reprinted in Force, *Tracts*, Vol. III, No. 14, and *Narratives of Early Maryland*, pp. 277-307.

Hamor, Ralph. *A True Discourse of the Present Estate of Virginia*. . . . London, 1615.

Hariot, Thomas. *A Briefe and True Report of the New Found Land of Virginia*. . . . London, 1588.

Harrower, John. Diary, 1773-1776. *American Historical Review*, VI, 65-107.

Hartwell, Henry, James Blair, and Edward Chilton. *The Present State of Virginia and the College*. ·London, 1727.

Hawkins, Benjamin. Letters, 1796-1806. Georgia Historical Society, *Collections*, Vol. IX. Savannah, 1916.

Hayne, Colonel Isaac. Records Kept by Colonel Isaac Hayne. *South Carolina Historical and Genealogical Magazine*, X-XII, *passim*.

Helton, John. *Reasons for Quitting the Methodist Society; being a Defence of Barclay's Apology*. . . . 3rd ed. Philadelphia, 1784.

Herrman, Augustine. Journal of the Dutch Embassy to Maryland, 1659. *Narratives of Early Maryland*, pp. 309-33.

Heth, Major William. Orderly Book, 1777. Edited by R. A. Brock. Virginia Historical Society, *Collections*, New Series, XI, 317-76.

Hewatt, Alexander. *An Historical Account of the Rise and Progress of the Colonies of South Carolina and Georgia.* 2 vols. London, 1779.

Hilton, William. A Relation of a Discovery, 1664. *Narratives of Early Carolina*, pp. 31-61.

Historical Collections of South Carolina. Ed. B. R. Carroll. 2 vols. New York, 1836.

Horne, Robert. A Brief Description of the Province of Carolina . . . Wherein is set forth . . . the great pleasure and profit will accrue to those that shall go thither. . . . London, 1666. *Historical Collections of South Carolina*, II, 2-18.

Hotten, John Camden (ed.). *The Original Lists of Persons of Quality, Emigrants; Religious Exiles, Political Rebels; Serving Men Sold for a Term of Years; Apprentices; etc. Who Went from Great Britain to the American Plantations, 1600-1700*. . . . London, 1874.

Howard, McHenry. Some Abstracts of Old Baltimore County Records. *Maryland Historical Magazine*, XVIII, 1-22.

Hume, George. Letters to and from George Hume of Virginia, formerly of Wedderburn, Scotland (1743-1754). *Virginia Magazine of History and Biography*, XX, 381-421.

Hume, Sophia. *An Exhortation to the Inhabitants of the Province of South Carolina. . . . In which is inserted some Account of the Author's Experience in the Important Business of Religion, (1747).* Bristol, 1750.

Hutson, Mrs. Mary, and Hugh Bryan. *Living Christianity Delineated, in the Diaries and Letters of Two Eminently Pious Persons lately deceased; viz. Mr. Hugh Bryan and Mrs. Mary Hutson, both of South Carolina*. . . . London, 1760.

Inscriptions from the Church Yard of Old Prince Frederick Winyah, at Brown's Ferry, Black River. *South Carolina Historical and Genealogical Magazine*, XVIII, 91-95.

Inscriptions from the Independent or Congregational (Circular) Church, Charleston, S. C. *South Carolina Historical and Genealogical Magazine*, XXIX, *passim.*

Inscriptions on Old Tombs in Gloucester County, Virginia. *William and Mary College Quarterly Magazine*, II, 219-36.

Inscriptions on the Gravestones at Sheldon Church. *South Carolina Historical and Genealogical Magazine*, XVIII, 180-83.

Inscriptions on the Tombstones at the Old Parish Church of St. James's Santee, near Echaw Creek. *South Carolina Historical and Genealogical Magazine*, XII, 153-58.

Institution of the Discipline. *Friends' Library*, I, 109-41.

Iredell, James. *See* McRee, Griffith J.

Izard, Mrs. Ralph. Letters from Mrs. Ralph Izard to Mrs. William Lee (1781-1782). *Virginia Magazine of History and Biography*, VIII, 16-28.

Jackson, Thomas. *Recollections of My Own Life and Times.* Ed. Reverend B. Frankland. London, 1873.

Jefferson, Thomas. *The Writings of Thomas Jefferson.* Ed. Paul Leicester Ford. 10 vols. New York, 1892-1899.

Jerdone, Francis. Letter Book, 1746-1759. *William and Mary College Quarterly Magazine,* First Series, XI, XIV, XVI, *passim.*

[Johnson, Robert]. New Life of Virginia: Declaring the Former Success and Present State of that Province, being the Second Part of Nova Britannia. Force, *Tracts,* I, No. 7.

———— Nova Britannia: Offering Most Excellent Fruits by Planting in Virginia. . . . London, 1609. Force, *Tracts,* Vol. I, No. 6.

Jones, Hugh. *The Present State of Virginia.* London, 1724. Reprinted for Joseph Sabin. New York, 1865.

Jones Papers. From the Originals in the Library of Congress. *Virginia Magazine of History and Biography,* XXVI, *passim.*

Journal of a French Traveller in the Colonies, 1765. *American Historical Review,* XXVI, XXVII, *passim.*

Journal of a Young Lady of Virginia, 1782. See Lee, Lucinda.

Kalm, Peter. *Travels into North America . . . 1748.* Translated by John Reinhold Forster. 3 vols. London, 1770-1771.

Keith, Reverend George. *A Journal of Travels from New-Hampshire to Caratuck. On the Continent of North America.* London, 1706.

Land Notes, 1634-1655, *Maryland Historical Magazine,* V-IX, *passim.*

Langford, John. Refutation of Babylon's Fall, 1655. *Narratives of Early Maryland,* pp. 247-74.

La Rochefoucauld Liancourt, Francois Alexander du Frederic, Duc de. *Travels through the United States of America . . . in the Years 1795, 1796, and 1797. . . .* 4 vols. London, 1799.

Laurens, Henry. Correspondence. Ed. Joseph W. Barnwell. *South Carolina Historical and Genealogical Magazine,* XXVIII-XXXI, *passim.*

———— Correspondence between Honorable Henry Laurens and his Son, John, 1777-1780. *South Carolina Historical and Genealogical Magazine,* VI, *passim.*

———— Letters from Hon. Henry Laurens to his Son John, 1773-1776. *South Carolina Historical and Genealogical Magazine,* III-V, *passim.*

Laurens, John. Letters from John Laurens to his Father, Hon. Henry Laurens, 1774-1776. *South Carolina Historical and Genealogical Magazine,* V, 197-208.

Lawes Resolutions of Womens Rights; Or, the Lawes Provision for Women. London, 1632.

Laws respecting Women, As they regard their Natural Rights, or their Connections and Conduct, in which their Interests and Duties as Daughters, Wards, Heiresses, Spinsters, Sisters, Wives, Widows, Mothers, Legatees, Executrixes, &c. are ascertained and enumerated. . . . In four Books. London, 1777.

Lawson, John. *The History of Carolina containing the Exact Description and Natural History of that Country, together with the Present State thereof.* . . . London, 1709, 1718. Later edition, Raleigh, 1860.

Lederer, John. *The Discoveries of John Lederer, in three Several Marches from Virginia to the West Coast of Carolina, and other Parts of the Continent; begun in March, 1669, and ended in September, 1670.* . . . *Collected and translated out of Latine from his discourse and writings.* By Sir William Talbot. London, 1672. Reprinted in Francis Lister Hawks, *History of North Carolina*, II, 43-53.

[Lee, Lucinda?]. *Journal of a Young Lady of Virginia, 1782.* Ed. Emily V. Mason. Baltimore, 1871.

Lee, Richard Henry. *The Letters of Richard Henry Lee, 1762-1794.* Ed. James Curtis Ballagh. 2 vols. New York, 1911-1914.

Letter from South Carolina . . . written by a Swiss Gentleman to his Friend at Bern. London, 1710. Reprinted in *University of North Carolina Magazine*, IV (September, 1855), 289-305.

Letters and Documents Relating to the Early History of the Lower Cape Fear. Ed. Kemp P. Battle. *James Sprunt Historical Publications*, No. 4. Chapel Hill, 1903.

Lucas, Eliza. *Journal and Letters of Eliza Lucas.* Ed. Harriott Pinckney Holbrook. Wormsloe, 1850.

Lyons, Judge Peter. Letters to his Granddaughter. *Tyler's Quarterly Historical and Genealogical Magazine*, VIII, 184-94.

McRee, Griffith J. *Life and Correspondence of James Iredell.* 2 vols. New York, 1857.

Manigault, Mrs. Ann. Extracts from the Journal of Mrs. Ann Manigault, 1754-1781. Ed. Mabel L. Webber. *South Carolina Historical and Genealogical Magazine*, XX, XXI, *passim*.

Manigault, Peter. Letters concerning Peter Manigault, 1773. *South Carolina Historical and Genealogical Magazine*, XXI, 39-49.

———— Peter Manigault's Letters. Ed. Mabel L. Webber. *South Carolina Historical and Genealogical Magazine*, XXXI, *passim*.

———— Six Letters. *South Carolina Historical and Genealogical Magazine*, XV, 113-23.

[Martyn, Benjamin]. An Account Showing the Progress of the Colony of Georgia in America from its First Establishment. London, 1741. Georgia Historical Society, *Collections*, II, 265-325.

———— An Impartial Inquiry into the State and Utility of the Province of Georgia. London, 1741. Georgia Historical Society, *Collections*, I, 153-201.

———— Reasons for Establishing the Colony of Georgia, with regard to the Trade of Great Britain, the Increase of our People, and the Employment and Support it will Afford to great Numbers of our own Poor, as well as foreign persecuted Protestants. . . . London, 1733. Georgia Historical Society, *Collections*, I, 203-38.

386   BIBLIOGRAPHY OF PRIMARY SOURCES

Maryland Gastronomic Accounts. Miscellaneous State Papers, Nos. 46 and 47. *Maryland Historical Magazine*, X, 55-57.

Maryland Medical Student and his Friends (Correspondence from the Letter Book of Dr. Richard Hopkins). *Maryland Historical Magazine*, XXIII, 279-92.

Maury, Ann. *Memoirs of a Huguenot Family: Translated and Compiled from the Original Autobiography of the Rev. James Fontaine, and other Family Manuscripts, comprising an original Journal of Travels in Virginia, New-York, etc. in 1715-1716.* New York, 1872.

Mazzei, Philip. Memoirs of the Life and Voyages of Doctor Philip Mazzei. *William and Mary College Quarterly Magazine*, Second Series, IX, X, *passim*.

Meacham, James. A Journal and Travel of James Meacham (1789-1797). Trinity College Historical Society, *Papers*, IX, X, *passim*.

Mereness, Newton Dennison (ed.). *Travels in the American Colonies.* New York, 1916.

Michel, Francis-Louis. Report of the Journey of Francis Louis Michel from Berne, Switzerland, to Virginia, October 2, 1701-December 1, 1702. Translated and edited by Prof. William J. Hinke. *Virginia Magazine of History and Biography*, XXIV, *passim*.

Middleton, Arthur. Correspondence of Honorable Arthur Middleton, Signer of the Declaration of Independence. Ed. Joseph W. Barnwell. *South Carolina Historical and Genealogical Magazine*, XXVI, XXVII, *passim*.

Milligan, Dr. George. A Short Description of the Province of South Carolina . . . written in the Year 1763. London, 1770. *Historical Collections of South Carolina*, II, 462-535.

Minutes of Several Conversations between The Rev. Thomas Coke, LL.D., The Rev. Francis Asbury, and Others, at a Conference, begun in Baltimore, in the State of Maryland, in Monday, the 27th of December, in the Year, 1784. Composing a Form of Discipline for the Ministers, Preachers, and other Members of the Methodist Episcopal Church in America. Philadelphia, 1785.

Minutes of the Philadelphia Baptist Association, from A. D. 1707 to A. D. 1807; Being the First One Hundred Years of its Existence. Ed. A. D. Gillette. Philadelphia, 1851.

Minutes of the Vestry of St. Helena's Parish, South Carolina, 1726-1812. Ed. A. S. Salley, Jr. Columbia, S. C., 1919.

Montgomery, Robert. A Discourse concerning the Designed Establishment of a New Colony to the South of Carolina, in the Most Delightful Country of the Universe. London, 1717. Force, *Tracts*, Vol. I, No. 1.

Moore, Francis. A Voyage to Georgia, begun in the Year 1735. . . . London, 1744. Georgia Historical Society, *Collections*, I, 80-152.

Moravian Diaries of Travels through Virginia. Eds. Rev. William J. Hinke and Charles G. Kemper. *Virginia Magazine of History and Biography*, XI, XII, *passim*.

Morrison, Alfred Jones (ed.). *Travels in Virginia in Revolutionary Times*. Lynchburg, Va., 1922.

Nairne, Thomas. *A Letter from South Carolina: Giving an Account of the Soils, Air, Products, Trade, Government, Laws, Religion, Military Strength, etc. of that Province. . . .* London, 1710.

Narrative of a Voyage to Maryland, 1705-1706. *American Historical Review*, XII, 327-41.

Narratives of Early Carolina, 1650-1708. Ed. A. S. Salley, Jr. New York, 1911.

Narratives of Early Maryland. Ed. Clayton Colman Hall. New York, 1910.

Nelson, William. Nelson Letter Book. *William and Mary College Quarterly Magazine*, VII, 25-30.

New Voyage to Georgia, by a Young Gentleman, Giving an Account of His Travels to South Carolina and Part of North Carolina (1733-34). 2d ed. London, 1737. Georgia Historical Society, *Collections*, II, 36-66.

Newe, Thomas. Letters of Thomas Newe from South Carolina, 1682. *American Historical Review*, XII, 322-27; *Narratives of Early Carolina*, pp. 181-87.

Norton, John. *John Norton & Sons, Merchants of London and Virginia. Being the Papers from their Counting House for the Years 1750 to 1795*. Ed. Frances Norton Mason. Richmond, 1937.

Norwood, Colonel Henry. A Voyage to Virginia. Force, *Tracts*, Vol. III, No. 10.

Observations in Several Voyages and Travels in America. From the *London Magazine*, July, 1746. *William and Mary College Quarterly Magazine*, XV, *passim*.

Oglethorpe, James Edward. Letters from General Oglethorpe, October, 1735 to August, 1744. Georgia Historical Society, *Collections*, III, 1-156.

——— New and Accurate Account of the Provinces of South Carolina and Georgia. . . . London, 1733. Georgia Historical Society, *Collections*, I, 42-78.

[Oldmixon, John]. *The British Empire in America containing the History of the Discovery, Settlement, Progress and State of the British Colonies on the Continent and Islands of America*. 2 vols. London, 1708. 2d ed., 1741.

——— The History of Carolina: being an Account of that Colony, Originally Published in the History of the British Empire in America. *Historical Collections of South Carolina*, II, 391-461.

Origin of the Whalebone-petticoat. A Satyr. Boston, 1714.

Parish Register of Christ Church, Middlesex County, Virginia, from 1653 to 1812, published by the National Society of the Colonial Dames of America in the State of Virginia. Richmond, 1897.

Percival, John (Earl of Egmont). An Impartial Enquiry into the State and Utility of the Province of Georgia. London, 1741. Georgia Historical Society, *Collections*, I, 153-201.

Percy, Master George. Observations gathered out of a Discourse of the Plantations of the Southern Colonie in Virginia by the English, 1606. Introduction to *Works of Captain John Smith*, Arber ed., pp. lvii-lxxiii.

Perfect Description of Virginia: being a Full and True Relation of the Present State of that Plantation, their Health, Peace, and Plenty. . . . London, 1649. Force, *Tracts*, Vol. II, No. 9.

Phillips, Daniel. *Vindiciae Veritatis: or an Occasional Defence of the Principles and Practices of the People called Quakers.* 1703.

Phillips, Ulrich Bonnell (ed.). *Plantation and Frontier, 1649-1863.* Vols. I-II of *A Documentary History of American Industrial Society.* Cleveland, 1910.

Pinckney, Mrs. Charles (Eliza Lucas). Letter to Harriott Horry. (Sept. 10, 1785.) *South Carolina Historical and Genealogical Magazine*, XVII, 101-2.

——— *Recipe Book of Eliza Lucas Pinckney, 1756.* Published by the South Carolina Society of Colonial Dames, Charleston, 1937.

——— *See also* Ravenel, Harriott Horry.

Pinckney, Roger. Letters from Richard Cumberland, Esq. to Roger Pinckney, Esq. *Documents connected with the History of South Carolina.* Ed. P. C. J. Weston.

Pleasants, Robert. Letters of Robert Pleasants, Merchant at Curles, 1771-1774. *William and Mary College Quarterly Magazine*, Second Series, I, *passim*.

Pory, John. Observations of Master John Pory. *Works of Captain John Smith*, Arber ed., pp. 567-71.

Powell, Leven. Letters to his Wife. *The John P. Branch Historical Papers of Randolph-Macon College*, Vol. I, No. 1, pp. 24-38.

Pringle, Robert. Journal, 1746-1747. Annotated by Mabel L. Webber. *South Carolina Historical and Genealogical Magazine*, XXVI, *passim*.

Proctor, William. Letters (1739-1740). *Virginia Magazine of History and Biography*, X, 298-301.

Purry, John Peter. A Description of the Province of South Carolina drawn up at Charles Town in September, 1731. . . . Force, *Tracts*, Vol. II, No. 11; *Historical Collections of South Carolina*, II, 121-40.

Quincy, Josiah. Journal of Josiah Quincy, Junior, 1773. Massachusetts Historical Society, *Proceedings*, XLIX (June, 1916), 424-81.

Ramsay, David. *Memoirs of the Life of Martha Laurens Ramsay . . . With an Appendix containing extracts from her Diary, Letters, and other Private Papers.* . . . 3rd ed. Boston, 1812.

Randolph and Tucker Letters (1786-1789). Contributed with Notes by Mrs. George P. Coleman. *Virginia Magazine of History and Biography*, XLII, 47-52.

Ravenel, Harriott Horry. *Eliza Pinckney*. New York, 1896.

Read, Mrs. Helen. My Mother. Copy of a Memoir of Mrs. Helen Read (in the State Library, Richmond, Va.) entitled *My Mother*, written from his Mother's Lips, by the late William Maxwell. *Lower Norfolk County Virginia Antiquary*, I-III, *passim*.

Reck, Philipp Georg Friedrich von. *See* Von Reck.

Reichel, Bishop. Extracts from the Travel Diary of Bishop Reichel, Mrs. Reichel, and Christian Heckwelder from Salem to Lititz, 1780. *Travels in the American Colonies* (ed. Mereness), pp. 585-613.

Relation of Maryland, 1635. *Narratives of Early Maryland*, pp. 63-112.

Richardson, John. *An Account of the Life of that Ancient Servant of Jesus Christ, John Richardson, Giving a Revelation of . . . his Services in the Work of the Ministry, in England, Ireland, America, etc.* London, 1757.

Robertson, Donald. Donald Robertson's School. King and Queen County, Va., 1758-1769. Extracts from his Account Book. *Virginia Magazine of History and Biography*, XXXIII, XXXIV, *passim*.

Robin, Claude C. (Abbé). *New Travels through North-America; in a Series of Letters . . . in the Year 1781*. Translated (by Philip Freneau) from the Original of Abbé Robin. Philadelphia, 1783.

Rochefoucauld Liancourt. *See* La Rochefoucauld Liancourt.

Rogers, Major Robert. *Concise Account of North America*. London, 1765.

Rolfe, John. Relation of the State of Virginia, 1616. *Virginia Historical Register*, I, 101-13.

Salmon, Thomas. *Modern History; or the Present State of all Nations. Describing their respective Situations, Persons, Habits, Buildings, Manners, Laws, and Customs, Religion and Policy, Arts and Sciences, Trades, Manufactures, and Husbandry. . . .* 4 vols. London, 1737.

[Schaw, Janet]. *Journal of a Lady of Quality; Being a Narrative of a Journey from Scotland to the West Indies, North Carolina, and Portugal, in the Years 1774 to 1776*. Edited by Evangeline Walker Andrews in collaboration with Charles McLean Andrews. New Haven, 1923.

Scheme for Providing an Annuity to Ministers Widows, and a Stock to their Children; Past and Resolved by the General Assembly of the Church of Scotland, met at Edinburgh the 12th of May, 1743. . . . Edinburgh, 1743.

Schoepf, Johann David. *Travels in the Confederation* (1783-1784). Translated and edited by Alfred J. Morrison. 2 vols. Philadelphia, 1911.

Scisco, Louis Dow. Baltimore County Records of 1665-1667, 1668-1669. *Maryland Historical Magazine*, XXIV, XXV, *passim*.

———— Earliest Records of Baltimore County. *Maryland Historical Magazine*, XXIV, 151-56.

Scotus Americanus (pseud.). Informations Concerning the Province of North Carolina, etc. Glasgow, 1773. Reprinted in *North Carolina Historical Review*, III, 591-621.

Shaftesbury Papers and Other Records relating to Carolina and the First Settlement on Ashley River prior to the year, 1676. South Carolina Historical Society, *Collections*, Vol. V.

Sharpe, Horatio. Correspondence of Governor Sharpe, 1753-1768. *Archives of Maryland*, Vols. VI, IX, XIV, XXXI.

Sherwood, Grace. Record of Grace Sherwood's Trial for Witchcraft in 1705 in Princess Anne County, Virginia. Virginia Historical and Philosophical Society, *Collections*, I, 75-98.

Shrigley, Nathaniel. A True Relation of Virginia and Mary-land; with the Commodities therein. . . . London, 1669. Force, *Tracts*, Vol. III, No. 7.

Smith, Captain John. *Works of Captain John Smith, 1608-1631.* Ed. Edward Arber. Birmingham, England, 1884.

Smith, Patrick. *A Preservative against Quakerism, or A Complication of Deism, Enthusiasm, and divers other Ancient and Modern dangerous Errors and Heresies.* . . . London, 1732.

Smyth, John Ferdinand D. *A Tour in the United States. Containing an Account of the Present Situation of that Country, the Population, Agriculture, Commerce, Customs & Manners of the Inhabitants, &c.* 2 vols. London, 1784.

Some Colonial Letters. *Virginia Magazine of History and Biography*, III-V, X, *passim*.

Some Family Letters of the Eighteenth Century. *Virginia Magazine of History and Biography*, XV, 432-36.

Some Old English Letters, with Notes by McHenry Howard. *Maryland Historical Magazine*, IX, 107-56.

Spelman, Henry. Relation of Virginia. Introduction to *Works of Captain John Smith*, Arber ed., pp. ci-cxiv.

Spotswood, Alexander. The Official Letters of Alexander Spotswood, Lieutenant-Governor of the Colony of Virginia, 1710-1722. Virginia Historical Society, *Collections*, New Series, Vols. I and II.

Stanton, Daniel. *A Journal of the Life, Travels, and Gospel Labours of a Faithful Minister of Jesus Christ, Daniel Stanton, late of Philadelphia.* Philadelphia, 1772.

State of Religion in New England, since the Reverend Mr. George Whitefield's Arrival there . . . *with an Appendix, Containing Proofs* . . . *of the Disorders* . . . *lately introduced into various Parts of New-England and Carolina* . . . . Glasgow, 1742.

[Stephens, Thomas, and Sir Richard Everhard]. A Brief Account of the Causes that have Retarded the Progress of the Colony of Georgia. . . . London, 1743. Georgia Historical Society, *Collections*, II, 87-161.

Stephens, William. A Journal of the Proceedings in Georgia, Beginning October 20, 1737. *Colonial Records of Georgia.* Vols. IV and IV Supplement.

———— A State of the Province of Georgia, Attested upon Oath, in the Court of Savannah, November 10, 1740. London, 1742. Force, *Tracts*, Vol. I, No. 3. Also in Georgia Historical Society, *Collections*, II, 67-85, and in *Colonial Records of Georgia*, IV, 663-80.

Stith, William. *The History of the First Discovery and Settlement of Virginia.* . . . Williamsburg, 1747. Reprinted for Joseph Sabin. New York, 1865.

Strachey, William. The Historie of Travaile into Virginia Britannia . . . 1612? Ed. R. H. Major. Hakluyt Society, *Publications*, VI. London, 1849.

Symonds, William. The Proceedings of the English Colonie in Virginia since their first beginning from England in the yeare of our Lord 1606, till this present 1612. . . . Oxford, 1612. Reprinted in *Works of Captain John Smith*, Arber ed., pp. 85-174.

Tailfer, Patrick, Hugh Anderson, and others. A True and Historical Narrative of the Colony of Georgia. . . . Containing the Most Authentic Facts, Matters, and Transactions therein. . . . Charles Town, S. C., 1741. Georgia Historical Society, *Collections*, II, 163-263, and Force, *Tracts*, Vol. I, No. 4.

Thomas, Reverend Samuel. Letters, 1702-1710. *South Carolina Historical and Genealogical Magazine*, IV, *passim.*

Thomas, Mrs. Samuel. Documents concerning Mrs. Samuel Thomas, 1707-1710. *South Carolina Historical and Genealogical Magazine*, V, 95-99.

Tilghman, Molly and Hetty. Letters of Molly and Hetty Tilghman, Eighteenth Century Gossip of Two Maryland Girls. Ed. J. Hall Pleasants. *Maryland Historical Magazine*, XXI, *passim.*

True Declaration of the Estate of the Colony in Virginia with a Confutation of Such Scandalous Reports as Have Tended to the Disgrace of so Worthy an Enterprise. London, 1610. Force, *Tracts*, Vol. III, No. 1.

Tucker, St. George. *Blackstone's Commentaries: with Notes of Reference, to the Constitution and Laws, of the Federal Government of the United States; and of the Commonwealth of Virginia.* In Five Volumes. . . . Philadelphia, 1803.

Vestry Book of King William Parish, Virginia, 1707-1750. Translated from the French and annotated by Prof. R. H. Fife. *Virginia Magazine of History and Biography*, XI-XIII, *passim.*

Vestry Books. *See* Chamberlayne, Churchill Gibson, and Brock, R. A.

Vestry Proceedings, St. Ann's Parish, Annapolis, Maryland. *Maryland Historical Magazine*, VI-X, *passim.*

Von Reck, Baron Philipp Georg Friedrich, and John Martin Bolzius. An Extract of the Journals of Mr. Commissary Von Reck, who Conducted the First Transport of Saltzburgers to Georgia: and of the

Reverend Mr. Bolzius, One of their Ministers. Giving an Account of their Voyage to, and happy Settlement in that Province. London, 1734. Force, *Tracts*, Vol. IV, No. 5.

Wansey, Henry. *An Excursion to the United States of America in the Summer of 1794.* Salisbury, 1796.

Warville, J. P. Brissot de. *See* Brissot de Warville.

Washington, George. *The Daily Journal of Major George Washington in 1751-1752; Kept while on a Tour from Virginia to the Island of Barbadoes.* ... Ed. J. M. Toner. Albany, N. Y., 1892.

—— *Diaries of George Washington, 1748-1799.* Ed. John Clement Fitzpatrick. 4 vols. Boston and New York, 1925.

—— Extracts from Washington's Domestic Letters. Written to Mr. William Pearce, Superintendent of Mount Vernon Estate, 1794, 1795, 1796. Originals in Archives of the Long Island Historical Society. *Magazine of American History*, IX, 125-33.

—— *George Washington, Colonial Traveller, 1732-1775.* Compiled by J. C. Fitzpatrick. Indianapolis, 1927.

—— *Letters and Recollections of George Washington. Being Letters to Tobias Lear and Others between 1790 and 1799, showing the First American in the Management of his Estate and Domestic Affairs. With a Diary of Washington's Last Days Kept by Mr. Lear.* Ed. Jared Sparks. New York, 1906.

—— *Letters to Washington and Accompanying Papers.* Ed. Stanislaus Murray Hamilton. 5 vols. Boston and New York, 1898-1902.

—— *Orderly Book of General George Washington . . . Kept at Valley Forge, May 18-June 11, 1778.* Ed. A. P. C. Griffin. Boston and London, 1898.

—— *The Writings of George Washington.* Collected and edited by Worthington Chauncey Ford. 14 vols. New York and London, 1889-1893.

—— *The Writings of George Washington; being his Correspondence, Addresses, Messages, and Other Papers, Official and Private, Selected and Published from the Original Manuscripts; with a Life of the Author.* ... Ed. Jared Sparks. 12 vols. Boston, 1834-1837.

—— *The Writings of George Washington from the Original Manuscript Sources, 1745-1799.* Ed. John Clement Fitzpatrick. 14 vols. Washington, D. C., 1931-1934.

Washington, Martha. Letters of Martha Washington. *Historical Magazine*, II, 135.

Waterhouse, Edward. *A Declaration of the State of the Colony and Affairs in Virginia. With a Relation of the Barbarous Massacre . . . And a Note of the Charges of Necessary Provisions fit for every Man that Intends to Goe to Virginia.* London, 1622.

Watson, Elkanah. *Men and Times of the Revolution; or, Memoirs of Elkanah Watson, including Journals of Travels in Europe and America from 1777 to 1842.* ... Ed. W. C. Watson. New York, 1856.

Webber, Mabel L. (ed.). *The Records of the Quakers in Charles Town.* South Carolina Historical and Genealogical Magazine, XXVIII, *passim.*

Webster, Pelatiah. Journal of a Voyage to Charleston in So. Carolina, by Pelatiah Webster in 1765. Ed. T. P. Harrison. Southern History Association, *Publications*, II, 131-48.

Wesley, Rev. John. Journal. Vols. III and IV of *Works*. New York, 1831.

White, Rev. Father Andrew. A Briefe Relation of the Voyage unto Maryland, 1634. *Narratives of Early Maryland*, pp. 25-45.

Whitefield, George. *A Journal of a Voyage from London to Savannah in Georgia . . . 1737-1738.* 5th ed. London, 1739.

—— *A Continuation of the Reverend Mr. Whitefield's Journal, from his Arrival at London, to his Departure from there on his way to Georgia, Dec. 8, 1738-June 3, 1739.* London, 1739.

—— *A Continuation of Reverend Whitefield's Journal, during the Time he was Detained in England by the Embargo* (June 4, 1739 to August 3, 1739). London, 1739.

—— *A Continuation of the Rev. Mr. Whitefield's Journal, from his Embarking after the Embargo, to his Arrival at Savannah in Georgia* (Aug. 4, 1739 to Jan. 9, 1740). London, 1740.

—— *A Continuation of the Reverend Mr. Whitefield's Journal after his Arrival at Georgia, to a Few Days after his Second Return thither from Philadelphia.* London, 1741.

—— *A Continuation of the Reverend Mr. Whitefield's Journal, from a Few Days after his Return to Georgia to his Arrival at Falmouth, on the 11th of March 1741. . . .* Seventh Journal. London, 1741.

Wilkinson, Eliza (Yonge). *Letters of Eliza Wilkinson during the Invasion and Possession of Charlestown, S. C. by the British in the Revolutionary War.* Arranged from the original manuscripts by Caroline Gilman. New York, 1839.

[Williams, Edward]. *Virgo Triumphans: or, Virginia more especially the South part thereof, richly and truly valued. . . .* London, 1650. Reprinted in Force, *Tracts*, Vol. III, No. 11.

Wilson, Rachel. *A Discourse delivered on Saturday, the 10th Day of August, 1769, at the Friends Meeting House, in Beekman's Precinct, Dutches County, in the Province of New-York. By the Celebrated Rachel Wilson (One of the People called Quakers.) To a numerous Audience of different Persuasions.* Taken in short hand, from the Mouth of the Speaker, by one of the Audience. New York, and Newport, R. I., 1769.

[Wilson, Samuel]. An Account of the Province of Carolina. . . . London, 1682. Reprinted in *Historical Collections of South Carolina*, II, 19-35.

Wingate, Edmund. *Maximes of Reason: or the Reason of the Common Law of England.* London, 1658.

Wingfield, Edward Maria. A Discourse of Virginia. . . . Edited with notes and Introduction by Charles Deane. American Antiquarian Society, *Transactions and Collections*, IV, 69-103.

Yong, Thomas. Extract of a Letter of Captain Thomas Yong to Sir Toby Matthew, 1634. *Narratives of Early Maryland*, pp. 47-61.

INDEX

ABERCROMBIE, violinist, 101

Abortion, 325-26

Accidence to the English Tongue, An, 202

Accomplished Housewife or Gentlewoman's Companion, 212

Accomplished Lady's Delight . . . , 210

Accomplished Woman . . . , 228n

Actresses, 259-63

Adams, Elizabeth, married at sixty-two, 161

Adams, Ezekiel, whipped, 342n

Adams, Mary, remedy for eye disorders, 269

Adams, Mrs., school teacher, 258

Adams, William, provision for daughter's tuition, 255

Adams, William, writing master, 258

Addison, Thomas, Jr., courtship, 147

Adultery, punishment for, 314-15, 319-21

Adventurers, women, 11, 232, 237

"Adventures of Harlequin and Scaramouch . . . ," 100

Alamode, silk material, 114

Albemarle, the, 12

Albemarle Point, settlement, 12

Alexander, Anthony, 47

Alexander, William, author, 228n

Alexander, William, Esq., guardian, 346

Alexandria (Va.), annual ball, 97; inns, 299

Alford, Elizabeth, marriage contract, 366

Alford, John, and wife, whipped, 338

Alimony. *See* Separate maintenance

Allen, Aidwith, apprentice, 189n

Allen, Sarah, landowner, 307

Alley, Mary, sexton, 304

All for Love, 230n

Allingham, Anne, innkeeper, 298

Alpaca, a dress material, 114

Alsop, George, encouragement of women emigrants, 137n

Alverson, Becknell, wife of, separate maintenance, 343

Ambrose, Alice, missionary, 250

American Company, the, 93

American Company of Comedians, 96-97

Ams, Elizabeth, bequeathed clothes, 126

Amusements, in seventeenth century, 85-86; in Maryland, 91-95; in Virginia, 95-97; in North Carolina, 97-98; in South Carolina, 98-101; in Georgia, 101; of gentlewomen in general, 107-9; of frontier women, 109-12

Anatomist, or Sham Doctor, 96

Anburey, Thomas, description of "Tuckahoe," 33; food in western Virginia, 82n

Anderson, Elizabeth, apprentice, 189n

Anderson, Elizabeth, proprietress of baking business, 287n

Anderson, Elizabeth, schoolmistress, 198

Anderson, Esther, white woman, burned alive, 336

Anglican Church, women in, 245-47

Annapolis, free school, 190; private schools, 199; gay social center, 91-93; ladies, admired, 92-93; theatre, 93

Antenuptial agreements, 160, 364-66

Apparel, large amount imported, 74-76, 75n, 129-31; made by seamstresses, 75; of slaves, 75, 78; bought by Franklin for his wife and daughter, 79n; of Annapolis ladies, 92; of seventeenth-century ladies, 113-16; advertised by colonial shopkeepers, 118, 119, 120-22, 123, 124-26; ordered for Mrs. Washington, 122, 124; for Patcy Custis, 124; ordered by husbands, 129-30; selected by wives of English merchants, 130; bequeathed in wills, 126-27, 352-53; of ladies at "Nomini Hall," 132-33; of little girls, 133; of servants, 133-34; of women of poorer classes, 133-34

ings, 39-40; Georgia residences, 39-40; backwoods homes, 46-41
Housewife, an accessory, 125
Housewifery manuals, 69-71, 209-12
Housewives, notable, 64-65; on plantations, 65-70; in towns, 80-81; on the frontier, 81-83
Houston, Lady, landowner, 307
Howard, Anne, innkeeper, 298
Howard, Anne, whipped and pilloried, 334-35
Howell, Blanch, matron, pilloried, 334
Hoyland, Maria, schoolmistress, brazier, and tinner, 198, 257, 288
Hubbard, Thomas, 145
Hudson, Ann, 273
Hudson, Phoeby, lessons in psalmody, 201n
Hughes, James, 352-53
Hughes, Mary, shopkeeper, 281n
Hughes, Mrs., doctress and midwife, 269, 274
Hume, Marie, milliner and shopkeeper, 283
Hume, Robert, 252
Hume, Sophia, preacher, 249n, 252-53
Hunt, Mrs. Elizabeth, midwife, 273
Hunter, Jane and Margaret, milliners and shopkeepers, 281n, 284, 285
Hunter, Miss, author, 230n
Hurst, John, marriage contract, 366
Husband, legal rights and liabilities, 340-42, 356-59
Husbands, care of household affairs, 78-80, 129-30; duties of, 163-64; infidelity of, 172-78; advice regarding, 215-17, 223-27
Husk, Rebecca, apprentice, 188
"Hypochondriac complaints," 74

ICE cream, at governor's dinner, 73n
Illegitimate children, 175. See Bastards
Illiteracy, of women, 187-88
Imer, Rev. Abraham, 258
Imer, Ann, 258-59, 293, 294
Immorality, sex, laws regarding, 314-23
Incestuous marriages, 141-43
Inch, Jane, silversmith, 288
Indentured servant women, 76, 133-34, 314, 317-18, 321-23

Indian massacre (1622), 10
Indian women, not taken as wives, 8; as concubines, 177-78
Indian queens, at public celebration, 86
Indigo, 308-10
Inducements, offered women colonists, 3, 11, 14-15, 16-17, 136-37
Inequality, in punishment of men and women, 320, 321, 335, 336-37, 339
Infant mortality, 47, 48, 49, 53-54
Infanticide, 273, 323-25, 327
Infidelity, of husbands, 172-78
Ingle, Richard, rebel, 238
Ingram, Hannah, sexton, 305
In-laws, advice regarding, 225
Innkeepers, women, 293-302
Inns, much used, 293, 302; description of, 301-2
Inoculation, for smallpox, 272
Insanity, 353n
Intestate estates, laws regarding, 349-50
Intoxicating liquors, sold by women, 277, 295, 297, 298, 300, 338
Iredell, James, reads to Edenton ladies, 107-8; as lover, 144, 148-49; comment on marriage of aged man, 160-61; affectionate letter to wife, 167, 175
Irving, Rebecca, 277

JACKSON, Jacob, incestuous marriage, 142n
Jackson, John, 319
Jacksonburgh (S. C.), school in, 201
Jailers, women, 304
James, Elizabeth, "a notorious strumpet," 323
James, John, 183
James Town, 3-7, passim; food in, 67; fashionable dress in, 113
Jane Shore, 261
Janney, Sary, Quakeress, 253
Jefferson, Marie (Polly), 51-52, 205
Jefferson, Martha, 205. See Randolph, Martha Jefferson
Jefferson, Thomas, idea on mission of woman, 45, 245; advice to daughter about to become a mother, 51; death of wife, 51-52; death of children, 54; as lover, 148; advice to daughter on

Parks, Eleanor, 263n

Parks, William, printer and journalist, 211n, 263n

"Parsons' schools," 186

Pastry shops, 287-88

Patches, 128

Pauldin, Jane, unmarried mother, 320

Pawly, Major, 309

Payton, Catherine, Quaker missionary, 252n

"Peace," 240

Peach, Mrs., tavern keeper, 296

Peacock, school dame, 185, 255

Peale, Charles Wilson, portrait painter, 262

Pearce, Mistress, early planter, 306

Pearce, Polly, 94, 135

"Pecatone," 106

Peisley, Mary, Quaker missionary, 252n

Penistone, a woolen material, 114, 133

Pennington, Lady Sarah, 221, 222

Percival, Andrew, 145

Percival, John, 18n

Perjury, punishment for, 334

Perry, Elizabeth, apprentice, 186n

Perry, Elizabeth, 130

Perry, Micajah, London merchant, 130

Persian, a dress material, 117, 131-32

Petersburg (Va.), 97, 301

Petit treason, 335

Petticoat Plotter, 230n

Petticoats, 114, 115, 117, 118, 126, 131, 133

Pewterer, a woman, 288

Peyton, Henry, 362

Philandering husband, advice regarding, 215, 216-17, 226-27

Phillips, Elizabeth, Charles Town midwife, 273

Phillips, Elizabeth, indentured servant, 322

"Physic and Chyrurgery," receipts in, 210

"Physick Garden," 210

Physicians, women, 267-69

Pianoforte, 102, 107, 203

Pierce, Jane, 4

Pierce, William, 4

Pigot, Sarah, 185

Pike, Mr., dancing master, 204n

Pillions, 88

Pillory, 331, 334-35

Pinckney, Col. Charles, hasty remarriage, 157, 206n, 310; visit to England, 206; death, 311

Pinckney, Eliza Lucas, an intelligent mother, 55, 59-60; on use of wet nurses, 56; pride in daughter's housewifery, 65; servants of, 77; on card playing, 108; lace for daughter, 122; visit to England, 206; learning of, 231. *See* Lucas, Eliza

Pinckney, Harriott, 56, 65, 122, 206

Pinckney, Roger, death of wife, 156

Pinkard, Mr., 106

Pinners, 122, 131, 134

Piscataway Emperor, 237

Pitt, Dr. George, 290

Pitt, Sarah, shopkeeper, 281n, 284, 289-90

Pitt, Thomas, 125

Plantation work, of women, 311-12

Planters, women, 305-311

Plato, Hester, apprentice, 58

Platonick Love, 230n

Platt, H., author, 210n

Players, 98. *See* Actresses; Dramatic performances

Playhouse. *See* Theatre

Plea of pregnancy, 326

Pocahontas, 6, 7

Pocket-books, 124

Pocket combs, 124

Poinsett, Catherine, innkeeper, 301, 302

Poinsett, Elisha, 301

Polite accomplishments, 202, 207, 241. *See* Carving; Dancing; Drawing; Music; Needlework; Writing

"Polite education," 198, 222

Polite Lady, 221, 223, 244n

Politics, for women, 243-45, 340

Polk, Mrs., schoolmistress, 199, 258

Pollard, Rebecca, nurse, 272

Pomatum, 122, 283

Pompons (for hair), 122

Pooley, Rev. Greville, courting of, 151

Porter, Eleanor, staymaker, 286

Portrait painters, 259

Port Royal, the, 12

Port Royal (S. C.), 12

Port Royal (Va.), 196

Port Tobacco (Md.), 298

Pory, John, 113
Posey, Capt. John, fortune-hunter, 155
Posey, Milley, at dancing school, 205
Postell, James, 156
Pothooks, 25, 323
Pott, Elizabeth, 233
Pott, Dr. John, physician, 50, 233
Powder. *See* Tooth powder; Hair powder
Powder-boxes, 283
Powder puffs, 128, 283
Powell, Mary, hanged for murder, 335n
Powhatan, 6, 7
Practical Discourse concerning Death, 209
Practice of Piety, 208
Pratt, Betty, drinks toast, 74; interest in theatricals, 96; education of, 195
Pratt, Henry, 180n
Preachers, women, 247-54
Pregnancy, plea of, 326
Presbyterians, ideas on education of girls, 197
Present for the Ladies, 227
Preston, William, 353
Price, Rachel, married woman, allowed income from own labor, 361
Primogeniture, 349, 353-55
Pringle, Robert, 126
Printers, women, 263-67
Prisbett, Bridgett, paraphernalia, 361
Pritchard, Catharine, sells rum, 277
Pritchard, Frances, wardrobe, 115
Pritchard, Miriam and Elizabeth, account for schooling of, 201n
Proctor, Mistress Alice, early heroine, 233
Property rights, of spinsters in early Maryland, 11; of women in early Georgia, 17; of married women, 359-61
"Provincial free school," in Charles Town, 294
Prunella, a durable material, 114, 115
Psalmody, 201n, 202
Public houses of entertainment, uses of, 302. *See* Inns; Ordinaries; Taverns
Public penance, punishment for adultery, 319-20; for slander, 332-33
Purdie, Alexander, journalist, 266

Puritans, in Maryland, 236; in England, 240
Purses, ladies', 124; for races, 91
Purton, John, 270

QUAKERS, oppose hasty remarriage, 157. *See* Friends
"Quaking pudding," 69
Quàsh, Sarah, staymaker, 286
Queen-like Closet . . ., 209
"Queen's dress cloaks," 119
Quilting parties, 110
Quincy, Josiah, on dinners in Charles Town, 73; St. Cecilia concert and ball, 100-1; cohabitation of planters with their slaves, 177

RAKE, Mary, aged woman, marriage of, 161
Raleigh, Sir Walter, 3
Ramsay, David, 48
Ramsay, Martha Laurens, as mother, 47-48, 55; reading of, 230-31. *See* Laurens, Martha
Ramsay, Mrs., tavern hostess, 296
Randolph, John, provision for wife, 165
Randolph, Judith, given jewelry, 126
Randolph, Martha Jefferson, 47, 162
Randolph, Susannah, 171n
Randolph, Col. Thomas Mann, marriage of, 162
Randolph, William, gives jewelry to daughters, 126
Rathell, Catherine, shopkeeper, 281n, 282, 283-84
Raymer, Sarah, tavern keeper, 302
Reading, taught girl apprentices, 186, 188, 189; taught in girls' schools, 197, 198, 199, 200, 201, 207; recommended for women, 212-13, 214, 219; of women in general, 230-31. *See* Books; Ladies' books
Reas Town Camp, 270
Recruiting Officer, 96
Redman, Alice, nurse, 271
Reed, Penelope, given separate estate, 363
Reed, Thomas, 363
Reflections on Courtship and Marriage . . ., 225n, 278